Applied Data Structures Using Pascal

Applied Data Structures Using Pascal

Guy J. Hale

Indiana State University

Richard J. Easton

Indiana State University

D. C. Heath and Company

Lexington, Massachusetts   Toronto

Acquisitions Editor: Pam Kirshen
Production Editor: Marret McCorkle
Designer: Cia Boynton
Production Coordinator: Michael O'Dea

Microsoft is a registered trademark of Microsoft Corporation. CDC and Cyber are trademarks of Control Data Corporation. PDP/11 and VAX/11 are trademarks of Digital Equipment Corporation. Turbo Pascal is a trademark of Borland International, Inc. UCSD is a trademark of the Regents of the University of California.

Cover: "Indian Amish Baskets" Roberta Horton, Berkeley, California, quilting by Mary Mashuta, Berkeley, California. Photo: Sharon Risedorph and Lynn Kellner. Photo courtesy of C & T Publishing.

Published simultaneously in Canada.

Printed in the United States of America.

International Standard Book Number: 0-669-07579-5

Library of Congress Catalog Card Number: 85-81813

This book is dedicated to our parents,
Eva Mae Hale, Lester Wayne Hale,
Norma Jensen Easton, and Ray Robert Easton,
who have influenced our lives
in so many ways.

Preface

Applied Data Structures Using Pascal

Applied Data Structures Using Pascal may be used for a one-semester data structures class, a two-semester (or two-quarter) data structures sequence, or the second course in the computer science curriculum as recommended by the ACM. The only prerequisite assumed is a previous introductory course using the Pascal language.

The text develops the definitions, concepts, and algorithms expected in a data structures text. However, it goes beyond other data structures texts by integrating especially selected applications. These applications, along with a readable writing style and thorough explanations, lead the student to an in-depth understanding of the subject.

Features

After teaching data structures for several years, we are convinced that it is much easier for students to learn the important concepts in data structures when these concepts are reinforced with meaningful applications. The old phrase that "a picture is worth a thousand words" could well be modified to "an appropriate programming application is worth a thousand definitions and vague explanations." Throughout the text we use such applications to introduce and develop important concepts and algorithms. In this way students gain a much better and more meaningful understanding of basic data structures and, at the same time, learn how to apply them. In selecting the applications used in the text, we decided to use "real-life" examples rather than many of the old, traditional data structures examples, which provide little more than mental exercises. Certain examples appear in more than one chapter as various types of data structures are developed. In this way, students can see the advantages and disadvantages of using different structures and methods for a specific application.

A second objective of the text is readability and understanding. To accomplish this, an easy-to-read writing style, step-by-step explanations and walk-throughs, and an extensive use of figures guide the student through basic structures and algorithms.

The text is filled with fully developed procedures and programs that are coded using the Pascal language. For the more involved procedures and programs, we develop pseudocode prior to developing the actual Pascal code. It is often quite difficult to understand the whole picture if only bits and pieces of it are given. Thus, in addition to pseudocoding and the coding of individual procedures, there are a large number of completely coded Pascal programs that illustrate how individual procedures are linked to form a complete application program.

The Pascal code utilized in the text is as close to "standard Pascal" as possible. Appendix A includes discussions and comparisons of several Pascal compilers. These discussions concentrate on differences in the handling of file names, input and output, and strings. In addition, variations in Pascals that apply to specific applications are discussed (when appropriate) throughout the text.

A major difference from many other texts is the extensive use of the Pascal pointer type. The dynamic pointer in Pascal is a very powerful and natural tool to use with linked lists, trees, and other structures. Since it seems illogical to teach data structures using the Pascal language and not use this built-in pointer type, the text makes extensive use of dynamic pointers to introduce and develop major concepts and structures. However, since at some point the student may be asked to develop data structures while using a language that does not include the pointer type, we also include the use of static arrays for major data structures such as lists and trees. This should provide the student with a very complete data structures background.

Extensive lists of exercises appear throughout, with summary exercises at the end of each chapter. These exercises vary widely in both type and depth. A significant number of them involve either modifications to example procedures and programs or the complete development of new procedures and programs. Other exercises include general questions relating to major concepts and structures or require students to walk through procedures and/or programs and explain what happens at each step of the process. These walk-through exercises are excellent tools in developing thorough understanding. Answers to selected exercises appear at the end of the text. The exercises for which answers are provided are those that test basic concepts and/or promote overall understanding such as walk-throughs.

An *Instructor's Guide* is available with selected answers to exercises, sample test items, transparency masters, and brief descriptions and insights on each chapter.

Organization and Content

Chapter 1 introduces the study of data structures. It leads students through the development of a fairly large applications program that uses arrays as the structure in which the data is stored. This applications program maintains a collection of employee data that is stored in a text file. It allows the user to add data to or delete data from the collection, modify any record of employee data, and obtain a printout of the collection. In its development, we show how to use top down design, modular development, and testing. The Pascal language is reviewed throughout the process. As we write the program, we point out the problems encountered when the static data structure (array) is used. These problems are again referred to when dynamic data structures are discussed in Chapters 2 and 3.

Chapter 2 provides a good introduction to dynamic data structures. The chapter introduces the pointer data type in Pascal and shows how to use linked lists. The applications program from Chapter 1 is rewritten using the linked list as the data structure to store the data from the file. Data is added, deleted, modified, and sorted. The important stack and queue data structures are also introduced.

Chapter 3 continues the discussion of dynamic data structures. Stacks and queues are studied in detail along with the basic procedures needed in order to be able to use them. These structures are used in the development of long integer addition and in the evaluation of arithmetic expressions. The chapter introduces other linked lists, the ring, the doubly linked list, and the doubly linked ring. The doubly linked list is used by rewriting some of the basic procedures from the employee program from Chapter 2. After a thorough study of dynamic data structures using linked lists, these ideas are implemented using arrays. Some of the basic procedures for the employee program are again rewritten to illustrate them.

Chapter 4 covers searching and sorting. The linear and binary search techniques are developed and compared. Sorting is introduced by investigating several simple sorting techniques in detail. Following the development of the bubble sort, the selection sort, and the insertion sort, these techniques are modified to lead to ones that are more efficient: the bubble sort with flag, the modified selection sort, and the binary insertion sort. The chapter also contains a detailed analysis of how to measure the efficiency of these various sorting techniques.

Chapter 5 is devoted to developing a firm understanding of recursion and the use of recursive functions and procedures. To accomplish this, the reader is led through the recursive process for both recursive functions and recursive procedures. Each of these detailed discussions includes not only a walkthrough for the Pascal coding but also a detailed, step-by-step analysis of the run-time stack for each stage of the recursive process. Thus this chapter provides the in-depth understanding of the recursive process mandatory for any programmer who plans to use recursion.

Chapter 6 provides an excellent introduction to the tree data structure. Beginning with basic definitions, the chapter develops several very interesting applications of binary trees. These include an inventory program, a cross-reference table generator program, and a message decoding program. The trees in these applications are created using the Pascal pointer type. The last section in the chapter develops the use of trees by using static arrays rather than the Pascal pointer type.

In Chapter 7 the development of trees continues with the investigation of several advanced topics. These include threaded trees, balanced AVL trees, and B-trees. The extensive discussions and explanations relating to each of these topics provide the reader with step-by-step walk-throughs. The objective is a thorough understanding of each of the topics.

Chapter 8 includes several advanced sorting techniques, including the shellsort, tree selection sort, heapsort, and quicksort. In order to help students understand each of the sorts, we have included step-by-step walk-throughs and numerous figures.

The study of files in Chapter 9 reviews the basic file of characters (text) used in Pascal; it also discusses other types of files and compares them with text files. Some of the procedures for the employee program from Chapters 1 and 2 are rewritten using a more general file of records. Since files can store collections of data too large to store in internal memory, we include a discussion of some external sorting techniques, including merging of files. We also introduce the important topic of hashing and develop some hashing functions and techniques. The use of these techniques is illustrated with an application to the employee program. Finally, we use Microsoft Pascal to introduce the topic of random access files. Some of the basic procedures from the employee program are rewritten to illustrate the use of these files.

The last chapter (Chapter 10) introduces graphs and uses Pascal and the Pascal pointer type to create and manipulate them. An airline example helps the reader to understand the techniques involved in creating and deleting arcs and then searching for paths within the graph. Obviously, a complete study of graphs and graph theory would require much more than a single chapter. However, the chapter should sufficiently motivate the reader to continue study in this fascinating and very useful area of computer science.

Acknowledgments

The authors are grateful to the many people who helped with the development of this text. First of all, we would like to express our thanks to our families who put up with us during the hundreds of hours required for writing, rewriting, editing, and proofing. We certainly wish to express our thanks to Pam Kirshen and Marret McCorkle at D. C. Heath.

We also would like to acknowledge those who reviewed the manuscript: Carter Bays, University of South Carolina; Thomas Copeland, Middlebury College; Henry A. Etlingler, Rochester Institute of Technology; Michael A. Grajek, Hiram College; John A. Koch, Wilkes College; Ronald Peterson, Weber State College; Edwin D. Reilly, State University of New York at Albany; R. Waldo Roth, Taylor University; David Stemple, University of Massachusetts; and Chip Weems, University of Massachusetts.

G. J. H.
R. J. E.

Contents

Applied Data Structures Using Pascal

Introduction

In this chapter we introduce the study of data structures. An introduction to the study of data structures could begin with a brief outline and review of the syntax in Pascal. However, very little new is ever learned by just doing a quick review of individual Pascal statements, functions, etc. Also, no computer language is worthwhile unless it can be applied to actual programming applications, and Pascal is no exception. Thus we have not taken the review approach in this first introductory chapter.

Since the phrase "a picture is worth a thousand words" is certainly applicable in computer science, this first chapter will introduce data structures through a specific application program. We will write a program to maintain a collection of employee data that is stored in a file. While writing the program we will illustrate modular development and testing. Throughout the example we will review much of the Pascal language. This example and most others in the text were developed and tested on a Cyber computer system using the Pascal 6000 compiler developed at the Federal Institute of Technology in Zurich, Switzerland. The programs have since been rewritten to reflect the current style.

As you probably already know, there are several different Pascal compilers available for various computer systems. Since no specific national or international standards exist for the Pascal language, there are differences in syntax among these various compilers. Also, there are wider variations among the various computer systems with regard to JCL, character sets, word size, etc. Thus you may have to make software- and hardware-dependent changes in the code included in this text so that the code can be run on your particular system. By JCL (Job Control Language) we mean the operating system commands that are needed to write, compile, run, etc., Pascal programs. In many situations, we will point out where different Pascal compilers may vary. Several Pascal compilers will be discussed in Appendix A. As much as possible, the examples in this text will be coded so that the standard syntax of Pascal, as suggested by Wirth, is used. Thus in most situations very few changes will have to be made in the code for different compilers and systems. However, codes for such functions as clearing the screen, reversing video on the screen, reading from files, printing files, etc., will vary depending on the software and the hardware that you have available to use for writing and testing these various programs, examples, and exercises. One of the major differences among the various versions of Pascal is in how each of them handles files. Some of these differences will be pointed out in Appendix A.

Most of the programs that you have written in previous classes have probably been fairly short ones. These programs were usually written to illustrate new programming concepts. In this section we will illustrate the steps that should be taken in writing a larger application program. In order to facilitate debugging, large programs should be written using the concepts of modular design and modular testing. We have all seen large programs (such as operating systems) that are put into use in spite of bugs that programmers are still trying to fix. Many times, projects that have consumed years of effort are discarded because it is impossible to discover why they will not work. The difficulty of debugging a program increases rapidly with the size of the program. Throughout this text we will be introducing you to new data structures by writing and testing subprograms (modules) that can be used in our application-programming example.

A computer is a tool that allows people to manipulate large amounts of data. The study of computer science teaches us how to use computers and how to organize the data so that they can be manipulated by a program. For a collection of data to be maintained by a computer program, the data must be organized and stored so that the program is able to access the information. The programmer must choose a data structure that can be built by the program to store some or all of the data while they are being modified or updated. By a *data structure* we simply mean a structure that can be used to store a given collection of data.

This text will concentrate on introducing you to various data structures available in the Pascal language, showing you how they are built and how they are used in programs. The text will also discuss how you can decide which data structures are appropriate for a given program. Some of these structures, such as the array, the record, and the file, you should have already seen and used. We will review these structures and will show how Pascal can be used to build other data structures, such as the linked list and the tree.

In this text we will also discuss various techniques, or algorithms, that can be used to maintain data after they have been stored in a data structure. You will be led through the development of each algorithm and shown how each algorithm can be used with a specific example.

The program that we will write in this chapter will allow the user to maintain information on a collection of employees. This information will be stored in a file. The program will allow the user to add information to the collection, delete information from the collection, change any of the information, and obtain a printout of the data. Each of these procedures will be discussed in more detail in the section where we write the subprogram appropriate for the particular task.

The array is the one data structure that is available in most languages and, as we have stated, is the structure that we will use in our program. As we write the program that will allow the user to maintain the collection of data, we will point out some of the problems that we encounter when arrays are used to store the data. Some of the newer languages, such as Pascal, have a feature that allows us to build structures that will help us overcome some of these problems. This feature is the pointer data type. The pointer and the structures that we can build using pointers will be discussed in detail in later chapters.

The files that we will be using to store the data for our application program will be character files, which are called text files in Pascal. The data are stored in a file of this type as characters, using the character coding system for the particular computer. The character code may be ASCII, EBCDIC, or another code developed for a particular computer system (such as was done on the Cyber).

This text will introduce you to a programming method that many students have found to be the most useful for developing and writing a large program. Following the concept of top-down design, the more difficult modules of the programs will be outlined in pseudocode before they are written. A technique for testing program modules is described, and you will be asked to write and test some of the modules on your computer system.

The pseudocode that we will be using will consist of a sequence of English-like sentences that outline a given program or subprogram. We will make use of all of the structures that are built into the Pascal programming language, including the case structure. The outline will be written in such a way that the translation to a programming language that utilizes all the programming structures will be straightforward. The structures that are used in the pseudocode will be presented in upper-case letters, and the variable identifiers that are to be used in the program will be presented in boldface.

All of the programs in this text will be written in lower case, with upper-case and lower-case letters used for the comments, identifiers, and program and procedure names. You may want to use all upper-case, all lower-case, or some mixture of upper-case and lower-case letters depending on what you like to use. The choice of which style to use is certainly a minor aspect of programming; it depends on the specific likes of the programmer and on the computer system that is being used to write and run the programs.

1.1 Maintaining Employee Data

Let us assume that a collection of data for the employees of a given company is stored in a file. Assume that the file has at most 50 lines of data, that each line contains the data for one employee, and that the data are stored in the following format.

$$\begin{array}{lll} \text{Columns} & 1\text{–}20 & \text{Name} \\ & 21\text{–}31 & \text{Social Security Number} \\ & 40\text{–}44 & \text{Pay Rate} \end{array}$$

We will use the record structure in Pascal to store the data for each employee and an array of records to store the entire collection of data from the file. We will store the names and the social security numbers as arrays of characters; we will store the pay rates as reals. We will use packed arrays for all of the arrays of characters. (Packed arrays will be discussed in the next section.) We will need the following declarations.

```
const
  Max = 50;                              { Maximum number of
                                           employee records   }
type
  String11 = packed array[1..11] of char;  { One soc. sec. num }
  String20 = packed array[1..20] of char;       { One name }
  EmpInfo = record                          { One employee rec. }
              Name : String20;
              SsNum : String11;
              PayRate : real
            end;
                                            { Array of records }
  EmpArray = packed array[1..Max] of EmpInfo;
var
  Count : integer;                       { Number of records stored }
  Choice : char;                           { User input for choice }
  Done : boolean;                        { To exit program when done }
  Employees : EmpArray;                    { Array for employee data }
  PrtFile,                                 { File for employee report }
  Master : text;                         { Master file of employee data }
```

The program that we will write will allow the user to do the following.

1. Add employee records to the collection.
2. Delete employee records from the collection.
3. Sort the collection of data by name.
4. Search for an employee record with a given social security number and, if it is found, print the information of the employee to the screen.
5. Print a complete list of the employee information to a file in report format.

The program will present the list of options to the user through the use of a menu. We will now outline the program using pseudocode.

Pseudocode

EmployeeList Program

Print sign on message.
Open **Master** file for input.
IF **Master** not empty THEN
    Read data from the file, count the number of employee
      records, and store data in an array of records.
    Set **Done** to false.
    REPEAT
      Print menu.
      Input **Choice**.
      WHILE **Choice** not acceptable
        Print error message.
        Input **Choice**.
      END WHILE.
      CASE **Choice** OF
        'A' : Call procedure to add employee record to array.
        'D' : Call procedure to delete employee record from
            array.
        'S' : Call procedure to sort array of records by name.
        'P' : Call procedure to print report of all employee data
            to a file.
        'O' : Call procedure to search for record with given
            social security number.
        'E' : Set **Done** to true.
      END CASE.
    UNTIL **Done**.
    Open **Master** file for output.
    Write array of records back to **Master** file.
    Print instructions of how to replace old
      Master file with new **Master** file.
    Print instructions of how to obtain printed report.
ELSE
    Print error message.
END IF.

We will write separate procedures to do each of the following.

1. Open the master file for input. Read the data, count the number of records, and store the data in the array of records.
2. Print the menu.
3. Sort the data by name.

4. Add an employee record.
5. Delete an employee record.
6. Locate an employee record with a given social security number.
7. Print a report of all of the employee data to a file.
8. Open the master file for output. Write data from an array back to the master file.
9. Print instructions for replacing the master file. Print instructions for obtaining the employee report.

Before we code the main program using the outline given above, let us discuss what information needs to be passed between the procedures and the calling program. Some of the procedures, such as the procedure to print a sign-on message, will not have to pass any information. Other procedures, such as the procedure to read the data from the file, will have to pass the array to store the data from the file, the count for the number of records stored, and the master file of employee data. We will discuss the parameters for each of the procedures, and then we will code and test the main program.

The procedure to read the data from the file will be called **ReadData**. This procedure will pass the file **Master** as a parameter, since the procedure must read all of the information on the collection of employees. The array of records, **Employees**, will be passed, since the data from the file will be stored in this array. We will also need to pass the parameter **Count**, since the procedure is to count the number of employees and pass this number back to the main program. Thus a call to the **ReadData** procedure will be done with the following statement.

```
ReadData(Master, Employees, Count);
```

The procedure to sort the data by name will be called **SortData**. This procedure will have to pass the array of records, **Employees**, and the number of records stored in the array, **Count**, as parameters. Therefore, a call to the **SortData** procedure will be done with the statement

```
SortData(Employees, Count);
```

The procedure to write the data that is stored in the array **Employees** back to the file **Master** is called **WriteData**. It will have to pass the file, the array of records, and the number of records stored in the array as parameters. Thus a call to the **WriteData** procedure will be done with the statement

```
WriteData(Master, Employees, Count);
```

The procedures to add an employee record to the collection and to delete an employee record from the collection are similar. The procedures are called **AddEmployee** and **DeleteEmployee**, respectively. These procedures need to pass the array of employee records, **Employees**, and the number of records stored in the array, **Count**, as parameters. Thus calls to these procedures will be done with the statements

```
AddEmployee(Employees, Count);
```

and

```
DeleteEmployee(Employees, Count);
```

The procedure to locate an employee record with a given social security number is called **FindOne**. This procedure will need access to the array of employee records, **Employees**, and the number of records stored in the array, **Count**. Therefore a call to this procedure will be done with the statement

```
FindOne(Employees, Count);
```

The procedure to print a master report to the file **PrtFile** is called **PrintData**. This procedure needs to pass the file **PrtFile** as a parameter, along with the array of employees, **Employees**, and the number of records stored in the array **Count**. Thus a call to this procedure will be done with the statement

```
PrintData(PrtFile, Employees, Count);
```

The rest of the procedures simply print information to the user at the screen. These procedures do not have to pass any information and therefore do not need any parameters. The procedure to print a sign-on message is called **SignOn**. The procedure to print the menu of options is called **PrintMenu**. The procedure to print the instructions on how to save the new master file and on how to obtain a copy of the printed report is called **FinalInstructions**. These procedures will be called with the statements

```
SignOn;
PrintMenu;
FinalInstructions;
```

We can now code the main program. We will simply indicate where the declarations and the procedures are to be placed in the program.

```
program EmployeeList(input, output, Master, PrtFile);
{*****************************************************************}
{*          Type and var declarations go here.              *}
{*****************************************************************}
{*              Procedures go here.                         *}
{*****************************************************************}
```

```
begin
  SignOn;
  Reset(Master);
  if not eof(Master) then begin
    ReadData(Master, Employees, Count);
    Done := false;
    repeat
      PrintMenu;
      writeln('Please input your choice.');
      readln(Choice);
      while not (Choice in ['A', 'D', 'S', 'O', 'P', 'E']) do begin
        writeln('The character ', Choice, ' was not acceptable.');
        writeln('Please try again.');
        PrintMenu;
        writeln('Please input your choice.');
        readln(Choice)
      end; { while }
      case Choice of
        'A' : if Count < Max then
                 AddEmployee(Employees, Count)
              else
                 writeln('Sorry, there is no room in the array.');
        'D' : DeleteEmployee(Employees, Count);
        'S' : SortData(Employees, Count);
        'P' : PrintData(PrtFile, Employees, Count);
        'O' : FindOne(Employees, Count);
        'E' : Done := true
      end { case }
    until Done;
    WriteData(Master, Employees, Count);
    FinalInstructions
  end {if}
  else
    writeln('error!! - Master file is empty.')
  {end else}
end.
```

One of the nice features of Pascal is the set structure that is available for use in this type of program. When the user inputs a particular choice, the program must check to make sure that what was input was one of the available choices. If not, the user is to input another choice. Rather than having to use a long, nested, if-then-else structure, we can simply ask whether or not what was input belongs to a set that contains these values. For example, in the above program the choices were the characters 'A', 'D', 'S', 'O', 'P', and 'E'. The set containing these choices is simply coded as

```
['A', 'D', 'S', 'O', 'P', 'E']
```

If **Choice** is the identifier where the user input is stored, we can ask whether or not **Choice** is one of the allowable values with the statement

```
Choice in ['A', 'D', 'S', 'O', 'P', 'E']
```

This statement returns a value of true or false.

In the above discussion we have only used capital letters for the choices that can be input by the user. You can easily modify the code so that it allows either upper-case or lower-case letters for each of the choices. We will ask you to do this as one of the exercises.

As was discussed in the introduction, writing error-free programs is much more difficult when the programs are large. However, if a large program is built in such a way that each module of the program can be tested separately, locating and eliminating bugs is much easier. To test the main program as a module, we first need to write as stubs all of the subprograms (procedures) that are called. A *stub* is a procedure whose main body consists of a single **writeln** statement saying that the procedure has been entered. For example, the **SortData** procedure would be written as a stub as follows.

```
procedure SortData(Emps3 : EmpArray; Ct3 : integer);
begin
   writeln('The SortData procedure was entered.')
end;
```

In this text, whenever the parameters for a given procedure are declared, as was just done, the identifier name that is used will not be the same as the global identifier that was used in the **var** paragraph in the main program. Thus in the above procedure header **Emps3** is used instead of the global **Employees**. The global is used when the procedure is called. In the stubbed procedures all of the parameters will be defined as value parameters. Later in this chapter we will discuss the necessary changes that must be made to code and test individual procedures. At that time we will also discuss how to decide which parameters should be variable parameters and which should be value parameters. We will also consider how these two types of parameters are handled in Pascal.

The stubbed procedures will need to be added to the main program where indicated. After the main program has been written and the stubs have been added, the program is compiled and run. When the program is run, all of the options (procedures) need to be executed. When each of the procedures is called, a message will be printed to the screen saying that the given procedure has been executed. We will ask you to perform this test as one of the exercises.

In the next section we will discuss how the individual procedures are written and tested.

1.2 Pascal and Basic Procedures

In Section 1.1 we discussed the **const**, **type**, and **var** declarations that were needed to define a data structure to store the collection of employee data from a file. The main **EmployeeList** program was written and tested. In this section we will discuss and write some of the procedures that will be needed for the program. We will also review and discuss some features of Pascal and point out which of these features are different on different Pascal compilers.

In the declarations in Section 1.1, we used packed arrays to store the names and the social security numbers. Packed arrays of characters were used for the following reasons.

1. The characters will be stored in memory, with a maximum number of characters stored in a word. Therefore the use of packed arrays will conserve memory.
2. Packed arrays of the same type can be compared directly instead of character by character.
3. Packed arrays can be written an array at a time instead of character by character.
4. On some compilers packed arrays can be read an array at a time instead of character by character.

These ideas will be illustrated when we write some of our procedures. The Pascal compilers on the Cyber and on the Vax will not allow us to read the packed array with one statement. We must read the data one character at a time.

Some of the procedures that we will write for this program will be either the same or nearly the same as the procedures that we will want to write for other programs in later chapters. We will write these procedures in this section and then simply refer back to this section as necessary. The procedures that we will write are **SignOn**, **PrintMenu**, **PrintData**, and **FinalInstructions**. We begin with the **SignOn**\procedure.

The **SignOn** procedure will simply print a series of messages to the screen. These messages can be as fancy as the programmer cares to make them. The sign-on message we develop here will be very simple, and in the exercises we will ask you to rewrite the procedure so that it will work using your compiler. At that time you can write a more sophisticated sign-on message. We outline the procedure using pseudocode.

Pseudocode

SignOn Procedure

Clear screen.
Ring bell.
Enter reverse video.
Print the message
        Employee List

> Program
> centered and enclosed in stars.
> Exit reverse video.
> Ask user to enter any character to continue.
> Input a character.

Compilers differ as to the strings of characters that must be printed or special procedures that must be called to do each of the following.

Enter reverse video.
Clear screen.
Ring bell.
Exit reverse video.

For the Infoton terminal and the Pascal compiler that were used to run these programs, the strings that are listed below were used. These strings will be given as **const** declarations in the main program. The declarations are as follows.

```
const
   EnterVideo  = ':I^>^B';
   ClearScreen = ':I^=';
   RingBell    = ':I^*';
   ExitVideo   = ':I^>^A';
```

As one of the exercises, you will be asked to find out from the terminal manual what strings or special procedures should be used on your computer system and compiler for the above terminal control statements.

Since treatment of interactive input and end-of-line is one place where Pascal compilers generally differ, we will discuss this problem in more detail in Appendix A. We can now code the **SignOn** procedure.

```
{*****************************************************************}
{* SignOn - Procedure to print a SignOn message to the screen. *}
{*          The SignOn message will remain on the screen until  *}
{*          the user inputs any character.                      *}
{*      Parameters -                                            *}
{*          None.                                               *}
{*****************************************************************}
procedure SignOn;
var
   Ch : char;                                    { For user input }
begin
   writeln(ClearScreen);
   writeln(RingBell);
   writeln; writeln; writeln; writeln; writeln;
   writeln; writeln; writeln; writeln; writeln;
   writeln(EnterVideo);
```

```
     writeln('   ****************************************************');
     writeln('   *                                                  *');
     writeln('   *                                                  *');
     writeln('   *                  Employee List                   *');
     writeln('   *                                                  *');
     writeln('   *                     Program                      *');
     writeln('   *                                                  *');
     writeln('   *                                                  *');
     writeln('   ****************************************************');
     writeln(ExitVideo);
     writeln; writeln; writeln; writeln;
     writeln('   Input any character to continue.');
     readln(Ch)
end; { SignOn }
```

The procedure to print the menu will be similar to the one that was just written; therefore we omit the outline.

```
{*******************************************************************}
{* PrintMenu - Procedure to print the user options to the        *}
{*             screen.                                            *}
{*       Parameters -                                            *}
{*             None.                                             *}
{*******************************************************************}
procedure PrintMenu;
begin
  writeln(ClearScreen);
  writeln(RingBell);
  writeln; writeln; writeln; writeln; writeln;
  writeln; writeln; writeln; writeln;
  writeln(EnterVideo);
  writeln('   ****************************************************');
  writeln('   *                                                  *');
  writeln('   *                  Employee List                   *');
  writeln('   *                     Options                      *');
  writeln('   *   A - Add an employee to the list.               *');
  writeln('   *   D - Delete an employee from the list.          *');
  writeln('   *   S - Sort the list of employees by name.        *');
  writeln('   *   P - Print the list of employees to a file.     *');
  writeln('   *   O - Print the record for one employee to the   *');
  writeln('   *       screen.                                    *');
  writeln('   *   E - Exit the program.                          *');
  writeln('   *                                                  *');
  writeln('   ****************************************************');
  writeln(ExitVideo);
  writeln; writeln; writeln; writeln
end; { PrintMenu }
```

The next procedure will be the procedure to print a formatted listing of all of the employee records to a file. This procedure will allow the user to obtain a hard copy of the employee information. The procedure will need the following parameters.

1. The array of employee records will need to be passed to the procedure. This could be done using a value parameter. Recall, however, that when Pascal uses a value parameter, it makes a complete new copy of the information in memory. Since the array of records could be fairly large, we will pass the array of records using a variable parameter.
2. The number of employee records will also need to be passed to the procedure, and this will be done with a value parameter.
3. We will need to write the formatted printout to a file, and all file names must be passed using variable parameters.

When Pascal is used with a printer that accepts carriage controls, in order for a line to be printed at the top of a new page the first character of the line must be a one (1). Most Pascal compilers have a built-in **page** procedure that is used to move the next line of printed output to the top of a new page, however, the **page** procedure is not available on the Pascal compiler on the Cyber. When a file is sent to a printer, the first character of each line is used as a carriage control by the printer and is not printed. The following is a list of typical carriage-control characters.

'1'	Top of a new page.
' '	Single space.
'0'	Double space.
'-'	Triple space.
'+'	Carriage return only, no line feed.

You should review whether or not your printers use carriage controls. We can now code the procedure.

```
{******************************************************************}
{* PrintData - Procedure to print a formatted list of all       *}
{*             employee records to a file.                      *}
{*      var parameters -                                        *}
{*          Pt : Text file to which the formatted list is to    *}
{*               be printed.                                    *}
{*          Ems : Array of employee records.                    *}
{*      value parameters -                                      *}
{*          Cnt : Integer number of employee records.           *}
{******************************************************************}
procedure PrintData(var Pt : text; var Ems : EmpArray;
                    Cnt : integer);
var
  I : integer;                                    { Loop index }
begin
  rewrite(Pt);                             { Open file for input }
  writeln(' Master list of employee data being written ');
  writeln(' to the file. Please wait. ');
  writeln(Pt, '1', ' ' : 56, 'Master Employee List');
  writeln(Pt, ' ', ' ' : 56, '****** ******** ****');
  writeln(Pt); writeln(Pt);
```

```
      writeln(Pt, ' ', ' ' : 35, 'Employee Name', ' ' : 12,
            'Employee SsNum', ' ' : 7, 'Employee Pay Rate');
      writeln(Pt);
      for I := 1 to Cnt do begin
         write(Pt, ' ', ' ' : 35, Ems[I].Name);
         write(Pt, ' ', ' ' : 5, Ems[I].SsNum);
         write(Pt, ' ', ' ' : 51, Ems[I].PayRate : 5 : 2);
         writeln(Pt)
      end { for }
end; { PrintData }
```

The final procedure that we will code in this section is the procedure **FinalInstructions**. This procedure will instruct the user how to obtain a copy of the master list that was printed to the file **Prtfile**. It will also instruct the user how to replace the old master data file that is stored in main memory with the new master data file that has been created by the program. This new master data file contains all of the additions and changes; it is missing the records that were deleted from the array. As before, this procedure is written for the Cyber, and you are asked to rewrite this procedure for your system as one of the exercises. Since the procedure is similar to the **SignOn** procedure, we will omit the outline.

```
{*****************************************************************}
{* FinalInstructions - Procedure to inform the user of how to   *}
{*                     obtain a copy of the master employee     *}
{*                     list if it was printed to the file. It   *}
{*                     also informs the user of how to replace  *}
{*                     the old master file with the new master  *}
{*                     file created by the EmployeeList         *}
{*                     program.                                 *}
{*       Parameters -                                          *}
{*             None.                                            *}
{*****************************************************************}
procedure FinalInstructions;
var
   Ch : char;                            { Character for user input }
begin
   writeln(ClearScreen);
   writeln(RingBell);
   writeln(EnterVideo);
   writeln('  ***********************************************');
   writeln('  *                                           *');
   writeln('  *             Final Instructions            *');
   writeln('  *                                           *');
   writeln('  *      ***   BEFORE LOGGING OFF    ***      *');
   writeln('  *                                           *');
   writeln('  *    In order to obtain a copy of the master *');
   writeln('  *    employee list, you need to send the file *');
   writeln('  *    PrtFile to the printer. This is done   *');
   writeln('  *    with the system command                *');
   writeln('  *            ROUTE,PRTFILE,TC = #           *');
   writeln('  *    # is the number of the printer.        *');
   writeln('  *                                           *');
```

```
   writeln('  *     In order to replace the old master file   *');
   writeln('  *     with the new master file, you need to use  *');
   writeln('  *     the system command                         *');
   writeln('  *            REPLACE,MASTER                       *');
   writeln('  *                                                *');
   writeln('  **************************************************');
   writeln(ExitVideo);
   writeln;
   writeln(' Enter any character to continue.');
   readln(Ch)
end; { FinalInstructions }
```

In order to test a procedure that we have written, we write a program that consists of the minimum amount of code needed to run the procedure. This program is called a **driver**. For example, a driver to test the **SignOn** procedure would be the following. The documentation is omitted to save space.

```
program Driver1(output);
{*          ***   type and variable declarations go here. *** *}
{*          ***   SignOn procedure goes here. ***             *}
begin
   SignOn
end.
```

The driver program is then compiled and run; and the SignOn message should appear on the screen.

Exercises

1.1 Look in your terminal manual and find the strings of characters that have to be printed or special procedures that must be called in order to perform the options that were used in the **SignOn** procedure.

1.2 Rewrite the **SignOn** procedure so that it uses the strings that you found in Exercise 1.1. Rewrite the sign-on message that was printed in our procedure so that it more closely resembles the sign-on messages that you have seen in other programs. Write a driver and test this procedure.

1.3 Rewrite the **PrintMenu** procedure so that it uses the strings that you located in Exercise 1.1. Write a driver and test this procedure.

1.4 Locate the system manual and find out what system commands are used to send a file to the printer and to replace a file that you have in permanent storage with the new file created by the program.

1.5 Rewrite the **FinalInstructions** procedure using what you found in Exercise 1.4 and Exercise 1.1. Write a driver and test this procedure.

1.6 Write all of the procedures that are called by the **EmployeeList** program as stubs. Code the program, including all of the stubbed procedures. Run and test the program.

1.7 Rewrite the main control module so that it allows the user to input either an upper-case or a lower-case character for each choice. If your computer system allows, test this new main control module.

1.3 The ReadData and WriteData Procedures

In order to use external files in a Pascal program on some computer systems, the files must be listed in the program statement, declared in the variable paragraph, and opened for input before any data can be read from the file. A file must be opened for output before any data can be written back to the file. We will be using **Master** as the file that contains the data for the collection of employees and **PrtFile** as the file for our employee-list printout. In order to have a program that allows input from the keyboard and output to the screen and uses text files **Master** and **PrtFile**, we will need the following program statement.

```
program EmployeeList(input, output, Master, Prtfile);
```

We will have to declare **Master** and **PrtFile** as files of characters with the declaration

```
var
   Master, Prtfile : text;
```

The word **text** is a built-in type identifier that stands for the declaration

```
text = file of char;
```

Thus each element of a text file is a single character.

In order for the data from the file **Master** to be read, the file must be opened for input with the statement

```
reset(Master);
```

reset is the built-in Pascal procedure for opening a file for input on some computer systems, such as the Vax and the Cyber. When the reset statement is executed in the program, the following happens.

1. The file pointer is moved to the first element (character) of the file.
2. The first element (character) of the file is moved to the file window.
3. If **Master** is not empty, the Boolean functions **eof(Master)** and **eoln(Master)** are set to false.

Since the file **Master** is to contain data in the format

Columns 1–20 Name
21–31 Social Security Number
40–44 Pay Rate

on each line of the file, the program will read the name and the social security number one character at a time as character data. The pay rate will be read as a real number. As was pointed out in Section 1.1, the data will be stored in an array of records where each record will store one line of data from the file. If **Emps1** is the array of records, the Ith line of data is read into the Ith component of the array, **Emps1[I]**. If the file pointer is at the first character of the Ith line, the name is read and stored in the **Name** field of **Emps1[I]** with the code

```
for J := 1 to 20 do
  read(Master, Emps1[I].Name[J]);
```

The file pointer is now at the twenty-first character of the line, which is the first character of the social security number. The code to read and store this data item is the following.

```
for J := 1 to 11 do
  read(Master, Emps1[I].SsNum[J]);
```

When a numeric is read, blanks are skipped, so even though the file pointer is at the thirty-second position and the pay rate is in columns 40 through 44, the pay rate is read with the code

```
read(Master, Emps1[I].PayRate);
```

In order to move the file pointer to the first character of a new line, if it exists, and to check for end-of-file, the following statement is used.

```
readln(Master);
```

This statement will set the Boolean function **eof(Master)** to true if there is not another line in the file. The two statements

```
read(Master, Emps1[I].PayRate);
readln(Master);
```

can be replaced with the single statement

```
readln(Master, Emps1[I].PayRate);
```

Furthermore, if the **with** statement is used, the above code can be replaced with the following block of code.

```
with Emps1[I] do begin
  for J := 1 to 20 do
    read(Master, Name[J]);
  for J := 1 to 11 do
    read(Master, SsNum[J]);
  read(Master, PayRate)
end; {* with *}
readln(Master);
```

Note that the record **Emps1[I]** does not have to be referenced directly in any of the **read** statements. The **with** statement will be used when we code the **ReadData** procedure, and the last **read** and the **readln** will not be replaced with a single **readln** statement. In order to emphasize the steps in the **ReadData** procedure, we prefer to code these statements separately. We can now outline the procedure.

Pseudocode

> **ReadData Procedure**
>
> Set **Count** to 0.
> WHILE not end of file
>   Increment **Count**.
>   Read name and store in **Name** field of **Emps1(Count)**.
>   Read social security number and store in **SsNum** field of
>   **Emps1(Count)**.
>   Read pay rate and store in **PayRate** field of
>   **Emps1(Count)**.
>   Move file pointer to next line and check for end of file.
> END WHILE.

The procedure needs to pass the file name as a parameter (recall that file names must be passed as variable parameters in Pascal). The data that are to be stored in the array need to be returned to the calling program, and so does the count of the number of records that has been read from the file. Thus the array and the count will be passed using variable parameters. The procedure is written assuming that the main program opens the data file and checks for an initial end of file. We can now code the procedure.

```
{*****************************************************************}
{* ReadData - Procedure to read the data from a text file,      *}
{*            store it in an array of records, and count the    *}
{*            number of records. It expects the data in the     *}
{*            format:  Columns   1 - 20   Name                  *}
{*                              21 - 31   Social Security Num    *}
{*                              40 - 44   Pay rate               *}
{*      var parameters -                                         *}
{*          Mas1 : Text file containing the data.               *}
{*          Emps1 : Array of records to return the data.        *}
{*          Ct1 : Integer to return the number of records.      *}
{*      value parameters -                                       *}
{*          None.                                               *}
{*****************************************************************}
procedure ReadData(var Mas1 : text; var Emps1 : Emparray;
                var Ct1 : integer);
var
  I : integer;                              { Loop index }
begin
```

```
Ct1 := 0;
while not eof(Mas1) do begin            { Loop to read data }
  Ct1 := Ct1 + 1;
  with Emps1[Ct1] do begin
    for I := 1 to 20 do
      read(Mas1, Name[I]);
    { end for }
    for I := 1 to 11 do
      read(Mas1, SsNum[I]);
    { end for }
    read(Mas1, PayRate)
  end; { with }
  readln(Mas1)                          { Move to new line and
                                          check for end of file }

end { while }
end; { ReadData }
```

Once the data have been read and stored in the array of records, they can be modified as needed by the user. After the user is done with any needed modifications, the data are to be written back to the file in exactly the same format as originally stored. Since we are using packed arrays of characters for the name, the address, and the social security number, these strings can be written an array at a time. If the file pointer is at the first position of the Ith line, the name can be written in columns 1–20 with the statement

```
write(Mas2, Emps2[I].Name);
```

The social security number can be written in columns 21–31 with the statement

```
write(Mas2, Emps2[I].SsNum);
```

Since the file pointer is now at position 32 of the line and the pay rate is to be printed in the form XX.XX in columns 40–44, the following statement is used.

```
write(Mas2, Emps2[I].PayRate : 12 : 2);
```

This statement prints the pay rate right justified with two decimal places in the twelve-place field. The end-of-line marker is then inserted with the statement

```
writeln(Mas2);
```

The file name needs to be passed as a variable parameter. The array of records and the number of records will also have to be passed as parameters; however, since they are not to be changed, they can be passed as value parameters. Since an array of records is being passed, it will be passed as a variable parameter in order to save memory (recall the discussion from Section 1.2). We can now code the procedure.

```
{***********************************************************}
{* WriteData - Procedure to write the data back to a text file *}
{*            from an array of records. The data are to be     *}
{*            written in the following format.                 *}
{*            Columns  1 - 20   Name                           *}
{*                     21 - 31  Social Security Number         *}
{*                     40 - 44  Pay Rate                       *}
{*        var parameters -                                     *}
{*            Mas2 : Text file where data are to be written.   *}
{*            Emps2 : Array of records containing the data     *}
{*        value parameters -                                   *}
{*            Ct2 : Integer containing number of records.      *}
{***********************************************************}
procedure WriteData(var Mas2 : text; var Emps2 : EmpArray;
                    Ct2 : integer);
var
  I : integer;                                    { Loop index }
begin
  rewrite(Mas2);                          { Open file for output }
  for I := 1 to Ct2 do begin              { Write records to file }
    with Emps2[I] do begin
      write(Mas2, Name);
      write(Mas2, SsNum);
      write(Mas2, Pay Rate : 13 : 2)
    end; { with }
    writeln(Mas2)                         { Insert end of line }
  end { for }
end; { WriteData }
```

Now that we have written the two procedures **ReadData** and **WriteData**, we will want to write a driver to test these two procedures. As we discussed in Section 1.2, this means that we will want to write a short program that will simply call these two procedures. We will need to create a file, **Master**, of data. The testing procedure will do the following.

1. Obtain a listing of **Master**.
2. Run the driver program.
3. Obtain a listing of **Master**.

We will then compare the two listings to make sure that they are identical. We can use the following as a driver to test the two procedures. To conserve space we will omit the program documentation for this driver.

```
program Driver2(Master);
{*       *** Type and variable declarations go here. ***    *}
{*       *** ReadData procedure goes here. ***              *}
{*       *** WriteData procedure goes here. ***             *}
begin
  ReadData(Master, Employees, Count);
  WriteData(Master, Employees, Count)
end.
```

We will ask you to perform this test as one of the exercises.

Exercises

1.8 Check to see if your compiler allows you to read a whole array at a time if it is a packed array of characters. If so, rewrite the **ReadData** procedure to make use of this idea.

1.9 Code the program **Driver2** and test the **ReadData** and **WriteData** procedures.

1.10 Write a driver and test the **PrintData** procedure from Section 1.2. You will have to use the data file that you created to test the **ReadData** and **WriteData** procedures. You will use the **ReadData** procedure and do a test similar to the one you did in Exercise 1.6.

1.4 Sort, Add, Delete, and FindOne Procedures

The ability to maintain a large collection of data virtually depends on the ability to have the data sorted according to some key. The key will be one of the fields of the data record. For our collection of employee data, we will probably want to use either the **Name** field or the **SsNum** field. We will use one of the fields in this discussion and ask you to use the other field in the exercises. Certainly we can use many different techniques to sort data, and many of these will be discussed in Chapters 4 and 8 of this text. In this section we will simply pick one of the elementary, less efficient techniques with which you are probably familiar. We will write a procedure to sort the data so that the names are in nondecreasing order.

Use of packed arrays will allow us to compare the names directly, a string at a time, without having to compare them character by character. We will now outline the sort procedure, which uses the selection sort technique that will be discussed in more detail in Chapter 4.

Pseudocode

> **SortData Procedure**
>
> FOR **I** = 1 to **Count** − 1
>   FOR **J** = **I** + 1 to **Count**
>   IF **Emps3(I)(Name)** > **Emps3(J)(Name)** THEN
>   switch **Emps3(I)** with **Emps3(J)**.
>   END IF.
>   END FOR.
> END FOR.

In order to perform the statement

switch **Emps3(I)** with **Emps3(J)**.

we need a temporary identifier of the same type, say **Temp** of type **Emp-Info**, and we use the three statements

Move **Emps3(I)** to **Temp**.
Move **Emps3(J)** to **Emps3(I)**.
Move **Temp** to **Emps3(J)**.

We will need to pass the array of records as a variable parameter, since the data in the array are to be changed. The number of records in the array will be passed as a value parameter. We can now code the procedure.

```
{**********************************************************************}
{* SortData - Procedure to sort the data contained in an array *}
{*            of records into nondecreasing order by name.     *}
{*      var parameters -                                       *}
{*          Emps3 : Array of employee records.                 *}
{*      value parameters -                                     *}
{*          Ct3 : Integer number of records in Emps3.          *}
{**********************************************************************}
procedure SortData(var Emps3 : EmpArray; Ct3 : integer);
var
   I, J : integer;                              { Loop indices }
   Temp : EmpInfo;                           { Temporary storage }
begin
   for I := 1 to Ct3 - 1 do
     for J := I + 1 to Ct3 do
       if Emps3[I].Name > Emps3[J].Name then begin
         Temp := Emps3[I];                      { Switch records }
         Emps3[I] := Emps3[J];
         Emps3[J] := Temp
       end { if }
     { end for }
   { end for }
end; { SortData }
```

The next procedure that we want to discuss is the procedure to allow the user to add an employee record to the collection of data. The data will be entered from the keyboard. The procedure will be written so that it allows the user to enter one employee record. In order for an employee record to be added, the data need to be entered from the keyboard and then the record needs to be inserted into the array of records in order by name. We will use the following basic technique: If the data are to be inserted into the Ith position in the array, all of the records in the array from the Ith position to the last position will be moved down one position in the array. (This technique is unfortunately very inefficient, since a number of moves must be made in order to insert a single element into the structure. This inefficiency is another of the problems that we encounter using arrays for our data structures.) After the elements of the array have been moved, the new element can be inserted into the array. The main program will check to make sure that **Count** < **Max** before the procedure is called. We begin by outlining the procedure.

Pseudocode

AddEmployee Procedure

Input name.
Input social security number.
Input pay rate.
Store data in record **Temp**.
Set **I** to 1.
WHILE (**Name** > **Emps4(I)(Name)**) and (**I** < **Count**)
    Increment **I**.
END WHILE.
IF **Name** < **Emps4(I)(Name)** THEN
    FOR **K** = **Count** DOWNTO **I**
        Move **Emps4(K)** to **Emps4(K + 1)**.
    END FOR.
    Move **Temp** to **Emps4(I)**.
    Increment **Count**.
ELSE
    Increment **Count**.
    Move **Temp** to **Emps4(Count)**.
END IF.

The procedure will pass the array as a variable parameter, since the data in the array will be changed. The count will also be passed as a variable parameter, since it too will change values. We can now code the procedure.

```
{***************************************************************}
{* AddEmployee - Procedure to add an employee record to the    *}
{*               array of employee records in order by name.   *}
{*               It assumes that the array of records has been  *}
{*               sorted in nondecreasing order by name.        *}
{*      var parameters -                                        *}
{*          Emps4 : Array of employee records.                 *}
{*          Ct4 : Integer number of employee records.          *}
{*      value parameters -                                      *}
{*          None.                                               *}
{***************************************************************}
procedure AddEmployee(var Emps4 : EmpArray; var Ct4 : integer);
var
  I,K : integer;                             { Loop index }
  Temp : EmpInfo;                    { Temporary employee record }
begin
  with Temp do begin
                                             { Input the name }
    writeln('Please input employee name.');
    writeln('  XXXXXXXXXXXXXXXXXXXX');
    for I := 1 to 20 do
      read(Name[I]);
    { end for }
    readln;
```

```
                                              { Input the social
                                                security number   }
   writeln('Please input the social security number.');
   writeln('   XXX-XX-XXXX');
   for I := 1 to 11 do
     read(SsNum[I]);
   { end for }
   readln;
                                         { Input the pay rate }
   writeln('Please input the pay rate.');
   writeln('   XX.XX');
   readln(PayRate)
 end; { with }
                                   { Find position to insert
                                     new employee record       }
 I := 1;
 while (Temp.Name > Emps4[I].Name) and (I < Ct4) do
   I := I + 1;
 { end while }
 if Temp.Name < Emps4[I].Name then begin
   for K := Ct4 downto I do                { Move records down }
     Emps4[K + 1] := Emps4[K];
   { end for }
   Emps4[I] := Temp;
   Ct4 := Ct4 + 1
 end { if }
 else begin
   Ct4 := Ct4 + 1;
   Emps4[Ct4] := Temp
 end { else }
end; { AddEmployee }
```

We must remember that since we are using an array of records as the data structure for our program, we have a maximum number of components in the array that we can use to store data. Recall that this number is declared at the beginning of the program and cannot be changed while the program is running. This is another of the problems that is encountered when arrays are used for the data structures in a program. The main program must keep track of how many records have been stored to make sure that the user does not try to add too many records. In order for the program to keep track, the add option in the main program was written as follows.

'A' : If **Count** < **Max** THEN
    Call **AddEmployee**.
ELSE
    Print message that there are no more storage locations
        available.

There are other ways in which the new employee records can be added to the collection of data. We will consider some of these in the exercises.

We will now consider the procedure to delete an employee record from the array of employee records. To delete an employee record, we must first search for the record that we want to delete. If the record is found, the procedure should delete the record from the array. If the record is not found, an error message should be printed and the user should then be given the option of trying again. The record will be located using the name of the employee. The name is to be entered from the keyboard by the user. In order to make the routine one that we can modify fairly easily, we will write a separate procedure to search for the record. This procedure will be called **FindEmployee** and will accept a name, the array of records, the number of records in the array, and a Boolean variable as parameters. The Boolean variable will be used to indicate whether or not the record was found. We begin by outlining the procedure.

Pseudocode

DeleteEmployee Procedure

REPEAT
   Input name.
   Call procedure **FindEmployee**.
   IF **Found** THEN
     IF **Num** <> **Count** THEN
       FOR **I** = **Num** to **Count** − 1
         Move **Emps5(I + 1)** to **Emps5(I)**.
       END FOR.
     END IF.
     Decrement **Count**.
   ELSE
     Print message that record not found.
     Ask user if wants to try again.
     Input **Choice**('Y' - Yes, 'N' - No).
UNTIL **Found** or (**Choice** = 'N').

Note that this procedure simply moves the records in the array from **Num** + 1 through **Count** down one position in the array. This removes the record that was in the **Num** position and leaves a free record at the **Count** position. The number of employees, **Count**, is then decremented. For the special case in which the record to be deleted is in the **Count** position, **Count** merely has to be decremented. The procedure will pass the array and the count as variable parameters, since they may possibly change values. Notice that again our procedure is relatively inefficient, since a number of moves may have to be made in order to delete a single element from the array.

```
{*********************************************************}
{* DeleteEmployee - Procedure to delete one employee record   *}
{*               from the array of employee records.          *}
```

```
{*        var parameters -                                    *}
{*            Emps5 : Array of employee records.              *}
{*            Ct5 : Integer number of employee records.       *}
{*        value parameters -                                  *}
{*            None.                                           *}
{**************************************************************}
procedure DeleteEmployee(var Emps5 : EmpArray;
                         var Ct5 : integer);
var
  Num,
  I : integer;                        { Integer for position }
  Ch : char;                                { Loop index }
  Found : boolean;                     { Input user choice }
  Tname : String20;               { boolean for record found }
                                       { Input name for search }
begin
  repeat
    Ch := 'Y';
    writeln(ClearScreen);
                                             { Input name }
    writeln('Please input the name of the employee.');
    writeln('Input 20 characters, no special characters.');
    writeln('Last name initial first name.');
    writeln('   XXXXXXXXXXXXXXXXXXXX');
    for I := 1 to 20 do
      read(Tname[I]);
    { end for }
    readln;
    FindEmployee(Emps5, Ct5, Tname, Num, Found);    { Search for
                                                      employee }

    if Found then begin
      writeln('Name found, record being deleted.');
      if Num <> Ct5 then        { Element not last element }
        for I := Num to Ct5 - 1 do
          Emps5[I] := Emps5[I+1];
        { end for }
      { end if }
      Ct5 := Ct5 - 1
    end { if }
    else begin
      writeln('Employee ', Tname, ' not found.');
      writeln('Do you wish to try again?');
      writeln('Enter Y - Yes, N - No');
      readln(Ch)
    end; { else }
  until Found or (Ch = 'N')
end; { DeleteEmployee }
```

We will now write the **FindEmployee** procedure. The method that we will use to search for the record with the given name will be a simple linear search. By a linear search we mean that we simply make a pass through the array of records, looking at each name. If we find the record with the given name, we assign the position of the record to **Num** and set **Found** to true. We can now outline the procedure.

Pseudocode

FindEmployee Procedure

Set index to 0.
Set Boolean to false.
FOR **J** = 1 to **Ct6**
   IF **TName** = **Emps6**[**J**] THEN
      Set index to **J**.
      Set Boolean to true.
   END IF.
END FOR.

We will pass the array of records as a variable parameter (in order to save space), the number of records as a value parameter, the name of the employee that we are searching for as a value parameter, the position in the array as a variable parameter, and the Boolean variable as a variable parameter. We can now code the procedure.

```
{*********************************************************}
{* FindEmployee - Procedure to search the given array of  *}
{*               employee records for the given name. If the *}
{*               name is found, the position in the array is *}
{*               returned and the boolean Fnd is returned as *}
{*               true. If the name is not found, the boolean *}
{*               is returned as false.                    *}
{*      var parameters -                                  *}
{*          Emps6 : Array of employee records.            *}
{*          Num6 : Integer position of given record in array *}
{*               if found, and 0 if not found.            *}
{*          Fnd : Boolean returned as true if found, and as *}
{*               false if not found.                      *}
{*      value parameters -                                *}
{*          Ct6 : Integer number of records in the array. *}
{*          Name6 : String containing name to look for.   *}
{*********************************************************}
procedure FindEmployee(var Emps6 : EmpArray; Ct6 : integer;
                       Name6 : String20; var Num6 : integer;
                       var Fnd6 : boolean);
var
  J : integer;                                  { Loop index }
begin
  Num6 := 0;
  Fnd := false;
  for J := 1 to Ct6 do                  { Linear search loop }
    if Name6 = Emps6[J].Name then begin
      Num6 := J;
      Fnd6 := true
    end { if }
  { end for }
end; { FindEmployee }
```

Instead of using a Boolean variable to keep track of whether or not the employee record was found, we can use the temporary index, which is initially set to 0. When the record is located, the temporary index is set to that index. Thus we can tell whether or not the record was located by examining the value of the temporary index. Either a method that uses a Boolean variable or a method that uses the index is acceptable.

The **FindOne** procedure is similar to the **FindEmployee** procedure that we have just written. This procedure will need the array of records and the number of employees passed by the calling program. The social security number will be input by the user and this is done in the procedure. The procedure will then search for an employee record with the social security number and, if it is found, print the information of the employee to the screen. We will write this procedure as one of the exercises.

Exercises

1.11   Write a driver program to test the **SortData** procedure.

1.12   Write a driver program to test the **AddEmployee** procedure.

1.13   Write a driver program to test the **DeleteEmployee** procedure.

1.14   Before character data are sorted, we must make sure that they contain allowable characters and are in the proper format. How would each of the following names have to be modified in order to be included in our data file?

SMITH, ALBERT   Smith George
SMITH AL   Smith, Alec G
SMITH ALICE   Smith J. R.

1.15   Rewrite the **AddEmployee** procedure so that it allows the user to add as many employee records as the user wishes. The procedure should make sure that the user does not try to add so many records that the total number exceeds **Max**. The records can be added at the end of the list of records, and then the **SortData** procedure can be called to move the records to the correct positions. Write a driver and test this procedure.

1.16   Rewrite the **FindEmployee** procedure so that it does not use a Boolean identifier. The procedure should return the index with a value of 0 if the record was not found. Write a driver to test this procedure.

1.17   After all of the procedures and the main program have been modified to run on your Pascal compiler, code and run the **EmployeeList** program.

1.18   One procedure that can be added to the **EmployeeList** program is a procedure to allow the user to modify any of the data fields on any of the employee records. Write a procedure that will allow the user to do this. Write a driver to test this procedure.

1.19   Write the **FindOne** procedure. Write a driver and test this procedure.

Summary

In this beginning chapter we have discussed in detail the creation of a rather large applications program that we have written in Pascal. We have reviewed some of the features of Pascal and how these features help us design and write this kind of a program. The programs were created using top-down design. The only structures that were used in this program are the array, the record, and the set structure. The array is a static data structure because the size of the structure must be declared at the beginning of the program and cannot be changed while the program is running. In fact, the program must be modified in order to change the size of the structure. In Chapters 2 and 3 we will study structures that can be used where the size of the structure can be changed by the program. These data structures are called *dynamic data structures*.

The main program was then written and tested, and the subroutines were written one at a time. As we developed the program, we pointed out some of the differences in Pascal compilers. This was done so that you will be aware of some of the things you must check for before starting to write a program using a compiler with which you are not familiar.

We pointed out some of the limitations and inefficiencies that a programmer would encounter using static data structures to code this type of a program. In Chapters 2 and 3 we will see how these limitations can be overcome if we build dynamic data structures to store data.

The only files that we have used in this chapter are text files (that is, files of characters). In Chapter 9 we will see how we can use other files (including binary files) to store our data. We will do some comparisons to see how much faster data can be accessed from a binary file than from a text file.

Chapter Exercises

Program 1   A file is to contain at most 100 records of inventory data. Each record of data is stored on one line of a text file in the following format.

Columns		
1– 7	Inventory Number	7 characters
8–27	Description	20 characters
30–32	Quantity on Hand	Integer
35–36	Reorder Number	Integer
40–45	Cost of Item	Real
50–55	Selling Price	Real

The next few exercises involve writing a program that will allow the user to maintain the above collection of data.

1.20   Write the constant, type, and variable declarations that are needed to build an array of records as the data structure to store the data from the file.

1.21   In order to permit maintenance of the collection of inventory data, the program should allow the user to choose any of the following options:
(a) Sort the data by inventory number.
(b) Add an inventory record to the collection.
(c) Delete an inventory record from the collection.
(d) Modify an inventory record by changing any of the fields.
(e) Post the data from the sales at the end of a day.
(f) Post the data from orders received.
(g) Print out an inventory report.
(h) Print out a list of items to be reordered.
Using pseudocode, outline the program that will allow the user to do all of the above.

1.22   Using the outline from Exercise 1.20, write and test the main control module. All of the called procedures should be written as stubs.

1.23   Write the procedure that will read the data from the file, count the number of records, and store the data in the array of records. Write the procedure that will write the data stored in the array back to the same master file. Write a driver and test the two procedures.

1.24   Write the procedure that will allow the user to add an inventory record to the array. Write a driver and test this procedure.

1.25   Write the procedure that will allow the user to delete an inventory record from the array. Write a driver and test this procedure.

1.26   Write the procedure that will allow the user to modify an inventory record by changing any of the fields. Write a driver and test this procedure.

1.27   Write a procedure that will print out an inventory report. The report should be printed to a file. Write a driver and test this procedure.

1.28   Write a procedure that will print out a list of all of the inventory items that need to be ordered. The list should include the number on hand, the reorder number, and the inventory number for each of the items. Write a driver and test this procedure.

1.29   Write a procedure that will allow the user to post the sales and the orders received. This can be done with one procedure if the number sold is entered as a negative integer and the number received is entered as a positive integer. Write a driver and test this procedure.

1.30   Once you have written and tested each of the modules for the program, write and test the complete program.

Program 2   A file is to contain at most 100 records of data from an address book. Each line of the file contains a record of data in the following format.

Columns	1–20	Name	20 characters
	21–64	Address	Record
	21–35	Street	15 characters
	36–49	City	14 characters
	50–59	State	10 characters
	60–64	Zip Code	5 characters
	65–76	Telephone Number	12 characters

1.31   Write the constant, type, and variable declarations that are needed to build an array of records as the data structure to store the data from the file.

1.32   In order to permit maintenance of this collection of address data, the program should allow the user to choose any of the following options.
(a) Sort the data by name.
(b) Add an address to the collection.
(c) Delete an address from the collection.
(d) Modify an address by changing any of the fields.
(e) Print out a list of all of the records with a given zip code.
(f) Print out a list of all of the records with a given city.
(g) Print out a complete list of addresses.
Using the same ideas that were explained in detail in Program 1 of this set of exercises, write and test each of the individual modules of the program and then put these modules together to form the final program.

CHAPTER 2

Linked Lists

A *static data structure* is a data structure that remains fixed throughout its lifetime. As we have seen, the Pascal types **array** and **record** allow us to define static data structures. For example, the declarations

```
const
  Max = 25;

var
  Nums1, Nums2 : array[1..Max] of integer;
```

define static data structures **Nums1** and **Nums2**, each of which stores a maximum of 25 integers. The memory for these structures is set aside before the program begins execution, and the size of this allocation cannot be changed while the program is running.

A *dynamic data structure*, on the other hand, is a structure that can change in size while the program is running. In this chapter we will discuss dynamic data structures that we can build and use in place of arrays.

In order to see why dynamic data structures are useful, let us refer back to Chapter 1, where we considered the problem of maintaining the information for a collection of employees. The data for a single employee were stored in a record that was defined with the following **type** declarations.

```
type
  String11 = packed array[1..11] of char;
  String20 = packed array[1..20] of char;
  EmpInfo = record
              Name : String20;
              SsNum : String11;
              PayRate : real
            end;
```

In Chapter 1 we used an array of these records as the data structure in the program to store the data. We had to decide in advance the maximum number of records of information that the array should hold. This amount of memory was set aside for use by the program, even if the file contained only four or five records of information.

Other problems were encountered in Chapter 1 when records of data were being added or deleted from the list. Since an array was used as the data structure, deleting an element from the list involved either leaving a gap in the array of data or moving all of the remaining elements in the list up one position. When elements were to be added to the array and the array did not contain any gaps, it was necessary to search for the position where each element would be inserted. After the correct position for an element had been located, all of the elements from that position on in the array were moved down one position. The element was then inserted into the array. As we pointed out, this method is inefficient in terms of the number of moves that have to be made to insert a single record of data.

In order to solve these problems efficiently, we need a data structure that will allow new elements to be created as they are needed and old elements to be disposed of when they are no longer needed by the program. We would also like to be able to insert a new element directly into the list in its proper location without having to move the other elements of the list. The tool that will allow us to create such a data structure is the *pointer*. The pointer is available in Pascal and in other languages such as PL/1 and C; but it is not, however, available in all high-level languages.

In this chapter we will study the pointer and how it can be used to build dynamic data structures.

2.1 Pointer Variables

The type *pointer* is a simple Pascal data type. It is simple in the sense that it cannot be broken down into smaller components. A pointer variable is used to create another variable of a given data type. The new variable is called a *dynamic variable*. In the following paragraphs we will look at how pointer variables are used to create dynamic variables. We should point out that the word *pointer* is not a reserved word in Pascal, since it is not used in defining a pointer variable or in creating dynamic variables.

Pointer variables are defined as follows.

```
type
   Item = (some data type);
   Link = ↑Item;
```

On some computer systems and many printers, the up arrow, ↑, is not available. For this reason, most compilers allow the alternative declaration

```
   Link = ^Item;
```

We will use the second declaration throughout this text. This declaration reads as follows.

The type **Link** is a pointer to an identifier of type **Item**

We declare a variable **Pt1** of type **Link** in the usual way:

```
var
    Pt1 : Link;
```

This declaration causes the compiler to name a memory location **Pt1**, the contents of which will be a memory address. As usual, the contents or value of **Pt1** is not yet defined.

Pt1

Even though the pointer variable **Pt1** exists, the corresponding dynamic variable has not yet been created. In order to create a dynamic variable that is to correspond to **Pt1**, the built-in Pascal procedure **new** must be used. The statement

```
new(Pt1);
```

would be used in the program. When this statement is executed a dynamic variable of type **Item** is created, and we say that it is *pointed to* by the pointer variable **Pt1**. The dynamic variable that is created is called **Pt1^**. When the statement **new(Pt1)** is executed, a block of memory is set aside for the new dynamic variable **Pt1^** that is created. The address of this block of memory (that is, of **Pt1^**) is stored at **Pt1**. This point is illustrated in Figure 2.1. The block of memory that is set aside for **Pt1** when it is defined in the variable paragraph is normally one or two words, since this is what is needed to store one address. When the dynamic variable is created with the statement

```
new(Pt1);
```

in a program, the block of memory set aside will vary depending on the **type** declaration for **Item**. Setting aside memory for an identifier in this way (that is, while the program is running) is known as *dynamic memory allocation*.

Figure 2.1

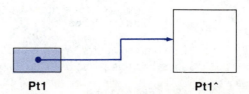

Pt1   **Pt1^**

It is important to understand the distinction between the pointers and the identifiers that they reference. Suppose we have, as before,

```
type
   Item = (some data type);
   Link = ^Item;
var
   P, Q : Link;
```

and we create two new dynamic variables **P^** and **Q^** with the statements

```
new(P);
new(Q);
```

Furthermore, suppose that we have stored appropriate data items at **P^** and **Q^** with the statements

```
P^ := data1;
Q^ := data2;
```

Since the dynamic variables **P^** and **Q^** are pointed to by **P** and **Q**, respectively, the preceding statements give us the situation shown in Figure 2.2.

Figure 2.2

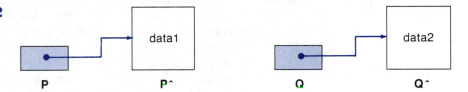

The assignment

```
P := Q;
```

moves the address of **Q^** to **P** so that we have the situation depicted in Figure 2.3. Note that the block of memory containing **data1** is no longer pointed to by a pointer and therefore cannot be referenced by any variable name. On the other hand, the block of memory containing **data2** is pointed to by both **P** and **Q**, so it is referenced by both **P^** and **Q^**.

Figure 2.3

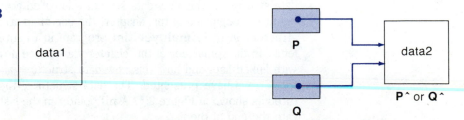

If we had made the assignment

```
P^ := Q^;
```

then we would have the situation shown in Figure 2.4.

Figure 2.4

As we will see, there are times when we will want or need a pointer that does not point to any object. We can create this special situation by using the Pascal built-in constant identifier **nil** and the assignment

```
P := nil;
```

This assignment stores a special value at **P** so that the Pascal compiler knows that there is no block of memory referenced by **P^**. It is meaningless to try to use **P^** in the program as long as **P** is assigned this special value.

Once a dynamic variable is no longer needed in a program, there is no longer any reason to reserve the block of memory that is set aside for it. Most Pascal compilers provide a built-in procedure called **dispose**, which can be used to return (release) this block of memory so that it can be assigned again in the program if it is needed. We can return the block of memory that has been assigned to the dynamic variable **Pt1** by using the statement

```
dispose(Pt1);
```

The Pascal compiler has a block of memory set aside to use for allocation to dynamic pointer variables as they are created with the **new** statement. This block of memory is known as the *Pascal heap*. As each new pointer variable is created with the **new** statement, a portion of the Pascal heap is assigned to this variable. When the **dispose** statement is used, the block of memory that was assigned to the pointer variable is returned to the heap and can be used again in the program.

We will now illustrate how these ideas can be used to build a new kind of data structure. This new data structure is called a *linked list*. As we pointed out at the beginning of this chapter, the use of an array of records as the data structure in the **EmployeeList** program in Chapter 1 caused some problems. In the remainder of this chapter we will see how arrays can be replaced with linked lists and how this new data structure takes care of the problems that arrays have presented. The data structure, the linked list, can be pictured as shown in Figure 2.5. A **nil** pointer in the last element is used to indicate the end of the list.

Figure 2.5

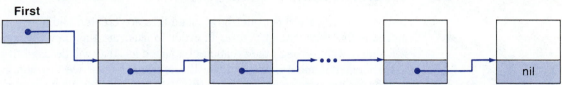

In order to build this structure, we need to generate an object that consists of two components. One of the components holds the data that we want to store in the list, and the other component must be a pointer to another element of the same type. We can create such an object with the type declarations

```
type
   DataType = record
                      Some record of data
              end;
   Item = record
            Data : DataType;
            Next : ItemPtr
          end;
```

where **ItemPtr** must be defined as a pointer type to an object of type **Item**.

We now find ourselves faced with a dilemma: Which do we define first, **ItemPtr** (the pointer to the **Item**) or **Item** (which has **ItemPtr** as one of its components)? When the Pascal language was designed, this problem was, of course, anticipated, and the compiler was written to allow the user to define a pointer to an object before defining the object itself. Therefore, the pointer **ItemPtr** would be defined before **Item**, where **Item** is the element to which **ItemPtr** will point. We would therefore have the following.

```
type
   DataType = record
                      Some record of data
              end;
   ItemPtr = ^Item;
   Item = record
            Data : DataType;
            Next : ItemPtr
          end;
var
   First, P, Q, : ItemPtr;
```

Notice that the data to be stored in the elements of the linked list will vary from program to program. The choice of an identifier name for the pointer field of **Item** is of course up to the programmer. Two commonly used identifier names are **Next** and **Link**.

2.2 Linked Lists—Creation

In this section we will consider how linked lists are created and how data are stored in this new data structure. In order to illustrate this new concept, we will simply walk through the creation of a linked list that will be used to store three integer numbers. We will use the techniques that we develop in this section for our employee data in Section 2.4. The list that we want to create in this section is shown in Figure 2.6.

Figure 2.6

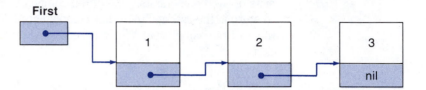

To create this linked list, we must first have the appropriate **type** and **var** declarations. Since the data to be stored in the list are integer data, we need the following declarations.

```
type
  ItemPtr = ^Item;
  Item = record
           Data : integer;
           Next : ItemPtr
         end;
var
  First,                      { Pointer to first element }
  P, Q : ItemPtr;                { General pointers }
```

We begin the creation of the list by creating the first element, storing the first data item, and marking the first element of the list with the pointer **First**. The element is created with the statement

```
new(P);                      { Create first element }
```

which produces the situation illustrated in Figure 2.7. The two components of the object **P^** are referenced by the identifiers **P^.Data** and **P^.Next**. The first data item is stored in the list element with the statement

```
P^.Data := 1;                { Store first data item }
```

Figure 2.7

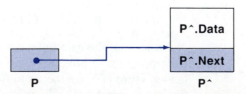

This will give us the situation in Figure 2.8.

Figure 2.8

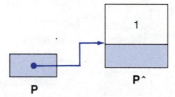

We now want to use the pointer variable **First** to mark the first element of the list. In order to do this, we make **First** point to the first element that we have just created. Therefore we assign the address of **P^** to **First**. Since the address of **P^** is stored at **P**, we mark the head of the list with the statement

```
First := P;            { Mark first element of list }
```

creating the situation shown in Figure 2.9.

Figure 2.9

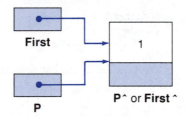

The three statements above can be replaced with the two statements

```
new(First);
First^.Data := 1;
```

The second element is then created, as shown in Figure 2.10, with the statement

```
new(Q);                            { Create second element }
```

The second data item is stored in this new element with the assignment

```
Q^.Data := 2;               { Store second data item }
```

Figure 2.10

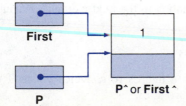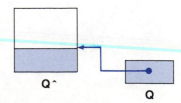

giving us the two elements shown in Figure 2.11.

Figure 2.11

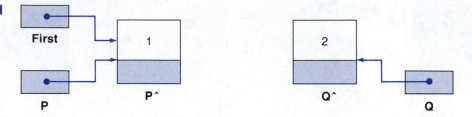

The two list elements now need to be hooked together to form the first two elements in the linked list. In order to hook the two elements together, we must store the address of **Q^** in the address component of **P^**, that is, in **P^.Next**. It is clear that we need a minimum of two pointer variables, one to each element, in order to hook the two elements together. The pointer **P** is pointing to the first element, and the pointer **Q** is pointing to the second element. Since the address of **Q^** is stored at **Q**, the hookup is done with the statement

```
P^.Next := Q;                    { Hook element Q^ to P^ }
```

We now have the list depicted in Figure 2.12.

Figure 2.12

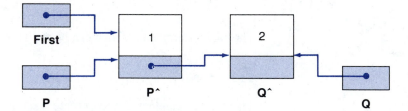

We next move our pointer **P** to the second element of the list so that we can use **Q** to create the third and last element of the list. Since **P** is pointing to the first element of the list and **Q** is pointing to the next element of the list, **P** can be moved with the statement

```
P := Q;                  { Move P to next element }
```

Since **P^** is also pointing to the next element, **P** could also be moved with the statement

```
P := P^.Next;
```

Draw the appropriate figures to convince yourself that the preceding statement results in Figure 2.13.

Figure 2.13

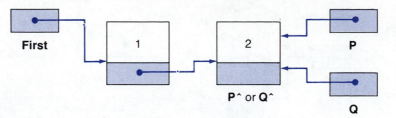

We create the third and last element with the statement

```
new(Q);                        { Create third element }
```

resulting in Figure 2.14. The third data item is stored with the statement

```
Q^.Data := 3;                  { Store third data item }
```

and this last element is hooked into the list with the statement

```
P^.Next := Q;                  { Hook element to list }
```

This gives Figure 2.15.

Figure 2.14

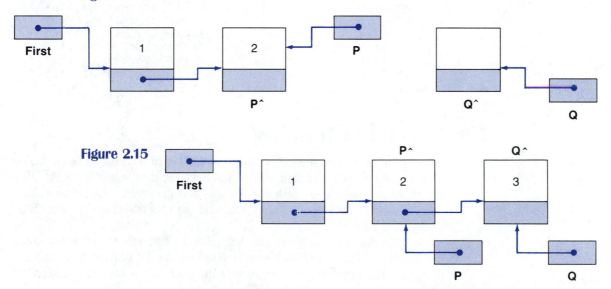

Figure 2.15

The last step in creating the list is to mark the end of the list. This is done with the statement

```
Q^.Next := nil;                   { Mark end of list }
```

creating the completed list illustrated in Figure 2.16.

Figure 2.16

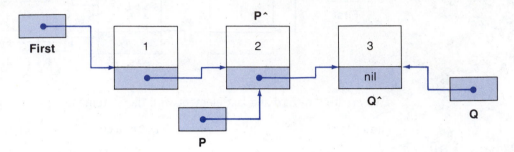

We now write the complete block of code that is needed to build the list and store the data.

```
begin
  new(P);                      { Create first element }
  First := P;                    { Mark head of list }
  P^.Data := 1;              { Store first data item }
  new(Q);                    { Create second element }
  Q^.Data := 2;             { Store second data item }
  P^.Next := Q;        { Hook second element to list }
  P := Q;                     { Move P to next element }
  new(Q);                      { Create last element }
  Q^.Data := 3;              { Store third data item }
  P^.Next := Q;         { Hook third element to list }
  Q^.Next := nil               { Mark end of list }
end.
```

2.3 Linked List Traversal

Once we have created the list, we need to be able to traverse through the list to search for a particular data item or print out the data stored in the list. We will illustrate these ideas with the list that was created in the previous section. We assume that the list is created and the data are stored as illustrated in Figure 2.16.

We will write the statements that will print the data stored in this list to the screen. We will need a pointer to move through the list of data. If the pointer is **P**, then **P** is set to the first element of the list with the following statement.

```
P := First;      { Set P to first element of list }
```

The first data item is written to the screen with the statement

```
writeln(P^.Data);    { Print first data to screen }
```

The pointer is moved to the second element of the list with the statement

```
P := P^.Next;        { Move P to next element }
```

The second data item is printed to the screen with the statement

```
writeln(P^.Data);    { Print second data to screen }
```

The pointer is moved to the last element of the list with the statement

```
P := P^.Next;        { Move P to next element }
```

The last data item is printed to the screen with the statement

```
writeln(P^.Data);    { Print last data to screen }
```

We can tell when the pointer **P** is at the last element of the list by checking to see if the following statement is true.

```
P^.Next = nil;       { Check for end of list }
```

We can move the pointer through the list, stopping at the last element, with the code

```
while P^.Next <> nil do       { Move P through list }
   P := P^.Next;
```

We will illustrate these new concepts with some examples.

Example   Write a procedure to print out the data contained in the list in Figure 2.16. Assume that the list is not empty and contains an arbitrary number of elements.

We will first outline the procedure by writing the pseudocode.

Pseudocode

> **PrintData Procedure**
>
> Set pointer to the first element.
> Write data.
> WHILE pointer not at end of list
>   Move pointer.
>   Write data.
> END WHILE.

We can now code the procedure.

```
procedure PrintData;
var
  P : ItemPtr;                    { Pointer to move through list }
begin
  P := First;                     { Print data first element }
```

```
   writeln(P^.Data);
   while P^.Next <> nil do begin          { Loop for
                                             remainder of list }
      P := P^.Next;
      writeln(P^.Data)
   end    { while }
end; { PrintData }
```

Example   Write a procedure to search for a particular data item. If the data item is found, print out the data. If the data item is not found, print the message "Item not found." The procedure should pass the data item that we are searching for as a parameter.

We will again outline our procedure with pseudocode. As before, we are assuming that the list is not empty.

Pseudocode

FindData Procedure

Set pointer to first element.
WHILE (pointer(Data) <> Data) and (not end of list)
    Move pointer.
END WHILE.
IF Data found THEN
    Write Data.
ELSE
    Write message.
END IF.

We can now code the procedure.

```
procedure FindData(Dta : integer);
var
  P : ItemPtr;                    { Pointer to move through list }
begin
  P := First;
  while (P^.Data <> Dta) and              { Search loop }
        (P^.Next <> nil) do
    P := P^.Next;                             { Move P }
  { end while }
  if P^.Data = Dta then
     writeln('Data item found. ', P^.Data)
  else
     writeln('Data not found')
  { end if }
end; { FindData }
```

Exercises

2.1   Give the type and variable declarations necessary to do each of the following.
(a) Build a linked list to hold integer data items.
(b) Build a linked list to hold real data items.
(c) Build a linked list to hold character data items.

2.2   A file called **DataI** has several lines of data, and each line contains one integer data item. Write the block of code to read the data from the file, store the data in a linked list, and mark both the beginning and the end of the list.

2.3   Write the block of code that will traverse the linked list that was created in Exercise 2.2 and print out the integer data items that are stored in the list to the screen.

2.4   Using the declarations from Exercise 2.1(a), draw the figure that would result for the following block of code:

```
new(P);
Head := P;
P^.Data := 1;
for I := 2 to 5 do
  begin
    new(Q);
    P^.Next := Q;
    Q^.Data := I;
    P := P^.Next
  end;
P^.Next := nil;
```

2.5   Consider the following declarations.

```
var
   P1, P2 : ^integer;
```

(a) Illustrate what happens with each step for the following block of code.

```
new(P1);
new(P2);
P1^ := 5;
P2^ := 7;
```

(b) Illustrate what would now happen if we did

```
P1 := P2;
```

(c) Illustrate what would happen if we did

```
P1^ := P2^;
```

instead of the step in (b).

2.6   Assume that we have the following list created.

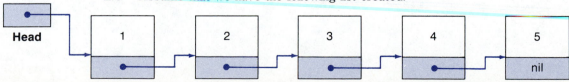

What would be generated for each of the following blocks of code?

(a)
```
P := Head;
for I := 1 to 4 do
begin
   writeln(P^.Data);
   P := P^.Next
end;
```

(b)
```
P := Head;
for I := 1 to 2 do
begin
   writeln(P^.Data);
   P := P^.Next;
   P := P^.Next
end;
```

(c)
```
P := Head;
while P^.Next <> nil do
begin
   writeln(P^.Data);
   P := P^.Next
end;
```

(d)
```
P := Head;
while P^.Next <> nil do
begin
   P := P^.Next;
   writeln(P^.Data)
end;
```

(e)
```
P := Head;
writeln(P^.Data);
while P^.Next <> nil do
   begin
      P := P^.Next;
      writeln(P^.Data)
   end;
```

2.7 Show what each of the following commands does to the indicated linked list.

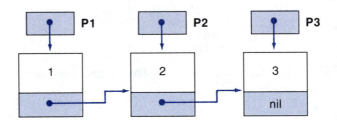

(a) `P1 := P2^.Next;`

(b) `P1 := P2^.Next^.Next;`

(c) `P1 := P3^.Next;`

(d) `P1^.Data := P2^.Data;`

(e) `P2^.Data := P2^.Next^.Data;`

(f) `P3^.Next := P1;`

2.8 A program is to be written to play a game that uses a deck of cards. Assume that each element of a linked list is to store the information for one card. Use the characters 'C', 'D', 'H', and 'S' for the suit values and the integer values 1, 2, ..., 13 for the card values of ace through king. Give the **type** and **var** declarations that are needed for this program.

2.9 How would an element be created and the data for the "ace of spades" be stored using the declarations from Exercise 2.8?

2.4 Procedure Parameters

In the previous section the procedure **PrintData** was written without using any parameters, and the procedure **FindData** was written using only the data item as a parameter. In order to write procedures that deal with linked lists, we must consider the problem of passing the appropriate parameters. Since we have no type declarations that reference the whole list, we have what appears to be a different situation from those we have encountered so far. Recall from Chapter 1, however, that even when we were passing an array as a parameter, we were using the array variable name in order to pass the whole array in and out of the procedure. The array name in a program is identified in the computer with the address of the first word of the memory reserved for the structure. This means that, in terms of how the computer handles the structure, arrays present us with exactly the same situation as linked lists. Therefore, for linked lists, all that has to be passed into the procedure is the address of the first element of the linked list. For example, a procedure to create a linked list would need the following heading.

```
procedure CreateList(var First : ItemPtr);
```

The pointer to the first element of the list is passed as a variable parameter so that the address of the first element of the created list will be passed back to the calling program. When this address is passed back, the procedure has in essence passed back the whole list. Similarly, in our procedures to print out the data in a linked list, the list information will be passed into the procedure by passing the pointer to the first element of the list. Since this information is not to be changed, the pointer to the first element of the list will be passed as a value parameter.

```
procedure PrintData(First : ItemPtr);
```

We will illustrate this technique for passing a list with some examples. Suppose we have a data file that contains an unknown number of lines with one integer data item per line. We will write a procedure to read the data from the file and store it in a linked list that is being created. Each element of the linked list will contain one integer from the file. We will assume that we have the declarations from Section 2.1 in our main program. As before, we begin by outlining the procedure using pseudocode. These procedures assume that the main program opens the data file and checks for an initial end of file. If the file is empty, the procedure is not called.

Pseudocode

CreateList Procedure

Create the first element.
Mark beginning of list.
Get one line of data.
Store data.

> WHILE not end of file
>   Create an element.
>   Get one line of data.
>   Store data.
>   Hook up element.
>   Move pointer.
> END WHILE.
> Mark end of list.

We can now code the procedure. We will omit the procedure documentation.

```
procedure CreateList(var DFile : text; var First : ItemPtr);
var
  P, Q : ItemPtr;                         { General pointers }
begin
  new(P);                                 { First element }
  First := P;
  readln(DFile, P^.Data);
  while not eof(DFile) do begin           { Loop for rest of list }
    new(Q);
    readln(DFile, Q^.Data);
    P^.Next := Q;                         { Hook element into list }
    P := Q
  end; { while }
  P^.Next := nil                          { Mark end of list }
end; { CreateList }
```

As the next example, we will code a procedure to write out the data stored in the linked list. The data are to be written to a file, one integer per line. As before, the main program will not call this procedure if the original data file is empty and we have an empty list. We omit the documentation.

```
procedure PrintData(var PFile : text; First : ItemPtr);
var
  P : ItemPtr;                        { Pointer to move through list }
begin
  rewrite(PFile);                         { Open file for output }
  P := First;                             { First element }
  writeln(PFile,P^.Data : 1);
  while P^.Next <> nil do begin       { Loop for remainder of list }
    P := P^.Next;
    writeln(PFile, P^.Data : 1)
  end { while }
end; { PrintData }
```

We will now illustrate these new concepts by returning to the program that was written in Chapter 1. The employee data were stored in the file in the following format.

Columns 1–20 Employee Name
          21–31 Social Security Number
          40–44 Pay Rate

We will write a procedure that will create a linked list containing the data from the file. We will also write a procedure that will write the data from a linked list back to a file in exactly the same format as originally stored.

Since each element of the list will have to contain one record of data from the file, we will need the following type declarations.

```
type
   String20 = packed array[1..20] of char;
   String11 = packed array[1..11] of char;
   EmpInfo = record
               Name : String20;
               SsNum : String11;
               PayRate : real
             end;
   ItemPtr = ^Item;
   Item = record
             Data : EmpInfo;
             Next : ItemPtr
          end;
```

In order to write the **CreateList** procedure, we will use the pseudocode outline prepared earlier. In order to perform the statement

Get one line of data.

from the outline, we will write a separate procedure **ReadData** that will read one line of data from the file, store it in a record, and return the record to the calling procedure.

The parameters that we will want to pass in this **CreateList** procedure are the file that contains the data and the pointer to the first element of the list. Both parameters will be variable parameters. We can now code the procedure. The main program will open the data file and check to make sure that it is not empty before calling any of the following procedures.

```
{***************************************************************}
{* CreateList - Procedure to create a linked list to store the *}
{*             data from an employee file. The procedure calls*}
{*             ReadData to return one record of data from the *}
{*             file.                                          *}
{*      var parameters -                                      *}
{*          Dt : Text file containing the data.               *}
{*          Hd : Pointer to the head of the list.             *}
{*      value parameters -                                    *}
{*          None.                                             *}
{***************************************************************}
procedure CreateList(var Dt : text; var Hd : ItemPtr);
var
   P, Q : ItemPtr;                          { General pointers }
```

```
begin
  new(P);                                        { First element }
  ReadData(Dt, P^.Data);
  Hd := P;
  while not eof(Dt) do begin         { Loop for remainder of list }
    new(Q);
    ReadData(Dt, Q^.Data);
    P^.Next := Q;
    P := Q
  end; { while }
  P^.Next := nil
end; { CreateList }
```

We will now code the **ReadData** procedure. The data file and a record to hold one line of data will be passed as variable parameters.

```
{*******************************************************************}
{* ReadData - Procedure to read one line of data from a file,    *}
{*            store it in a record, and return the record to     *}
{*            the calling program. Data in the file are          *}
{*            expected in the following format.                  *}
{*            Columns  1 - 20 Name                               *}
{*                    21 - 31 Social Security Number             *}
{*                    40 - 44 Pay Rate                           *}
{*        var parameters -                                       *}
{*            Infile : Text file containing the data.            *}
{*            DtRec  : Record to pass the data back to the       *}
{*                     calling program.                          *}
{*        value parameters -                                     *}
{*            None.                                              *}
{*******************************************************************}
procedure ReadData(var Infile : text; var DtRec : EmpInfo);
var
  I : integer;                                   { Loop index }
begin
  with DtRec do
    begin
      for I := 1 to 20 do                        { Read Name }
        read(Infile, Name[I]);
      { end for }
      for I := 1 to 11 do                        { Read Ssnumber }
        read(Infile, Ssnum[I]);
      { end for }
      read(Infile, PayRate)                      { Read PayRate }
    end; { with }
  readln(Infile)                          { New line, check for eof }
end; { ReadData }
```

We will now write the procedure **WriteList** that will print the data stored in the linked list back to a file. The data will be printed to the file in exactly the same format as they were stored in the data file. We can use the pseudocode outline we used for the **PrintData** procedure in Section 2.3.

We will write a separate procedure **WriteData** to perform the statement

Write the data to the file.

The output file and the pointer to the first element of the list will be passed as parameters in the **WriteList** procedure. We can now code the procedure.

```
{*****************************************************************}
{* WriteList - Procedure to write the data stored in a linked *}
{*             list to a file. The procedure WriteData is      *}
{*             called to write one record of data to one line  *}
{*             of the file.                                    *}
{*       var parameters -                                      *}
{*           Rst : Text file to which data are written.        *}
{*       value parameters -                                    *}
{*           Hd2 : Pointer to the head of the list.            *}
{*****************************************************************}
procedure WriteList(var Rst : text; Hd2 : ItemPtr);
var
  P2 : Itemptr;                    { Pointer to move through list }
begin
  rewrite(Rst);                         { Open file for output }
  P2 := Hd2;                                  { First element }
  WriteData(Rst, P2^.Data);
  while P2^.Next <> nil do begin  { Loop for remainder of list }
    P2 := P2^.Next;
    WriteData(Rst, P2^.Data)
  end { while }
end; { WriteList }
```

We can now code the **WriteData** procedure. The parameters that are passed are the output file and one record to hold one line of data for the file.

```
{*****************************************************************}
{* WriteData - Procedure to write one record to a file. The   *}
{*             record will be printed to one line of the       *}
{*             file in the following format.                   *}
{*             Columns  1 - 20 Name                            *}
{*                     21 - 31 Social Security Number          *}
{*                     40 - 44 Pay Rate                        *}
{*       var parameters -                                      *}
{*           Outfile : Text file to which the record of data   *}
{*                     is written.                             *}
{*       value parameters -                                    *}
{*           DtRec1 : Record containing the data.              *}
{*****************************************************************}
procedure WriteData(var Outfile : text; DtRec1 : EmpInfo);
begin
  with DtRec1 do begin                       { Write one record }
    write(Outfile, Name);
    write(Outfile, Ssnum);
    write(Outfile, ' ' : 8,
          PayRate : 5 : 2)
  end; { with }
  writeln(Outfile)                         { Write line to file }
end; { WriteData }
```

We have written the procedure this way for clarity. The procedure could have been written using the one statement

```
begin
   writeln(Outfile, DtRec1.Name, DtRec1.Ssnum,
                  ' ' : 8, DtRec1.PayRate : 5 : 2)
end; { WriteData }
```

Once these procedures have been written, they should be tested, as was done in Chapter 1. Writing a driver to test these four procedures is left as one of the exercises.

2.5   Forward- and Backward-Pointing Linked Lists

The linked lists that we have used in the preceding sections all have the form shown in Figure 2.17. Because of the way these lists were created, the first data item of the file is stored at the beginning of the list. Therefore, when we print the data back out of the list, the first data item read in will be the first data item printed back out, and the last item read in will be the last item printed out. This type of a data structure is known as a queue. A *queue* is a list where the First item In is the First item Out and the Last item In is the Last item Out. These phrases are shortened to *FIFO* and *LILO*. We will use one other term in reference to this type of a linked list; since when the list is built the head of the list will be generated first and the end of the list will be generated last, we will also refer to this list as a *forward-pointing linked list*. We will study forward-pointing linked lists as queues in more detail in Chapter 3.

Figure 2.17

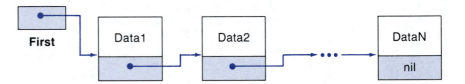

The other way to create a simple linked list is as follows: When the first element of the list is created, mark it as the end of the list. When the last element of the list is created, mark it as the beginning of the list. Assuming that the main program checks for end of file, the outline for this process would be as follows.

Pseudocode

CreateBPList Procedure

Create an element.
Get data.
Store data.
Mark end of list.

> WHILE not end of file
>   Create an element.
>   Get data.
>   Store data.
>   Insert element into list.
>   Move pointer.
> END WHILE.
> Mark beginning of list.

We can now write the procedure.

```
procedure CreateBPList(var DFile : text; var First : ItemPtr);
var
  P, Q : ItemPtr;                          { General pointers }
begin
  new(P);                                    { First element }
  readln(DFile, P^.Data);
  P^.Next := nil;
  while not eof(DFile) do         { Loop for remainder of list }
  begin
    new(Q);
    readln(DFile, Q^.Data);
    Q^.Next := P;
    P := Q
  end; { while }
  First := P
end; { CreateBPList }
```

A linked list created by this procedure would look like Figure 2.18.

Figure 2.18

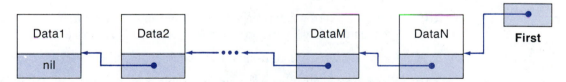

This list is created so that the first item of the data file is stored at the end of the list and the last item of the data file is stored at the beginning of the list. Thus when the data is read back out of the list, the first item in will be the last item out and the last item in will be the first item out. This type of data structure is called a stack. A *stack* is a structure in which the First item In is the Last item Out (*FILO*) and the Last item In is the First item Out (*LIFO*). Since the end of the list is generated first and the beginning of the list is generated last, we will also refer to these structures as *backward-pointing linked lists*. Backward-pointing linked lists will be studied as stacks in Chapter 3.

We will conclude this section with the procedure to print the data stored in in a backward-pointing linked list to a file. Since the procedure is similar to what we have written previously, we will skip the outline and just code the procedure. We will also omit the documentation.

```
procedure PrintBPData(var PFile : text; First : ItemPtr);
var
  P : ItemPtr;                        { Pointer to move through list }
begin
  rewrite(PFile);                          { Open file for output }
  P := First;                                   { First element }
  writeln(PFile, P^.Data : 1);
  while P^.Next <> nil do begin    { Loop for remainder of list }
    P := P^.Next;
    writeln(PFile, P^.Data : 1)
  end { while }
end; { PrintBPData }
```

We will normally represent a backward-pointing linked list as shown in Figure 2.19. You should satisfy yourself that it is the same linked list as was represented in Figure 2.18.

Figure 2.19

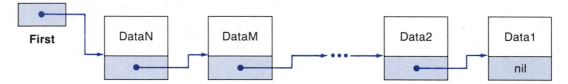

Exercises

2.10   Using a forward-pointing linked list and the appropriate parameters, write the procedure that will perform the tasks described in Exercise 2.2.

2.11   Rewrite Exercise 2.10 using a backward-pointing linked list.

2.12   Write a procedure that will count the number of data items stored in a linked list and return this number to the calling program. Write a program to test this procedure.

2.13   Write a procedure that will find and return the average of the integer data items stored in a linked list. Write a program to test this procedure.

2.14   Write a function that will find and return the maximum integer number stored in a linked list. Write a program to test this procedure.

2.15   A file called **dataC** has several lines of data. Each line contains one sentence consisting of several words. Write a procedure that will read one line of the file and store the data in a forward-pointing linked list, one character per element. Include all blanks.

2.16 Write the procedure that will print the list of data stored by Exercise 2.15. The data should be printed to the screen. Write a program and test these two procedures.

2.17 Using the list that was generated in Exercise 2.15, write a procedure that will count the number of blanks stored in the list and will return this number to the calling program. Write a program to test this procedure.

2.18 Using the list from Exercise 2.15, write a procedure that will count the number of words stored in the list and return this number to the calling program. Write a program to test this procedure.

2.19 Write driver programs and test each of the procedures **CreateList**, **WriteList**, **ReadData**, and **WriteData** written in this section. Refer back to Chapter 1 where we discussed how drivers were written to test procedures.

2.6 Insertion and Deletion

In this section we will consider the problems of inserting and deleting elements from a linked list that has already been created. Then we will write the procedures that can be used with the **EmployeeList** program.

Suppose we have the linked list shown in Figure 2.20 and a new element P^. We want to insert the new element P^ into the list at a particular position. The first thing we must do is move a pointer down the list until we find the element after which the new element is to be inserted. If we call the pointer **Q**, then after positioning **Q** at the appropriate element we would have the situation depicted in Figure 2.21.

Figure 2.20

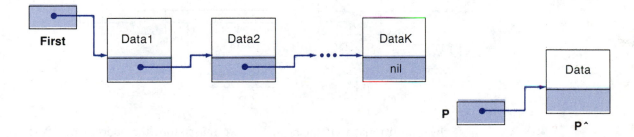

Figure 2.21

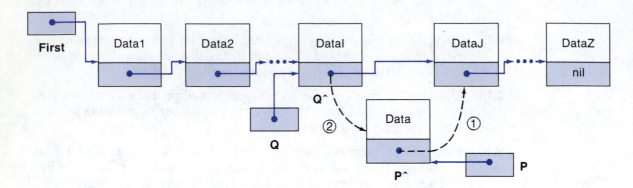

The insertion can now be done in two steps. We must make sure that we do these two steps in exactly the right order. As illustrated in Figure 2.21, the two steps are the following.

1. Make **P^** point to the element following **Q^**.
2. Make **Q^** point to **P^**.

In order to make **P^** point to the element following **Q^**, we must store the address of this element in **P^.Next**. Since **Q^.Next** contains this address, we simply do

```
P^.Next := Q^.Next;          { P point to
                               element following Q^ }
```

This gives us Figure 2.22.

Figure 2.22

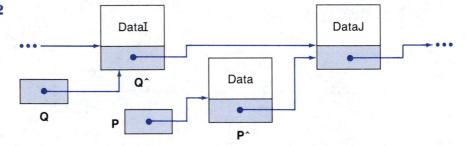

In order to make **Q^** point to **P^**, we must store the address of **P^** in **Q^.Next**. As before, since **P** contains this address, we simply do

```
Q^.Next := P;                    { Q^ point to P^ }
```

This gives us Figure 2.23, and the insertion is complete.

Figure 2.23

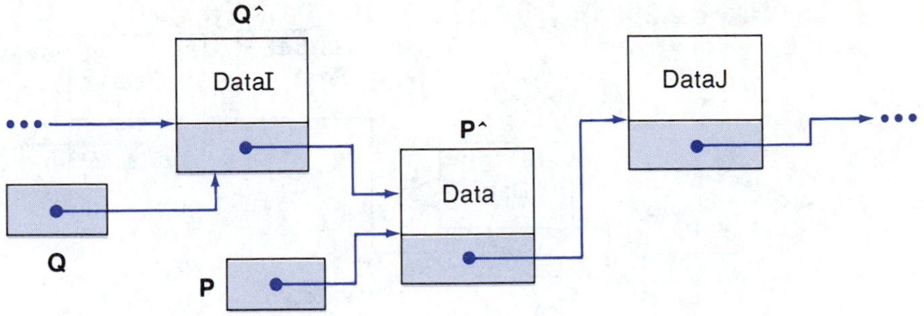

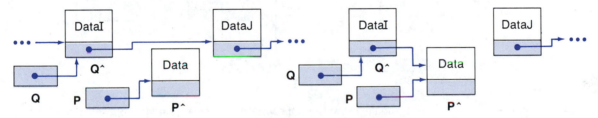

Let us consider what would happen if we did the two steps in the other order. If we did

```
Q^.Next := P;
P^.Next := Q^.Next;
```

the first instruction would cause the left-hand figure in Figure 2.24 to change to the right-hand figure. We can clearly see that the second instruction could not possibly hook up the list, since **Q^.Next** does not contain the right address. We have lost the reference to the next element of the list.

Figure 2.24

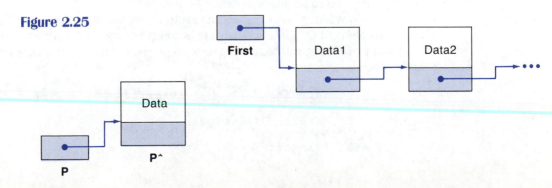

We must consider as a special case the situation in which **P^** is to be inserted at the beginning of the list. In this case we would not have an element **Q^** after which to insert **P^** (see Figure 2.25). In order to do this insertion, we simply make **P^** point to the first element and then mark **P^** as the new first element of the list. To make **P^** point to the first element, we assign the address of the first element, which is stored in **First**, to **P^.Next**.

Figure 2.25

Figure 2.26

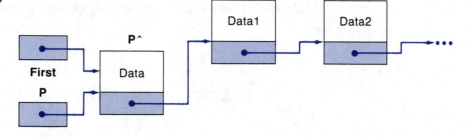

```
P^.Next := First;          { P^ point to first element }
```

This gives us Figure 2.26. We next make **First** point to **P^** with the statement

```
First := P;                { Mark P^ as new first element }
```

which gives us Figure 2.27.

Figure 2.27

You should draw the appropriate figures to satisfy yourself that the two statements

```
P^.Next := Q^.Next; { P^ point to element following Q^ }
Q^.Next := P;                        { Q^ point to P^ }
```

will also take care of the case in which **Q^** is the last element in the linked list. Thus the insertion of the new element at the end of the list does not have to be treated as a special case.

We will now write the procedure to insert the new element **P^** after the list element **Q^**. The special case in which **P^** must be inserted at the beginning of the list will be handled separately; we will discuss this case in the next section.

```
procedure Insert(P, Q : ItemPtr);
begin
  P^.Next := Q^.Next;
  Q^.Next := P
end; { Insert }
```

We will consider this procedure again in the next section when we discuss the problem of creating a sorted linked list.

The problem of deleting an element from a linked list is a little bit more complicated. Let us assume that we have a linked list with a pointer **P** pointing to the element that we want to delete, as in Figure 2.28. In order to remove **P^** from the list, all we have to do is make the element before **P^** point to the element following **P^**. This gives us Figure 2.29. We can then release the memory reserved for **P^** with the statement

```
dispose(P);
```

Figure 2.28

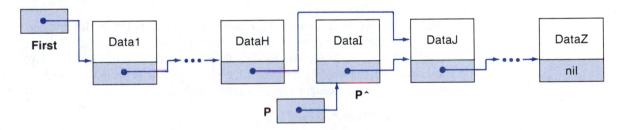

Figure 2.29

In order to accomplish the above, however, we must have a pointer to the element of the list right before **P^**. We can get this pointer by setting a pointer **Q** to the beginning of the list and moving **Q** down the list until the list element **Q^** and the pointer **P** point to the same element, that is, until

```
Q^.Next = P
```

The block of code that we need to get the pointer **Q** to point to the element right before **P^** is the following.

```
Q := First;
while Q^.Next <> P do
  Q := Q^.Next;
{ end while }
```

This would give us Figure 2.30. Now, in order to make the list element **Q^** point to the list element following **P^**, we simply do the assignment

```
Q^.Next := P^.Next;
```

Figure 2.30

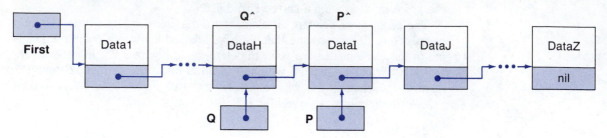

Figure 2.31

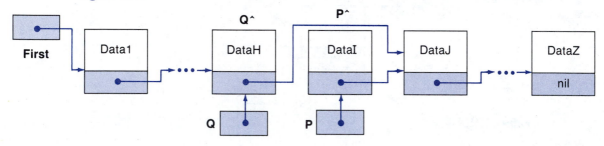

We now have Figure 2.31.

As before, we must look at the special case in which **P^** is the first element of the list. In this case, of course, there is no element before **P^** in the list, as in Figure 2.32. As we can see, all we have to do in this case is move the marker for the head of the list to the next element. This is done with either of the following assignments.

```
First :=First^.Next;
```

or

```
First :=P^.Next;
```

Figure 2.32

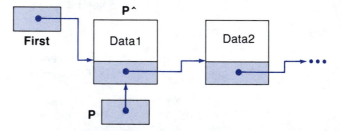

We then have Figure 2.33. Finally, we can dispose of the old first element with

```
dispose(P);
```

Figure 2.33

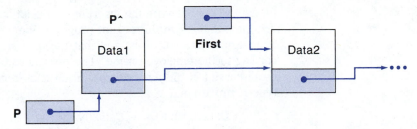

The outline for the procedure to delete an element from the list is as follows.

Pseudocode

> **Delete Procedure**
>
> IF **P** is first element THEN
>   Move beginning list pointer to second element.
> ELSE
>   Set **Q** to first element.
>   WHILE (list element **Q^** and pointer **P** not pointing at the
>   same element)
>   Move **Q**.
>   END WHILE.
> Unhook **P**.
> END IF.
> Release memory of **P^**.

Before writing the procedure we need to consider the parameters that we would pass. We will need to pass the pointer to the element that is to be removed from the list as a value parameter. From the preceding discussion, we can also see that the pointer to the first element of the list needs to be passed as a variable parameter because its value can possibly change during the deletion process.

We can now code the procedure to delete an element from a linked list. We will omit the documentation here and write it when we code this procedure for use in our **EmployeeList** program.

```
procedure Delete(var First1 : ItemPtr; P1 : ItemPtr);
var
   Q1 : ItemPtr;                       { Pointer to move through list }
begin
   if P1 = First1                              { If first element }
      then First1 :=First1^.Next                   { Remove P1^ }
      else begin                        { Else find element before P1^ }
      Q1 := First1;
      while Q1^.Next <> P1 do
         Q1 := Q1^.Next;
      { end while }
      Q1^.Next := P1^.Next                             { Remove P1^ }
   end; { else }
   dispose(P1)                                      { Release memory }
end; { Delete }
```

We will now rewrite the insertion and deletion procedures so that we can use them in our **EmployeeList** program. We will assume that the data have been stored in a linked list and that the data are stored in sorted order according to the employee name. The procedure that will do this ordering will be discussed in the next section. Each data item **DataI** will be a record of type **EmpInfo** and

$$\text{Data1(Name)} <= \text{Data2(Name)} <= \ldots <= \text{DataK(Name)}$$

We assume that an element **P^** has been created and the data for a new employee have been stored in this element. We will also assume that there is a pointer **Q**, pointing to the list element **Q^** after which the new element **P^** is to be inserted. We will discuss how the element **Q** is positioned in the next section. An outline of the procedure to insert the new element follows. As before, the case in which the new element is to be inserted at the beginning of the list will be discussed separately.

Pseudocode

InsertEmployee Procedure

Make new employee element point to element following list element.
Make list element point to new employee element.

We can now code the **InsertEmployee** procedure.

```
{***********************************************************************}
{* InsertEmployee - Procedure to insert an element that          *}
{*                  contains the data for an employee into a     *}
{*                  linked list.                                 *}
{*      var parameters -                                         *}
{*          None.                                                *}
{*      value parameters -                                       *}
{*          P : Pointer to the element to be inserted.           *}
{*          Q : Pointer to the element of the list after         *}
{*              which P^ is to be inserted.                      *}
{***********************************************************************}
procedure InsertEmployee(P, Q : ItemPtr):
begin
  P^.next := Q^.next;                        { Insert P^ after Q^ }
  Q^.next := P
end; { InsertEmployee }
```

In order to delete an element from the list, we will want to have a pointer **P** pointing to that element in the list. We will write a procedure, **FindEmployee**, to set the pointer. We will assume that we have a name stored in an identifier, **EmpName**. The procedure will search our list for an element containing this name. If the name is not found, the procedure will print the message "EMPLOYEE NOT FOUND" on the screen and return with the pointer **P** pointing to the last element of the list. If the name is found, the procedure will print the message "EMPLOYEE FOUND" on the screen and return with the pointer **P** pointing to the appropriate element. A Boolean will be returned set to true if the element is found and to false if the element is not found. The pseudocode for this procedure is as follows.

Pseudocode

FindEmployee Procedure

Set pointer **P** to head of the list.
WHILE (**P** not at end of list) and (**P(Name)** <> **EmpName**)
   Move **P**.
END WHILE.
IF **P(Name)** = **EmpName** THEN
   Write "EMPLOYEE FOUND."
   Set **Found** to true.
ELSE
   Write "EMPLOYEE NOT FOUND."
   Write "P POINTS TO LAST ELEMENT."
   Set **Found** to false.
END IF.

We will need to pass a pointer to the head of the list, a pointer to the element of the list, a Boolean for **Found**, and the **Name** as parameters. Since the pointer to the element of the list and the Boolean are to be returned, they are passed as variable parameters. We can now code the procedure.

```
{**************************************************************}
{* FindEmployee - Procedure to search the list for an element  *}
{*                containing the data for an employee. It will  *}
{*                search for an element with a given name.      *}
{*      var parameters -                                        *}
{*          P3 : Pointer to the element to the list contain-    *}
{*               ing the data if found, or to the last         *}
{*               element of the list if not found.             *}
{*          Fnd : Boolean to return true if the element is      *}
{*                found and false if it is not found.           *}
{*      value parameters -                                      *}
{*          Hd3 : Pointer to the head of the list.             *}
{*          EmpName : String containing the name of the        *}
{*                    employee for which we are searching.      *}
{**************************************************************}
procedure FindEmployee(var P3 : ItemPtr; Hd3 : ItemPtr;
                       EmpName : string20; var Fnd : boolean);
begin
  P3 := Hd3;
                                              { Search loop }
  while (P3^.Next <> nil) and (P3^.Data.Name <> EmpName) do
    P3 := P3^.Next;
  { end while }
```

```
      if P3^.Data.Name = EmpName then begin          { Name found }
        Fnd := true;
        writeln('Employee found.')
      end { if }
      else begin                                    { Name not found }
        Fnd := false;
        writeln('Employee not found.');
        writeln('Pointer at last element of list.')
      end { else }
end; {FindEmployee }
```

We will now write the procedure **DeleteEmployee** to delete an element from the list, based on the earlier pseudocode outline for the **Delete** procedure. The procedure will pass the pointers **Pt4** and **Hd4** as parameters. The pointer **Pt4** will point to the element of the list that is to be deleted, and the pointer **Hd4** will point to the first element of the list. Since the value of **Hd4** can possibly change, **Hd4** will be passed as a variable parameter.

```
{******************************************************************}
{* DeleteEmployee - Procedure to delete an element from a list *}
{*                  that contains the data for a particular    *}
{*                  employee.                                   *}
{*      var parameters -                                        *}
{*          Hd4 : Pointer to the head of the list.             *}
{*      value parameters -                                     *}
{*          Pt4 : Pointer to the element of the list to be     *}
{*                deleted.                                      *}
{******************************************************************}
procedure DeleteEmployee(var Hd4 : ItemPtr; Pt4 : ItemPtr);
var
  Q4 : ItemPtr;                    { Pointer to move through list }
begin
  if Pt4 = Hd4 then                         { If first element }
    Hd4 := Hd4^.next
  else begin
    Q4 := Hd4;
    while Q4^.Next <> Pt4 do                        { Search loop }
      Q4 := Q4^.Next;
    { end while }
    Q4^.Next := Pt4^.Next                       { Remove element }
  end; { else }
  dispose(Pt4)                                 { Release memory }
end; { DeleteEmployee }
```

In Section 2.8 we will discuss the use of these procedures in rewriting the **EmployeeList** program using a linked list.

Exercises

2.20 Rewrite the **Insert** procedure. Assume that a pointer **Q** points to an element of the list and that the element **P^** is to be inserted before **Q^**. Write the procedure. Hint: Insert **P^** after **Q^** and then switch the data of **P^** with the data of **Q^**.

2.21   Rewrite the **InsertEmployee** procedure so that it uses the same algorithm as that in Exercise 2.20.

2.22   Rewrite the **FindEmployee** procedure so that it returns a pointer **Q** to an element of the list after which we can insert the element **P^**.

2.23   Assume that **Head1** and **Head2** are pointers to two forward-pointing linked lists of the same type. Write a procedure that will concatenate the two lists, that is, attach one of the lists at the end of the other list. Return a pointer to this new list to the calling program. Write a program to test this procedure.

2.24   Assuming that the two lists with pointers **Head1** and **Head2** are created so that the data are in nondecreasing order and so that the data can be compared directly, write a procedure that will merge the two lists into one list where the data are again in nondecreasing order. Return a pointer to this new list to the calling program. Write a program to test this procedure.

2.25   Assume that we have created a list with a pointer **Head** to the first element of the list. If we have an element of the list that is pointed to by the pointer **P**, write a procedure that will remove the element P^ from the list and attach it at the end of the list. Write a program to test this procedure.

2.26   Using the same list that we discussed in Exercise 2.25, assume that we also have a pointer **Q** pointing to another element of the list. Write a procedure that will interchange these two elements in the list. Write a program to test this procedure.

2.27   Write a procedure that will reverse the order of the elements of a linked list. The procedure should change the forward-pointing linked list

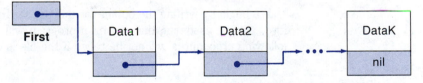

into the backward-pointing linked list.

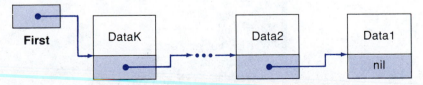

Write a program to test this procedure.

2.7 Maintaining Sorted Linked Lists

We have seen that one of the things that we must be able to do with data, once they are stored in a data structure, is to sort them according to some key, that is, one of the fields of the records. Let us now consider how this can be done when the data structure is a linked list. We could, of course, do what we did when our data structure was an array — simply write a procedure to sort an existing linked list that already contains the data. This approach is more difficult than it first appears; we will use this method in the exercises.

In this section we will approach the sorting problem from a different direction. We will create an element and store the data. Then, instead of simply inserting the element at one end of the list, we will insert the element into the list so that the data are in the appropriate order. In order to make this process a little easier, we will make one other modification in our list. We will create a dummy element at the beginning of the list. This element will not contain any of the data, but will simply serve the purpose of allowing us to avoid the special case in which the element has to be inserted at the beginning of the list. With the addition of a dummy element (see Figure 2.34), it will always be possible to find an element in the list after which the new element can be inserted.

Figure 2.34

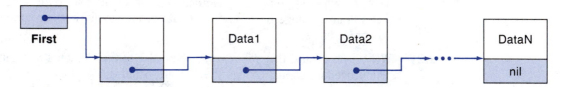

We begin by writing the outline for the **CreateInOrder** procedure. As before, we are assuming that the main program will open the file and that the following procedures will not be called if the file is empty.

Pseudocode

> **CreateInOrder Procedure**
>
> Create dummy element.
> Mark head of list.
> Mark end of list.
> WHILE not end of file
>   Create an element.
>   Get data.
>   Store data.
>   Find list element after which we will insert new element.
>   Insert new element after list element.
> END WHILE.

Before we attempt to code the procedure, two observations should be made. First, once we create the dummy element for the first element of the list, both the head and the end of the list are marked. Thus, if the element that is to be inserted happens to go at the end of the list, the end of list marker (pointer = **nil**) will automatically be moved to the new element. Second, we will have to write separate procedures to perform each of the following.

Find list element after which we will insert new element.

and

Insert new element after list element.

If we assume that the pointer **P** points to the element that we want to insert into the list and that the pointer **Q** points to the element of the list after which we will insert **P^**, the above two statements can be rewritten as follows.

Find element **Q^** after which we will insert **P^**.
Insert **P^** after **Q^**.

We will write the code for the **CreateInOrder** procedure and then proceed with our top-down design by writing the two procedures **FindElement** and **InsertElement** that are called by the **CreateInOrder** procedure. We will want to pass the data file containing the data and the pointer that will mark the head of the list as parameters in this procedure.

```
procedure CreateInOrder(var DtFile : text; var Head : ItemPtr);
var
  P, Q : ItemPtr;                              { General pointers }
begin
  new(P);                                      { Create dummy element }
  Head := P;
  P^.Next := nil;
  while not eof(DtFile) do begin               { Loop to store data }
    new(P);
    ReadData(DtFile, P^.Data);                 { Get and store data }
    FindElement(Q, P, Head);                        { Find element }
    Insert(P, Q)                                    { Insert element }
  end { while }
end; { CreateInOrder }
```

In order to write the procedure **FindElement**, we need to make some additional assumptions. We will assume that we are able to compare the data that we have stored in the list directly and that the data are nondecreasing, that is,

$$\text{Data1} <= \text{Data2} <= \text{Data3} \ldots$$

A little thought will show that we must have two pointers to move through the list, since the pointers cannot be moved backwards. One pointer will look for the first element of the list that has data greater than or equal to the data stored in the new element or for the end of the list, whichever comes first.

The second pointer will be one element behind the first so that it will point to the element after which the new element is to be inserted. We must worry about two special cases:

1. If the element is the first element to be inserted into the list.
2. If the element is to be inserted at the end of the list.

In the first case, when both pointers are set to the beginning of the list, they are also at the end of the list. Therefore, we simply return the pointer pointing to the first element. In the second case, the first pointer will arrive at the end of the list without encountering any data greater than or equal to the data in the new element. Since the pointer that we want to return is one element behind, it is moved one more element.

We will now write the pseudocode. Carefully think through these special cases to make sure that this outline is exactly what we want.

Pseudocode

FindElement Procedure

Set **P1** to first element.
Set **P2** to first element.
WHILE (**P1** not at end of list)
    Move **P1**.
    IF **P1(Data)** < **NP(Data)** THEN
        Move **P2**.
    END IF.
END WHILE.

We are using **P1** and **P2** as pointers that move through the list, with **P2** being the one that we want to return. We are using **NP** as the pointer to the element that is to be inserted. We will have to have parameters for **NP** to be passed into the procedure and for **P2** to be passed back to the calling program. We will also have to have a parameter for the pointer to the head of the list to be passed into the procedure. The pointer **P1** will be a local identifier. We can now code the procedure.

```
procedure FindElement(var P2 : ItemPtr; NP, Hd : ItemPtr);
var
  P1 : ItemPtr;                                 { General pointer }
begin
  P1 := Hd;
  P2 := Hd;
  while P1^.Next <> nil do begin                { Search loop }
    P1 := P1^.Next;
    if P1^.Data < NP^.Data then
      P2 := P2^.Next
    { end if }
  end { while }
end; { FindElement }
```

Once again you should draw the appropriate figures and walk through the procedure to make sure that it takes care of all of the special cases.

We now consider the procedure to insert the new element **P^** into the list after the element **Q^**. The new element **P^** is pointed to by **P**, and the list element **Q^** is pointed to by **Q**. This is exactly what we did in the previous section. You should refer back to where the **Insert** procedure is written. We will not rewrite this procedure; however, we do need to discuss the parameters that we are using. The fact that we can pass **P** and **Q** as value parameters is rather subtle, but it should be understood. Since **P** is a pointer, it will point to the same block of memory (location of **P^**) whether it is passed as a value parameter or as a variable parameter. Therefore, when we assign an address to **P^.Next** it is going to be known to the calling program, since this assignment is to the pointer part of **P^**. The same argument holds for **Q**.

We will now rewrite these procedures so that they can be used in our **EmployeeList** program. Recall that we are assuming that we want to sort the data by name in nondecreasing order. We begin by rewriting the **CreateInOrder** procedure based on the **CreateInOrder** pseudocode outline; the new version will be called **EmployeeInOrder**. We can use the **ReadData** procedure that we wrote in Section 2.4 to perform the statements

Get data.
Store data.

We can now code the procedure.

```
{******************************************************************}
{* EmployeeInOrder - Procedure to store the data, for a        *}
{*                   collection of employees, in a linked list *}
{*                   in nondecreasing order by name.           *}
{*      var parameters -                                       *}
{*          Dt3 : Text file containing the collection of       *}
{*                data for the employees.                      *}
{*          Hd3 : Pointer to the first element of the list.    *}
{*      value parameters -                                     *}
{*          None.                                              *}
{******************************************************************}
procedure EmployeeInOrder(var Dt3 : text; var Hd3 : ItemPtr);
var
  P3, Q3 : ItemPtr;                        { General pointers }
begin
  new(P3);                                 { Create dummy element }
  Hd3 := P3;
  P3^.Next := nil;
  while not eof(Dt3) do begin              { Create loop }
    new(P3);
    ReadData(Dt3, P3^.Data);               { Get and store data }
    FindEmpElement(Q3, P3, Hd3);           { Find element }
    InsertEmployee(P3, Q3)                 { Insert element }
  end { while }
end; { EmployeeInOrder }
```

In order to code the **FindEmpElement** procedure, we refer back to the outline for **FindElement**. We will pass **R2**, the pointer to be returned, as a variable parameter; the pointer **Hd**, the pointer to the first element of the list, as a value parameter; and the pointer **NP**, the pointer to the new element, as a value parameter. The pointer **R1** will be a local variable. You should compare this procedure with the **FindEmployee** procedure written above. You should clearly understand the difference between the two procedures and why two different procedures were written.

```
{***********************************************************}
{* FindEmpElement - Procedure to find the element of the   *}
{*                  list after which the new element can    *}
{*                  be inserted.                            *}
{*       var parameters -                                   *}
{*           R2 : Pointer to element after which the new    *}
{*                element NP^ is to be inserted.            *}
{*       value parameters -                                 *}
{*           NP : Pointer to the element to be inserted.    *}
{*           Hd : Pointer to the first element of the list.*}
{***********************************************************}
procedure FindEmpElement(var R2 : ItemPtr; NP, Hd : ItemPtr);
var
  R1 : ItemPtr;                 { Pointer to move through list }
begin
  R1 := Hd;
  R2 := Hd;
  while R1^.Next <> nil do begin              { Search loop }
    R1 := R1^.Next;
    if R1^.Data.Name < NP^.Data.Name
      then R2 := R2^.Next
    { end if }
  end { while }
end; { FindEmpElement }
```

The procedure to insert the element into the list is called **Insert-Employee** and is written in Section 2.6.

This concludes the basic procedures on linked lists that we will need to write the **EmployeeList** program using linked lists. In the next section we will conclude this chapter with a discussion of the **EmployeeList** program.

Exercises

2.28 Create a file of three integer data items. Walk through the creation of a sorted linked list using the procedures that we have written in this section. The file should contain the integers in the reverse order from that of the list.

2.29 Repeat Exercise 2.28 using a file in which the integer data items are in the same order as they are to be stored in the list.

2.30 Repeat Exercise 2.28 for a random ordering of the integer data items in the file.

2.31 Write a subprogram that will sort integer data items that are already stored in a linked list. Duplicate a bubble sort: when two elements of the list are out of order, simply switch the data stored in the elements. You may have to refer to Chapter 4 where this sorting algorithm is discussed.

2.32 Write a subprogram that will sort integer data items that are already stored in a linked list. Duplicate a selection sort. You may have to refer to Chapter 4 where this sorting algorithm is discussed.

2.8 EmployeeList Program

In this section we will discuss how the procedures that we have written in the previous sections of this chapter can be used to rewrite our **EmployeeList** program from Chapter 1. We will be utilizing dynamic data structures (linked lists) rather than the static data structures (arrays) that were used in Chapter 1. We begin by asking you to review the pseudocode for the main control module from Chapter 1. We will have to make the following modifications.

1. We will replace the step

    Read data from the file . . . and store data in an array of records.

    with

    Create the list in order.

2. We will replace the **AddEmployee** procedure that we wrote in Chapter 1 with the procedure that utilizes our procedure **InsertEmployee**.

The pseudocode for our new program is as follows.

Pseudocode

> **EmployeeList Program**
>
> Open **Master** file for input.
> IF not end of file THEN
>   Call **EmployeeInOrder** procedure.
>   Call **SignOn** procedure.
>   Call **PrintMenu** procedure.
>   Input **Choice**.
>   Trap **Choice**.
>   WHILE **Choice** <> 'E'
>   CASE **Choice** OF
>   'A' : Call **AddEmployee**.
>   'D' : Call **DeleteEmployee**.
>   'P' : Call **PrintMasterList**.
>   'O' : Call **PrintOne**.
>   END CASE.

```
                    Call PrintMenu procedure.
                    Input Choice.
                    Trap Choice.
                 END WHILE.
                 Open Master file for output.
                 Call WriteList procedure.
                 Inform user.
              ELSE
                 Print error message.
```

The procedures **SignOn** and **PrintMenu** will be the same procedures that were written for the program in Chapter 1. The procedures **Delete-Element**, **ReadData**, **WriteData**, **WriteList**, **InsertEmployee**, **Find-Employee**, **FindEmpElement**, and **EmployeeInOrder** have all been written in the previous sections of this chapter. We will need to write the procedures **AddEmployee**, **DeleteEmployee**, **PrintMasterList**, and **PrintOne** that are called in the **case** statement in the main control module of the program. We will write outlines for some of these procedures and ask you to write and test the procedures as exercises. The outline for the procedure **AddEmployee** is the following.

Pseudocode

AddEmployee Procedure

```
Input the name.
Input the social security number.
Input the pay rate.
Create element.
Store data in element.
Call FindEmpElement.
Call InsertEmployee.
```

The following is the outline for the **DeleteEmployee** procedure.

Pseudocode

DeleteEmployee Procedure

```
REPEAT
   Input the name.
   Call FindEmployee.
   IF Found THEN
      Call DeleteElement.
      Write message "Employee Deleted."
   ELSE
      Write message "Employee Not Found."
      Ask user if wishes to input the name again.
```

> Input **Answer**.
> END IF.
> UNTIL (**Found** or **Answer** = 'No').

We can now code the **EmployeeList** program.

```
{********************************************************************}
{* EmployeeList - Program to maintain information on a group    *}
{*               of employees. The program interacts with       *}
{*               the user. The user can add an employee to       *}
{*               the list, delete an employee from the list,    *}
{*               print out the complete list of information      *}
{*               to a file, and print out the information        *}
{*               on any one employee to the screen.             *}
{*       files -                                                *}
{*            Master : Text file containing employee data.      *}
{*            List : Text file to which the list of             *}
{*                   employee information is written.           *}
{********************************************************************}
program EmployeeList(Input, Output, Master, List);
const
  ClearScreen = ':I^=';                        { Infoton terminal }
  RingBell = ':I^*';
{********************************************************************}
{**              Type declarations go here                    **}
{********************************************************************}
var
  Master,                                { File of employee data }
  List : text;                        { File for list of employees }
  Head,                                { Pointer for head of list }
  P, Q : ItemPtr;                          { General pointers }
  Choice : char;                         { User menu input }
  Allowable : set of 'A'..'Z';             { User choices }
{********************************************************************}
{**    Insert PrintMenu, SignOn, DeleteElement, ReadData,      **}
{**    WriteData, WriteList, InsertEmployee, FindEmployee,     **}
{**    FindEmpElement, EmployeeInOrder, AddEmployee,           **}
{**    DeleteEmployee, PrintMasterList, PrintOne, and          **}
{**    FinalInstructions procedures here.                      **}
{********************************************************************}
begin                                    { Main control module }
  reset(Master);
  if not eof(Master) then begin
    EmployeeInOrder(Master, Head);
    SignOn;
    PrintMenu;
    writeln('Please input your choice.');
    readln(Choice);
    Allowable := ['A', 'D', 'P', 'O', 'E'];
```

```
      while not (Choice in Allowable) do begin      { Trap choice }
        writeln('Choice not acceptable, please input again.');
        PrintMenu;
        readln(Choice)
      end; { while }
      while Choice <> 'E' do begin
        case Choice of
          'A' : AddEmployee(Head);
          'D' : DeleteEmployee(Head);
          'P' : PrintMasterList(List, Head);
          'O' : PrintOne(Head)
        end; { case }
        PrintMenu;
        writeln('Please input your choice.');
        readln(Choice);
        while not (Choice in Allowable) do begin      { Trap choice }
          writeln('Choice not acceptable.');
          writeln('Please input another choice.');
          PrintMenu;
          readln(Choice)
        end { while }
      end; { while }
      rewrite(Master);
      WriteList(Master, Head);
      FinalInstructions
    end { if }
    else
      writeln('Error!! - Master file is empty.')
    { end else }
  end.
```

You should compare the modules that we have written in the last few sections and the modules that are written as exercises with the modules written in Chapter 1. Make sure that you clearly understand the differences between how arrays are used and how linked lists are used. The advantages of dynamic data structures should also be clearly understood. We will be using linked lists again in Chapter 3 to build and use other useful dynamic data structures.

Exercises

2.33 Write a driver and test the main control module for the **EmployeeList** program.

2.34 Write each of the procedures, **AddEmployee**, **DeleteEmployee**, **Print-One**, and **PrintMasterList**. Write drivers and test each of these procedures.

2.35 The main control module for the **EmployeeList** program could have been written more efficiently using the following pseudocode.

Open **Master** file for input.
If not end of file THEN
    Call **EmployeeInOrder** procedure.

    Call **SignOn**.
    Set **Done** to false.
    WHILE not **Done**
      PrintMenu
      Input **Choice**.
      Trap **Choice**.
      CASE **Choice** OF
        'A' : Call **AddEmployee**.
        'D' : Call **DeleteEmployee**.
        'P' : Call **PrintMasterList**.
        'O' : Call **PrintOneEmployee**.
        'E' : Set **Done** to true.
      END CASE.
    END WHILE.
    Open **Master** file for output.
    Call **WriteList** procedure.
    Inform user.
ELSE
    Print error message.
Rewrite the main control module to match this pseudocode.

2.36 Explain why the algorithm in Exercise 2.35 is more efficient than the original algorithm.

2.37 Replace the while loop in Exercise 2.35 with a repeat-until structure. Rewrite the main control module to match this pseudocode.

2.38 Rewrite the pseudocode for the main control module for a language that does not have the case structure available. Rewrite the main control module to match this pseudocode.

2.39 Write a subprogram to add to the **EmployeeList** program to allow the user to change any of the information on any of the employees in the list. Print a menu to allow the users to choose the piece of information they would like to change.

Summary

Dynamic data structures and linked lists are very fascinating subjects and are extremely useful tools for programmers. We have seen how the pointer in Pascal allows linked lists to be built and used. We have worked through a fairly large applications program using and developing these ideas. We have pointed out how some of the problems involved in using arrays can be overcome by using linked lists.

    The lists that we have studied have been simple linked lists. These lists can be traversed in only one direction. We will continue the study of linked lists in Chapter 3.

Chapter Exercises

Program 1 A file is to contain several records of inventory data in the same format as was discussed in Chapter 1, Program 1. The next few exercises are designed to write a program that will allow the user to maintain this collection of data. The program will utilize a dynamic data structure (linked list) as the structure to store the data from the file.

2.40 Write the constant, type, and variable declarations that are needed to build a linked list to store the data from the file.

2.41 In order to permit maintenance of the collection of inventory data, the program should allow the user to choose any of the following options.
(a) Add an inventory record to the collection.
(b) Delete an inventory record from the collection.
(c) Modify an inventory record by changing any of the fields.
(d) Post the data from the sales at the end of the day.
(e) Post the data from orders received.
(f) Print out an inventory report.
(g) Print out a list of items to be reordered.
Outline the program, using pseudocode, that will allow the user to do all of the above.

2.42 Using the outline from Exercise 2.41, write and test the main control module. All of the called procedures are to be written as stubs.

2.43 Write and test the procedure that will read the data from the file, create a linked list, and store the data from the file in this linked list. Each element of the linked list should contain one record of inventory data from the file. This exercise should be done along with Exercise 2.44.

2.44 Write and test the procedure that will write the data stored in the linked list back to the master file in exactly the same format as originally stored.

2.45 Write a procedure that will allow the user to add an inventory record to the linked list. Write a driver and test this procedure.

2.46 Write a procedure that will read the data from the file and store them in a linked list in order by inventory number. Write a driver and test this procedure.

2.47 Modify the add procedure so that it will add the inventory record to the linked list in order by inventory number. Write a driver and test this procedure.

2.48 Write a procedure that will allow the user to delete an inventory record from the linked list. Write a driver and test this procedure.

2.49 Write a procedure that will allow the user to modify an inventory record by changing any of the fields. Write a driver and test this procedure.

2.50   Write a procedure that will print out an inventory report. The report should be printed to a file. Write a driver and test this procedure.

2.51   Write a procedure that will print out a list of all of the inventory items that need to be reordered. The list should include the number on hand, the re-order number, and the inventory number for each of the items. Write a driver and test the procedure.

2.52   Write a procedure that will allow the user to post the sales and the orders received. The data entered should include the inventory number and the number sold (negative) or the number received (positive). These data should be stored in another linked list. Write a driver and test this procedure. The driver can print the data stored in the linked list to the screen.

2.53   Write a procedure that will update the data stored in the main linked list using the data stored in the linked list that is created by the post procedure. Write a driver and test this procedure; again the data from the updated list can be printed to the screen.

2.54   Once you have written and tested each of the modules for the program, make the necessary changes in the main control module, and write and test the complete inventory program.

Program 2   A file is to contain several records of data from an address book. The data are stored in the same format as was discussed in Program 2 from Chapter 1.

2.55   Write the constant, type, and variable declarations that are needed to build a linked list as the data structure to store the data from the file.

2.56   In order to permit maintenance of this collection of address data, the program should allow the user to choose any of the following options.
(a) Add an address to the collection.
(b) Delete an address from the collection.
(c) Modify an address by changing any of the fields.
(d) Print out a list of all of the records with a given zip code.
(e) Print out a list of all of the records with a given city.
(f) Print out a complete list of addresses.
Using the same ideas that were explained in detail in Program 1 of this set of exercises, write and test each of the individual modules of the program. After each of the modules has been written and tested, put these modules together to form the final program.

CHAPTER 3

Stacks, Queues, and Other Linked Lists

Chapter 2 discussed the basic data structures stacks and queues and pointed out how these structures can be built using simple linked lists. In this chapter we will write the procedures that are needed in order to use these structures in our programs and then use the structures and the procedures in some applications.

As we saw in Chapter 2, modifications can be made to the linked-list structure to make some of the procedures easier to write. In this chapter we will develop some of these modifications and discuss the different types of linked lists that can be built using these modifications. The use of some of these structures will be illustrated with examples.

Although students often find it easier to learn how to build and use stacks and queues if these structures are introduced using pointers, not all languages have the pointer available for use in building dynamic data structures. Pointers are available in PASCAL, PL/1, SNOBOL, C, and ADA, but are not available in FORTRAN, BASIC, COBOL, and many other computer languages. Because some languages do not provide the pointer mechanism, programmers must be able to build dynamic data structures without using that powerful tool. Section 3.5 will discuss using arrays to build stacks and queues.

3.1 Stacks and Queues

One of the most useful concepts in computer science is that of a stack. Since stacks and queues are very similar concepts, in this section we will study both of these simple data structures. We will develop the basic procedures that we will need to use these structures in the next few sections.

A stack is a list structure that can be described using the terms

First On–Last Off
Last On–First Off

Items are inserted ("pushed") onto and deleted ("popped") off the same end of the list. A stack can be represented by the backward-pointing linked list in Figure 3.1. The data item **DataK** is the last item pushed onto the stack and is at the beginning of the list. The beginning of the list is also the *top* of the stack, and therefore **DataK** will be the first data item popped off the stack.

Figure 3.1 *Stack*

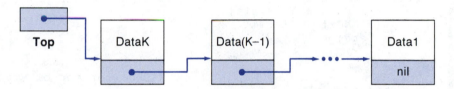

A queue, on the other hand, is a structure that can be described using the terms

First On–First Off
Last On–Last Off

Items are pushed onto and popped off opposite ends of the list. A queue can be represented by the forward-pointing linked list shown in Figure 3.2. The data item **Data1** is the first item pushed onto the queue and is at the beginning of the list. The beginning of the list is also called the *top* or *front* of the queue. Since **Data1** is on the top of the queue, it will be the first data item popped off the queue. In order to eliminate some of the special cases, we will modify both of these lists to build the stacks and queues that we will use in this text.

Figure 3.2 *Queue*

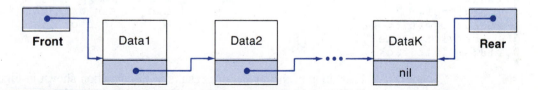

In Section 2.5 we wrote procedures to create forward-pointing and backward-pointing linked lists. The linked lists thus created are the structures that we will use to represent stacks and queues. Stacks and queues are important basic programming tools. Therefore, we will now write the basic procedures needed to implement these structures.

Basic Procedures: Stacks

1. Initialize procedure: Create an empty stack.
2. Push procedure: Push one data item onto the top of the stack.
3. Pop procedure: Pop one data item off the top of the stack.

We will need the following **type** and **var** declarations.

```
type
   ItemData = record

                   Some data type

           end;
   ItemPtr = ^Item;
   Item = record
             Data : ItemData;
             Next : ItemPtr
          end;

var
   Top,                          { Marker for top of stack }
   P : ItemPtr;
   Empty : boolean;              { Empty or nonempty stack }
   OneItem : ItemData;       { Data for one element of stack }
```

The initialize procedure will simply create a first element for the top of the stack, mark this element as the top of the stack, mark the end of the list, and initialize the Boolean identifier **Empty** to true. We will call this procedure **InitStack**.

```
{*****************************************************************}
{* InitStack - Procedure to create the first element for the  *}
{*             stack.                                          *}
{*        var parameters -                                     *}
{*            Top1 : Pointer to first element.                 *}
{*            Empty1 : Boolean for empty stack.                *}
{*        value parameters -                                   *}
{*            None.                                            *}
{*****************************************************************}
procedure InitStack(var Top1 : ItemPtr; var Empty1 : boolean);
begin
   new(Top1);                            { Create and mark top }
   Top1^.Next := nil;                    { Mark end of list }
   Empty1 := true
end; { InitStack }
```

Execution of this procedure results in the situation shown in Figure 3.3.

The **PushStack** procedure will do the following. If the stack is not empty, an element is created, the data item is stored, and the element is inserted onto the top of the stack. If the list is empty, the data item is stored in the first element and the Boolean **Empty** is set to false. We will assume that we have a **ReadData** procedure to get the data item and store it at **OneItem**. If

Figure 3.3

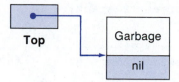

P is the pointer to the newly created element, the following two steps will insert the new element on top of the stack.

```
P^.Next := Top;
Top  := P;
```

The insertion is illustrated in Figure 3.4.

Figure 3.4

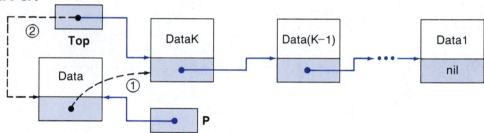

The pseudocode for the **PushStack** procedure is as follows.

Pseudocode

> **PushStack Procedure**
>
> IF stack empty THEN
>   Set **Empty** to false.
> ELSE
>   Create element.
>   Insert element.
> END IF.
> Store data.

We will use a parameter **DtItem** to pass the data stored at **OneItem** to the procedure. The parameter **DtItem** will be a value parameter. We will also need to pass variable parameters **Top2** for the top of the stack and **Empty2** for the empty or nonempty stack.

```
{***********************************************************}
{* PushStack - Procedure to store one data item on top of the  *}
{*            stack.                                            *}
{*       var parameters -                                       *}
{*            Top2 : Pointer to top of stack.                   *}
```

```
{*             Empty2 : Boolean for empty stack.                *}
{*        value parameters -                                    *}
{*             DtItem : Data to be pushed onto the stack.       *}
{**************************************************************}
procedure PushStack(DtItem : ItemData; var Top2 : ItemPtr;
                    var Empty2 : boolean);
var
  P2 : ItemPtr;                                    { List pointer }
begin
  if Empty2 then                                   { Empty stack }
    Empty2 := false
  { end if }
  else begin                                       { Stack not empty }
    new(P2);
    P2^.Next := Top2;
    Top2 := P2
  end; { else }
  Top2^.Data := DtItem                             { Store data }
end; { PushStack }
```

After the stack is initialized, a call to **PushStack** will result in a change from the figure on the left in Figure 3.5 to the figure on the right.

Figure 3.5

The **PopStack** procedure will get the data from the element on top of the stack and assign the data item to the data identifier. If the data item was from the last element on the stack, the Boolean **Empty3** is set to true. Otherwise the element is removed from the stack and the memory is released. The pseudocode for the **PopStack** procedure is as follows. We will assume that the calling program will check to make sure that the stack is not empty before calling the procedure.

Pseudocode

PopStack Procedure

Get data from top of stack.
IF last element THEN
    Set **Empty3** to true.
ELSE
    Point to new top.
    Remove old top.
    Release memory.
END IF.

We will pass the top of the stack as a variable parameter, the Boolean for the empty stack as a variable parameter, and the data from the stack as a variable parameter.

```
{**************************************************************}
{* PopStack - Procedure to get the data from the top element  *}
{*            of the stack.                                    *}
{*      var parameters -                                       *}
{*          DtItemЭ : Return the data from top of the stack.   *}
{*          TopЭ : Pointer to the top of the stack.           *}
{*          EmptyЭ : Boolean for empty stack.                  *}
{*      value parameters -                                     *}
{*          None.                                              *}
{**************************************************************}
procedure PopStack(var DtItemЭ : ItemData; var TopЭ : ItemPtr;
                   var EmptyЭ : boolean);
var
  PЭ : ItemPtr;                                { List pointer }
begin
  DtItemЭ := TopЭ^.Data;                          { Get data }
  if TopЭ^.Next = nil then                     { Last element }
    EmptyЭ := true
  else begin
    PЭ := TopЭ;                               { Remove element }
    TopЭ := TopЭ^.Next;
    dispose(PЭ)                               { Release memory }
  end { if }
end; { PopStack }
```

The next section will discuss how stacks are used by compilers to evaluate arithmetic expressions. Stacks will be used in Chapter 5 when we study recursion and again in Chapter 10 when we study graphs.

Like stacks, queues arise quite naturally. One of the most common uses of queues is for the computerized scheduling of jobs. In batch processing the jobs are *queued up* as they are read in, and then executed one after another in the order in which they were read. This descrption is, of course, a simplification of what really takes place in most systems, since it ignores the existence of priorities; when priorities are used, usually a queue exists for each priority category.

Queues are also familiar from everyday life. Any time you wait in line for something, you are waiting in a queue: The first person in is the first person out, and the last person in is the last person out. Queues will be used in Chapter 8 when we study advanced sorting techniques and again in Chapter 10 when we study graphs.

The queues that we will build as linked lists are forward-pointing linked lists in which all insertions are made at one end and all deletions are made from the other end. We will use the same **type** and **var** declarations as we did for our stack procedures, with the addition of a marker for the rear of the list. The basic procedures for queues are as follows.

Basic Procedures: Queues

1. Initialize procedure: Create first element.
2. Push procedure: Push one data item onto the rear of the queue.
3. Pop procedure: Pop one data item off the front of the queue.

The **InitQueue** procedure will create a first element for the queue, mark the front and the rear of the queue, and set the Boolean **Empty** to true. A call to this procedure produces the situation illustrated in Figure 3.6.

Figure 3.6

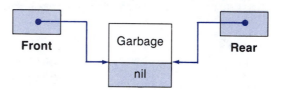

Since we are going to be popping from one end of the queue and pushing from the other end, we will mark the ends of the list using the pointers **Front** and **Rear**. These pointers will need to be added as global identifiers of type **ItemPtr** in the variable section of the main program. We therefore need the following **var** declarations in the main program.

```
var
   Front,                       { Marker for front of queue }
   Rear,                        { Marker for rear of queue }
   P : ItemPtr;
   Empty : boolean;             { Empty or nonempty queue }
   OneItem : ItemData;   { Data for one element of queue }
```

We can now code the **InitQueue** procedure.

```
{*********************************************************}
{* InitQueue - Procedure to create the first element for a    *}
{*             queue.                                         *}
{*        var parameters -                                    *}
{*            Front1 : Pointer to front of the queue.         *}
{*            Empty1 : Boolean for empty queue.               *}
{*            Rear1 : Pointer to rear of the queue.           *}
{*        value parameters -                                  *}
{*            None.                                           *}
{*********************************************************}
procedure InitQueue(var Front1, Rear1 : ItemPtr;
                    var Empty1 : boolean);
begin
   new(Front1);                        { Create element, mark front }
   Rear1 := Front1;                        { Mark rear of queue }
   Front1^.Next := nil;                       { Mark end of list }
   Empty1 := true
end; { InitQueue }
```

The procedures for pushing and popping elements from a queue are similar to the corresponding procedures for a stack. However, some differences should be noted. We will be marking both ends of the forward-pointing linked list. Elements are pushed onto the rear of the list, so the pointer **Rear** will be passed as a variable parameter in the **PushQueue** procedure. Elements are popped from the front of the list, so the pointer **Front** will be passed as a variable parameter in the **PopQueue** procedure. The Boolean **Empty** will be passed as a variable parameter in both procedures.

```
{***************************************************************}
{* PushQueue - Procedure to push a data item on the rear of a *}
{*             queue.                                          *}
{*       var parameters -                                      *}
{*            Rear2 : Pointer to rear of queue.                *}
{*            Empty2 : Boolean for empty queue.                *}
{*       value parameters -                                    *}
{*            DtItem2 : Data to be pushed onto the queue.      *}
{***************************************************************}
procedure PushQueue(var Rear2 : ItemPtr; DtItem2 : ItemData;
                    var Empty2 : boolean);
var
  P2 : ItemPtr;                               { List pointer }
begin
  if Empty2 then                              { Queue empty }
    Empty2 := false
  else begin                                  { Queue not empty }
    new(P2);
    P2^.Next := Rear^.Next;
    Rear^.Next := P2;
    Rear := P2
  end; { else }
  Rear^.Data := DtItem2                        { Store data }
end; { PushQueue }
```

After the queue is initialized, a call to **PushQueue** results in a change from the figure on the left in Figure 3.7 to the figure on the right.

Figure 3.7

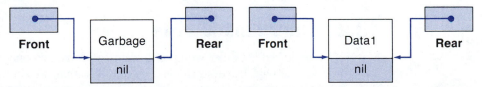

For the **PopStack** procedure, a variable parameter, **DtItem3**, is passed to return the data. The pointer, **Front3**, to the front of the list and the boolean, **Empty3**, are also passed as variable parameters. We can now code the procedure.

```
{***********************************************************}
{* PopQueue - Procedure to get one data item from the front of *}
{*           a queue.                                        *}
{*      var parameters -                                     *}
{*           DtItem∃ : Return the data.                      *}
{*           Empty∃ : Boolean for empty queue.               *}
{*           Front∃ : Pointer to front of queue.             *}
{*      value parameters -                                   *}
{*           None.                                           *}
{***********************************************************}
procedure PopQueue(var Front∃ : ItemPtr; var DtItem∃ : ItemData;
                   var Empty∃ : boolean);
var
  P∃ : ItemPtr;                                  { List pointer }
begin
  DtItem∃ := Front∃^.Data;                          { Get data }
  if Front∃^.Next = nil then                     { Last element }
    Empty∃ := true
  else begin
    P∃ := Front∃;                               { Remove element }
    Front∃ := Front∃^.Next;
    dispose(P∃)                                 { Release memory }
  end { else }
end; { PopQueue }
```

Exercises

3.1 Describe what is meant by each of the following.
(a) static data structure   (c) stack
(b) dynamic data structure   (d) queue

3.2 Give the **type** and **var** declarations needed to define a queue in which each data item is a single character.

3.3 Give the **type** and **var** declarations needed to define a queue in which each data item is a record containing a name of 20 characters, a social security number of 11 characters, a real pay rate, and an integer insurance code.

3.2 Other Linked Lists

The linked lists that we have studied so far contain only one pointer field, so we can only traverse the lists in one direction, as shown in Figure 3.8. As you may have already realized, some of our procedures would have been easier to code if we had been able to traverse the list in both directions. In order to be able to traverse both ways, we simply need to design the elements of the list so that they can have both forward and backward pointers. The elements of the list will each need to have three components, one component to hold the data and two additional components, one to point to the

Figure 3.8

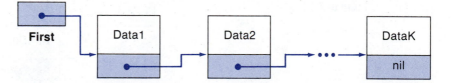

preceding element in the list and the other to point to the next element in the list. Each element will look like the element in Figure 3.9. Our list, after it has been created, will look like Figure 3.10. This type of a list is called a *doubly linked list*. Note that we have marked both ends of the list with the **nil** pointer and still have the first pointer at the beginning of the list.

Figure 3.9

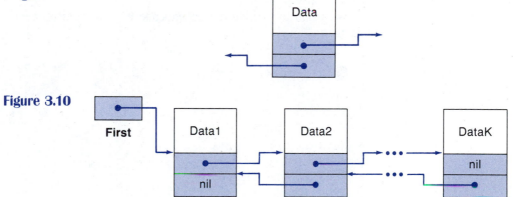

Figure 3.10

To define a single element of our list, we will have to modify our **type** declarations as follows.

```
type
   ItemData = record

                    |  Some data type

              end;
   ItemPtr = ^Item;
   Item = record
             Data : ItemData;
             RPtr,
             LPtr : ItemPtr
          end;
```

As we have seen, if **Pt** is an identifier of type **ItemPtr**, the statement

```
new(Pt);
```

creates an element whose three components are referenced by the identifiers indicated in Figure 3.11.

Figure 3.11

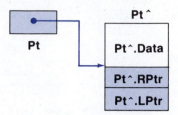

As an example of the use of a doubly linked list, let us consider the problem of creating a list in order as we did in Section 2.7. We will rewrite the procedures that we wrote in that section. However, this time we will use a doubly linked list for our structure. As before, we are assuming that the main program will open the data file and that the procedure will not be called if the file is empty.

We begin by writing the pseudocode for our main procedure, **Create2-InOrder**.

Pseudocode

Create2InOrder Procedure

Create an element.
Mark as first element.
Mark head of list.
Mark end of list.
WHILE not end of file
    Create an element.
    Get data.
    Store data.
    Find element after which new element is inserted.
    Insert new element.
END WHILE.

We will write the procedures to store the collection of employee data using doubly linked lists. As before, the list is created so that the data are stored in nondecreasing order by name. We now code the procedure called **Emp2InOrder**.

```
{*******************************************************************}
{* Emp2InOrder - Procedure to store the data for a collection  *}
{*              of employees in a doubly linked list in        *}
{*              nondecreasing order by name.                   *}
{*      var parameters -                                        *}
{*          DFile : Text file containing the data.             *}
{*          First : Pointer to the first element of the list.  *}
{*      value parameters -                                      *}
{*          None.                                               *}
{*******************************************************************}
```

```
procedure Emp2InOrder(var DFile : text; var First : Itemptr);
var
   P, Q : ItemPtr;                              { List pointers }
begin
   new(P);                                      { First element }
   First := P;
   P^.LPtr := nil;
   P^.RPtr := nil;
   while not eof(DFile) do begin                { Loop to store data }
      new(P);
      ReadData(DFile, P^.Data);
      Find2(Q, P, First);
      Insert2(P, Q)
   end   { while }
end; { Emp2InOrder }
```

There is only a slight difference between the code for this procedure and the code for the procedure for a singly linked list: When the first element is created in **Create2InOrder**, the **First** pointer is assigned to this element and both of the pointers **LPtr** and **RPtr** are set to **nil**. Compare the above code with the code using a simple linked list in Section 2.7.

Let us continue our top-down design by writing the pseudocode for the **Insert2** procedure. This procedure will insert the element pointed to by **P** into the list after the element pointed to by **Q**. This insertion is always possible, since we have created our list with a dummy element at the beginning of the list. We do, however, have to consider two special cases, one when there is an element of the list after the one pointed to by **Q**, and the other when **Q** points to the last element of the list. When there is another element in the list after the one pointed to by **Q**, we have the situation shown in Figure 3.12.

Figure 3.12

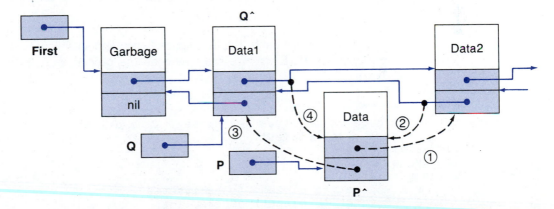

The insertion requires the establishment of the four pointers indicated in the figure. If **Q** is at the end of the list, only three steps are needed, as indicated in Figure 3.13.

Figure 3.13

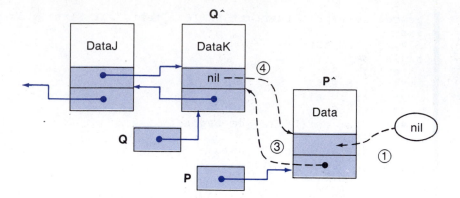

Satisfy yourself that Step 1 in Figure 3.13 is also accomplished by Step 1 in Figure 3.12. When **Q** is the last element and **P** is inserted, note how the end of the list is marked (**nil** is moved to **P**) when Step 1 is performed. Study both figures carefully. The pseudocode for this procedure is as follows.

Pseudocode

> **Insert2 Procedure**
>
> Make new element point to element following list element.
> Make new element point to list element.
> IF end of list THEN
>   Make list element point to new element.
> ELSE
>   Make element following list element point to new element.
>   Make list element point to new element.
> END IF.

If **Q** is the pointer to the list element, the element following can be referenced by **Q^.RPtr**. We can now code the procedure that we will call **Insert2**.

```
{*********************************************************}
{*  Insert2 - Procedure to insert a new element into a list    *}
{*            after a given element.                           *}
{*        var parameters -                                     *}
{*            None.                                            *}
{*        value parameters -                                   *}
{*            P : Pointer to element to be inserted.           *}
{*            Q : Pointer to element of the list.              *}
{*********************************************************}
procedure Insert2(P, Q : ItemPtr);
begin
  P^.RPtr := Q^.RPtr;
```

```
    P^.LPtr := Q;
    if Q^.RPtr = nil then              { Last element }
      Q^.RPtr := P
    else begin                         { Not last element }
      Q^.RPtr^.LPtr := P;
      Q^.RPtr := P
    end { else }
end; { Insert2 }
```

The **Find2** procedure will be a little bit different from procedure **Find** in Chapter 2, since the pointer can be moved in either direction in the list. For one thing, a single pointer **Q** can be used to find the element after which **P^** is to be inserted. The basic idea, however, is the same as in the earlier procedure. A single pointer, **Q**, is set to the beginning of the list. This pointer is moved through the list until the first element with data greater than or equal to the data stored in **P^** is found or until the end of the list is encountered. If, at the end of the list the data stored at **Q^** are still less than or equal to the data stored at **P^**, then **Q** is pointing at the right element. Otherwise, the pointer **Q** is moved back one element in the list.

We now code the procedure.

```
{**********************************************************}
{* Find2 - Procedure to find the element in the list after *}
{*         which the new element is to be inserted.        *}
{*      var parameters -                                   *}
{*          Q2 : Pointer to the element of the list.       *}
{*      value parameters -                                 *}
{*          First2 : Pointer to first element of list.     *}
{*          P2 : Pointer to element to be inserted.        *}
{**********************************************************}
procedure Find2(var Q2 : ItemPtr; P2, First2 : ItemPtr);
begin
  Q2 := First2;
  if Q2^.RPtr <> nil then begin
    while (Q2^.RPtr <> nil) and          { Loop to find element }
          (Q2^.Data.Name < P2^.Data.Name) do
      Q2 := Q2^.RPtr;
    { end while }
    if Q2^.Data.Name > P2^.Data.Name
      then Q2 := Q2^.LPtr
    { end if }
  end { if }
end; { Find2 }
```

Several other possible structures exist for linked lists. For now we will look at two of the many possibilities; several others will be considered in the exercises at the end of the chapter. One possible structure is known as a *circular linked list* or *ring* (see Figure 3.14). Note that with this structure we do not have an end of the list. The last element created is simply hooked back to the first element of the list, and this connection creates the ring. We do have a pointer to the first element so that we can enter the list.

Figure 3.14   *Ring*

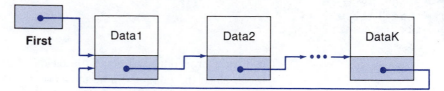

Such a structure would be helpful in a program that uses the days of the week. The program, for example, could print out the calendar for a month or for a whole year. The days of the week could be stored in a ring so that as the calendar was being created, the program would simply travel around the ring as many times as was needed. The ring would look like Figure 3.15. We will ask you to use this idea in the exercises.

Figure 3.15   *Weekly ring*

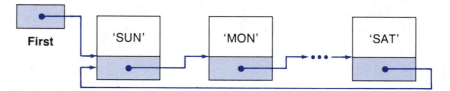

A second structure is known as a *doubly linked circular list* or a *doubly linked ring*. It is similar to the ring, but it is created with forward and backward pointers (see Figure 3.16).

Figure 3.16

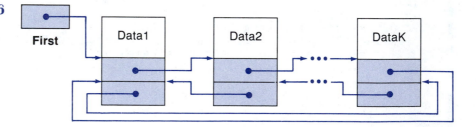

Exercises

3.4   Give the **type** and **var** declarations needed to create a doubly linked list of data. The data consist of a name with 20 characters, a social security number with 11 characters, a real pay rate, and an integer age.

3.5   Write a procedure that will use the declarations from Exercise 3.4. The procedure should read the data from a file and store them in a doubly linked list.

3.6 Write a procedure that will print the data that were stored in the list in Exercise 3.5 back to a file in exactly the same format.

3.7 Write a procedure that will write the data that were stored in the list in Exercise 3.5 back to a file in exactly the same format. The data should be written to the file in the reverse order from that in which they were originally stored.

3.8 Write a procedure that will use the declarations in Exercise 3.4. The procedure should read the data from a file and store them in a doubly linked circular list.

3.9 Write a program that will create a ring containing the days of the week. The days can be stored as strings of three characters.

3.10 Write a procedure that will print out a calendar for any given month using the procedure written in Exercise 3.9. The procedure should accept the number of days in the month, the first day of the month, and a pointer to an element of the list from the calling program.

3.3 Long Integers

In this section we will look at the use of a stack in an application. One problem that programmers must be aware of is that each computer system allows integers of only a specific maximum length. The compiler usually limits this length based on the word size of a particular machine. For example, an 8-bit machine may allow integers up to 5 digits in length, whereas a large computer like the Cyber may allow integers up to 13 digits in length.

In this section we will develop a method for storing positive integers of arbitrary length and will build a function that will add and return the sum of two such integer numbers. Recall that any time we add two integer numbers we traverse the string of digits from right to left, adding corresponding digits along with the carry from the sum of the two previous digits. Therefore, we will need to build a structure to store the individual digits of long integer numbers.

The digits of the numbers will be stored as characters, and they will be stored from right to left. The first component of the structure we build will hold the rightmost digit, and the last component will hold the leftmost digit. Since integer numbers are read from left to right and numbers are added from right to left, we need a process in which the first digit read will be the last digit added and the last digit read will be the first digit added. Thus we will use stacks for the structures to store our long integer numbers.

To build the necessary structure we will need the following **type** declarations:

```
type
   ItemData = char;
   ItemPtr = ^Item;
```

```
Item = record
         Data : ItemData;
         Next : ItemPtr
      end;
```

Let us now consider the basic operations that we will use to obtain the digits of an integer so that we can store these digits as characters in a list. We will illustrate this process with a simple three-digit integer. Consider the integer

$$492$$

Using integer division to divide this integer by 10,

$$
\begin{array}{r}
49 \\
10\overline{)492} \\
490 \\
\hline
2
\end{array}
$$

we find that our first digit will be 2, the remainder. Since we want to store the corresponding character, '2', the character is obtained by using the built-in Pascal function **chr**. The statement

```
chr(2 + ord('0'));
```

returns the character '2'. We need to use 2 + **ord**('0') as the argument because the function **chr** expects the ordinal value of the character it is to return. The ordinal value of a character is simply the position number of the character in the sequence of characters used by a given computer system. Since the sequence of digits 0, . . . , 9 is always in order and **ord**('0') returns the position number of 0, the position number of any digit will be given by

$$\text{digit} + \mathbf{ord}('0')$$

We repeat this process, dividing the new quotient by 10:

$$
\begin{array}{r}
4 \\
10\overline{)49} \\
40 \\
\hline
9
\end{array}
$$

This time we obtain our second integer digit, 9. We can compute and store the corresponding character digit in the list. We again divide the new quotient by 10:

$$
\begin{array}{r}
0 \\
10\overline{)4} \\
0 \\
\hline
4
\end{array}
$$

We obtain our next digit, 4, and our process is over since the quotient that we obtain is 0. If **Num** is the integer identifier that is assigned the integer number 492, then

```
Num mod 10
```

will return the remainder and

```
Num div 10
```

will return the new quotient.

We also need to be able to compute the integer value that corresponds to a given character digit. In order to do so, we again use the built-in Pascal function **ord**. If **Digit** is any character digit, the integer value of **Digit** is given by the following expression:

```
ord(Digit) - ord('0');
```

We now consider the problem of finding the sum of two long integer numbers that are stored in two stacks. The process will be illustrated with short integer numbers in order to save space. Suppose that we have the lists depicted in Figure 3.17. The problem is to build a function that will find the sum of **Num1** and **Num2**, which means that the function must accept the two stacks, compute the sum, store this sum in another stack, and return the sum stack to the calling program. The stack that is to be returned in this example will be the one in Figure 3.18.

Figure 3.17

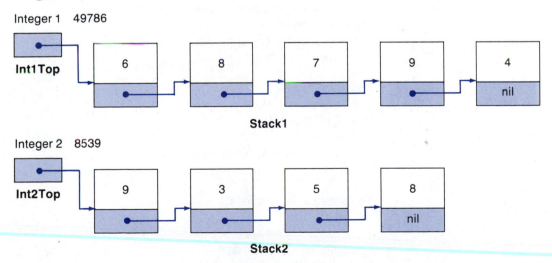

Integer 1   49786

Int1Top   Stack1

Integer 2   8539

Int2Top   Stack2

Figure 3.18

Integer Sum   58325

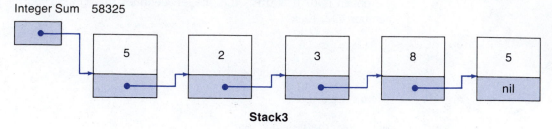

Stack3

Note that we must obtain each digit for the sum by adding the corresponding integer digits of the two character digits that are stored on **Stack 1** and **Stack 2**, along with the carry that was generated in the previous addition. After we do this addition, we must compute the character digit that is to be stored and we must compute the new carry to be used in the next addition. We will illustrate this process by walking through the first two steps in the above example.

Pop **Digit1**, '6', off **Stack 1**.
Compute integer **Digit1**, 6.
Pop **Digit2**, '9', off **Stack 2**.
Compute integer **Digit2**, 9.
Add the 6 and the 9 to obtain 15.
Compute the integer digit for the sum by dividing by 10 and computing the remainder.

$$15 \textbf{ mod } 10 = 5$$

Compute the corresponding character digit, '5'.
Push '5' on **Stack 3**.
Compute the carry by computing the quotient.

$$15 \textbf{ div } 10 = 1$$

Pop '8' off **Stack 1**.
Compute integer digit 8.
Pop '3' off **Stack 2**.
Compute integer digit 3.
Add the two integers along with the carry.

$$8 + 3 + 1 = 12$$

Compute the integer for the sum.

$$12 \textbf{ mod } 10 = 2$$

Compute the character digit '2'.
Push '2' on **Stack 3**.
Compute the new carry.

$$12 \textbf{ div } 10 = 1$$

As we can see, this process will end when we run out of data in either list. We must then proceed to the end of the other list, adding the integer and the carry, computing the new integer, computing the character digit to be stored, and computing the new carry. We can now outline the process using pseudocode.

Pseudocode

LongIntSum Function

Initialize Stack 3.
Set **Carry** to 0.
WHILE (not **Empty1**) and (not **Empty2**)
  Pop character corresponding to digit 1 off stack 1.
  Compute integer 1.
  Pop character corresponding to digit 2 off stack 2.
  Compute integer 2.
  Find sum of integer 1 + integer 2 + **Carry**.
  Compute integer digit.
  Compute character corresponding to digit.
  Compute new **Carry**.
  Push character corresponding to digit on stack 3.
END WHILE.
WHILE not **Empty1**
  Pop character corresponding to digit 1 off stack 1.
  Compute integer 1.
  Find sum of integer 1 + **Carry**.
  Compute integer digit.
  Compute character corresponding to digit.
  Compute **Carry**.
  Push character corresponding to digit on stack 3.
END WHILE.
WHILE not **Empty2**
  Pop character corresponding to digit 2 off stack 2.
  Compute integer 2.
  Find sum of integer 2 + **Carry**.
  Compute integer digit.
  Compute character corresponding to digit.
  Compute **Carry**.
  Push character corresponding to digit on stack 3.
END WHILE.
IF **Carry** <> 0 THEN
  Compute character corresponding to digit of **Carry**.
  Push character corresponding to digit on stack 3.
END IF.

Since the pseudocode is straightforward, we can now code the function.

```
{***********************************************************}
{* LongIntSum - Function to compute the sum of two long integer*}
{*              numbers that are stored in two stacks. The      *}
{*              numbers are stored one character digit per      *}
{*              element. The sum is to be stored in a third     *}
{*              stack one character digit per element.          *}
{*      value parameters -                                      *}
{*           Int1Top : Pointer to top of first stack.           *}
{*           Int2Top : Pointer to top of second stack.          *}
{*           Empty1 : Boolean for empty first stack.            *}
{*           Empty2 : Boolean for empty second stack.           *}
{***********************************************************}
function LongIntSum(Int1Top, Int2Top : ItemPtr;
                    Empty1, Empty2 : boolean) : ItemPtr;
var
  IntSumTop : ItemPtr;                        { Stack pointer }
  IntSum, IntDigit, Carry,                    { Integers for
                                                arithmetic   }
  IntDig1, IntDig2 : integer;
  ChrDig1, ChrDig2, Chrdigit : char;          { Digits from stacks }
  EmptySum : boolean;                         { Empty stack for sum }
begin
  InitStack(IntSumTop, EmptySum);
  Carry := 0;
  while (not Empty1) and (not Empty2) do begin    { Loop to
                                                  compute sum }

    PopStack(ChrDig1, Int1Top, Empty1);
    IntDig1 := ord(ChrDig1) - ord('0');
    PopStack(ChrDig2, Int2Top, Empty2);
    IntDig2 := ord(ChrDig2) - ord('0');
    IntSum := IntDig1 + IntDig2 + Carry;
    IntDigit := IntSum mod 10;
    ChrDigit := Chr(IntDigit + ord('0'));
    Carry := IntSum div 10;
    PushStack(ChrDigit, IntSumTop, EmptySum)
  end; { while }
  while not Empty1 do begin                       { Loop for list1 }
    PopStack(ChrDig1, Int1Top, Empty1);
    IntDig1 := ord(ChrDig1) - ord('0');
    IntSum := IntDig1 + Carry;
    IntDigit := IntSum mod 10;
    ChrDigit := chr(IntDigit + ord('0'));
    Carry := IntSum div 10;
    PushStack(ChrDigit, IntSumTop, EmptySum)
  end; { while }
  while not Empty2 do begin                       { Loop for list2 }
    PopStack(ChrDig2, Int2Top, Empty2);
    IntDig2 := ord(ChrDig2) - ord('0');
    IntSum := IntDig2 + Carry;
    IntDigit := IntSum mod 10;
    ChrDigit := Chr(IntDigit + ord('0'));
    Carry := IntSum div 10;
    PushStack(ChrDigit, IntSumTop, EmptySum)
```

```
   end; { while }
   if Carry <> 0 then begin                        { Last carry }
      ChrDigit := chr(Carry + ord('0'));
      PushStack(ChrDigit, IntSumTop, EmptySum)
   end; { if }
   LongIntSum := IntSumTop
end; { LongIntSum }
```

You will be asked to test this function in the exercises. You will also be asked to write a procedure to store a long integer number in a stack, with each digit stored as a character. Also as an exercise you will be asked to consider what can be done if one or both of the long integer numbers is negative.

Exercises

3.11 Write the procedure that will allow the user to input a long integer number from the keyboard. The integer is to be stored in a stack, with one character digit stored in each element.

3.12 Write a program that will use the procedure written in Exercise 3.11. The program is to test the function **LongIntSum**. The program should allow the user to input two long integer numbers from the keyboard. The sum is to be computed using the function **LongIntSum**, and the result is to be printed back to the screen.

3.13 In order to be able to handle the case in which one of the long integers is negative, we will use complements to represent these numbers. Write a procedure that will allow the user to input either a positive or a negative long integer number from the keyboard. When the integer is negative, the procedure should compute and store the 10s complement of the number. For example, the 10s complement of 273 is found by first finding the three-digit 9s complement, 726, and then adding 1. The three-digit number 727 is the 10s complement of 273.

3.14 Write a program that will use the procedure from Exercise 3.13 and the function **LongIntSum** to compute the sum of any two long integer numbers. The sum should then be printed to the screen.

3.15 Rewrite the function **LongIntSum** so that each element of the linked list can store three-digit integer numbers.

3.16 Rewrite the procedures from Exercises 3.11 and 3.12 so that the long integer number that is input from the keyboard is stored as one three-digit integer number per element.

3.17 Write a program to test the subprograms written in Exercises 3.15 and 3.16.

3.4 Arithmetic Expressions

In this section we will consider one of the most common applications of stacks: the evaluation of arithmetic expressions. Some BASIC interpreters, for example, contain a stack for this purpose, and many advanced pocket calculators use stacks for expression evaluation. Some Hewlett-Packard calculators have a stack to carry out their arithmetic. They use postfix (reverse Polish) notation, and if you have ever used one of these calculators, you are already familiar with the convenience of this notation and stack storage since it eliminates parentheses from complicated expressions.

Consider the simple arithmetic expression A + B. We have three possibilities for the positioning of the operator with respect to the operands A and B. We can position the operator before the operands:

$$+ \ A \ B$$

which is called *prefix notation*. We can position the operator between the operands:

$$A + B$$

which is called *infix notation*. We can position the operator after the operands:

$$A \ B \ +$$

which is called *postfix notation*.

Prefix notation was invented by the Polish logician Lukasiewicz and is known as *Polish notation*. Postfix notation is also known as *reverse Polish notation*.

Let us consider how to convert a standard infix expression to postfix notation. We apply the rules of precedence and convert the portion of the expression that is to be evaluated first, positioning the operator after that portion's operands for postfix conversions. The conversion is done in stages. Consider the following example.

A + B * C	Original expression
A + (B * C)	Parentheses for emphasis
A + (B C *)	Convert the multiplication
A (B C *) +	Convert the addition
A B C * +	Final result

The rules for this conversion are as follows:

1. The operations with highest precedence are converted first.
2. After a portion of the expression has been converted, it is treated as a single operand.

In order to convert the same expression to prefix notation, we use the two rules just listed but position the operator before the operands:

A + B * C	Original expression
A + (B * C)	Parentheses for emphasis

$$A + (* B \ C)$$ Convert the multiplication
$$+ A \ (* B \ C)$$ Convert the addition
$$+ A * B \ C$$ Final result

Notice that one of the advantages prefix and postfix notation have over infix notation is that in prefix and postfix notations, neither parentheses nor operator priorities are required in order to determine the order in which the operators are to be applied. In prefix notation, an operator can only be applied to the two operands that immediately follow it. In postfix notation, the operator applies only to the two immediately preceding operands. For example, consider the two infix expressions

$$A + (B * C) \quad \text{and} \quad (A + B) * C$$

In these expressions, parentheses are used to show how the infix expressions are to be evaluated. Converting these expressions to postfix notation, we obtain the following.

$$A + (B * C) \qquad (A + B) * C$$
$$A + (B \ C *) \qquad (A \ B +) * C$$
$$A \ (B \ C *) + \qquad (A \ B +) \ C *$$
$$A \ B \ C * + \qquad A \ B + C *$$

Notice the following important points. First, the two infix expressions, which differ only in the positioning of the parentheses, translate into two different postfix expressions. Thus we do not need the parentheses to distinguish between the two once they have been converted to postfix notation. Second, the postfix expression determines the order in which the operators will be applied. In the expression

$$A \ B \ C * +$$

we cannot apply the operation '+' first, since the operator can only apply to the two operands that immediately precede it. Only the '*' is preceded by two operands, and hence it must be applied first.

Even though Pascal does not have the operation of exponentiation built into the language, we will use all of the operations of addition, subtraction, multiplication, division, and exponentiation in the longhand conversions of the examples that follow. We will use the standard symbols for the first four operations (+, −, *, /), and we will use ∧ for exponentiation. For these binary operations, the following is the order of precedence, highest to lowest.

∧	exponentiation
*, /	multiplication, division
+, −	addition, subtraction

We will also use the standard convention that when unparenthesized operators of the same precedence are scanned, the order of precedence will be from left to right except in the case of exponentiation, where it will be from right to left. Thus

A + B − C	means	(A + B) − C
A / B * C	means	(A / B) * C
A ^ B ^ C	means	A ^ (B ^ C)

Consider the following examples.

Example   Convert each of the following infix expressions to postfix.

Expression1	*Expression2*	*Expression3*
A − B + C	A * (B − C)	(A + B) * (C − D)
(A − B) + C	A * (B C −)	(A B +) * (C D −)
(A B −) + C	A (B C −) *	(A B +) (C D −) *
(A B −) C +	A B C − *	A B + C D − *
A B − C +		

Example   Convert each of the following infix expressions to postfix.

Expression1

A − B ^ C + D / E − F
A − (B C ^) + (D E /) − F
(A (B C ^) −) + (D E /) − F
((A (B C ^) −) (D E /) +) − F
(A B C ^ − D E / +) − F
A B C ^ − D E / + F −

Expression2

(B ^ 2 − 4 * A * C) ^ (1 / 2)
((B 2 ^) − (4 A *) * C) ^ (1 2 /)
((B 2 ^) − (4 A * C *)) ^ (1 2 /)
(B 2 ^ 4 A * C * −) ^ (1 2 /)
B 2 ^ 4 A * C * − 1 2 / ^

Example   Convert each of the following infix expressions to prefix.

Expression1	*Expression2*	*Expression3*
A − B + C	A * (B − C)	(A + B) * (C − D)
(− A B) + C	A * (− B C)	(+ A B) * (− C D)
+ (− A B) C	* A (− B C)	* (+ A B) (− C D)
+ − A B C	* A − B C	* + A B − C D

Example   Convert each of the following infix expressions to prefix.

Expression1

$$A - B \wedge C + D / E - F$$
$$A - (\wedge B C) + (/ D E) - F$$
$$(- A \wedge B C) + (/ D E) - F$$
$$(+ - A \wedge B C / D E) - F$$
$$- + - A \wedge B C / D E F$$

Expression2

$$(B \wedge 2 - 4 * A * C) \wedge (1 / 2)$$
$$((\wedge B 2) - (* 4 A) * C) \wedge (/ 1 2)$$
$$((\wedge B 2) - (* * 4 A C)) \wedge (/ 1 2)$$
$$(- \wedge B 2 * * 4 A C) \wedge (/ 1 2)$$
$$\wedge - \wedge B 2 * * 4 A C / 1 2$$

Evaluating Postfix and Prefix Expressions

In order to evaluate a postfix expression, we need the following rules.

1. Scan the expression from left to right.
2. Each time an operator is encountered, apply it to the two immediately preceding operands.
3. Replace the operands and the operator with the result.
4. Continue scanning to the right.

We illustrate with some examples.

Example

Infix Expression		*Postfix Expression*
$3 + 4 * 5$	$\longrightarrow$	$3\ 4\ 5\ *\ +$

Evaluation

$$3\ 4\ 5\ *\ +$$
$$3\ (\ 4\ 5\ *\ )\ +$$
$$3\ 20\ +$$
$$23$$

Example

Infix Expression		*Postfix Expression*
$(\ 7 + 2\ ) * 3$	$\longrightarrow$	$7\ 2\ +\ 3\ *$

Evaluation

$$7\ 2\ +\ 3\ *$$
$$(\ 7\ 2\ +\ )\ 3\ *$$
$$9\ 3\ *$$
$$27$$

As another example, let us evaluate the following expression, which is already in postfix notation.

Example

Expression	Evaluation
2 3 4 5 6 7 + * + * +	(6 7 +)
2 3 4 5 13 * + * +	(5 13 *)
2 3 4 65 + * +	(4 65 +)
2 3 69 * +	(3 69 *)
2 207 +	
209	

We can evaluate expressions that are written in prefix notation similarly. Here are the corresponding rules.

1. Scan the expression from right to left.
2. When an operator is encountered, apply it to the two operands that immediately follow the operator in the string.
3. Replace the operands and the operator with the result.
4. Continue scanning the expression to the left.

We illustrate with some examples.

Example

Infix Expression		*Prefix Expression*
3 * (2 − 6)	⟶	* 3 − 2 6

Evaluation

* 3 − 2 6
* 3 (− 2 6)
* 3 (−4)
−12

Example

Infix Expression		*Prefix Expression*
(2 + 3) * (6 − 4)	⟶	* + 2 3 − 6 4

Evaluation

* + 2 3 (− 6 4)
* + 2 3 2
* (+ 2 3) 2
* 5 2
10

As these examples show, postfix and prefix notation can be used equally well to handle the evaluation of arithmetic expressions. We will concentrate on postfix notation and ask you to do some additional problems using prefix notation in the exercises.

Using a Stack

The most appropriate structure to use in a Pascal program for evaluating postfix expressions is a stack, as the following discussion will make clear. Here is the process that we will use in our program:

1. Scan the expression from left to right.
2. Each time an operand (digit) is encountered, convert it to an integer and push it onto the stack.
3. Each time an operator is encountered, pop the top two operands (integers) off the stack, evaluate the binary expression, and push the result (integer) back onto the stack.

Let us consider some examples. The stack is horizontal, with the top of the stack on the right. The elements on the stack are separated by commas.

Example

Expression	*Stack*	*Evaluation*
2 4 5 * +	2	
4 5 * +	2, 4	
5 * +	2, 4, 5	
* +	2, 20	4 * 5 = 20
+	22	2 + 20 = 22

Example

Expression	*Stack*	*Evaluation*
7 2 + 3 *	7	
2 + 3 *	7, 2	
+ 3 *	9	7 + 2 = 9
3 *	9, 3	
*	27	9 * 3 = 27

We will begin to develop a procedure to evaluate a postfix expression by first writing the pseudocode. We will make the following assumptions:

1. The expression is stored in a buffer of 20 characters.
2. The buffer contains only allowable characters, blanks, digits, and operators.
3. The only operators in the expression are '+', '−', '*', and '/'.
4. The operands in the expression are single-digit integers.

We will call this procedure **PostFixEval**.

Pseudocode

PostFixEval Procedure

Initialize the stack.
FOR **I** = 1 to 20
   IF **Buff(I)** <> blank THEN
     IF **Buff(I)** is a digit THEN
       Convert to integer.

```
                Push integer on stack.
            ELSE
                Pop Val1 off stack.
                Pop Val2 off stack.
                Operation = Buff(I).
                Evaluate (Val2, operation, Val1)
                Push computed value on stack.
            END IF.
        END IF.
    END FOR.
    Pop final value off stack.
```

If a character represents one of the digits, we need to use the following statement to convert the digit from its character value to its corresponding integer value.

```
ord(character) - ord('0');
```

Since we are assuming that our expressions are made up of single-digit integer numbers, in order to obtain integer output we will use the Pascal operator **div** any time the operator '/' is encountered in an expression. This process will be generalized in the exercises.

We can make use of the procedures that we already have written for stacks, **InitStack**, **PushStack**, and **PopStack**, but we will have to write a new procedure, **Evaluate**, to evaluate the expression

Val2 Operator **Val1**

The array containing the postfix expression will be passed as a value parameter. The final computed value will be passed back to the calling program using a variable parameter. We now code the procedure.

```
{*******************************************************************}
{* PostFixEval - Procedure to compute the integer value for a    *}
{*               postfix expression. It is assumed that each      *}
{*               operand is a single integer digit and that       *}
{*               the expression contains only legal characters.*}
{*        var parameters -                                        *}
{*            FinalVal : Return the computed value.               *}
{*        value parameters -                                      *}
{*            Buff - Array containing the postfix expression.     *}
{*******************************************************************}
procedure PostFixEval(Buff : string20; var FinalVal : integer);
var
   Top : Itemptr;                           { Stack pointer }
   Empty : boolean;                         { For empty stack }
   Val1, Val2, Val, CharVal : integer;      { For evaluation }
```

```
begin
   InitStack(Top, Empty);
   for I := 1 to 20 do begin              { Scanning loop }
      if Buff[I] <> ' ' then
         if Buff[I] in ['0'..'9'] then begin     { Digit }
            CharVal := ord(Buff[I]) - ord('0');
            PushStack(CharVal, Top, Empty)
         end { if }
         else begin                       { Operator }
            PopStack(Val1, Top, Empty);
            PopStack(Val2, Top, Empty);
            Evaluate(Val, Val2, Buff[I], Val1);
            PushStack(Val, Top, Empty)
         end  { else }
      { end if }
   end; { for }
PopStack(FinalVal, Top, Empty)            { Final value }
end; { PostFixEval }
```

To write the procedure **Evaluate**, we need to check to make sure that the character read is one of the four operators '+', '−', '∗', or '/'. If it is, we need to use the appropriate expression to evaluate

Val2 Operator **Val1**

The computed value will be assigned to **Val** and passed back to be pushed onto the stack. The use of the **case** structure will make this coding easier. We need to worry about division by 0: if **Val1** = 0, the expression **Val2** / **Val1** will be assigned the value of 0, so that the program will continue to run, and a warning message will be issued.

```
{*****************************************************************}
{* Evaluate - Procedure to compute the integer value of    *}
{*          (V1 Oper V2). If "Oper" is "/" and V2 is 0,    *}
{*          a warning message is printed and 0 is assigned *}
{*          as the computed value.                          *}
{*      var parameters -                                    *}
{*          Result : Integer for computed value             *}
{*      value parameters -                                  *}
{*          V1 : First operand.                             *}
{*          Oper : Operator.                                *}
{*          V2 : Second operand.                            *}
{*****************************************************************}
procedure Evaluate(var Result : integer; V1 : integer;
                   Oper : char;  V2 : integer);
   begin
      if Oper in ['+', '-', '*', '/'] then          { Operator }
         case Oper of                        { Compute value }
            '+' : Result := V1 + V2;
            '-' : Result := V1 - V2;
            '*' : Result := V1 * V2;
            '/' : begin
```

```
          if V2 <> 0 then
             Result := V1 div V2
          { end if }
          else begin                      { Division by zero }
             writeln('Warning! Division by zero.');
             Result := 0;
          end { else }
       end
    end  { case }
  { end if }
  else
     writeln('Invalid operator')
  { end else }
end;  { Evaluate }
```

Converting Infix to Postfix

Let us now consider the problem of developing a procedure to convert an expression from infix notation to postfix notation. If we study the expressions that were converted previously,

Infix	*Postfix*
A + (B * C)	A B C * +
(A + B) * C	A B + C *
(A + B) * (C − D)	A B + C D − *

we notice that the order of the operands is the same in both notations. However, the operators are positioned differently and even their order may be changed. Our job, then, is to reposition and reorder the operators if necessary. We can accomplish this task by again making use of a separate stack to store the operators. Each operator from the infix expression is pushed onto the stack before being placed in the postfix expression. Also, before an operator is pushed onto the stack, any operator having higher priority is popped off the stack and placed in the postfix expression. More explicitly, the rules that we will follow for transforming an infix expression to a postfix expression are the following:

1. Scan the infix expression from left to right.
2. When an operand is encountered, move it directly to the postfix expression.
3. When an operator is encountered:
   (a) If the stack is empty, push the operator onto the stack.
   (b) If the stack is not empty, pop the operators off the stack one at a time and place them in the postfix expression. This process continues until one of the following happens:
   (i) the stack is empty;
   (ii) the priority of the element from the stack is less than the priority of the operator from the infix expression;
   (iii) a left parenthesis is encountered.

If this process terminates when the stack is empty, push the operator from the infix expression onto the stack. In the other two cases, push the last element from the stack back onto the stack, and then push the operator from the infix expression onto the stack.

4. When a left parenthesis is encountered, push it onto the stack.
5. When a right parenthesis is encountered, unstack the operators and place them in the postfix expression until a matching left parenthesis is found on the stack. Both parentheses are discarded and the process continues.
6. When the entire infix expression has been processed, remove any remaining operators from the stack and place them in the postfix expression.

When a left parenthesis is encountered in the infix expression, the parenthesis is placed on the stack and a new substack is started. The bottom of this new stack is the left parenthesis. The expression inside the parentheses is translated using this substack and the above set of rules. When the matching right parenthesis is encountered, the substack is emptied and the parentheses are discarded. Let us consider some examples.

Example

Infix Expression	Postfix Expression	Operator Stack
A + B * C	empty	empty
+ B * C	A	empty
B * C	A	+
* C	A B	+
C	A B	+ *
empty	A B C	+ *
empty	A B C *	+
empty	A B C * +	empty

Example

Infix Expression	Postfix Expression	Operator Stack
A * B + C	empty	empty
* B + C	A	empty
B + C	A	*
+ C	A B	*
C	A B *	+
empty	A B * C	+
empty	A B * C +	empty

Example

Infix Expression	Postfix Expression	Operator Stack	
(A + B) * C	empty	empty	
A + B) * C	empty	(	sub
+ B) * C	A	(	.
B) * C	A	(+	.
) * C	A B	(+	stack
* C	A B +	empty	
C	A B +	*	
empty	A B + C	*	
empty	A B + C *	empty	

Example

Infix Expression	Postfix Expression	Operator Stack
A * (B * C + D) + E	empty	empty
* (B * C + D) + E	A	empty
(B * C + D) + E	A	*
B * C + D) + E	A	* (sub
* C + D) + E	A B	* (.
C + D) + E	A B	* (* .
+ D) + E	A B C	* (* .
D) + E	A B C *	* (+ .
) + E	A B C * D	* (+ stack
+ E	A B C * D +	*
E	A B C * D + *	+
empty	A B C * D + * E	+
empty	A B C * D + * E +	empty

Notice that in the last example, the expression in parentheses,

$$(B * C + D)$$

is translated on a substack that begins with the left parenthesis. The '*' (below the left parenthesis) remains on the stack until the expression in parentheses has been translated.

Let us now write the pseudocode for the procedure to convert an expression from infix notation to postfix notation. We will assume that the infix expression is stored in a buffer of 20 characters. The operands will be single digits, and each of the characters in the expression will be separated by one blank. The buffer will be padded with blanks. The conversion procedure will convert the infix expression, which is stored in the buffer called **InBuff**, to the postfix expression, which will be stored in a buffer called **PostBuff**. The buffer **PostBuff** will also be an array of 20 characters.

Pseudocode

Convert Procedure

Initialize the stack.
FOR **I** = 1 to 20
    IF **InBuff**(**I**) is a digit THEN
        Put digit in **PostBuff**.
        Put blank in **PostBuff**.
    END IF.
    IF **InBuff**(**I**) is a left parenthesis THEN
        Push left parenthesis onto stack.
    END IF.
    IF **InBuff**(**I**) is a right parenthesis THEN
        Pop character off stack.
        WHILE character <> left parenthesis

```
                    Put character in PostBuff.
                    Put blank in PostBuff.
                    Pop character off stack.
                END WHILE.
            END IF.
        IF InBuff(I) is an operation THEN
            IF stack is empty THEN
                Push InBuff(I) onto stack.
            ELSE
                Pop character off stack.
                WHILE (Priority(character) >= Priority
                        (InBuff(I))* and (stack not empty)
                        and (character <> left parenthesis)
                    Put character in PostBuff.
                    Put blank in PostBuff.
                    Pop character off stack.
                END WHILE.
                IF character <> left parenthesis THEN
                    IF Priority(InBuff(I)) <= Priority(character)
                        THEN
                        Put character in PostBuff.
                        Put blank in PostBuff.
                        Push InBuff(I) onto stack.
                    ELSE
                        Push character onto stack.
                        Push InBuff(I) onto stack.
                    END IF.
                ELSE
                    Push character onto stack.
                    Push InBuff(I) onto stack.
                END IF.
            END IF.
        END IF.
    END FOR.
    WHILE stack not empty
        Pop character off stack.
        Put character in PostBuff.
        Put blank in PostBuff.
    END WHILE.
```

*In order for our program to be able to evaluate this condition, the **Priority** function will have to be defined when the character is an operator or a left parenthesis.

In order to write the **Convert** procedure, we will need to use a stack in which the data field of each element in the linked list is a single character. For the buffer we will simply use an array of 20 characters. There are certainly other possible choices for a structure, and some of these will be covered in the exercises. The **type** declarations that we will need for this procedure are as follows:

```
type
   ItemPtr1 = ^Item1;
   Item1 = record
              Data : char;
              Next : ItemPtr1
           end;
   CharBuffer = array[1..20] of char;
```

We can now write our procedure. The procedure will need a value parameter **InBuff** to pass in the infix expression and a variable parameter **PostBuff** to pass back out the converted postfix expression.

```
{**************************************************************}
{* Convert - Procedure to convert an infix expression to a    *}
{*           postfix expression.                              *}
{*      var parameters -                                       *}
{*          PostBuff : Array to return postfix expression.    *}
{*      value parameters -                                     *}
{*          InBuff : Array containing infix expression.        *}
{**************************************************************}
procedure Convert(InBuff : CharBuffer;
                  var PostBuff : CharBuffer);
var
  Top : ItemPtr1;                          { Stack pointer }
  Empty : boolean;                         { Empty stack }
  I, J : integer;                  { Array and loop indices }
  Ch : char;                              { Stack data }
begin
  InitStack(Top, Empty);
  J := 1;
  for I := 1 to 20 do begin                { Convert loop }
    if InBuff[I] in ['0'..'9'] then begin         { Digit }
      PostBuff[J] := InBuff[I];
      J := J + 1;
      PostBuff[J] := ' ';
      J := J + 1
    end; { if }
    if InBuff[I] = '(' then              { Left parenthesis }
      PushStack(InBuff[I], Top, Empty);
    { end if }
    if InBuff[I] = ')' then begin        { Right parenthesis }
      PopStack(Ch, Top, Empty);           { Convert substack }
      while Ch <> '(' do begin
        PostBuff[J] := Ch;
        J := J + 1;
```

```
            PostBuff[J] := ' ';
            J := J + 1;
            PopStack(Ch, Top, Empty)
         end { while }                              { End substack }
      end; { if }
   if InBuff[I] in ['+', '-', '*', '/'] then        { Operator }
      if Empty then
         PushStack(InBuff[I], Top, Empty)
      else begin
         PopStack(Ch, Top, Empty);
         while (Priority(Ch) >= Priority(InBuff[I]))
               and (not Empty) and (Ch <> '(') do begin
            PostBuff[J] := Ch;
            J := J + 1;
            PostBuff[J] := ' ';
            J := J + 1;
            PopStack(Ch, Top, Empty)
         end; { while }
         if Ch <> '(' then
            if Priority(InBuff[I]) <= Priority(Ch) then begin
               PostBuff[J] := Ch;
               J := J + 1;
               PostBuff[J] := ' ';
               J := J + 1;
               PushStack(InBuff[I], Top, Empty)
            end { if }
            else begin
               PushStack(Ch, Top, Empty);
               PushStack(InBuff[I], Top, Empty)
            end { else }
         else begin
            PushStack(Ch, Top, Empty);
            PushStack(InBuff[I], Top, Empty)
         end { else }
      end { else }
   { end if }
   end; { for }
   while not Empty do begin                          { Loop to empty stack }
      PopStack(Ch, Top, Empty);
      PostBuff[J] := Ch;
      J := J + 1;
      PostBuff[J] := ' ';
      J := J + 1
   end { while }
end; { Convert }
```

Continuing with top-down design, we now have to code a subprogram to compute the priority of any of the operators that are used by the procedure. Since we are using the four operators '+', '-', '*', and '/', we can simply write a function that will return an integer value that will be used for the priority of the given operator. The function will return the value of 2 if the operator is either '*' or '/' and return the value of 1 if the operator is either '+' or '-'. We have pointed out that the **Priority** function will also have to be defined when the character is a left parenthesis. In this case the function will return a value of 0. Even though this will make the condition

```
(Ch <> '(')
```

redundant in the **while** loop, we will leave the condition in for clarity. The priority function can now be written using the **case** statement.

```
{***************************************************************}
{* Priority - Function to compute the priority of a given      *}
{*            operator.                                         *}
{*      value parameters -                                     *}
{*          Ch1 : Given operator.                              *}
{***************************************************************}
function Priority(Ch1 : char) : integer;
begin
  case Ch1 of
    '*', '/' : Priority := 2;
    '+', '-' : Priority := 1;
    '('      : Priority := 0
  end { case }
end; { Priority }
```

The other procedures that are called by the **Convert** procedure, **InitStack**, **PopStack**, and **PushStack**, were all written in Section 3.1.

Exercises

3.18 Convert each of the following infix expressions to a postfix expression.
(a) $3 + 7 * 8 - 5$
(b) $3 * 7 - 4 / 2$
(c) $(3 + 7) * 8 - 5$
(d) $(6 + 9) * (2 - 8)$
(e) $(3 + 4) * 8 - (7 * 3 - 4)$
(f) $A - B * (C - D) / E$
(g) $(A - B) * (C - D + E) / F$
(h) $A * (B - C / D) - (E - F)$

3.19 Convert each of the infix expressions in Exercise 3.18 to a prefix expression.

3.20 Evaluate each of the following postfix expressions.
(a) $3\ 7\ 8 * + 5 -$
(b) $3\ 4 * 2\ 5 * 6 - +$
(c) $7\ 3\ 8\ 2 + * 5 - -$
(d) $8\ 2 - 3 / 4\ 5 * -$
(e) $3\ 7 + 8\ 5 - *$
(f) $4\ 7\ 3\ 5 + 2 * - - 4 -$
(g) $2\ 3\ 8\ 4 - * + 5\ 3\ 4 + + * -$
(h) $3\ 4\ 5 + 6\ 3 * - - 2 +$

3.21 Evaluate each of the following prefix expressions.
(a) $* - 2\ 3\ 5$
(b) $* + 5\ 4 - 8\ 3$
(c) $+ 2 * 3 - 8\ 4$
(d) $- 4 * 3 - 5 / 4\ 2$
(e) $- / - 8\ 2\ 3 * 4\ 5$
(f) $- * - 5\ 4 - 6\ 3\ 7$
(g) $- / 8\ 2 - 5 * + 4\ 3\ 2$
(h) $- + 2 * 3 - 8\ 4 * 5 + 3\ 4$

3.22   Create a data file containing several postfix expressions, one per line. Write a program that uses the **PostFixEval** procedure and other necessary subprograms. The program should evaluate each of the expressions and write the results back to the screen.

3.23   Rewrite the **PostFixEval** procedure so that the operands are allowed to be real numbers. The **Evaluate** procedure will also have to be modified.

3.24   Write a procedure to evaluate prefix expressions.

3.25   Write a procedure to convert an infix expression to a prefix expression.

3.26   Write a procedure to convert an infix expression to a postfix expression. The procedure should allow the integer operands to have more than one integer digit.

3.27   Write a procedure to convert a postfix expression to a corresponding infix expression. The infix expression should include all parentheses. For example, the postfix expression A B * would be converted to the expression (A * B). The postfix expression A B C + * would be converted to the expression (A * (B + C)).

3.28   Write a procedure to convert a prefix expression to a corresponding infix expression. The infix expression should include all parentheses. For example, the prefix expression + * A B C would be converted to ((A * B) + C).

3.29   Write a procedure to evaluate a postfix expression in which the expression is stored in a linked list.

3.30   Write a procedure to convert an infix expression to a postfix expression. The infix expression should be stored in a linked list, and the postfix expression that is returned should also be stored in a linked list.

3.5 Stacks Using Arrays

Since a stack is an ordered collection of items and an array is a structure that is also an ordered collection of items, it is possible to use arrays to build a stack to use in a given program. It is critical for programmers to understand how this is done, since there are languages in which the array is the only structure available. Now that you thoroughly understand what stacks are and how they are used, it should be fairly easy to apply this knowledge to the use of arrays.

It is tempting simply to define a type identifier called a stack as an array of an appropriate number of the appropriate data items. A little thought, however, leads to the realization that a stack and an array are really two different objects. For one thing, an array is a static data structure: The number of elements in the array is fixed. A stack, on the other hand, is a dynamic data structure, whose size is changing as items are pushed onto and popped off the stack.

In spite of this difference, we can use an array as a structure to contain our stack. The array will have to be declared so that it is large enough to hold the stack when it is at its maximum size. While the program is running, the stack will grow and shrink within the array that contains it. The array size remains fixed. We will place the bottom of the stack at one end of the array and allow the top of the stack to move as items are pushed and popped. In order to keep track of the current position of the top of the stack, we will use an additional field. The stack will be a record containing two fields: the first field will be an array to hold the elements of the stack, and the second field will be an integer that simply keeps track of the position of the top of the stack. The stack is defined with the following declarations.

```
const
  Size = 100;
type
  Data = record
              ↓        Some data type

           end;
  Stack = record
              Item : array[1..Size] of Data;
              Top : 0..Size
           end;
var
  S : Stack;
```

The elements of the stack will be stored in the components of the array **S.Item**. These elements will be of type **Data,** and the stack can contain no more than **Size** items. In this example, **Size** is set at 100. The position of the top of the stack will be an integer from 0 to **Size** and will be assigned to the integer identifier **S.Top**. When the stack is empty, **S.Top** will be assigned to 0. If the stack contains four items, they will be stored in **S.Item[1]**, **S.Item[2]**, **S.Item[3]**, and **S.Item[4]**, and **S.Top** will be 4. If an item is pushed onto the stack, it will be stored in **S.Item[5]** and **S.Top** will be changed to 5. If we then pop an item off the stack, the item will be the one stored in **S.Item[5]** and the value of **S.Top** will be changed to 4. During the execution of the program, the stack will be empty if **S.Top** is equal to 0 and will be full if **S.Top** is equal to **Size**.

We can now build some of the basic procedures that will be needed to utilize a stack as outlined above. We begin by writing a function to determine whether the stack is **Empty** or not. The procedures that we will write in this section are either procedures that we have previously written or procedures that we could easily have written for linked lists using pointers.

```
function Empty(S1 : Stack) : boolean;
begin
  if S1.Top = 0 then
    Empty := true
  { end if }
```

```
    else
       Empty := false
    { end else }
end; { Empty }
```

Once we have written this function, we can test for an empty stack in a program with a block of code such as the following:

```
if Empty(S) then begin
              ↓
end { if }
else begin
              ↓
end; { else }
```

Similarly, we can write a function to check to see if a stack is full:

```
function Full(S2 : Stack) : boolean;
begin
   if S2.Top = Size then
      Full := true
   { end if }
   else
      Full := false
   { end else }
end; { Full }
```

When the stack is full and we want to push another data item onto the stack, we say that we have *stack overflow*.

We will now code the two procedures that are used to push data onto the stack and to pop data off the stack. We will call these two procedures **PushStk** and **PopStk**. The parameters that we pass will be the same ones we used in our procedures for linked lists. For the **PushStk** procedure we will pass the stack as a variable parameter and the data item that is to be pushed onto the stack as a value parameter.

```
procedure PushStk(var S3 : Stack; Dt : Data);
begin
   if not Full(S3) then begin
      S3.Top := S3.Top + 1;
      S3.Item[S3.Top] := Dt
   end { if }
   else begin
      writeln('Warning! Stack overflow.');
      writeln('Data not pushed onto the stack.')
   end { else }
end; { PushStk }
```

For the **PopStk** procedure, we will pass the stack as a variable parameter and the data item that is to be popped off the stack as another variable parameter.

```
procedure PopStk(var S4 : Stack; var Dt4 : Data);
begin
  if not Empty(E4) then begin
    Dt4 := S4.Item[S4.Top];
    S4.Top := S4.Top - 1
  end { if }
  else begin
    writeln('Warning! Stack underflow.');
    writeln('Data not popped off the stack.')
  end { else }
end; { PopStk }
```

The problem of stack overflow is not a condition that is applicable to a stack as an abstract data structure. In theory, it should always be possible to push an element onto the stack, since a stack is an ordered collection with no theoretical limit as to how many elements it can contain. In practice, however, the size of the stack will be limited either by the amount of memory allocated to the program or, in the case of arrays, by the number of elements in the array that contains the stack. When we are using arrays, we can easily check for stack overflow with the function that we have written above. When we are using pointers, as in the previous sections, the program cannot check for stack overflow, since overflow would be caused by the program memory allocation. When we are using arrays, it may very well be the case that the algorithm used by the program is correct and the amount of data to be stored on the stack is too large. In this case we can simply increase the constant **Size** in the program to correct the problem.

However, in a large percentage of the cases an overflow does indicate an error in the program and not simply a lack of space. The program may be in an infinite loop in which elements are simply being pushed onto the stack faster than they are being popped off the stack. In this case, the stack will overflow no matter how large we make **Size**, if we are using arrays, or no matter how much memory is allocated to our program, if we are using pointers and linked lists. Before simply changing the size of the array, the programmer should always check to make sure that an infinite loop is not the problem.

Some languages provide neither pointers nor records for use in storing data. These languages make available as a data structure only the array. In these cases, an array can be used to contain the structure and a separate integer identifier to keep track of the top of the stack. We need the following **type** and **var** declarations:

```
const
  Size = 100;
type
  Data = {some simple data type or array}
  Stack = array[1..Size] of Data;
var
  S : Stack;
  Top : integer;
```

We can now rewrite our functions **Empty** and **Full** as well as our procedures **PopStk** and **PushStk** to utilize the above structures.

```
function Empty(Top1 : integer) : boolean;
begin
  if Top1 = 0 then
    Empty := true
  { end if }
  else
    Empty := false
  { end else }
end; { Empty }

function Full(Top2 : integer) : boolean;
begin
  if Top2 = Size then
    Full := true
  { end if }
  else
    Full := false
  { end else }
end; { Full }

procedure PushStk(var S3 : Stack; var Top3 : integer;
                  Dt3 : Data);
begin
  if not Full(Top3) then begin
    Top3 := Top3 + 1;
    S3[Top3] := Dt3
  end { if }
  else begin
    writeln('Warning! Stack overflow.');
    writeln('Data not pushed onto the stack.')
  end { else }
end; { PushStk }

procedure PopStk(S4 : Stack; var Top4 : integer;
                 var Dt4 : Data);
begin
  if not Empty(S4) then begin
    Dt4 := S4[Top4];
    Top4 := Top4 - 1
  end { if }
  else begin
    writeln('Warning! Stack underflow.');
    writeln('Data not popped off the stack.')
  end { else }
end; { PopStk }
```

In the case in which the data items contain more than one field, we will have to use a separate stack for each field. For example, if our data contain a 20-character **Name** along with an integer **Age**, we would want to have the following declarations.

```
const
  Size = 100;
type
  Name = array[1..20] of char;
  Age = integer;
  StackN = array[1..Size] of Name;
  StackA = array[1..Size] of Age;
var
  SN : StackN;
  SA : StackA;
  Top : integer;
```

The **Empty** and **Full** procedures will remain the same; however, the **PushStk** procedure would have to be modified as follows.

```
procedure PushStk1(var SN3 : StackN; var SA3 : StackA;
                   var Top3 : integer; DtN3 : Name; DtA3 : Age);
begin
  if not Full(Top3) then begin
    Top3 := Top3 + 1;
    SN3[Top3] := DtN3;
    SA3[Top3] := DtA3
  end { if }
  else begin
    writeln('Warning! Stack overflow.');
    writeln('Data not pushed onto the stack.')
  end { else }
end; { PushStk }
```

The **PopStk1** procedure can be modified in a similar way.

In order to illustrate the above ideas, let us return to the problem of writing a procedure for evaluating a postfix expression. We will assume that the only structure we have available in our language is the array. As before, we will assume that the postfix expression is stored in an array of 20 characters. The expression is made up of only blanks, digits, and the operators '+', '-', '*', and '/'. Our numbers will be only single-digit integers, and when the operator '/' is encountered in an expression, the Pascal operator **div** will be used so that the value obtained will be an integer. We will need the following declarations:

```
const
  Size = 15;
  BSize = 20;
type
  Data = integer;
  Stack = array[1..Size] of Data;
  Buffer = array[1..BSize] of char;
var
  ValStack : Stack;
  Buff : Buffer;
  Top : integer;
```

The pseudocode for the procedure to evaluate a postfix expression is the same as the one developed in Section 3.4. This version of the procedure will be called **PostEval**. As before, we will first code the **PostEval** procedure and then code the procedures that it calls. The documentation is omitted.

```
procedure PostEval(Buff : Buffer; Num : integer;
                   var FinalVal : integer);
var
  Top : integer;                        { Top of stack }
  ValStack : Stack;                { Stack for evaluation }
  Val1, Val2, CharVal : integer;     { For computations }
begin
  for I := 1 to Num do begin
    if Buff[I] <> ' ' then
      if (Buff[I] <> '+') and (Buff[I] <> '-')
          and (Buff[I] <> '*')
          and (Buff[I] <> '/') then begin
            CharVal := ord(Buff[I]) - ord('0');
            PushStk(ValStack, Top, CharVal)
        end { if }
      else begin
        PopStk(ValStack, Top, Val1);
        PopStk(ValStack, Top, Val2);
        Evaluate(Val, Val2, Buff[I], Val1);
        PushStk(ValStack, Top, Val)
      end { else }
    { end if }
  end; { for }
  PopStk(ValStack, Top, FinalVal)
end; { PostEval }
```

We can now code the procedures that are called by the **PostEval** procedure, **InitStack**, **PushStk**, **PopStk**, and **Evaluate**. To code the procedure **InitStack**, we need to initialize the integer **Top** to 0. Thus we have the following:

```
procedure InitStack(var TopI : integer);
begin
  TopI := 0
end; { InitStack }
```

The procedures **PushStk** and **PopStk** will use the functions **Full** and **Empty** and will be coded as follows:

```
procedure PushStk(var Stk : Stack; var Tp : integer; Dt : integer);
begin
  if not Full(Tp) then begin
    Tp := Tp + 1;
    Stk[Tp] := Dt;
  end { if }
  else begin
    writeln('Warning! Stack overflow.');
    writeln('Data not pushed onto the stack.');
```

```
   end { else }
end; { PushStk }


procedure PopStk(Stk1 : Stack; var Tp1 : integer; Dt1 : integer);
begin
  if not Empty(Tp1) then begin
    Dt1 := Stk1[Tp1];
    Tp1 := Tp1 - 1
  end { if }
  else begin
    writeln('Warning! Stack underflow.');
    writeln('Data not popped off the stack.')
  end { else }
end; { PopStk }
```

The **Evaluate** procedure will be exactly the same as the one we wrote in Section 3.4. In the exercises you will be asked to write a program that will test the above procedures.

Exercises

3.31 Give the **type** and **var** declarations needed to define a queue if the only data structure available is an array. The queue should store integer data items.

3.32 Write **Empty** and **Full** functions for the queues defined in Exercise 3.31.

3.33 Write **PushQueue** and **PopQueue** procedures for the queues defined in Exercise 3.31.

3.34 Give the **type** and **var** declarations needed to write a function to perform long-integer addition. The long integers are to be stored in arrays.

3.35 Create a data file containing several postfix expressions. Write a program that will use the procedures written in Section 3.5. The program should evaluate each of the postfix expressions in the file and print out the expression along with the computed value.

Summary

In this chapter we studied the very important structures stacks and queues and saw how these data structures are used in examples. Pascal pointers and linked lists were used to introduce these structures since this approach to building and using stacks and queues seems to be the easiest one to learn. After several examples, stacks and queues were introduced using arrays. The example involving evaluation of a postfix expression was rewritten using arrays so that the two implementations could be compared. This example again illustrates the limitations that we encounter when using arrays. The size of the stack (or queue) is limited by the size of the array and cannot be changed while the program is running. Using linked lists, however, the size of the stack (or queue) is limited only by the amount of memory that has been allocated to the program. The basic procedures for stacks and queues that we have written in this chapter will be used again in Chapter 5 when we study recursion and in Chapter 10 when we study graphs.

Other linked lists were also introduced: rings, doubly linked lists, and doubly linked rings. The example from Chapter 2 involving creation of a linked list and storage of data from the file containing employee records was rewritten using a doubly linked list. This example illustrated the advantage of being able to move a pointer both directions in a doubly linked list.

The discussion concerning the evaluation of arithmetic expressions illustrated the advantages of using either postfix or prefix notation in place of the standard infix notation. The procedures that were written allowed us to convert an infix expression to a postfix expression by scanning the infix expression only one time. The corresponding postfix expression can also be evaluated by scanning this expression only once. The evaluation of infix expressions requires repeated scanning. Postfix and prefix expressions also have the advantage that they can be written without the use of parentheses.

Chapter Exercises

3.36 Each line of a data file **DataF** contains a record of data in the following format.

Columns		
1– 7	Inventory number	(7 characters)
8–27	Description	(20 characters)
30–32	Quantity on hand	(Integer)
35–36	Reorder number	(Integer)
40–45	Cost of item	(Real)
50–55	Selling price	(Real)

Give the **const**, **type**, and **var** declarations that are needed to define a doubly linked list to store the data from the file for use in a program.

3.37 Write a procedure that will read the data from the file and store the data in the linked list defined in Exercise 3.36. The data should be stored in order by inventory number. Write a driver and test this procedure. The driver should print the data stored in the list to the screen.

3.38 Write a procedure to add an inventory record to the collection of inventory data. The record should be added to the linked list in order by inventory number. Write a driver and test this procedure.

3.39   Each line of a data file **Dfile** contains a record of data in the following format:

Columns	1–20	Name	(20 characters)
	21–64	Address	Record
	21–35	Street	(15 characters)
	36–49	City	(14 characters)
	50–59	State	(10 characters)
	60–64	Zip code	(5 characters)
	65–76	Telephone no.	(12 characters)

Write the **const**, **type**, and **var** declarations needed to define a doubly linked list to store the data from the file for use in a program.

3.40   Write a procedure that will read the data from the file and store it in the structure defined in Exercise 3.39. The data should be stored in the list in order by name. Write a driver and test this procedure. The driver should print the data stored in the linked list to the screen.

3.41   Write a procedure to add an address record to the collection of data in Exercise 3.39. The record should be added to the linked list in order by name. Write a driver and test this procedure.

3.42   Rewrite the procedure to convert an infix expression to a postfix expression. Replace the arrays containing the two expressions with queues. This will allow the procedure to convert expressions without the restriction imposed by the size of the array. Write **PopQueue** and **PushQueue** procedures to be called by this **Convert** procedure. Write a driver and test this procedure.

3.43   Using the ideas from Exercise 3.42, write a procedure to convert an infix expression to a prefix expression. Write a driver and test this procedure.

CHAPTER 4

Elementary Searching and Sorting Techniques

Searching through and sorting data are among the most common programming processes; they are essential parts of a great number of data processing programs. Searching and sorting are also processes that people commonly encounter in their daily routines. Consider, for example, the process of finding a word in a dictionary or a name in a telephone directory. The *search* for the particular item is simplified considerably by the fact that the words in the dictionary and the names in the telephone directory are *sorted* in alphabetical order.

In this chapter we will discuss some of the basic terminology applying to these processes, and we will also develop some elementary searching and sorting techniques. We will analyze the development of these routines and discuss how we can modify them in an attempt to improve their efficiency. Our study of the sorting algorithms will demonstrate the necessity of a performance analysis of these algorithms as well as introduce some of the basics of performance analysis.

After the search and sort techniques have been developed, we will write the procedures that will allow us to apply these ideas to the **EmployeeList** example from Chapter 1. The chapter will conclude with the results from test runs of the procedures using large, randomly generated lists of data. These results are included to provide some idea of the relative efficiencies of various sorting algorithms. We will be able to compare these results with the more advanced sorting techniques that we will discuss in Chapter 8.

Sorting data consists of rearranging a collection of data so that it is in some order with respect to one of the fields of the elements of the collection. For example, each element of the collection of data in a phone book has a name field, an address field, and a telephone-number field. The collection as a whole is arranged in order with respect to the name field. A collection of data to be sorted may be stored in a file, an array, a linked list, or a tree. (The term *list* refers to any and all of these structures.) If the data are stored in a file, one of the other structures may be used in writing a procedure to re-arrange the data. When the data are sorted while stored in a file, the sorting process is called an *external sort*. Sorting data stored in an array, a linked list, or a tree is called an *internal sort*.

Each element of the collection of data is called a *record*, and each record can have one or more *fields* of information. For example, the telephone directory contains many records, each record containing three fields: the name field, the address field, and the telephone-number field. A *key K* is associated with each record and is usually one of the fields. A list is said to be *sorted on the key K* if the list is in either ascending or descending order with respect to this key. The list is said to be in *ascending (nondecreasing) order* if

$$i < j \qquad \text{implies} \qquad K(i) \le K(j)$$

and is said to be in *descending (nonincreasing) order* if

$$i < j \qquad \text{implies} \qquad K(i) \ge K(j)$$

for all elements in the list. For the telephone book example, the list is sorted in ascending order on the key K where $K(i)$ is the name field of the ith record.

4.1 Searching Techniques

In this section we will study two elementary techniques for searching a list of data for a particular item. We will assume that the list of data is stored in an array of records and that we are looking for a particular record that contains in one of its fields a given piece of information. The searching process that we will use will look for a particular data item and will return the position in the list of the element corresponding to that data item if the element exists.

Usually the data will be sorted in either ascending or descending order on some key so that the searching process can be carried out efficiently. Consider how nearly impossible it would be to find a particular name in a tele-phone book or word in a dictionary if the data were not sorted.

The simplest technique to use to search a list of data is simply to look at each item one at a time, starting with the first element of the list. If the list contains the element sought, this process should return the position of the element in the list. This very inefficient method is known as a *linear search* or a *sequential search*. Let us write the procedure that will perform a linear search on our list of data from Chapter 1. Recall that we had the following **type** declarations.

```
const
  Max = { some integer value };
```

```
type
   String20 = packed array[1..20] of char;
   String11 = packed array[1..11] of char;
   EmpInfo = record
                Name : String20;
                SSNum : String11;
                PayRate : real
             end;
   EmpArray = packed array[1..Max] of EmpInfo;
```

Let us assume that we are searching the list for a record that contains a name stored in an identifier called **TName**. Since the procedure will return the position of the data item in the list (if the item exists), this integer value will be assigned to an identifier called **Position**. **Position** will be initialized to 0, and if the data item is found during the search, **Position** will be assigned a new integer value equal to the index in the array of the record in which **TName** was found. At the end of the search, if **Position** still has the value 0, we will know that the data item was not found in the list. We will also assume that we have **Count** employee records stored in the array **EmpList**. We begin by outlining the procedure using pseudocode.

Pseudocode

LinSearch Procedure

Set **Position** to 0.
FOR **I** = 1 TO **Count**
   IF **EmpList(I)(Name)** = **TName** THEN
      Assign **I** to **Position**.
   END IF.
END FOR.

We can now code the procedure.

```
{*******************************************************}
{* LinSearch - Procedure to search an array of records for   *}
{*          a record containing a given name.               *}
{*      var parameters -                                    *}
{*          Position : If the name is found, Position re-   *}
{*                     turns the index of the record con-   *}
{*                     taining this name. If not, zero is   *}
{*                     returned.                            *}
{*      value parameters -                                  *}
{*          EmpList - The array of employee records.        *}
{*          TName -   Name for which we are searching.      *}
{*          Count -   Number of records in the array.       *}
{*******************************************************}
procedure LinSearch(EmpList : EmpArray; TName : String20;
             Count : integer; var Position : integer);

var
   I : integer;                          { Loop index }
```

```
begin
  Position := 0;
  for I := 1 to Count do                          { Search loop }
    if EmpList[I].Name = TName then
      Position := I;
    { end if }
  { end for }
end; { LinSearch }
```

If the list is empty, **Count** is 0 and the **for** loop is not entered. The parameter **Position** returns the value of 0.

We can easily make our linear search procedure a little more efficient by stopping the process once we have found the element for which we are looking. In order to do this, we need to replace the **for** loop with either a **repeat-until** loop or a **while-do** loop which will allow us to exit the loop once the data item has been found. We will use the **repeat-until** structure. We will also introduce a Boolean identifier **Found**. The outline for this new procedure, which we will call a *modified linear search*, follows. The actual coding of the procedure is left as an exercise at the end of the chapter. In the exercises we will also ask the student to write the procedure using a **while-do** structure and to compare these two procedures.

Pseudocode

ModLinSearch Procedure

Set **Found** to false.
Set **Position** to 0.
Set **I** to 1.
REPEAT
   IF **EmpList(I)(Name)** = **TName** THEN
      Set **Position** to **I**.
      Set **Found** to True.
   END IF.
   Increment **I**.
UNTIL **Found** or (**I** > **Count**).

We do not return **Found** in the procedure.

A linear search is certainly only suitable for short lists of data. For long lists of data it is hopelessly inefficient. For example, imagine looking up a word in the dictionary by starting on page 1 and looking at every word until you come up with the one you want. If words in the dictionary were printed in arbitrary or random order, a linear search would be the only alternative. However, because the words are in alphabetical order, use of a more efficient search method is possible. You start by opening the dictionary to a page you think might be close to where the word you are looking for will be located, thereby dividing the dictionary into two parts. You repeat this process on whichever part of the dictionary contains your word.

One of the most efficient methods of searching an ordered list, called a *binary search*, is based on the above algorithm. Since a binary search is more complicated than a linear search, we will illustrate a binary search with an array of integers before outlining and coding the procedure for our list of employees. We will use an array of 50 integers that have been sorted into ascending order. Two variables, **First** and **Last**, will hold the values of the lower and upper indices of the portion of the array that remains to be searched. Initially, **First** will be assigned the value of 1 and **Last** will be assigned the value of 50. At each step, the components of the array **Nums** that remain to be searched are **Nums[First]** through **Nums[Last]**. We begin the binary search by examining the middle element of the list. The index of the middle element can be computed using the expression

$$\textbf{Mid} := (\textbf{First} + \textbf{Last}) \ \textbf{div} \ 2;$$

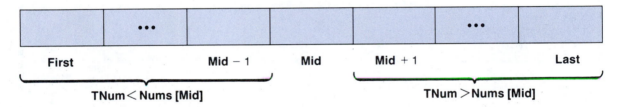

If the data item that we are searching for is stored in the identifier **TNum**, we compare **Nums[Mid]** with **TNum**. If the two values are equal, our search is over. If

$$\textbf{TNum} < \textbf{Nums[Mid]}$$

TNum must be found in the part of the array,

$$\textbf{Nums[First]} \qquad \text{through} \qquad \textbf{Nums[Mid} - 1]$$

if it is in the array at all. In this case we would set **Last** to the position **Mid** − 1. On the other hand, if

$$\textbf{TNum} > \textbf{Nums[Mid]}$$

we would search the other part of the array for **TNum**; that is, from

$$\textbf{Nums[Mid} + 1] \qquad \text{through} \qquad \textbf{Nums[Last]}$$

In this case we would set **First** to **Mid** + 1. If the value **TNum** appears in the list, this process of resetting **First** and **Last** will terminate when **TNum** and **Nums[Mid]** are equal. On the other hand, if the value **TNum** does not appear in the list, we must consider how we can terminate the above process. At each step, either the value of **First** is increased or the value of **Last** is decreased. If the value that we are looking for is not found, the values that are assigned to **First** and **Last** must eventually pass each other. Thus we can terminate the search when

$$First > Last$$

We can now code the procedure which will only return position.

```
{*****************************************************************}
{* BinSearch - Procedure to search an array of records for a *}
{*             given name.                                    *}
{*        var parameters -                                    *}
{*            Position1 : Returns the index of the record     *}
{*                        containing the name, if found,      *}
{*                        and 0 if not found.                 *}
{*        value parameters -                                  *}
{*            EList : Array of employee records.              *}
{*            TName1 : Name for which we are searching.       *}
{*            Count1 : Number of records stored in the array. *}
{*****************************************************************}
procedure BinSearch(EList : EmpArray; TName1 : String20;
                    Count1 : integer; var Position1 : integer);
var
  First, Last, Mid : integer;           { Indices for search }
begin
  Position1 := 0;                       { Initialize indices }
  First := 1;
  Last := Count1;
  repeat                                { Search loop }
    Mid := (First + Last) div 2;
    if TName1 < EList[Mid].Name then
      Last := Mid - 1;
    { end if }
    if TName1 > EList[Mid].Name then
      First := Mid + 1
    { end if }
  until (TName1 = EList[Mid].Name) or (First > Last);
  if TName1 = EList[Mid].Name then      { If found }
    Position1  := Mid
  { end if }
end; { BinSearch }
```

To compare the two preceding search algorithms, we need to evaluate the relationship between a value n, called the size of the algorithm, and a value t, the computer time needed to produce the answer. The value of n is simply a measure of the size of the problem to be solved. For example, when the problem is to search for a particular element of a list, a natural measure of the size of the problem is the number of elements in the list. With the sequential-search method, the worst case (in which the item is at the end of the list or not in the list at all) requires looking at all n items of the list in order to find the desired item or to determine that the item is not in the list. Thus the relationship between t and n is given by

$$t = k * n$$

where k is some constant based on the internal speed of the machine performing the search and the number of machine instructions to look at one item of the list.

The preceding formula is not used to compute the exact timing of a search method because the value of the constant k is frequently difficult to obtain. We can, however, use this formula as a general guideline in evaluating and comparing algorithms. We use what is called *O-notation*:

$$t = O[f(n)]$$

This formula is read "t is of the order of $f(n)$," which means formally that there exist constants M and N such that if

$$t = O[f(n)]$$

then

$$t < M * f(n)$$

for all $n > N$. This definition simply says that the computing time of the algorithm grows no faster than a constant times $f(n)$. Thus as the problem gets bigger (n increases), the time needed to solve the problem increases at a rate approximated by the function $f(n)$.

For the sequential-search algorithm,

$$t = O(n)$$

since, in the worst case, we would have to look at each of the n items in the list. If the size of the list were to double, the time needed to search the list would also double.

In the binary-search algorithm, with each comparison we halve the size of the list under consideration. Since n is the size of the list, the consecutive sizes of the lists under consideration in the succeeding comparisons will be

$$n/2, \; n/4, \; n/8, \; \ldots$$
$$n/2^1, \; n/2^2, \; n/2^3, \; \ldots$$

The process will terminate when the size becomes less than or equal to 1. Therefore, if k is the greatest number of comparisons, then

$$n/2^k < 1$$

or

$$n < 2^k$$

If we take the logarithm to the base 2 of both sides, we have

$$\log_2 n < k$$

Thus the order of the binary search can be written as

$$O(\log_2 n)$$

which is a lower-order algorithm than the linear-search algorithm, as can be seen in Figure 4.1, which compares these two functions graphically.

Figure 4.1

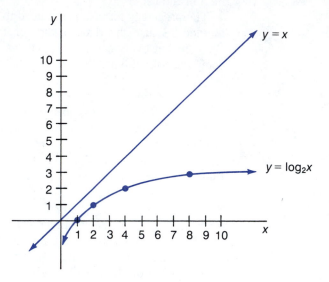

Therefore the larger the list, the more time is saved by using a binary search instead of a linear search. For a list of 50,000 items, the linear search would, in the worst case, require 50,000 comparisons, whereas the binary search would never require more than $\log_2 50{,}000$, or about 16, comparisons.

Notice, however, that for the binary search to work correctly, the list being searched must be sorted. The linear search, on the other hand, works for both sorted and unsorted lists. In order to get a true comparison of these two methods, we would need to add the time required to sort a list to the time required to do a binary search. We will discuss the times required for various simple sorting techniques in the remainder of this chapter. More advanced sorting techniques will be discussed in Chapter 8.

Exercises

4.1   Code the **ModLinSearch** procedure using the pseudocode from this section. Write a driver and test this procedure.

4.2   Rewrite the **ModLinSearch** procedure using a while-do structure instead of a repeat-until structure. The procedure should handle the case when the array is empty. What are the advantages and the disadvantages of using the while-do structure instead of the repeat-until structure?

4.3   Write a driver and test the **BinSearch** procedure that was written in this section.

4.4   Consider the following list of the first 50 positive integers.

$$1, 2, 3, \ldots, 50$$

Walk through the **LinSearch** procedure and count the number of moves and the number of compares in a search for the integer 27. Repeat the above process in a search for the integer 55 that is not in the list. Repeat the above process for the **ModLinSearch** procedure, once for the integer 27 and again for the integer 55.

4.5 Consider the same list of integers as in Exercise 4.4. Repeat the walk through once for the integer 27 and again for the integer 55. Use the **BinSearch** procedure.

4.2 The Selection Sort

The sorting technique that we will discuss in this section is referred to as the *selection sort*. We will be sorting lists of data into ascending order based on some key. The basic idea of the selection sort is to find the smallest element in the list and move it to the first position, then find the next smallest element and move it to the second position, and continue this process until the next to the last position is filled. When the correct element is in the next to the last position, the sort is finished because the last element, which is the only one left, must be the largest element. Let us look at a specific example of a selection sort before we attempt to write the code. Suppose that we have the following.

$$
\begin{array}{lll}
A[1] & : & 5 \\
A[2] & : & 13 \\
A[3] & : & -2 \\
A[4] & : & 10 \\
A[5] & : & 2
\end{array}
$$

In order to get the smallest element in the first position, we compare what is stored at $A[1]$ with each of the other elements, $A[2]$, $A[3]$, $A[4]$, and $A[5]$, and each time we find a smaller value we switch. We will refer to this process as pass no. 1. It takes four comparisons to complete the sort. In the tables that follow, **I** will be the index of the fixed element and **J** will range over the indices of the elements with which $A[I]$ is compared.

Pass No. 1: I = 1

	Comparison 1 (J = 2)	Comparison 2 (J = 3)	Comparison 3 (J = 4)	Comparison 4 (J = 5)	
SORTED					
A[1]	5	5	−2	−2	−2
UNSORTED					
A[2]	13	13	13	13	13
A[3]	−2	−2	5	5	5
A[4]	10	10	10	10	10
A[5]	2	2	2	2	2

We now have the smallest element in the first position, and we are ready for pass no. 2. We compare what is stored at **A[2]** with what is stored at **A[3]**, **A[4]**, and **A[5]**, and each time we find a smaller value we switch the positions of the elements.

Pass No. 2: I = 2

	Comparison 1 (J = 3)	Comparison 2 (J = 4)	Comparison 3 (J = 5)	
SORTED				
A[1]	−2	−2	−2	−2
A[2]	13	5	5	2
UNSORTED				
A[3]	5	13	13	13
A[4]	10	10	10	10
A[5]	2	2	2	5

We repeat the passes until all the elements have been sorted.

Pass No. 3: I = 3

	Comparison 1 (J = 4)	Comparison 2 (J = 5)	
SORTED			
A[1]	−2	−2	−2
A[2]	2	2	2
A[3]	13	10	5
UNSORTED			
A[4]	10	13	13
A[5]	5	5	10

Pass No. 4: I = 4

	Comparison 1 (J = 5)	
SORTED		
A[1]	−2	−2
A[2]	2	2
A[3]	5	5
A[4]	13	10
A[5]	10	13

The process just illustrated can be described as follows:

1. Make four passes through the array: **I** = 1, 2, 3, 4.
2. For pass no. 1 (**I** = 1), do four comparisons (**J** = 2, 3, 4, 5): **A**[1] with **A**[2], **A**[1] with **A**[3], **A**[1] with **A**[4], and **A**[1] with **A**[5].
3. For pass no. 2 (**I** = 2), do three comparisons (**J** = 3, 4, 5): **A**[2] with **A**[3], **A**[2] with **A**[4], and **A**[2] with **A**[5].
4. For pass no. 3 (**I** = 3), do two comparisons (**J** = 4, 5): **A**[3] with **A**[4] and **A**[3] with **A**[5].
5. For pass no. 4 (**I** = 4), do one comparison (**J** = 5): **A**[4] with **A**[5].

The number of passes can be controlled by a **for** loop

$$\text{FOR } \mathbf{I} = 1 \text{ TO } 4$$

and each sequence of comparisons can be controlled by an inside **for** loop in which **J** runs from the value of **I** plus 1 to 5:

$$\text{FOR } \mathbf{J} = \mathbf{I} + 1 \text{ TO } 5$$

We can now write the procedure for the selection sort. We will write the procedure for the data from our **EmployeeList** program from Chapter 1. The procedure will sort the list of data in ascending order by name.

```
{****************************************************************}
{* SelectionSort - Procedure to sort an array of records       *}
{*                  into ascending order by name.               *}
{*        var parameters -                                      *}
{*            DtList : Array of employee records.               *}
{*        value parameters -                                    *}
{*            N : Number of records stored in the array.        *}
{****************************************************************}
procedure SelectionSort(var DtList : EmpArray; N : integer);
var
  I, J : integer;                          { Loop indices }
  Temp : EmpInfo;                          { Temporary storage }
begin
  for I := 1 to N - 1 do
    for J := I + 1 to N do
      if DtList[I].Name > DtList[J].Name then begin
        Temp := DtList[I];                 { Switch elements }
        DtList[I] := DtList[J];
        DtList[J] := Temp
      end { if }
    { end for }
  { end for }
end; { SelectionSort }
```

The following observation will help us improve the efficiency of this sorting technique. In the procedure as written, a switch that requires three moves is made each time an element is found to be out of order in the list. However, the same sort can be accomplished by finding the element in the list that belongs in the position to be filled and moving the element to that position at the end of the pass. With this approach, the computer need only keep track of the data and the index number of the out-of-place element in each comparison, rather than switch it; the number of moves at each step is therefore reduced from three to two. Although this algorithm requires additional moves at the beginning and end of each pass to move the data, the number of moves saved is nearly one-third of the total number required by procedure **SelectionSort**. We will use **Index** to save the position and **Temp** to save the record of data stored at position **Index**.

The complete sort will take $N - 1$ passes, and the pseudocode for this sort will be as follows. We will refer to this sorting technique as the modified selection sort.

Pseudocode

ModSelectSort Procedure

```
FOR I = 1 to N − 1
    Move I to Index.
    Move DtList(I) to Temp.
    FOR J = I + 1 to N
        IF DtList(J) < Temp THEN
            Move J to Index.
            Move DtList(J) to Temp.
        END IF.
    END FOR.
    Move DtList(I) to DtList(Index).
    Move Temp to DtList(I).
END FOR.
```

Note that this algorithm sorts the data into ascending order. You should write the corresponding code to sort the data into descending order. We can now code the procedure.

```
{*******************************************************************}
{* ModSelectSort - Procedure to sort an array of employee       *}
{*                 records into ascending order by name.         *}
{*      var parameters -                                         *}
{*          DtList : Array of employee records.                  *}
{*      value parameters -                                       *}
{*          N : Number of records in the array.                  *}
{*******************************************************************}
procedure ModSelectSort(var DtList : EmpArray; N : integer);
var
  I, J,                                      { Loop indices }
  Index : integer;                           { Save element index }
  Temp : EmpInfo;                            { Save array element }
begin
  for I := 1 to N − 1 do begin
    Index := I;                              { Save index }
    Temp := DtList[I];                       { Save element }
    for J := I + 1 to N do
```

```
        if DtList[J].Name < Temp.Name then begin
          Index := J;                          { Save new index }
          Temp := DtList[J]          { Save smaller element }
        end; { if }
      { end for }
      DtList[Index] := DtList[I];          { Complete the switch }
      DtList[I] := Temp
    end { for }
end; { ModSelectSort }
```

We will see in Section 4.5 that the modified selection sort is much more efficient than the selection sort. For an array of 500 randomly generated real numbers, the modified selection sort is about 40 percent more efficient.

Exercises

4.6   Consider the following list of integers:

$$5\ 9\ 1\ 7\ 4\ 3\ 2\ 6$$

Show how the list appears after each pass of the selection sort, sorting in ascending order. Count the number of comparisons and the number of moves for each pass. Count the total number of comparisons and the total number of moves.

4.7   Consider the list of integers in Exercise 4.6. Show how the list appears after each pass of the modified selection sort. Count the number of comparisons and the number of moves for each pass. Count the total number of comparisons and the total number of moves.

4.8   In an attempt to develop a more efficient sorting technique, the following modification of the selection sort was developed: On each pass through the array, instead of locating the smallest element and moving it to its appropriate position in the array, the compiler copies the successive smallest values to a second array. As these values are copied to the second array, they are replaced with a value that is clearly not one of the data items. Write a procedure that will use this technique to sort an array of integer data items, and use the built-in Pascal constant **Maxint** as the replacement value.

4.9   Consider the list of integers in Exercise 4.6. Perform the same type of analysis you did in Exercise 4.6 for the technique that was developed in Exercise 4.8. What are the advantages and the disadvantages of this technique?

4.10   The manager of a local airport has a file of data in which each line contains one record of information that is in the following format:

Columns		
1–10	Airline name	(Character string)
11–25	Arriving from	(Character string)
26–40	Departing to	(Character string)
45–50	Flight number	(Character string)
60–64	Arrival time	(Integer; e.g., 0930)
70–74	Departure time	(Integer; e.g., 1720)

The data need to be sorted by flight number and then written back to the file in exactly the same format. Assume that there are at most 500 such records in the file. Write a procedure that will perform the sort using the selection-sort algorithm. Write a program that will use the procedure to sort the data and will then write the sorted data back to the file.

4.11 Repeat Exercise 4.10 using the modified selection-sort technique.

4.12 The airport manager now needs the program modified so that a list sorted either by arrival time or by departure time can be printed. Write the necessary procedures and modify either the program that was written in Exercise 4.10 or the one written in Exercise 4.11 so that the user can obtain the desired printout.

4.3 The Bubble Sort

The second of the elementary sorting techniques that we will study is the *bubble sort*. As before, our examples will involve sorting a list of data into ascending order.

The basic idea of the bubble sort is to compare consecutive elements on each pass through the array. Each time a comparison is made, the elements are switched if they are out of order. As before, in order to illustrate the algorithm, we will consider an array **A** with five integer data values. Pass no. 1 involves four comparisons of the consecutive elements: **A**[1] with **A**[2], **A**[2] with **A**[3], **A**[3] with **A**[4], and **A**[4] with **A**[5]. In the tables that follow, **I** will be the value of the pass, and **J** will range over the indices of the elements that are compared. The **J**th element is compared with the (**J** + 1)st element.

Pass No. 1: I = 1

	Comparison 1 (J = 1)	Comparison 2 (J = 2)	Comparison 3 (J = 3)	Comparison 4 (J = 4)	
UNSORTED					
A[1]	13	5	5	5	5
A[2]	5	13	-2	-2	-2
A[3]	-2	-2	13	10	10
A[4]	10	10	10	13	2
SORTED					
A[5]	2	2	2	2	13

After the first pass, the largest element is in the last position. Pass no. 2 involves three comparisons: **A**[1] with **A**[2], **A**[2] with **A**[3], and **A**[3] with **A**[4].

Pass No. 2: I = 2

	Comparison 1 (J = 1)	Comparison 2 (J = 2)	Comparison 3 (J = 3)	
UNSORTED				
A[1]	5	−2	−2	−2
A[2]	−2	5	5	5
A[3]	10	10	10	2
SORTED				
A[4]	2	2	2	10
A[5]	13	13	13	13

After pass no. 2, the next largest element is in the next to the last position. Pass no. 3 involves two comparisons: **A[1]** with **A[2]** and **A[2]** with **A[3]**.

Pass No. 3: I = 3

	Comparison 1 (J = 1)	Comparison 2 (J = 2)	
UNSORTED			
A[1]	−2	−2	−2
A[2]	5	5	2
SORTED			
A[3]	2	2	5
A[4]	10	10	10
A[5]	13	13	13

After pass no. 3 the last three elements are in order. Pass no. 4 involves only one comparison: **A[1]** with **A[2]**.

Pass No. 4: I = 4

	Comparison 1 (J = 1)	
SORTED		
A[1]	−2	−2
A[2]	2	2
A[3]	5	5
A[4]	10	10
A[5]	13	13

The process we just walked through can be described as follows:

1. Make four passes through the array: **I** = 1, 2, 3, 4.
2. For pass no. 1 (**I** = 1), make four comparisons (**J** = 1, 2, 3, 4): **A**[1] with **A**[2], **A**[2] with **A**[3], **A**[3] with **A**[4], and **A**[4] with **A**[5].
3. For pass no. 2 (**I** = 2), make three comparisons (**J** = 1, 2, 3): **A**[1] with **A**[2], **A**[2] with **A**[3], and **A**[3] with **A**[4].
4. For pass no. 3 (**I** = 3), make two comparisons (**J** = 1, 2): **A**[1] with **A**[2] and **A**[2] with **A**[3].
5. For pass no. 4 (**I** = 4), make one comparison (**J** = 1): **A**[1] with **A**[2].

Again, the number of passes can be controlled by a **for** loop

$$\text{FOR } \mathbf{I} = 1 \text{ TO } 4$$

and each sequence of comparisons can be controlled by an inside **for** loop in which **J** runs from 1 to 5 minus the particular value of **I**. For each of the above passes, we had the following.

$\mathbf{I} = 1$	$\mathbf{J} = 1, 2, 3, 4$	$5 - \mathbf{I} = 4$
$\mathbf{I} = 2$	$\mathbf{J} = 1, 2, 3$	$5 - \mathbf{I} = 3$
$\mathbf{I} = 3$	$\mathbf{J} = 1, 2$	$5 - \mathbf{I} = 2$
$\mathbf{I} = 4$	$\mathbf{J} = 1$	$5 - \mathbf{I} = 1$

Thus the inside **for** loop to control each pass would be

$$\text{FOR } \mathbf{J} = 1 \text{ TO } 5 - \mathbf{I}$$

We can now write the procedure that will perform a bubble sort on the list of employees. As before, the list will be sorted in ascending order by name.

```
{*****************************************************************}
{* BubbleSort - Procedure to sort an array of employee records *}
{*              into ascending order by name.                   *}
{*       var parameters -                                       *}
{*           DtList : Array of employee records.                *}
{*       value parameters -                                     *}
{*           N : Number of records stored in the array.         *}
{*****************************************************************}
procedure BubbleSort(var DtList : EmpArray; N : integer);
var
   I, J : integer;                              { Loop indices }
   Temp : EmpInfo;                           { Temporary storage }
begin
   for I := 1 to N - 1 do
     for J := 1 to N - I do
       if DtList[J].Name > DtList[J + 1].Name then begin
          Temp := DtList[J];                  { Switch elements }
          DtList[J] := DtList[J + 1];
          DtList[J + 1] := Temp
       end { if }
     { end for }
   { end for }
end; { BubbleSort }
```

The bubble-sorting technique compares consecutive elements of the list; therefore if a pass is made through the list and no switching occurs, the list must be in order. We can make use of this idea to modify the bubble-sort procedure in an attempt to make it more efficient. Since this modified sort will be a variation of the bubble sort, we will refer to this variation as the *bubble sort with flag*.

To make use of the above idea, we must replace the outside **for** loop with either a **repeat-until** loop or a **while-do** loop. Also, since the final value, **N − I**, of the inside **for** loop depends on **I**, which is the value of the particular pass, a counter will be needed to keep track of the number of the current pass. Finally, a Boolean identifier **Sorted** will be set to true at the beginning of each pass and set back to false if two data items are switched. We begin by writing the pseudocode, which will use the **repeat-until** structure.

Pseudocode

> **BubbleFlagSort Procedure**
>
> Set **I** to 1.
> REPEAT
>   Set **Sorted** to true.
>   FOR **J** = 1 to **N − I**
>   IF **DtList(J).(Name)** > **DtList(J + 1).(Name)** THEN
>   Switch **DtList(J)** with **DtList(J + 1)**.
>   Set **Sorted** to false.
>   END IF.
>   END FOR.
>   Increment **I**.
> UNTIL **Sorted** OR (**I** > **N − 1**).

A little thought shows that we need the condition **I** > **N** − 1 in order to save the procedure from making one extra pass when a switch is made on the (**N** − 1)st pass. We can convert the pseudocode to the procedure.

```
{*****************************************************************}
{* BubbleFlagSort - Procedure to sort an array of employee       *}
{*                  records into ascending order by name.        *}
{*      var parameters -                                         *}
{*          DtList : Array of employee records.                  *}
{*      value parameters -                                       *}
{*          N : Number of records in the array.                  *}
{*****************************************************************}
procedure BubbleFlagSort(var DtList : EmpArray; N : integer);
var
  I, J : integer;                              { Loop indices }
  Temp : EmpInfo;                           { Temporary storage }
  Sorted : boolean;                          { Flag for sorted }
begin
  I := 1;
```

```
repeat
   Sorted := true;
   for J := 1 to N - I do
      if DtList[J].Name > DtList[J + 1].Name then begin
         Temp := DtList[J];                        { Switch records }
         DtList[J] := DtList[J + 1];
         DtList[J + 1] := Temp;
         Sorted := false
      end; { if }
   { end for }
   I := I + 1
   until Sorted or (I > N - 1)
end; { BubbleFlagSort }
```

As we will see in Section 4.5, our attempt at creating a more efficient sorting technique has not really accomplished what we thought it would. For lists of data that are almost in order to begin with, this technique is more efficient than the original bubble sort. However, for lists of data that are in random order, this technique is actually much more inefficient. When we inserted the statement

```
Sorted := false;
```

we increased the number of steps in each switch from three to four. As we can see from this example, it is important that we conduct a performance analysis for each of the sorting algorithms. We will do this in Section 4.5.

Exercises

4.13   Consider the list of integers in Exercise 4.6. Show how the list appears after each pass of the bubble sort. Count the number of comparisons and the number of moves for each pass. Count the total number of comparisons and the total number of moves.

4.14   Consider the list of integers in Exercise 4.6. Show how the list appears after each pass of the bubble sort with flag. Count the number of comparisons, the number of moves, and the number of times the flag is set for each pass. Count the total number of comparisons, the total number of moves, and the total number of times the flag is set.

4.15   One attempt to improve on the bubble sort has successive passes go in opposite directions. This modification is sometimes referred to as the *shaker sort*. Write an outline of this procedure using pseudocode.

4.16   Consider the list of integers in Exercise 4.6. Perform the same type of walk-through analysis you did in Exercise 4.13 for the shaker sort discussed in Exercise 4.15.

4.17   Write a procedure that will use the algorithm for the shaker sort. The procedure should sort the array of employee records into ascending order by name.

4.4 The Insertion Sort

The third elementary sorting technique we will study is the *insertion sort*. This technique is one used by card players who are arranging their hands. The items to be sorted are considered as a sequence $A(1), \ldots, A(N)$. At each step, starting with $I = 2$ and incrementing by 1, the **I**th element of the sequence is removed from the sequence and reinserted back in the sequence in the appropriate position. For example,

A[1]	5	5	-2	-2	-2
A[2]	13	13	5	5	2
A[3]	-2	-2	13	10	5
A[4]	10	10		13	10
A[5]	2	2			13

The first step in developing an algorithm for this sort is to notice that for $I = 2$ to N, the **I**th element is removed from the list and inserted back in the appropriate position in the array $A[1]..A[I]$. We will walk through the first few steps of the algorithm:

1. For $I = 1$, the first element is left unchanged.
2. For $I = 2$, the element is moved to a temporary storage location called **Temp**. The data item stored at **Temp** is compared with the data item stored at **A[1]**.
   (a) If **Temp** $<$ **A[1]**, then **A[1]** is moved to **A[2]** and **Temp** is moved to **A[1]**. The element is inserted.
   (b) If **Temp** $>=$ **A[1]**, then **Temp** is moved to **A[2]** and the element is inserted.
3. For $I = 3$, the element **A[3]** is moved to **Temp**. The data item stored at **Temp** is compared with the data item stored at **A[2]**.
   (a) If **Temp** $<$ **A[2]**, then **A[2]** is moved to **A[3]**, **Temp** is compared to **A[1]**, and the processes in 2(a) and 2(b) are repeated.
   (b) If **Temp** $>=$ **A[2]**, then **Temp** is moved to **A[3]** and the element is inserted.

Before we outline the procedure using pseudocode, we make the following observations.

1. The complete insertion sort takes $N - 1$ passes. This is controlled by letting **I** range over 2..N.
2. For each **I**, the data item stored in **A[I]** is moved to the storage location **Temp**.
3. The data item stored at **Temp** is compared with the data items that are stored in the locations $A[I - 1], A[I - 2], \ldots$.
4. The insertion of the element stored at **Temp** will terminate when the data item stored at **Temp** is greater than or equal to the data item stored at **A[J]** or when we reach the first element in the array.

5. At each step either **A[J]** is moved to **A[J + 1]** and the comparisons continue or **Temp** is moved to **A[J + 1]**. The insertion of **Temp** will also be complete when **A[J]** is moved to **A[J + 1]** for **J** = 1. In this case **Temp** is moved to **A[1]**.

When we have a repetition that is to terminate when either one of two conditions occurs, we can introduce a Boolean flag. We can now write our pseudocode.

Pseudocode

InsertionSort Procedure

FOR **K** = 2 to **N**
    Move **DtList(K)** to **Temp**.
    Set **I** to **K − 1**.
    Set **Found** to false.
    WHILE (**I** >= 1) and (not **Found**)
        IF **Temp(Name)** < **DtList(I)(Name)** THEN
            Move **DtList(I)** to **DtList(I + 1)**.
            Decrement **I**.
        ELSE
            Set **Found** to true.
        END IF.
    END WHILE.
    Move **Temp** to **DtList(I + 1)**.
END FOR.

We can now code the procedure.

```
{***************************************************************}
{* InsertionSort - Procedure to sort an array of employee      *}
{*                 records into ascending order by name.       *}
{*       var parameters -                                      *}
{*           DtList : Array of employee records.               *}
{*       value parameters -                                    *}
{*           N : Number of records in the array.               *}
{***************************************************************}
procedure InsertionSort(var DtList : EmpArray; N : integer);
var
   I,                                      { Position index }
   K : integer;                             { Loop index }
   Temp : EmpInfo;                       { Temporary storage }
   Found : boolean;                        { Position flag }
begin
   for K := 2 to N do begin                    { Insert loop }
     Temp := DtList[K];                     { Save element }
     I := K - 1;
     Found := false;
     while (I >= 1) and (not Found) do    { Search for position }
```

```
    if Temp.Name < DtList[I].Name then begin
      DtList[I + 1] := DtList[I];
      I := I - 1
    end { if }
    else
      Found := true;
    { end else }
  { end while }
    DtList[I + 1] := Temp                    { Store element }
  end  { for }
end;  { InsertionSort }
```

One attempt to improve on the algorithm for **InsertionSort** would be the following. We note that when the **I**th element, **A[I]**, is removed from the list, the sequence of elements

$$A[1], A[2], \ldots, A[I-1]$$

is sorted. Thus instead of using a linear search to find where to insert **A[I]**, we can use a binary search, which is much more efficient. This modification will give us a sorting technique that is called a *binary insertion sort*. We outline this technique using pseudocode. You may want to review the technique that was described when we discussed the binary search in Section 4.1.

Pseudocode

BinaryIntSort Procedure

```
FOR K = 2 to N
   Move A(K) to Temp.
   Set First to 1.
   Set Last to K − 1.
   WHILE First <= Last
      Compute Mid = middle index.
      IF Temp(Name) < A(Mid)(Name) THEN
         Set Last to Mid − 1.
      ELSE
         Set First to Mid + 1.
      END IF.
   END WHILE.
   FOR J = K − 1 DOWNTO First
      Move A(J) to A(J + 1).
   END FOR.
   Move Temp to A(First).
END FOR.
```

We can now code the procedure.

```
{******************************************************************}
{* BinaryIntSort - Procedure to sort an array of employee        *}
{*                 records into ascending order by name.          *}
{*        var parameters -                                        *}
{*            DtList : Array of employee records.                 *}
{*        value parameters -                                      *}
{*            N : Number of records in the array.                 *}
{******************************************************************}
procedure BinaryIntSort(var DtList : EmpArray; N : integer);
var
  I, K,                                      { Loop indices }
  First, Last, Mid : integer;        { Binary-search indices }
  Temp : EmpInfo;                       { Temporary storage }
begin
  for K := 2 to N do begin                { Insertion loop }
    Temp := DtList[K];                     { Save element }
    First := 1;                            { Binary search }
    Last := K - 1;
    while First <= Last do begin
      Mid := (First + Last) div 2;
      if Temp.Name < DtList[Mid].Name then
        Last := Mid - 1
      else
        First := Mid + 1;
      { end if }
    end; { while }
    for J := K - 1 downto First do      { Loop to move elements }
      DtList[J + 1] := DtList[J];
    { end for }
    DtList[First] := Temp                { Store saved element }
  end { for }
end; { BinaryIntSort }
```

In Section 4.7 we will do run-time comparisons of the various sort techniques, and we will see that this modification improves the run-time efficiency of the insertion sort in some cases by almost 50 percent.

The techniques that we have just studied can also be used to read the data from a file and place them in an array in the appropriate order. The approach is similar to the one we used in Chapter 2 with the **CreateInOrder** procedures for linked lists. We will write this procedure so that we can obtain some run-time comparisons for this file-reading insertion sort and the **CreateInOrder** procedure.

A file-reading insertion sort will differ from the previous insertion sorts in the following ways:

1. The data item stored in **Temp** is to be read from the file.
2. The position into which the data item stored in **Temp** is to be inserted is located before any of the items in the array are moved.

We can now write the pseudocode.

Pseudocode

FileInsertSort Procedure

Open data file.
Set **I** to 0.
WHILE (not end of file) and (**I** < **Size**)
    Read(**Item**) from data file.
    Set **J** to 1.
    Set **Found** to false.
    WHILE (**J** <= **I**) and (not **Found**)
        IF **Item**(**Name**) < **A**(**J**)(**Name**) THEN
            Set **Found** to true.
        ELSE
            Increment **J**.
        END IF.
    END WHILE.
    FOR **K** = **I** DOWNTO **J**
        Move **A**(**K**) to **A**(**K** + 1).
    END FOR.
    Move **Item** to **A**(**J**).
    Increment **I**.
END WHILE.

We can now code the procedure.

```
{******************************************************************}
{* FileInsertSort - Procedure to read the data from a file       *}
{*                  and place them in an array of records in      *}
{*                  ascending order by name.                      *}
{*      var parameters -                                          *}
{*          DtFile : Text file of data.                           *}
{*          DtList : Array of records to store the data           *}
{*                   from the file.                               *}
{*          Num : Number of records read from the file.           *}
{*      value parameters -                                        *}
{*          Size : Size of the array.                             *}
{******************************************************************}
procedure FileInsertSort(var DtFile : text;
                         var DtList : EmpArray; Size : integer;
                         var Num : integer);
var
  J, K : integer;                          { Loop indices }
  Item : EmpInfo;                          { Temporary storage }
  Found : boolean;                         { Position flag }
begin
  reset(DtFile);
  Num := 0;
                                           { Insert loop }
  while (not eof(DtFile)) and (Num < Size) do begin
    ReadOne(DtFile, Item);                 { Get first item }
    J := 1;
```

```
      Found := false;
                                             { Loop to find position }
      while (J <= Num) and (not Found) do
        if Item.Name < DtList[J].Name then
          Found := true
        else
          J := J + 1;
        { end if }
      { end while }
      for K := Num downto J do                { Move elements }
        DtList[K + 1] := DtList[K];
        { end for }
      DtList[J] := Item;                      { Insert element }
      Num := Num + 1;
    end { while }
end; { FileInsertSort }
```

This procedure can also be modified to a binary file insertion sort by using the techniques for a binary insertion sort developed in this section. We will leave this as one of the exercises.

Exercises

4.18 Consider the list of integers in Exercise 4.6. Show how the list appears after each pass of the insertion sort. Count the number of comparisons and the number of moves for each pass. Count the total number of comparisons and the total number of moves.

4.19 Repeat the walk-through process described in Exercise 4.18 using the binary insertion sort.

4.20 Refer to the data described in Exercise 4.10. Write a procedure that will sort the data by flight number using the insertion-sort technique. Write a program to test the procedure.

4.21 Repeat Exercise 4.20 using the binary insertion sort technique.

4.22 Assume that the data from Exercise 4.10 have been sorted by flight number. Write a procedure that will allow the airport manager to search for the record containing a specified flight number. If the record is contained in the list, the data should be printed to the screen with appropriate headings. Otherwise an error message should be printed. The user should have the option of repeating the search with a new flight number. Use a linear search. Write a program and test the procedure.

4.23 Write a procedure that will do what is described in Exercise 4.22 using a binary search. Write a program and test the procedure.

4.24   A large firm has plants in five different cities. The firm has a large file that contains data in the following format:

Columns 1–20	Name	(Character string)
21–30	City	(Character string)
34–35	Age	(Integer)
40–45	Pay rate	(Real)

Write a procedure that will sort the data by name using a file insertion sort. Assume that the file has at most 500 records. Write a program and test this procedure.

4.25   Repeat Exercise 4.24 using a binary insertion sort.

4.26   The president of the firm discussed in Exercise 4.24 would like a printed list of employee information that is sorted by city and by name within each city. Write a procedure that will sort the data in this manner; you may use any of the sorting techniques. Write a program that will test this procedure.

4.27   Write a program that will compare run times for the file insertion sort using arrays written in this section with the **CreateInOrder** procedure from Chapter 2. Use a file of randomly generated real numbers.

4.28   Write a modification of the file insertion sort so that the procedure will perform a binary insertion sort. Write a program and test this procedure.

4.29   Write a program that will compare run times for the file insertion sort with the binary file insertion sort. Use a file of randomly generated real numbers. Compare the two sorts for the best and worst cases.

4.5   Some Comparisons

Because of the relationship between sorting and searching, the first question a programmer should ask is whether or not it pays to sort the given data before searching. Sometimes there will be less work involved in searching a list of data for a particular item than in sorting the entire list and then searching for the particular item. Most applications programs, however, will be more efficient if the list of data is sorted in order on some key before a search is performed. Anytime a printed list of the data in order on some key is required, the data eventually have to be sorted on that key anyway.

A programmer must be able to recognize when a particular sort is inefficient in comparison to other sorting techniques that could be used. If an inefficient sort is used in a given program, the programmer must be able to justify that use. Too often, programmers take the easy way out and code an inefficient sort. When the program is then incorporated into a larger program in which the sort becomes a key component, the larger program becomes grossly inefficient. A programmer should know a wide range of sorting techniques and be cognizant of the advantages and disadvantages of each. When the need for a sort arises, the programmer can then supply a sorting technique that is appropriate for a given program.

One measure of the efficiency of a sorting technique is obtained by counting the number of comparisons, C, and the number of moves, M, of the items in the list. Each of these numbers is a function of the number of items in the list, N. We will compare sorting techniques by estimating the number of comparisons made by a sort on an array of N elements. We will say that a given sort requires on the order of N^2 comparisons if, when we estimate C, we obtain a polynomial of degree N^2. In Chapter 8 we will consider sorting techniques in which the estimated number of comparisons is of the order of N log N. In this chapter we will see that all of the techniques that we have studied are of the order of N^2. As we will see, for large N, N log N is much smaller than N^2. All of the sorting techniques in this section are referred to as *simple methods*. We are studying these simple methods before proceeding to the faster and more efficient techniques for the following reasons:

1. Simple methods are particularly well suited for presenting the basic ideas used in sorting techniques.
2. The simple methods are fairly easy to understand and to code. They are relatively short so they do not occupy very much memory.
3. Although the more sophisticated methods require fewer operations, they are usually more complex in their design. Therefore, for sufficiently small N the simple methods are almost as efficient as the more advanced techniques.

The efficiency consideration that we will focus on in this section is the time required for a given technique to sort a list of data. We are interested in the change in the amount of time that the technique takes to sort a list of N elements as N changes. We are also interested in a comparison of the times that different sorting techniques take to sort the same list of N elements.

In order to understand how the change in time is measured in comparison to the change in the number, N, of elements in the list, we need to discuss the following ideas. We say that Y is *proportional to* X if multiplying X by a constant multiplies Y by the same constant. Thus if Y is proportional to X, doubling the value of X will double the value of Y and multiplying the value of X by 5 will also multiply the value of Y by 5. Similarly, if Y is proportional to X^2, doubling X will multiply the value of Y by 4 and multiplying the value of X by 5 will multiply the value of Y by 5^2, or 25.

If T is the time required for a given sorting technique to sort a given list with N elements, the mathematical analysis that is needed to obtain an estimate of the relationship between T and N is usually very involved and complicated. Since T is certainly directly determined by the number of comparisons, C, and the number of moves, M, that a given sort performs, we will indicate how estimates are obtained for C in terms of N and for M in terms of N for some of the simple sorting techniques that we have discussed. One of the estimates that we will derive is given by the following formula.

$$C = (1/2)(N^2 - N)$$

The following table illustrates how C is affected by a change in N, according to the preceding formula:

N	$(1/2)N^2$	$(1/2)N$	$C = (1/2)(N^2 - N)$
10	50	5	45
100	5000	50	4950
1000	500,000	500	499,500

Clearly, as N becomes larger and larger, the number of comparisons, C, becomes more and more closely proportional to N^2. Because of this, we say that the number of comparisons is on the *order of* N^2 and we write $O(N^2)$. For most of the classic sorts, the number of comparisons, C, and the number of moves, M, are $O(N^2)$ or $O(N \log N)$.

It can be shown that the base of the logarithm used is irrelevant in determining the order of the sort. In computer science, however, we use base 2 for the analysis of sorting algorithms. The following table shows the comparison between N^2 and $N \log_2 N$ for a range of values of N.

N	$N \log_2 N$	N^2
2	2	4
16	64	256
128	896	16,384

The table makes clear that for larger and larger N, N^2 increases at a much more rapid rate than $N \log_2 N$. We will now estimate C and M for some of the sorts that we have discussed.

Selection Sort

The number of comparisons for the selection sort is independent of the initial order of the elements in the list. We recall that for each pass the comparisons are made and the data may or may not be switched depending on the relative order of the data elements. We have seen that for a list of N elements the sorting process requires $N - 1$ passes. The number of comparisons for each of these passes is as follows.

Pass	*Number of Comparisons*
1	$N - 1$
2	$N - 2$
3	$N - 3$
↓	↓
$N - 1$	1

Thus the total number of comparisons is

$$1 + 2 + 3 + \cdots + (N - 3) + (N - 2) + (N - 1)$$
$$= (N - 1)(N)/2 = (1/2)(N^2 - N)$$

The number of moves for this sort is certainly dependent on the initial order of the elements in the list and ranges from a minimum of zero moves, if the elements of the list are initially in order, to a maximum of three moves for each of the $(1/2)(N^2 - N)$ comparisons, if the elements of the list are initially in reverse order. We have three moves for each comparison because three steps are needed to switch the data stored in the two locations. Thus we have the following estimates for the minimum, the maximum, and the average number of moves needed in a selection sort:

$$M_{min} = 0$$
$$M_{max} = 3 * (1/2)(N^2 - N)$$
$$= (3/2)(N^2 - N)$$
$$M_{aver} = (M_{min} + M_{max})/2$$
$$= [0 + (3/2)(N^2 - N)]/2$$
$$= (3/4)(N^2 - N)$$

Bubble Sort

Just as for the selection sort, the number of comparisons for the bubble sort is independent of the initial order of the elements in the list. For a list of N elements, the sorting process requires $N - 1$ passes, and the number of comparisons is exactly the same as it was for the selection sort. The number of comparisons on each pass is given below.

Pass	*Comparisons*
1	N − 1
2	N − 2
3	N − 3
↓	↓
N − 1	1

Thus the total number of comparisons is

$$1 + 2 + 3 + \cdots + (N - 3) + (N - 2) + (N - 1) = (1/2)(N^2 - N)$$

Furthermore, the number of moves for the bubble sort certainly depends on the initial order of the elements in the list. The number of moves ranges from a minimum of zero moves to a maximum of three moves for each comparison.

Thus the minimum, the maximum, and the average number of moves for the bubble sort are also given by the formulas

$$M_{min} = 0$$

$$M_{max} = (3/2)(N^2 - N)$$

$$M_{aver} = (3/4)(N^2 - N)$$

Insertion Sort

The analysis of the insertion sort is a little more complicated. The number of comparisons at the Ith step is at most $I - 1$ and at least 1. Thus, on the average, the number of comparisons is

$$[(I - 1) + 1]/2 = I/2$$

The total number of comparisons is

$$C_{max} = \sum_{I=2}^{N} (I - 1)$$

$$= 1 + 2 + \cdots + (N - 1)$$

$$= (N - 1)(N)/2$$

$$= (N^2 - N)/2$$

$$C_{min} = \sum_{I=2}^{N} (1)$$

$$= 1 + 1 + \cdots + 1 \qquad (N - 1) \text{ times}$$

$$= N - 1$$

$$C_{aver} = (C_{max} + C_{min})/2$$

$$= [(N^2 - N)/2 + (N - 1)]/2$$

$$= (1/4)(N^2 + N - 2)$$

In the case of the maximum number of comparisons, the number of moves is one for each comparison, plus one initial move, plus one final move. If M_I denotes the number of moves for the Ith step and C_I denotes the number of comparisons for the Ith step, then

$$M_I = C_I + 2$$

Thus the maximum number of moves is given by

$$M_{max} = \sum_{I=2}^{N} (C_I + 2)$$

$$= \sum_{I=2}^{N} [(I - 1) + 2]$$

$$= 3 + 4 + 5 + \cdots + (N + 1)$$

$$= (N + 1)(N + 2)/2 - 3$$

$$= (1/2)(N^2 + 3N - 4)$$

For the minimum number of moves, two moves are made for each comparison because the **while** loop is never entered. Thus we have

$$M_{min} = \sum_{I=2}^{N} 2$$

$$= 2 + 2 + 2 + \cdots + 2 \qquad (N - 1) \text{ times}$$

$$= 2(N - 1)$$

Furthermore, for the average number of moves, we must note that for each step I, the number M_I of moves taken is again given by

$$M_I = C_I + 2$$

Therefore, the average number of moves is given by

$$M_{aver} = \sum_{I=2}^{N} M_I$$

$$= \sum_{I=2}^{N} (C_I + 2)$$

$$= \sum_{I=2}^{N} C_I + \sum_{I=2}^{N} 2$$

$$= C_{aver} + 2(N - 1)$$

$$= (1/4)(N^2 + N - 2) + 2(N - 1)$$

$$= (1/4)(N^2 + 9N - 10)$$

Binary Insertion Sort

The analysis of the binary insertion sort is quite complicated. In order to estimate the number of comparisons, we note that one comparison is made for each pass of the binary search process through the part of the list that is already sorted. Since each pass cuts the search interval in half, we know from the discussion in Section 4.1 that the process can take at most

$$\log_2 I$$

steps, where I is the number of elements in the search interval. Furthermore, since the binary search process does not terminate until

$$\text{First} > \text{Last}$$

the search process takes $\log_2 I$ steps, regardless of the initial order of the elements in the list. Thus the number of comparisons is given by

$$C = \sum_{I=2}^{N} \log_2 I$$

It can be shown that this can be approximated by

$$C = N(\log_2 N - k) + k$$

where

$$k = \log_2 (e)$$

The value of k is approximately

$$k = 1.44269$$

The computation of the above formula for C is complicated. If you are interested in the derivation of the formula, see D. E. Knuth, *Sorting and Searching* (Addison-Wesley, Reading, Mass., 1973).

The number of moves is a little bit harder to estimate. The minimum number of moves would be required if the data were initially in order. In such a case two moves would be made for each of the elements inserted. Thus the minimum number of moves is given by

$$M_{min} = \sum_{I=2}^{N} (2)$$
$$= 2(N - 1)$$

To estimate the maximum number of moves, we note that in the worst case each of the data items in the sorted list will have to be moved up one position and the new data item inserted at the front of the list. One additional move will be needed for each element when it is moved to the temporary storage location. Thus each I requires I + 1 moves. This gives us the estimate

$$M_{max} = \sum_{I=2}^{N} (I + 1)$$
$$= 3 + 4 + 5 + \cdots + (N + 1)$$
$$= (1/2)(N + 1)(N + 2) - 3$$
$$= (1/2)(N^2 + 3N - 4)$$

The average is now given by the estimate

$$M_{aver} = (M_{max} + M_{min})/2$$
$$= [N^2/2 + 3N/2 - 2(N - 1)]/2$$
$$= (N^2 + 7N/2 - 4)/2$$
$$= (1/4)(N^2 + 7N - 8)$$

Although the binary insertion-sort technique improves on the number of comparisons that the insertion sort has to make, the improvement is not quite what we anticipated. One reason for this is that a move takes more time to perform than does a comparison. Another reason is that since the time involved is a function of both the number of moves and the number of comparisons, if either of these is $O(N^2)$, the sorting technique is also of that same order.

Bubble Sort with Flag

A complete analysis of the bubble sort with flag is also very involved. What we can easily derive is the following. Since the sort must make one pass through the list, the minimum number of comparisons is given by

$$C_{min} = N - 1$$

The maximum number of comparisons is the same as it was for the bubble sort. Thus

$$C_{max} = (1/2)(N^2 - N)$$

We can also see that the minimum number of moves is zero,

$$M_{min} = 0$$

and the maximum number of moves is three times the maximum number of comparisons,

$$M_{max} = (3/2)(N^2 - N)$$

The average number of comparisons and the average number of moves have been computed by Knuth. He finds that the average number of passes is proportional to

$$N - K_1\sqrt{N}$$

From this estimate Knuth arrives at the following estimate for the average number of comparisons:

$$C_{aver} = (1/2)[N^2 - N(K_2 + \log_2 N)]$$

The values for K_1 and K_2 are computed by Knuth. Since the average number of moves is just three times the average number of comparisons, we have

$$M_{aver} = (3/2)[N^2 - N(K_2 + \log_2 N)]$$

Modified Selection Sort

A complete analysis of the modified selection sort is also very involved. We refer the reader to Knuth for the analysis.

Conclusion

To conclude our discussion of these simple sorting techniques, we will try to compare their effectiveness. Each of these techniques needs one block of memory for the array and the additional element. They are all of $O(N^2)$ and are fairly easy to code. In Table 4.1, N will denote the number of items to be sorted, C will stand for the number of comparisons, and M will stand for the number of moves.

Table 4.1   Simple Sorting Techniques

	Minimum	*Average*	*Maximum*
SELECTION SORT			
Comparisons	$C = (N^2 - N)/2$	$(N^2 - N)/2$	$(N^2 - N)/2$
Moves	$M = 0$	$(3/4)(N^2 - N)$	$(3/2)(N^2 - N)$
MODIFIED SELECTION SORT			
Comparisons	$C = (N^2 - N)/2$	$(N^2 - N)/2$	$(N^2 - N)/2$
Moves	$M = 3(N - 1)$	$N(\log_2 N + 0.57)$	$(1/4)(N^2 + 12N - 12)$
BUBBLE SORT			
Comparisons	$C = (N^2 - N)/2$	$(N^2 - N)/2$	$(N^2 - N)/2$
Moves	$M = 0$	$(3/4)(N^2 - N)$	$(3/4)(N^2 - N)$
BUBBLE SORT WITH FLAG			
Comparisons	$C = N - 1$	$(1/2)(N^2 - N(K_2 + \log_2 N))$	$(N^2 - N)/2$
Moves	$M = 0$	$(3/2)(N^2 - N(K_2 + \log_2 N))$	$(3/2)(N^2 - N)$
INSERTION SORT			
Comparisons	$C = N - 1$	$(1/4)(N^2 + N - 2)$	$(N^2 - N)/2$
Moves	$M = 2(N - 1)$	$(1/4)(N^2 + 9N - 10)$	$(1/2)(N^2 + 3N - 4)$
BINARY INSERTION SORT			
Comparisons	$C = (1/2)[N \log_2 N + (k - 1)(N - 1)]$	Same	Same
Moves	$M = 2(N - 1)$	$(1/4)(N^2 + 7N - 8)$	$(1/2)(N^2 + 3N - 4)$

This table of formulas merely provides a rough measure of the performance of each of the sorting techniques as a function of N. These formulas do not take into account the computational effort expended on loop control, for example. As a final comparison of the techniques, Table 4.2 gives the times required for each of the sorts to sort a list of real data items. The sorting procedures were run on a CDC 170 computer, using the Pascal 2.3 compiler. The times were generated for lists of 512 and 2500 randomly generated real numbers. The best times were obtained for the lists when they were initially in order and the worst times when they were initially in the reverse order. The times are expressed in seconds. Figures 4.2–4.4 show best case, worst case, and random case for 512 elements.

Table 4.2   Run-Time Comparisons

	512			2500		
	Random	*Best*	*Worst*	*Random*	*Best*	*Worst*
Bubble sort	5.654	3.751	7.396	131.618	88.419	171.132
Bubble sort with flag	5.713	0.018	7.808	135.469	0.072	183.683
Selection sort	5.967	4.038	7.896	137.526	92.352	180.410
Modified selection sort	3.389	3.350	4.019	77.480	76.616	91.716
Insertion sort	3.018	0.036	5.755	66.554	6.170	134.245
Binary insertion sort	1.453	0.230	0.229	30.361	1.365	1.400

Figure 4.2

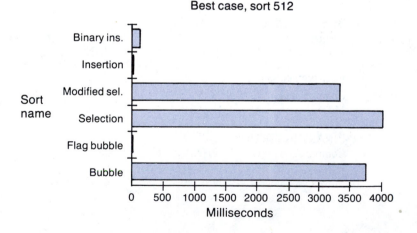

Best case, sort 512

Figure 4.3

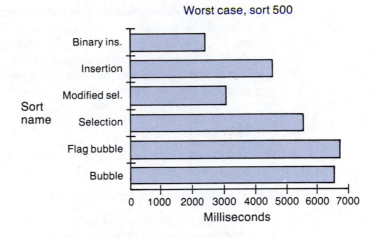

Worst case, sort 500

Figure 4.4

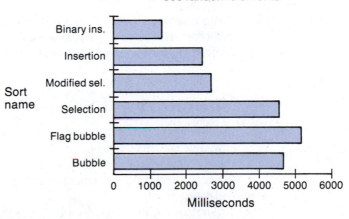

500 random elements

Notice the following:

1. The selection sort is the worst of the sorting methods that we have compared. The bubble sort is almost as bad.
2. The bubble sort with flag is only better if the array is almost in order and is actually worse than the bubble sort generally.
3. The modified selection sort is a big improvement over the selection sort and is one of the best techniques overall.
4. The insertion sort is one of the best methods overall. The binary insertion sort is even better. In the case in which the list is almost in order, however, its performance is worse than that of the bubble sort with flag.

Keep in mind that the data to be sorted by a program will seldom be simply a list of numbers. Most of the time they will be a list of records with several fields. In the exercises you will be asked to do a run-time analysis of the various sorting techniques written in this chapter. This analysis will probably show the modified selection sort and the binary insertion sort performing significantly better than the other sorts, with the modified selection sort emerging as the best of the simple sorting methods. In Chapter 8 we will discuss some of the more advanced sorting techniques. For large collections of data, these advanced techniques are much more efficient than the simple approaches discussed in this chapter.

Exercises

4.30   How many comparisons are necessary to find the maximum element in an array of N elements?

4.31   Show that if a given sorting technique is $O(N \log_2 N)$, it is also $O(N \log_{10} N)$.

4.32   A sorting technique is said to be *stable* if the relative order of the items with equal keys remains unchanged by the sorting process. Which of the sorting techniques in this chapter are stable?

4.33   Write a program that will do a run-time analysis for the sorting techniques in this chapter. The program can be similar to the program in Section 4.5. This analysis, however, should be for an array of records.

Summary

In this chapter we investigated some of the simple array-sorting methods. We saw that for small arrays, there is very little difference in the efficiency of these techniques. For larger arrays, however, the modified selection sort and the binary insertion sort emerged as the most efficient of these simple sorting methods.

The sorting times required by these simple methods to sort arrays of 512 and 2500 randomly generated real numbers are summarized in the following table.

	512 elements	*2500 elements*
Bubble sort	5.654 seconds	131.618 seconds
Bubble sort with flag	5.713 seconds	135.469 seconds
Selection sort	5.967 seconds	137.526 seconds
Modified selection sort	3.389 seconds	77.480 seconds
Insertion sort	3.018 seconds	66.554 seconds
Binary insertion sort	1.453 seconds	30.361 seconds

Very little memory beyond that needed for the array itself is required by any of the simple sorts. All of these simple sorting techniques are fairly easy to code.

Some of the techniques and analyses involved in developing a sorting technique were introduced, as were the ways algorithms are analyzed and modified in an attempt to make them more efficient. In Chapter 8 we will continue the study of sorting with a look at some of the more advanced and more efficient sorting techniques.

Chapter Exercises

4.34   Each line of a data file **DataF** contains a record of data in the following format:

Columns	1– 7	Inventory number	(Character string)
	8–27	Description	(Character string)
	30–32	Quantity on hand	(Integer)
	35–36	Reorder number	(Integer)
	40–45	Cost of item	(Real)
	50–55	Selling price	(Real)

(a) Write a program that reads the data into an array and then calls an insertion sort procedure to sort the data into ascending order according to inventory number. The program should then write the sorted data to a file.

(b) Write the insertion sort procedure to sort the data into ascending order according to the description instead of according to inventory number. The program should then write the sorted data to a file.

4.35   Redo Exercise 4.34 using the other sorting algorithms developed in this chapter:

> Bubble sort
> Bubble sort with flag
> Selection sort
> Modified selection sort
> Binary insertion sort

Compare the sorting times.

4.36   Each line of a data file **DFile** contains a record of data in the following format:

Columns	1–20	Name	(Character string)
	21–64	Address	(Character string)
	65–76	Phone number	(Character string)

(a) Write a program that reads the data into an array and then calls an insertion sort procedure to sort the data into ascending order according to name. The program should then write the sorted data to a file.

(b) Write the insertion sort procedure to sort the data into ascending order according to phone number instead of according to name. The program should then write the sorted data to a file.

4.37 Redo Exercise 4.36 using the other sorting procedures developed in this chapter:

Bubble sort
Bubble sort with flag
Selection sort
Modified selection sort
Binary insertion sort

Compare the sorting times.

CHAPTER 5

Recursion

In previous chapters we have written and called procedures and functions to perform particular programming tasks. In this chapter we will investigate the process of having a procedure or function call itself. This technique, which is called *direct recursion*, is a very powerful programming tool that, if used appropriately, can reduce greatly the number of lines of code required to write a particular program. Recursion can be used for a wide range of programming applications including some of the fastest sorting techniques.

Direct recursion means that a function or procedure calls itself. Indirect forms of recursion may also be used. In *indirect recursion* a procedure (or function) **A** calls another procedure (or function), **B**, which then may either call **A** again or call other procedures or functions that in turn call **A**. Thus the procedure (or function) **A** indirectly calls itself through other procedures or functions. Recursion is not possible in all high-level languages; however, it is available in Pascal.

Recursion can be a very powerful programming tool. However, for recursion to be used appropriately, it must be thoroughly understood. Included in this understanding must be a knowledge of exactly how recursion works and also when and where it should and can be used. Too often, programmers attempt to use recursion in their programs by merely copying an example of recursion written in another program without knowing how recursion works or why they are using it.

The main objective of this chapter is to provide a thorough understanding of how recursion works and when to use it. This understanding will be developed through the very careful analysis of rather simple recursive programming examples, which will include both recursive function calls and recursive procedure calls. This chapter will provide the in-depth understanding of recursion needed to progress through the major applications of recursion that appear throughout the remaining chapters of the text.

5.1 The Run-Time Stack

Before we begin our development of recursion, we need to take a close look at how Pascal handles calls to procedures and functions. Let us consider the following small program, which calls a function to compute the square of an integer number.

```
{********************************************************************}
{* CallFunction - Program which calls a function to compute the *}
{*                square of a number.                           *}
{********************************************************************}
program CallFunction(output);
var
  Num : integer;                            { Integer number }
  NumSq : integer;                        { Square of the number }
{********************************************************************}
{* Square - Function to compute the square of a number.       *}
{*      value parameters -                                    *}
{*            N : Integer number to be squared.               *}
{********************************************************************}
function Square(N : integer) : integer;
begin
  Square := N * N                         { Find the function value }
end;  { Square }
{********************************************************************}
{*                    Main Control Module                     *}
{********************************************************************}
begin
  Num := 2 + 1;
  NumSq := Square(Num);                   { Call to Square function }
  writeln(Num : 12, NumSq : 20)
end.   { CallFunction }
```

To understand the techniques Pascal uses in executing this program, we must look at the run-time stack (or stacks). Pascal uses at least one stack during execution of any program to store values for variables, constants, parameters, and return addresses. Let us take a look at how Pascal manages its run-time stack during execution of program **CallFunction**. Various Pascal compilers handle their stacks in slightly different manners during program execution. However, the techniques we will investigate are representative of the methods used, and the effective results will be the same. We will assume that our compiler uses only one run-time stack, and we will investigate how this stack is actually used.

First of all, when the program starts to execute, space is allocated on the stack for the main program (see Figure 5.1). Included in this allocated space are locations for each of the global variables, **Num** and **NumSq**. When the Pascal compiler compiles the first executable statement

```
Num := 2 + 1
```

Figure 5.1   *Allocation of run-time stack space for the main program.*

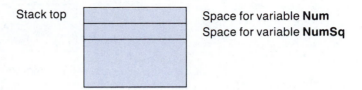

the resultant machine code must perform two steps in order to execute the statement:

1. Evaluate 2 + 1.
2. Assign the value found to the variable **Num**.

Now let us take a look at what happens on the run-time stack during execution. To accomplish Step 1, the value 2 is first pushed onto the top of the stack [see Figure 5.2(a)]. The value 1 is then pushed onto the top of the stack [see Figure 5.2 (b)]. The top two values from the stack (1 and 2) are then popped in order to perform the binary addition operation, +, on the two numbers. The result, 3, is then pushed back onto the stack (see Figure 5.3).

Figure 5.2

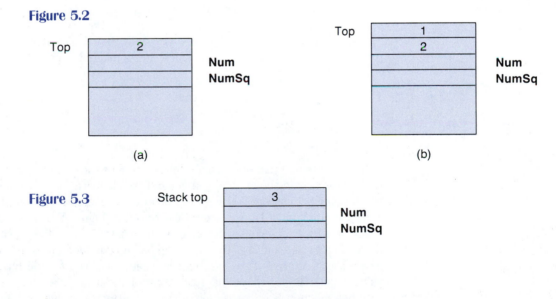

We have now accomplished Step 1 of the statement

```
Num := 2 + 1
```

which was to find the value of 2 + 1. The resultant value is now on top of the stack. To now do Step 2, which was to assign the value 3 to the variable **Num**, the top value (3) is popped from the stack and stored in the space reserved for variable **Num** (see Figure 5.4).

Figure 5.4

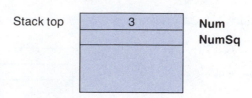

Notice that the assignment step merely takes the top value off the top of the stack and stores it in the correct stack location. Execution of the main program now goes to the statement

```
NumSq := Square(Num)
```

Again, since this is an assignment statement, execution consists of two steps.

1. Find the value for **Square(Num)**.
2. Assign the value found to the variable **NumSq**.

Step 1 requires a call to function **Square** to find the value for **Square**(3). Now, how should the function return the value it finds to the main program? This is easily understood if we remember that Step 2 assumes that the value to be assigned is on the top of the stack. Thus all we have to do is make sure that function **Square** returns the value on the top of the stack immediately` above the space reserved for the variables in the main program. How will this be accomplished?

Each time a procedure or function is called, Pascal allocates space for that module on the top of the run-time stack. For a function, space is allocated for each of the following.

1. The function value (to be returned)
2. Value parameters (if any)
3. The return address
4. Local variables (if any)

We will assume that our Pascal compiler pushes these items onto the stack in the order given above. Thus, in general, stack space for a function call will be allocated as illustrated in Figure 5.5. For our example program the space is allocated for function **Square** as illustrated in Figure 5.6. Notice that the space allocation for function **Square** is immediately above the stack area for the main program and that the stack top has now moved up to the top of the newly allocated area. Also note that the space reserved for the final function value is immediately above the stack area for the main program.

When function **Square** is called, the space for the value parameter **N** is filled with its value of 3, and the return address location is filled with the address of the machine code in the main program that will proceed with Step 2 of the assignment statement. Remember that once the function value has been found and returned, the main program must complete the assignment statement

```
NumSq := Square(Num)
```

Figure 5.5   *Stack space allocation for a function call.*

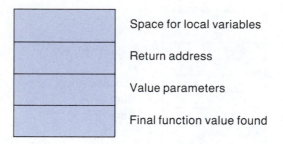

Space for local variables

Return address

Value parameters

Final function value found

Figure 5.6

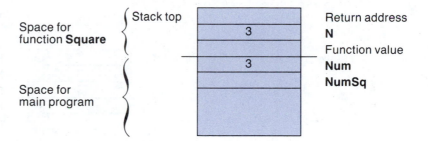

Space for function **Square**

Space for main program

Stack top

3	Return address
	N
	Function value
3	**Num**
	NumSq

by storing the value found on the right side of the statement. It will store this value in the stack location reserved for **NumSq**. We must also remember that Step 2 in the assignment statement will assume that the value for **Square(Num)** is on top of the stack when we return from the function call.

After the call to the function is made, after the stack space is allocated, and after the parameter and return address values are put into their correct stack locations, the execution of function **Square** may begin. The only executable statement is

```
Square := N * N
```

This statement requires that we find the value for **N** ∗ **N** and then assign the value found to the function name **Square**. This means that we will store the value found in the location reserved for the function value. To compute **N** ∗ **N** we will get the value for **N** from the stack location for **N** and *push* its value of 3 onto the top of the stack. Before the multiplication operation can be performed a second copy of **N** must be pushed onto the stack. Thus another value of 3 is pushed onto the top of the stack [see Figure 5.7(a)].

The top two stack values are now popped, the ∗ operation is performed, and the answer (9) is pushed back onto the stack [see Figure 5.7(b)]. To now complete Step 2 of the assignment statement, we *pop* the answer from the top of the stack and store it at the location allocated for the function value. The stack should now appear as illustrated in Figure 5.8.

Figure 5.7

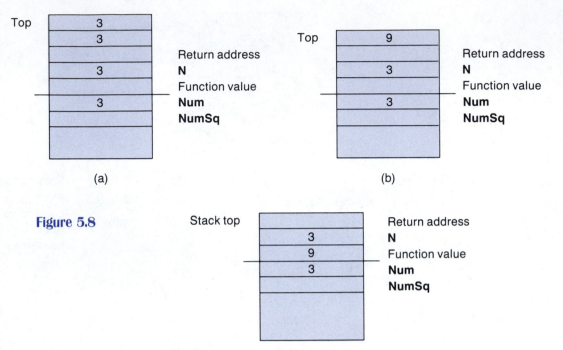

(a)   (b)

Figure 5.8

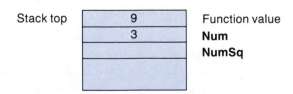

Since all statements in function **Square** have now been executed, execution now returns to the main program. This return is accomplished with the following two steps.

1. Using the return address saved in the stack we return to the next executable machine-code instruction in the main program.
2. The stack space for function **Square** (except for the space for the function value) is now released. Note that the function value is now on top of the stack (see Figure 5.9).

Figure 5.9

Execution of the main program now continues with Step 2 of the assignment statement

```
NumSq := Square(Num)
```

which is to assign the value found [for **Square(Num)**] to **NumSq**. This is accomplished by popping the value from the top of the stack and inserting it inside of the stack at the location reserved for **NumSq** (see Figure 5.10).

Figure 5.10

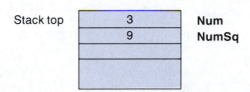

This example illustrates that a function call for our Pascal compiler simply involves allocating space on the run-time stack for that function and then making sure that the value returned will be *on top of the stack* when execution returns to the calling module. All of this is controlled by the machine code that the Pascal compiler created during compilation.

5.2 Recursive Function Calls

Now that we have an understanding of how Pascal can handle function calls on the run-time stack, we will proceed to an example which will involve a Pascal function calling itself. Thus we will see how a recursive function call works.

As our example, suppose that we wish to write a Pascal function that will find the sum of the first **N** positive integers. That is, if **N** is 5, we want to find the value of

$$5 + 4 + 3 + 2 + 1$$

A formula for this sum can be expressed as follows.

$$\textbf{IntSum(N)} = \textbf{N} + (\textbf{N} - 1) + (\textbf{N} - 2) + \cdots + 1$$

Thus,

$$\textbf{IntSum}(5) = 5 + 4 + 3 + 2 + 1$$

However, this sum can also be expressed as

$$\textbf{IntSum}(5) = 5 + \textbf{IntSum}(4)$$

since

$$\textbf{IntSum}(4) = 4 + 3 + 2 + 1$$

This leads us to another type of definition for **IntSum**.

$$\textbf{IntSum(N)} = \textbf{N} + \textbf{IntSum(N} - 1) \qquad \text{if } \textbf{N} > 1$$
$$\textbf{IntSum(N)} = 1 \qquad \text{if } \textbf{N} = 1$$

Notice that our definition includes the special case where **N** = 1. Using this definition, consider now the steps required to evaluate **IntSum**(4).

1. **IntSum**(4) = 4 + **IntSum**(3)
2.   **IntSum**(3) = 3 + **IntSum**(2)
3.   **IntSum**(2) = 2 + **IntSum**(1)
4.   **IntSum**(1) = 1

We still do not have the value for **IntSum**(4). However, notice what happens when we now reverse the above four steps and substitute values when we find them.

4. **IntSum**(1) = 1
3. **IntSum**(2) = 2 + **IntSum**(1) = 2 + 1 = 3
2. **IntSum**(3) = 3 + **IntSum**(2) = 3 + 3 = 6
1. **IntSum**(4) = 4 + **IntSum**(3) = 4 + 6 = 10

Thus we may find the value for **IntSum(N)** by continuously using our definition until we reach the limiting case where **N** = 1 and then reverse our steps until we find the final value. This is an example of what is called a recursive definition. It is recursive for the following two reasons.

1. The definition is written such that the value is defined in terms of a simpler form. In our example, **IntSum(N)** is defined in terms of **IntSum** **(N − 1)**, which is a simpler form.
2. The definition includes a simple limiting case. In our example, **IntSum(N)** = 1 when **N** = 1.

Now that we understand the definition, let us write a Pascal function **IntSum** that uses this definition. Function **IntSum** will have only the one integer parameter **N**. Primarily all the function must do is check to see if **N** = 1. If so, the function should assign the value of 1 to **IntSum**; otherwise, our definition implies that we must find the value for **N** + **IntSum(N − 1)**. We can do this in our function with the assignment statement.

```
IntSum := N + IntSum(N - 1);
```

where **IntSum(N − 1)** is another call to **IntSum**.

```
{*******************************************************************}
{* IntSum - Recursive function to find the sum of the first N   *}
{*          positive integers.                                  *}
{*      value parameters -                                      *}
{*          N : Positive integer number.                        *}
{*******************************************************************}
function IntSum(N : integer) : integer;
begin
  if N = 1 then
    IntSum := 1
  { end if }
  else
    IntSum := N + IntSum(N - 1)      { Recursive call to IntSum }
  { end else }
end;  { IntSum }
```

Notice that we are using direct recursion since

```
IntSum(N - 1)
```

is a call to function **IntSum**. That is, the function calls itself. Now suppose that we call function **IntSum** from some main program as follows.

```
begin
      .
      .
      .
   Num := 3;
   Sum := IntSum(Num);
      .
      .
      .
end.
```

If we are to thoroughly understand how the process of recursion works in Pascal, we need to carefully follow step by step what happens when the above call is executed. Let us examine both the order of the statements as they will be executed and, also, the run-time stack. First of all, execution of the assignment statement

```
Sum := IntSum(Num)
```

in the main program is interrupted by the call to function **IntSum**.

```
Num := 3;
Sum := IntSum(Num);

              First interruption call

         function IntSum(N : integer) : integer;
         begin
            if N = 1 then
               IntSum := 1
            { end if }
            else
               IntSum := N + IntSum(N - 1)
```

Assume that the interruption call to **IntSum** has been made, but the execution of the statements in function **IntSum** has not yet started. At this point the run-time stack should appear as illustrated in Figure 5.11(a).

Figure 5.11

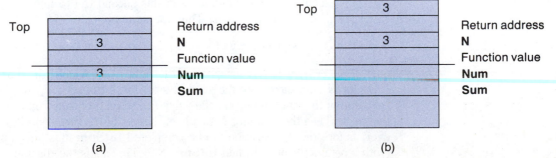

(a)   (b)

Now, let us look at the execution of the statements in this first call to function **IntSum**. Since **N** is not equal to 1, the statement

```
IntSum := N + IntSum(N - 1);
```

must be executed.

Remember that the first step in execution of this statement must be the evaluation of the right side. This evaluation requires first getting the value for **N** from within the stack and pushing it onto the top of the stack [see Figure 5.11(b)]. Before the + operation can be performed, the value of **IntSum(N − 1)** must be pushed onto the top of the stack. However, **IntSum(N − 1)** is a recursive call to function **IntSum** with a parameter value of 2. Thus we have our second interruption call.

```
Num := 3;
Sum := IntSum(Num);
                        First interruption call

        function IntSum(N : integer) : integer;
        begin
          if N = 1 then
            IntSum := 1
          { end if }
          else
            IntSum := N + IntSum(N - 1)
                                            Second interruption call

        function IntSum(N : integer) : integer;
        begin
          if N = 1 then
            IntSum := 1
          { end if }
          else
            IntSum := N + IntSum(N - 1)
```

After function **IntSum** is called the second time, but before the start of the execution of function **IntSum**, the run-time stack should appear as illustrated in Figure 5.12(a).

When execution of the statements in this second call to function **IntSum** starts, **N** is again not equal to 1. Thus the statement

```
IntSum := N + IntSum(N - 1);
```

must again be executed. Evaluation of the right side begins with a push of the value for **N** onto the top of the stack. Since this is the second call of function **IntSum** on the run-time stack, the value for **N** will be taken from this area of the stack. Thus the value for **N** that is pushed is 2 [see Figure 5.12(b)]. However, before the + operation can be completed **IntSum** must again be called (with a parameter of 1) to find **IntSum(N − 1)**. This is the third interruption call to **IntSum**.

Figure 5.12

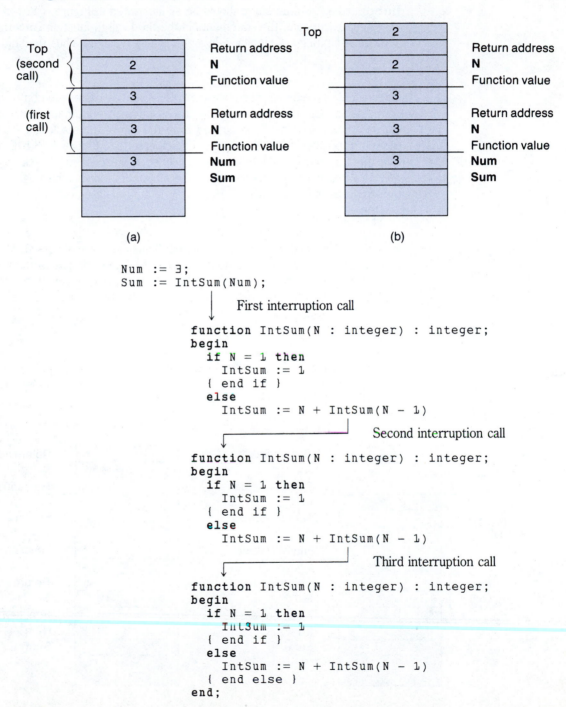

(a)   (b)

```
Num := 3;
Sum := IntSum(Num);
```
        First interruption call

```
function IntSum(N : integer) : integer;
begin
   if N = 1 then
      IntSum := 1
   { end if }
   else
      IntSum := N + IntSum(N - 1)
```
                    Second interruption call

```
function IntSum(N : integer) : integer;
begin
   if N = 1 then
      IntSum := 1
   { end if }
   else
      IntSum := N + IntSum(N - 1)
```
                    Third interruption call

```
function IntSum(N : integer) : integer;
begin
   if N = 1 then
      IntSum := 1
   { end if }
   else
      IntSum := N + IntSum(N - 1)
   { end else }
end;
```

After the third call to function **IntSum**, but before execution of function **IntSum**, the run-time stack should be as illustrated in Figure 5.13(a).

When execution of the statements in the third call to function **IntSum** now starts, the limiting case in which **N** = 1 is finally reached. Thus the statement

```
IntSum := 1
```

is executed. To execute this statement, the value of 1 is pushed onto the top of the stack, and then, to complete the assignment statement (**IntSum** :=
1), the top stack value (1) is popped from the top of the stack and stored as the function value within the third call stack area [see Figure 5.13(b)]. Notice that the first function value has now finally been stored in the stack.

Now what happens? Execution of the statements in the third call to function **IntSum** must be finished. However, after the statement

```
IntSum := 1
```

is executed the **end** statement is reached. Thus execution of this third call to function **IntSum** has been completed. Execution now returns to the instruction where the function was called. That is, we must now return to the second call to function **IntSum**. More specifically, the return will be to the completion of the assignment statement

```
IntSum := N + IntSum(N - 1)
```

in the second call. This return is made through the return address on the stack. When the return is made, all run-time stack locations used for the third

Figure 5.13

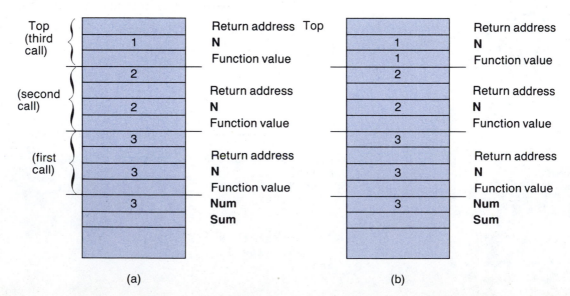

(a)   (b)

function call are deallocated except for the function-value location. Note that it is important that the function value be left on the *top of the stack. This is how the function value is returned.* See Figure 5.14.

Figure 5.14

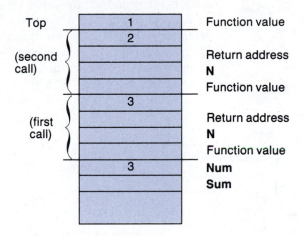

Now, what happens when the return is made to the second call to function **IntSum**?

```
Num := 3;
Sum := IntSum(Num);
```

First interruption call

```
function IntSum(N : integer) : integer;
begin
  if N = 1 then
    IntSum := 1
  { end if }
  else
    IntSum := N + IntSum(N - 1)
```

Second interruption call

```
function IntSum(N : integer) : integer;
begin
  if N = 1 then
    IntSum := 1
  { end if }
  else
    IntSum := N + IntSum(N - 1)
```

Return from third call

Remember, the call to **IntSum** was made to find **IntSum(N − 1)** in the line

```
IntSum := N + IntSum(N - 1)
```

That value has now been found and returned on the top of the stack. Therefore, to complete the right side of the assignment statement, the top two numbers are popped from the stack (from the stack in Figure 5.14), the two numbers are added and the result (3) is pushed back onto the stack [see Figure 5.15(a)]. The program is now ready to complete Step 2 of the assignment statement, which is to assign the value found to **IntSum**. Since this is the function name, this value is assigned by popping the top value from the stack (3) and storing it in the location for the function value (in the second call area of the stack). See Figure 5.15(b).

Figure 5.15

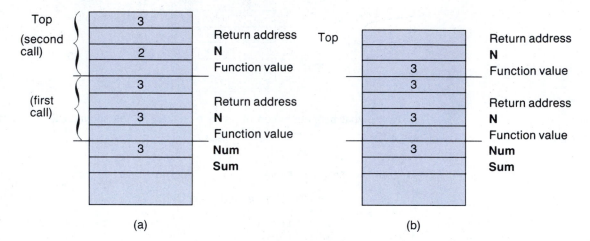

(a)   (b)

Since the **end** statement is next in function **IntSum**, the execution of the second call to the function has now been completed, and execution may now return to the statement from which the function was called:

```
Num := 3;
Sum := IntSum(Num);
```
        ↓   First interruption call

```
        function IntSum(N : integer) : integer;
        begin
          if N = 1 then
            IntSum := 1
          { end if }
          else
            IntSum := N + IntSum(N - 1)
```
                        ↑
                        └──Return from second call

Execution returns to the address that was saved on the stack and except for the returned function value, the stack space used by the second function call is deallocated (see Figure 5.16).

Figure 5.16

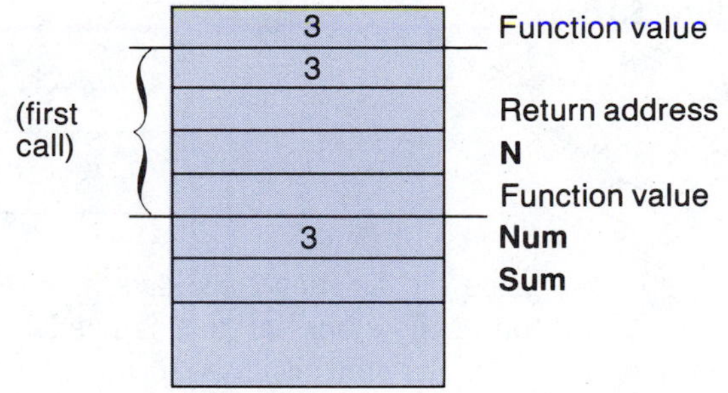

Note that again the return is to the assignment statement

```
IntSum  :=  N + IntSum(N - 1)
```

in function **IntSum**. So again we must pop the two top stack values, add them, and push the sum (6) back onto the stack [see Figure 5.17(a)]. We complete the assignment by popping this top stack value (6) and storing it for the function value [see Figure 5.17(b)].

Figure 5.17

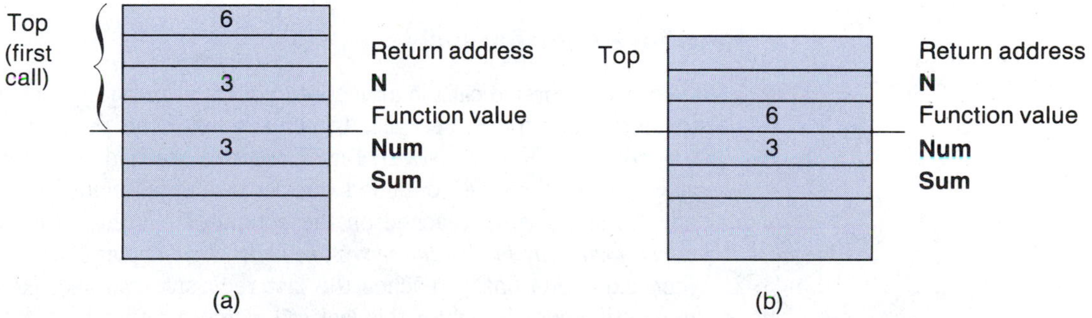

After the assignment statement has been completed, the **end** of the **IntSum** function is again encountered. Thus execution returns to the point from which the function was called.

```
Num := 3;
Sum := IntSum(Num);
          ↑
          └─Return from first call
```

As you can see, this is back to the call from the main program. As before, upon return, the stack space for the function call is deallocated except for the function value (see Figure 5.18).

Now once we are back to the main program, we will complete the assignment statement

```
Sum := IntSum(N)
```

Figure 5.18

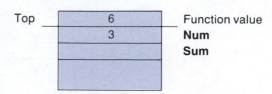

Top   6   Function value
        3   **Num**
             Sum

Since the function calls have now returned the value for **IntSum(N)** on the top of the stack, all that is needed is to pop this value from the top of the stack and store it in the location for **Sum** (see Figure 5.19).

Figure 5.19

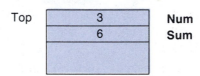

Top   3   **Num**
        6   **Sum**

We have gone through this example in great detail in order to develop an in-depth understanding of just exactly how recursive function calls work. Now that we have finished let us make some important observations about recursive function calls.

Recursive Function Calls

1. If you use recursive calls in a function, you must provide at least one stopping check for these calls. In our example, the recursive calls stopped when $N = 1$. Notice that if we had not had this stopping value, we would have continued our recursive calls indefinitely (or until the limits were reached on the computer system). *Be sure to provide for a way to stop the recursion calls at some point.*

2. When execution finally reaches the last recursive call and executes the function completely for this last call, it must return back through each previous call made. Each time execution returns to a previous function call, all remaining statements in the function (if any) must be executed, before control can return to the previous call. Thus execution must backtrack through each of the recursive calls in reverse order of the calls.

3. As execution backtracks through the previous recursive calls, the final function value at each stage is returned to the previous call. This value is always put on top of the stack when the return is made.

4. The values for variables and value parameters used at any stage of recursion are the values of those variables and parameters at *that particular stage*. Notice in our example that an **N** value was put onto the stack for *each* call of the function. For each recursive stage the **N** value for that particular stage was the value used. The importance of this fact will become more evident in the next example.

5. Local copies (on the stack) are made only for *value* parameters. If a parameter is a *var* parameter, then no local copies will be made for each recursive stage. Therefore, if previous values of a parameter are needed as execution backs out through previous recursive calls, then that parameter should be declared a value parameter.

Before we leave our present example, let us write a program that will not only use our recursive function, but also traces the execution of the program during the process of recursion. In order to trace the execution, we will insert **writeln** statements within the function subprogram so that we can see not only what is going on during the recursive calls but also what happens when the limiting case is reached and the program starts backtracking through the previous recursive calls.

```
{********************************************************************}
{* SumDemo - Program to demonstrate recursive function calls to a  *}
{*           function that finds the sum of the first N positive   *}
{*           integer numbers. As an added feature, the recursive   *}
{*           process will be traced with the use of writeln        *}
{*           statements.                                           *}
{********************************************************************}
program SumDemo(output);
var
  Num,
  Sum : integer;
{********************************************************************}
{* IntSum - Recursive function to find the sum of the first N      *}
{*          positive integers.                                     *}
{*       value parameters -                                        *}
{*            N : Positive integer number.                         *}
{********************************************************************}
function IntSum(N : integer) : integer;
begin
  writeln('Call to function IntSum with N = ', N:0);
  if N = 1 then
    IntSum := 1
  { end if }
  else
    IntSum := N + IntSum(N-1);              { Recursive call to IntSum }
  { end else }
  writeln;
  writeln('Finishing function IntSum when N = ', N:0)
end;   { IntSum }
{********************************************************************}
{*                        Main Control Module                      *}
{********************************************************************}
begin
  Num := 3;
  Sum := IntSum(Num);                       { Call to function IntSum }
  writeln;
  writeln('The sum of the first ', Num:0, ' pos. integers is ', Sum:0)
end.    { SumDemo }
```

Notice in the program that each time the **IntSum** function is called, a message will be printed indicating that the function was called along with the value for **N** at the time of the call. Thus when this program is run, we should see three of these messages printed one after another until the value for **N** becomes 1. When this finally occurs, we will reach the terminating condition for the **if** structure. Thus, we will finally be able to complete the remaining statements in the **IntSum** function. The last **writeln** statement will print out the value for **N** at this point. After completion of this statement, execution then starts backtracking through the previous calls to the function, as we discussed earlier. Thus we should see all of the values for **N** printed in reverse order until **N** becomes 3. Execution will then return to the main program, which will print the value for **Sum**. A printout of a run of this program follows.

```
Call to function IntSum with N = 3
Call to function IntSum with N = 2
Call to function IntSum with N = 1

Finishing function IntSum when N = 1

Finishing function IntSum when N = 2

Finishing function IntSum when N = 3

The sum of the first 3 pos. integers is 6
```

This method of tracing the recursive process can be a very valuable tool not only for getting an understanding of the recursive process, but also for debugging programs that use recursion.

Exercises

5.1   Write a program that calls a recursive function to find the sum of just the even integers from a starting positive even integer **N** down to 2. That is,

$$\textbf{EvenSum} = \textbf{N} + (\textbf{N} - 2) + (\textbf{N} - 4) + \cdots + 2$$

Include a check to make sure that **N** is positive and even; if it is not, print an error message.

5.2   For the program in Exercise 5.1, assume that **N** = 6. Illustrate what the run-time stack looks like for each recursive call and also what the run-time stack looks like as the program backs through the previous recursive calls.

5.3   Write a program that calls a recursive function to find the factorial value for a nonnegative integer **N**. **N** factorial is defined as follows: $\textbf{N}! = \textbf{N} * (\textbf{N} - 1) * (\textbf{N} - 2) * \cdots * 1$ if $\textbf{N} > 0$, and $0! = 1$.

5.4   For the program in Exercise 5.3, assume that **N** = 4, and illustrate what the run-time stack looks like for each recursive stage.

5.5 Write a program that calls a recursive function to find x^n where x and n are positive integer numbers.

5.6 Modify the program in Exercise 5.5 so that n may be any integer number and x may be any real number.

5.3 Recursive Procedure Calls

Now that we know how recursive function calls work, let us turn to the use of recursive procedure calls. In one way recursive procedure calls are simpler, since no function value is returned to the calling module. Thus when stack space is allocated for a procedure call, no space is required for the function return value. However, for each procedure call space will still be allocated for value parameters, a return address, and all local variables, as illustrated in Figure 5.20.

Figure 5.20 *Stack space allocation for a procedure call.*

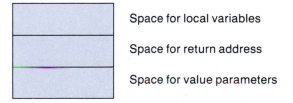

Space for local variables

Space for return address

Space for value parameters

No space is allocated for **var** parameters. Why not? Well, remember that value parameters may change value within the procedure, but the changed value will not be sent back to the calling module; therefore, during execution a local copy of each value parameter is made so that if its value changes then the change will be made in the local copy only and not sent back. However, for **var** parameters any changes are supposed to be sent back: therefore, no local copies are made and changes are made in the original variable memory locations.

Let us approach an example of recursive procedure calls in a different way than we did in our recursive-function example. We will look at a small program that uses recursive procedure calls before we know what the program is supposed to do, and then we will analyze the recursive process in order to determine what the program actually does.

```
{ ************************************************************ }
{ *                     Program RecEx                        * }
{ ************************************************************ }
program RecEx(DataF, output);
var
   DataF : text;
```

```
{*******************************************************************}
{*                      Procedure ProcChar                        *}
{*******************************************************************}
procedure ProcChar;
var
  OneCh : char;                                     { One character }
begin
  read(DataF, OneCh);                        { Read one character }
  if not (eoln(DataF)) then
    ProcChar;                                { Recursive call to
                                               procedure ProcChar }
  { end if }
  write(OneCh)                               { Print one character }
end;  { ProcChar }


{*******************************************************************}
{*                      Main Control Module                       *}
{*******************************************************************}
begin
  reset(DataF);
  if not (eoln(DataF)) then
    ProcChar;                                { Call procedure ProcChar }
  { end if }
  writeln
end.    { program RecEx }
```

Assuming that our program will read its data from data file **DataF**, the main control module will first check for an immediate end of line. If the input file is not at an end of line, procedure **ProcChar** is called. Assuming that the first character in the data line is an 'A', the

```
read(DataF, OneCh)
```

statement in **ProcChar** will read this character and store it in the run-time stack, as illustrated in Figure 5.21.

Figure 5.21

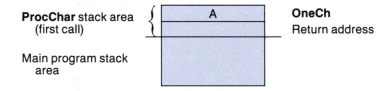

Now, assuming that an end of line still has not been reached, the

```
if not (eoln(DataF))
```

check will be true, and we will have a recursive call to **ProcChar**. The procedure will read the next character, put it in the run-time stack, and again check for the end of the line. The recursive calls to **ProcChar** will continue until **eoln(DataF)** becomes true.

Figure 5.22

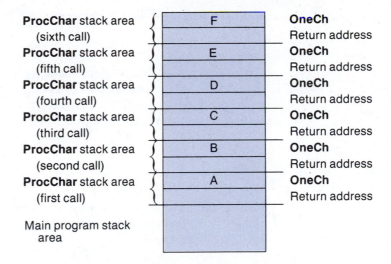

ProcChar stack area (sixth call) — F — OneCh / Return address
ProcChar stack area (fifth call) — E — OneCh / Return address
ProcChar stack area (fourth call) — D — OneCh / Return address
ProcChar stack area (third call) — C — OneCh / Return address
ProcChar stack area (second call) — B — OneCh / Return address
ProcChar stack area (first call) — A — OneCh / Return address
Main program stack area

If we assume that our data line contains the characters

'ABCDEF'

then after the last character, 'F', is read, the run-time stack should appear as illustrated in Figure 5.22.

After the last character, 'F', is read in the sixth call to **ProcChar**, the **eoln(DataF)** condition will become true. Thus, execution will finally get past the **if** condition and be able to complete this present call to **ProcChar**. The

```
write(OneCh)
```

statement will now print the character 'F' (since 'F' is the present value for **OneCh**). Having completed this sixth call to **ProcChar**, the program will now return to the previous call to **ProcChar** and also release the stack area allocated for the sixth call (see Figure 5.23).

Figure 5.23

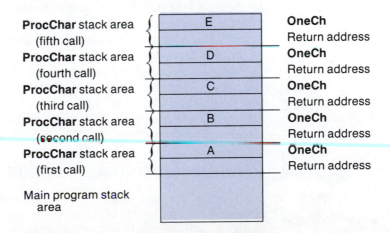

ProcChar stack area (fifth call) — E — OneCh / Return address
ProcChar stack area (fourth call) — D — OneCh / Return address
ProcChar stack area (third call) — C — OneCh / Return address
ProcChar stack area (second call) — B — OneCh / Return address
ProcChar stack area (first call) — A — OneCh / Return address
Main program stack area

In order to finish the fifth call to **ProcChar** the statement

```
write(OneCh)
```

will be executed. Therefore, the character 'E' which is the value for **OneCh** for this fifth call, will be printed. It should now be apparent what will happen as we continue to go back through the previous calls to **ProcChar**. All of the characters that were read from the data line will be printed in reverse order.

```
FEDCBA
```

Thus we have written a program that reads characters from a data line and then prints these characters in reverse order. This example should again illustrate the importance of understanding how the backtracking out through the previous recursive calls works. We could easily put a trace in **ProcChar** by merely inserting a

```
writeln(OneCh)
```

statement immediately after

```
read(DataF, OneCh)
```

The output would then be

```
A
B
C
D
E
F
FEDCBA
```

The ability to access data items and then process them in reverse order can be used in many different types of applications. For example, if we want to create a singly linked list of data items, we now have an easy method of accessing and printing the data in both the normal order and the reverse order. This and other applications will be included in the exercises at the end of the next section.

As indicated earlier, value parameters (if any) are also kept on the run-time stack for each recursive procedure call. However, this is not true for **var** parameters. Thus if we want parameters kept on the stack for each recursive call, we must make sure that they are value parameters.

5.4 Print-in-Reverse Application

Suppose that a special inventory file is maintained, sorted in ascending order according to quantity sold. Each record of the file contains a 20-character description, a 10-character code number, and the quantity that has been sold.

Assume that we have been asked to code a procedure that will print the data in reverse order so that the item with the largest quantity sold will be first. We will need the following declaration.

```
type
   String20 = packed array[1..20] of char;
   String10 = packed array[1..10] of char;
   Datatype = record
                 Description : String20;
                 CodeNo : String10;
                 QuanSold : integer
              end;
```

The coding of the **PrintInReverse** procedure should be practically identical to that of the recursive procedure in Section 5.3. The primary differences will be that the procedure will read one record for each recursive call and will continue the recursive calls until EOF.

```
{**********************************************************************}
{*   PrintInReverse - Recursive procedure that reads all records from  *}
{*                    an inventory file and prints the data in reverse *}
{*                    order. Each record contains a 20-character       *}
{*                    description, a 10-character code number, and the *}
{*                    quantity sold.                                   *}
{*       var parameters -                                              *}
{*           DataF : Text data file.                                   *}
{*       value parameters -                                            *}
{*           None.                                                     *}
{**********************************************************************}
procedure PrintInReverse(var DataF : text);
var
   OneRecord : DataType;                          { One data record }
begin
   ReadRecord(DataF, OneRecord);                  { Read one record }
   if not (eof(DataF)) then
     PrintInReverse(DataF);                        { Recursive call
                                                     to PrintInReverse }

   { end if }
   PrintRecord(OneRecord)                          { Print one record }
end;  { PrintInReverse }
```

Before calling this procedure, the calling module should test for immediate EOF. Once called, the procedure calls a procedure **ReadRecord** which reads one complete record from the data file **DataF**. If EOF has not now been reached, a recursive call is made back to procedure **PrintInReverse** which reads the next record. For each recursive call, the entire record **OneRecord** will be put on the run-time stack for that call. These recursive calls continue until EOF is finally reached. When this occurs the **PrintRecord** procedure then prints the data for the last record read. Then as the program backs through the previous recursive calls, **PrintRecord** prints each of the previous records, but in reverse order, as we wanted.

It should be obvious that if the file is large, a large amount of memory will be required for the run-time stack. The programmer should always keep in mind the memory required as a result of recursive calls.

Exercises

5.7 Assume that each line of a data file contains one integer number. Write a program to do the following:
(a) Read each number from the data file until EOF.
(b) Print the values for the integer numbers in reverse order from that in which they were read.

5.8 For the program in Exercise 5.7, assume that the data file contains four integer numbers — 1, 2, 3, and 4. For each recursive stage illustrate the run-time stack.

5.9 Each line of a simple personnel file contains a name (20 characters), social security number (11 characters), address (36 characters), hourly rate, and number of hours worked. Write a program that reads each line of data until EOF and then prints out the data in reverse order.

5.10 For the same data file as in Exercise 5.7, write a program to do the following:
(a) Call a procedure that reads each integer number from the data file into a linked list until EOF.
(b) Call a procedure that reads the data from the linked list and prints them in the order in which they were read.
(c) Call a procedure that reads the data from the linked list and then prints each integer number in the reverse order from that in which it was read.
(Notice that this allows a singly linked list to be traversed in either direction just as with a doubly linked list.)

5.5 Recursive Binary Search

In Chapter 4 we discussed the development of a procedure to do a binary search of employee data that were sorted and stored in an array of records. Let us reconsider that example and attempt to rewrite the search procedure using recursion. However, instead of having the array sorted according to name, let us assume that the array is sorted according to the social security number. We will attempt, then, to write a recursive binary-search procedure that searches the array for a particular social security number. However, before we attempt this procedure, we will review some of the important concepts regarding the binary-search process.

Recall that in a binary search a middle location in the array is selected, and the value at that location is compared with the search value. If the two values are equal, the correct array element is found. Otherwise the value (if it exists in the array) is either in the first half of the array or the second half. After selecting the correct half, the search continues by checking a middle location in this subarray and repeating the process. The repetitiveness of the same process on smaller and smaller subarrays certainly suggests the possible use of recursion.

As a specific example, suppose array **Nos** is a nine-element array of integer numbers that has been sorted in ascending order as follows:

$$\textbf{Nos}[1] = 2$$
$$\textbf{Nos}[2] = 6$$
$$\textbf{Nos}[3] = 8$$
$$\textbf{Nos}[4] = 11$$
$$\textbf{Nos}[5] = 12$$
$$\textbf{Nos}[6] = 15$$
$$\textbf{Nos}[7] = 20$$
$$\textbf{Nos}[8] = 21$$
$$\textbf{Nos}[9] = 25$$

Assume that we wish to search for the value of 8. The first step in the first call to our search procedure will be to find the middle array index using the formula

$$\textbf{Mid} = (\textbf{First} + \textbf{Last}) \ \textbf{div} \ 2 \qquad \text{(integer division)}$$

Since the first array index is 1 and the last array index is 9,

$$\textbf{Mid} = (1 + 9) \ \textbf{div} \ 2 = 5$$

Since **Nos**[5] > 8, the value 8 must be in the first half of the array (if it is in the array). We now want to repeat the above process with **First** being 1 and **Last** being **Mid** − 1 = 4. This will be the second call to our search procedure.

Second Call to Search Procedure

$$\textbf{Nos}[1] = 2$$
$$\textbf{Nos}[2] = 6$$
$$\textbf{Nos}[3] = 8$$
$$\textbf{Nos}[4] = 11$$

In this second call, **Mid** will be (1 + 4) **div** 2 = 2, and it will be found that **Nos**[2] < 8. Therefore, the second half of the subarray should be selected for the next procedure call. **First** should be **Mid** + 1 = 3, and **Last** should be 4.

Third Call to Search Procedure

$$\textbf{Nos}[3] = 8$$
$$\textbf{Nos}[4] = 11$$

In the third call, **Mid** will be (3 + 4) **div** 2 = 3. Since **Nos**[3] = 8, the search is now complete. Normally, the search procedure will pass back the value 3, since this is the index of the location in the array where the value was found.

In previous examples using recursion, we were very careful to include terminating conditions. Otherwise, the recursive calls would never end. Obviously, one terminating condition would be finding the value. However, suppose the value is not in the array. In this case, what should be the terminating condition?

To investigate this last question, suppose that in the **Nos** array, we search for the value 9. In the third call to the search procedure, **Nos**[3] < 9. Therefore, a fourth call to the search procedure must be made with **First** = **Mid** + 1 = 4 and **Last** = 4.

Fourth Call to Search Procedure

$$\textbf{Nos}[4] = 11$$

In this fourth call, **Mid** = 4; since **Nos**[4] > 9, a fifth call must be made with **First** = 4 and **Last** = **Mid** − 1 = 3.

Fifth Call to Search Procedure

Note that we now have the strange condition that **First** > **Last**. This condition will occur only if the value searched for is not found in the array. Thus we can use this condition as our second terminating condition.

An understanding of this example leads rather directly into a coding of the recursive binary-search procedure. However, since an array consisting of only integer numbers is not very typical, let us write our procedure for the more practical example of searching an array of employee records for a given social security number in an array of type **DataList**.

Pseudocode

BinSearch Procedure

```
IF First > Last THEN
    Set Position to 0.
ELSE
    Compute Mid = integer division value of (First + Last)/2.
    IF SearchNum = SSNum at array index Mid THEN
        Set position to Mid.
    ELSE
        IF SearchNum < SSNum at array index Mid THEN
            Set Last to Mid − 1.
            Call BinSearch again.
        ELSE
            Set First to Mid + 1.
            Call BinSearch again.
        END IF.
    END IF.
END IF.
```

Notice that the following two terminating conditions are included in the pseudocode:

1. IF **First** > **Last**
2. IF **SearchNum** = **SSNum** at array index **Mid**

The first condition occurs if the value is not found in the array, and the second condition occurs if the value is found. The actual Pascal coding follows directly from the pseudocode.

```
{*****************************************************************}
{* BinSearch - Recursive procedure that searches a sorted array of   *}
{*            records for the index of the record that contains a    *}
{*            particular social security number.                     *}
{*      var parameters -                                             *}
{*         EList : Entire data array.                               *}
{*         Position : If the social security number is found,       *}
{*                  the index of the record that contains the       *}
{*                  number will be returned as Position; if not     *}
{*                  found, Position will be returned as 0.           *}
{*         SearchNum : Social security number to be found.          *}
{*      value parameters -                                          *}
{*         First : Lowest index in the array (or subarray).         *}
{*         Last : Largest index in the array (or subarray).         *}
{*****************************************************************}
procedure BinSearch(var EList : DataList; var SearchNum : String11;
                    First, Last : integer; var Position : integer);
var
  Mid : integer;                              { Middle array index }
begin
  if First > Last then                        { If value not
                                                found in the array }

    Position := 0
  { end if }
  else begin
    Mid := (First + Last) div 2;
    if SearchNum = EList[Mid].SSNum then       { If value is found }
      Position := Mid
    { end if }
    else
      if SearchNum < EList[Mid].SSNum then begin
              { Search first half of subarray }
        Last := Mid - 1;
        BinSearch(EList, SearchNum, First, Last, Position)
      end  { if }
      else begin
              { Search second half of subarray }
        First := Mid + 1;
        BinSearch(EList, SearchNum, First, Last, Position)
      end  { else }
  { end else }
  end  { else }
end;    { BinSearch }
```

The list of parameters is important to this procedure. **EList** is the sorted array, **SearchNum** is the social security number for which we are searching, and **First** and **Last** are the beginning and ending array indices. **Position** returns an array index that is 0 if the social security number is not found or the correct location in the array if it is found.

Obviously, **Position** must be a **var** parameter in order to return its value to the calling module. Why **EList** and **SearchNum** were declared as **var** parameters, however, is less clear. Remember that recursive calls are being made to this procedure and that copies of all value parameters are saved on the run-time stack for *each* recursive call. Thus, if these were value parameters, then we would be saving several copies of them on the stack. Are these copies necessary? Not for this example, since it is different from our previous examples of recursion in one important way. There are *no* executable statements following either of the recursive call statements in **BinSearch**, so when execution finishes making recursion calls and starts backing through each preceding call, the end of the procedure is reached immediately. This means that we do not need to print or in any other way use any of the values stored locally on the stack for each recursive call as execution backs out through each previous call.

First and **Last** could have been declared as either **var** or value parameters. Normally, in recursive calls, parameters should be made value parameters if it is necessary to keep local copies of their values on the stack so that as the program backs out through previous recursive calls the old values may be restored and used. However, when backing through previous recursive calls to procedure **BinSearch**, the intermediate values for **First** and **Last** are not needed. Thus this was not the reason for making **First** and **Last** value parameters in procedure **BinSearch**. They were made value parameters for the sake of the calling program. In this way, the calling program may send either constants or variables for **First** and **Last**. Recall that constants may not be sent as values for **var** parameters. Also remember that if variables are sent to value parameters, then even if these values are changed in procedure **BinSearch**, the changed values will not be sent back to the calling program. Thus, if the calling program involves subsequent uses of these variables, then the original values will not have to be reassigned.

In this example, as in many others, it is possible to handle the parameters by using nested procedures. Suppose that we call a procedure **BinSearch** that includes the normal list of parameters. We can then nest a second procedure **BSearch** inside of **BinSearch** that really does the searching. In this way the nested procedure may be relatively free of parameters. In this situation, **BinSearch** is considered the *control procedure*.

```
{*************************************************************************}
{* BinSearch - Procedure that searches a sorted array of              *}
{*             records for the index of the record that contains a    *}
{*             particular social security number.                     *}
{*       var parameters -                                             *}
{*             EList : Entire data array.                             *}
```

```
{*              Position : If the social security number is found, the    *}
{*                         index of the record that contains the number   *}
{*                         will be returned as Position; if not found,     *}
{*                         Position will be returned as 0.                  *}
{*              SearchNum : Social security number to be found.            *}
{*         value parameters -                                              *}
{*              First : Lowest index in the array (or subarray).           *}
{*              Last : Largest index in the array (or subarray).           *}
{***************************************************************************}
procedure BinSearch(var EList : DataList; var SearchNum : String11;
                    First, Last : integer; var Position : integer);
var
  Mid : integer;                                      { Middle array index }
{***************************************************************************}
{* BSearch - Recursive procedure that searches an array of records       *}
{*           for the index of the record that contains a particular      *}
{*           social security number.                                     *}
{***************************************************************************}
procedure BSearch;
begin
  if First > Last then                                { If value not found }
    Position := 0
  { end if }
  else begin
    Mid := (First + Last) div 2;
    if SearchNum = EList[Mid].SSNum then              { If value is found }
      Position := Mid
    { end if }
    else
      if SearchNum < EList[Mid].SSNum then begin
                { Search first half of subarray }
        Last := Mid - 1;
        BSearch                                       { Call BSearch procedure }
      end  { if }
      else begin
                { Search second half of subarray }
        First := Mid + 1;
        BSearch                                       { Call BSearch procedure }
      end  { else }
    { end else }
  end { else }
end; { BSearch }

begin { BinSearch }
  BSearch                                             { Call BSearch }
end; { BinSearch }
```

Notice that **BinSearch** still has the same list of parameters. However, **BSearch** has no parameters. When **BinSearch** is called, the value parameters **First** and **Last** will be put on the run-time stack just as before. Since **BSearch** is a procedure nested within **BinSearch**, **BSearch** may access **First** and **Last** as well as all other parameters from **BinSearch** as global variables. Also, **Mid**, which is a variable local to **BinSearch**, is global to **BSearch**. We are now free to call **BSearch** without using a parameter list.

Thus each time **BSearch** is called, no space is required on the run-time stack for value parameters. Also, since **BSearch** has no local variables, no run-time space is required for them.

This nesting process has certainly minimized the run-time stack space required for each recursive call, a factor that can be extremely important if memory is limited. Another advantage to using this type of control procedure to call the recursive procedure is the ability to include tests for special cases within the control procedure. For example, if we need to check for EOF before proceeding, a test can be included in the control procedure. This method also allows the calling module to pass either constant values or variables (which will not be changed) to the control procedure.

Exercises

5.11 Make up a data file for the employee-array example. Select an arbitrary social security number from the list and follow logically the binary-search procedure to find this social security number. List the values for **First**, **Last**, and **Mid** for each stage.

5.12 Select a social security number that is not in the list for Exercise 5.11, and then follow logically through the search procedure. List the values for **First**, **Last**, and **Mid** for each stage.

5.13 Assume that the data file for the employee-array example is sorted according to name instead of social security number. Then rewrite the recursive binary-search procedures to search for a given name.

5.14 For Exercise 5.13, write a program to do the following:
(a) Read all data into an array.
(b) Ask the user for a name.
(c) Call a recursive binary-search procedure to search for the name. If the name is found, all data for that record should be printed. If the name is not found, a message should be printed.

5.15 A small airline creates a file for each flight such that each data line contains a 20-character name, a 12-character phone number, and the seat number (integer). Assume that the file is sorted according to the seat number. Write a program to do the following:
(a) Read all data into an array.
(b) Ask the user if a seat number search is desired.
(c) If the response to the preceding question is Y, ask for the number of the seat to be found. Call a binary-search procedure to search for the seat number. If it is found, print out all data for that record. If it is not found, print out a message indicating that the seat is still vacant. Then go back to Step (b).
(d) If the response to the question in (b) was N, exit the program.

5.6 Recursion—Pros and Cons

Recursion is certainly a powerful programming tool. However, we should not attempt to use it in every program we write. Thus we need some guidelines regarding the pros and cons of recursion and also, when and when not to use it.

Important Guidelines for Using Recursion

1. First of all, never use recursion unless there is a way to terminate the recursive calls. The programmer must include checks for all possible limiting cases for termination of the recursive calls. Also, be sure that, for the data used, at least one of these terminating cases will be encountered.
2. If a process can be defined in terms of a simpler form of itself, as in sums, factorials, etc., recursion should be considered.
3. If a process calls for repeated calls to a procedure, the saving of variable values at each stage, and then a processing of the variables saved in reverse order, recursion is usually applicable.
4. The number of programming steps may be reduced greatly using a recursive process. Also program design may be simplified greatly. For example, in Chapter 6 we will find that traversing a tree is remarkably simpler with the use of recursion than without.
5. Each recursive call requires the allocation of stack space for all local variables, value parameters, and a return address. Therefore, each call uses memory. This may become an important consideration and suggests that recursion not be used when memory space is limited.
6. If there is no specific advantage to using recursion, do not use it. Recursion can have high overhead because of the memory required, and the number of calls involved.

As we will see in Chapter 8, recursive techniques may be used to speed up the sorting process greatly. However, even in these programs a limitation of memory can force us to use other techniques. Thus even though a design that uses recursion may be the best and the simplest, practical limitations may force the use of other alternatives. Although the Pascal programmer has in recursion a powerful tool, it must be used only where applicable and practical.

In the next section we will investigate an interesting, but often challenging, possibility: the simulation of recursion. A study of the simulation of recursion will not only strengthen understanding of recursion, but illustrate a viable programming process. Because of the overhead involved with recursive calls, it is sometimes advantageous to use regular programming techniques to simulate recursive design. Such techniques can sometimes cut down on the memory required, or, reduce the execution time.

5.7 Simulation of Recursion

Many languages such as BASIC and FORTRAN do not support recursion. However, the simplest design for a program may be recursive, and there is a way to accomplish recursive techniques with languages that do not allow recursive function or procedure calls. Even in languages that allow recursion, such as Pascal, the programmer may wish to improve the efficiency and/or memory requirements in a recursively designed program.

In our development of recursion, we carefully went through the steps involved in the recursive process. We can simulate recursion if we can carry out the same steps using nonrecursive programming techniques.

Certainly, recursion involves the use of at least one stack. We must remember that *each* recursive call to a function or procedure means the pushing of data involved with *that* particular call onto the stack. Similarly, when a program backs out of the recursive calls, each time a particular call is completed the data for that call must be popped off the stack. Thus, especially for procedure calls, it would seem appropriate to define a record that would include *all* data for a particular call. Then the entire record can be pushed or popped at once.

As an example, consider the rather simple procedure developed in Section 5.3 which reads in a string of characters from a data line and printed them in the reverse order. Each time this procedure was called, space was allocated on the stack for the character read and the return address. One way to simulate these recursive procedure calls would be to declare a stack in which each element is a record containing a character and the return address.

```
type
  StackEltType = record
                   OneCh : char;
                   Address : integer
                 end;
```

However, **Address** presents us with a problem. Remember that a return address is used to return to the correct location in order to complete the remaining executable statements for each of the recursive calls as the program backs through the previous calls. Also remember that recursion involves two major stages. The first stage is when recursive calls are repeatedly made to the procedure until the limiting condition is reached. The second stage involves the return to each previous procedure call to complete the remaining statements. The return addresses are used to accomplish this second stage. If we can design our code to accomplish the two stages, we will not need to worry about these return addresses. Our present example will be used to illustrate how this can be done.

In our example, the first stage consists of reading in the characters one at a time and pushing them onto a stack as they are read. The second stage consists of popping one character at a time from the stack and printing it. Each stage can be accomplished with a relatively simple loop structure. We will call our simulation procedure **PtInRevSim**.

Pseudocode

> **PtInRevSim Procedure**
>
> IF not end of line THEN
>   Initialize stack.
>   WHILE not end of line
>   Read one character from data line.
>   Push character onto stack.
>   END WHILE.
>   WHILE stack is not empty
>   Pop one character from stack.
>   Print character.
>   END WHILE.
> END IF.

The first **while** loop takes care of the first stage, and the second **while** loop takes care of the second stage. Since the need for return addresses has been eliminated, the stack consists of only the single characters. The Pascal coding for this procedure follows directly from the pseudocode. We will call the basic procedures for stacks that we developed in Chapter 3.

```
{ ***************************************************************** }
{ * PtInRevSim - Recursive simulation procedure that reads a string  * }
{ *              of characters from one data line and prints the      * }
{ *              characters in reverse order.                         * }
{ *      calls -                                                      * }
{ *          InitStack : Procedure to initialize stack.               * }
{ *          PushStack : Procedure to add element to top of stack.    * }
{ *          PopStack : Procedure to remove element from top of       * }
{ *                      stack.                                        * }
{ ***************************************************************** }
procedure PtInRevSim;
var
  OneCh : char;                                { One character }
  StTop : StackPtr;                            { Stack top pointer }
  Empty : boolean;                             { Stack empty flag }
begin
  if not eoln(DFile) then begin
    InitStack(StTop, Empty);                   { Initialize the stack }
    while not eoln(DFile) do begin
      read(DFile, OneCh);
      PushStack(OneCh, StTop, Empty)           { Push character }
    end;  { while }
    while not Empty do begin
      PopStack(OneCh, StTop, Empty);           { Pop character }
      write(OneCh)                             { Print the character }
    end  { while }
  end  { if }
end; { PtInRevSim }
```

As a second simulation example, we will consider the recursive **IntSum** function developed in Section 5.2. Recall that each recursive call to **IntSum** involved the allocation of run-time stack space for **N**, the return address, and the final function value. Therefore, we could define a stack in which each element is a record consisting of these three items. As we discovered in our first simulation example, however, it is possible to eliminate the return address; the values for **N**, though, will still need to be pushed onto the stack.

How should we handle the final function values? In general, when a function call is completed and the stack space deallocated, the final function value must be kept. As we discussed in Section 5.1, this value may be left on the stack. Thus, even though all other data associated with the function call are popped, the function value should remain. Therefore, this final function value is rather separate from the rest of the function data. For simulation, this suggests the general practice of keeping the main data records on one stack and the final function values on another stack. This approach eliminates the problem of having different data types on the same stack. For languages that do not allow record data types, several parallel stacks may be used with each stack holding one simple data type item.

Now let us turn to the simulation of the recursive **IntSum** function. To do this we will develop a new nonrecursive procedure, **SimIntSumFn**. (Note: This could also be developed as a nonrecursive function instead of a procedure. This will be included in the exercises.) Assume that we create two stacks. One stack will hold the values for **N**, and the other will hold the final function values (as found in the recursive function **IntSum**). After the stacks are initialized, the decreasing values for **N** will be pushed onto the first stack and 0 values will be pushed onto the second stack until **N** becomes 1. The 0 values are pushed onto the second stack temporarily until they are replaced with the final function values as these values are found.

Pseudocode

SimIntSumFn Procedure

Initialize stack 1.
Initialize stack 2.
WHILE **N** is not 1
    Push the value for **N** onto stack 1.
    Push the value 0 onto stack 2.
    Decrement the value of **N** by 1.
END WHILE.
Set **Sum** to 1.
Push the value 1 onto stack 2.
WHILE stack 1 is not empty
    Pop the value for **Sum** from stack 2.
    Pop the value for **N** from stack 1.
    Compute the new value for **Sum** as **N** + **Sum**.
    Pop the place holder 0 value from stack 2.
    Push the new **Sum** value onto stack 2.
END WHILE.

Notice that the second **while** loop gets the last **Sum** value from stack 2, gets the value for **N** from the top of stack 1, finds **Sum** = **N** + **Sum**, and then pushes this new **Sum** value onto stack 2. Before each new **Sum** value is pushed onto stack 2, the temporary 0 value that was used as a place holder on stack 2 is removed.

It should be obvious that some steps in the second **while** loop can be eliminated. One simplification will be to keep just one function value on stack 2 instead of several. That is, the first function value can be pushed, but when the next function value is found the old value will be replaced with the new. Thus stack 2 will contain only one element.

Pseudocode

> **SimIntSumFn Procedure (Second Form)**
>
> Initialize stack 1.
> Initialize stack 2.
> WHILE **N** is not 1
>   Push the value for **N** onto stack 1.
>   Decrement the value of **N** by 1.
> END WHILE.
> Set **Sum** to 1.
> Push the value 1 onto stack 2.
> WHILE stack 1 is not empty
>   Pop the value for **Sum** from stack 2.
>   Pop the value for **N** from stack 1.
>   Compute the new value for **Sum** as **N** + **Sum**.
>   Push the new **Sum** value onto stack 2.
> END WHILE.

In fact, since we are now dealing with only one value for **Sum**, we could simplify our process even more by eliminating the stack for the function value and just using the variable **Sum**.

Pseudocode

> **SimIntSumFn Procedure (Third Form)**
>
> Initialize stack.
> WHILE **N** is not 1
>   Push the value for **N** onto stack.
>   Decrement the value of **N** by 1.
> END WHILE.
> Set **Sum** to 1.
> WHILE stack is not empty
>   Pop the value for **N** from stack.
>   Compute the new value for **Sum** as **N** + **Sum**.
> END WHILE.

Thus all that needs to be put onto the stack for each recursive-call simulation step is the value for **N**. The variable **Sum** takes care of the function value. In this way we save the stack space required in normal recursion for the final function value for each recursive call. This is one example in which simulation of recursion can reduce memory requirements. The coding in Pascal for this simulation will be left as an exercise.

In situations in which memory space is limited and/or execution time is critical, a programmer may design and write a program in several different ways, run benchmarks (timed test runs), and then choose the best method. Depending on the application, the best method may be recursion, a simulation of recursion, or a nonrecursive process such as simple iteration. For example, to find our integer sum, we could use a normal iterative technique involving a **for**, **while**, or **repeat** loop. For example,

```
Sum := 1;
for Num := N downto 2 do
  Sum := Num + Sum;
{ end for }
```

Our integer sum example is certainly a simple problem; however, the techniques we have discussed can be applied to relatively difficult situations also. Realize, however, that recursive simulation may be much more involved in more elaborate recursive programs.

Exercises

5.16   Write the Pascal code for procedure **SimIntSumFn** (Third Form) based on the pseudocode in this section and write a program to test it. Then rewrite **SumIntSumFn** as a nonrecursive function.

5.17   Rewrite the program in Exercise 5.7 so that the recursive procedure is replaced by a procedure that simulates recursion.

5.18   Rewrite the program in Exercise 5.1 using simulation of the recursive function.

5.19   Rewrite the program in Exercise 5.3 using simulation of the recursive function.

5.8   Evaluation-of-Expressions Application

In Chapter 3 we discussed the conversion of expressions from normal infix notation to postfix notation so that the value of the expression can be calculated. Recall that an expression in infix form is difficult to evaluate because of the ordering of the operands (numbers) and the arithmetic operations.

Let us now approach the evaluation of expressions in a different manner. For the time being, assume that our expressions involve only single-digit integer numbers and the arithmetic operations of +, −, *, and /. Also assume that parentheses are not included and that / stands for integer division. Later we will investigate the evaluation of more complicated expressions.

In any expression we will call any unsigned single-digit integer number a *factor* of the expression. Thus each of the following is a factor:

$$3$$
$$7$$
$$0$$

A *term* is defined to be either a single factor or two or more factors separated by * or / operations. Each of the following is called a term:

$$3$$
$$3 * 4$$
$$4 / 2$$
$$2 * 5 * 4 / 3$$
$$9 / 3 / 2$$

An *expression* is either a single term or two or more terms separated by + or − operations. An expression may be preceded by a + or − sign. Each of the following is an expression:

$$3$$
$$-3$$
$$+3$$
$$3 + 2$$
$$-3 + 2$$
$$4 - 3$$
$$2 + 3 + 4$$
$$5 - 3 - 1 - 1$$
$$-3 * 4 + 2 * 3$$
$$4 * 3 / 2 + 4 * 5 * 2 - 8 / 3 / 2$$

As usual, * and / will have higher priority than + or −. Thus,

$$3 * 4 + 2 * 3 = 18$$

From the above definitions we see that expressions are defined in terms of terms, and terms are defined in terms of factors. For example, the expression

$$3 * 4 + 4 * 5 + 6 / 3$$

consists of the following three terms:

$$3 * 4$$
$$4 * 5$$
$$6 / 3$$

Included in these three terms are six factors: 3, 4, 4, 5, 6, and 3.

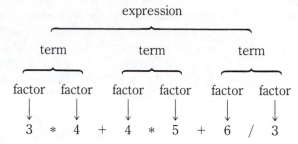

The definitions suggest that we can write a procedure **Expression** which calls a procedure **Term** to evaluate each term. Similarly, the procedure **Term** will call a procedure **Factor** to process each factor. We will also write a control procedure **EvalExp** to handle parameters and a procedure **GetCh** that gets one character at a time from the expression (which we will assume is on one line in a data file).

We will use a stack to hold the factors as we read them and also to hold intermediary arithmetic results. Thus we will need our **InitStack**, **PushStack**, and **PopStack** procedures from Chapter 3. The overall structure for the procedure **EvalExp** will be as follows:

```
{****************************************************************}
{* EvalExp - Control procedure for the evaluation of an arithmetic  *}
{*           expression that is in normal infix notation and is in   *}
{*           one line of a data file.                                *}
{*      var parameters -                                             *}
{*           DataF : Data file.                                      *}
{*           ValidExp : Boolean variable returned as true if a value *}
{*                      for the expression is found; otherwise,      *}
{*                      returned as false.                           *}
{*           ExpVal :  Value for the expression if it is found;      *}
{*                      otherwise, returned as 0.                     *}
{*      value parameters -                                           *}
{*           None.                                                   *}
{****************************************************************}

procedure EvalExp(var DataF: text; var ExpVal : integer;
                  var ValidExp : boolean);
var
  StTop : StackPtr;                              { Stack top pointer }
  Empty : boolean;                               { Stack empty flag }
  Num,
  Num1,
  Num2 : integer;                                { Integer numbers }
  Ch : char;                                     { One character }
  procedure GetCh;
       .
       .
       .
  end;  { GetCh }
  procedure Expression;
```

```
        .
        .
        .
    procedure Term;
        .
        .
      procedure Factor;
          .
          .
      end;  { Factor }
          .
          .
    end;  { Term }
        .
        .
  end;  { Expression }
      .
      .
end;  { EvalExp }
```

Since an expression is defined in terms of terms, procedure **Term** may be nested within procedure **Expression**. Likewise, since each term is defined in terms of factors, procedure **Factor** may be nested within procedure **Term**. Note that the variables **Num**, **Num1**, **Num2**, **Ch**, **StTop**, and **Empty** will be global to all of the procedures nested within **EvalExp**.

Now let us turn to the development of the individual procedures. If we assume that the expression is in a data file, then in its simplest form the **GetCh** procedure will read just one character at a time from the data file. We will also echo the character as it is read. The pseudocode for **GetCh** follows (the Pascal coding of **GetCh** will be assigned in the exercises).

Pseudocode

GetCh Procedure

Read one character of the expression from the data file.
Print the character.

The **Factor** procedure will push the integer value for one factor onto the stack and call **GetCh** to get the next character. Note that it is assumed that the factor character has been read *before* procedure **Factor** is called. Since the factor is read as character data, we will convert it to an integer value before it is pushed onto the stack.

Pseudocode

Factor Procedure

Compute integer value for factor character read.
Push integer value onto stack.
Call **GetCh** to read next character.

To compute the integer value for the character read, we will use the Pascal **ord** function. The Pascal coding for the **Factor** procedure follows.

```
{************************************************************}
{* Factor - Procedure to find integer factor value and push onto   *}
{*          the stack. The procedure then calls the GetCh procedure *}
{*          to read the next character.                             *}
{************************************************************}
procedure Factor;
begin
   Num := ord(Ch) - ord('0');              { Compute integer
                                             value for character read  }
   PushStack(Num, StTop, Empty);              { Push integer value }
   GetCh                                   { Call GetCh to
                                             read the next character }

end;  { Factor }
```

Notice that regardless of the character coding used, as long as the codes for the digits are in sequence, **ord(Ch)** − **ord**('0') will return the correct integer value.

Procedure **Term** must first call **Factor** to get the first factor value pushed onto the stack. Then if the next character read is an * or /, we will save the operation under a local variable, get the next character, and call **Factor** again. The two top stack values are then popped, and the arithmetic operation, which was previously saved, is performed on the two numbers. Finally, the result is pushed back onto the stack. The process continues until the next character read is not an * or /.

Pseudocode

Term Procedure

Call procedure **Factor** to get factor value and push onto stack.
WHILE character read is * or /
   Save character read as local variable **FactOp**.
   Call **GetCh** to read next factor character.
   Call procedure **Factor** to get factor value and push onto stack.
   Pop two top numbers from stack.
   Perform operation **FactOp** on the two numbers.
   Push result onto stack.
END WHILE.

Notice that the local variable **FactOp** is used to save the operation (* or /) until the second number is pushed onto the stack. Then the two numbers may be popped from the stack, the operation performed on the two numbers, and the result pushed back onto the stack. If another * or / operation follows, the process will be repeated. The actual Pascal coding follows.

```
{*******************************************************************}
{* Term - Procedure to find the value for one term and push the value *}
{*       onto the stack. The procedure then calls the GetCh          *}
{*       procedure to read the next character.                       *}
{*******************************************************************}
procedure Term;
var
  FactOp : char;                                  { Factor operation }
begin
  Factor;                                   { Call Factor to get factor
                                            value and push onto stack }

  while Ch in ['*', '/'] do begin
    FactOp := Ch;
    GetCh;
    Factor;                                 { Call Factor to get factor
                                            value and push onto stack }

    PopStack(Num2, StTop, Empty);               { Pop the 2nd factor }
    PopStack(Num1, StTop, Empty);               { Pop the 1st factor }
    if FactOp = '*' then
      Num := Num1 * Num2
    { end if }
    else
      Num := Num1 div Num2;
    { end else }
    PushStack(Num, StTop, Empty)                     { Push result }
  end    { while }
end;  { Term }
```

The **Expression** procedure is rather similar to **Term** except that the connecting operations are + and −, and we connect terms instead of factors. One added consideration is the possibility of a leading + or − sign in front of the expression. If a leading sign exists, its value is saved under a local variable name and the value of the following term is pushed onto the stack. If the sign is a −, the value for the term is popped from the stack, its sign reversed, and then its value pushed back onto the stack.

Pseudocode

Expression Procedure

IF first character is a + or − THEN
    Save sign as local variable **Sign**.
    Call **GetCh** to read next character.
    Call **Term** to get term value and push onto stack.
    IF sign saved for **Sign** was a − THEN
        Pop top stack value.
        Compute negative of this value.
        Push this negative value back onto stack.
    END IF.
ELSE
    Call **Term** to get term value and push onto stack.
END IF.

WHILE character is a + or −
    Save operation (+ or −) as local variable **TermOp**.
    Call **GetCh** to read next character.
    Call **Term** to push value of the next term onto stack.
    Pop top two stack values.
    Perform operation **TermOp** on these two numbers.
    Push result back onto stack.
END WHILE.

Note that the techniques used in the **while** loop here are nearly identical to those used in the **while** loop in the **Term** procedure. The Pascal coding for procedure **Expression** follows directly from the pseudocode.

```
{********************************************************************}
{* Expression - Procedure to evaluate an expression and push the    *}
{*              resulting value onto the stack.                      *}
{********************************************************************}
procedure Expression;
var
  Sign,                                      { + or - sign preceding
                                               an expression (if any) }
  TermOp : char;                               { Operation on terms }
begin
  if Ch in ['+', '-'] then begin           { If first
                                             character is a + or - }
    Sign := Ch;
    GetCh;
    Term;                                  { Call Term to get term
                                             value and push onto stack }
    if Sign = '-' then begin
      PopStack(Num, StTop, Empty);
      Num := -Num;
      PushStack(Num, StTop, Empty)
    end  { if }
  end   { if }
  else
    Term;                                  { Call Term to get term
                                             value and push onto stack }
  { end else }
  while Ch in ['+', '-'] do begin
    TermOp := Ch;
    GetCh;
    Term;
    PopStack(Num2, StTop, Empty);                        { Pop 2nd term }
    PopStack(Num1, StTop, Empty);                        { Pop 1st term }
    if TermOp = '+' then
      Num := Num1 + Num2
    { end if }
    else
      Num := Num1 - Num2;
    { end else }
```

```
      PushStack(Num, StTop, Empty)                          { Push result }
   end;  { while }
end;   { Expression }
```

Notice that the final value for the expression is pushed onto the stack. This should be the only value left on this stack. Our last procedure to consider is the control procedure, **EvalExp**. This procedure is supposed to pass the value found for the expression back as the parameter **ExpVal**. If no expression is found in the file, the Boolean parameter **ValidExp** will be set to false; otherwise, if the expression results in a valid value, **ValidExp** will be set to true. **EvalExp** must initialize the stack and read the first character of the expression from the data file.

Pseudocode

EvalExp Procedure

IF not end of file THEN
    Initialize stack.
    Initialize **ValidExp** to true.
    Call **GetCh** to read first character.
    Call **Expression** to get expression value and push onto
        stack.
    Pop stack and assign value to **ExpVal**.
ELSE
    Set **ValidExp** to false.
END IF.

The complete Pascal coding for **EvalExp** follows.

```
{*******************************************************************}
{* EvalExp - Control procedure for the evaluation of an arithmetic *}
{*           expression that is in normal infix notation and is in  *}
{*           one line of a data file.                               *}
{*      var parameters -                                            *}
{*          DataF : Data file.                                      *}
{*          ValidExp : Boolean variable returned as true if a value *}
{*                     for the expression is found; otherwise,      *}
{*                     returned as false.                           *}
{*          ExpVal :  Value for the expression if it is found;      *}
{*                     otherwise, returned as 0.                    *}
{*      value parameters -                                          *}
{*          None.                                                   *}
{*******************************************************************}

procedure EvalExp(var DataF: text; var ExpVal : integer;
                  var ValidExp : boolean);
var
  StTop : StackPtr;                              { Stack top pointer }
  Empty : boolean;                               { Stack empty flag }
  Num,
```

```
      Num1,
      Num2 : integer;                                    { Integer numbers }
      Ch : char;                                         { One character }
```

Insert procedures **InitStack**, **PushStack**, **PopStack**
GetCh, **Expression**, **Term**, and **Factor** here

```
begin
   if not eof(DataF) then begin
      InitStack(StTop, Empty);                     { Initialize the stack }
      ValidExp := true;
      GetCh;                                  { Call GetCh to
                                                read the first character }
      Expression;                      { Call Expression to
                                         find the expression
                                         value and push onto the stack }
      PopStack(ExpVal, StTop, Empty)         { Pop stack and
                                               assign value to ExpVal }
   end  { if }
   else begin                                             { else, eof }
      ValidExp := false;
      ExpVal := 0
   end  { else }
end;  { EvalExp }
```

As yet, no checks for invalid data have been made. Also, we have assumed that no blanks are within the expression. These limitations will be discussed in the exercises. However, in its present form **EvalExp** also has no provisions for dealing with pairs of parentheses within the expression. For example, suppose we wish to evaluate the expression

$$(2 + 3 * 4 + 5) * 4 + (6 * 2 - 8 / 2)$$

which has the following three factors:

$$(2 + 3 * 4 + 5)$$
$$4$$
$$(6 * 2 - 8 / 2)$$

To find the value for the factor

$$(2 + 3 * 4 + 5)$$

we must find the value for the expression

$$2 + 3 * 4 + 5$$

within the parentheses. Thus procedure **Factor** can call procedure **Expression** to find the value for the expression and then return to **Factor**. This is an *indirect* recursive call, since procedure **Expression** calls procedure **Term**, which calls procedure **Factor**, which then calls procedure **Expression** again.

To allow the inclusion of pairs of parentheses we must modify procedure **Factor** so that it checks for a left parenthesis. If one is found, procedure **Ex-**

pression is called. After the expression is terminated by the right parenthesis, execution then returns to procedure **Factor**.

Pseudocode

> **Factor Procedure**
>
> IF character is a left parenthesis THEN
>   Call **GetCh** to read next character.
>   Call **Expression** to get expression value and push onto
>   stack.
> ELSE
>   Compute integer value for character (integer digit) read.
>   Push integer value onto stack.
> END IF.
> Call **GetCh** to read next character.

```
{*****************************************************************}
{* Factor - Procedure to find factor value and push onto the stack.  *}
{*          Also, calls GetCh to read the next character.            *}
{*****************************************************************}
procedure Factor;
begin
  if Ch = '(' then begin
    GetCh;
    Expression                        { Call Expression to evaluate the
                                        expression and push onto stack  }

  end  { if }
  else begin                                      { If normal factor }
    Num := ord(Ch) - ord('0');           { Compute integer value
                                          for the character read }

    PushStack(Num, StTop, Empty)
  end;  { else }
  GetCh
end;  { Factor }
```

Procedure **Expression** will terminate when the next character is not a + or −. Thus **Expression** will terminate when a right parenthesis is found. However, we should check to make sure that the terminating character is really a right parenthesis. This, along with other error checking, will be included in the exercises.

Exercises

5.20 Write the Pascal code for the **GetCh** procedure. This procedure should read one character from the data file into the global variable **Ch**. Write a driver program that calls **EvalExp** to find the values for expressions in a data file.

Assume that each line of the data file contains one expression. Print the value for each expression.

For Exercises 5.21 through 5.25, write a driver program for each exercise as in Exercise 5.20. Alter the data file used in order to thoroughly test all requirements specified in each exercise.

5.21 Modify the **GetCh** procedure so that blanks may be embedded in the expression.

5.22 Make necessary changes so that multiple-digit integer numbers may be used instead of just single-digit integer numbers.

5.23 Make necessary changes so that an expression may be on several data lines and terminated with a semicolon.

5.24 Make necessary changes so that a check is made for the right parenthesis. If it is not found where it should be, set **ExpVal** to 0 and **ValidExp** to false.

5.25 Make necessary changes so that data checks are made for invalid characters. If any error occurs, set **ExpVal** to 0 and **ValidExp** to false.

Summary

In this chapter we have investigated the process of recursion. We have seen that recursion is a very powerful programming tool that can reduce the number of lines of code quite significantly. For example, the amount of code for the recursive simulation procedure **PtInRevSim** (including the required **InitStack**, **PushStack**, and **PopStack** procedures) is *much* greater than the very short recursive **PrintInReverse** procedure. However, it is certainly true that unless the programmer thoroughly understands the recursive process and is quite careful, it is easy to produce disastrous results.

In Section 5.6 we discussed some guidelines with regard to the use of recursion. You should review that section now and at any time in the future when the possibility of using recursion is being considered.

The appropriateness of the use of recursion should be considered before it is used. Then, if recursion is used, the programmer must be *very careful to provide terminating conditions in order to stop the recursive calls*. It is quite easy to get into an infinite loop if these terminating conditions are not included.

Some programming languages do not permit recursion. Therefore a programmer may wish to pseudocode a program using recursive techniques and then simulate the use of recursion using nonrecursive code. Even in a language that permits the use of recursion (such as Pascal), the programmer may wish to attempt to reduce the overhead involved in the recursive process by simulating recursion.

Chapter Exercises

5.26 What is the difference in the way **var** and value parameters are handled in recursive calls?

5.27 Write a program to compute the greatest common divisor, **GCD**, of two positive integers. If $M >= N$, a recursive definition for the **GCD** is

$$GCD = \begin{cases} M \text{ if } N = 0 \\ \qquad \text{or} \\ GCD \text{ (N, M modulo N) if } N <> 0 \end{cases}$$

The program should allow the user to input the values for **M** and **N** from the console. A recursive function is then called to compute the **GCD**. The program should then print the value for the **GCD**. (If the user inputs a value for **M** that is less than **N**, the program is responsible for switching the values.)

5.28 Create a small inventory file such that each line contains a 22-character description, a 10-character code number, a 20-character supplier, and a quantity (integer). Assume that the data file is not sorted. Write a program to do the following:
(a) Read all data into an array.
(b) Call a procedure to sort the records in the array so that the code numbers are in ascending order.
(c) Ask the user if he or she wishes to search for a particular code number.
(d) If the response to the preceding question is Y, ask for the code number and call a binary-search procedure to search for the code number. If it is found, print all data for that record. If it is not found, print a message to that effect. Then go back to Step (c).
(e) If the response to the question in (c) is N, exit the program.

5.29 Use the same data file as in Exercise 5.28. Write a program to do the following:
(a) Read all data into an array.
(b) Call a procedure to sort the records in the array so that the descriptions are in ascending order.
(c) Follow Steps (c), (d), and (e) from Exercise 5.28 except search for a particular description.

5.30 Rewrite the program in Exercise 5.9 using simulation of the recursive procedure.

5.31 Modify Exercise 5.25 so that an error message is printed indicating the type of data error. (Hint: Assign a value to an error-code variable and call an error procedure.)

CHAPTER 6

Introduction to Trees

In previous chapters in this text, various types of linked lists were discussed and then used for many different types of applications. Another very important data structure is the tree. In a normal linked list each node points to just one other node. In a tree structure, however, each node may point to several other nodes, and then each of these nodes may point to several other nodes (which may then point to several other nodes, etc.). Thus a tree is a very flexible and powerful data structure that can be used for a wide variety of applications.

For example, suppose that we wish to use a data structure to represent a person and all of his or her descendants. Assume that the person's name is John and that he has three children, Linda, Bonnie, and Lester. Also suppose that Linda has two children, April and Nicole; Bonnie has three children, Eva Mae, Clifford, and Horace; and Lester has one child, Guy. We can represent John and his descendants quite naturally with the tree structure in Figure 6.1. Notice that each tree node contains a name for data and one or more pointers to other tree nodes.

Although the nodes in a general tree may contain any number of pointers to other tree nodes, a large number of data-structure applications involve trees in which each node can have at most two pointers to other tree nodes. This type of tree is called a *binary tree*. In this chapter we will discuss several very interesting applications of binary trees, including a tree sort, an inventory tree, a tree search, the representation of arithmetic expressions in a tree, a cross-reference table generator, and a message decoder. In Chapter 7 we will continue our work with binary trees and also investigate some non-binary trees.

Figure 6.1   *Tree representation for John and his descendants.*

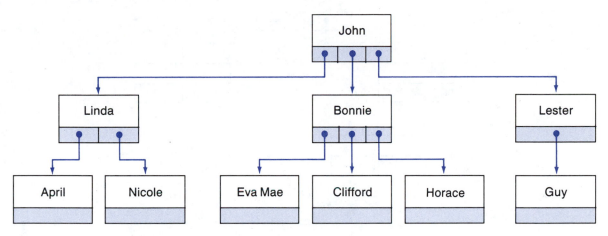

6.1   Binary Trees

Let us begin our study of binary trees by discussing some basic concepts and terminology. A simple binary tree is illustrated in Figure 6.2. Each node in a binary tree normally contains data and may contain at most two pointers to other tree nodes. Basic entry into the tree is through node A which is called the *root*. The left pointer of A points to the *successor node* B, and the right pointer of A points to successor node C. Similarly, the left and right pointers of B and C point to successor nodes D, E, F, and G. B and C are said to be *immediate successors* of A, and A is the *immediate predecessor* of B and C. D, E, F, and G are successors of A, but not immediate successors. B and C are also called *children* of A, and A is said to be the *parent* of B and C. A is also called an *ancestor* of nodes B, C, D, E, F, and G. Also, B is an ancestor of D and E, and C is an ancestor of F and G.

The root is said to be at level 0 in the tree, nodes B and C are at level 1, and nodes D, E, F, and G are at level 2. The *height* of the tree is defined to be the highest level in the tree. Thus the height of the tree in Figure 6.2 is 2.

Figure 6.2

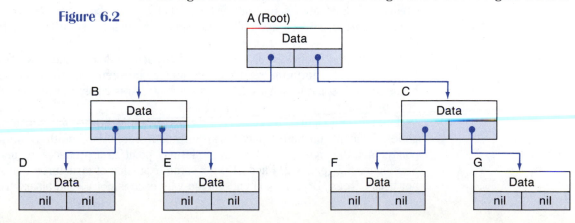

Figure 6.3

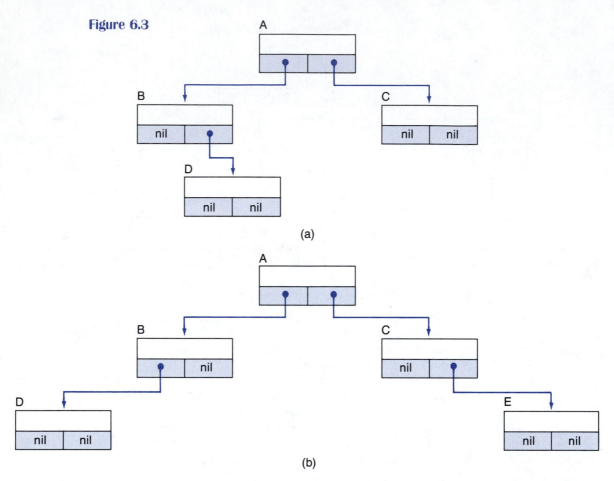

(a)

(b)

Any node with no successors is called a *leaf* or a *terminal node*. Thus nodes D, E, F, and G are all leaves, or terminal nodes, in the tree. A binary tree is said to be *balanced* if each node has exactly two children or has no children and if every leaf is at the same level. Thus the tree in Figure 6.2 is balanced. Figure 6.3 illustrates some binary trees that are not balanced. However, these unbalanced trees are still quite usable, as will be seen later in this chapter.

In Figure 6.4, nodes B, D, and E form the *left subtree* of the tree. Similarly, C, F, and G form the *right subtree*. As may be seen from the definitions in the preceding paragraphs, each of these subtrees is really a tree if considered by itself.

The left and right subtrees of a binary tree must be disjoint subsets of nodes. That is, no nodes may be in both subtrees. Also, neither the left pointer nor the right pointer of any node may point to a predecessor node. See Figure 6.5 (pages 214 and 215) for some examples of structures that are not binary trees. Be sure you understand why each is not a valid binary tree.

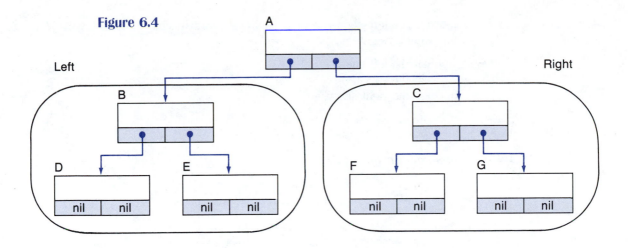

Figure 6.4

Now that we have an understanding of what a binary tree really is, let us formulate a definition.

> A *binary tree* is a set of nodes that is either empty or consists of a root node and two disjoint binary trees called the left subtree and the right subtree.

This definition emphasizes the fact that a binary tree is a recursive type of data structure. That is, each subtree is defined as a simpler tree. The recursive nature of the binary tree helps simplify programming with binary trees. For example, as we will see in the next section, because of the recursive nature of the binary tree, the procedures to access the data in the nodes of a tree require very few lines of code.

One aspect of trees that makes them very valuable as data structures is the flexibility they allow in accessing the data in the tree. For example, in Figure 6.4 we could start at the root (A), then follow the left pointer to the root's left child (B), and finally follow the right pointer in node B to node E. Similarly, we could follow other paths starting at the root.

More commonly, however, we use one of several standard methods for accessing *all* of the nodes of a tree in various specified orders. This process of accessing or visiting the nodes of a tree is usually referred to as *traversing* the tree. Three of the most commonly used methods for traversing a tree are the following.

Preorder (or node-left-right) (or NLR)
Inorder (or left-node-right) (or LNR)
Postorder (or left-right-node) (or LRN)

None of these are difficult to learn. Let us begin our discussion with the inorder (or left-node-right) (or LNR) traversal. This method involves the following three steps.

1. Visit the left subtree (L)
2. Visit the root (N)
3. Visit the right subtree (R)

Figure 6.5   *Structures that are not binary trees.*

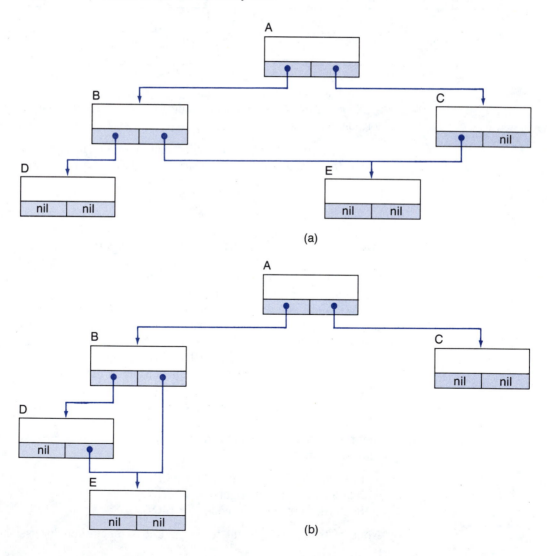

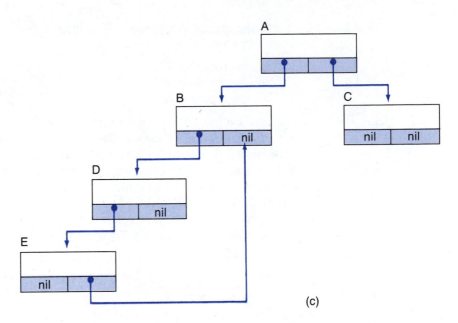

(c)

We begin an inorder traversal of the tree in Figure 6.6 by looking at the left subtree. Since this subtree (consisting of nodes B, D, and E) is itself a tree with node B as its root, we follow the LNR order by visiting D (left) first, then B (node or root), and finally E (right). After the visit to this left subtree, we visit the root, A (node), and finally we visit the right subtree of A, which consists of the nodes C, F, and G. In following the LNR order for this right subtree, we visit F (left) first, then C (node or root), and finally G (right). Notice that the N in LNR refers to the root; we use N because R is used to stand for right. Thus the inorder traversal order for the tree in Figure 6.6 is D-B-E-A-F-C-G.

Figure 6.6

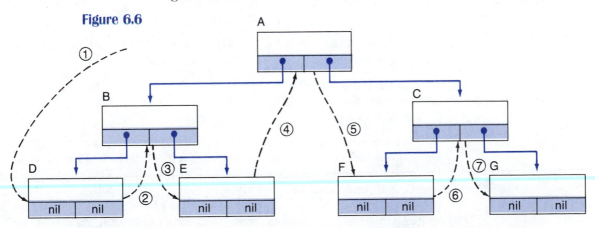

For the preorder (or node-left-right) (or NLR) traversal, the following three steps are followed.

1. Visit the root (N)
2. Visit the left subtree (L)
3. Visit the right subtree (R)

If we use preorder traversal for the tree in Figure 6.7, we will visit the root, A (node), first. Then we will visit the left subtree of A, which consists of the nodes B, D, and E. Since this subtree is itself a tree, we will visit the nodes using the NLR order. Thus we will visit B (node) first, then D (left), and finally E (right). We now go to the right subtree of A, which is a tree containing the nodes C, F, and G. Again, following the NLR order, we will visit C (node) first, then F (left), and finally G (right). Thus the preorder traversal order for the tree in Figure 6.7 will be A-B-D-E-C-F-G.

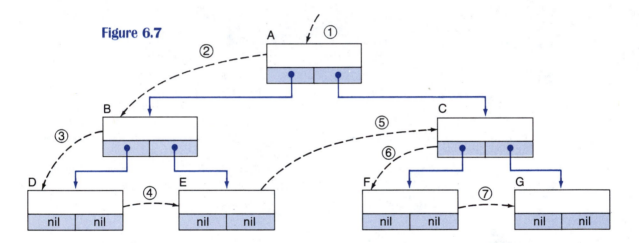

Figure 6.7

For the postorder (or left-right-node) (or LRN) traversal the following three steps are required.

1. Visit the left subtree (L)
2. Visit the right subtree (R)
3. Visit the root (N)

If we use postorder traversal for the tree in Figure 6.8, we will visit the left subtree of A first. This subtree (which is a tree) consists of the nodes B, D, and E. There we will follow the LRN order and visit D (left) first, then E (right), and finally B (node). We will next visit the right subtree of A, which consists of the nodes C, F, and G. Following the LRN order for this tree, we will visit F (left) first, then G (right), and finally C (node). Finally we will visit the root, A (node). Thus the postorder traversal order for the tree in Figure 6.8 will be D-E-B-F-G-C-A.

Figure 6.8

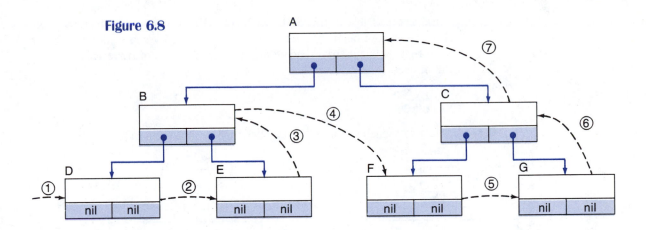

Suppose we now insert one integer number as data for each node in the tree (see Figure 6.9). The order in which the data will be read from the tree will certainly depend on the traversal technique used. You should verify the following reading orders.

For inorder (LNR) the order is 8, 12, 14, 15, 17, 20, 25.
For preorder (NLR) the order is 15, 12, 8, 14, 20, 17, 25.
For postorder (LRN) the order is 8, 14, 12, 17, 25, 20, 15.

Figure 6.9

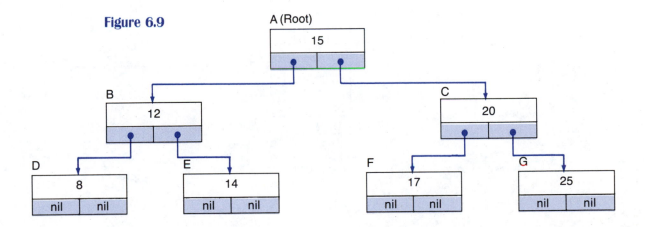

It should be emphasized that the only variation among the three different traversal methods is in the order in which the node (or root) is visited. For preorder traversal we visit the node first; for inorder traversal we visit the node second; and for postorder traversal we visit the node last. Note that for each of these tree traversal methods, the left subtree is always visited before the right subtree.

It is also possible to use RNL, RLN, or NRL traversals in which the right subtree is visited before the left subtree. However, by convention (and since left-to-right is our natural reading order), these orders of traversals are very seldom used.

Exercises

6.1   Explain why each of the following structures is not a binary tree.

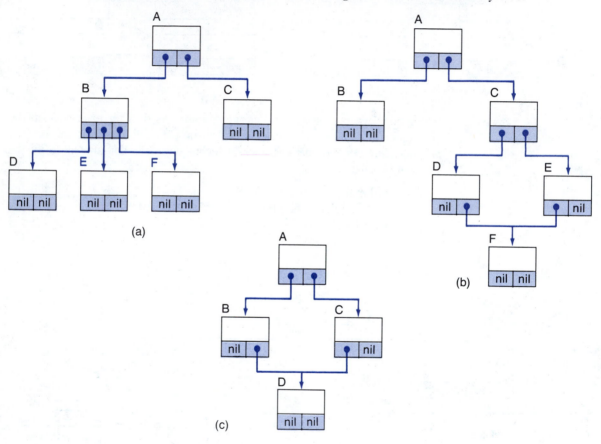

(a)

(b)

(c)

6.2 Consider the following tree.
  (a) What is the height?
  (b) Is the tree balanced? Why or why not?
  (c) List all leaf nodes.
  (d) What is the immediate predecessor (parent) for node U?
  (e) List the children of node R.
  (f) List all successors for node R.

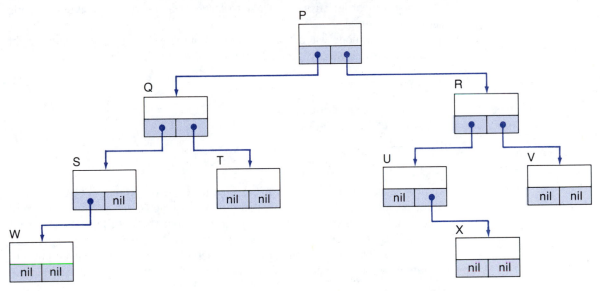

6.3 List the order of the nodes if the following tree is
  (a) traversed using inorder traversal.
  (b) traversed using preorder traversal.
  (c) traversed using postorder traversal.

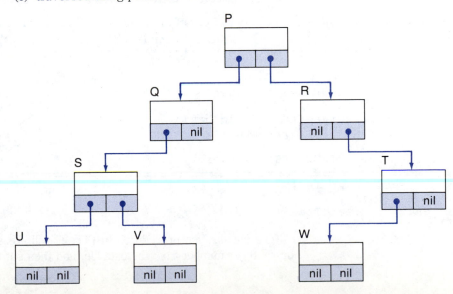

6.2 Binary-Tree Creation

Now that we have considered the commonly used tree-traversal methods, let us take a look at how we can create a tree. Assume that we have created a data file in which each line contains a single integer number. Let us create a tree in which the data item in each node will be one of the numbers. We will insert each of the numbers into a separate node of the tree so that they will be in sorted order (from smallest to largest) if the tree is traversed using inorder traversal.

Since each node will contain an integer number, a left pointer, and a right pointer, the following **type** declarations will be used.

```
type
   NodePtr = ^TrNode;
   TrNode = record
             Data : integer;
             LeftPtr : NodePtr;
             RightPtr : NodePtr
           end;
```

The main control module for the **CreateTree** program will begin with an initialization of the tree. This initialization will involve the creation of a root node and the insertion of the first number from the data file into this root node. Following the initialization of the tree, each remaining integer number will be read from the file one at a time. Each of these numbers will be put into a new node, and this node will then be inserted into the correct location in the tree.

The Pascal code for the main control module will involve calls to two procedures. One of these procedures, **InitTree**, will initialize the tree, and the second procedure, **InsertInTree**, will insert each integer number into a new node and place it in the correct location in the tree.

```
{*****************************************************************}
{*                    Main Control Module                       *}
{*****************************************************************}
begin
  reset(DFile);
  if not eof(DFile) then begin
    InitTree(Root);                             { Initialize the tree }
    while not eof(DFile) do begin
      readln(DFile, Number);                    { Read one number
                                                  from the data file }
      InsertInTree(Root, Number)                { Insert number
                                                  into the tree }
    end  { while }
  end { if }
end.   { CreateTree }
```

The initialization procedure, **InitTree**, will create a root node, read the first integer number from the data file, and then put this number into the root node. **InitTree** should also set the left and right pointers in the root node to **nil**. The Pascal code for **InitTree** is quite easy to write. Notice, however, that the parameter **TreeRoot** is a **var** parameter so that the pointer to the tree root, which is created in **InitTree**, can be returned to the main program.

```
{ ***************************************************************** }
{ * InitTree - Procedure to initialize a tree by creating the root    * }
{ *            node, inserting the first integer data value into the   * }
{ *            root node, and setting the LeftPtr and RightPtr         * }
{ *            pointers to nil.                                         * }
{ *       var parameters -                                             * }
{ *           TreeRoot : Pointer to the root node.                     * }
{ *       value parameters -                                           * }
{ *           None.                                                    * }
{ ***************************************************************** }
procedure InitTree(var TreeRoot : NodePtr);
begin
  new(TreeRoot);                     { Create the tree root node }
  readln(DFile, Number);             { Read one integer number }
  TreeRoot^.Data := Number;             { Insert number
                                           into the root node }

  TreeRoot^.LeftPtr := nil;
  TreeRoot^.RightPtr := nil
end;   { InitTree }
```

Before we attempt to code the **InsertInTree** procedure, let us examine the techniques that we will use in creating the tree. Assume that the first number read and then stored in the root node is 15. If the next number read is 10, a new node will be created. Since 10 is less than 15, the new node will be put into the left subtree by having the left pointer of the root point to this new node (see Figure 6.10).

Figure 6.10

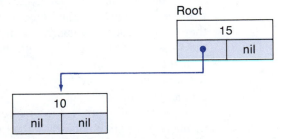

If the next number read is 25, a new node is created and put in the right subtree (see Figure 6.11).

Now suppose the next number read is 18. Since 18 > 15, we know that 18 will be put in the right subtree. Thus we compare 18 with 25. Since 18 < 25, the 18 should be inserted in a new node pointed to by the left pointer of the node containing 25 (see Figure 6.12).

Figure 6.11

Figure 6.12

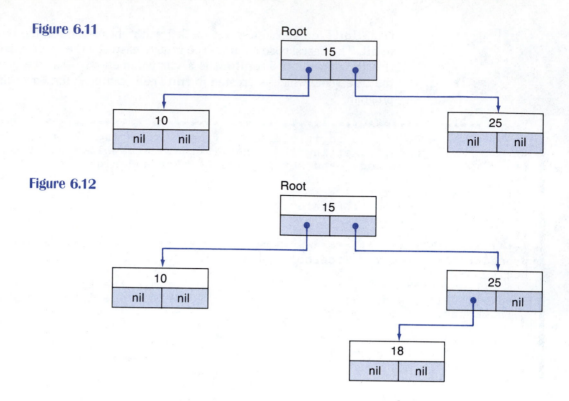

The process will be continued until all numbers have been read and inserted into the tree. This illustration suggests a method for inserting each new number into the tree. First the new number is compared with the number in the tree root node. If the new number is smaller, then we know that the number should be put in the root's left subtree. Therefore, we check the root's left pointer. If it is **nil**, the root's left pointer is patched to point to the new node, and the job is complete. However, if the root's left pointer is not **nil**, then we move to the node (say B) pointed to by this left pointer. We then compare our new number with the number in this node. We are now at the same point that we were with the original tree root.

If the comparison of the new number with the number in any node shows the new number to be larger, then instead of going to the left subtree, we should go to the right subtree.

Thus the entire process is a matter of comparing the new number with the numbers in existing nodes and then going to the left or to the right subtree after each comparison until a **nil** pointer is found. At this point, the **nil** pointer is replaced with a pointer to the new node (which contains the new number).

Now let us look at the pseudocode for procedure **InsertInTree**.

Pseudocode

InsertInTree Procedure

Create new tree node **NewNode**.
Initialize Boolean variable **Inserted** to false.
Initialize pointer variable **OneNode** to point to tree root.
WHILE new data number has not been inserted into tree
    IF new data number <= data in **OneNode** THEN
        IF **LeftPtr** of **OneNode** not **nil** THEN
            Set **OneNode** to **OneNode^.LeftPtr**.
        ELSE
            Set **LeftPtr** of **OneNode** to **NewNode**.
            Set **Inserted** to true.
        END IF.
    ELSE
        IF **RightPtr** of **OneNode** not nil THEN
            Set **OneNode** to **OneNode^.RightPtr**.
        ELSE
            Set **RightPtr** of **OneNode** to **NewNode**.
            Set **Inserted** to true.
        END IF.
    END IF.
END WHILE.
Insert new data number into **NewNode**.
Set **LeftPtr** of **NewNode** to **nil**.
Set **RightPtr** of **NewNode** to **nil**.

Study this pseudocode carefully. Note that the first **if** statement in the **while** loop checks to see if the new node should be put into the left or the right subtree of **OneNode**. If the pointer to that particular subtree is not **nil**, then we continue looking down that subtree by moving the pointer **OneNode** to the next node in the subtree. However, if the pointer to the subtree is **nil**, the place where the new node goes has been found; thus the **nil** pointer is changed to point to **NewNode** and **Inserted** is set to true. When this occurs, the **while** loop is exited, the data item is inserted into **NewNode**, and the left and right pointers of **NewNode** are set to **nil**. The Pascal code for the **InsertInTree** procedure follows.

```
{*****************************************************************}
{* InsertInTree - Procedure to insert one integer number into the    *}
{*               tree such that when the tree is traversed using      *}
{*               inorder traversal, the numbers will be sorted in     *}
{*               ascending order.                                     *}
{*      var parameters -                                              *}
{*          None.                                                     *}
```

```
{*        value parameters -                                   *}
{*            TreeRoot : Pointer to the tree root.             *}
{*            Num : Integer number to be inserted into the tree.  *}
{*****************************************************************}
procedure InsertInTree(TreeRoot : NodePtr; Num : integer);
var
   Inserted : boolean;                    { Boolean flag to indicate
                                            insertion into the tree  }
   OneNode,                                   { Tree-node pointer }
   NewNode : NodePtr;                         { Tree-node pointer }
begin
   new(NewNode);                          { Create a new tree node }
   Inserted := false;
   OneNode := TreeRoot;
   while not Inserted do begin
     if Num <= OneNode^.Data then
       if OneNode^.LeftPtr <> nil then
         OneNode := OneNode^.LeftPtr
       { end if }
       else begin
         OneNode^.LeftPtr := NewNode;
         Inserted := true
       end  { else }
     { end if }
     else
       if OneNode^.RightPtr <> nil then
         OneNode := OneNode^.RightPtr
       { end if }
       else begin
         OneNode^.RightPtr := NewNode;
         Inserted := true
       end  { else }
     { end else }
   end; { while }
   NewNode^.Data := Num;                        { Insert number }
   NewNode^.LeftPtr := nil;
   NewNode^.RightPtr := nil
end;    { InsertInTree }
```

Following is the Pascal coding for program **CreateTree**, which initializes a tree and then inserts all of the numbers from the data file into the tree in their correct locations.

```
{*****************************************************************}
{*  CreateTree - Program to create a tree in which each node contains *}
{*              one integer number as data. The numbers are inserted *}
{*              into the tree so that when the tree is traversed      *}
{*              using inorder traversal, the numbers will be sorted   *}
{*              in ascending order.                                   *}
{*****************************************************************}
program CreateTree(output, DFile);
type
   NodePtr = ^TrNode;
   TrNode = record
```

```
                    Data : integer;
                    LeftPtr : NodePtr;
                    RightPtr : NodePtr
                end;
var
   Root : NodePtr;                              { Tree-root pointer }
   Number : integer;                            { One integer number }
   DFile : text;                                       { Data file }

            ****************************************
            **  Insert InitTree and InsertInTree  **
            **  procedures here.                  **
            ****************************************

{*****************************************************************}
{*                  Main Control Module                         *}
{*****************************************************************}
begin
   reset(DFile);
   if not eof(DFile) then begin
      InitTree(Root);                           { Initialize the tree }
      while not eof(DFile) do begin
         readln(DFile, Number);                 { Read one integer number }
         InsertInTree(Root, Number)             { Insert number into tree }
      end   { while }
   end   { if }
end.   { CreateTree }
```

The search in the **InsertInTree** procedure is binary in the sense that if the new number, **Num**, is less than or equal to the data in the test node, the procedure checks the left subtree; otherwise, the procedure checks the right subtree. The check of the subtree is also binary. If the subtree is empty, the location where the new node is to be inserted has been found; otherwise the search must continue down that subtree.

Now that we have created our tree, our next major objective is to traverse the tree and print the data. If we use inorder traversal, the data will be printed in ascending order. Thus in this section we have developed a new sorting method, the tree sort. After all of the data have been inserted into the tree in the correct tree locations, then all that remains to be done is to traverse the tree using inorder traversal and print the data from each node. We will see how this is done in the next section.

Exercises

6.4 Change the **InsertInTree** procedure so that the numbers will be in descending order (from largest to smallest) if the tree is traversed using inorder traversal.

6.5 Create a data file such that each line contains an 11-character social security number. Change the **CreateTree** program to read each line of the data file and insert the social security numbers into a tree so that they will be sorted in ascending order (for inorder traversal).

6.6   Create a data file such that each line contains a name (20-character maximum). Change the **CreateTree** program to read these names and insert them into a tree so that the names will be sorted in ascending order (for inorder traversal).

6.3 Tree-Traversal Procedures

The procedures used to traverse a tree can be kept quite short if we understand the recursive nature of a binary tree. Recall that a tree is recursive in that each subtree is really a tree in itself.

Suppose that we wish to use inorder traversal to traverse the tree and print the data from each node. As we saw earlier, to use the inorder traversal for a tree, we must first look at the left subtree. Since this left subtree is itself a tree, we look at its left subtree. Again, since the left subtree is a tree, we look at its left subtree. This suggests a recursive procedure in which we first follow the pointers down the left-most nodes until a left **nil** pointer is reached. Then the data item for this last leftmost node (L) is printed. The inorder procedure dictates that next the data item for the parent node (N) is printed. After this, the right subtree for this node (if there is one) must be traversed. If there is a right subtree, its left subtree must be examined first.

This inorder traversal process should certainly suggest the use of a recursive procedure. Let us look at the pseudocode for procedure **TravInOrder** first. The only parameter we need is a pointer to a tree node. When first called, the procedure will send the pointer to the root of the tree as the value for this parameter.

Pseudocode

TravInOrder Procedure

IF node pointer is not **nil** THEN
    Call procedure **TravInOrder** again, sending the left pointer
       from the node as the new parameter.
    Print the node data.
    Call procedure **TravInOrder** again, sending the right
       pointer from the node as the new parameter.
END IF.

The Pascal coding for procedure **TravInOrder** is quite short. We will assume that the data item in each node is a single integer number. After the listing, we will continue our discussion of how the procedure really works.

```
{*****************************************************************}
{* TravInOrder - Recursive procedure to traverse a tree using inorder *}
{*               traversal and print the integer numbers stored as    *}
{*               data in the tree nodes. Each tree node contains one   *}
{*               number.                                               *}
{*        var parameters -                                             *}
{*               None.                                                 *}
{*        value parameters -                                           *}
{*               TreeNode : Tree-node pointer (initially sent as the tree *}
{*                          root).                                     *}
{*****************************************************************}
procedure TravInOrder(TreeNode : NodePtr);
begin
  if TreeNode <> nil then begin
    TravInOrder(TreeNode^.LeftPtr);                    { Left subtree }
    writeln(TreeNode^.Data);                           { Print node data }
    TravInOrder(TreeNode^.RightPtr)                    { Right subtree }
  end { if }
end;  { TravInOrder }
```

Notice that the recursive calls **TravInOrder(TreeNode^.LeftPtr)** will result in a traversal down the leftmost nodes until a **nil** pointer is reached. Assume that in the small tree in Figure 6.13 the left nodes A, B, and D have been traversed by calling **TravInOrder** three times. When **TravInOrder** is called for the fourth time with the left **nil** pointer from node D, the **if TreeNode <> nil** condition will become false, causing an immediate jump to the end of the procedure. At this point, execution will start backing through the previous recursive calls. When it backs up to the third call, the remaining statements in **TravInOrder** will be executed. The next statement to be executed is

```
writeln(TreeNode^.Data);
```

Figure 6.13

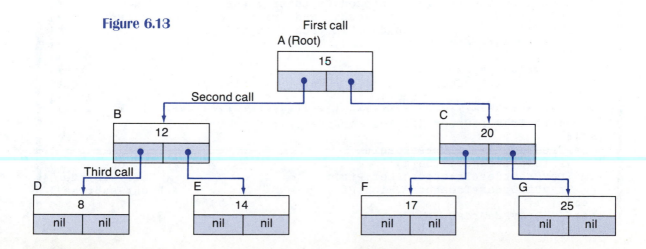

This statement will print the integer number 8 from node D. The next statement to be executed is

```
TravInOrder(TreeNode^.RightPtr)
```

This calls the procedure again to look at the right subtree for node D. Since the right pointer in D is **nil**, the end of the procedure is immediately reached. Therefore, the next step is a return to the second recursive call to execute the

```
writeln(TreeNode^.Data)
```

statement; however, note that in this second call the node pointer points to B. Thus the number 12 from node B will be printed. Now the

```
TravInOrder(TreeNode^.RightPtr)
```

statement is executed. This statement calls the procedure to look at the right subtree of node B.

It should be apparent that our small procedure is doing a lot of work. However, it should also be apparent that the procedure is doing exactly what we wanted it to do. In the exercises you will be asked to continue the walk-through of **TravInOrder** that we have started, making sure you understand the process.

Now that we have a procedure for traversing a tree using inorder traversal, what must we change in order to use a preorder or postorder traversal? All we really need to change is the order of the statements. Thus the preorder procedure will print the node data first, then go to the left subtree, and finally go to the right subtree. The **TravPreOrder** procedure follows.

```
{**********************************************************************}
{* TravPreOrder - Recursive procedure to traverse a tree using       *}
{*                preorder traversal and print the integer number     *}
{*                stored as data in each tree node.                    *}
{*      var parameters -                                               *}
{*          None.                                                      *}
{*      value parameters -                                             *}
{*          TreeNode : Tree-node pointer (initially sent as the tree  *}
{*                     root).                                          *}
{**********************************************************************}
procedure TravPreOrder(TreeNode : NodePtr);
begin
  if TreeNode <> nil then begin
    writeln(TreeNode^.Data);                        { Print node data }
    TravPreOrder(TreeNode^.LeftPtr);                { Left subtree }
    TravPreOrder(TreeNode^.RightPtr)                { Right subtree }
  end { if }
end; { TravPreOrder }
```

The coding is similar for the **TravPostOrder** procedure; only a change in order of the three statements is required. The procedure goes to the left subtree first, then goes to the right subtree, and finally prints the node data.

```
{****************************************************************}
{* TravPostOrder - Recursive procedure to traverse a tree using *}
{*                 postorder traversal and print the integer number *}
{*                 stored as data in each tree node.            *}
{*      var parameters-                                         *}
{*          None.                                              *}
{*      value parameters -                                     *}
{*          TreeNode : Tree-node pointer (initially sent as the tree *}
{*                     root.)                                  *}
{****************************************************************}
procedure TravPostOrder(TreeNode : NodePtr);
begin
  if TreeNode <> nil then begin
    TravPostOrder(TreeNode^.LeftPtr);      { Left subtree }
    TravPostOrder(TreeNode^.RightPtr);     { Right subtree }
    writeln(TreeNode^.Data)                { Print node data }
  end { if }
end;  { TravPostOrder }
```

Exercises

6.7 Complete the walk-through of the **TravInOrder** procedure for the tree in Figure 6.13.

6.8 Walk through the **TravPreOrder** procedure for the tree in Figure 6.13.

6.9 Walk through the **TravPostOrder** procedure for the tree in Figure 6.13.

6.10 Assume that a tree has been created so that the data (integer numbers) will be in ascending order if inorder traversal is used. Modify the **TravInOrder** procedure so that the data will be printed in descending order instead of ascending order. Remember that the order of output is controlled by the order of the statements in the recursive traversal procedures.

6.4 Tree Sort

Now that we know how to traverse a tree and print the data stored in the tree nodes, we are in a position to write a complete program to use a tree to do a numerical sort. This can be accomplished by adding the appropriate traversal procedure from Section 6.3 to the tree-creation program in Section 6.2. Since the tree-creation program in Section 6.2 inserted the data so that they would be in sorted order when inorder traversal was used, we should use the **TravInOrder** procedure. The complete program **TreeSort** follows.

```
{*****************************************************************}
{* TreeSort - Program to create a tree in which each node contains  *}
{*            one integer number as data. The numbers are inserted  *}
{*            into the tree so that when the tree is traversed using *}
{*            inorder traversal, the numbers will be sorted in       *}
{*            ascending order. After the tree is created, the data   *}
{*            will be printed, one number per line.                  *}
{*****************************************************************}
program TreeSort(output, DFile);
type
   NodePtr = ^TrNode;
   TrNode = record
              Data : integer;
              LeftPtr : NodePtr;
              RightPtr : NodePtr
            end;
var
   Root : NodePtr;                           { Pointer to the tree root }
   Number : integer;                         { One integer number }
   DFile : text;                             { Data file }


          *********************************************
          **   Insert InitTree, InsertInTree, and  **
          **   TravInOrder procedures here.         **
          *********************************************

{*****************************************************************}
{*                    Main Control Module                        *}
{*****************************************************************}
begin
   reset(DFile);
   if not eof(DFile) then begin
      InitTree(Root);                              { Initialize the tree }
      while not eof(DFile) do begin
         readln(DFile, Number);              { Read one integer number }
         InsertInTree(Root, Number)          { Insert number into tree }
      end; { while }
      TravInOrder(Root)                             { Traverse tree
                                                and print the data }

   end { if }
end.   { TreeSort }
```

A tree sort can be quite efficient in comparison to the sorts we discussed in Chapter 4. In fact, if the tree is close to being balanced, the sorting time is of order N log N. Recall from Chapter 4 that a sort of order N log N is much faster than sorts of order N^2 for larger files or arrays.

However, there is a potential pitfall to the tree sort. If the tree is far from being balanced, the efficiency of the tree sort suffers greatly. In fact, the order can degenerate down to $O(N^2)$. For example, if the file is already sorted in ascending order, then when the tree is initialized the value put in the root will be the first (and smallest) one. The next data value will be put in

Figure 6.14

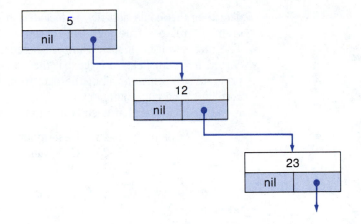

the right subtree. In fact, all remaining values will always be put in right subtrees. Thus the tree will be completely unbalanced and will really be nothing more than a linked list. We lose the efficiency normally resulting from a balanced binary tree, since the tree is no longer binary in structure. The same unbalanced situation will occur if the data are in reverse order.

Except for these extreme cases, however, the tree sort is a relatively efficient sorting method, and for large random files it is certainly superior to the sorting methods discussed in Chapter 4.

Exercises

6.11 Create a data file in which each line contains one real number. Read the data into a tree so that the numbers will be sorted (in ascending order) if traversed using inorder traversal. After printing a centered heading on a new page, print out the numbers one per output line so that the numbers are sorted in descending order (highest to lowest).

6.12 Add an inorder traversal procedure to the program in Exercise 6.5 and print out the sorted social security numbers.

6.13 Add an inorder traversal procedure to the program in Exercise 6.6 and print out the sorted names.

6.5 Inventory Tree

The program in Section 6.4 is interesting but not very typical of practical examples. An actual situation will usually involve several data items in each data record rather than just a simple integer number.

Suppose that a company keeps an inventory file in which each data record contains an item description, a code number, and a quantity. Obviously, more data than this could actually be included in each record. We will write a program to create a tree and insert one complete data record into each node. The nodes will be inserted into the tree so that the code numbers will be sorted from smallest to largest if the tree is traversed inorder. Finally, the program will print out all of the data from the tree (which is now sorted according to the code number).

We will assume that each line in the data file is formatted as follows:

Columns	1–16	Description	(Character string)
	17–28	Code number	(Character string)
	29–33	Quantity	(Integer)

Since the data consist of more than one item, we will make the following declarations.

```
type
  String16 = packed array[1..16] of char;
  String12 = packed array[1..12] of char;
  DataType = record
                Description : String16;
                CodeNo : String12;
                Quantity : integer
             end;
  NodePtr = ^TrNode;
  TrNode = record
              Data : DataType;
              LeftPtr : NodePtr;
              RightPtr : NodePtr
           end;
```

Very few changes will have to be made in the **InitTree** and **InsertInTree** procedures that we used in Section 6.4. Each node of the tree will contain a complete inventory record instead of just one integer number. Therefore, we will have the **InitTree** procedure call a procedure named **ReadRec** to read an entire data record from the file. This entire record will then be put into the root node.

The **InsertInTree** procedure will also call **ReadRec** to read each data record. **InsertInTree** must compare the code numbers of the data records instead of just single integer numbers as it did for the program in Section 6.4.

In addition to including the new procedure **ReadRec** to read one record at a time, we will also use a new procedure **PrintRec** to print an entire record. We have inserted the procedures in alphabetical order (as is good practice). Since **InitTree** calls **ReadRec**, we have inserted a **forward** declaration for **ReadRec**.

The complete program **InvSort** follows.

```
{*****************************************************************}
{* InvSort - Program to use a binary tree to sort an inventory file   *}
{*           according to code numbers and then print the data.       *}
```

```
{*        Data file format -                                      *}
{*            Columns 1 - 16   Description   (Character string)   *}
{*                    17 - 28  Code number   (Character String)   *}
{*                    29 - 33  Quantity      (Integer)            *}
{*        Output print format -                                   *}
{*            Columns 11 - 22  Code number  (Character string)    *}
{*                    36 - 51  Description  (Character string)    *}
{*                    65 - 69  Quantity     (Integer)             *}
{****************************************************************}
program InvSort(output, DFile);
type
   String16 = packed array[1..16] of char;
   String12 = packed array[1..12] of char;
   DataType = record
                 Description : String16;
                 CodeNo : String12;
                 Quantity : integer
              end;
   NodePtr = ^TrNode;
   TrNode = record
                 Data : DataType;
                 LeftPtr : NodePtr;
                 RightPtr : NodePtr
            end;
var
   Root : NodePtr;                            { Tree-root pointer }
   OneRec : DataType;                    { One complete data record }
   DFile : text;                                    { Data file }
                 { Forward procedure declarations }
procedure ReadRec(var DataF : text; var DataRec : DataType); forward;
                 { End of forward procedure declarations }
{****************************************************************}
{* InitTree - Procedure to initialize the tree. The root node is   *}
{*            created and the first data record is inserted into the *}
{*            root node.                                            *}
{*        var parameters -                                         *}
{*            TreeRoot : Pointer to the root node.                 *}
{*        value parameters -                                       *}
{*            None.                                                *}
{****************************************************************}
procedure InitTree(var TreeRoot : NodePtr);
begin
   new(TreeRoot);                            { Create the root node }
   ReadRec(DFile, OneRec);                   { Read one data record }
   TreeRoot^.Data := OneRec;                      { Insert data
                                               record into root }

   TreeRoot^.LeftPtr := nil;
   TreeRoot^.RightPtr := nil
end;   { InitTree }


{****************************************************************}
{* InsertInTree - Procedure to insert one data record into the tree  *}
{*                such that the inventory code numbers will be in    *}
{*                ascending order if inorder traversal is used to    *}
{*                print the data.                                     *}
```

```
{*        var parameters -                                        *}
{*             None.                                              *}
{*        value parameters -                                      *}
{*             TreeRoot : Pointer to the root node.               *}
{*             DataRec : One inventory data record.               *}
{****************************************************************************}
procedure InsertInTree(TreeRoot : NodePtr; DataRec : DataType);
var
  Inserted : boolean;                         { Flag to indicate if
                                               node has been inserted }
  OneNode,                                       { One tree node }
  NewNode : NodePtr;                             { New tree node }
begin
  new(NewNode);                                 { Create one node }
  Inserted := false;
  OneNode := TreeRoot;
  while not(Inserted) do begin
    if DataRec.CodeNo <= OneNode^.Data.CodeNo then
      if OneNode^.LeftPtr <> nil then
        OneNode := OneNode^.LeftPtr
      { end if }
      else begin
        OneNode^.LeftPtr := NewNode;
        Inserted := true
      end   { else }
    { end if }
    else
      if OneNode^.RightPtr <> nil then
        OneNode := OneNode^.RightPtr
      { end if }
      else begin
        OneNode^.RightPtr := NewNode;
        Inserted := true
      end   { else }
    { end else }
  end;     { while }
  NewNode^.Data := DataRec;                     { Insert data
                                               record into new node }
  NewNode^.LeftPtr := nil;
  NewNode^.RightPtr := nil
end;   { InsertInTree }


{****************************************************************************}
{* PrintHeadings - Procedure to print a main heading and column     *}
{*                 headings.                                        *}
{****************************************************************************}
procedure PrintHeadings;
begin
  writeln('Inventory for ABC Company':52);
  writeln;
  writeln('Code No.':20, 'Description':28, 'Quantity':23);
  writeln;
  writeln;
end;   { PrintHeadings }
```

```
{***********************************************************************}
{* PrintRec - Procedure to print one line of data according to the   *}
{*            following format:                                       *}
{*                    Columns 11 - 22  Code number  (Character string) *}
{*                            36 - 51  Description  (Character string) *}
{*                            65 - 69  Quantity     (Integer)          *}
{*       var parameters -                                             *}
{*           None.                                                    *}
{*       value parameters -                                           *}
{*           DataRec : One data record.                              *}
{***********************************************************************}
procedure PrintRec(DataRec : DataType);
begin
  with DataRec do
    writeln(CodeNo:22, ' ':13, Description:16, Quantity:18)
end;  { PrintRec }


{***********************************************************************}
{* ReadRec - Procedure to read one data record from the data file,   *}
{*           DataF, according to the following format:               *}
{*                    Columns 1 - 16  Description  (Character string) *}
{*                           17 - 28  Code number  (Character String) *}
{*                           29 - 33  Quantity     (Integer)          *}
{*       var parameters -                                            *}
{*           DataF : Data file.                                      *}
{*           DataRec : One complete data record.                     *}
{*       value parameters -                                          *}
{*           None.                                                   *}
{***********************************************************************}
procedure ReadRec;
var
  I : integer;                                              { Index }
begin
  with DataRec do begin
    for I := 1 to 16 do
      read(DataF, Description[I]);
    { end for }
    for I := 1 to 12 do
      read(DataF, CodeNo[I]);
    { end for }
    readln(DataF, Quantity)
  end  { with }
end;  { ReadRec }


{***********************************************************************}
{* TravInOrder - Recursive procedure to traverse the tree using      *}
{*               inorder traversal and then print the inventory      *}
{*               records stored as data in the tree nodes. Each tree *}
{*               node contains one inventory record.                 *}
{*       var parameters -                                            *}
{*           None.                                                   *}
{*       value parameters -                                          *}
{*           TreeNode : Tree-node pointer (initially sent as the tree *}
{*                      root).                                        *}
{***********************************************************************}
```

```
procedure TravInOrder(TreeNode : NodePtr);
begin
  if TreeNode <> nil then begin
    TravInOrder(TreeNode^.LeftPtr);                    { Left subtree }
    PrintRec(TreeNode^.Data);                       { Print node data }
    TravInOrder(TreeNode^.RightPtr)                    { Right subtree }
  end   { if }
end;   { TravInOrder }


{***********************************************************************}
{*                        Main Control Module                         *}
{***********************************************************************}
begin
  reset(DFile);
  PrintHeadings;                                      { Print headings }
  if not eof(DFile) then begin
    InitTree(Root);                                { Initialize the tree }
    while not eof(DFile) do begin
      ReadRec(DFile, OneRec);                     { Read one data record }
      InsertInTree(Root, OneRec)              { Insert record into tree }
    end;   { while }
    TravInOrder(Root)                               { Traverse tree
                                                      and print the data }

  end   { if }
end.   { InvSort }
```

Exercises

6.14   Create a data file in which each line contains the following.

Columns	1–20	Name	(Character string)
	21–31	Social security number	(Character string)
	32–78	Address	(Character string)

Write a program to read each data record into a tree so that when the tree is traversed using inorder traversal, the social security numbers will be sorted in ascending order. Print a heading "EMPLOYEE DATA SORTED AC-CORDING TO SOCIAL SECURITY NOS." Then print the tree data using the following output format:

Columns	1–11	Social security number	(Character string)
	25–44	Name	(Character string)
	58–104	Address	(Character string)

6.15   Alter the program in Exercise 6.14 so that the social security numbers will be printed in descending order.

6.16   Create an inventory data file in which each data line contains the following data.

Columns	1–12	Code number	(Character string)
	13–32	Description	(Character string)

33–36	Present quantity	(Integer)
38–41	Quantity sold this year	(Integer)
43–49	Cost	(Real)
51–57	Selling price	(Real)

Write a Pascal program to read each data record into a tree so that the data will be sorted according to the quantity sold this year (if inorder traversal is used). Print an appropriate heading and then print all data, sorted by the quantity sold this year, according to the following output format.

Columns	1–12	Code number	(Character string)
	27–36	Description	(Character string)
	51–54	Present quantity	(Integer)
	69–72	Quantity sold this year	(Integer)
	87–93	Cost	(Real)
	108–114	Selling price	(Real)

6.6 Tree Search

Once a tree containing our data has been created, we may wish to search the tree for a specified data item. In fact, a binary tree that is created such that the data are in sorted order (when traversed) is commonly called a *binary search tree*.

Searching the tree should be a relatively simple task, since the techniques needed to do a search should be very similar to the methods used to insert a new data item. A procedure to perform a search should return the pointer to the data item if the item is found. If the item is not found, the procedure should so indicate by some means such as returning a **nil** pointer. Since just one value is being returned, we could use a Pascal function instead of a procedure. (Writing this search as a function instead of a procedure will be covered in the exercises.)

Let us design our search procedure **SearchTree** so that the tree root and the data key item for which we are searching are value parameters and the pointer to the node containing the found data is a **var** parameter. The procedure will indicate that the data item was not found by returning a **nil** pointer for this last parameter. First we will write the pseudocode for this procedure.

Pseudocode

> **SearchTree Procedure**
>
> Initialize Boolean variable **Found** to false.
> Initialize **OneNode** to tree root.
> WHILE not **Found** and **OneNode** is not **nil**
>   IF data key is at **OneNode** THEN
>   Set **Found** to true.
>   ELSE

```
        IF data key is <= OneNode^.Data THEN
            Set OneNode to OneNode^.LeftPtr.
        ELSE
            Set OneNode to OneNode^.RightPtr.
        END IF.
    END IF.
END WHILE.
```

Note that if the data item is found, the procedure will return with the **OneNode** pointer pointing to the node containing our data; otherwise, **OneNode** will be returned as **nil**.

Now let us write the Pascal code for the **SearchTree** procedure. Assume that we wish to search for a node with a specific inventory-item code number in the tree that was created in Section 6.5. The code number to be searched for will be passed to the procedure as the value for parameter **SearCode**.

```
{***********************************************************************}
{* SearchTree - Procedure to search a tree for a given inventory-item *}
{*              code number. If the item is found, the procedure      *}
{*              returns with the parameter, OneNode, pointing to the   *}
{*              found node. If the item is not found, the procedure    *}
{*              returns with OneNode set to nil.                       *}
{*      var parameters -                                               *}
{*          OneNode : Node where code number was found or nil if not   *}
{*                    found.                                           *}
{*      value parameters -                                             *}
{*          RootNode : Tree-root pointer.                              *}
{*          SearCode : Code number to be found.                        *}
{***********************************************************************}
procedure SearchTree(RootNode : NodePtr; SearCode : String12;
                     var OneNode : NodePtr);
var
   Found : boolean;                            { Flag indicating if
                                                 code number is found }

begin
   Found := false;
   OneNode := RootNode;
   while not(Found) and (OneNode <> nil) do begin
     if SearCode = OneNode^.Data.CodeNo then
       Found := true
     { end if }
     else
       if SearCode < OneNode^.Data.CodeNo then
         OneNode := OneNode^.LeftPtr
       { end if }
       else
         OneNode := OneNode^.RightPtr
       { end else }
     { end else }
   end { while }
end;   { SearchTree }
```

Any program or procedure that calls **SearchTree** will only need to check the **OneNode** pointer to see whether or not it is **nil**. If it is not **nil**, then **OneNode** is the pointer to the node containing the data, and the data may then be accessed.

This procedure is specific in that it is used to find a particular type of data item within the data records. However, only minor changes are required to search for different types of data items.

Exercises

6.17   Write **SearchTree** as a Pascal function rather than a procedure.

6.18   Alter the **InvSort** program in Section 6.5 to meet the following specifications.
(a) After the tree has been created, do not print out all data.
(b) Interactively, ask the user if he or she wishes to print out all data for a given inventory item. If the response is "Y," ask the user for the code number, and then print out all data for that particular inventory item. Include this process in a loop so that an exit will be made only after the user responds "N" to the prompt question.

6.19   Do the same as in Exercise 6.18 except use the data file and the tree from Exercise 6.14. Search for given social security numbers.

6.7   Tree Insertions and Deletions

In addition to techniques for searching a tree for specified data, practical examples call for techniques for inserting new data into a tree and deleting data from a tree.

It should be relatively easy to insert new items into an existing tree since we have already written the **InsertInTree** procedure to insert each new item into the tree while the tree is being created. After the tree has been created, this same procedure may be used to insert additional items at any time. As before, the new data item is passed to this procedure, and the procedure inserts the new item into the tree.

Now let us turn our attention to the process of deleting a node from a tree. Assume that we will pass the specified data item that we wish to delete to the **DeleteNode** procedure. There are four possible cases that we need to consider.

Case 1   No node in the tree contains the specified data.
Case 2   The node containing the data has no children.
Case 3   The node containing the data has exactly one child.
Case 4   The node containing the data has two children.

For case 1 we merely need to print a message that the data item is not in the tree.

As an example of case 2, suppose that we wish to delete node E from the tree in Figure 6.15 (Before). Since node E does not point to any other nodes, all we have to do to delete node E is change the pointer to E in node B to **nil** [see Figure 6.15, (After)].

Figure 6.15

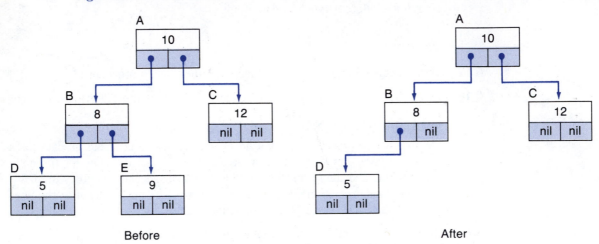

Before   After

As an example of case 3, suppose that the node to be deleted has one child, as node B does in Figure 6.16 (Before). The solution is again rather simple. We patch the pointer in node A (the parent of B) so that it now points to D. B is thereby deleted from the tree [see Figure 6.16, (After)].

Figure 6.16

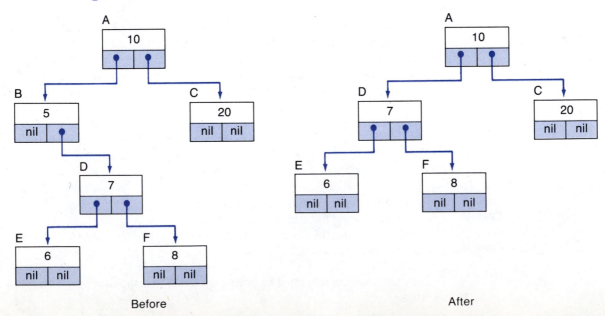

Before   After

For case 4, in which the node has two children, the solution is more involved. Consider node C in Figure 6.17 (Before). Suppose we follow the pointers down the rightmost path of the left subtree of node C until we find

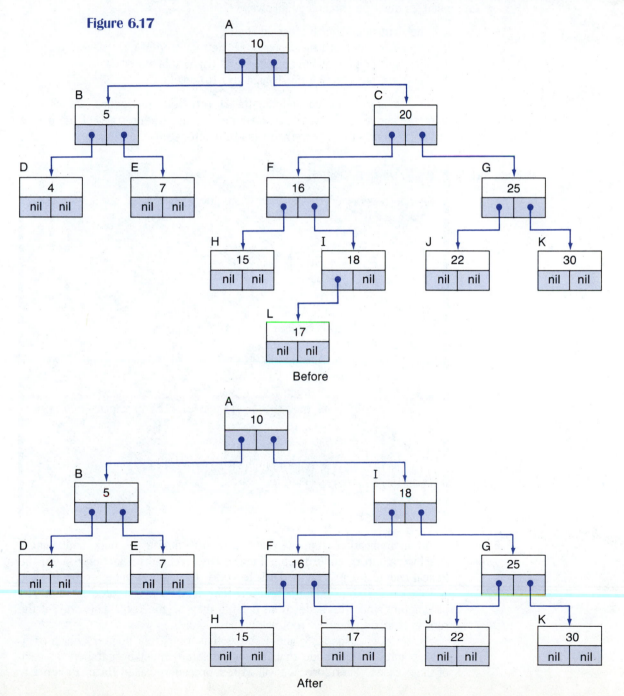

Figure 6.17

Before

After

node I. Note that 18 is the largest value (in the left subtree of C) smaller than 20 (the value in node C). Thus we should be able to replace node C with node I, as shown in Figure 6.17 (After). In order to make this replacement, four pointers must be patched as follows.

1. The right pointer of F must point to L.
2. The left pointer of I must point to F (left subtree of C).
3. The right pointer of I must point to G (right subtree of C).
4. The right pointer of A must point to I (to delete C).

In designing the pseudocode for the **DeleteNode** procedure, we will consider the above four cases one at a time. We must keep track of the parent node that points to the node we wish to delete.

Pseudocode

DeleteNode Procedure

Search tree for node to be deleted and pointer to node's parent.
IF not found THEN
    Print message.
ELSE
    IF node to be deleted has no children THEN
        Patch parent pointer to **nil**.
    ELSE
        IF node to be deleted has one child THEN
            Patch parent pointer to point to this child.
        ELSE (for two children)
            Search down rightmost path of left child of node to be
                deleted.
            Patch replacement node's pointers.
            Patch old pointer that previously pointed to replace-
                ment node.
            Patch parent node to point to replacement node.
        END IF.
    END IF.
    Dispose of node to be deleted.
END IF.

As an application, suppose that we wish to delete the node containing a specific inventory code number for the tree created in Section 6.5. In the Pascal coding for procedure **DeleteNode**, the code number to be deleted will be passed as a value parameter. The tree root will need to be a **var** parameter, since the node to be deleted may be the root. This way, if the root is changed, the new root will be passed back.

A review of cases 2, 3, and 4 shows that the parent pointer (which originally pointed to the node that is being deleted) must be patched for each of these cases. Therefore, we will write a procedure called **PatchParentPtr** to patch the parent pointer. This procedure will be nested within the **DeleteNode** procedure and have as a value parameter the new pointer **NewParPtr**, which will be put in the parent node in place of the pointer to the node that is being deleted.

For the **PatchParentPtr** procedure we must consider the case in which the node to be deleted is the tree root. In this case, **NewParPtr** will be assigned as the new tree root. Another concern in **PatchParentPtr** is whether the pointer in the parent node to the node to be deleted is the left pointer or the right pointer. After the procedure checks to see which pointer it is, that particular pointer is changed to **NewParPtr**.

We can now write the Pascal code for the **DeleteNode** procedure and also its nested procedure **PatchParentPtr**. The coding of **DeleteNode** for cases 1, 2, and 3 is rather quick. However, the coding for case 4 is more involved. We will discuss the coding for case 4 in detail following the listing.

```
{*****************************************************************}
{* DeleteNode - Procedure to delete the tree node containing a   *}
{*              selected data item. The data item is a specific  *}
{*              inventory-item code number. If the code number is not *}
{*              found in the tree, a message will be printed and the  *}
{*              tree left unchanged. The code number will be sent in  *}
{*              the parameter DelCode.                           *}
{*      var parameters -                                         *}
{*          TreeRoot : Tree-root pointer.                        *}
{*      value parameters -                                       *}
{*          DelCode : Code number to be deleted.                 *}
{*****************************************************************}
procedure DeleteNode(var TreeRoot : NodePtr; DelCode : String12);
var
  DelNode,                                { Node to be deleted }
  ParNode,                               { Parent node of DelNode }
  Node1,
  Node2,
  Node3 : NodePtr;                        { Temporary pointers }
  Found : boolean;                         { Boolean to
                                           indicate if found }
{*****************************************************************}
{* PatchParentPtr - Procedure to patch the pointer in ParNode (the *}
{*                  parent node).                                *}
{*      var parameters -                                         *}
{*          None.                                                *}
{*      value parameters -                                       *}
{*          NewParPtr : Pointer to be inserted in ParNode.       *}
{*****************************************************************}
procedure PatchParentPtr(NewParPtr : NodePtr);
begin
  if ParNode = nil then
    TreeRoot := NewParPtr
  { end if }
  else
    if ParNode^.LeftPtr = DelNode then
      ParNode^.LeftPtr := NewParPtr
```

```
                { end if }
        else
          ParNode^.RightPtr := NewParPtr
        { end else }
      { end else }
end;   { PatchParentPtr }

begin   { DeleteNode }
  Found := false;
  DelNode := TreeRoot;
  ParNode := nil;
        { Search tree for the node to delete and the parent node }
  while(not Found) and (DelNode <> nil) do begin
    if DelCode = DelNode^.Data.CodeNo then
      Found := true
    { end if }
    else begin
      ParNode := DelNode;                      { Move down the tree }
      if DelCode < DelNode^.Data.CodeNo then
        DelNode := DelNode^.LeftPtr
      { end if }
      else
        DelNode := DelNode^.RightPtr
      { end else }
    end   { else }
  end;   { while }
  if not Found then
    writeln('Code number ', DelCode, ' was not found.')     { Case 1 }
  { end if }
  else begin
    if DelNode^.LeftPtr = nil then
      if DelNode^.RightPtr = nil then                            { Case 2 }
        PatchParentPtr(nil)               { If no children then
                                       patch parent pointer to nil }

      { end if }
      else
        PatchParentPtr(DelNode^.RightPtr)                        { Case 3 }
                                          { Patch parent left
                                            pointer around DelNode }

      { end else }
    { end if }
    else
      if DelNode^.RightPtr = nil then                            { Case 3 }
                                          { Patch parent right
                                            pointer around DelNode }

        PatchParentPtr(DelNode^.LeftPtr)
      { end if }
      else begin                                                 { Case 4 }
            { Search down rightmost path of left
                child of DelNode to find the node to replace DelNode }
        Node1 := DelNode;
        Node2 := DelNode^.LeftPtr;
        Node3 := Node2^.RightPtr;
        while Node3 <> nil do begin
              { Move the temporary pointers down }
```

```
            Node1 := Node2;
            Node2 := Node3;
            Node3 := Node3^.RightPtr
        end;  { while }
                    { Patch pointers for Case 4 }
        if Node1 <> DelNode then begin
          Node1^.RightPtr := Node2^.LeftPtr;
          Node2^.LeftPtr := DelNode^.LeftPtr
        end;  { if }
        Node2^.RightPtr := DelNode^.RightPtr;
        PatchParentPtr(Node2)
      end;  { else }
    { end else }
    dispose(DelNode)
  end { else }
end;  { DeleteNode }
```

Notice that in procedure **PatchParentPtr** the statement "**if ParNode = nil** ..." takes care of the special case in which the root of the tree is the node to be deleted.

Let us take a closer look at case 4 (in which **DelNode** has two children). Remember that we agreed to traverse down the rightmost path of the left subtree of **DelNode** until a leaf was found. This is done in procedure **DeleteNode** by using the three temporary pointer variables **Node1**, **Node2**, and **Node3**. **Node1** is initialized to **DelNode**; **Node2** is initialized to the **LeftPtr** of **DelNode**; and **Node3** is initialized to the **RightPtr** of **Node2**. Then as the rightmost nodes in the left subtree of **DelNode** are traversed, the pointers move down until **Node3** becomes **nil**. After this traversal, **Node2** is pointing to the rightmost leaf.

This last leaf will take the place of **DelNode**. As indicated earlier, several pointer patches must be made. These patches are indicated in Figure 6.18. Patch 1 sets the right pointer of F to L so that node I can replace node C. This patch is coded in **DeleteNode** as

```
Node1^.RightPtr := Node2^.LeftPtr;
```

Patch 2 sets the **LeftPtr** of I to F. F was the original root of the left subtree of **DelNode**. This patch is coded in **DeleteNode** as

```
Node2^.LeftPtr := DelNode^.LeftPtr
```

Patch 3 sets the **RightPtr** of I to G. G was the original root of the right subtree of **DelNode**. This patch is coded in **DeleteNode** as

```
Node2^.RightPtr := DelNode^.RightPtr
```

Patch 4 sets the parent pointer (in A) to node I. Node I has now taken the place of **DelNode**. This patch is coded in **DeleteNode** as

```
PatchParentPtr(Node2)
```

Figure 6.18

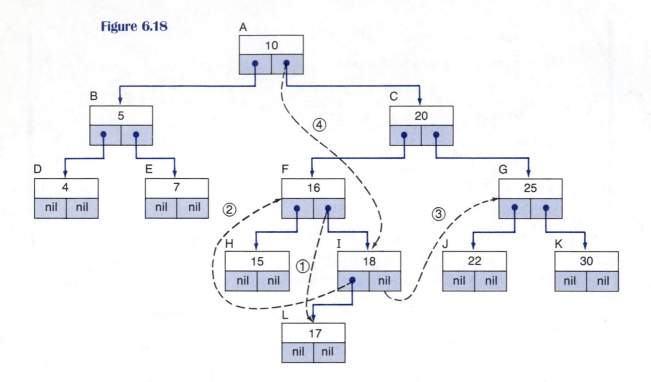

What is the purpose of the statement "**if Node <> DelNode** ..." in procedure **DeleteNode**? Note that this will only be true if **Node3** (or **Node2^.RightPtr**) is **nil** when the temporary pointers **Node1**, **Node2**, and **Node3** are initialized. As may be seen in Figure 6.19, this situation will occur if the procedure immediately reaches the rightmost leaf in the left subtree of node C (**DelNode**). In this situation, patching is simple. We need to make only two patches instead of four. The **RightPtr** of F must point to G, and the **RightPtr** of A must point to F. The resulting tree (after node C has been deleted) is illustrated in Figure 6.20.

Exercises

6.20   Alter the **InvSort** program in Section 6.5 so that after the data are entered into the tree, a menu of available options is printed for the user. The menu should include the following options.
   (a) Print all data for all inventory items.
   (b) Search for a particular item by code number, and then print all data for that item.
   (c) Insert a new inventory item into the tree.
   (d) Delete an old item from the tree.
   (e) Write all tree data to a new inventory file, **NewData**.
   (f) Exit the program.

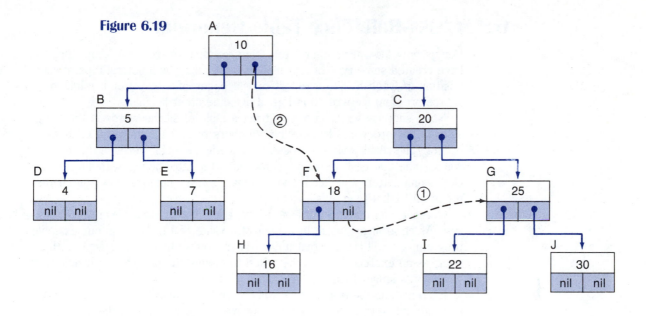

Figure 6.19

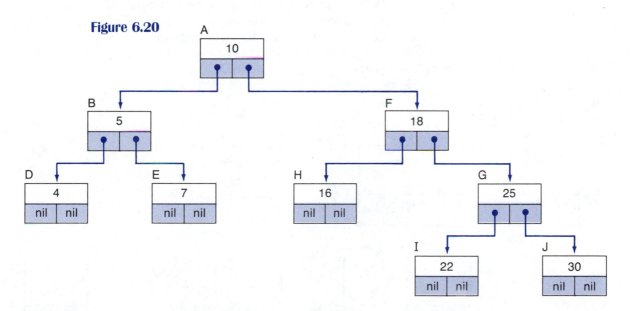

Figure 6.20

After the menu is printed, ask the user what he or she wants to do. Then execute the request. Include this process in a loop that can be terminated by a user request of option "f".

6.21 Add to Exercise 6.20 the option to alter any of the data in any inventory item.

6.8 Cross-Reference Table Generator

Let us now look at another interesting example of trees. Assume that we have created some type of text file. This file might be a normal type of composition in English (like a report or the pages of a book) or it might be a source program file written in Pascal or some other language.

Now, suppose we wish to construct a table of all the words in the file in alphabetical order and list the line numbers of all lines in which each word occurs. The result will be a cross-reference listing of all words in the file. We will assume that each word to be entered in the table begins with a letter, includes only letters and digits, and terminates with a nonletter/nondigit character or an EOLN (end of line) marker.

One decision that we will have to make is what maximum word size to allow. As an arbitrary value let us select a value of 14. Thus, in our example program, we will assume that no words are longer than 14 characters. However, as an exercise you will be asked to modify the program to handle text with words longer than 14 characters.

Each node in the tree that we will create will contain a word as well as left and right pointers to other nodes. However, keeping track of the numbers of the lines where each of the words occurs presents a problem. A rather obvious solution to this problem is to keep a linked list of all the line numbers in the order encountered. Therefore each tree node will also need to contain a pointer to the beginning of the list for that word. For example, suppose the word "for" occurs in lines 4, 8, 23, and 30 of our text file. Then for this one tree node we would have the situation depicted in Figure 6.21.

Figure 6.21

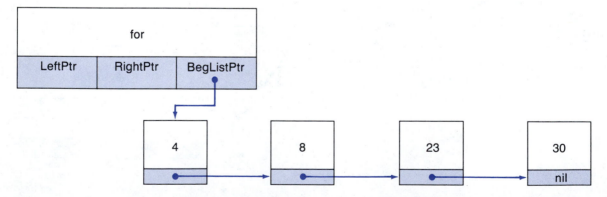

The tree we will be creating is not a normal binary tree because each node will contain one extra pointer. However, this extra pointer does not point to another tree node. Thus the operational characteristics will still be those of a binary tree. The functions of the left and right pointers are still the same. Main program declarations will include the following.

```
const
  MaxWordSize = 14;
type
  String14 = packed array[1..MaxWordSize] of char;
  NodePtr = ^Node;
  ListEltPtr = ^ListElt;
  Node = record
          Word : String14;
          LeftPtr : NodePtr;
          RightPtr : NodePtr;
          BegListPtr :ListEltPtr
        end;
  ListElt = record
              LineNo : integer;
              ListPtr : ListEltPtr
            end;
```

Our cross-reference table–generator program will begin by initializing the tree. It will then read one word at a time from the text file. If the word is not already in the tree, the word will be put into the tree along with the line number for the text line where the word was found. If the word is already in the tree, the new line number where the word was found will be added to the end of the linked list of line numbers for that particular word. After all words from the text file have been processed, a procedure will be called to print a cross-reference listing of all words and all the numbers of the lines where each word was found.

In the following pseudocode for the main control module, we will assume that a procedure will be written to get one word at a time from the text file. This procedure will set the global variable **WordFound** to false if no legitimate word was found. Thus, the main control module must check for the value of **WordFound**. As we will see shortly, the procedure to initialize the tree will also assign a boolean value to **WordFound**.

Pseudocode

CrossRefGen Program
Main Control Module

IF not at end of file THEN
    Initialize line number to 1.
    Initialize tree.
    WHILE a word was found and not at end of file
        Get one word from text file.
        IF a word was found THEN
            Put in tree.
        END IF.
    END WHILE.
    Print cross-reference listing of words and line numbers.
END IF.

We will make the following global variable declarations.

```
var
   WordFound : boolean;
   Root : NodePtr;
   OneLineNo : integer;
   OneWord : String14;
   DFile : text;
```

The Pascal code for the main control module follows.

```
{***************************************************************************}
{*                         Main Control Module                           *}
{***************************************************************************}
begin
  reset(DFile);
  if not eof(DFile) then begin
    OneLineNo := 1;
    InitTree(Root);                                    { Initialize the tree }
    while WordFound and (not eof(DFile)) do begin
      GetWord(DFile, OneWord, OneLineNo);      { Get word from text file }
      if WordFound then
        PutInTree(Root, OneWord, OneLineNo)          { Put word into tree }
      { end if }
    end; { while }
    PrintCrossRefListing(Root);                        { Print the cross-
                                                         reference listing }
  end  { if }
end.  { CrossRefGen }
```

The **InitTree** procedure will create the tree root node, get the first word (if there is one) and insert it in the root node, and set **LeftPtr** and **RightPtr** to **nil**. (If a word is found, **WordFound** will be set to true; otherwise, **WordFound** will be set to false.) In addition, the procedure must create the first node of the linked list for this particular word, set the **BegListPtr** to point to this node, insert the number of the line where the word was found into this first node, and set the pointer in this first list node to **nil**. The Pascal code for **InitTree** will be as follows.

```
{***************************************************************************}
{* InitTree - Procedure to initialize the tree.                          *}
{*       var parameters -                                                 *}
{*            RootNode : Tree-root pointer.                               *}
{*       value parameters -                                               *}
{*            None.                                                       *}
{***************************************************************************}
procedure InitTree(var RootNode : NodePtr);
var
  OneListNode : ListEltPtr;                            { One list node }
 begin
  new(RootNode);                                  { Create the root node }
  GetWord(DFile, OneWord, OneLineNo);                   { Get one word }
```

```
   if WordFound then begin
      RootNode^.Word := OneWord;               { Put word into root node }
      RootNode^.LeftPtr := nil;
      RootNode^.RightPtr := nil;
      new(OneListNode);                        { Create a new list node }
      RootNode^.BegListPtr := OneListNode;
      OneListNode^.LineNo  := OneLineNo;          { Put line number
                                                    into list node }

      OneListNode^.ListPtr := nil
   end { if }
end;  { InitTree }
```

Each word is retrieved from the text file by a procedure named **GetWord**. Recall that a legitimate word begins with a letter and includes only letters and digits. A word is terminated with a nonletter/nondigit character or an EOLN marker. The **GetWord** procedure will initialize **WordFound** to false. If a legitimate first character for a word is found, **WordFound** will be set to true. Then the procedure will continue getting word characters until a word terminator is located. The word characters will be put into the variable **PresWord**.

The Pascal coding for **GetWord** is a little tricky because of EOLN markers and the EOF marker.

```
{ **************************************************************** }
{* GetWord - Procedure to get one word from the data file DataF  *}
{*           and return it in the parameter PresWord. If a word is *}
{*           found, the global variable WordFound will be set to  *}
{*           true; otherwise, it will be set to false.            *}
{*       var parameters -                                         *}
{*           DataF : Datafile                                     *}
{*           PresWord : One word read from the data file.         *}
{*           PresLineNo : Line number in file where word is found. *}
{*       value parameters -                                       *}
{*           None.                                                *}
{ **************************************************************** }
procedure GetWord(var DataF : text; var PresWord : String14;
                  var PresLineNo : integer);
var
   GoodCh : boolean;                           { Good character-
                                                 true or false   }
   OneCh : char;                               { One character }
   I : integer;                                      { Index }
begin
   WordFound := false;
   PresWord := '                 ';           { Init. PresWord to blanks }
                        { Search for the first word character }
   while (not WordFound) and (not eof(DataF)) do begin
      if eoln(DataF) then begin
         PresLineNo := PresLineNo + 1;
         readln(DataF)
      end; { if }
      if not eof(DataF) then begin
         read(DataF, OneCh);                    { Read one character }
```

```
        if Onech in ['a'..'z'] then
           WordFound := true
           { end if }
      end { if }
   end;  { while }
  if WordFound then begin
    I := 1;
    PresWord[I] := OneCh;                   { Put first word
                                              character into PresWord }

    repeat
      GoodCh := false;
      if not eoln(DataF) then begin
        read(DataF, OneCh);                 { Get next file character }
        if Onech in ['a'..'z', '0'..'9'] then begin
         GoodCh := true;
         I := I + 1;
         PresWord[I] := OneCh
        end { if }
      end; { if }
    until not GoodCh                         { Until end of word }
  end { if }
end;  { GetWord }
```

Notice that in **GetWord** we must be very careful with EOLN and EOF markers. If **GetWord** reaches an EOLN marker, the procedure increments the line number counter, **PresLineNo**, and jumps to the beginning of the next text file line. You should study the procedure carefully and note the detail. The procedure returns with the global variable **WordFound** set to either true or false depending on whether or not a word was found. The above procedure allows only lower-case letters. Expanding the procedure to include upper-case letters will be left as an exercise.

The **PutInTree** procedure will search the tree for the word and, if the word is already in the tree, the procedure will insert the new line number at the end of the list of line numbers for the word. If the word is not already in the tree, the procedure will create a new node for the word, initialize a list for the line numbers, and insert the number of the line where the word was found into the first element in the list. The tree structure was selected as the data structure for this program because of its faster binary searching capability (as compared to a sequential search in a linked list). Thus, the time required to insert a new word or a new line number for an existing word will be much less than if we had chosen a list structure.

Pseudocode

PutInTree Procedure

Initialize **Found** to false.
Search tree for node containing word.
IF not **Found** THEN
    Create new tree node.
    Patch parent node pointer to point to this node.
    Set **RightPtr** and **LeftPtr** to **nil**.

> Put word in **PresWord** into node.
> Create new list node.
> Set pointer **BegListPtr** to this list node.
> Put word's line number into this list node.
> Set **ListPtr** in this node to **nil**.
> ELSE
> Traverse line number list in word-node linked list to find last item in list.
> Create new list node.
> Change pointer in previous last list node to point to this new last node.
> Insert new line number into this list node.
> Set **ListPtr** in this node to **nil**.
> END IF.

The Pascal code for procedure **PutInTree** follows directly.

```
{**************************************************************************}
{* PutInTree - Procedure to update the tree by inserting a new word      *}
{*             or, if the word already exists, to update the list of     *}
{*             line numbers.                                             *}
{*      var parameters -                                                 *}
{*          None.                                                        *}
{*      value parameters -                                               *}
{*          TreeRoot : Tree-root pointer.                                *}
{*          PresWord : The present word.                                 *}
{*          PresLineNo : Line number for word.                           *}
{**************************************************************************}
procedure PutInTree(TreeRoot : NodePtr; PresWord : String14;
                    PresLineNo : integer);
var
  Found : boolean;                              { Boolean flag }
  OneTreeNode,                                  { One tree node }
  ParNode,                                      { Parent node }
  NewTreeNode : NodePtr;                        { New tree node }
  OneListNode,                                  { One list node }
  NewListNode : ListEltPtr;                     { New list node }
begin
  Found := false;
                { Search tree for node containing the word }
  OneTreeNode := TreeRoot;
  ParNode := nil;
  while (OneTreeNode <> nil) and (not Found) do begin
    if PresWord = OneTreeNode^.Word then
      Found := true
    { end if }
    else begin
      ParNode := OneTreeNode;
      if PresWord < OneTreeNode^.Word then
        OneTreeNode := OneTreeNode^.LeftPtr
      { end if }
```

```
      else
         OneTreeNode := OneTreeNode^.RightPtr
      { end else }
   end  { else }
end;  { while }
if not Found then begin
   new(NewTreeNode);                               { Create new tree node }
   if PresWord < ParNode^.Word then           { Patch parent-node pointer }
      ParNode^.LeftPtr := NewTreeNode
   { end if }
   else
      ParNode^.RightPtr := NewTreeNode;
   { end else }
   NewTreeNode^.LeftPtr := nil;
   NewTreeNode^.RightPtr := nil;
   NewTreeNode^.Word := PresWord;                  { Put word into node }
   new(NewListNode);                             { Create new list node }
   NewTreeNode^.BegListPtr := NewListNode;
   NewListNode^.LineNo := PresLineNo;              { Insert line number }
   NewListNode^.ListPtr := nil
end  { if }
else begin                                            { For old node }
      { Search list of line numbers for last list element }
   OneListNode := OneTreeNode^.BegListPtr;
   while OneListNode^.ListPtr <> nil do
      OneListNode := OneListNode^.ListPtr;
   { end while }
   new(NewListNode);                             { Create new list node }
   OneListNode^.ListPtr := NewListNode;
   NewListNode^.LineNo := PresLineNo;              { Insert line number }
   NewListNode^.ListPtr := nil
end  { else }
end;  { PutInTree }
```

The work involved in traversing the list of line numbers just to find its end could be eliminated if we kept a pointer, **EndListPtr**, which points to the last node of the list of line numbers for each word. This extra pointer would be kept in each node for that particular word. This change will be included in the exercises.

The **PrintCrossRefListing** procedure should not be difficult to write. If we want to print one word per line followed by the numbers of the lines where the word occurs, we will have to decide how many numbers will be printed per line. Suppose we decide on the following print format:

The word in columns 1–14
Blanks in columns 15–20
The first line number in columns 21–28
The second line number in columns 29–36

$$\vdots$$

The seventh line number in columns 69–76

If more than seven line numbers exist, the extras will be printed on the following lines, lined up under the previous line numbers.

In the Pascal coding of the **PrintCrossRefListing** procedure, the recursive inorder traversal procedure, **TravTreeInOrder**, will be called to print the data from the tree. This **TravTreeInOrder** procedure will be the normal inorder tree-traversal procedure plus a section to print the node data. This section will print the word and then up to seven line numbers on the same line. (Recall our output format for the line numbers.) If there are more than seven line numbers, the procedure will jump to the next line to continue printing the line numbers. All of this is a little tricky to code, but it is not difficult.

```
{*******************************************************************}
{* PrintCrossRefListing - Procedure to print the words and the line  *}
{*                      numbers where the words exist in the data     *}
{*                      file.                                         *}
{*      var parameters -                                             *}
{*          None.                                                    *}
{*      value parameters -                                           *}
{*          TreeRoot : Tree-root pointer.                            *}
{*******************************************************************}
procedure PrintCrossRefListing(TreeRoot : NodePtr);
var
  Counter : integer;
  OneListNode : ListEltPtr;                              { One list node }

{*******************************************************************}
{* TravTreeInorder - Procedure to traverse the tree using inorder   *}
{*                 traversal and print the words and line numbers.   *}
{*      var parameters -                                            *}
{*          None.                                                   *}
{*      value parameters -                                          *}
{*          TreeRoot : Tree-root pointer.                           *}
{*******************************************************************}
procedure TravTreeInorder(TreeRoot : NodePtr);
begin
  if TreeRoot <> nil then begin
    TravTreeInorder(TreeRoot^.LeftPtr);                { Left subtree }
    write(TreeRoot^.Word, '      ');                   { Print the word }
    Counter := 0;
    OneListNode := TreeRoot^.BegListPtr;
    while OneListNode <> nil do begin
      if Counter < 7 then begin
        Counter := Counter + 1;
        write(OneListNode^.LineNo : 8);                { Print line number }
        OneListNode := OneListNode^.ListPtr
      end  { if }
      else begin                                       { If Counter = 7 }
        Counter := 0;                                  { Reset Counter to 0 }
        writeln;
        write(' ':20)
```

```
         end { else }
      end; { while }
      writeln;
      TravTreeInorder(TreeRoot^.RightPtr)                { Right subtree }
   end { if }
end;   { TravTreeInorder }

begin { PrintCrossRefListing }
   writeln('CROSS-REFERENCE TABLE LISTING OF WORDS':60);
   writeln;
   writeln;
   TravTreeInorder(TreeRoot)                        { Traverse tree
                                                      and print listing }
end;   { PrintCrossRefListing }
```

The complete listing for the **CrossRefGen** program follows:

```
{**************************************************************************}
{* CrossRefGen - Cross-reference table-generation program to list all *}
{*               words in a data file in alphabetical order and list   *}
{*               the numbers of the lines where each word occurs.      *}
{**************************************************************************}
program CrossRefGen(output, DFile);
const
   MaxWordSize = 14;                                { Maximum word size }
type
   String14 = packed array[1..MaxWordSize] of char;
   NodePtr = ^Node;
   ListEltPtr = ^ListElt;
   Node = record
             Word : String14;
             LeftPtr : NodePtr;
             RightPtr : NodePtr;
             BegListPtr : ListEltPtr
          end;
   ListElt = record
                LineNo : integer;
                ListPtr : ListEltPtr
             end;
var
   WordFound : Boolean;                         { Flag to indicate if
                                                 word is found in the tree }
   Root : NodePtr;                                { Tree-root pointer }
   OneLineNo : integer;                           { One line number }
   OneWord : String14;                              { One word }
   DFile : text;                                   { Data file }

          ****************************************************
          ** Insert GetWord, InitTree, PrintCrossRefListing, **
          ** and PutInTree procedures here.                 **
          ****************************************************

{**************************************************************************}
{*                      Main Control Module                            *}
{**************************************************************************}
```

```
begin
   reset(DFile);
   if not eof(DFile) then begin
      OneLineNo := 1;
      InitTree(Root);                                  { Initialize the tree }
      while WordFound and (not eof(DFile)) do begin
         GetWord(DFile, OneWord, OneLineNo);    { Get word from text file }
         if WordFound then
            PutInTree(Root, OneWord, OneLineNo)      { Put word into tree }
         { end if }
      end; { while }
      PrintCrossRefListing(Root);                       { Print cross-
                                                         reference listing }
   end   { if }
end.  { CrossRefGen }
```

To illustrate the results of the use of this cross-reference generator, the following simple version of the **InitTree** procedure was used as a source file.

```
procedure inittree(var rootnode : nodeptr);
var
   onelistnode : listeltptr;
begin
   new(rootnode);
   getword(dfile, oneword, onelineno);
   if wordfound then begin
      rootnode^.word := oneword;
      rootnode^.leftptr := nil;
      rootnode^.rightptr := nil;
      new(onelistnode);
      rootnode^.beglistptr := onelistnode;
      onelistnode^.lineno  := onelineno;
      onelistnode^.listptr := nil
   end
end;
```

The output from the cross-reference generator was the following.

```
CROSS-REFERENCE TABLE LISTING OF WORDS

begin              4        7
beglistptr        12
dfile              6
end               15       16
getword            6
if                 7
inittree           1
leftptr            9
lineno            13
listeltptr         3
listptr           14
new                5       11
nil                9       10       14
nodeptr            1
onelineno          6       13
```

onelistnode	3	11	12	13	14
oneword	6	8			
procedure	1				
rightptr	10				
rootnode	1	5	8	9	10	12
then	7				
var	1	2			
word	8				
wordfound	7				

It may also be desirable to print the original text file together with a line number in front of each line in the text file before printing the cross-reference listing. This can be done with a **PrintFile** procedure; you will be asked to write this procedure in the exercises.

Exercises

6.22 Modify the **CrossRefGen** program to include upper-case letters and to allow words up to a maximum of 20 characters. Also, add a procedure called **Print-File** to print the original text file along with line numbers before each line. (Print the text file before you print the cross-reference listing.)

6.23 In **CrossRefGen** (as it is presently written) each node contains a pointer to the beginning of the list of line numbers for that particular word. Each time a new line number is added to the list, a traversal of the list from beginning to end is required. This traversal could be eliminated if each node also had a pointer that pointed to the end of its list. Rewrite program **CrossRefGen** so that each node also contains a pointer to the end of its list (of line numbers), and then use this pointer when inserting new line numbers into the list.

6.24 The **CrossRefGen** program will include a line number more than once in the list of line numbers if any word occurs more than once on the same line. Rewrite the program so that a line number will not be repeated regardless of how many times the word occurs on any line.

6.9 Arithmetic Expressions in a Binary Tree

As another interesting example of binary trees, we will examine the storage of arithmetic expressions in a tree. For a simple binary arithmetic operation consisting of a number, an operator, and another number, the operator will be stored in the root and the two numbers will be stored in the left and right immediate successor nodes. For example, 3 ∗ 4 would be stored as shown in Figure 6.22.

For more complicated expressions, we merely expand the tree so that if it is traversed using inorder traversal the result will be the given expression. For example, (3 ∗ 4) + 5 would be stored as shown in Figure 6.23. Notice that the left subtree will be 3 ∗ 4. Thus when we traverse the tree inorder, we will get (3 ∗ 4) + 5.

Figure 6.22

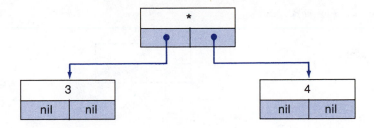

Figure 6.23

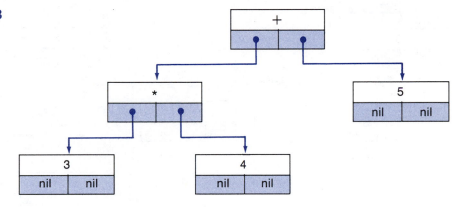

Taking a more complicated example, let us store the expression

$$(3 - (4 - 5)) * (6 + 7)$$

The resulting tree is illustrated in Figure 6.24. Notice that the placement of the parentheses is extremely important in an infix form for an arithmetic expression. For example, if we changed our expression to

$$3 - (4 - 5) * 6 + 7$$

our tree would change dramatically (see Figure 6.25).

Thus, if we traverse a tree inorder and ignore parentheses when we list the node data, the results may or may not be correct. For example, if we traverse the tree in Figure 6.24 and list the node data (ignoring parentheses), we get

$$3 - 4 - 5 * 6 + 7$$

which equals -24. Similarly, if we traverse the tree in Figure 6.25 and list the node data (again ignoring parentheses), we get

$$3 - 4 - 5 * 6 + 7$$

which is again equal to -24. Therefore, it is obvious that if inorder traversal of a tree is used to list the node data, parentheses must be inserted correctly. The required parentheses will be dictated by the structure of the tree.

Figure 6.24

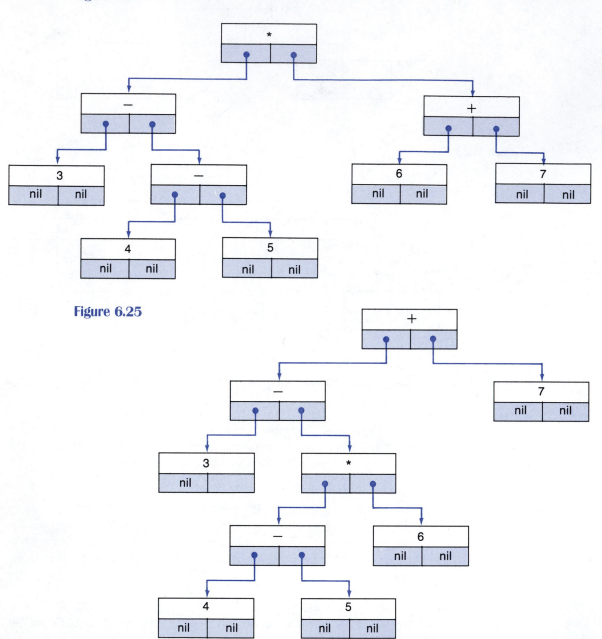

Figure 6.25

Now let us see what happens if we traverse the trees using preorder rather than inorder traversal. For example, for the tree in Figure 6.24 we get

$$* - 3 - 4\ 5 + 6\ 7$$

which equals 52. As you may have noticed, we now have the expression written in prefix form and the result is obviously correct. Similarly, a preorder traversal of the tree in Figure 6.25 gives

$$+ - 3 * - 4\ 5\ 6\ 7$$

which equals 16. This prefix form also gives the correct result, again illustrating the fact that prefix notation does not require parentheses.

Now let us turn our attention to postorder traversal of the tree. Postorder traversal should result in postfix forms for the arithmetic expressions. The tree in Figure 6.24 will result in

$$3\ 4\ 5 - - 6\ 7 + *$$

which equals 52. Similarly, the tree in Figure 6.25 will result in

$$3\ 4\ 5 - 6 * - 7 +$$

which equals 16. Thus postorder traversal leads to correct postfix forms.

Exercises

6.25   For the following tree:

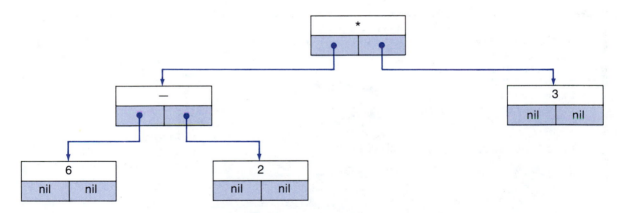

(a) What is the resulting prefix expression if the tree is traversed using preorder traversal?
(b) What is the resulting postfix expression if the tree is traversed using postorder traversal?

6.26   Draw a tree for which inorder traversal will give the following expression in infix form.

$$4 * 3 - 2$$

Explain the problem with using inorder traversal for expressions.

6.27   Draw a tree for which preorder traversal will give the following expression in prefix form.

$$* + 2\ 5 + 3\ 6$$

6.28   Draw a tree for which preorder traversal will give the following expression in prefix form.

$$+ - 2\ 3 * + 7\ 2\ 8$$

6.29   What will be the resulting postfix expression if the tree in Exercise 6.28 is traversed using postorder traversal?

6.10   Message Decoder

Another interesting program to write is one that decodes messages written in a dot (.) and dash (–) code (such as the Morse Code). The program consists of two major parts. The first part reads a file containing the dot-and-dash codes and the character that each code represents and then inserts these data into a tree. The second part reads a source file containing a coded message (in dots and dashes) and decodes it into the characters that the coded message represents.

The Pascal code for the main control module will be as follows.

```
{****************************************************************}
{*                     Main Control Module                     *}
{****************************************************************}
begin
  reset(Codes);
  reset(CodeMes);
  PrintHeading;                           { Print the main heading }
  CrCodeTree(Codes, Root);         { Read the codes and
                                     the corresponding
                                     characters into the tree }
  DecodeMessage(CodeMes, Root);       { Decode and print
                                        the decoded message }
  writeln
end.  { Decode }
```

The **CrCodeTree** procedure will read the codes and their corresponding characters into a tree. Each line of the data file **Codes** will consist of one dot-and-dash code (sequence of dots and dashes), a blank, and the character the code represents.

The major concern will be how to insert the codes into the tree. Basically, all codes beginning with a dot will go into the left subtree, and all codes beginning with a dash will go into the right subtree. If we let the dot-and-dash codes vary in length to allow flexibility in the code, we can structure the tree so that each level of nodes contains codes of a specific length. For example, all nodes in level 2 might contain just single-character (. or –) codes; all nodes in level 3 would then contain all two-character codes (for example, . – or ..);

all nodes in level 4 would contain three-character codes (for example, we might have . – . or – – –); etc. If we follow this scheme, the root node will contain no data.

We will make the following declarations.

```
type
   NodePtr = ^Node;
   Node = record
            Data : char;
            LeftPtr,
            RightPtr : NodePtr
          end;
   Direction = (Left, Right);
var
   Root : NodePtr;                        { Tree-root pointer }
   Codes : text;                  { File of codes and
                                    corresponding characters }
   CodeMes : text;                   { File containing
                                       message to decode }
```

Notice that the only data in any node will be the single character that the dot-and-dash code represents. We do not have to include the dot-and-dash codes in the nodes that correspond to the included character because of the way we are structuring the tree. Thus a tree node for the character C will be just

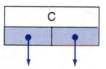

There is no requirement with respect to the order in which the dot-and-dash codes and their equivalent characters are put in the source **Codes** file. For example, this file may appear as follows.

```
.  E
–  T
.. – U
–.–– Y
.–.–.– ?
```
etc.

Assuming our **Codes** file is as above, let us follow the logic involved in inserting these nodes into the tree. Remember, a . means go to the left subtree, and a – means go to the right subtree. First the root node (with no data) is created, and the **LeftPtr** and the **RightPtr** of the root node are set to **nil**. Now the first character is read from the **Codes** file, a dot (.). Thus the left subtree is examined. Since the **LeftPtr** of the root is **nil**, a new node (node B in Figure 6.26) must be created and its pointers set to **nil**. Now the next character from **Codes** is read, and a blank is found. Thus the correct node in the tree has been reached. The next character (E) is read from **Codes** and inserted in node B.

Figure 6.26

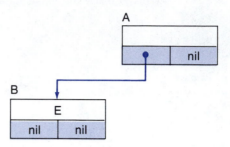

Now the first character (. or –) from data line 2 is read. Since it is a –, the right subtree of the tree is examined. Again, since the **RightPtr** of the root is **nil**, a new node, C, must be created and its pointers set to **nil**. The next data file character is read, and a blank is found. Thus, the correct tree location in which to insert the data character has again been found quickly. The next character (T) is read from **Codes** and inserted in node C. See Figure 6.27.

Figure 6.27

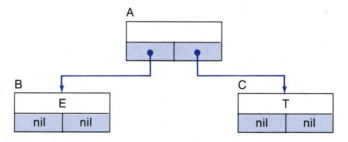

For the code in the third data line, the following steps are taken (see Figure 6.28).

Step 1 Read the first code character (which is a dot).
Step 2 Start down the left subtree (with temporary pointer) and stop at the next level (node B).
Step 3 Read the next code character (which is a dot).
Step 4 Since the **LeftPtr** of B is **nil**, create a new node D and set its pointers to nil.
Step 5 Read the next code character (which is a dash).
Step 6 Since the **RightPtr** of D is **nil**, create a new node E and set its pointers to nil.
Step 7 Read the next code character (which is a blank).
Step 8 Read the next file character (U) and insert this character into node E.

Notice that the process continues down the tree one level per code character. If at any stage a node does not already exist, it is created. If a node already exists the temporary pointer is moved down to this node. The process

Figure 6.28

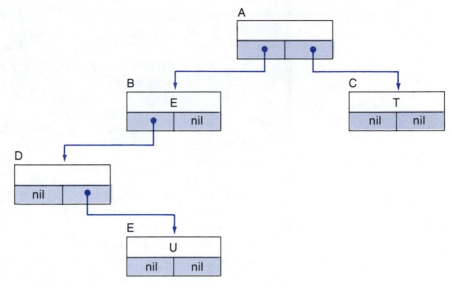

continues until the code string is done. At that point in the tree the one data character is inserted.

As indicated previously, the structuring of the tree in this method fixes the location in the tree of a specific dot-and-dash code sequence. Thus it is not necessary to store the dot-and-dash sequences in the tree nodes. The pseudocode for the **CrCodeTree** procedure follows.

Pseudocode

> **CrCodeTree Procedure**
>
> Create root node.
> Set **LeftPtr** and **RightPtr** to **nil** in root node.
> WHILE not at end of file for file **Codes**
>   Read one character.
>   Initialize Boolean variable **Inserted** to false.
>   Initialize **PresNode** pointer to root.
>   WHILE NOT **Inserted**
>   IF character is a . THEN
>   IF **PresNode^.LeftPtr** <> NIL THEN
>   Set **PresNode** to **PresNode^.LeftPtr**.
>   ELSE
>   Create new node **NewNode** as left child of
>   **PresNode**.
>   Set **PresNode** to **NewNode**.
>   END IF.
>   ELSE
>   IF character is a – THEN

```
                    IF PresNode^.RightPtr <> NIL THEN
                        Set PresNode to PresNode^.RightPtr.
                    ELSE
                        Create new node NewNode as right child of
                            PresNode.
                        Set PresNode to NewNode.
                    END IF.
                ELSE
                    Print bad-code-character message.
                    Abort.
                END IF.
                Read next code character.
                IF character is a blank THEN
                    Read next character.
                    Put character into PresNode.
                    Set Inserted to true.
                    Jump to next line in data file.
                END IF.
            END IF.
        END WHILE.
END WHILE.
```

Study the above pseudocode carefully in order to see how it relates to our previous discussion. If a bad code is found while the tree is being created, a message will be printed and the program will abort. The process to abort will vary according to the programmer's desires and the version of the Pascal compiler being used. In the following Pascal code for the **CrCodeTree** procedure, the abort is included only as a comment. The actual coding for the abort will be assigned in the exercises. The name of the codes data file will be passed to **CrCodeTree** as a **var** parameter. Note that the initialization of the tree is included as part of the **CrCodeTree** procedure. This initialization certainly could be a separate procedure as it was in previous programs.

```
{*****************************************************************}
{* CrCodeTree - Procedure to read the codes and the corresponding  *}
{*              characters into a tree.                            *}
{*        var parameters -                                         *}
{*            DataF : Name of file containing codes.               *}
{*            RootNode : Tree-root pointer.                        *}
{*        value parameters -                                       *}
{*            None.                                                *}
{*****************************************************************}
procedure CrCodeTree(var DataF : text; var RootNode : NodePtr);
var
  NewNode,                                          { New tree node }
  PresNode : NodePtr;                               { Present tree node }
```

```
   Inserted : boolean;                    { Flag to indicate if
                                            code has been inserted }
   Ch : char;                                    { One character }
begin
   new(RootNode);                        { Create the tree root node }
   RootNode^.LeftPtr := nil;
   RootNode^.RightPtr := nil;
   while not eof(DataF) do begin
      read(DataF, Ch);                          { Get one
                                            character from DataF }

      Inserted := false;
      PresNode := RootNode;                      { Set PresNode
                                            to the tree root }

      while not Inserted do begin
         if Ch = '.' then
            if PresNode^.LeftPtr <> nil then
               PresNode := PresNode^.LeftPtr
            { end if }
            else begin
               CrTreeNode(PresNode, Left, NewNode);    { Create new tree
                                            node as left child }

               PresNode := NewNode
            end { else }
         { end if }
         else
            if ch = '-' then
               if PresNode^.RightPtr <> nil then
                  PresNode:=PresNode^.RightPtr
               { end if }
               else begin
                  CrTreeNode(PresNode, Right, NewNode);{ Create new tree
                                            node as right child }

                  PresNode := NewNode
               end { else }
            { end if }
            else begin
               writeln('Bad code');
                     { ABORT }
            end; { else }
         { end else }
         read(DataF, Ch);                      { Read next character }
         if ch = ' ' then begin
            read(DataF, Ch);
            PresNode^.Data := Ch;
            Inserted := true;
            readln(DataF)
         end { if }
      end { while }
   end { while }
end; { CrCodeTree }
```

Notice again that if a bad code character (not . and not –) is found, a message is printed and the program is aborted by some method. For example, if the Microsoft Pascal compiler is used, an **abort** statement can be used. Since the nature of this program abort will depend on the Pascal compiler being used, writing the code is left as an exercise.

Also, note that the program assumes that if EOLN is ignored, the character read at EOLN will be a blank (as is true on some Pascal compilers including the Cyber). This handling of EOLN must be modified for other types of Pascal compilers.

We will need to write procedure **CrTreeNode**, which creates a new tree node. Parameters to this procedure will include the present parent-node pointer, the direction for the new node from the present parent node (left or right), and the pointer to the newly created node. This pointer to the new node will be a **var** parameter so that it will be sent back to the calling procedure.

Pseudocode

> **CrTreeNode Procedure**
>
> Create new node.
> If parent node's pointer direction is left THEN
>   Set parent node's **LeftPtr** to new node.
> ELSE
>   Set parent node's **RightPtr** to new node.
> END IF.
> Set **LeftPtr** and **RightPtr** for new node to NIL.

The Pascal code for procedure **CrTreeNode** follows.

```
{***********************************************************************}
{* CrTreeNode - Procedure to create a new tree node, patch the parent *}
{*              pointer to point to this new node, and set the new     *}
{*              node's LeftPtr and RightPtr values to nil.             *}
{*      var parameters -                                               *}
{*          NewN : New node.                                          *}
{*      value parameters -                                            *}
{*          OldN : Parent node.                                       *}
{*          PtrDir : Direction of pointer from the parent node to     *}
{*                   the new node.                                    *}
{***********************************************************************}
procedure CrTreeNode(OldN : NodePtr; PtrDir : Direction;
                     var NewN : NodePtr);
begin
  new(NewN);                                      { Create new node }
  if PtrDir = Left then
    OldN^.LeftPtr := NewN                { Set parent node's
                                          LeftPtr to the new node }
  { end if }
  else
    OldN^.RightPtr := NewN;              { Set parent node's
                                          RightPtr to the new node }
```

```
  { end else }
  NewN^.LeftPtr := nil;
  NewN^.RightPtr := nil
end; { CrTreeNode }
```

The coding of the **DecodeMessage** procedure is not as difficult as it might seem. This procedure reads a coded message from a data file **CodeMes** that is written in dot-and-dash codes and prints out the decoded message. We will assume that at least one blank will separate each coded character in **CodeMes** (and that the EOLN character is a blank). To be more flexible, we will allow any number of blanks between the individual codes in **CodeMes**. Therefore we will call a procedure called **SkipBlanks** to skip over any blanks.

The basic approach in **DecodeMessage** for each dot-and-dash code will be to go left if a dot is encountered and go right if a dash is found. A blank will indicate that the correct tree node has been found and all that remains to be done is to get the letter from that node and print it.

Pseudocode

> **DecodeMessage Procedure**
>
> Skip over blanks in file **CodeMes** to find first nonblank character.
> WHILE not at end of file **CodeMes**
>   WHILE not decoded
>   IF character is a . THEN
>   Move down to the left in tree.
>   ELSE
>   IF character is a — THEN
>   Move down to the right in tree.
>   ELSE
>   Print bad-code-character message.
>   Abort.
>   END IF.
>   Read next character.
>   IF character is a blank THEN
>   Write out decoded character for code (data from present tree node).
>   END IF.
>   END IF.
>   END WHILE.
>   Skip blanks until first nonblank character is found.
> END WHILE.

Again, notice that the procedure will abort if it finds a character that is not . or – or blank. We are assuming that the EOLN character is read as a blank.

For versions of Pascal in which a blank is not read at EOLN, the EOLN will have to be handled differently.

The corresponding Pascal coding is as follows.

```
{*****************************************************************}
{* DecodeMessage - Procedure to read a message in code from a data   *}
{*                 file, decode the message, and print the decoded   *}
{*                 message.                                           *}
{*       var parameters -                                             *}
{*           DataF : Name of message file.                           *}
{*       value parameters -                                          *}
{*           RootNode : Root-node pointer.                            *}
{*****************************************************************}
procedure DecodeMessage(var DataF : text; RootNode : NodePtr);
var
  Ch : char;                                    { One character }
  ChDecoded : boolean;                      { Flag to indicate if
                                            character is decoded }
  PresNode : NodePtr;                       { Present tree node }
begin
  read(DataF, Ch);                          { Read one character }
  SkipBlanks(DataF, Ch);                    { Skip over any blanks }
  while not eof(DataF) do begin
    ChDecoded := false;
    PresNode := RootNode;
    while not (ChDecoded) do begin
      if Ch = '.' then                      { If character is a dot }
        PresNode := PresNode^.LeftPtr
      { end if }
      else
        if Ch = '-' then                    { If character is a dash }
          PresNode := PresNode^.RightPtr
        { end if }
        else begin
          writeln('Ord of bad character is ', ord(Ch));
          writeln('Bad code in coded file');
          { ABORT }
        end; { else }
      { end else }
      read(DataF, Ch);                      { Get next character }
      if Ch = ' ' then begin
        ChDecoded := true;
        write(PresNode^.Data);              { Print character }
      end { if }
    end { while };
    SkipBlanks(DataF, Ch)                   { Skip blanks }
  end { while }
end; { DecodeMessage }
```

The complete **Decode** program follows.

```
{********************************************************************}
{* Decode - Program that reads dot-and-dash codes and the characters  *}
{*          they represent into a tree. It then decodes messages writ-*}
{*          ten in dots and dashes into the corresponding characters. *}
{********************************************************************}
program Decode(output, Codes, CodeMes);
type
   NodePtr = ^Node;
   Node = record
             Data : char;
             LeftPtr,
             RightPtr : NodePtr
          end;
   Direction = (Left, Right);
var
   Root : NodePtr;                           { Tree-root pointer }
   Codes : text;                         { File of codes and their
                                          corresponding characters }
   CodeMes : text;                            { File containing
                                               a coded message }


                    { Forward procedure declarations }
procedure CrCodeTree(var DataF : text; var RootNode : NodePtr);
                     forward;
procedure CrTreeNode(OldN : NodePtr; PtrDir : Direction;
                     var NewN : NodePtr); forward;
procedure DecodeMessage(var DataF : text; RootNode : NodePtr); forward;
procedure PrintHeading; forward;
procedure SkipBlanks(var DataF : text; var Ch : char); forward;
                    { End of forward procedure declarations }

                 **********************************************
                 **   Insert CrCodeTree, CrTreeNode, and   **
                 **   DecodeMessage procedures here.        **
                 **********************************************


{********************************************************************}
{* PrintHeading - Procedure to print the main heading.              *}
{********************************************************************}
procedure PrintHeading;
begin
   writeln;
   writeln('Decode program':47);
   writeln;
   writeln
end;  { PrintHeading }


{********************************************************************}
{* SkipBlanks - Procedure to skip over blanks until a nonblank      *}
{*              character is found or until eof is reached. The non- *}
{*              blank character is returned in parameter Ch.         *}
{*       var parameters -                                            *}
{*             DataF : Data file.                                    *}
{*             Ch : Nonblank character read.                         *}
```

```
{*        value parameters -                                          *}
{*            None.                                                   *}
{*********************************************************************}
procedure SkipBlanks;
begin
  while (Ch = ' ') and (not eof(DataF)) do
    read(DataF, Ch)
  { end while }
end;  { SkipBlanks }


{*********************************************************************}
{*                      Main Control Module                          *}
{*********************************************************************}
begin
  reset(Codes);
  reset(CodeMes);
  PrintHeading;                                { Print the main heading }
  CrCodeTree(Codes, Root);                  { Read the codes and
                                              the corresponding
                                              characters into the tree }
  DecodeMessage(CodeMes, Root);             { Decode and print
                                                 the decoded message }
  writeln
end.  { Decode }
```

As written, this version of the program ignores the length of the output decoded message. Thus if it is longer than one line in length, there will be a problem. The correction of this problem is left as an exercise.

Exercises

6.30   Alter program **Decode** so that the output can be any number of lines.

6.31   Complete the code for the abort in procedure **CrCodeTree** so that the program will terminate if a bad code is found in the codes file.

6.32   Complete the code for the abort in procedure **DeCodeMessage** so that the program will terminate if a bad code is found in the message file.

6.33   Modify procedure **CrCodeTree** so that it checks for lines with identical codes in the codes file. If a code is found that is identical to an earlier code, the program should terminate.

6.34   Modify program **Decode** so that if a code in the message file was not included in the codes file, the program terminates.

6.11   Using Trees Without Using the Pascal Pointer Type

Many languages do not allow the Pascal pointer type and the record data type that we have been using in our examples with trees. However, this does not mean that a programmer cannot use tree structures with these languages.

Let us take a look at how the inventory-tree program **InvSort** in Section 6.5 could be written in Pascal without using the pointer and record types. First of all, we will use parallel arrays to hold our data and pointers. We call the arrays parallel because corresponding items will be held in different arrays at the same index locations (see Figure 6.29).

Figure 6.29

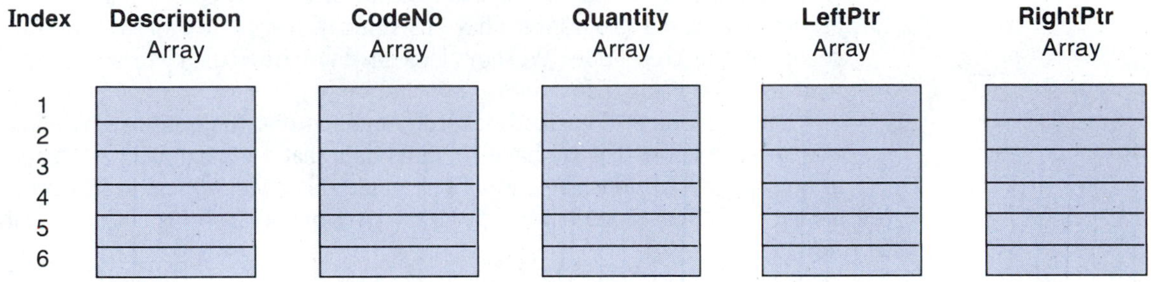

Index	Description Array	CodeNo Array	Quantity Array	LeftPtr Array	RightPtr Array
1					
2					
3					
4					
5					
6					

For example, if the tree node is stored using index value 1, the description will be in the **Description** array at **Description**[1], the code number will be in **CodeNo**[1], the left pointer will be in **LeftPtr**[1], and the right pointer will be in **RightPtr**[1].

The pointers stored in the **LeftPtr** and **RightPtr** arrays will actually be array indices. That is, a pointer will point to the specific index in the parallel arrays where the next node's values are stored. Thus our pointers will be integer values. Since arrays are static structures, we must declare the size of the arrays. This is certainly a disadvantage of using arrays rather than dynamic pointer types.

A major concern in creating a tree is how to get the next available array index as we are creating the tree and inserting new nodes. To handle this problem, we will begin our program by initializing a new array, **Avail-Indices**, that, in essence, will be nothing but a list of available indices. Assuming that the maximum number of elements in each of our arrays is 100, we will initialize the array as pictured in Figure 6.30. This initialization can be accomplished quite easily by the following code.

```
for I := 1 to 99 do
   AvailIndices[I] := I + 1;
{ end for }
AvailIndices[100] := 0;
```

Figure 6.30

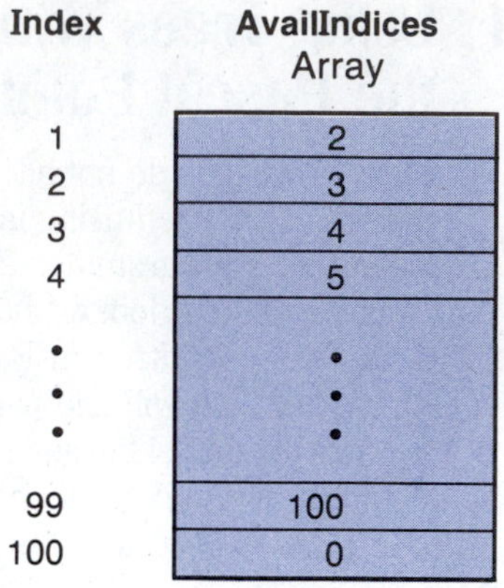

Index	AvailIndices Array
1	2
2	3
3	4
4	5
•	•
•	•
•	•
99	100
100	0

We put a 0 in the last element to indicate that no more are available. Now, assume that in our program we have used array index 1 to store our first data record in the tree node. We now look in **AvailIndices**[1] to see that the next available array index will be 2.

When we look at **AvailIndices**[100] and find that the next available index is 0, we will know that we have so much data that we have filled all locations in our arrays. We must be careful to include this check in our programming.

Let us begin our rewrite of program **InvSort** with the required declarations.

```
const
  MaxElts = 100;                               { Max. num. of elements }
type
  String16 = packed array[1..16] of char;
  String12 = packed array[1..12] of char;
var
  Root : integer;                              { Tree-root index }
  Description : array[1..MaxElts] of String16;   { Description
                                                    array }
  CodeNo : array[1..MaxElts] of String12;      { Code-number array }
  Quantity : array[1..MaxElts] of integer;     { Quantity array }
  LeftPtr,                                      { Left pointer }
  RightPtr,                                     { Right pointer }
  AvailIndices : array[1..MaxElts] of integer;  { Available-
                                                  indices array }
  OneDesc : String16;                          { One description }
  OneCodeNo : String12;                        { One code number }
  OneQuant,                                     { One quantity }
  PresIndex : integer;                         { The present
                                                  index being used }
  TooMuchData : Boolean;                       { Flag to indicate
                                                 if out of array space }
  DFile : text;                                { Data file }
```

The new main control module will be similar to that in program **InvSort** except for some of the parameters and the use of the Boolean flag **TooMuchData**. This flag will be set to true if we run out of array space.

```
{*****************************************************************}
{*                      Main Control Module                     *}
{*****************************************************************}
begin
  TooMuchData := false;
  PrintHeadings;                                { Print main heading }
  reset(DFile);
  if not eof(DFile) then begin
    InitTree(Root);                             { Initialize the tree }
    while (not eof(DFile)) and (not TooMuchData) do begin
      ReadRec(OneDesc, OneCodeNo, OneQuant);       { Read one record }
      InsertInTree(Root, OneDesc, OneCodeNo, OneQuant)    { Insert
                                                            into tree }
    end; { while }
    if not TooMuchData then
      TravInorder(Root);                           { Traverse tree
                                                      and print data }
    { end if }
  end   { if }
end.   { InvSort2 }
```

The **InitTree** procedure will be different in this implementation in that we will first initialize the **AvailIndices** array and initialize the global variable **PresIndex** to 1. Then we will create the root node.

Pseudocode

> **InitTree Procedure**
>
> FOR I = 1 TO **MaxElts** − 1
>   **AvailIndices**[I] = I + 1.
> END FOR.
> Set **AvailIndices[MaxElts]** to 0.
> Initialize **PresIndex** to 1.
> Set root to **PresIndex**.
> Read one record of data from data file.
> Put data in respective arrays in root node.
> Set root node **LeftPtr** and **RightPtr** to 0.

The Pascal coding of **InitTree** is quite straightforward.

```
{*****************************************************************}
{* InitTree - Procedure to initialize the tree:                 *}
{*            1. Initialize the AvailIndices array.             *}
{*            2. Initialize PresIndex to 1.                     *}
{*            3. Initialize Root to 1.                          *}
{*            4. Read the first data record.                    *}
{*            5. Insert data into the root node.                *}
{*            6. Set the root pointers to 0.                    *}
{*      var parameters -                                        *}
{*          TreeRoot : The tree root (Index)                   *}
{*      value parameters -                                      *}
{*          None.                                               *}
{*****************************************************************}
```

```
procedure InitTree(var TreeRoot : integer);
var
  I : integer;                                          { Index }
begin
  for I := 1 to MaxElts - 1 do
    AvailIndices[I] := I + 1;
  { end for }
  AvailIndices[MaxElts] := 0;
  PresIndex := 1;
  TreeRoot := PresIndex;
  ReadRec(DFile, OneDesc, OneCodeNo, OneQuant); { Read one data record }
  Description[1] := OneDesc;                    { Put data into arrays }
  CodeNo[1] := OneCodeNo;
  Quantity[1] := OneQuant;
  LeftPtr[1] := 0;
  RightPtr[1] := 0
end;   { InitTree }
```

We will add to our inventory program a new subroutine called **GetNext-Index**, which will get the value of the next available index (for global variable **PresIndex**) and set the value of **TooMuchData** to true if no more indices are available.

Pseudocode

> **GetNextIndex Procedure**
>
> Get next available index.
> IF no more indices are available THEN
>   Set **TooMuchData** to true.
>   Print message "NO MORE SPACE LEFT."
> END IF.

Again, the Pascal code is quite simple.

```
{*******************************************************************}
{* GetNextIndex - Procedure to get the next available index into the *}
{*                variable PresIndex. If no more indices are          *}
{*                available, print a message and set TooMuchData to   *}
{*                true.                                               *}
{*******************************************************************}
procedure GetNextIndex;
begin
  PresIndex := AvailIndices[PresIndex];         { Get next available index }
  if PresIndex = 0 then begin                   { If no more
                                                  indices are available }

    TooMuchData := true;
    writeln('No more space left!!!!!')
  end { if }
end;   { GetNextIndex }
```

The Pascal coding for procedure **InsertInTree** will be similar to program **InvSort** except for the creation of the node and the check for **TooMuch-**

Data. Note carefully how data are inserted into the node. Remember that a pointer to any node is now an array index. For example,

```
OneNode^.LeftPtr := nil
```

will now become

```
LeftPtr[OneNode] := 0
```

The Pascal coding for the **InsertInTree** follows.

```
{***************************************************************}
{* InsertInTree - Procedure to insert one data record into the tree.  *}
{*               Data will be inserted so that inorder traversal       *}
{*               will result in the data being sorted in ascending     *}
{*               order according to the code number.                   *}
{*      var parameters -                                               *}
{*          None.                                                      *}
{*      value parameters -                                             *}
{*          TreeRoot : Tree-root index.                                *}
{*          NewDesc : Description to be inserted.                      *}
{*          NewCodeNo : Code number to be inserted.                    *}
{*          NewQuant : Quantity to be inserted.                        *}
{***************************************************************}
procedure InsertInTree(TreeRoot : integer; NewDesc : String16;
                   NewCodeNo : String12; NewQuant : integer);
var
   Inserted : boolean;                   { Flag to indicate when
                                           data have been inserted }

   OneNode,                              { One tree node }
   NewNode : integer;                    { New tree node }
begin
   GetNextIndex;                                 { Get the next
                                                   available index }

   if not TooMuchData then begin
      NewNode := PresIndex;
      Inserted := false;
      OneNode := TreeRoot;
                          { Insert new node }
      while not Inserted do begin
        if NewCodeNo < CodeNo[OneNode] then
          if LeftPtr[OneNode] <> 0 then
            OneNode := LeftPtr[OneNode]
          { end if }
        else begin
          LeftPtr[OneNode] := NewNode;
          Inserted := true;
        end { else }
        { end if }
        else
          if RightPtr[OneNode] <> 0 then
            OneNode := RightPtr[OneNode]
          { end if }
```

```
        else begin
          RightPtr[OneNode] := NewNode;
          Inserted := true
        end { else }
      { end else }
    end; { while }
                     { Insert data record into NewNode }
    Description[NewNode] := OneDesc;
    CodeNo[NewNode] := OneCodeNo;
    Quantity[NewNode] := OneQuant;
    LeftPtr[NewNode] := 0;
    RightPtr[NewNode] := 0
  end { if }
end; { InsertInTree }
```

Now let us take a look at the Pascal coding for the **TravInorder** procedure. Remember that this procedure traverses the tree and prints the data inorder. The changes to Program **InvSort** will be minor. The only parameter is **TreeNode**. When **TravInorder** is called from the main program, the tree-root index will be sent as the value for **TreeNode**.

```
{****************************************************************}
{* TravInorder - Procedure to traverse the tree using inorder  *}
{*               traversal and print the data.                 *}
{*      var parameters -                                       *}
{*          None.                                              *}
{*      value parameters -                                     *}
{*          TreeNode : Tree node index.                        *}
{****************************************************************}
procedure TravInorder(TreeRoot : integer);
begin
  if TreeRoot <> 0 then begin
    TravInorder(LeftPtr[TreeRoot]);                { Left subtree }
    PrintRec(Description[TreeRoot], CodeNo[TreeRoot],
             Quantity[TreeRoot]);                  { Print the node data }
    TravInorder(RightPtr[TreeRoot])                { Right subtree }
  end { if }
end; { TravInorder }
```

Again, only minor changes need to be made in the **ReadRec** and **Print-Rec** procedures in program **InvSort** from Section 6.5, and no changes are required for procedure **PrintHeadings**. The complete **InvSort2** program is rewritten as follows.

```
{****************************************************************}
{* InvSort2 - Program to use a tree to sort an inventory file  *}
{*            according to code numbers and print the data. Pascal *}
{*            pointer and record types will not be used.       *}
{*      data file format -                                     *}
{*          Columns  1 - 16  Description (Character string)    *}
{*                  17 - 28  Code number (Character string)    *}
{*                  29 - 33  Quantity    (Integer)             *}
```

```
{*      output print format -                                    *}
{*         Columns 11 - 22  Code number  (Character string)      *}
{*                 36 - 51  Description  (Character string)       *}
{*                 65 - 69  Quantity     (Integer)                *}
{***************************************************************}
program InvSort2(output, DFile);
const
  MaxElts = 100;                          { Max. num. of elements }
type
  String16 = packed array[1..16] of char;
  String12 = packed array[1..12] of char;
var
  Root : integer;                          { Tree-root index }
  Description : array[1..MaxElts] of String16;  { Description array }
  CodeNo : array[1..MaxElts] of String12;  { Code number array }
  Quantity : array[1..MaxElts] of integer;  { Quantity array }
  LeftPtr,                                  { Left pointer }
  RightPtr,                                 { Right pointer }
  AvailIndices : array[1..MaxElts] of integer;  { Available
                                                  indices array }
  OneDesc : String16;                       { One description }
  OneCodeNo : String12;                     { One code number }
  OneQuant,                                 { One quantity }
  PresIndex : integer;                      { The present
                                              index being used }

  TooMuchData : boolean;                    { Flag to indicate
                                              if out of array space }

  DFile : text;                             { Data file }

                { Forward procedure declarations }
procedure ReadRec(var DataF : text; var OneDesc : String16;
               var OneCodeNo : String12;
               var OneQuant : integer); forward;
            { End of forward procedure declarations }


            ****************************************
            **  Insert GetNextIndex, InitTree, and  **
            **  InsertInTree procedures here.       **
            ****************************************

{***************************************************************}
{* PrintHeadings - Procedure to print a main heading and column  *}
{*                 headings.                                      *}
{***************************************************************}
procedure PrintHeadings;
begin
  writeln('INVENTORY FOR ABC COMPANY':52);
  writeln('Code No.':20, 'Description':28, 'Quant.':23);
  writeln;
  writeln
end; { PrintHeadings }
```

```
{*****************************************************************}
{* PrintRec - Procedure to print one line of data.            *}
{*      var parameters -                                        *}
{*           None.                                              *}
{*      value parameters -                                      *}
{*           OneDesc : Description.                             *}
{*           OneCodeNo : Code number.                          *}
{*           OneQuant : Quantity.                              *}
{*****************************************************************}
procedure PrintRec(OneDesc : String16; OneCodeNo : String12;
                   OneQuant : integer);
begin
   writeln(OneCodeNo:22, ' ':13, OneDesc:16, OneQuant:18)
end; { PrintRec }


{*****************************************************************}
{* ReadRec - Procedure to read one data record from the data file. *}
{*      var parameters -                                        *}
{*           DataF : Data file.                                 *}
{*           OneDesc : Description.                             *}
{*           OneCodeNo : Code number.                          *}
{*           OneQuant : Quantity.                              *}
{*      value parameters -                                      *}
{*           None.                                              *}
{*****************************************************************}
procedure ReadRec;
var
   I : integer;
begin
   for I := 1 to 16 do
      read(DataF, OneDesc[I]);
   { end for }
   for I := 1 to 12 do
      read(DataF, OneCodeNo[I]);
   { end for }
   readln(DataF, OneQuant)
end; { Readrec }


            *****************************************
            ** Insert TravInorder procedure here **
            *****************************************


{*****************************************************************}
{*                   Main Control Module                        *}
{*****************************************************************}
begin
   TooMuchData := false;                        { Initialize
                                                  TooMuchData to false }
   PrintHeadings;                               { Print main headings }
   reset(DFile);
   if not eof(DFile) then begin
      InitTree(Root);                           { Initialize the tree }
      while (not eof(DFile)) and (not TooMuchData) do begin
         ReadRec(DFile, OneDesc, OneCodeNo, OneQuant);  { Read one record }
```

```
      InsertInTree(Root, OneDesc, OneCodeNo, OneQuant)        { Insert
                                                                into tree }
   end;  { while }
   if not TooMuchData then
      TravInorder(Root);                                    { Traverse tree
                                                              and print data }
     { end if }
  end   { if }
 end.  { InvSort2 }
```

To get a better understanding of exactly how the program works, let us
see how the following first three lines of data from an inventory file would be
inserted into the tree using arrays.

19″ TV	342-236-1234	10
15″ TV	123-472-3122	5
25″ TV	476-435-7892	12

When the program executes, the **InitTree** procedure will create the root
node by inserting the first line of data into the respective arrays with an index
of 1 (**PresIndex**). **LeftPtr**[1] and **RightPtr**[1] will both be set to 0.

Index	Description Array	CodeNo Array	Quantity Array	LeftPtr Array	RightPtr Array
1	19″ TV	342-236-1234	10	0	0

The second line of data is now read by **ReadRec**. Then the **InsertInTree**
procedure calls the **GetNextIndex** procedure to get the next available index
from **AvailIndices**[1]. The value is 2, and it is assigned to **PresIndex**.
InsertInTree now finds that the code number in the second data line is
smaller than the code number in the root. Thus the second line of data should
be put into the left subtree of the root. Therefore, the root's **LeftPtr**[1] is
assigned the value of 2 (**PresIndex**). The second line of data is put into the
respective arrays at index 2, and **LeftPtr**[2] and **RightPtr**[2] are set to 0.

Index	Description Array	CodeNo Array	Quantity Array	LeftPtr Array	RightPtr Array
1	19″ TV	342-236-1234	10	2	0
2	15″ TV	123-472-3122	5	0	0

The program is now ready to get the third line of data. After the line is
read by **ReadRec**, the **InsertInTree** procedure calls **GetNextIndex** to find
the new **PresIndex** value. The value is found in **AvailIndices**[2] to be 3.
InsertInTree then finds that the code number in the third line of data is

larger than the code number in the root. Thus the third line of data should be placed in the right subtree of the root. Therefore, the **RightPtr**[1] value is now set to 3. The data from line 3 is put into the respective arrays at index 3 (**PresIndex**), and **LeftPtr**[3] and **RightPtr**[3] are set to 0.

Index	Description Array	CodeNo Array	Quantity Array	LeftPtr Array	RightPtr Array
1	19" TV	342-236-1234	10	2	3
2	15" TV	123-472-3122	5	0	0
3	25" TV	476-435-7892	12	0	0

In the exercises, you will be asked to make up at least three more lines of data and discuss how these lines would be inserted into the tree.

How difficult is it to delete a tree node in an application program if we cannot use Pascal pointer types? Assuming that the **AvailIndices** array has been created as in this last inventory example, deleting a node is not very hard to do. After deletion, the index of the deleted node is returned to the **AvailIndices** list of indices. If the index of the deleted node is called **DelNode**, the following two steps can be followed (see Figure 6.31).

Figure 6.31

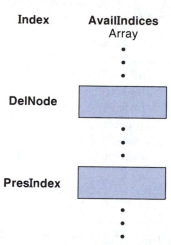

Index   AvailIndices
         Array

DelNode

PresIndex

1. Put the value of **AvailIndices**[**PresIndex**] into **AvailIndices** [**DelNode**].
2. Put the value of **DelNode** into **AvailIndices**[**PresIndex**].

Note that what is being done is merely inserting **DelNode** as the next available index. For example, assume that **NextIndex** is 77, **Avail-Indices**[77] is 78, and **DelNode** is 3 (see Figure 6.32). The next index to be used will be 3; then, the next will be 78.

Figure 6.32

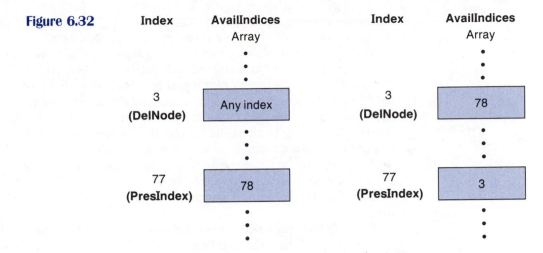

The above discussion illustrates possibilities for programming trees without the Pascal pointer and record types; the fact that a language does not allow these types does not prohibit the use of tree structures. However, a major disadvantage to this approach is the requirement that array sizes be predeclared, which may result in wasted memory space. Also, programming is obviously more complicated when the Pascal record types cannot be used.

Exercises

6.35 Make up at least three additional lines of inventory data and explain how these would be inserted into the inventory sort tree by **InvSort2**.

6.36 Rewrite the program in Exercise 6.14 using arrays instead of the Pascal pointer type. Do use the Pascal record type.

6.37 Rewrite the program in Exercise 6.36 without using the Pascal record type.

6.38 Rewrite the program in Exercise 6.16 using arrays instead of the Pascal pointer type. Do use the Pascal record type.

6.39 Rewrite the program in Exercise 6.38 without using the Pascal record type.

Summary

In this chapter the tree data structure was introduced and developed. This very powerful structure can be used for a wide variety of programming applications.

The most commonly used tree structure is the binary tree, in which a parent node may point to zero, one, or two children. A binary tree can be used efficiently to hold data that is sorted in some specified order. This structure, which is commonly called a binary search tree, can be traversed to print out the sorted data or can be easily searched for a specified item.

In addition to procedures for creating and searching trees, we investigated various procedures for inserting and deleting nodes. As a typical application we developed a program to create and process a tree that held inventory data. We also developed a cross-reference table generator that printed a listing of all words in a file and the numbers of the lines where the words occurred. Another quite interesting application investigated was the use of a binary tree to decode messages written in a dot-and-dash code.

At some time you will probably have to use a language that does not allow the use of dynamic pointers or record types. Therefore the last section in the chapter discussed the development of binary trees without these valuable tools.

Although this chapter has covered many aspects of the tree, much more can be done with the tree structure. In Chapter 7 we will continue our discussion of trees and investigate other potential uses for this powerful data structure.

Chapter Exercises

6.40 For what type(s) of data structuring applications is the tree a better choice than a linked list? Why is it a better choice?

6.41 What will happen in a tree structure if the data read into the tree are already sorted? Can this problem be solved?

6.42 Assume that we wish to create a small data base in which we use a tree structure to hold and process inventory data. Write a program that prints a sign-on message and then prints a menu with the following choices.
(a) Print the menu
(b) Create an inventory data base (all data input from the console)
(c) Create an inventory data base (all data input from a data file)
(d) Write all inventory data to a file (sorted by inventory number)
(e) Print all inventory data (sorted)
(f) Search for an inventory item (by inventory number)
(g) Insert a new inventory item
(h) Delete an inventory item (given the inventory number)
(i) Exit
Each inventory data record will include the following.

Inventory number	(7 characters)
Description	(20 characters)
Quantity on hand	(integer)
Reorder quantity	(integer)
Cost of item	(real)
Selling price	(real)

Write all procedures that allow the above choices. The user should be allowed to continue making selections and having them executed until choice (i) is selected.

6.43 Add the following choices to the program in Exercise 6.42.
(i) Modify any field in a given inventory item
(j) Print all inventory items for which the quantity on hand is less than the reorder quantity
(k) Exit

CHAPTER 7

More Trees

Trees are such a valuable data structure that we will continue in Chapter 7 to develop the concepts and applications introduced in Chapter 6.

Since binary-tree traversal is used in about every application involving binary trees, we will investigate the possibility of improving the recursive traversal procedures we wrote in Chapter 6 by rewriting these procedures using nonrecursive code. We will also investigate what are called *threaded trees* in which normally worthless **nil** pointers are replaced with very helpful pointers that point back up to ancestor nodes.

Since the efficiency of the basic binary-tree operations of search, insertion, traversal, and deletion depend heavily on the balance of the tree, we will develop procedures to guarantee that the tree is relatively balanced. We will also rewrite the insertion procedure so that during creation the tree will remain relatively balanced regardless of the order of the data inserted. This will solve the problems involved in creating a tree with data that are already in order or in reverse order. Recall from Chapter 6 that using sorted data will otherwise result in a horribly unbalanced tree and highly inefficient tree operations. We will also revise the node-deletion procedure from Chapter 6 so that after any node is deleted, the tree will retain its relative balance.

In addition, we will take a look at nonbinary trees in which any node may contain more than two pointers. Finally, we will develop procedures for a type of tree called a *B-tree*. This type of nonbinary tree has relatively strict growth requirements that make it quite useful for the paging of data and, especially, the paging of keys for external files.

7.1 Nonrecursive Binary-Tree Traversal

In Chapter 6 we wrote inorder, preorder, and postorder traversal routines as recursive procedures. Since these routines are an important part of programs involving binary trees, we should investigate the possibility of rewriting them using nonrecursive code. By using a nonrecursive approach we may be able to improve the speed and/or memory requirements of these routines. This approach will also provide the understanding necessary to write these routines using a nonrecursive language such as FORTRAN.

Let us first look back at the coding for the recursive procedure to traverse a tree using inorder traversal.

```
{*******************************************************************}
{* TravInorder - Recursive procedure to traverse a tree using inorder *}
{*               traversal and print the integer numbers stored as    *}
{*               data in the tree nodes. Each tree node contains one   *}
{*               integer number.                                       *}
{*      var parameters -                                               *}
{*          None.                                                      *}
{*      value parameters -                                             *}
{*          TreeNode : Tree-node pointer (initially sent as the        *}
{*                     root).                                          *}
{*******************************************************************}
procedure TravInorder(TreeNode : NodePtr);
begin
  if TreeNode <> nil then begin
    TravInorder(TreeNode^.LeftPtr);          { Left subtree }
    writeln(TreeNode^.Data);                 { Print node data }
    TravInorder(TreeNode^.RightPtr)          { Right subtree }
  end { if }
end; { TravInorder }
```

At this point, be sure to review the discussion in Chapter 6 on how this procedure works. Also, recall that a recursive call such as the

```
TravInorder(TreeNode^.LeftPtr)
```

statement saves the parameter **TreeNode^.LeftPtr** on a stack. Thus when the procedure starts backing through the previous recursive calls, the node pointers can be retrieved and used. Remember that when a left **nil** pointer is reached, the statement

```
writeln(TreeNode^.Data)
```

will print the data for the last node encountered. The procedure then looks at the right subtree for this node with the statement

```
TravInorder(TreeNode^.RightPtr)
```

After processing the right subtree for the node, the procedure backs up to the previous parent node, prints its data, and then processes its right subtree.

The same results can be accomplished if the pointers to the nodes are pushed onto a stack and then retrieved as needed. For example, for the tree in Figure 7.1, a variable **Ptr** to the tree root (A) is initialized. Then *while* **Ptr** is not **nil**, the left subtree is descended and the pointers to each of the nodes are pushed onto a stack until a **nil** pointer is reached (the **nil** pointer is not pushed onto the stack). Thus the process so far is

1. Push the pointer to A onto the stack.
2. Push the pointer to B onto the stack.
3. Reach the left **nil** pointer in node B.

Figure 7.1

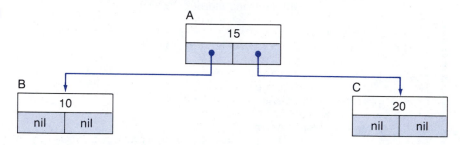

Now the pointer to B is popped from the stack and the data from node B are printed. Next, the right pointer in node B is examined and found to be **nil**. Since B has no right subtree, the pointer to A is popped from the stack and the data from node A are printed. The next step is to look at the right pointer in A. Since it is not **nil** and points to node C, this pointer (to C) is pushed onto the stack. Then the left pointer in C is examined. Since it is **nil**, there is no left subtree. Thus the pointer to C is popped and the data from C are printed. Finally, since the right pointer in C is **nil**, the process is done.

Following this example, we should now be able to write the pseudocode for a nonrecursive inorder traversal procedure, which we will call **NonRecInorderTraversal**.

Pseudocode

NonRecInorderTraversal Procedure

Initialize stack.
Set local variable **Ptr** to tree root.
REPEAT
    WHILE **Ptr** is not **nil**
        Push value for **Ptr** onto stack.
        Set **Ptr** to left pointer of **Ptr**.
    END WHILE.
    IF stack is not empty THEN
        Pop value for **Ptr** from stack.
        Print data from node pointed to by **Ptr**.
        Set **Ptr** to right pointer of **Ptr**.
    END IF.
UNTIL (stack is empty) and (**Ptr** is **nil**).

Notice that the procedure will be finished only when the stack is empty and the last **Ptr** value is **nil**. The Pascal code follows directly from the pseudocode. Assume that for an application program the data item in each node is a record consisting of a name, a social security number, and an address.

```
{*******************************************************************}
{* NonRecInorderTraversal - Nonrecursive procedure to traverse a   *}
{*                          binary tree using inorder traversal and *}
{*                          print the data from each node.          *}
{*        var parameters -                                          *}
{*            None.                                                 *}
{*        value parameters -                                        *}
{*            TreeRoot : Pointer to the tree root.                  *}
{*******************************************************************}
procedure NonRecInorderTraversal(TreeRoot : NodePtr);
var
  Ptr : NodePtr;                              { Tree-node pointer }
  StTop : StackPtr;                             { Stack pointer }
  Empty : boolean;                            { Stack empty flag }
begin
  InitStack(StTop, Empty);                   { Initialize the stack }
  Ptr := TreeRoot;
  repeat
    while Ptr <> nil do begin
      PushStack(Ptr, StTop, Empty);          { Push the value
                                               for Ptr onto the stack }
      Ptr := Ptr^.LeftPtr
    end;  { while }
    if not Empty then begin
      PopStack(Ptr, StTop, Empty);           { Pop the value for
                                               Ptr from the stack }
                                             { Print node data }
      with Ptr^.Data do
        writeln(Name, SocSecNo:20, Address:50);
      { end with }
      Ptr := Ptr^.RightPtr
    end  { if }
  until (Empty) and (Ptr = nil)
end;  { NonRecInorderTraversal }
```

We could improve the execution speed and memory requirements for the above procedure by entering the codes for procedures **InitStack**, **Push-Stack**, and **PopStack** directly into the procedure instead of calling them as separate procedures. This will be left as an exercise.

The coding of nonrecursive procedures to do preorder and postorder traversals is extremely similar to that for the inorder traversal. The development of these traversal procedures will be included in the exercises.

It should be obvious that the nonrecursive traversal procedures can be used in any tree application program in place of the normal recursive procedures. For example, with a simple modification to procedure **Non-RecInorderTraversal** it could replace the **InorderTraversal** procedure in the **InventorySort** program in Section 6.4. This simple modification is to the **writeln** statement, which must be changed so that the data output is an inventory record. You will be asked to do this in the exercises.

Exercises

7.1 Create an array of 50 randomly generated integer numbers. Create a binary tree by inserting each of these integer numbers into the tree such that if the tree is traversed using inorder traversal, the integers will be sorted in ascending order. Rewrite procedure **NonRecInorderTraversal** to traverse this tree and print out the data. Try the program to make sure it works. Then increase the number of elements in the array to 2500. Remove the **writeln** statement from **NonRecInorderTraversal**, insert statements to print the system clock before and after **NonRecInorderTraversal** is called, and run the program to create and traverse the tree. You can now determine the traversal time for procedure **NonRecInorderTraversal**.

7.2 Repeat the determination of the traversal time for the 2500-element tree in Exercise 7.1 using the recursive **TravInorder** procedure instead of **NonRecInorderTraversal**. Compare the times.

7.3 Rewrite **NonRecInorderTraversal** so that the codes for the procedures **InitStack**, **PushStack**, and **PopStack** are entered directly rather than called as separate procedures. Again, determine the traversal time for the 2500-element tree. Compare this time with those found in Exercise 7.1 and Exercise 7.2.

7.4 Write the nonrecursive procedure to traverse a binary tree using preorder traversal. Create any small tree (in which each node contains one integer number) and call this procedure to print the data using preorder traversal.

7.5 Write the nonrecursive procedure to traverse a binary tree using postorder traversal. As in Exercise 7.4, create any small tree (in which each node contains one integer number) and call this procedure to print the data using postorder traversal.

7.6 Rewrite program **InvSort** in Section 6.6 so that it calls procedure **NonRecInorderTraversal** instead of procedure **TravInorder**. Make the required modification to procedure **NonRecInorderTraversal** as discussed in this section.

7.7 Rewrite the **CrossRefGen** program in Section 6.8 using a nonrecursive traversal procedure rather than a recursive procedure.

7.2 Threaded Trees

Both our recursive and our nonrecursive procedures for binary-tree traversal have required that pointers to all of the tree nodes be kept temporarily on a stack. It is possible to write binary-tree–traversal procedures that do not re-

Figure 7.2

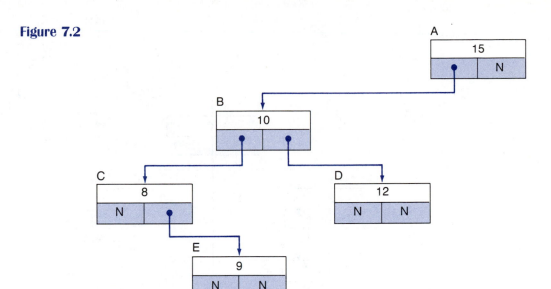

quire that any pointers to the nodes be put on a stack. Such procedures eliminate the overhead (time and memory) involved in initializing, pushing, and popping with stacks.

In order to get an idea of how such binary-tree–traversal procedures work, let us look at the tree in Figure 7.2. (Note that N stands for **nil** pointer.) First we follow the left pointers until we reach node C, without, however, pushing the pointers to A, B, and C onto a stack. For inorder traversal the data for node C are then printed, after which C's right pointer is followed to node E. Then the data from node E are printed.

The next step in our inorder traversal is to go back to node B and print its data; however, we did not save any pointers. But suppose that when we created the tree we had replaced the **nil** right pointer in node E with a pointer back to node B. We could then easily follow this pointer back to node B (see Figure 7.3).

Similarly, suppose we replace the normal **nil** right pointer of D with a pointer back up to A, as in Figure 7.4. Then after printing the data in D, we can easily jump up to A and print its data.

These pointers back up to previous nodes are called *right threads*. Each right thread replaces a normal right pointer in a tree node. The only problem with threads is that the coding requires that we know whether a right pointer is a normal right pointer to a child or a right thread that points back to a prior ancestor node. One solution to this problem is to add to the data in each tree node another field that indicates whether the right pointer in that node is a normal right pointer or a right thread. For example, this field might be a Boolean variable, **Thread**, that is true if the right pointer is a thread and false if it is a normal right pointer. See Figure 7.5 for two additional binary trees in which right threads have been inserted.

Figure 7.3

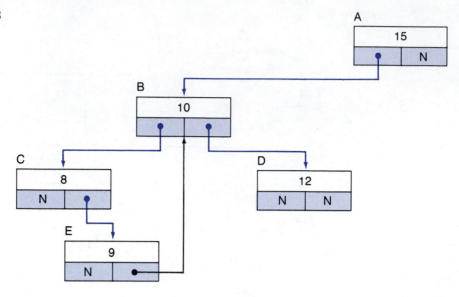

Figure 7.4

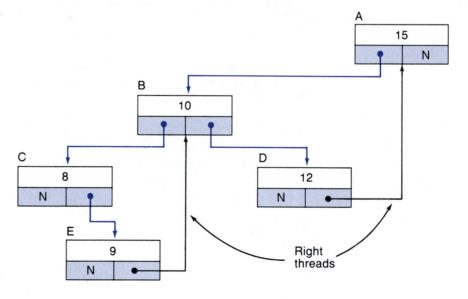

Figure 7.5   *Binary trees with right threads inserted.*

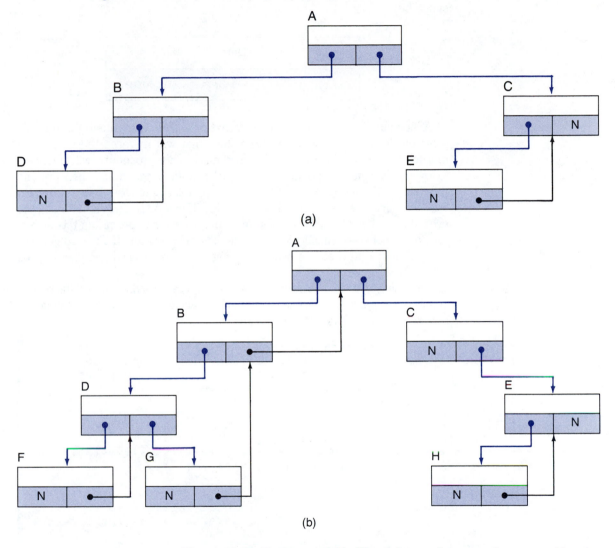

(a)

(b)

If we add the Boolean variable **Thread** to each tree node, we would make the following **type** declaration for **TreeNode**.

```
type
  TreeNode = record
               Data : DataType;
               LeftPtr : NodePtr;
               Thread : boolean
               RightPtr : NodePtr
             end;
```

Thus each node would contain data, a left pointer, a true or false value for **Thread**, and a right pointer (see Figure 7.6). It should be noted that on many computers a Boolean variable requires very little memory (in many cases, a single bit).

Figure 7.6

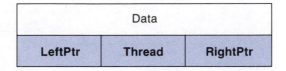

Assuming that we have already created a tree with the right threads inserted, let us investigate the procedure that will traverse the tree using inorder traversal and print all the tree data. This procedure will begin by following the leftmost pointers until a **nil** pointer is found and then printing the data for the leftmost node. Next, the procedure gets the right pointer for this node and checks the Boolean value for **Thread**. If **Thread** is true, the procedure follows the thread back up to the ancestor node, prints this ancestor node's data, and then looks at this node's right pointer. If **Thread** is false, the procedure proceeds as usual by going to the right child and checking its left subtree.

Assuming that each tree node for our application contains a data record consisting of a name, social security number, and address, the Pascal code for procedure **ThreadInorderTraversal** is as follows.

```
{ *************************************************************** }
{ * ThreadInorderTraversal - Procedure to traverse a right-threaded  * }
{ *                          tree using inorder traversal and print  * }
{ *                          the data for each node.                 * }
{ *      var parameters -                                            * }
{ *          None.                                                   * }
{ *      value parameters -                                          * }
{ *          TreeRoot : Pointer to the tree root.                    * }
{ *************************************************************** }
procedure ThreadInorderTraversal(TreeRoot : NodePtr);
var
  Ptr : NodePtr;
  RightThread : boolean;                      { Local variable to
                                                save the value for Thread }
begin
  Ptr := TreeRoot;
  while Ptr^.LeftPtr <> nil do
    Ptr := Ptr^.LeftPtr;
  { end while }
  while Ptr <> nil do begin
    with Ptr^.Data do                         { Print the node data }
      writeln(Name, SocSecNo:20, Address:50);
    { end with }
    RightThread := Ptr^.Thread;               { Save the value for Thread }
    Ptr := Ptr^.RightPtr;
    if (Ptr <> nil) and (not RightThread) then
      while Ptr^.LeftPtr <> nil do
        Ptr := Ptr^.LeftPtr;
```

```
      { end while }
   { end if }
 end { while }
end;   { ThreadInorderTraversal }
```

Now let us consider the process required to create a tree that will include the right threads. As in Chapter 6, the tree can be created by using an insert procedure to insert one node after the other until all the data have been put into the tree. We will write a new procedure, **InsertWithRightThreads**, that will insert one new node into the tree so that if inorder traversal is used, the data will be sorted in ascending order according to some key.

However, before we attempt to write the procedure, let us walk through a process we could use to create the five-element tree in Figure 7.2. We begin by creating the root, inserting the first data record into this root, setting the left and right pointers of the root to **nil**, and setting **Thread** to false. As in Chapter 6, we can do all this in an **InitTree** procedure. In Figure 7.7 we have abbreviated false to F and **nil** to N.

The next value, 10, will be inserted into the left subtree. As usual, a new node (B) is created, the data are inserted into this node, the left pointer in the root is set to point to this node, and the left pointer in the node is set to **nil**. However, since we will need to get back up to the root during inorder traversal, the right pointer in the new node will be set to point back up to the root. Finally, **Thread** (in this new node) will be set to true (abbreviated as T). See Figure 7.8.

If 8 is the next value to be inserted, a new node (C) is created, 8 is inserted into this node, the left pointer in B is set to point to the new node, and the left pointer in C is set to **nil**. Now, as with node B, the right pointer in C is set to point back up to B and **Thread** (in C) is set to true (see Figure 7.9).

To insert 12 into the tree, a new node (D) is created, 12 is inserted into this node, and the left pointer in D is set to **nil**. The right pointer, however, presents a problem. During inorder traversal, after printing the data in D, we

Figure 7.7

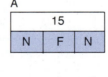

Figure 7.8

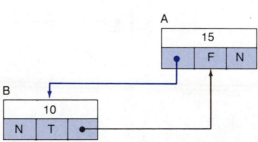

need to go back to the root. However, the pointer to the root has already been saved in B as its right pointer. Therefore the right pointer in D can be set to the right pointer in B and the value of **Thread** in D can be set to true. Finally, the right pointer in B will be set to point to D and the value of **Thread** in B will be set to false (see Figure 7.10).

Insertion of the last value 9 into node E will follow the same process as was followed for the insertion of node D. See Figure 7.11.

Insertion of nodes into the right subtree would follow the same pattern as above. A walk-through of the insertion of right subtree nodes for this example will be assigned as an exercise.

Figure 7.9

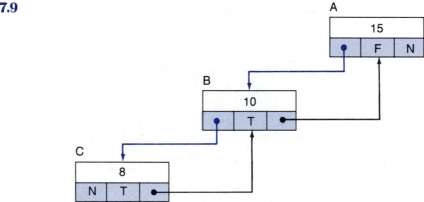

Figure 7.10

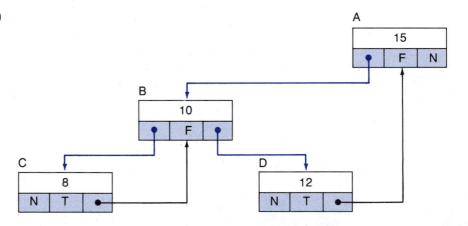

Figure 7.11

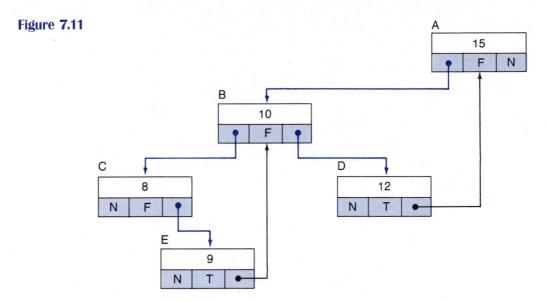

With the above example as a guide, writing the Pascal coding for procedure **InsertWithRightThreads** is not difficult. As with the **Thread-InOrderProcedure**, assume that for our application program, each tree node contains a data record consisting of a name, social security number, and address.

```
{**********************************************************************}
{* InsertWithRightThreads - Procedure to insert one data record node *}
{*                          into a tree so that if inorder traversal *}
{*                          is used, the data will be sorted in      *}
{*                          ascending order according to the social  *}
{*                          security numbers. Right threads are in-  *}
{*                          serted.                                  *}
{*     var parameters -                                              *}
{*          None.                                                    *}
{*     value parameters -                                            *}
{*          TreeRoot : Pointer to the root.                          *}
{*          NewRecord : New data record to be inserted.              *}
{**********************************************************************}
procedure InsertWithRightThreads(TreeRoot : NodePtr;
                                 NewRecord : DataType);
var
  Inserted : boolean;                      { Flag to indicate when the
                                           new node has
                                           been inserted into the tree }
  OneNode,                                        { Tree-node pointer }
  NewNode : NodePtr;                              { New-node pointer }
begin
  new(NewNode);                            { Create a new tree node }
  NewNode^.Data := NewRecord;
  NewNode^.LeftPtr := nil;
  Inserted := false;
```

```
      OneNode := TreeRoot;
      while not Inserted do begin
        if NewRecord.SocSecNo <= OneNode^.Data.SocSecNo then
          if OneNode^.LeftPtr <> nil then
            OneNode := OneNode^.LeftPtr
          { end if }
          else begin
            OneNode^.LeftPtr := NewNode;
            NewNode^.RightPtr := OneNode;
            NewNode^.Thread := true;
            Inserted := true
          end  { else }
        { end if }
        else
          if (OneNode^.RightPtr <> nil) and (not OneNode^.Thread) then
            OneNode := OneNode^.RightPtr
          { end if }
          else begin
            NewNode^.RightPtr := OneNode^.RightPtr;
            OneNode^.RightPtr := NewNode;
            OneNode^.Thread := false;
            NewNode^.Thread := true;
            Inserted := true
          end  { else }
        { end else }
      end  { while }
    end;  { InsertWithRightThreads }
```

As an application, we will now write a complete program to read employee records and insert them into a tree using procedure **InsertWithRightThreads** so that the social security numbers will be in ascending order if the tree is traversed using the **ThreadInorderTraversal** procedure.

```
{***********************************************************************}
{* PersonnelSort - Program to use a threaded tree to sort a personnel *}
{*                 file in ascending order according to social        *}
{*                 security numbers and then print all the data.      *}
{*       data file format -                                           *}
{*             Name                - Columns 1 - 20                    *}
{*             Social Security No. -         21 - 31                   *}
{*             Address             -         32 - 78                   *}
{*       output print format -                                        *}
{*             Social Security No. - Columns 1 - 11                    *}
{*             Name                -         25 - 44                   *}
{*             Address             -         58 - 114                  *}
{***********************************************************************}
program PersonnelSort(output,DFile);
type
   String20 = packed array [1..20] of char;
   String11 = packed array [1..11] of char;
   String47 = packed array [1..47] of char;
   DataType = record
```

```
                      Name : String20;
                      SocSecNo : String11;
                      Address : String47
                end;
  NodePtr = ^TreeNode;
  TreeNode = record
                Data : DataType;
                LeftPtr : NodePtr;
                RightPtr : NodePtr;
                Thread : boolean;
             end;
var
  Root : NodePtr;                          { Tree-root pointer }
  OneRec : DataType;                  { One complete data record }
  DFile : text;                              { Data file }
                  { Forward procedure declarations }
procedure ReadRec(var DataF : text; var DataRec : DataType); forward;
                { End of forward procedure declarations }

{***************************************************************}
{* InitTree - Procedure to initialize the tree. The root node is    *}
{*            created and the first data record is inserted into the *}
{*            root node.                                             *}
{*     var parameters -                                              *}
{*            TreeRoot : Pointer to the root node.                   *}
{*     value parameters -                                            *}
{*            None.                                                  *}
{***************************************************************}
procedure InitTree(var TreeRoot : NodePtr);
begin
  new(TreeRoot);                           { Create the root node }
  ReadRec(DFile,OneRec);                   { Read one data record }
  TreeRoot^.Data := OneRec;                  { Insert data
                                            record into root }
  TreeRoot^.LeftPtr := nil;
  TreeRoot^.RightPtr := nil
end;   { InitTree }

          ***************************************************
          * Insert InsertWithRightThreads procedure here. *
          ***************************************************

{***************************************************************}
{* ReadRec - Procedure to read one data record from a data file    *}
{*           according to the following format:                    *}
{*              Name              - Columns 1 - 20                  *}
{*              Social Security No. -     21 - 31                   *}
{*              Address           -       32 - 78                   *}
{*     var parameters -                                            *}
{*           DataF : Data file.                                    *}
{*           DataRec : One complete data record.                   *}
{*     value parameters -                                          *}
{*           None.                                                 *}
{***************************************************************}
```

```
procedure ReadRec;
var
  I : integer;                                          { Index }
begin
  with DataRec do begin
    for I := 1 to 20 do
      read(DataF,Name[I]);
    { end for }
    for I := 1 to 11 do
      read(DataF,SocSecNo[I]);
    { end for }
    for I := 1 to 47 do
      read(DataF,Address[I])
    { end for }
  end;  { with }
  readln(DataF)
end;  { ReadRec }

          *****************************************************
          * Insert ThreadInorderTraversal procedure here. *
          *****************************************************

{***************************************************************************}
{*                         Main Control Module                           *}
{***************************************************************************}
begin
  reset(DFile);
  if not eof(DFile) then begin
    InitTree(Root);                               { Initialize the tree }
    while not eof(DFile) do begin
      ReadRec(DFile,OneRec);                      { Read one data record }
      InsertWithRightThreads(Root,OneRec)     { Insert record into tree }
    end;  { while }
    ThreadInorderTraversal(Root)                     { Traverse tree
                                                   and print the data }
  end  { if }
end.  { PersonnelSort }
```

This is not the only application for which threaded trees can be used. Any binary-tree application that involves the insertion of data into a tree and then uses inorder traversal to traverse the tree can use the threaded tree procedures we have developed in this section. The use of these threaded tree procedures in other applications will be included in the exercises.

Inorder traversal is certainly used much more than either preorder or postorder traversal. However, since the preorder traversal procedure is surprisingly easy to write for a right-threaded tree, we will investigate its coding.

We begin a preorder traversal of the five-element tree in Figure 7.10 by printing the root data, printing the data for node B, and printing the data for node C. Since node C has no left child, the data for its right child, E, are then printed. Finally, we go to node D and print its data. But how do we get to node D? Remember that the right thread of E will take us back to node B. We can then use the right pointer of B to get to D. Thus the preorder-traversal process is not difficult if we use the right thread to get back to the appropriate ancestor node and then use the right pointer for that node to get to the right subtree (if it has a right subtree).

The pseudocode for procedure **ThreadPreorderTraversal** (which will do preorder traversal of a tree with right threads) follows.

Pseudocode

```
ThreadPreorderTraversal Procedure

Set local variable Ptr to tree root.
WHILE Ptr is not nil
    Print data in node pointed to by Ptr.
    IF left pointer in Ptr is not nil THEN
        Set Ptr to left pointer of Ptr.
    ELSE
        IF (right pointer in Ptr is not nil) and (Thread is not
            true) THEN
            Set Ptr to right pointer of Ptr.
        ELSE
            WHILE Thread in Ptr is true
                Set Ptr to right pointer of Ptr.
            END WHILE.
            Set Ptr to right pointer of Ptr.
        END IF.
    END IF.
END WHILE.
```

Notice that the

```
WHILE Thread in Ptr is true
    Set Ptr to right pointer of Ptr.
END WHILE.
```

loop follows the right threads back up to a node in which the right pointer is not a thread. The next statement,

```
Set Ptr to right pointer of Ptr.
```

then moves us to the right subtree so that its data can be printed.

The Pascal coding of procedure **ThreadPreorderTraversal** follows easily from the pseudocode and will be covered in the exercises. The coding of a procedure to do postorder traversal of a tree with right threads is also possible. However, it is more involved than that of either the inorder or the preorder traversal.

Instead of inserting right threads in a tree, we could insert left threads that point back up to ancestor nodes. However, left threads do not help us nearly as much as do right threads. For example, in inorder traversal, right threads are the perfect choice. When the traversal of any left subtree is complete (indicated when the last right pointer is normally **nil**), all we have to do is follow the right thread (which replaced the normally **nil** right pointer) back up to the parent node (for this left subtree).

It is also possible to include both left and right threads in a tree. The most common technique, however, is to use only the right threads, as emphasized in this section. Remember that threading eliminates the necessity for saving the pointers to ancestor nodes by either using recursion or pushing onto a stack. This certainly saves stack space. However, in our procedures we included a new variable, **Thread**, for each tree node. Thus the tree itself will take slightly more memory space.

Suppose that instead of using the Pascal pointer type and the dynamic allocation of nodes, we used a normal array to hold our tree. We could then get by without introducing the new variable thread for each node. Remember from Chapter 6 that tree-node pointers for trees stored in an array are nothing more than array indices. Since array indices are just integer numbers, we could indicate that a pointer is a thread merely by entering the negative value for the index. Thus if a pointer (array index) is negative, it represents a thread; otherwise it represents a normal pointer (array index). This strategy eliminates the need to use the Boolean variable **Thread** to indicate whether a pointer is a normal pointer or a thread.

As an example of the second way to handle threads, consider the tree in Figure 7.12 in which the pointers are array indices. Notice that the array index for each node is printed above the node. **Nil** pointers are indicated with a 0 index value, and right threads are entered as negative indices.

Figure 7.12

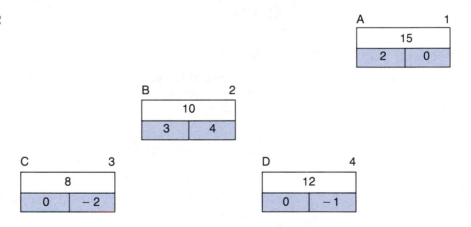

Exercises

7.8 Make up 6 employee records containing random social security numbers. Walk through the **InsertWithRightThreads** Pascal code to insert the data and right threads. (Assume that the first record will be put into the root using an initialization procedure.)

7.9   Write a program assuming that each data record is an inventory-item record consisting of a description, code number, and quantity as described at the beginning of Section 6.5. Insert records into the tree so that when the tree is traversed using inorder traversal, the code numbers will be sorted in ascending order.

7.10   Rewrite procedures **InsertWithRightThreads** and **ThreadInorderTraversal** to handle data records that consist of just one integer number. Create a file of 500 randomly generated integer numbers. Then write a program to do the following.

    (a) Initialize a tree by creating the tree root and then inserting the first integer number into the root.

    (b) Read each of the remaining integer numbers from the data file and insert them into the tree using procedure **InsertWithRightThreads**.

    (c) Call procedure **ThreadInorderTraversal** to print the sorted numbers.

7.11   In the program you created in Exercise 7.10 insert statements to print the system clock before and after the traversal, once the tree has been created. Also, remove the **writeln** statements from the **ThreadInorderTraversal** procedure so that I/O time is not included in the traversal. Record the traversal time.

7.12   Repeat Exercise 7.11 using the normal insertion and inorder traversal procedures (from Chapter 6). Compare the traversal time with that found in Exercise 7.11.

7.13   Walk through the pseudocode for procedure **ThreadPreorderTraversal** to traverse the tree in Figure 7.10.

7.14   Write the Pascal code for procedure **ThreadPreorderTraversal** assuming that each data record consists of a single integer number. Create a data file consisting of the integer numbers 1, 2, 3, ... , 20. Rerun Exercise 7.10 using preorder traversal. Make sure your results are correct for preorder traversal.

7.15   Rewrite procedure **ThreadPreorderTraversal** to handle data records consisting of employee records. Then redo Exercise 7.8 using preorder traversal. Make sure your output is correct.

7.16   Rewrite procedures **InsertWithRightThreads** and **ThreadInorderTraversal** using arrays to hold the tree (rather than using the dynamic Pascal pointers) and inserting right threads as negative indices (as discussed in the text). Assume the data file consists of 500 randomly generated integer numbers. Repeat Exercise 7.10 using your new procedures.

7.17   Write the pseudocode and the Pascal code for a procedure **ThreadPostOrderTraversal** that will use postorder traversal to print the data from a tree created with right threads. Using the data file from Exercise 7.10, redo Exercise 7.10 using your new procedure to traverse the tree.

7.3 Balanced and AVL Trees

In Chapter 6 we discussed the creation of binary trees by inserting data items in such a way that if inorder traversal is used, then the data will be printed in sorted order. Later insertion into these trees could be done by the same insertion process used during creation. We also discussed how we could search for and/or delete specified data from the trees.

These insertion, deletion, search, and traversal processes are quite efficient for trees that are relatively balanced. (Review the definition for a balanced tree in Chapter 6.) However, the more unbalanced the tree, the less efficient the insertion, deletion, and search processes will be. For example, the tree in Figure 7.13 is nothing more than a linked list. Thus the binary nature of the tree is lost, and the insertion, deletion, and search processes are no better than for a linked list. In fact, they are less efficient than linked-list processes because they must deal with the left **nil** pointers. This type of tree will arise when a tree is created from an already sorted file. Assuming that we have a file such as

$$2 \quad 3 \quad 4 \quad 5 \quad 6 \quad 7 \quad 8 \quad 9$$

for which the normal tree-creation process would result in a highly unbalanced tree, is it possible to vary the tree-creation process so that the tree is balanced? The answer is "yes" — if we ease the degree of balance required. Let us define an *AVL (Adelson, Velsky, and Landis) tree* as a tree in which the difference in the heights of the right and left subtrees for each tree node is not greater than 1. Thus for any node the heights of the subtrees may be the same, the height of the right subtree may be at most 1 more than the height of the left subtree, or the height of the left subtree may be at most 1 more than the height of the right subtree. Examples of AVL trees are shown in Figure 7.14; Figure 7.15 shows some non-AVL trees.

Figure 7.13

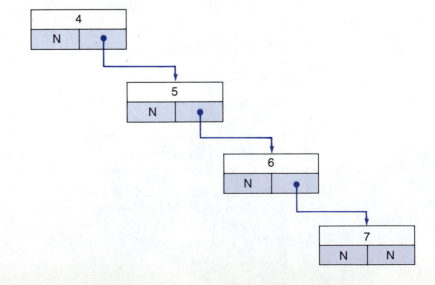

Figure 7.14 *Examples of AVL trees.*

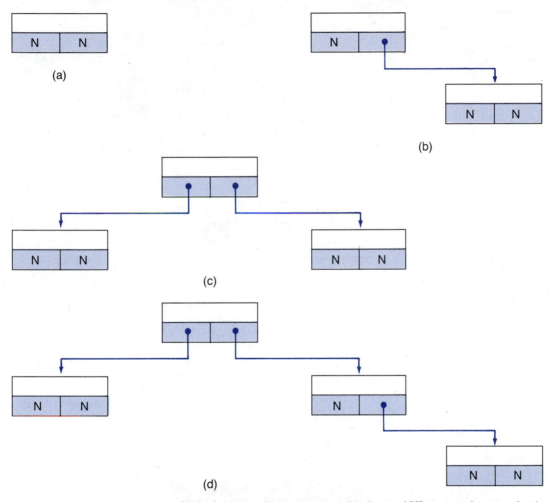

If during creation we can maintain an AVL tree, the standard tree processes of insertion, deletion, search, and traversal will be more efficient. In order to maintain this balance, we need to introduce a new variable field into each tree node. This new variable, which we will call **BalVal** (short for *balance value*), will specify the balance for that particular node. For each node,

BalVal = height of right subtree − height of left subtree

In order to include the value for **BalVal** in each node, we will make the following **type** declaration:

```
type
   TreeNode = record
                 Data : DataType;
                 LeftPtr : NodePtr;
                 BalVal : integer;
                 RightPtr : NodePtr
              end;
```

(a)

(b)

Thus each node will be of the form shown in Figure 7.16.

Since the height of the right subtree and the height of the left subtree of the tree in Figure 7.17 are both 1, the value of **BalVal** for root A is 0. Since the heights of the right and left subtrees for nodes B and C are both 0, the value of **BalVal** for both B and C is 0.

For the non-AVL tree in Figure 7.18

BalVal for node A = right subtree height − left subtree height
$$= 3 - 0 = 3$$
BalVal for node B = 0 − 2 = −2
BalVal for node C = 0 − 1 = −1

If the value of **BalVal** is −1, the node is *left-heavy*; if the value for **BalVal** is 1, the node is *right-heavy*; and if the value for **BalVal** is 0, the node is balanced. If the value for **BalVal** is greater than 1, the node is *out of balance on the right*; if the value for **BalVal** is less than −1, the node is *out of balance on the left*.

Figure 7.16

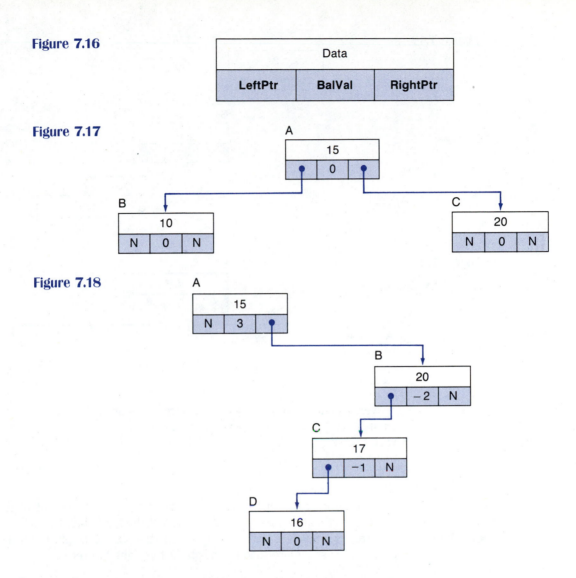

Figure 7.17

Figure 7.18

To get an idea of what we can do during tree creation to maintain an AVL tree, let us consider the file

$$2 \quad 3 \quad 4 \quad 5 \quad 6 \quad 7 \quad 8$$

Suppose that we insert 2 into the root node and insert 3 and 4 into the right subtree as usual except that we will insert the value for **BalVal** into each node (see Figure 7.19).

Obviously the tree is out of balance on the right, since the value for **BalVal** in the root is greater than 1. We can restore balance by rotating the tree to the left. Just think of rotating the tree 45 degrees to the left so that B becomes the new root (see Figure 7.20). The tree has now been transformed into an AVL tree. Similarly, if both B and C had been placed in the left subtree, we could have rotated the tree to the right.

Figure 7.19

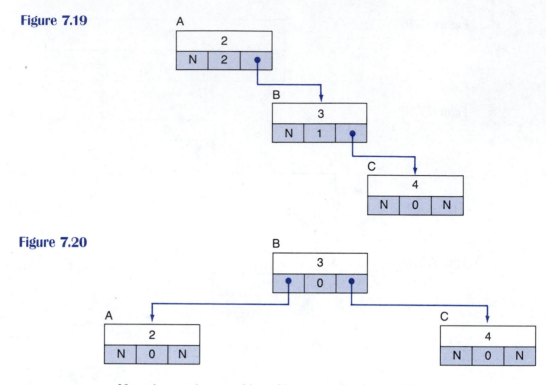

Figure 7.20

Now that we have an idea of how to maintain an AVL tree, let us formally examine all possible cases and what we can do for each case. Suppose we wish to insert a new node into an AVL tree. The insertion will produce one of three possible results:

Case 1   The tree is still an AVL tree.
Case 2   The tree is now out of balance on the right (that is, the height of the right subtree is at least 2 more than the height of the left subtree).
Case 3   The tree is now out of balance on the left (that is, the height of the left subtree is at least 2 more than the height of the right subtree).

For case 1 there is no problem, and we do not have to make any adjustments. However, for case 2 and case 3, we want to adjust the tree so that it returns to being an AVL tree.

Let us consider case 2 in detail. Suppose that the original tree (before the insertion of the new node) was the tree in Figure 7.21. If we insert the number 4 into the tree, we have the non-AVL tree in Figure 7.22. The tree is clearly out of balance on the right. As we discussed earlier, to correct this unbalance we rotate the tree to the left so that E is the new root (see Figure 7.23).

Figure 7.21

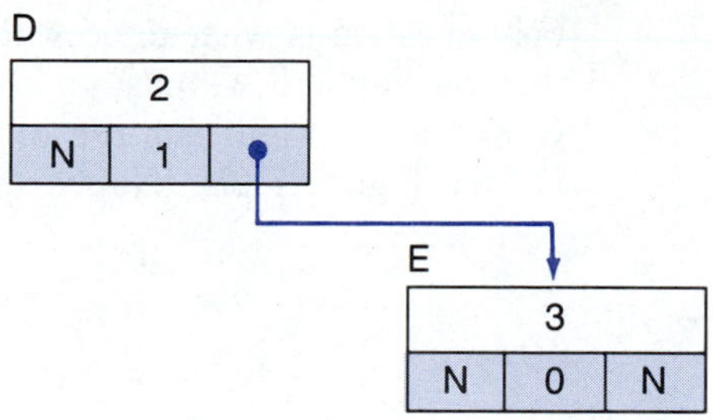

D
	2	
N	1	●

E
	3	
N	0	N

Figure 7.22

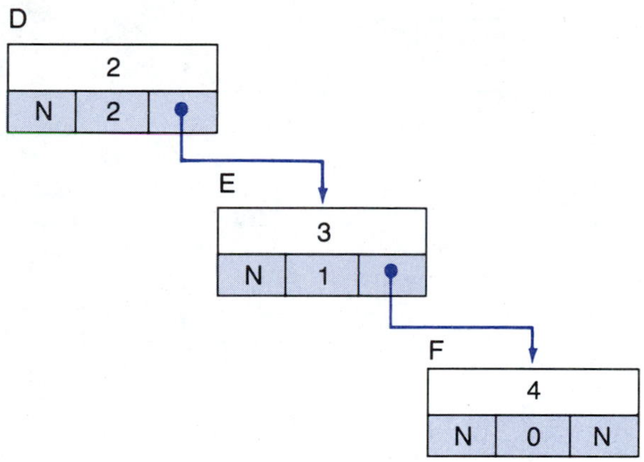

D
	2	
N	2	●

E
	3	
N	1	●

F
	4	
N	0	N

Figure 7.23

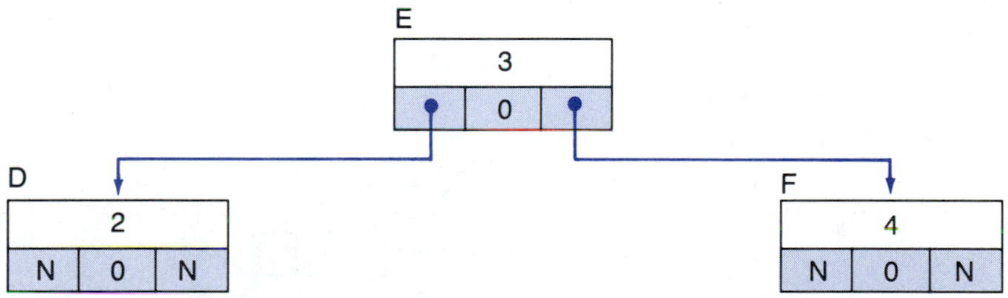

E
	3	
●	0	●

D
	2	
N	0	N

F
	4	
N	0	N

We will call this type of adjustment case A (of case 2). For case A,

1. **BalVal** in the root was 1 before the insertion of the new node and is 2 after the insertion.
2. **BalVal** in the root of the right subtree was 0 before the insertion and is 1 after the insertion.

The tree we used above for case A is extremely simple. However, the left rotation will still work for a more complex tree that satisfies conditions 1 and 2 above. Consider the tree in Figure 7.24 (after node I has been inserted). This tree satisfies condition 1 because **BalVal** in the root was 1 before the insertion of node I and is 2 after. It satisfies condition 2 because **BalVal** in F was 0 before the insertion and is 1 after. As before, we will rotate the tree to the left so that F becomes the new root and D moves to the left subtree. The only question is what to do with node G. Since the data key in G is smaller than the key in F, G must go into the left subtree of F. Since before insertion G was in the right subtree of D, it should remain in the right subtree of D (see Figure 7.25). Notice that the tree has now been adjusted into an AVL tree.

Figure 7.24

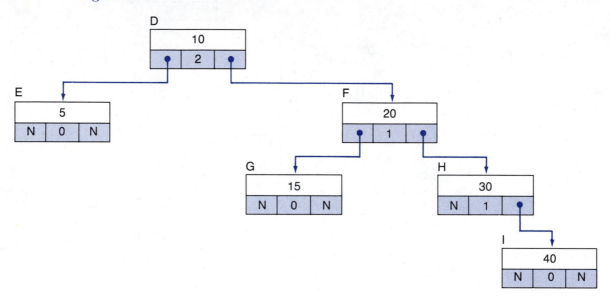

Figure 7.25

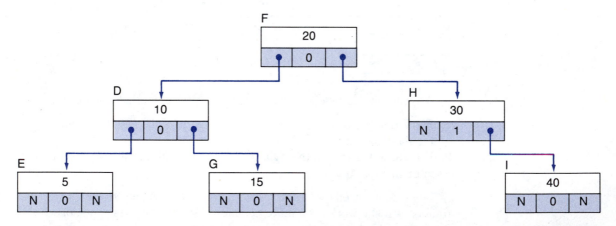

Let us now write the pseudocode for case A of procedure **RightUnbalanceRestore**. We will send the root pointer to the procedure in **var** parameter **Ptr**. (Since the rotation will change the root, the new value for the root must be sent back. Therefore **Ptr** must be a **var** parameter.)

Pseudocode

> **RightUnbalanceRestore Procedure (Case A)**
>
> Assign right pointer of **Ptr** to **SecPtr**.
> IF case A THEN
>   Assign left pointer of **SecPtr** to right pointer of **Ptr**.
>   Assign **Ptr** to left pointer of **SecPtr**.
>   Set **BalVal** in node **Ptr** to 0.
>   Set **BalVal** in node **SecPtr** to 0.
>   Assign **SecPtr** to **Ptr**.
> END IF.

As an illustration, consider the steps needed to convert the unbalanced tree in Figure 7.26 to the AVL tree in Figure 7.25. We first assign the right pointer of **Ptr** to **SecPtr** as in Figure 7.26.

We then assign the left pointer of **SecPtr** to the right pointer of **Ptr**. (See Figure 7.27).

Next, **Ptr** is assigned to the left pointer of **SecPtr** as illustrated in Figure 7.28.

Finally, **BalVal** in **Ptr** and **SecPtr** is set to 0, and **SecPtr** is assigned to **Ptr**. The result is illustrated in Figure 7.29, which is the balanced tree that was shown in Figure 7.25.

Figure 7.26

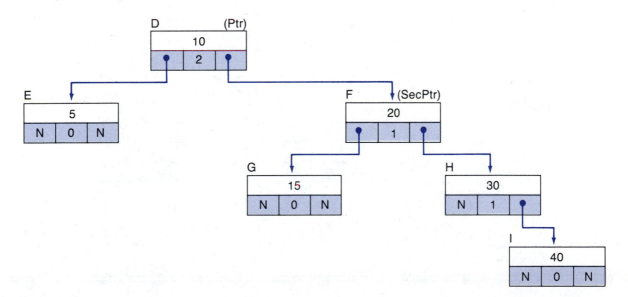

Figure 7.27

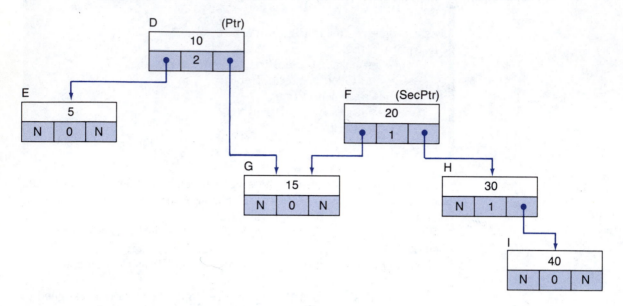

Figure 7.28

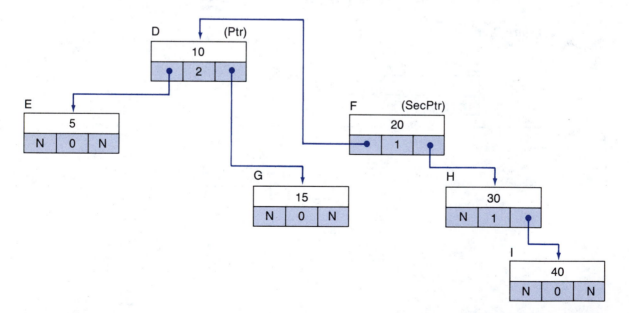

Figure 7.29

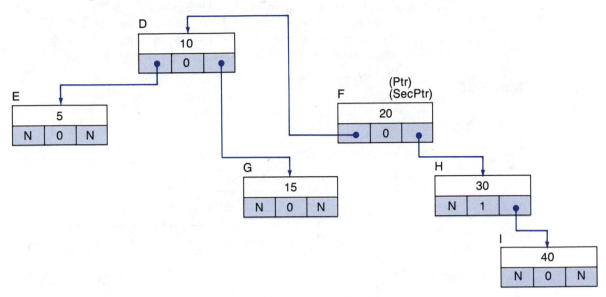

There is one more case of right unbalance that we need to consider. Suppose that after insertion of node F we have the non-AVL tree in Figure 7.30. Just as for case A, the tree is now unbalanced on the right. **BalVal** for the root was 1 before insertion and is 2 after the insertion. This is the same condition 1 we had for case A. However, **BalVal** for the root of the right subtree (E) is not the same as it was in case A. For this tree, **BalVal** was 0 before the insertion and is −1 after the insertion. We will call this type of situation, case B. The two conditions for case B (of case 2) are

1. **BalVal** in the root was 1 before the insertion of the new node and is 2 after the insertion.
2. **BalVal** in the root of the right subtree was 0 before the insertion and is −1 after the insertion.

Figure 7.30

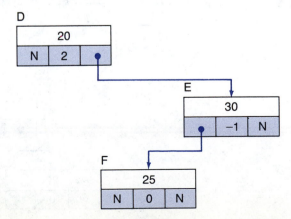

For case B, a simple left rotation will not work; two rotations are necessary. The first will be a right rotation on the right subtree only. This will rotate F up so that it becomes the new root for the right subtree (see Figure 7.31). Notice that the tree is now in the form for case A. Thus we now do a left rotation of the entire tree and F becomes the new root (see Figure 7.32).

Figure 7.31

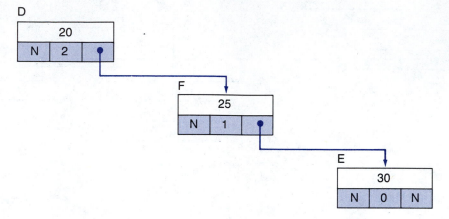

Figure 7.32

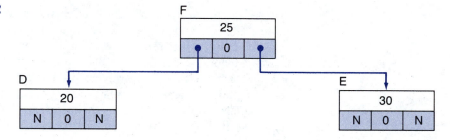

Figure 7.33

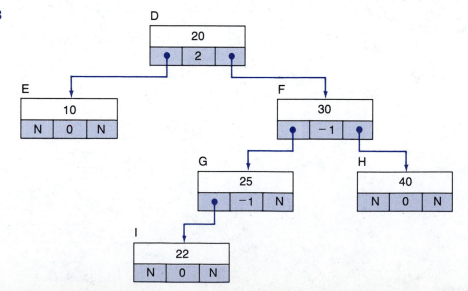

We have now restored our tree to being an AVL tree. These same two rotations will also work for more complex trees satisfying case B. Consider the tree in Figure 7.33 after the insertion of node I. We should first rotate the right subtree only so that G becomes the new root of the right subtree (see Figure 7.34). Next, we will rotate the entire tree to the left (see Figure 7.35).

Figure 7.34

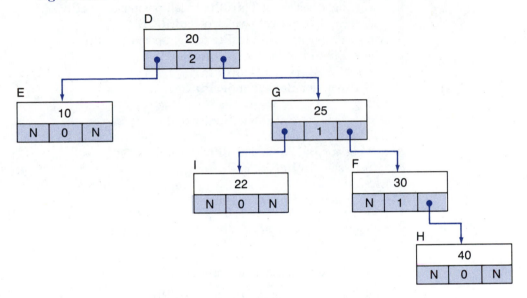

Figure 7.35

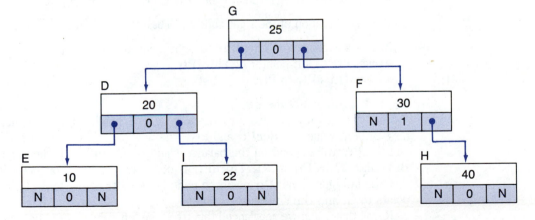

Let us now take a look at the pseudocode for case B of procedure **Right-UnbalanceRestore**. Recall from case A that the root pointer is sent as **var** parameter **Ptr**.

Pseudocode

> **RightUnbalanceRestore Procedure**
> **(Case B)**
>
> Assign left pointer of **SecPtr** to **ThirdPtr**.
> Assign right pointer of **ThirdPtr** to left pointer of **SecPtr**.
> Assign **SecPtr** to right pointer of **ThirdPtr**.
> Assign left pointer of **ThirdPtr** to right pointer of **Ptr**.
> Assign **Ptr** to left pointer of **ThirdPtr**.
> IF value for **BalVal** in **ThirdPtr** is −1 THEN
>   Set value for **BalVal** in **SecPtr** to 1.
> ELSE
>   Set value for **BalVal** in **SecPtr** to 0.
> END IF.
> IF value for **BalVal** in **ThirdPtr** is 1 THEN
>   Set value for **BalVal** in **Ptr** to −1.
> ELSE
>   Set value for **BalVal** in **Ptr** to 0.
> END IF.
> Assign **ThirdPtr** to **Ptr**.

In the above pseudocode for case B, the statements

Assign left pointer of **SecPtr** to **ThirdPtr**.
Assign right pointer of **ThirdPtr** to **LeftPtr** of **SecPtr**.
Assign **SecPtr** to right pointer of **ThirdPtr**.

do the right rotation of the right subtree. Then the statements

Assign left pointer of **ThirdPtr** to right pointer of **Ptr**.
Assign **Ptr** to left pointer of **ThirdPtr**.
Assign **ThirdPtr** to **Ptr**.

do the left rotation of the tree.

The last two if-then-else structures in case B handle the assignment of new **BalVal** values for **SecPtr** and **Ptr**. The new balance values for both **Ptr** and **SecPtr** will depend on the balance value of **ThirdPtr**. If the value for **BalVal** in **ThirdPtr** is −1, **ThirdPtr** is heavy on the left. For example, in the tree in Figure 7.36, **Ptr** points to node D, **SecPtr** points to F, **ThirdPtr** points to G, and **BalVal** equals −1 in G.

Recall that when we rebalanced this tree, the left subtree of G became the right subtree of the old root, D, after it was rotated to the left. D was then balanced. Also F became heavy on the right (Figure 7.35). Thus if the value for **BalVal** in **ThirdPtr** is −1, the value for **BalVal** in **Ptr** should become 0, and the value for **BalVal** in **SecPtr** should become 1.

Now let us make a change in the original unbalanced tree (Figure 7.32) by putting node I into the right subtree of G (instead of the left subtree). Thus **BalVal** for G is now 1 instead of −1 (see Figure 7.37). When balanced, the right subtree of G becomes the left subtree of F (see Figure 7.38).

Figure 7.36

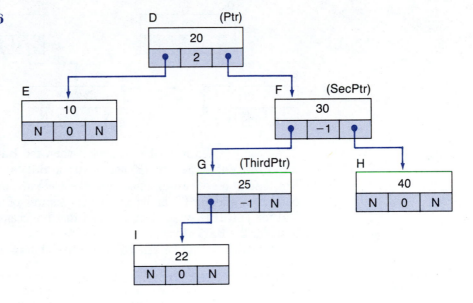

Figure 7.37

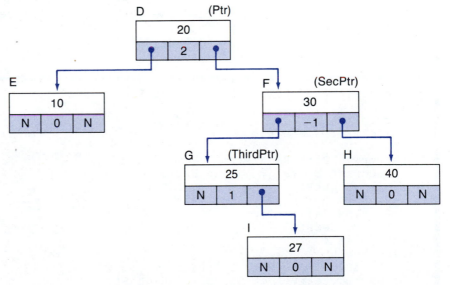

Figure 7.38

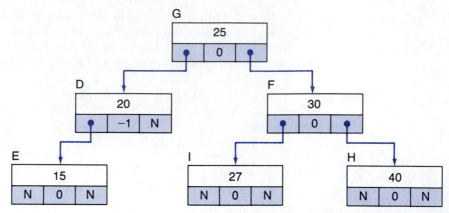

As can be seen from this example, when the **BalVal** for **ThirdPtr** (G) was 1, **BalVal** for **SecPtr** (F) became 0 and **BalVal** for **Ptr** (D) became −1. Notice from these two examples that the **BalVal** values for **Ptr** and **SecPtr** depend on whether I is in the left or right subtree of G (that is, whether **BalVal** for **ThirdPtr** was −1 or 1). Note that the change in position of I is the basis for the **BalVal** values.

The Pascal coding for procedure **RightUnbalanceRestore** follows.

```
{********************************************************************}
{* RightUnbalanceRestore - Procedure to restore a tree to an AVL tree *}
{*                         after the insertion of a node that caused  *}
{*                         the tree to become unbalanced on the right.*}
{*      var parameters -                                              *}
{*          Ptr : Pointer to tree node.                              *}
{*      value parameters -                                            *}
{*          None.                                                     *}
{********************************************************************}
procedure RightUnbalanceRestore(var Ptr : NodePtr);
var
  SecPtr,                                        { Tree-node pointer }
  ThirdPtr : NodePtr;                            { Tree-node pointer }
begin
  SecPtr := Ptr^.RightPtr;
  if SecPtr^.BalVal = 1 then begin               { Case A }
    Ptr^.RightPtr := SecPtr^.LeftPtr;
    SecPtr^.LeftPtr := Ptr;
    Ptr^.BalVal := 0;
    Ptr := SecPtr
  end  { if }
  else begin                                     { Case B }
    ThirdPtr := SecPtr^.LeftPtr;
    SecPtr^.LeftPtr := ThirdPtr^.RightPtr;
    ThirdPtr^.RightPtr := SecPtr;
    Ptr^.RightPtr := ThirdPtr^.LeftPtr;
    ThirdPtr^.LeftPtr := Ptr;
    if ThirdPtr^.BalVal = -1 then
      SecPtr^.BalVal := 1
    { end if }
```

```
      else
        SecPtr^.BalVal := 0;
      { end else }
      if ThirdPtr^.BalVal = 1 then
        Ptr^.BalVal := -1
      { end if }
      else
        Ptr^.BalVal := 0;
      { end else }
      Ptr := ThirdPtr
    end; { else }
  Ptr^.BalVal := 0
end; { RightUnbalanceRestore }
```

Now that we have written the code to restore a tree that is unbalanced on the right to an AVL tree (case 2), it should not be difficult to consider case 3. Recall that in case 3 the tree becomes unbalanced on the left when we add a new node. The coding for procedure **LeftUnbalancRestore** is very similar to procedure **RightUnbalanceRestore** because of tree symmetry. We can think of the nodes on the left as being a mirror image of those on the right. With this in mind let us write the Pascal code for **LeftUnbalanceRestore**. Again, as with **RightUnbalanceRestore**, the pointer to the root will be passed as **var** parameter **Ptr**. Be sure to note the symmetry in corresponding statements in procedures **RightUnbalanceRestore** and **LeftUnbalanceRestore**.

```
{**************************************************************************}
{* LeftUnbalanceRestore - Procedure to restore a tree to an AVL tree    *}
{*                        after the insertion of a node that caused     *}
{*                        the tree to be unbalanced on the left.        *}
{*      var parameters -                                                *}
{*           Ptr : Pointer to tree node.                                *}
{*      value parameters -                                              *}
{*           None.                                                      *}
{**************************************************************************}
procedure LeftUnbalanceRestore(var Ptr : NodePtr);
var
  SecPtr,                                          { Tree-node pointer }
  ThirdPtr : NodePtr;                              { Tree-node pointer }
begin
  SecPtr := Ptr^.LeftPtr;
  if SecPtr^.BalVal = -1 then begin                { Case A }
    Ptr^.LeftPtr := SecPtr^.RightPtr;
    SecPtr^.RightPtr := Ptr;
    Ptr^.BalVal := 0;
    Ptr := SecPtr
  end { if }
  else begin                                       { Case B }
    ThirdPtr := SecPtr^.RightPtr;
    SecPtr^.RightPtr := ThirdPtr^.LeftPtr;
    ThirdPtr^.LeftPtr := SecPtr;
    Ptr^.LeftPtr := ThirdPtr^.RightPtr;
    ThirdPtr^.RightPtr := Ptr;
```

```
    if ThirdPtr^.BalVal = 1 then
       SecPtr^.BalVal := -1
    { end if }
    else
       SecPtr^.BalVal := 0;
    { end else }
    if ThirdPtr^.BalVal = -1 then
       Ptr^.BalVal := 1
    { end if }
    else
       Ptr^.BalVal := 0;
    { end else }
    Ptr := ThirdPtr
  end;  { else }
  Ptr^.BalVal := 0
end;   { LeftUnbalanceRestore }
```

Now that we know how to restore the balance of an AVL tree, let us turn to the coding of the complete procedure to insert a new node into an AVL tree and then restore its balance if necessary.

As usual, in order to insert a new node, we will set a temporary pointer to the root of the tree and then move down the tree until we find the location where the new node should be inserted. After we insert the new node, we must restore the balance of each subtree as necessary. The procedures we have written will be used to restore the balance for any tree with a particular node as the root. That is, the procedures will be used to restore AVL balance to subtrees within the entire tree.

As the tree grows larger and larger, any unbalance will occur farther and farther down the tree. Since we want the tree to remain an AVL tree, we must restore balance to *each* node. This means that after insertion we must back up to each ancestor node, check the value for **BalVal**, restore balance if necessary, and then update the **BalVal** values.

This suggests that we use a recursive search process to find the new node's location. Such a recursive process will save the pointers to ancestor nodes on a stack so that these ancestor nodes can be returned to for balancing.

Suppose that we are creating a large tree by inserting new nodes and that an unbalance occurs way down in the tree. Probably the quickest way to correct this unbalance is to back up (from the inserted node) and check the balance as we go. Assuming that we have an imbalance, we can back up to the nearest ancestor node that is the root of a subtree which is now out of balance. We can then use our balancing procedures to restore balance to this subtree.

For example, in Figure 7.39 assume that the new node I has just been inserted into the tree. However, the **BalVal** values in the ancestor nodes have not yet been changed, and no rebalance has as yet been attempted. Assume that in our insert procedure a Boolean flag **NewInsert** is set to true as soon as the new node I is inserted. Then, by using the recursively saved pointers we can back up to node H. Since **NewInsert** is true, and since the new node was inserted in the left subtree of H, the value of **BalVal** in H will change from 0 to −1 (see Figure 7.40).

Figure 7.39

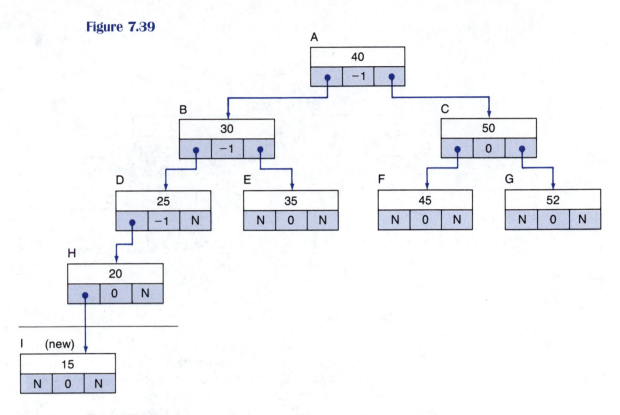

Figure 7.40

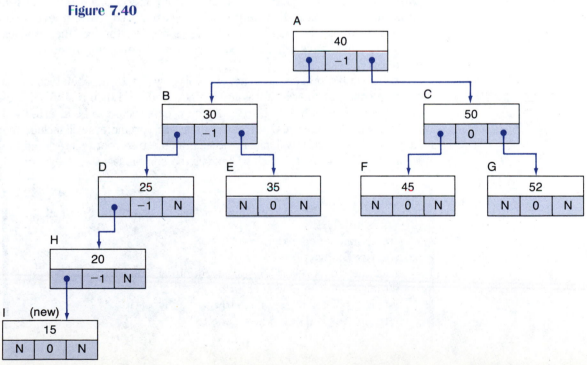

Figure 7.41

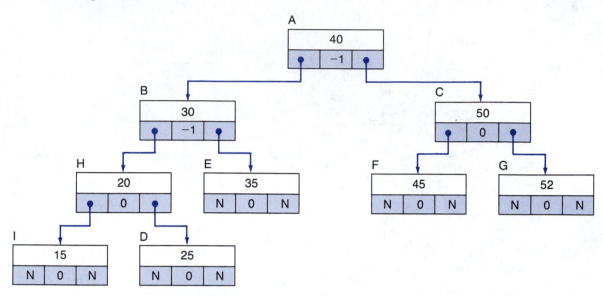

Since **NewInsert** is still true, we now back up to node D. Because the value for **BalVal** in D is −1 and the value for **BalVal** in H is −1, the procedure can do a right rotation on the subtree consisting of D (**Ptr**), H (**SecPtr**), and I using **LeftUnbalanceRestore** (see Figure 7.41).

Note that procedure **LeftUnbalanceRestore** has changed the values in both D and H to 0. Since balance has now been restored, **NewInsert** is set to false, and the process is complete. (As we back up through the previous recursively saved ancestor node pointers B and A, nothing is done since **NewInsert** is false.)

With the above process in mind, we will now write the pseudocode for procedure **InsAndBal**, which will insert a new node and then restore, if necessary, the balance of the AVL tree. The new data record to be inserted will be sent as value parameter **OneRecord**. The **var** parameters will include the node pointer **Ptr**, which will initially be sent as the tree-root pointer, and the Boolean flag **NewInsert**, which will initially be sent as false.

Pseudocode

> **InsAndBal Procedure**
>
> IF **Ptr is nil** THEN
>   Create a new node, **Ptr**.
>   Set **NewInsert** to true.
>   Insert new data record **NewRecord** into new node.
>   Set left pointer in new node to **nil**.
>   Set right pointer in new node to **nil**.
>   Set value for **BalVal** in new node to 0.

```
ELSE
    IF new data key is less than or equal to data key in node Ptr
        THEN
        Make recursive call to InsAndBal with left pointer in
            node Ptr sent to parameter Ptr, OneRecord sent to
            parameter OneRecord, and NewInsert sent to
            parameter NewInsert.
        IF NewInsert is true THEN
        CASE Ptr^.BalVal OF
            0: Set value for BalVal in Ptr to −1.
            −1: Call procedure LeftUnbalanceRestore with
                Ptr sent to parameter Ptr.
                Set NewInsert to false.
            1: Set value for BalVal in Ptr to 0.
                Set NewInsert to false.
        END CASE.
        END IF.
    ELSE
        Make recursive call to InsAndBal with right pointer in
            node Ptr sent to parameter Ptr, OneRecord sent to
            parameter OneRecord, and NewInsert sent to
            parameter NewInsert.
        IF NewInsert is true THEN
        CASE Ptr^.BalVal OF
            0: Set value for BalVal in Ptr to 1.
            −1: Set value for BalVal in Ptr to 0.
                Set NewInsert to false.
            1: Call procedure RightUnbalanceRestore with
                Ptr sent to parameter Ptr.
                Set NewInsert to false.
        END CASE.
        END IF.
    END IF.
END IF.
```

Comments on details will follow the Pascal listing for procedure **InsAnd-Bal**. We will use a control procedure called **InsertIntoAVL** that will accept the tree root as a **var** parameter and the new data record as a value parameter. The control procedure will then call procedure **InsAndBal** and pass the tree root into **var** parameter **Ptr**, the new data record into value parameter **NewRecord**, and a value of false into **var** parameter **NewInsert**. The control program will free the main calling program from having to set a variable to false and then pass it directly to **InsAndBal**. Assume for our application that each data item contains a name, social security number, and address. Also, assume that we wish to insert the data records into the tree so that if the tree is traversed using inorder traversal then the social security numbers will be sorted in ascending order.

```
{******************************************************************}
{* InsertIntoAVL - Control procedure for the InsAndBal procedure.  *}
{*      var parameters -                                           *}
{*          TreeRoot : Tree-root pointer.                          *}
{*      value parameters -                                         *}
{*          NewRecord : New data record that is to be inserted.    *}
{******************************************************************}
procedure InsertIntoAVL(var TreeRoot : NodePtr; NewRecord : DataType);
var
  Inserted : boolean;
{******************************************************************}
{* InsAndBal - Procedure to insert a new data item into an AVL tree *}
{*          and then, if necessary, rebalance the tree in order to *}
{*          restore it to an AVL tree.                             *}
{*      var parameters -                                           *}
{*          Ptr : Tree-node pointer (initially sent as the root).  *}
{*          NewInsert : Boolean flag to indicate new node insertion *}
{*                      (initially sent as false).                 *}
{*      value parameters -                                         *}
{*          NewRecord : New data record that is to be inserted.    *}
{******************************************************************}
procedure InsAndBal(var Ptr : NodePtr; NewRecord : DataType;
                    var NewInsert : Boolean);
begin
  if Ptr = nil then begin
    new(Ptr);                                  { Create a new tree node }
    NewInsert := true;
    Ptr^.Data := NewRecord;
    Ptr^.LeftPtr := nil;
    Ptr^.RightPtr := nil;
    Ptr^.BalVal := 0;
  end  { if }
  else
    if NewRecord.SocSecNo <= Ptr^.Data.SocSecNo then begin
      InsAndBal(Ptr^.LeftPtr, NewRecord, NewInsert);
      if NewInsert then
        case Ptr^.BalVal of
          0:  Ptr^.BalVal := -1;
          -1:  begin
                 LeftUnbalanceRestore(Ptr);
                 NewInsert := false
               end;  { begin }
          1:  begin
                Ptr^.BalVal := 0;
                NewInsert := false
              end  { begin }
        end  { case }
    { end if }
    end  { if }
    else begin
      InsAndBal(Ptr^.RightPtr, NewRecord, NewInsert);
```

```
      if NewInsert then
        case Ptr^.BalVal of
          0:  Ptr^.BalVal := 1;
         -1:  begin
                Ptr^.BalVal := 0;
                NewInsert := false
              end;  { begin }
          1:  begin
                RightUnbalanceRestore(Ptr);
                NewInsert := false
              end;  { begin }
        end  { case }
      { end if }
    end  { else }
  { end else }
end;  { InsAndBal }

begin  { InsertIntoAVL }
  Inserted := false;
  InsAndBal(TreeRoot, NewRecord, Inserted)
end;  { InsertIntoAVL }
```

It might not be clear how, in procedure **InsAndBal**, the pointer in the parent of the newly inserted node is patched to point to the new node. Since **Ptr** is a **var** parameter, any new value for **Ptr** will be sent back to the corresponding argument in the call. For example, suppose an initialization procedure has already created the root node and has also inserted the first data record into the root node. (For simplicity, assume the data item is just a single integer number. See Figure 7.42.) Procedure **InsertIntoAVL** is now called to insert the next data value (say, 10). When **InsertIntoAVL** and then **InsAndBal** are called, **Ptr** will point to the root. Now, since 10 is less than 15, the code for case 2 will make a recursive call to **InsAndBal** and the argument **Ptr^.LeftPtr** will be sent to the **var** parameter **Ptr**. When execution now jumps to the beginning of **InsAndBal**, **Ptr** will be **nil**; thus a new node will be created pointed to by **Ptr**. Its data and pointers are entered as in Figure 7.43.

Figure 7.42

Figure 7.43

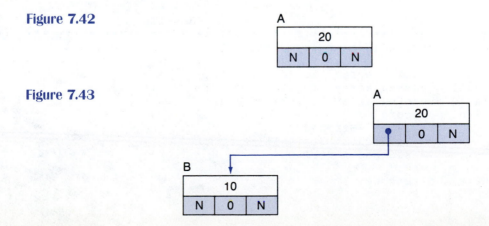

Execution then returns to the statement following the recursive call. However, at this point the new value of **Ptr** (the pointer to node B) will be sent back to the argument **Ptr^.LeftPtr** (where the value of **Ptr** at that stage was the root pointer). Thus the left pointer in the root will be changed to the new pointer value (for the new node). The procedure, therefore, has succeeded in patching the parent's pointer to point to the new node.

Also, note in the **case** structure for the insertion of a new left node that if the value of **BalVal** in the parent node (**Ptr**) is 1, the insertion of the new left node will cause the parent node to be balanced (**BalVal** = 0). Thus in this case **NewInsert** is also set to false. If the original value for **BalVal** in the parent node was 0, the new value for **BalVal** will be −1. However, in this case the procedure must still check the parent of the parent node to see if rebalancing is needed; therefore **NewInsert** cannot as yet be set to false. The final possibility in the **case** structure is when the value for **BalVal** in the parent node is −1. Since a new *left* node has been added, there will definitely be an unbalance on the left. Thus **LeftUnbalanceRestore** must be called to restore the balance. The **case** structure for adding a new right node is basically the same if we remember that it should be a mirror image of the left insertion.

As an application of AVL trees, we will modify the **PersonnelSort** program in Section 7.2 so that the employee records will be inserted into an AVL tree. By using the AVL tree procedures, AVL balance may be maintained as each record is inserted into the tree.

```
{*******************************************************************}
{* AVLPersonnelSort - Program to use an AVL tree to sort a         *}
{*                    personnel file in ascending order according to *}
{*                    social security numbers and then print all the *}
{*                    data.                                         *}
{*       data file format -                                        *}
{*             Name                 Columns  1 - 20                *}
{*             Social Security No.          21 - 31                *}
{*             Address                      32 - 78                *}
{*       output print format -                                     *}
{*             Social Security No.  Columns  1 - 11                *}
{*             Name                         25 - 44                *}
{*             Address                      58 - 114               *}
{*******************************************************************}
program AVLPersonnelSort(output,DFile);
type
  String20 = packed array [1..20] of char;
  String11 = packed array [1..11] of char;
  String47 = packed array [1..47] of char;
  DataType = record
               Name : String20;
               SocSecNo : String11;
               Address : String47
             end;
  NodePtr = ^TreeNode;
```

```
    TreeNode = record
                Data : DataType;
                LeftPtr : NodePtr;
                BalVal : integer;
                RightPtr : NodePtr
              end;
var
  Root : NodePtr;                               { Tree-root pointer }
  OneRec : DataType;                        {One complete data record }
  DFile : text;                                    {Data file }
                 { Forward procedure declarations }
procedure ReadRec(var DataF : text; var DataRec: DataType); forward;
                 { End of forward procedure declarations }

{*****************************************************************}
{* InitTree - Procedure to initialize the tree. The root node is   *}
{*            created and the first data record is inserted into the *}
{*            root node.                                           *}
{*      var parameters -                                          *}
{*          TreeRoot : Pointer to the root node.                  *}
{*      value parameters -                                        *}
{*          None.                                                 *}
{*****************************************************************}
procedure InitTree(var TreeRoot : NodePtr);
begin
  new(TreeRoot);                        { Create the root node }
  ReadRec(DFile,OneRec);                { Read one data record }
  TreeRoot^.Data := OneRec;
  TreeRoot^.LeftPtr := nil;
  TreeRoot^.BalVal := 0;
  TreeRoot^.RightPtr := nil
end;   { InitTree }


          **************************************************
          * Insert InsertIntoAVL, LeftUnbalanceRestore,   *
          * ReadRec, and RightUnbalanceRestore procedures *
          * here.                                         *
          **************************************************


{*****************************************************************}
{* TravInorder - Recursive procedure to traverse the tree using   *}
{*               inorder traversal and then print the employee     *}
{*               records stored as data in the tree nodes. Each tree *}
{*               node contains one employee record.               *}
{*      var parameters -                                          *}
{*          None.                                                 *}
{*      value parameters -                                        *}
{*          TreeNode : Tree-node pointer (initially sent as the tree *}
{*                     root).                                     *}
{*****************************************************************}
procedure TravInorder(TreeNode : NodePtr);
begin
  if TreeNode <> nil then begin
```

```
      TravInorder(TreeNode^.LeftPtr);                    { Left subtree }
      with TreeNode^.Data do
         writeln(Name, SocSecNo:20, Address:50);     { Print node data }
      TravInorder(TreeNode^.RightPtr)                    { Right subtree }
   end   { if }
end;   { TravInorder }

{*******************************************************************}
{*                      Main Control Module                       *}
{*******************************************************************}
begin
   reset(DFile);
   if not eof(DFile) then begin
      InitTree(Root);                               { Initialize the tree }
      while not eof(DFile) do begin
         ReadRec(DFile,OneRec);                    { Read one data record }
         InsertIntoAVL(Root,OneRec)             { Insert record into tree }
      end;   { while }
      TravInorder(Root)                                 { Traverse tree
                                                    and print the data }
   end   { if }
end.   { AVLPersonnelSort }
```

It should be obvious that the AVL procedures can be used in any tree application program in which it is desirable to maintain a balanced tree.

Exercises

7.18 Make up 6 employee records with random social security numbers. Walk through the creation of an AVL tree using the **InsertIntoAVL** procedure. Assume that an initialization procedure has previously created the root and inserted the first record into this root.

7.19 Using an employee record file, write a program to do the following.
(a) Initialize an AVL tree by creating the root and inserting the first data record into the root.
(b) Read and insert each remaining data record into the tree using procedure **InsertIntoAVL** so that the names will be in ascending order if inorder traversal is used.
(c) Call a **TraverseInorder** procedure to traverse the tree and print all of the tree data.

7.20 Rewrite **InsertIntoAVL** assuming that each data record is a single integer number. Walk through the creation of the AVL tree in Figure 7.30 using procedure **InsertIntoAVL**. Assume an initialization procedure creates the tree root and inserts the first number into the root.

7.21 Write a program to do the following.
(a) Initialize an AVL tree by creating the root and inserting the first integer number from a file of 500 randomly generated integer numbers.

(b) Read and insert each of the remaining integer numbers into the tree using the **InsertIntoAVL** procedure that you wrote for Exercise 7.20.

(c) Call a **TraverseInorder** procedure to traverse the tree using inorder traversal and print the sorted numbers.

7.22 Repeat Exercise 7.21 with the following changes: first, do not print the data in the **TraverseInorder** procedure; second, insert statements to print the system clock before and after traversal. Record the traversal time.

7.23 Repeat Exercise 7.22 using a standard procedure to insert a node, like the one used in Chapter 6 (just insert — do not balance). Compare the traversal time with that found in Exercise 7.22.

7.24 Rewrite **InsertIntoAVL** assuming that each record is an inventory data record like the one described in Section 6.5. Then write a program to do the following.

(a) Initialize a tree by creating the root node and inserting the first inventory record (from a data file) into the root.

(b) Read and insert each remaining inventory record from the data file into the tree so that if inorder traversal is used, the code numbers will be in ascending order.

(c) Call a **TraverseInorder** procedure to traverse the tree and print all of the tree data.

7.4 Node Deletion in AVL Trees

Like insertion, deletion of a node from an AVL tree may require rebalancing of the tree so that it remains an AVL tree. The actual process for deleting a node containing given data will follow the same steps as the ones we used in Section 6.7. That is, there are four cases:

Case 1 No node in the tree contains the data to be deleted.
Case 2 The node to be deleted has no children.
Case 3 The node to be deleted has one child.
Case 4 The node to be deleted has two children.

For case 1 we will just print a message indicating that the data item was not found. As an example of case 2, suppose that we wish to delete node F in the tree in Figure 7.44.

Since node F has no children, its actual deletion is rather simple. We just change the left pointer in C to **nil** and dispose of node F (see Figure 7.45). However, the subtree has now become unbalanced. To restore it to an AVL tree, we can do a left rotation on the subtree with root C (see Figure 7.46). Thus for this deletion example, a single rotation restored the AVL balance.

For any of the three actual deletion cases (2, 3, and 4), we may have to use any one of the four rebalancing cases discussed in Section 7.3. That is, we may have a single rotation to the left or right, or we may have either one of the two double rotations.

Figure 7.44

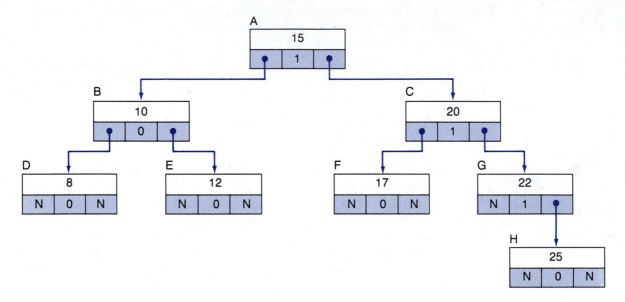

Figure 7.45

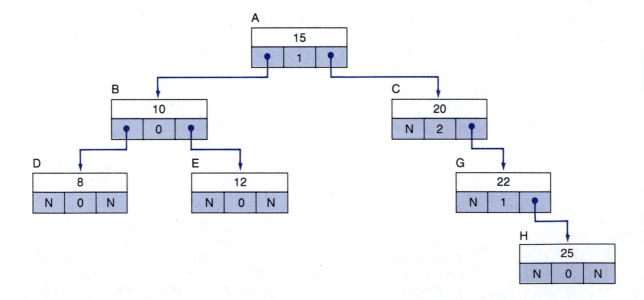

Figure 7.46

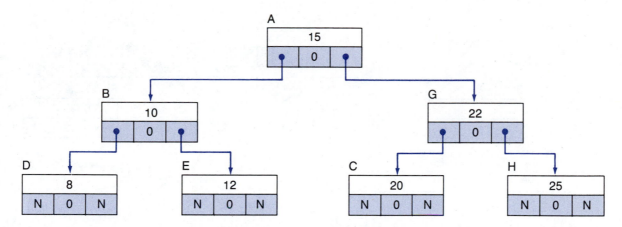

As a second example, suppose we wish to delete node C from the tree in Figure 7.47. After deletion, the tree is obviously unbalanced, as shown in Figure 7.48. To restore the tree to an AVL tree, we will follow the double rotation process from Section 7.3. We first rotate the subtree with B as its root to the left to get the tree in Figure 7.49. Then we rotate the tree with root A to the right (see Figure 7.50).

Figure 7.47

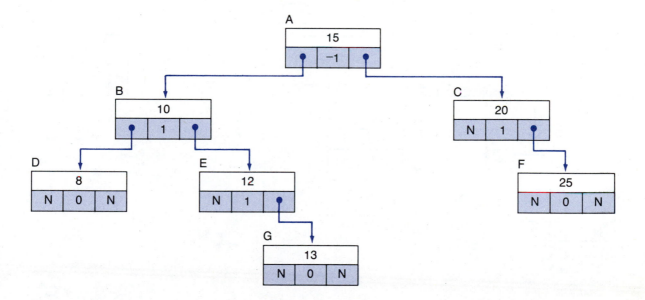

Figure 7.48

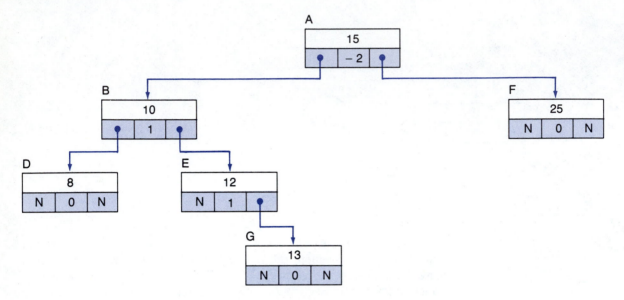

Figure 7.49

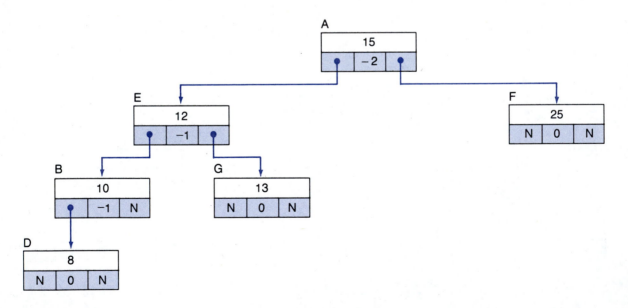

Figure 7.50

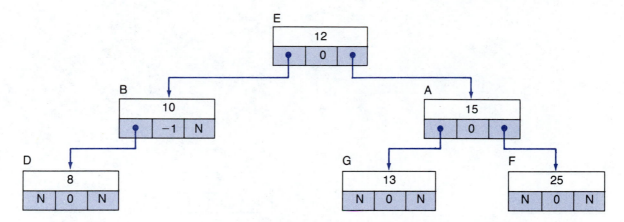

Remember that for any deletion case any of the rebalancing processes may be needed, or rebalancing may not be required. As a final deletion example, suppose we wish to delete node A from the tree in Figure 7.51. Remember from Section 6.7 that to delete a node with two children, we search for the rightmost node in the left subtree of the node. For the tree in Figure 7.51 this will be node E. We then make E the new root (see Figure 7.52). For this deletion, no rebalancing is required; the tree in Figure 7.52 is an AVL tree.

Figure 7.51

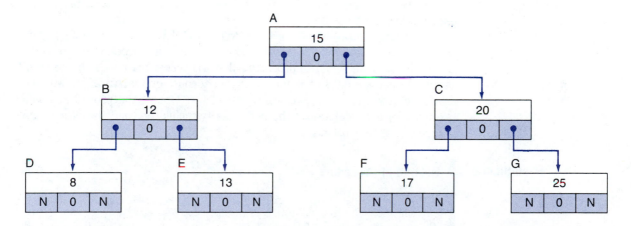

Figure 7.52

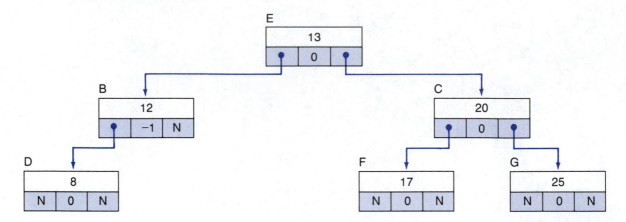

Let us now turn to the coding of the procedure to delete a node and then, if necessary, rebalance to restore the tree to an AVL tree. It should be rather obvious that we must incorporate the ideas from Sections 6.7 and 7.3. In order to keep track of previous pointers during the search process, we will write the procedure recursively. This will be done so that as execution backs through previous calls, we can back up through the previous ancestor nodes. Using recursion will help in both deletion and rebalancing. Just as we defined the Boolean variable **InsertNew** for the insertion procedure, we will define **OldDeleted** for the deletion procedure to be a Boolean variable that will be set to true when a node is deleted and then not returned to false until all necessary rebalancing has been done.

This deletion procedure, which we will call **DelAndBal**, will have a **var** node-pointer parameter **Ptr** and the Boolean **var** parameter **OldDeleted**. Later we will write a control procedure that will accept the data to be deleted as a value parameter. In the following pseudocode for **DelAndBal**, we will call three procedures that we will discuss later. One of the procedures will take care of node deletion if the node has two children, and the other two procedures are for balancing.

Pseudocode

> **DelAndBal Procedure**
>
> IF **Ptr** is **nil** THEN
>   Print message that data item is not in tree.
>   Set **OldDeleted** to false.
> ELSE
>   IF data key to be deleted is less than data key in node **Ptr**
>   THEN
>   Make recursive call to **DelAndBal** with left pointer of
>   **Ptr** sent to parameter **Ptr**.

```
      IF OldDeleted is now true THEN
         Call procedure to restore right unbalance (if any).
      END IF.
   ELSE
      IF data key to be deleted is greater than data key in Ptr
         THEN
         Make recursive call to DelAndBal with right pointer
            of Ptr sent to parameter Ptr.
         IF OldDeleted is now true THEN
            Call procedure to restore left unbalance (if any).
         END IF.
      ELSE
         Set temporary pointer OneNode to Ptr.
         IF right pointer in OneNode is nil THEN
            Assign left pointer in OneNode to Ptr.
            Set OldDeleted to true.
         ELSE
            IF left pointer in OneNode is nil THEN
               Assign right pointer in OneNode to Ptr.
               Set OldDeleted to true.
            ELSE
               Call procedure to delete node Ptr, which we
                  now know has two children. Send value of
                  right pointer in Ptr to procedure.
               IF OldDeleted is now true THEN
                  Call procedure to restore left unbalance (if
                     any).
               END IF.
            END IF.
         END IF.
      END IF.
   END IF.
END IF.
Dispose of OneNode.
```

Notice that if **Ptr** is **nil**, a message will be printed indicating that the data item was not found. The next two **if** sections search for the node. Then the **if** section starting with the

IF right pointer in **OneNode** is NIL THEN

condition takes care of deleting a node with no children or a node with only a left child. The next **if** section takes care of a node with only a right child. The next section takes care of deleting a node with two children by calling a separate procedure to do this. Note that in each case one of two balancing procedures is called if **OldDeleted** has been set to true. It is important to note that if a node is deleted from the left subtree, the unbalance (if any) will occur on the right. Similarly, if a node is deleted from the right subtree, the unbalance (if any) will occur on the left.

As mentioned earlier, we will code a Pascal control procedure called **DeleteFromAVL** that accepts the root of the data tree into the procedure's **var** parameter, **TreeRoot**, and a social security number to be deleted into its value parameter, **DeleteData**. Procedure **DeleteFromAVL** will set a Boolean variable **Deleted** to false and then call procedure **DelAndBal**. Assume that each data record is an employee item consisting of a name, social security number, and address.

```
{*****************************************************************}
{* DeleteFromAVL - Control procedure for the DelAndBal procedure.  *}
{*       var parameters -                                          *}
{*           TreeRoot : Tree-root pointer.                         *}
{*       value parameters -                                        *}
{*           DeleteData : social security number to be deleted.    *}
{*****************************************************************}
procedure DeleteFromAVL(var TreeRoot : NodePtr; DeleteData : String11);
var
  Deleted : boolean;
{*****************************************************************}
{* DelAndBal - Procedure to delete a specified social security number *}
{*            from an AVL tree and then restore the balance of the *}
{*            AVL tree (if necessary).                             *}
{*       var parameters -                                          *}
{*           Ptr : Node pointer.                                   *}
{*           OldDeleted : boolean                                  *}
{*       value parameters -                                        *}
{*           None.                                                 *}
{*****************************************************************}
procedure DelAndBal(var Ptr : NodePtr; var OldDeleted : Boolean);
var
  OneNode : NodePtr;                         { Temporary node pointer }

      *************************************************************
      **   Insert RestoreLeftUnbalance, RestoreRightUnbalance, **
      **   and DeleteNodeWith2Children procedures here.        **
      *************************************************************

begin  { DelAndBal }
  if Ptr = nil then begin
    writeln('Data item to be deleted is not in the tree.');
    OldDeleted := false
  end  { if }
  else
     { If data key to be deleted is less than the data key in Ptr }
    if DeleteData < Ptr^.Data.SocSecNo then begin
      DelAndBal(Ptr^.LeftPtr, OldDeleted);
      if OldDeleted then
        RestoreRightUnbalance(Ptr, OldDeleted)    { Restore right
                                                    unbalance (if any) }

      { end if }
    end  { if }
```

```
      else
            { If data key is greater than the data key in Ptr }
        if DeleteData > Ptr^.Data.SocSecNo then begin
          DelAndBal(Ptr^.RightPtr, OldDeleted);
          if OldDeleted then
            RestoreLeftUnbalance(Ptr, OldDeleted)      { Restore left
                                                          unbalance (if any) }
          { end if }
        end   { if }
        else begin                                      { Node is found;
                                                          so delete it }

          OneNode := Ptr;
          if Ptr^.RightPtr = nil then begin
            Ptr := Ptr^.LeftPtr;
            OldDeleted := true
          end   { if }
          else                                          { 2 children }
            if Ptr^.LeftPtr = nil then begin
              Ptr := Ptr^.RightPtr;
              OldDeleted := true
            end   { if }
            else begin
              DeleteNodeWith2Children(Ptr^.LeftPtr, OldDeleted);
              if OldDeleted then
                RestoreRightUnbalance(Ptr, OldDeleted) { Restore
                                                          right unbalance }
              { end if }
            end; { else }
          { end else }
        end;  { else }
        Dispose(OneNode);
      { end else }
    { end else }
end;   { DelAndBal }

begin   { DeleteFromAVL }
  Deleted := false;
  DelAndBal(TreeRoot, Deleted)
end;   { DeleteFromAVL }
```

Note that if the record key to be deleted is less than the key at the present node, the procedure **DelAndBal** is called recursively to move the node pointer **Ptr** down to the left child of the present node. Similarly, if the record key to be deleted is larger than the key in the present node, the node pointer is moved to the right child of the present node. This way, access to all ancestor nodes is available as execution backs through the previous recursive calls.

Let us now discuss the coding for procedure **RestoreRightUnbalance**. Recall that this procedure is called when the node to be deleted is in the left subtree. Also, note that the previous values for **BalVal** (before deletion) are still in all the nodes. We will begin the procedure by checking the old value for **BalVal** in parameter **Ptr**. If the old **BalVal** value is -1 and the node was deleted from the left subtree, the new value for **BalVal** in **Ptr** will be 0. If the old value for **BalVal** is 0 and the node was deleted from the left subtree, the new value for **BalVal** will be 1. However, if the old value for **BalVal** is 1 and the node was deleted from the left, there will be an unbalance on the right. Therefore, just as in Section 7.3, either a single rotation or a double rotation is necessary. As in Section 7.3, we will declare two local temporary node pointers, **SecPtr** and **ThirdPtr**.

```
{*********************************************************************}
{* RestoreRightUnbalance - Procedure to restore AVL balance for node *}
{*                         Ptr (if necessary). This procedure is      *}
{*                         called when an unbalance in the right      *}
{*                         subtree is suspected.                      *}
{*      var parameters -                                              *}
{*          Ptr : Tree-node pointer.                                  *}
{*          OldDeleted : Boolean flag (true until rebalanced).        *}
{*      value parameters -                                            *}
{*          None.                                                     *}
{*********************************************************************}
procedure RestoreRightUnbalance(var Ptr : NodePtr;
                                var OldDeleted : boolean);
var
  SecPtr,                                    { Temporary node pointer }
  ThirdPtr : NodePtr;                        { Temporary node pointer }
  Balance2,                                 { Balance value for SecPtr }
  Balance3 : -1..1;                        { Balance value for ThirdPtr }
begin
  case Ptr^.BalVal of
    0: begin
         Ptr^.BalVal := 1;
         OldDeleted := false
       end; { begin }
   -1: Ptr^.BalVal := 0;
    1: begin
         SecPtr := Ptr^.RightPtr;
         Balance2 := SecPtr^.BalVal;
         if Balance2 >= 0 then begin
           Ptr^.RightPtr := SecPtr^.LeftPtr;
           SecPtr^.LeftPtr := Ptr;
           if Balance2 = 0 then begin
             Ptr^.BalVal := 1;
             SecPtr^.BalVal := -1;
             OldDeleted := false
           end  { if }
           else begin                              { Balance2 <> 0 }
             Ptr^.BalVal := 0;
             SecPtr^.BalVal := 0
           end;  { else }
           Ptr := SecPtr
         end  { if }
         else begin                                { Balance2 < 0 }
           ThirdPtr := SecPtr^.LeftPtr;
           Balance3 := ThirdPtr^.BalVal;
           SecPtr^.LeftPtr := ThirdPtr^.RightPtr;
```

```
         ThirdPtr^.RightPtr := SecPtr;
         Ptr^.RightPtr := ThirdPtr^.LeftPtr;
         ThirdPtr^.LeftPtr := Ptr;
         if Balance3 = -1 then
           SecPtr^.BalVal := 1
         { end if }
         else
           SecPtr^.BalVal := 0;
         { end else }
         if Balance3 = 1 then
           Ptr^.BalVal := -1
         { end if }
         else
           Ptr^.BalVal := 0;
         { end else }
         Ptr := ThirdPtr;
         ThirdPtr^.BalVal := 0
       end  { else }
     end  { case of BalVal = 1 }
  end  { case }
end;  { RestoreRightUnbalance }
```

The best way to thoroughly understand the procedure (especially the reassignment of **BalVal** values) is to walk through the deletion of different nodes. Such walk-throughs will be included in the exercises.

The coding for procedure **RestoreLeftUnbalance** should be symmetrically equivalent to that for **RestoreRightUnbalance**. Just remember that we are now working on a left unbalance rather than a right unbalance.

Pseudocode

RestoreLeftUnbalance Procedure

CASE **BalVal** value OF
  0: Set value for **BalVal** in **Ptr** to −1.
    Set **OldDeleted** to false.
  1: Set value for **BalVal** in **Ptr** to 0.
  −1: Set **SecPtr** to left pointer in **Ptr**.
    Set **Balance2** to value for **BalVal** in **SecPtr**.
    IF **Balance2** is larger than or equal to 0 THEN
      Set left pointer in **Ptr** to right pointer in **SecPtr**.
      Set right pointer in **SecPtr** to **Ptr**.
      IF **Balance2** is 0 THEN
        Set value for **BalVal** in **Ptr** to −1.
        Set value for **BalVal** in **SecPtr** to 1.
        Set **OldDeleted** to false.
      ELSE
        Set value for **BalVal** in **Ptr** to 0.
        Set value for **BalVal** in **SecPtr** to 0.
      END IF.
      Set **Ptr** to **SecPtr**.

```
        ELSE
            Set ThirdPtr to right pointer in SecPtr.
            Set Balance3 to BalVal value in ThirdPtr.
            Set right pointer in SecPtr to left pointer in
                ThirdPtr.
            Set left pointer in ThirdPtr to SecPtr.
            Set left pointer in Ptr to right pointer in ThirdPtr.
            Set right pointer in ThirdPtr to Ptr.
            IF Balance3 is −1 THEN
                Set value for BalVal in Ptr to 1.
            ELSE
                Set value for BalVal in Ptr to 0.
            END IF.
            IF Balance3 is 1 THEN
                Set value for BalVal in SecPtr to −1.
            ELSE
                Set value for BalVal in SecPtr to 0.
            END IF.
            Set Ptr to ThirdPtr.
            Set value for BalVal in Ptr to 0.
        END IF.
END CASE.
```

In the exercises you will be asked to walk through a deletion of nodes involving the use of the **RestoreLeftUnbalance** procedure. The Pascal coding of procedure **RestoreLeftUnbalance** is also left as an exercise.

Let us now code the **DeleteNodeWith2Children** procedure. Recall from Chapter 6 that to delete a node with two children, we follow the rightmost path of the left subtree until the rightmost node is found. We then replace the node we want to delete with this rightmost node. We will code this process recursively and include two **var** parameters. The first **var** parameter, **OnePtr**, will initially be sent the value **Ptr^.LeftPtr** in order to start us down the left subtree. The other **var** parameter will be **Old-Deleted**.

The procedure begins by checking to see if **OnePtr** is **nil**. If it is not, the procedure continues down the rightmost path in this left subtree by recursively calling **DeleteNodeWith2Children** and passing **OnePtr^.RightPtr** to parameter **OnePtr**. After return from the recursive call, the value for **OldDeleted** is checked. If it is true, **RestoreLeftUnbalance** is called, since a node from the right subtree will have been deleted.

If **OnePtr** is **nil**, the rightmost node has been found. The node is deleted by putting the data from the rightmost node into the node that is to have its data deleted and setting the pointer of the old rightmost node to the left child of this rightmost node, thus accomplishing the purpose of replacing the node we want deleted with the rightmost node (in the left subtree).

```
{****************************************************************}
{* DeleteNodeWith2Children - Procedure to delete a node with two *}
{*                           children from an AVL tree.          *}
{*       var parameters -                                        *}
{*          OnePtr : Node pointer (initially sent as the root of the *}
{*                   left subtree of the node (with 2 children) to *}
{*                   be deleted).                                *}
{*          OldDeleted : Flag to indicate if node has been deleted. *}
{*       value parameters -                                      *}
{*          None.                                                *}
{****************************************************************}
procedure DeleteNodeWith2Children(var OnePtr : NodePtr;
                                  var OldDeleted : Boolean);
begin
  if OnePtr^.RightPtr <> nil then begin
    DeleteNodeWith2Children(OnePtr^.RightPtr, OldDeleted);
    if OldDeleted then
      RestoreLeftUnbalance(OnePtr, OldDeleted)
    { end if }
  end   { if }
  else begin
    Ptr^.Data := OnePtr^.Data;            { Put data from node
                                            OnePtr into node Ptr }

    OnePtr := OnePtr^.LeftPtr;
    OldDeleted := true
  end   { else }
end;  { DeleteNodeWith2Children }
```

Now that we have completed the process to delete a node in an AVL tree, we have completed the basic processes for an AVL tree. Obviously, there is overhead in maintaining an AVL tree. However, if we are dealing with a file or list of data that is sorted in either normal or reverse order, these processes allow us to create and maintain a relatively balanced and efficient tree. This is certainly not true for the *normal* binary-tree processes.

Exercises

7.25 Write the Pascal code for procedure **RestoreLeftUnbalance**.

7.26 Walk through procedure **DeleteFromAVL** to delete the node D from the tree in Figure 7.40.

7.27 Add the following to the bottom of the program from Exercise 7.19.
(a) Read one data record at a time from a data file.
(b) Call procedure **DeleteFromAVL** to delete the data record from the tree. (Do steps a and b until EOF.)
(c) Traverse the tree and print all remaining data.

7.28 Rewrite **DeleteFromAVL** and its local procedures for the situation in which each record in the tree is an inventory data record like the one described at the beginning of Section 6.5. Then add the following to the bottom of the program from Exercise 7.24.

(a) Read one code number at a time from a data file.

(b) Delete the record containing the code number from the tree. (Do steps a and b until EOF.)

(c) Traverse the tree and print all remaining data records.

7.29 Add the following to the bottom of program **AVLPersonnelSort**.

(a) Ask the user if he or she wants to delete a data item.

(b) If the answer is "Y", ask the user for the social security number to be deleted, call **DeleteFromAVL** to delete the node containing the social security number (if it exists), and go back to step a. If the answer is "N", then go to step (c).

(c) Traverse the tree and print all remaining data.

7.5 Nonbinary Trees

So far in Chapter 6 and Chapter 7 we have used binary trees in which each node can have at most two children. However, suppose we want to create a tree in which any node may have more than two children. One approach to developing this type of tree would be to assume some maximum number of children for any node. For example, assuming that each node may contain a maximum of three children, we might have the descendant tree in Figure 7.53.

Figure 7.53 *John and his descendants.*

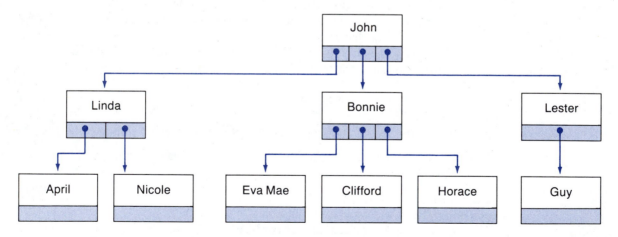

In order to use this type of tree, we could make the following **type** declarations.

```
type
   NodePtr = ^TreeNode;
   TreeNode = record
```

```
            Data : DataType;
            Ptr1,
            Ptr2,
            Ptr3 : NodePtr
         end;
```

Or, if we wish, we could vary the declarations to be

```
const
  Maxptrs = 3;
type
  NodePtr = ^TreeNode;
  TreeNode = record
               Data : DataType;
               Ptr : array[1..Maxptrs] of NodePtr
             end;
```

With the last declaration we would reference the pointers using an array subscript. In Section 7.6 we will discuss an important nonbinary tree application using this approach.

However these methods of handling multiple children can lead to two types of problems:

1. We must limit the number of children for any node to the specified maximum number (of children).
2. Each node must be statically declared to contain the maximum number of pointers even though many of the pointers will have a **nil** value. This can certainly waste a lot of memory if a large number of nodes contain fewer than the maximum number of children.

As another possible approach, suppose that we put just one child pointer in each node. This pointer will point to a linked list of children, where the children in this list could be arranged alphabetically, by age, etc. For example, in Figure 7.54, the nodes B, C, and D are the children of A; nodes E and F are the children of B; node G is the only child of C; and nodes H and I are the children of D. Notice that this approach involves using another pointer in each node. This other pointer points to the next child node. Therefore each node contains data, a pointer to a list of children, and a pointer to the next child (Figure 7.55).

The previous tree of John and his descendants would then become the tree in Figure 7.56.

To code this type of tree, we make the following **type** declarations.

```
type
  NodePtr = ^TreeNode;
  TreeNode = record
               Data : DataType;
               FirstChild,
               NextChild : NodePtr
             end;
```

Figure 7.54

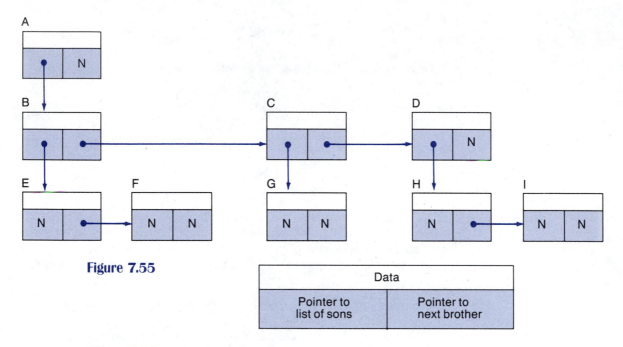

Figure 7.55

Data	
Pointer to list of sons	Pointer to next brother

Figure 7.56   *John and his descendants.*

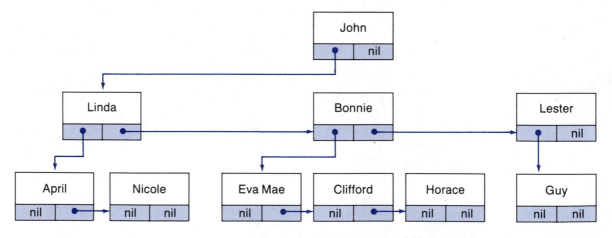

Suppose we decide to arrange our list of children by age from the youngest to the oldest. One procedure commonly used in the creation of a nonbinary tree is that of adding a new last (oldest) child to the list of children for a given parent node **Ptr**. This procedure, which we will call **InsertLastChild**, will have two value parameters, **Ptr** and **NewChildData**. **Ptr** will point to the parent node, and **NewChildData** will contain the data for the new last child. The procedure will traverse the list of children for **Ptr** and then insert the new last child at the end of the list.

```
{**********************************************************************}
{* InsertLastChild - Procedure to create a new last child for parent  *}
{*                   node Ptr and insert the data record sent in       *}
{*                   NewChildData into this last child node. An error  *}
{*                   message will be printed if Ptr is nil.            *}
{*       var parameters -                                              *}
{*           None.                                                     *}
{*       value parameters -                                            *}
{*           Ptr : Pointer to parent node.                            *}
{*           NewChildData : Data record to be inserted into the new    *}
{*                   last child node.                                 *}
{**********************************************************************}
procedure InsertLastChild(Ptr : NodePtr; NewChildData : DataType);
var
  NewChild,                                    { New child node pointer }
  OneChild : NodePtr;                               { Pointer to node }
begin
  if Ptr = nil then
    writeln('Invalid parent pointer.')
  { end if }
  else begin
    new(NewChild);                               { Create the new node }
    NewChild^.Data := NewChildData;
    NewChild^.FirstChild := nil;
    NewChild^.NextChild := nil;
    if Ptr^.FirstChild = nil then
      Ptr^.FirstChild := NewChild
    { end if }
    else begin
      OneChild := Ptr^.FirstChild;
      while OneChild^.NextChild <> nil do
        OneChild := OneChild^.NextChild;
      { end while }
      OneChild.NextChild := NewChild
    end   { else }
  end   { else }
end;   { InsertLastChild }
```

An easier procedure to write is one that inserts a new first (youngest) child into the list of children. Such a procedure is easy since the new child is merely inserted at the beginning of the list. This procedure, which we will call **InsertFirstChild**, will again have the two value parameters **Ptr** and **NewChildData**.

Pseudocode

InsertFirstChild Procedure

IF **Ptr** is **nil** THEN
    Print error message.
ELSE
    Create a new child node **NewChild**.
    Insert data record **NewChildData** into new node.
    Set **FirstChild** pointer in new node to **nil**.
    Set **NextChild** pointer in **NewChild** to **FirstChild** pointer
        in **Ptr**.
    Set **FirstChild** pointer in **Ptr** to **NewChild**.
END IF.

The Pascal coding of procedure **InsertFirstChild** will be included in the exercises.

To insert a new child into the middle of a list of children, it is necessary to have some way of determining where to insert the child. If the data record includes a name, the child could be inserted alphabetically according to the name. If we want to insert according to age, the data record in each node should include the child's age.

Exercises

7.30   Write the Pascal code for procedure **InsertFirstChild**.

7.31   Assume that the children for any parent node are arranged in alphabetical order according to **Name** (the only data item kept in each node is a 15-character-maximum **Name**). Write a procedure called **InsertChild** that accepts a pointer to the parent node, **Ptr**, and then inserts the data (**Name**) sent in **NewChildData** into a child node in the list of children (so that the list of children is still in alphabetical order according to **Name**).

7.32   Assume that the data record in each tree node consists of a 15-character-maximum **Name** and an integer value for **Age**. Also assume that the list of children for any parent node is arranged in ascending order according to **Age**. Write a procedure called **InsertChild** that accepts the pointer to the parent node, **Ptr**, and then inserts a data record sent in **NewChildData** into a child node in the list of children (so that the list of children is still in ascending order according to **Age**).

7.33   Assume that the children are arranged in alphabetical order as in Exercise 7.31. Write a procedure to delete a child node. Parameters for this procedure will include a pointer to the parent node, **Ptr**, and the data (**Name**) for the child to be deleted, **DeleteChildData**.

7.6 B-Trees

As a very useful example of a nonbinary tree, we will consider a tree structure called the *B-tree*. The usefulness of this type of tree is based on the grouping of data into pages and the control of the tree's growth patterns (as we will see shortly), which keep the tree well balanced and quite efficient to use. This type of tree is often employed in the structuring of keys for external files.

In this section we will investigate the basic concepts involved in creating and searching B-trees using normal data instead of file keys. In addition to being important in itself, the material in this section will also provide the basis for understanding the use of file keys in B-trees.

First of all, what is a B-tree? In a B-tree, data are considered to be grouped into pages, with both the number of data items in each page and the number of pages at each tree level controlled. For example, the tree in Figure 7.57 is a B-tree. Each box (node) represents a page of data. Thus page B contains two data items, 20 and 30, and page H contains four data items, 52, 54, 56, and 58.

Figure 7.57

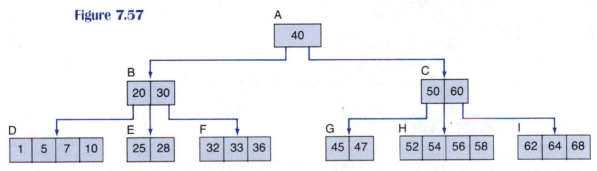

If every page of a B-tree (except possibly the root) contains at least N data items, but no more than 2 * N data items, then the B-tree is said to be of order N. Thus the tree in Figure 7.57 is of order 2, since each page contains between 2 and 4 data items. (Alternatively, the order of the tree may be considered to be 4 instead of 2. Using this terminology, if N is the order of the tree, each page must contain at least N **div** 2 elements. In our discussion, however, we will consider the order to be 2.) Furthermore, all leaf pages in a B-tree are at the same level. Also, each page of a B-tree that is not a leaf page has one more child than it does data items. For example, in the B-tree in Figure 7.57, page B contains 2 data items and 3 children (pages D, E, and F).

Thus we have the following characteristics for a B-tree of order N:

1. All leaf pages are at the same level.
2. Each page (except possibly the root page) contains at least N items but no more than 2 * N items.
3. If M is the number of data items in a nonleaf page, the page has M + 1 children.

The exception for the root page in condition 2 above does not mean that the root cannot contain from N up to 2 * N data items. It just excludes the root from this requirement. The tree in Figure 7.57 certainly satisfies condition 1. It satisfies condition 2, since each page (except the root) contains between 2 and 4 data items. Condition 3 is satisfied, because the root contains 1 data item and 2 children, B contains 2 data items and 3 children, and C contains 2 data items and 3 children.

Let us now consider the creation of a B-tree. First of all, we can make the following declarations for a B-tree of order 2 in which each data item is a single integer.

```
const
  N = 2;
  MaxElts = 4;
type
  DataType = integer;
  DataIndexRange = 1..MaxElts;
  PagePtr = ^OneTreePage;
  Item = record
           DataCount : integer;
           Data : DataType;
           RightPtr : PagePtr
         end;
  OneTreePage = record
                  NumOfItems : DataIndexRange;
                  FirstPtr : PagePtr;
                  ItemArray : array[DataIndexRange] of Item
                end;
var
  BTreeRoot : PagePtr;
  Num : DataType;
```

Let us look at the **OneTreePage** type first. **NumOfItems** is a count of the actual number of data items stored in that particular page. **ItemArray** holds an array of **Items**, and **FirstPtr** points to the child page in which all values are less than those on this page.

In addition to a data value, each **Item** contains a **DataCount** and a pointer to a page. The **DataCount** value is a count of the number of times that particular data value has been entered. This variable will ensure that we do not enter the same data values in separate locations: if an item is entered more than once, we merely increment the **DataCount** for that particular entry. Each item also contains a pointer, **RightPtr**, to a child page (this pointer will be discussed shortly).

Each page will be structured as shown in Figure 7.58. For example, page B from the B-tree in Figure 7.57 will actually look like Figure 7.59. Notice that **FirstPtr** (the pointer to page D) points to a page in which all data values are less than 20. **Ptr**[1] (the pointer to E) points to a page in which all data values are larger than 20 but less than 30, and **Ptr**[2] (the pointer to F) points to a page in which all data values are larger than 30. Thus the pointers are set up so that the data will be in sorted order.

Figure 7.58

NumOfItems				
FirstPtr	Data Count	Data Count	Data Count	Data Count
	Data [1]	**Data** [2]	**Data** [3]	**Data** [4]
	Ptr[1]	**Ptr**[2]	**Ptr**[3]	**Ptr**[4]

Figure 7.59

B

	2		
Ptr to page D	1	1	
	20	30	
	Ptr to page E	**Ptr** to page F	

Assume that we are now creating a B-tree in which we have inserted the first data value, 25 (from a file, etc.), into the root page. We have set **FirstPtr** to **nil**, **NumOfItems** to 1, **Data**[1] to 25, and **Ptr**[1] to **nil** (see Figure 7.60). If the next item read is 15, we move the 25 to the second array location, insert the 15 into the first array location, and increment **NumOfItems** to 2 (see Figure 7.61).

Figure 7.60

Root

	1	
nil	1	
	25	
	nil	

Figure 7.61

	2		
nil	1	1	
	15	25	
	nil	nil	

Suppose we next insert two more values, 20 and 30. The page in Figure 7.62 is now full, so to insert a new value of 17 into the tree we must split the page up into two pages and create a new root page. The new root page will contain the median (middle) value of the four old values (15, 20, 25, 30) and the new value 17. Thus the new root in Figure 7.63 will contain the value 20 (the median of 15, 17, 20, 25, 30), and we will have two child pages, each of which will contain two of the remaining values. The first child page will contain the two values less than the median, and the second page will contain the two values larger than the median (see Figure 7.64).

Note that **FirstPtr** (in the root) points to the page in which all data values are less than **Data**[1] (which is 20) in the root. **ItemArray**[1]**.RightPtr** (in the root) points to the page in which all data values are larger than **ItemArray**[1]**.Data** (in the root). Also notice that all requirements for the B-tree are still met.

Figure 7.62

	4			
	1	1	1	1
nil	15	20	25	30
	nil	nil	nil	nil

Figure 7.63

Root   (new)

	1	
	1	
nil	20	
	nil	

Figure 7.64

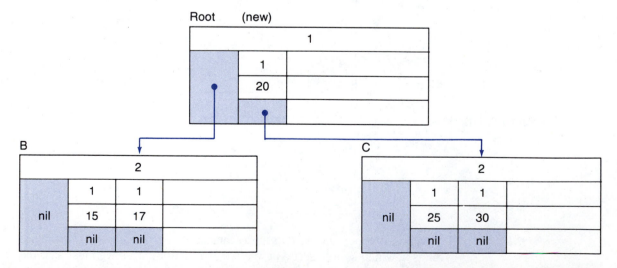

Suppose we now add values of 10 and 18. Since each of these is less than the value 20 in the root, each will go into page B (see Figure 7.65). Note that *as long as it will fit, each new data value is always inserted into the leaf pages.*

However, suppose we now want to insert the value 19 into the tree. Since 19 is less than 20 it should go into page B, but it will not fit. Therefore we will again have to split page B into two pages and move the median value up the tree. Earlier, when the root page became full, we split the root into two pages, and in order to move the median value up the tree we had to create a new root. However, now we *can* move the median value up the tree by inserting it as the second data value into the root. This median value will be the median for the four values already in B (10, 15, 17, and 18) and the new value, 19. Thus the median (which we will move *up* the tree) is 17. So that the figure will fit on the page, we will compress the two (split) pages (see Figure 7.66).

Figure 7.65

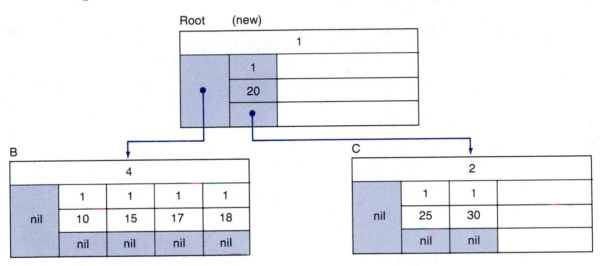

Figure 7.66

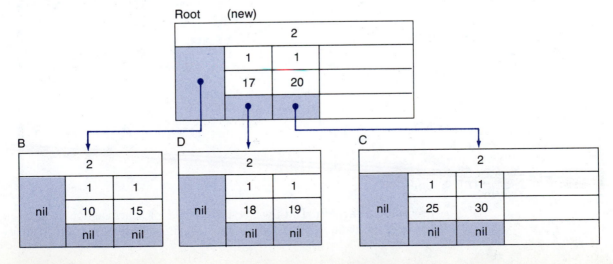

The root now has two data values and three pointers. Following this process, the B-tree can continue to grow either by inserting a node into an existing leaf, or, if the leaf is full, by splitting the leaf into two leaves and moving the median data value back up the tree to the parent page. The insertion of additional data values into the B-tree in Figure 7.66 will be considered in the exercises.

Now let us turn to the coding of the procedures to create a B-tree. We will assume that we will read one integer number at a time from a data file and insert it into a B-tree until EOF is reached. The main insertion procedure will be called **InsertIntoBTree**. This procedure will have one value parameter, **NewData** (the integer value to insert), and one **var** parameter, **Root** (the pointer to the tree root). In this procedure we will nest another procedure called **SearchForData** that, together with its nested procedures, will do most of the work.

```
{*****************************************************************)
{* InsertIntoBTree - Main insertion control procedure used to insert  *}
{*                   one data value into a B-tree. This procedure      *}
{*                   calls the SearchForData procedure, which          *}
{*                   searches for and then inserts the data value. If  *}
{*                   a new tree page is required, InsertIntoBTree       *}
{*                   will create it.                                    *}
{*      var parameters -                                                *}
{*          Root - Pointer to the root page.                           *}
{*      value parameters -                                             *}
{*          NewData : Data value to be inserted.                       *}
{*****************************************************************}
procedure InsertIntoBTree(var Root : PagePtr; NewData : DataType);
var
  OneItem : Item;                                      { One item }
  IncTree : boolean;                          { Flag to indicate
                                                if tree must grow }
  Index : DataIndexRange;                      { Index value
                                                for array location }
  NewRoot : PagePtr;                     { Newly created root pointer }
begin
  SearchForData(Root, NewData, OneItem, IncTree);
  if IncTree then begin                  { If a new root page is
                                           required, then create it }
    new(NewRoot);                            { Create new root page }
    with NewRoot^ do begin
      ItemArray[1] := OneItem;              { Insert item into new page }
      NumOfItems := 1;
      FirstPtr := Root;                       { Patch the
                                                pointers in the new root }
      Root := NewRoot
    end  { with }
  end { if }
end;  { InsertIntoBTree }
```

Procedure **SearchForData** will be responsible for searching for the position where the data value should be inserted into the tree. It accepts the pointer to the root as the initial value for value parameter **OnePage**. If **OnePage** is **nil**, it sets **IncTree** to true, inserts the correct values into item **AnItem,** and returns. Upon return to **InsertIntoBTree**, if **IncTree** is true, procedure **InsertIntoBTree** creates a new root page and inserts **OneItem** into the root as the root's first **Item**.

```
{***********************************************************************}
{* SearchForData - Recursive procedure to search for a given integer  *}
{*                 value. If the value is found, the DataCount value   *}
{*                 is incremented. Otherwise, the new value is in-     *}
{*                 serted into the B-tree. If the B-tree will not be   *}
{*                 complete without a new root page, IncTree will      *}
{*                 still be true.                                      *}
{*       var parameters -                                              *}
{*           AnItem : One item.                                        *}
{*           IncTree : Boolean variable to indicate that the tree     *)
{*                     must grow.                                      *}
{*       value parameters -                                            *}
{*           OnePage : Page pointer (initially sent as the root).      *}
{*           NewData : Data value to be inserted.                      *}
{***********************************************************************}
procedure SearchForData(OnePage : PagePtr; NewData : DataType;
                        var AnItem : Item; var IncTree : Boolean);
var
   Found : Boolean;
   Index : integer;
   NextPage : PagePtr;
   OneItem : Item;
begin
   if OnePage = nil then begin                            { Not found }
      IncTree := true;
      AnItem.Data := NewData;
      AnItem.DataCount := 1;
      AnItem.RightPtr := nil
   end  { if }
   else begin                                  { Search OnePage for the
                                                 new data value and
                                                 set the value for Index }

      with OnePage^ do begin
        if NewData < ItemArray[1].Data then begin
          Found := false;
          Index := 0
        end  { if }
        else begin
          Index := NumOfItems;
          while (Index > 1) and (NewData < ItemArray[Index].Data) do
            Index := Index - 1;
          { end while }
          if NewData = ItemArray[Index].Data then begin      { If found }
            Found := true;
            IncTree := false;
            ItemArray[Index].DataCount := ItemArray[Index].DataCount + 1
          end  { if }
          else
```

```
            Found := false
         { end else }
      end; { else }
      if not Found then begin                    { If not found,
                                                   set NewPage pointer }

         if NewData < ItemArray[1].Data then
            NextPage := FirstPtr
         { end if }
         else
            NextPage := ItemArray[Index].RightPtr;
         { end else }
         SearchForData(NextPage, NewData, OneItem, IncTree);
         if IncTree then
            PutInTree
         { end if }
      end { if }
   end { with }
 end { else }
end; { SearchForData }
```

In procedure **SearchForData**, if **OnePage** is not **nil**, **OnePage** is searched to see if the value (to be inserted) is already in the tree. If it is, its value for **DataCount** is incremented. If the value does not already exist, procedure **PutInTree** is called to do the insertion. Procedure **PutInTree** will be nested within procedure **SearchForData**. Note that the value for **Index** is the array index of the largest value that is smaller than the **NewData** value.

For example, suppose that we wish to insert the data value 75 into the page illustrated in Figure 7.67. Since 72 is the largest value that is less than 75, procedure **SearchForData** will set **Index** to the value of 2 (since 72 is in **ItemArray**[2]). Procedure **PutInTree** (which will be nested within procedure **SearchForData**) will first check to see if there is enough room in page **OnePage** to insert the new data item. If there is, the item will be inserted by using the value for **Index**. Since the new data item will be inserted right after array index **Index**, each item from location **NumOfItems** down to **Index** + 2 will be moved from its present array location up to the next location. This will allow the insertion of the new item at location **Index** + 1. Thus in Figure 7.67 the new data value of 75 will be inserted directly to the right of the 72 (see Figure 7.68).

Figure 7.67

3			
1	1	1	
70	72	80	

Figure 7.68

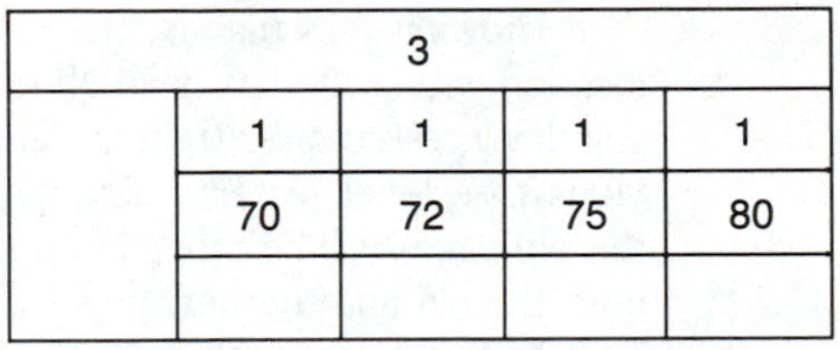

3			
1	1	1	1
70	72	75	80

```
{*******************************************************************}
{* PutInTree - If data in OneItem will fit in page OnePage this pro-  *}
{*             cedure will insert it immediately to the right of item *}
{*             ItemArray[Index]. If there is insufficient space in    *}
{*             page OnePage the nested procedure SplitInto2Pages will  *}
{*             be called.                                              *}
{*******************************************************************}
procedure PutInTree;
var
   J : DataIndexRange;
begin
   with OnePage^ do begin
      if NumOfItems < MaxElts then begin        { If item will fit on page }
         IncTree := false;
         NumOfItems := NumOfItems + 1;
         for J := NumOfItems downto Index + 2 do
           ItemArray[J] := ItemArray[J - 1];
         { end for }
         ItemArray[Index + 1] := OneItem
      end { if }
      else                                              { Else must
                                                         split into 2 pages }

         SplitInto2Pages;
      { end else }
   end { with }
end; { PutInTree }
```

However, if there is not enough room in page **OnePage**, then **OnePage** must be split into two pages. There are three cases to consider:

Case 1 If **Index** = N.
Case 2 If **Index** < N.
Case 3 If **Index** > N.

Recall that the maximum number of items in a page is $2 * N$. Thus think of the page as containing N items in the left-hand side (of the page) and N items in the right-hand side (of the page). Therefore, if **Index** = N, the new data value would go right in the middle if it were possible to put the value there. Since it is not possible to insert the value in the middle, the data value (note that it is the median) moves up to the previous level in the tree. A new page is created and the right-hand N items are moved from the old page to this new page. The left-hand N items remain in the old page. For both the old page and the new page, the value for **NumOfItems** will be set to N.

If **Index** is less than N, the new data value will be inserted into the correct location within the left-hand N items of the old page. However, this insertion will displace the old Nth item. This old Nth item will be moved up to the previous tree level. After a new page is created, the right-hand N items (from the old page) will be moved into the left-hand N positions of the new page. In both the old and the new page, the value for **NumOfItems** will be set to N.

If **Index** is larger than N, the item at array location N + 1 will be the one that should be moved up to the previous tree level. The new data value will be inserted into the correct location within the right-hand N items in the old page. Finally, as in the other two cases, a new page will be created and then the N right-hand elements will be moved from the old page into the left-hand N positions in this new page. The left-hand N elements will remain in the old page. In both the old page and the new page, the value for **NumOfItems** will be set to N. The coding of the **SplitInto2Pages** procedure will be assigned in the exercises.

Now that we know how to insert one data item at a time into a B-tree, we could certainly write a program to create an entire B-tree. However, in order to see what is in the tree during and/or after creation, let us write a small procedure to print the data from the tree. This procedure, which we will call **PrintBTreeData**, has only one value parameter. This parameter, **OnePage**, should initially be sent as the pointer to the tree root.

```
{***************************************************************************}
{* PrintBTreeData - Procedure to print the integer data stored in a     *}
{*                  B-tree.                                              *}
{*       var parameters -                                               *}
{*            None.                                                     *}
{*       value parameters -                                             *}
{*            OnePage : Page pointer (initially sent as the root).      *}
{***************************************************************************}
procedure PrintBTreeData(OnePage : PagePtr);
var
  J : integer;                                              { Index }
begin
  if OnePage <> nil then
    with OnePage^ do begin
      for J := 1 to NumOfItems do
        write(ItemArray[J].Data:6);             { Print each array element }
      { end for }
      writeln;
      writeln;
      PrintBTreeData(FirstPtr);                    { Print leftmost page }
      for J := 1 to NumOfItems do
        PrintBTreeData(Ptr[ItemArray[J].RightPtr])
                                         { Print each other child page }
      { end for }
    end   { with }
  { end if }
end;  { PrintBTreeData }
```

In what order will the procedure print the tree data? This question is included as an exercise.

As a program application, we will write a Pascal program that allows the user to input any number of integer numbers from the console. As each integer number is input, it is inserted into a B-tree. So that the user can see exactly how the tree is growing, we will have the program print out the contents of the tree after each insertion.

```
{***************************************************************}
{* CreateBTree - Program that creates a B-tree which contains integer *}
{*               numbers input from the console. The integers will be *}
{*               inserted so that they will be in ascending order.    *}
{***************************************************************}
program BTree(input,output);
const
  N = 2;
  MaxElts = 4;                        { Maximum number of items in each page }
type
  DataType = integer;
  DataIndexRange = 1..MaxElts;
  PagePtr = ^OneTreePage;
  Item = record
           DataCounts : integer;
           Data : DataType;
           RightPtr : PagePtr;
         end;
  OneTreePage = record
                  NumOfItems : DataIndexRange;
                  FirstPtr : PagePtr;
                  ItemArray : array [DataIndexRange] of Item
                end;
var
  BTreeRoot : PagePtr;                              { Root pointer }
  Num : DataType;                              { One integer number }

         ****************************************************
         * Insert InsertIntoBTree (and nested procedures)  *
         *        and PrintBTreeData procedures here.       *
         ****************************************************

{***************************************************************}
{*                    Main Control Module                      *}
{***************************************************************}
begin
  writeln('Beginning of B-Tree creation');
  writeln;
  write('Enter the first value (enter -9999 to terminate): ');
  readln(Num);
  writeln;
  while Num <> -9999 do begin
    InsertIntoBTree(BTreeRoot,Num);                  { Insert into B-tree }
    PrintBTreeData(BTreeRoot);                        { Print B-tree data }
    write('Enter the next value (enter -9999 to terminate): ');
```

```
      readln(Num);
      writeln
   end   { while }
end.
```

In the exercises, you will be asked to write applications in which each data item consists of a record rather than just a single integer number.

Now let us turn to the process of deleting a single data item from a B-tree. Recall that in insertion the new data value was first placed into a leaf. Similarly, in deletion we will want to remove one data item from a leaf (even though the item to be deleted is not in a leaf). We will see how this can be done shortly.

Deletion will fall into one of several cases. Let us consider one case at a time.

Case 1   The data value to be deleted is a duplicate. In this situation, all we have to do is decrement the **DataCount** counter by 1 and we are done.

Case 2   The data item to be deleted is not in a leaf. For this case, we delete the data item and replace it with the first array element in its child page.

As an example of case 2, suppose we want to delete the value of 30 in the B-tree in Figure 7.69. All we have to do is delete the 30 and replace it with the first array element from child D (35) (see Figure 7.70).

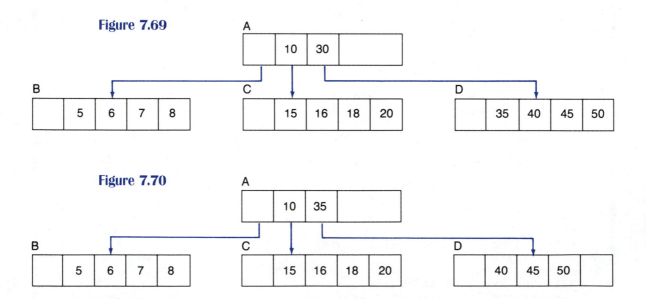

Figure 7.69

Figure 7.70

Case 3   The data item to be deleted is in a leaf that contains more than the minimum number of data items. For this situation, we just delete the item from the data array and move all other array items down one array location.

As an example of case 3, suppose we want to delete the value 16 from page C in Figure 7.70. We merely remove the array element 16 and then move the array elements 18 and 20 down one array location (see Figure 7.71).

Figure 7.71

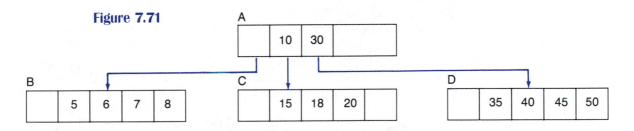

Case 4   The data item to be deleted is in a leaf that contains just the minimum number of data elements. In this case, we check the number of elements in adjacent children (or child). If one of these children has more than the minimum, then we can

1. Delete the value.
2. Move a value down from the parent page to replace the deleted value.
3. Move the appropriate value from the adjacent child page to replace the value that was moved from the parent.

As an example of case 4, suppose we wish to remove 40 from page D in Figure 7.72. First we delete the 40 from page D. Next we move 30 from the parent page down to page D. Then we move the 20 from page C to the parent page (A). (See Figure 7.73.)

Figure 7.72

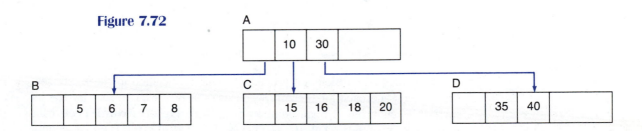

Figure 7.73

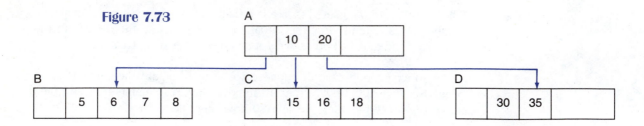

Case 5   The data item to be deleted is in a leaf that contains the minimum number of elements, and no adjacent child page contains more than the minimum number of elements. In this case, we delete the element and then combine the elements remaining with the elements in an adjacent child page to form just one page. We also move down one data value from the parent node. This value is also put in the combined page.

As an example of case 5, suppose we want to delete the value 35 from the B-tree in Figure 7.74. First we delete the 35. Then we combine 15, 16, and 40 into one page. We also delete 30 from the parent node and put it with the other three values (15, 16, and 40) in the new one page. (See Figure 7.75.)

Figure 7.74

Figure 7.75

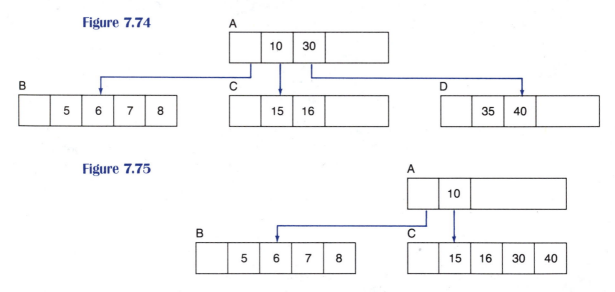

The coding of the deletion procedures will be included in the exercises. The general approach for these procedures is very similar to that for the insertion procedures. A main deletion procedure **DeleteFromBTree** calls a recursive procedure **TakeOutOfTree**. The **TakeOutOfTree** procedure can do much of the work. When execution returns from this procedure to

DeleteFromBTree, a check is made to see if the deletion of the node forces the deletion of the old root page. If so, **DeleteFromBTree** finishes by deleting the old root page.

Exercises

7.34   Using examples, illustrate the three different cases for splitting a page into two pages and moving the median value up to the previous tree level.

7.35   Walk through the logical process of inserting the following data values into the B-tree in Figure 7.62:

$$8, 40, 9, 45, 50, 55, 60$$

7.36   Write the Pascal code for the **SplitInto2Pages** procedure. Then, walk through the complete **InsertIntoBTree** procedure for the insertion of each item into the B-tree in Figure 7.60 through Figure 7.66.

7.37   In what order does **PrintBTreeData** print out the data?

7.38   Add to the bottom of the **CreateBTree** program the following.
(a) Ask the user if he or she wishes to search for a given integer number.
(b) If the answer in step (a) is "Y", then ask the user for the number and search the B-tree for this number. If it is found, then print a message indicating it was found; otherwise, print a message indicating it was not in the tree. Then go back to step (a). If the answer in step (a) was "N" then terminate the program.

7.39   Write a program which reads employee records from a data file and inserts them into a B-tree. Each employee record consists of a name (20 characters), a social security number (11 characters), and an address (47 characters). The records are to be inserted into the B-tree so that the names will be sorted in ascending order.

7.40   Write the procedure to delete a given integer value from a B-tree. Then add the following to the original **CreateBTree** program.
(a) Ask the user to input one integer number from the console.
(b) If the number is found, then delete it; otherwise print a message that it was not found.
(c) Call **PrintBTree** to print the data from the tree. (Do steps (a), (b), and (c) until the user inputs −9999.)

Summary

In this chapter several variations and uses of the very powerful and useful tree structures have been investigated. After writing some basic nonrecursive tree-traversal procedures, we discussed the use of threads in a binary tree. These threads use very little additional memory and provide the pointers necessary to jump back to previously visited parent nodes. Thus traversals can be performed easily without recursion.

We then investigated the use of AVL trees. Insertions and deletions can cause a normal binary tree to become extremely unbalanced, in which case the basic operations of traversal, insertion, deletion, searching, etc., become quite inefficient. If we can maintain the tree as an AVL tree, these operations are significantly more efficient.

The last sections of this chapter dealt with nonbinary trees. After developing some of the basic procedures involved, we turned to the development of B-trees. The B-tree structure is quite useful for the structuring of data into pages in external files. It is a very powerful, but challenging, type of tree structure.

Chapters 6 and 7 make it quite evident that trees are an extremely useful type of data structure that can be used in a wide variety of applications.

Chapter Exercises

7.41 What are some of the advantages of using AVL trees rather than normal trees? Disadvantages?

7.42 Rewrite the inventory data base creation program from Exercise 6.42 and Exercise 6.43, using an AVL tree instead of a regular tree. What are the advantages of this change? Disadvantages?

7.43 What are some of the advantages of using B-trees rather than normal trees? Disadvantages?

7.44 Rewrite the B-tree insertion procedures so that each data record will be an inventory record consisting of a description (16 characters), a code number (12 characters), and a quantity (integer). Insertion should be in ascending order according to the code numbers, and data should be read from a data file. Also, rewrite the **PrintBTreeData** procedure. Then write a program to create a B-tree and insert all records from the data file into the tree. Finally, print all data records in the B-tree.

7.45 Rewrite the program in Exercise 7.44 so that after the B-tree has been created, the user is allowed to search for records with specified code numbers. In each case, if the record is found, then all data for that record will be printed; otherwise a message indicating that the given code number does not exist will be printed.

7.46 Extend the program in Exercise 7.45 so that the user is allowed to input the code numbers for records which are to be deleted from the B-tree. If the code number is not found in the tree an appropriate message should be printed. After each deletion ask the user if all data from the tree is to be printed; if the response is "Y", then print all tree data.

CHAPTER 8

Advanced Sorting Techniques

In Chapter 4 we investigated some of the basic sorting techniques. For rather small arrays these basic sorts are relatively efficient, and since the coding for these sorts is not complex, they are used quite frequently. However, for large arrays, these basic sorts can be quite inefficient compared to more sophisticated sorts. Especially when the sorting of large arrays is done frequently, the time wasted by using an inefficient sorting technique can be substantial.

Thus for large arrays you need to be aware of more advanced sorting methods and be capable of using these techniques. The utilization of a more efficient sort for large arrays may result in saving of many hours of computer time if the program is used on a regular basis. The development of more efficient sorting techniques has been a continuing challenge for programmers, and the door is still open for the development of better methods.

In this chapter we will investigate four different sorting techniques: the Shellsort, the tree selection sort (tournament sort), the heapsort, and the quicksort. Each of these is more efficient than any of the elementary sorts discussed in Chapter 4.

8.1 The Shellsort

The *Shellsort*, which was named after its developer, D. L. Shell, is a type of modified insertion sort. In general, the first stage of the Shellsort involves the splitting up of the entire array to be sorted into subarrays. Each of these individual subarrays is then sorted using an insertion sort. For the second stage, the array is divided into *different* subarrays, and each of these subarrays is sorted. This process of division into subarrays and sorting may be repeated as many times as we wish; however, for the final sorting stage, the entire array is sorted as one large subarray.

For the first stage, an arbitrary number *k* of subarrays is selected from the entire array. For *each* of the *k* subarrays, the elements are selected so that they are each *k elements apart*. Thus one subarray will consist of the following elements.

element 1
element 1 + *k*
element 1 + 2*k*
element 1 + 3*k*
etc.

A second subarray will consist of

element 2
element 2 + *k*
element 2 + 2*k*
element 2 + 3*k*
etc.

A third subarray will consist of

element 3
element 3 + *k*
element 3 + 2*k*
element 3 + 3*k*
etc.

and so on.

As an example, assume we wish to sort the following 16-element **Nums** array.

Nums[1] = 80	**Nums**[9] = 12
Nums[2] = 32	**Nums**[10] = 6
Nums[3] = 38	**Nums**[11] = 40
Nums[4] = 19	**Nums**[12] = 7
Nums[5] = 36	**Nums**[13] = 72
Nums[6] = 45	**Nums**[14] = 90
Nums[7] = 21	**Nums**[15] = 50
Nums[8] = 16	**Nums**[16] = 15

Suppose that for the first sorting stage we select a value of $k = 7$ (later, we will discuss guidelines for selecting these k values). We split up the **Nums** array into 7 subarrays, with each subarray made up of elements that are 7 elements apart.

subarray 1 consists of **Nums**[1], **Nums**[8], **Nums**[15]
subarray 2 consists of **Nums**[2], **Nums**[9], **Nums**[16]
subarray 3 consists of **Nums**[3], **Nums**[10]
subarray 4 consists of **Nums**[4], **Nums**[11]
subarray 5 consists of **Nums**[5], **Nums**[12]
subarray 6 consists of **Nums**[6], **Nums**[13]
subarray 7 consists of **Nums**[7], **Nums**[14]

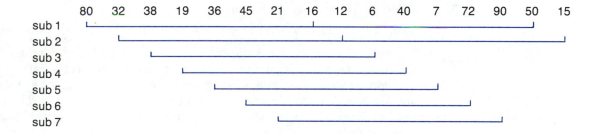

To complete stage one, we sort each of these subarrays separately using an insertion sort. (Although any sorting method could actually be used to sort the subarrays, the insertion sort is relatively efficient for small arrays.) For example, subarray 1 is sorted so that after the sort

Nums[1] = 16   **Nums**[8] = 50   **Nums**[15] = 80

The other subarrays are also sorted individually. After each of the other subarrays has been sorted separately, the array will be as follows.

After the First Stage of Sorting

16   12   6   19   7   45   21   50   15   38   40   36   72   90   80   32

After stage one is complete, we select another k value and repeat the process of dividing the array into subarrays and then sorting each subarray. However, the new k value should be less than the k value previously used. For the second sorting stage of the Shellsort, suppose that we select $k = 3$:

subarray 1 consists of **Nums**[1], **Nums**[4], **Nums**[7], **Nums**[10],
        Nums[13], **Nums**[16]
subarray 2 consists of **Nums**[2], **Nums**[5], **Nums**[8], **Nums**[11],
        Nums[14]
subarray 3 consists of **Nums**[3], **Nums**[6], **Nums**[9], **Nums**[12],
        Nums[15]

After each of these three subarrays has been sorted individually, the resulting array is

After the Second Stage of Sorting

16   7   6   19   12   15   21   40   36   32   50   45   38   90   80   72

For the third and final sorting stage, we select $k = 1$. That is, the entire array is sorted as one large subarray:

After the Third Stage of Sorting

6   7   12   15   16   19   21   32   36   38   40   45   50   72   80   90

The k value for the final stage of the Shellsort must be 1; this means that for the last stage, the entire array must be sorted as one large subarray.

There are two main reasons why the Shellsort is more efficient than a straight insertion sort for large arrays. First, the insertion sort is relatively efficient for small arrays, and the Shellsort certainly involves sorting smaller arrays in the form of small subarrays. Second, each sorting stage of the Shellsort causes the elements to be rearranged into a more sorted order, so when the entire array is sorted in the final stage, the elements are in a much better order than they were in the beginning. Thus the insertion sort is much more efficient for arrays that are more nearly sorted. It is not the purpose of this text to do a complete mathematical analysis of the Shellsort (or any of the other advanced sorting methods). However, it has been estimated that the Shellsort is of order $N^{1.2}$, which is much better than order N^2 (the order for the straight insertion sort) as is illustrated in the following table.

N	$N^{1.2}$	N^2
2	2.3	4
16	27.9	256
128	337.8	16,384

The selection of the k values can be rather arbitrary. However, each k selected must be less than the previous k value, and the final k value must be 1. It is a good idea to select the k values so that no k value is a multiple of the next k value chosen. That is, if one k value is 8, the next k value used should not be 4, since 8 is a multiple of 4. The rationale for this is to involve as much interaction among different subarrays as possible. One sequence for k values that has been frequently used is

1, 3, 7, 15, 31, . . .

in which each *k* value is twice the preceding *k* value plus 1. Note that this sequence is obviously in the reverse order from the way it is used in the Shellsort.

Now let us turn to the actual coding of the Shellsort. We will use a control procedure **ShellSort**, which accepts the **Nums** array and the number of elements in the array as parameters. This procedure will define the *k* values that will be used and the number of sorting stages. It will then call a procedure that we will name **ShSort**, which will do the actual sorting of the array.

```
{****************************************************************************}
{* ShellSort - Control procedure that calls the ShSort procedure to    *}
{*             perform a Shellsort on array Nums. The procedure         *}
{*             defines the k values to be used for the sort and the     *}
{*             number of sorting stages.                                *}
{*       var parameters -                                               *}
{*           Nums : Array of integer numbers.                           *}
{*       value parameters -                                             *}
{*           N : Number of array elements.                              *}
{****************************************************************************}
procedure ShellSort(var Nums : Arraytype; N : integer);
const
   NumStages = 3;
var
   KValues : array[1..NumStages] of integer;

                   *****************************************
                   **     Insert ShSort procedure here.   **
                   *****************************************
begin
   KValues[1] := 7;
   KValues[2] := 3;
   KValues[3] := 1;
   ShSort
end;
```

The actual sorting will be done by procedure **ShSort**. To code **ShSort**, we will use a **for** loop to control the different sorting stages and the different *k* values. At this point you should review the insertion sort in Chapter 4 and make sure that you understand it before proceeding.

Inside the outside **for** loop, we will use the insertion-sorting techniques to sort the elements within each subarray. Although it might appear that this sorting within each subarray would be difficult to code, it really is not. All we need to do is use an increment of *k* between the indices instead of the normal increment of 1 that is used in a straight insertion sort. Thus the coding will be very similar to that of the insertion sort.

Notations for **I**, **J**, and **K** are not exactly the same as they were for the insertion sort in Chapter 4. Minor changes were made primarily so that we could use **K** to stand for the number of subarrays (and also the increment in indices). Since **ShellSort** is a control procedure for the **ShSort** procedure, we will nest **ShSort** within **ShellSort**, as indicated above in the listing for **ShellSort**.

```
{****************************************************************}
{* ShSort - Procedure to sort the array Nums into ascending order   *}
{*          using a Shellsort.                                      *}
{****************************************************************}
procedure ShSort;
var
  I,                                              { Index }
  J,                                              { Index }
  K,                                    { Number of subarrays
                                          and index increment }

  Temp,                           { Temporary storage
                                    location for array element }
  Stage : integer;                 { The sorting stage number }
  Found : boolean;                        { Boolean flag }
begin
  for Stage := 1 to NumStages do begin
    K := KValues[Stage];                 { K value for this stage }
    for I := K + 1 to N do begin
      Temp := Nums[I];
      J := I - K;                    { Set J to index of
                                       previous subarray element }

      Found := false;
      while (J >= 1) and (not Found) do
        if Temp < Nums[J] then begin
          Nums[J + K] := Nums[J];          { Move element value to
                                             next subarray element }

          J := J - K                { Decrement J to
                                      the index of the
                                      previous subarray element }

        end  { if }
        else
          Found := true;
        { end else }
      { end while }
      Nums[J + K] := Temp
    end { for }
  end { for }
end;  { ShSort }
```

In order to test procedure **ShellSort** and procedure **ShSort**, we will write a main program **TestSort**. We will use a random number generator to generate an array **Nums** of 2500 random integer numbers from 1 to 2500. **TestSort** will then call **ShellSort** to sort the **Nums** array into ascending order. In order to determine the time required for sorting, we will print the system-clock value immediately before and immediately after sorting. [The following version of **TestSort** was written for the Cyber. You should use the random-number generator(s) available on your system. Also, the **clock** function is for the Cyber.]

```
{****************************************************************}
{* TestSort - Program to do the following                          *}
{*          1. Generate an array (Numbers) of 2500 random integer   *}
{*             numbers.                                            *}
```

```
{*                 2. Print the value for the system clock.           *}
{*                 3. Call the ShellSort procedure to sort array Numbers *}
{*                    into ascending order.                            *}
{*                 4. Print the value for the system clock.            *}
{*********************************************************************}
program TestSort(output);
{*$I'RANDOM' *}                                ( Cyber inclusion
                                                of Random-number
                                                generator from the library )

type
  ArrayType = array[1..2500] of integer;
var
  I : integer;
  Numbers : ArrayType;


                  *****************************************
                  **   Insert ShellSort procedure here.  **
                  *****************************************

begin
  Setran(1);                                  ( Seed the random-
                                                number generator )

                  ( Generate the random numbers )
  for I := 1 to 2500 do
    Numbers[I] := Trunc(2500 * Ran + 1);
  writeln(clock);                             ( Print system-clock
                                                value before sorting )

  ShellSort(Numbers, 2500);                   ( Call ShellSort
                                                to sort the array )

  writeln(clock)                              ( Print system-clock
                                                value after sorting )
end.
```

A test run of the above program resulted in a sorting time of 2.54 seconds. For this test run, eight sorting stages were used, with the k values being 255, 127, 63, 31, 15, 7, 3, and 1. How does this compare with a straight insertion sort? A test run of **TestSort** calling the **InsertionSort** procedure (which was developed in Chapter 4) resulted in a sorting time of 64.7 seconds. Thus the Shellsort is far more efficient than the straight insertion sort. The number of stages used in **ShellSort** does make a difference. Comparisons based on different numbers of stages will be included in the exercises.

A second test run of **ShellSort** was made on a randomly generated array of 512 integer elements. With six sorting stages (k values of 63, 31, 15, 7, 3, and 1), the sorting time was 0.370 second. We will compare this time, along with the time to sort 2500 elements, with the times required for the remaining sorts in this chapter.

Obviously, any programmer should make sure that a sort is working properly before making timed test runs as was done with program **TestSort**. It would be rather simple to insert loops before and after the sort to print the array elements before and after sorting in program **TestSort**. The resulting output would reveal whether the sort is working properly. However, for timed runs, we *do not* want to include I/O within the sorting times.

Summary: Shellsort Method

1. Select an integer value k. Partition the entire array into k disjoint subarrays such that the increment from one subarray element index to the next is k.
2. Sort each of the k subarrays using an insertion sort.
3. Repeat steps 1 and 2 as many times as desired. However, each k must be smaller than the previous k, and the final k value must be 1.

Exercises

Record all sorting times found for each of the following exercises. These times will be compared with times that will be found in later sections of this chapter.

8.1 Modify **ShellSort** so that the number of stages is 4 and the k values are 15, 7, 3, and 1. Run the **TestSort** program on your computer to check the time required to sort a 2500-element integer array.

8.2 Modify **ShellSort** so that the number of stages is 8 and the k values are 255, 127, 63, 31, 15, 7, 3, and 1. Run **TestSort** to find the sorting time. Then modify **ShellSort** so that the number of stages is 10 and the k values are 1023, 511, 255, 127, 63, 31, 15, 7, 3, and 1. Again, run **TestSort**.

8.3 Rewrite **TestSort** so that the 2500-element array will contain the elements 1, 2, 3, 4, ... Run **TestSort** on this sorted array and compare the sorting time with those above. Repeat for an array in reverse order. What observations can be made?

8.4 Rerun **TestSort** from Exercise 8.3 using a straight insertion sort instead of **ShellSort**. Compare the sorting times.

8.5 Redo Exercise 8.1 to sort a 512-element array of randomly generated integer numbers. Try different k values until you find the minimum sorting time. Then repeat the sort with an already sorted 512-element array. Finally, generate the array so that the numbers are in reverse order and repeat the sort. Record all sorting times.

8.6 Rewrite **ShellSort** and **ShSort** to sort social security numbers in a 2500-element array in which each record contains a name, a social security number, and an address. Use four sorting stages. Rewrite **TestSort** and create random social security numbers for the array. Insert **writeln** statements before and after sorting to make sure the sort works (use a small array for this). Then remove the **writeln** statements and record the actual sorting time for the 2500-element array. (*Note*: The data put in each record for the name and address may be constants for our purposes here. Just make sure the procedures move entire records at a time and not just the social security number.) (*Hint*: To create the random social security numbers, first call the random-number generator to generate each of the nine integer digits one at a time, then convert the integers to character digits and insert them into the social security numbers.)

8.7 Repeat Exercise 8.6 trying various numbers of sorting stages. Compare the sorting times.

8.8 Use a straight insertion sort to sort the array in Exercise 8.6. Compare the sorting time with times found using **ShellSort**.

8.9 Use a binary insertion sort to sort the array in Exercise 8.6. Compare the sorting times.

8.10 Create an inventory file with the same format as in Exercise 6.16 in Section 6.5. Rewrite **ShellSort** to sort a 500-element array in ascending order according to code number. Write a program that reads all records from the inventory file into an array, calls **ShellSort** to sort the data, and then prints the sorted inventory data (use the same output format as in Exercise 6.16, Section 6.5). Then remove the **writeln** statements and record the actual sorting time.

8.2 Tree Selection Sort (Tournament Sort)

In Chapter 6 we discussed binary-tree sorts in which a tree was initialized by inserting the first data item into the root node. We then inserted each new data item into the tree so that if the tree was traversed using inorder traversal, the data would be sorted according to some key.

Another type of tree sort is called the *tree selection sort* or, occasionally, the *tournament sort*. Assume that we have a small array, **Nums**, containing eight integer elements:

Nums[1] = 5
Nums[2] = 17
Nums[3] = 7
Nums[4] = 6
Nums[5] = 10
Nums[6] = 3
Nums[7] = 2
Nums[8] = 12

Now suppose that of the first two elements (**Nums**[1] and **Nums**[2]) we select the larger one. We do the same for the next pair, **Nums**[3] and **Nums**[4], and for the last two pairs.

Next we compare pairs of these selected numbers and again select the larger one.

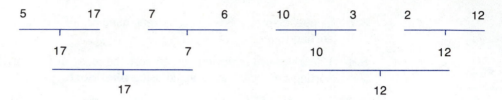

We then compare this last pair and select the larger number.

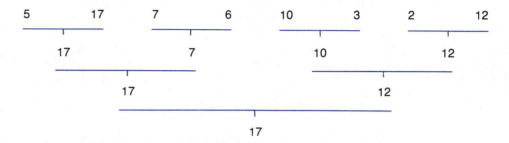

The above process resembles a tournament in which a winner emerges from each pair and then winning pairs continue to play until there is one final winner. In our example above, the final number is the largest array element.

The above process certainly results in a binary-tree type of structure. However, the process starts at the leaf nodes and works toward the root instead of the reverse. At the end of the above process, the root node obviously contains the largest number. However, how can we find the next largest number? As can be seen from the above example, we cannot assume that the next largest number will be at the next tree level.

Before we continue our sort, we should print the largest number, 17, or store it somewhere for future access. To find the next largest number, we have to go back to the original array and replace the data item in the leaf that contained the largest number. We will replace the 17 in this leaf with the smallest possible integer number, **−maxint** (**−maxint** is represented by **−M** in the tree).

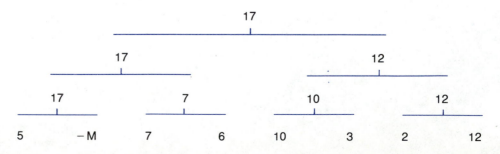

We can now repeat the previous comparison process to find the next largest element. However, we do not have to repeat *all* of the previous comparisons. The only nodes that may change in the upper levels (toward the root) of the tree are those that are ancestors of the leaf containing −**M**. Thus we first need to redetermine the value for the parent node for −**M**. Since 5 is larger than −**M**, the parent node should now contain 5.

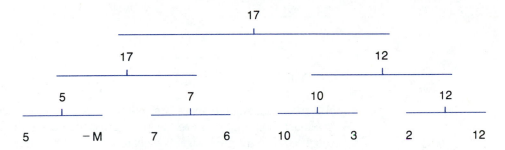

We now need to reevaluate the parent of this parent node. Since 7 is larger than 5, this node will now contain 7. Finally, we must reevaluate the root. Since 12 is larger than 7, the root will now contain 12.

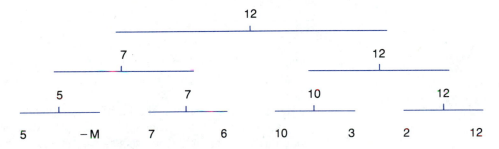

Thus we have found that 12 is the second largest number. We should now print the 12 or store it for future access, and replace the contents of the leaf that originally contained 12 with −**maxint**.

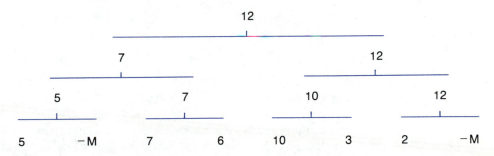

We must now reevaluate each ancestor node for this leaf, starting with its parent.

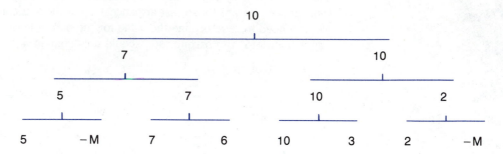

After reevaluating the ancestors, we find that 10 is the third largest number. We must then print or store the 10, replace the data in the leaf that contained the 10 with −**maxint**, and reevaluate its ancestor nodes.

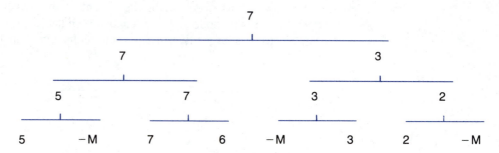

As the figure above shows, the fourth largest number is 7. We now print the 7 or store it somewhere and continue the preceding process. You should continue this walk-through. The process will terminate when we get the last leaf element (2) into the root node (see the following figure for the final tree).

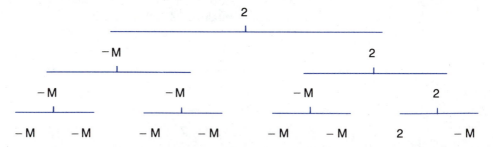

Surprisingly, the above sorting process is rather efficient; it is of order N log N. However, it has some disadvantages. In the example, we started with an array of eight elements that we had to copy into the eight leaf nodes of the tree. Then, in order to construct the ancestor nodes, we had to use seven other tree locations. Thus, a significant amount of memory is required.

Also, in order for it to be possible to construct all ancestor nodes up to the root as we did in this previous example, the number of leaves must be a power of 2; that is, the tree must be complete. If the number of elements in the array being used is not a power of 2, *additional leaves* must be created so that the total number of leaves is the next higher power of 2. These additional leaves should be filled with the smallest possible data value, as was done in our previous example with −**maxint**. We will see how this is done in our next example.

Let us consider one other question. If we attempt to code the tree selection sort, how should we construct the tree? Since the number of leaves will be a power of 2 and the tree is complete, we can store the tree nodes in an array and can reference parents or children without using left or right pointers. How can this be done? Suppose we number the nodes in a complete tree with eight leaves as depicted in Figure 8.1. The nodes of the tree will be stored in an array at the indices that correspond to the above numbering of the nodes. That is, the root will be stored in the first array location. The second-level nodes will be stored in array locations 2 and 3. The third-level nodes will be stored in array locations 4, 5, 6, and 7. Finally the leaves will be stored in array locations 8, 9, 10, 11, 12, 13, 14, and 15.

Figure 8.1

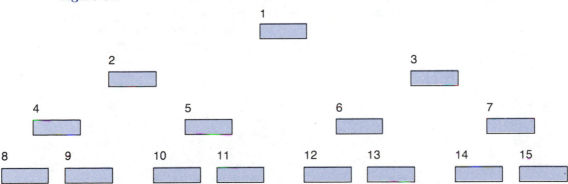

This method of storing the nodes leads to some nice access capabilities. Notice that the children of a node at index location I are always at index locations $2 * I$ and $2 * I + 1$. For example, the children of node 4 are nodes 8 and 9. Thus to find the children of a node (other than a leaf), all we need to know is the node's index location.

Can we find the parent for any node using a similar approach? The answer is yes, unless the node is the root (which has no parent). For a node at index location I, the parent will be at index I **div** 2. For example, the parent for node 14 will be at index 14 **div** 2 = 7. Likewise, the parent for node 15 will also be at index 15 **div** 2 = 7.

Thus we may go from parent to children or from children to parent just by using simple calculations on the indices. Because of this, we do not have to include right or left pointers within each tree node. Therefore, each tree node will just contain data.

Before we attempt to code the tree selection sort, let us look at a more practical problem than just sorting integer numbers. Suppose that we wish to sort an employee array of records according to social security number (assume that each record contains a name, social security number, and address). For demonstration purposes suppose the data array contains only seven elements. Each tree node will contain an entire record consisting of a name, social security number, and address. However, to simplify the figures, only the social security number will be shown.

Since 7 is not a power of 2, we will go up to the next power of 2, which is 8, as the number of leaves we will put in the tree array. The tree array will also have to have 7 additional elements to hold the ancestor nodes for the leaves. In general, if there are 2^N leaves in a complete tree, there will be $2^N - 1$ ancestor nodes for the leaves. Thus, the total number of tree nodes will be $2^N + (2^N - 1)$. The tree array for this example will contain 15 (the sum of 8 and 7) elements.

We will use an initialization procedure to copy the data from the original array into the leaf nodes of the tree array. The seven data records will be inserted into tree elements 8 through 14. Tree element 15 will be filled with the smallest possible social security number, 000-00-0000, along with any name and address. The array index for each tree node is printed above each node (see Figure 8.2). Remember that each node actually contains a name and an address in addition to the social security number.

Figure 8.2

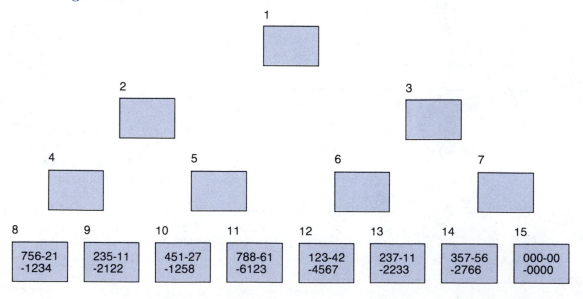

The initialization routine should also evaluate the data to be put into each of the ancestor nodes up to and including the root. The routine will therefore compare the social security numbers for pairs of children and put the record containing the larger social security number into the parent node.

Pseudocode

> **Initialize Procedure**
>
> Copy elements of original data array into leaves of tree array.
> IF necessary, fill additional leaves with smallest possible social
>   security number.
> END IF.
> Fill all ancestor nodes for leaves by comparing pairs of nodes
>   (starting at leaf level) and inserting data record with larger
>   social security number into parent node (for each pair).

Assume that **N** is the number of elements in the original array **Data-Array**, **NumOfLeaves** is the number of tree leaves, **NumOfTreeNodes** is the total number of nodes in the tree including leaves and ancestor nodes, **Tree** is the tree array, and **MinElement** is a data record containing the minimum social security number (000-00-0000), along with any name and address. A discussion of the methods used to fill the ancestor nodes will follow the Pascal listing for procedure **Initialize**.

Notice that if the data were originally in a data file, they could have been read directly from the file into the tree leaves.

```
{******************************************************************}
{* Initialize - Procedure to initialize the tree to be used in the  *}
{*              tree selection sort. All elements of the original    *}
{*              data array will be copied into the leaves of the     *}
{*              tree. Then each of the remaining empty tree leaves    *}
{*              will be filled with a data record containing the      *}
{*              smallest social security number (000-00-0000). The    *}
{*              data will be then inserted into all ancestor tree     *}
{*              nodes such that any parent node will contain the      *}
{*              larger social security number from its children.      *}
{******************************************************************}
procedure Initialize;
var
  L,                                                      { Index }
  I : integer;                                            { Index }
begin
        { Copy elements of original data array into the leaves of the
          tree array }
  for I := 1 to N do
    Tree[NumOfLeaves + I - 1] := DataArray[I];
{ end for }
        { Fill additional tree leaves with the minimum value }
  for I := NumOfLeaves + N to NumOfTreeNodes do
```

```
       Tree[I] := MinElement;
{ end for }
         { Fill all ancestor nodes for the leaves by comparing pairs
           of nodes (starting at the leaf level) and inserting the
           data record with the larger social security number into the
           parent node (for each pair) }
L := NumOfLeaves;
while L > 1 do begin                                  { While not at root }
   I := L;                                          { Set I to beginning
                                                      index for this level }
   while I <= (2 * L - 1) do begin                   { While on this level }
     if Tree[I].SocSecNo >= Tree[I + 1].SocSecNo then
       Tree[I div 2] := Tree[I]                      { Assign parent
                                                       data from left child }

     { end if }
     else
       Tree[I div 2] := Tree[I + 1];                 { Assign parent
                                                       data from right child }

     { end else }
     I := I + 2                                       { Increment I to point
                                                        to next pair of nodes }

   end;  { while }
   L := L div 2                                          { Jump to next level }
 end  { while }
end;  { Initialize }
```

The first **for** loop in procedure **Initialize** copies the data from array **DataArray** into the leaves of the tree. Notice that if **NumOfLeaves** is 8, the first data record will go into **Tree**[8]. The second **for** loop fills vacant nodes with **MinElement** (which contains the minimum social security number). The remaining statements take care of inserting data into the ancestor nodes. Notice that this is done level by level. The statement

```
   L := NumOfLeaves;
```

initializes **L** as the beginning index for the leaves level of the tree. The last statement in the following outside **while** loop divides the previous **L** value by 2. Thus **L** will be 4 the next time through the loop (4 is the beginning index for the nodes in the next previous level). When **L** finally becomes 1, we are at the root node and should stop. The inside **while** loop takes care of comparing pairs of nodes within each level and assigning maximums to the parent nodes. Note that if **L** is the beginning index for a level, then $2 * L - 1$ is the final index for that level.

After procedure **Initialize** has been executed for our example, the tree will appear as in Figure 8.3.

After the tree has been initialized, what should we do next? Since the record with the largest social security number is now in the root, we should store it for future access. The best place to put the record is definitely the last location in the original array (**DataArray**[7]), since it is then in its final sorted position in **DataArray**. After doing this, we should then replace the data in the leaf that contains this maximum social security number with a record containing the social security number 000-00-0000 (see Figure 8.4). Finally, the ancestor nodes for this leaf are reevaluated. The result is illustrated in Figure 8.5.

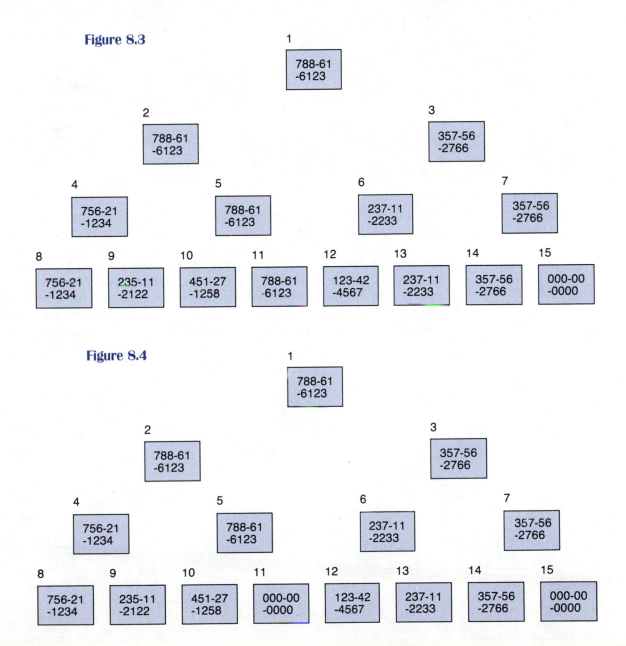

Figure 8.3

Figure 8.4

Figure 8.5

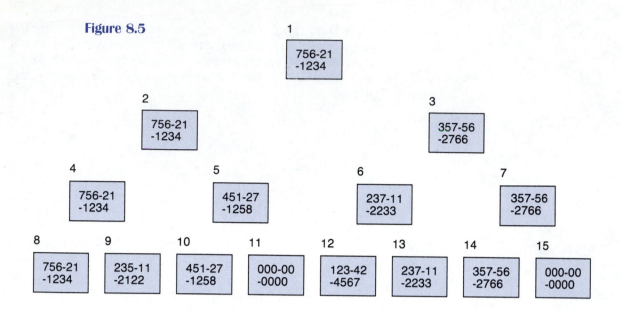

The record containing the second largest social security number is now in the root node. This record must be stored in the next to the last location in the original array (**DataArray**[6]). The next step is to replace the data in the leaf that contained this record with a record containing a 000-00-0000 social security number (see Figure 8.6). Then the ancestor nodes for this leaf should be reevaluated. This process is continued until the final value has been put into the root node. With this overall process in mind, we can now write the pseudocode for the complete **TreeSelectSort** procedure.

Figure 8.6

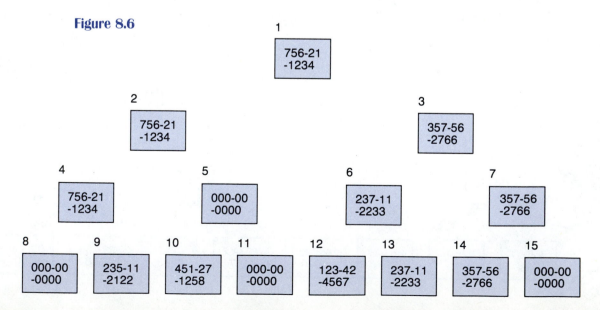

Pseudocode

> **TreeSelectSort Procedure**
>
> Initialize tree.
> FOR **M** values from **N** DOWNTO 2
>   Place root data into original array at index **M**.
>   Find index **K** of leaf that contains root data.
>   Replace data in this leaf with minimum data value.
>   Redo all ancestor nodes for this leaf.
> END FOR.
> Insert last root data value into first location of original array.

Before we write the Pascal code for procedure **TreeSelectSort**, let us discuss the coding for procedure **RedoAncestorNodes**, which will redo the ancestor nodes for a specific leaf (after the minimum value has been inserted into the leaf). Assume that the index **I** of the leaf is passed to **RedoAncestorNodes**. Since the minimum social security number has already been put into this leaf, the data from the sibling of this leaf can be selected for placement in the parent node. The sibling is easy to identify. Notice in our examples that left leaves have even indices and right leaves have odd indices. Thus if **I** is even, the leaf at index **I** + 1 will be the sibling, and if **I** is odd, the leaf at index **I** − 1 will be the sibling.

Pseudocode

> **RedoAncestorNodes Procedure**
>
> Set value in parent node to value in sibling leaf (sibling of leaf at
>   index **I**).
> Set **I** to index of parent node.
> WHILE **I** (index of node) is greater than 1
>   Find index for sibling node.
>   Put greater value of node and its sibling into parent node.
>   Set **I** to index of parent node.
> END WHILE.

The Pascal code for procedure **RedoAncestorNodes** is not difficult to write.

```
{****************************************************************}
{* RedoAncestorNodes - This procedure is called after one leaf node   *}
{*                     has been changed to the minimum value. It      *}
{*                     evaluates the data to be inserted into each     *}
{*                     ancestor node for this leaf.                    *}
{*      var parameters -                                               *}
{*            None.                                                    *}
{*      value parameters -                                             *}
{*            I : Index of leaf node that was changed prior to this    *}
{*                procedure.                                           *}
{****************************************************************}
```

```
procedure RedoAncestorNodes(I : integer);
var
  S : integer;                                    { Index - for sibling node }
begin
                { Set value in parent node to value in
                  sibling leaf (sibling of leaf at index I) }
  if odd(I) then
    Tree[I div 2] := Tree[I - 1]
  { end if }
  else
    Tree[I div 2] := Tree[I + 1];
  { end else }
  I := I div 2;                                   { Set I to index
                                                    of parent node }

  while I > 1 do begin
              { Find index for sibling node }
    if odd(I) then
      S := I - 1
    { end if }
    else
      S := I + 1;
    { end else }
            { Put the greater value of node
              and its sibling into parent node }
    if Tree[I].SocSecNo > Tree[S].SocSecNo then
      Tree[I div 2] := Tree[I]
    { end if }
    else
      Tree[I div 2] := Tree[S];
    { end else }
    I := I div 2                                  { Set I to index
                                                    of parent node }
  end { while }
end;  { RedoAncestorNodes }
```

We can now write the complete tree selection sort procedure, **Tree-SelectSort**. We will nest procedures **Initialize** and **RedoAncestorNodes** within **TreeSelectSort**. Let us increase the number of elements in the data array to 500. Thus we will need to declare **NumOfLeaves** to be 512, and the number of tree nodes, **NumOfTreeNodes**, will be $2 * 512 - 1 = 1023$.

```
{*****************************************************************************}
{* TreeSelectSort - Procedure to sort the elements in an array using    *}
{*                  a tree selection sort. The elements will be          *}
{*                  sorted in ascending order.                           *}
{*      var parameters -                                                 *}
{*          DataArray : Entire data array of type ArrayType              *}
{*      value parameters -                                               *}
{*          N : Number of array elements.                                *}
{*          MinElement : Array record containing the smallest            *}
{*                       possible social security number (000-00-        *}
{*                       0000).                                          *}
{*****************************************************************************}
```

```
procedure TreeSelectSort(var DataArray : ArrayType; N : integer;
                             MinElement : DataType);
const
   NumOfLeaves = 512;                            { Number of leaves }
   NumOfTreeNodes = 1023;                        { Number of tree nodes }
var
   Tree : array[1..NumOfTreeNodes] of DataType;
   M,                                                          { Index }
   K : integer;                                               { Index }

          *************************************************
          **   Insert Initialize and RedoAncestorNodes **
          **   procedures here.                        **
          *************************************************

begin
   Initialize;                                   { Initialize the tree }
   for M := N downto 2 do begin
      DataArray[M] := Tree[1];             { Place root data into
                                             original array at index M }
         { Find index K of leaf that contains root data }
      K := 1;
      while K < (NumOfTreeNodes div 2 + 1) do     { While in high level }
        if Tree[2 * K].SocSecNo = Tree[K].SocSecNo then
           K := 2 * K
        { end if }
        else
           K := 2 * K + 1;
        { end else }
      { end while }
      Tree[K] := MinElement;                     { Replace the data
                                                   in this leaf with
                                                   the minimum data value }

      RedoAncestorNodes(K)                     { Redo all ancestor nodes }
   end;  { for }
   DataArray[1] := Tree[1]                      { Insert last root value
                                                  into the first element
                                                  of the original array }

end;  { TreeSelectSort }
```

Notice that the code to find the index of the leaf that contains the root data is rather simple. The procedure starts at the root and follows the root data down to the leaf. The procedure stays in the loop as long as the tree level precedes the leaf level. The last index located will be the index in the leaf level. **NumOfTreeNodes div** 2 + 1 is the index of the first leaf.

In the exercises, you will be asked to complete the walk-through of **TreeSelectSort** for the seven-element personnel array that we used for our second example. In the exercises, you will also be asked to have the procedure determine the values to use for **NumOfLeaves** and **NumOfTreeNodes** mathematically instead of declaring them as the fixed values 512 and 1023 in procedure **TreeSelectSort**.

It can be shown that the tree selection sort is of order N log N. Remember from Chapter 4 that any sort of order N log N is much more efficient for larger arrays than are sorts of order N^2. Thus **TreeSelectSort** is significantly more efficient for larger arrays than are any of the basic sorts in Chapter 4. For comparison with the **ShellSort** procedure in Section 8.1, the **TreeSelectSort** procedure was modified to sort an array of integer numbers into ascending order. Test runs using the **TestSort** program resulted in sorting times of 0.487 second for a 512-element array and 3.171 seconds for a 2500-element array.

Summary: Tree Selection Sort Method

1. Define **NumOfLeaves** to be the smallest power of 2 that is greater than or equal to **N** (the number of array elements). Define **NumOfTreeNodes** to be 2 * **NumOfLeaves** − 1. Define **Tree** to be an array having **NumOfTreeNodes** elements.
2. Copy each element of the original data array into the **Tree** leaves, starting at index **NumOfLeaves**. If **N** is not a power of 2, fill all remaining leaves of **Tree** with the smallest possible array element.
3. For each pair of leaves (starting at index **NumOfLeaves**), copy the larger element into the parent node. Likewise, for each pair of parent nodes, copy the larger element into their parent node. Continue this process until the root is filled.
4. For values of **M** from **N** down to 2
   Copy the data that was put into the root node into the original array at index **M**.
   Insert the smallest possible data element into the leaf that originally contained the data that ended up in the root.
   Redo the data in each ancestor node for the leaf above so that the data in each ancestor are larger than or equal to the data in each of its children.
5. Copy the last root-node data into the first element of the original array.

Exercises

8.11 Complete the walk-through for procedure **TreeSelectSort** for the social security number sorting example.

8.12 Redo Exercise 8.6 using **TreeSelectSort** rather than **ShellSort** to sort the records. Have **TreeSelectSort** determine the values to be used for **NumOfLeaves** and **NumOfTreeNodes** rather than setting them to 512 and 1023. Compare the sorting time with that found for Exercise 8.6.

8.13 Rewrite **TreeSelectSort** so that it will sort an array **Nums** of integer numbers. Use program **TestSort** from Section 8.1 to generate an array of 512 random integer numbers and then call **TreeSelectSort** to sort the array into ascending order. Insert a **writeln** loop after the sort to make sure that the sort works. Then remove the **writeln** loop and check the sorting time. Compare this time with that found for **ShellSort**. Repeat for an array of 2500 random integer numbers.

8.14 Using the eight-element **Nums** array example at the beginning of this section, walk through the **TreeSelectSort** procedure that you wrote in Exercise 8.13.

8.15 Repeat Exercise 8.13 for integer arrays that are already in order. Compare the time with that found for **ShellSort**. Repeat for arrays that are in reverse order.

8.16 Redo Exercise 8.10 using the **TreeSelectSort** sorting procedure rather than the **ShellSort** procedure. Compare the sorting time with that found in Exercise 8.10.

8.3　Heapsort

The tree selection sort (tournament sort) is relatively efficient. However, it does have some problems. The primary problem is that a considerable amount of memory is used. The original array must be copied into the leaves of a tree, and if the number of elements in the array is not a power of 2, memory is wasted in filling additional tree leaves so that the number of leaves is a power of 2. Also, all ancestors for these leaves must be created. For example, if the original file contains 2050 elements, a total of 4096 leaves and 4095 ancestor nodes must be created. Thus the 2050-element array uses enough memory to hold 10,241 elements.

The *heapsort*, which we will discuss in this section, eliminates this waste of memory. The heapsort uses very little memory in addition to that required for the array itself.

A *heap* is a tree, but with special conditions. The first of these is that the contents of each node must be less than or equal to the contents of its parent. Although this condition was also true for the tree used in the tree selection sort, the tree selection sort required that the number of leaves be a power of 2. For a heap we may relax this requirement. In fact, for the heapsort that we will be discussing in this section, the number of leaves can be *any* number (odd or even).

Suppose that we wish to create a heap for a 10-element array of integers called **Nums**:

$$\begin{array}{ll}
\textbf{Nums}[1] = 12 & \textbf{Nums}[6] \ \ = 3 \\
\textbf{Nums}[2] = 15 & \textbf{Nums}[7] \ \ = 16 \\
\textbf{Nums}[3] = 10 & \textbf{Nums}[8] \ \ = 4 \\
\textbf{Nums}[4] = 6 & \textbf{Nums}[9] \ \ = 8 \\
\textbf{Nums}[5] = 11 & \textbf{Nums}[10] = 14
\end{array}$$

For the heapsort we will *not* begin by copying the elements into the leaves of a tree. Instead we will create a heap (tree) all within the original array as follows.

1. Form a one-element heap by making the first element in the array (**Nums**[1]) the root of a one-element tree.
2. Form a two-element heap by using **Nums**[1] and **Nums**[2]. (How this is done will be explained shortly.)
3. Form a three-element heap by using **Nums**[1], **Nums**[2], and **Nums**[3].
4. Form a four-element heap by using **Nums**[1] through **Nums**[4].
5. Continue this process of including one more element at a time, forming a heap at each step, until finally a heap containing all 10 elements of **Nums** has been formed.

Let us now discuss how the above steps are accomplished. For the first step we form a one-element heap that contains **Nums**[1] as the root of the one-element tree. (In Figure 8.7, the array index, 1, is placed above the node.) Remember that we are *not* copying the array elements into the tree. We will work with the elements as they are within the original array.

Figure 8.7

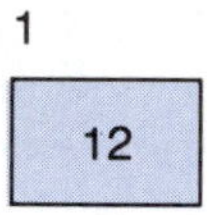

1

12

For Step 2, we want to form a two-element heap that contains the elements **Nums**[1] and **Nums**[2]. As they are in the array, **Nums**[1] and **Nums**[2] form the heap shown in Figure 8.8. Notice, however, that 15 is larger than 12. Thus the contents of the child (15) is larger than the contents of its parent (12). Therefore, the requirement in a heap that the contents of each node be less than or equal to the contents of its parent is not satisfied. To remedy this situation, we merely switch the contents of the child and the parent, as in Figure 8.9. We now have a two-element heap containing **Nums**[1] and **Nums**[2]. Thus Step 2 is complete.

Figure 8.8

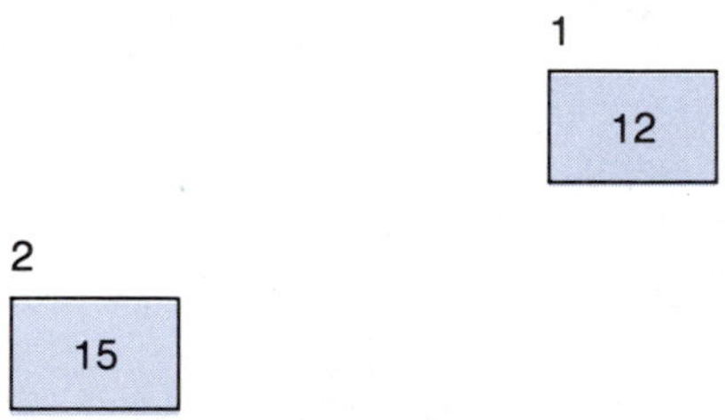

1

12

2

15

Figure 8.9

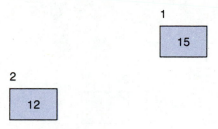

For Step 3 we want to include **Nums**[3] so that we have a three-element heap. We look at **Nums**[3] as it presently is in the array and check to see if we have to make any adjustments (see Figure 8.10). Since 10 is less than 15, the contents of the child (**Nums**[3]) is less than the contents of its parent (**Nums**[1]). Therefore, the three nodes form a heap without making any adjustments. Step 3 is now complete.

Step 4 requires that we add **Nums**[4] to the present heap and make any necessary adjustments so that we have a four-element heap. As **Nums**[4] is presently, we have the tree depicted in Figure 8.11. Since **Nums**[4] is less than its parent, **Nums**[2], no adjustments are required. Thus Step 4 is completed.

Figure 8.10

Figure 8.11

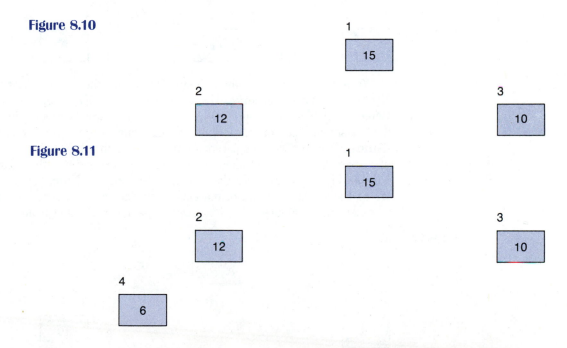

For **Nums**[5], which has a value of 11, we find that no adjustments are required in order to form a five-element heap (see Figure 8.12). We then find that everything is still okay when we add **Nums**[6] (see Figure 8.13).

Figure 8.12

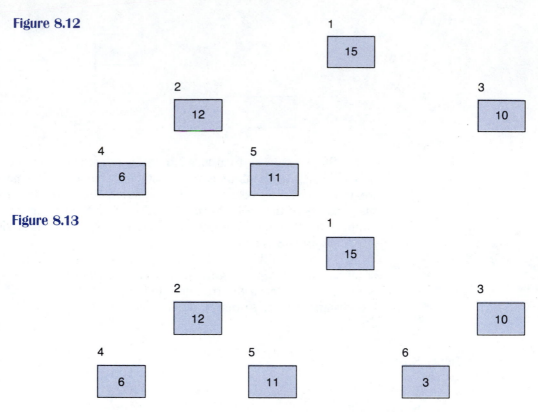

Figure 8.13

We now have a six-element heap. However, the present position for **Nums**[7] is not satisfactory. The value 16 of **Nums**[7] is greater than the value 10 of its parent (Figure 8.14), so we must make adjustments in order to have a seven-element heap. Thus we exchange the contents of the child (**Nums**[7]) with that of its parent (**Nums**[3]), as shown in Figure 8.15. This exchange, however, still does not give us a heap, because the contents of **Nums**[3] is now larger than the contents of its parent, **Nums**[1]. Therefore, we exchange the contents of the child with that of the parent, creating the tree depicted in Figure 8.16. We now have a seven-element heap.

Figure 8.14

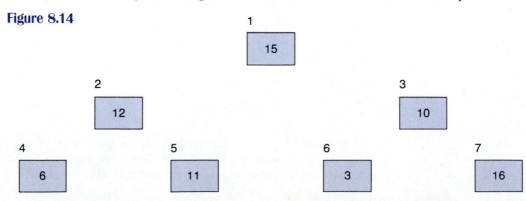

Figure 8.15

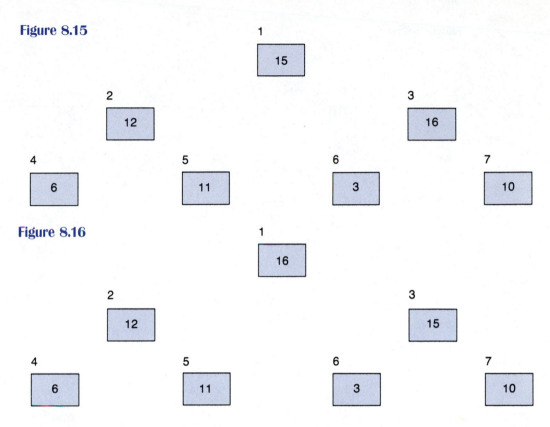

Figure 8.16

We check **Nums**[8] (which has a value of 4), and find that its present position is okay (Figure 8.17). However, **Nums**[9] is not in the correct location, since 8 is larger than 6 (Figure 8.18). Thus we exchange **Nums**[9] with **Nums**[4] (Figure 8.19).

Figure 8.17

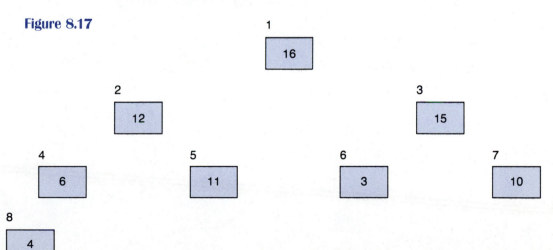

Figure 8.18

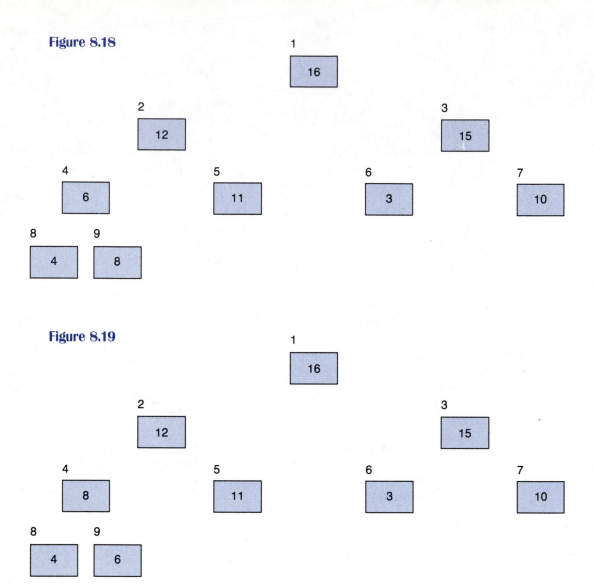

Figure 8.19

Nums[10], which has a value of 14, must be exchanged with its parent (**Nums**[5]) (Figure 8.20 and Figure 8.21). However, we still do not have a heap, because in its new position 14 is still larger than the contents of the parent node (**Nums**[2], with a value of 12). So we switch the contents of **Nums**[5] and **Nums**[2] (Figure 8.22).

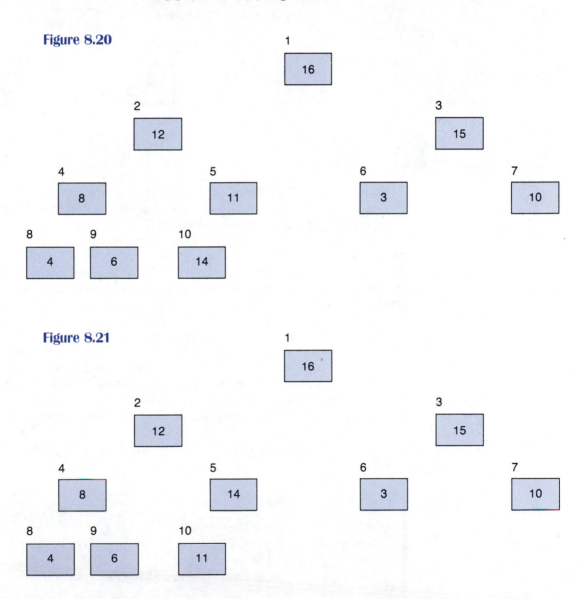

Figure 8.20

Figure 8.21

Figure 8.22

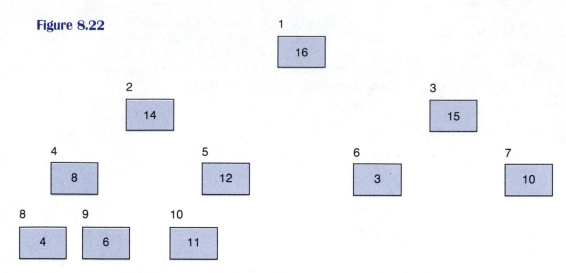

Nums[2] is less than Nums[1], so we have found the correct location for 14. We now have the complete 10-element heap that we wanted to construct. Obviously, the largest element is in Nums[1].

The process that we just walked through, for creating a heap containing all the array elements, is the first phase in the heapsort. We will code a procedure called **CreateHeap** to perform this creation. In pseudocoding this procedure we must remember that each time a new element is added to the previous heap, we must check to make sure that the new element is in its correct position. To do this we have to compare its contents with the contents of its parent. If the value of the contents of the parent is less, we must exchange the contents of new node with that in the parent node. After the exchange, we compare the node with its new parent. If the value of the contents of the new parent is less, we must again exchange. We must continue these comparisons of the node with its parent until the node reaches its correct location in the tree. Remember that all of the work is done within the original array.

In the following pseudocode we assume that **N** is the number of array elements.

Pseudocode

CreateHeap Procedure

FOR each array element from 2 TO **N**
 Initialize **I** to index of node.
 Initialize **F** to index of parent of node.
 WHILE **I** is not 1 and contents of node **I** is larger than contents of its parent node **F**
 Switch contents of node **I** with that of its parent **F**.
 Set **I** to index of its parent.
 IF **I** is larger than 1 THEN

                        Set **F** to index of parent of new node **I**.
            END IF.
        END WHILE.
    END FOR.

The condition in the **while** loop (**I** is not 1) makes sure that the process stops when the root is reached. The Pascal coding for procedure **CreateHeap** follows.

```
{**********************************************************************}
{* CreateHeap - Procedure to create an initial heap consisting of     *}
{*              all the elements in an array.                          *}
{**********************************************************************}
procedure CreateHeap;
var
  I,                                          { Index for node }
  F,                                          { Index for parent }
  M : integer;                                { Index for node }
begin
  for M := 2 to N do begin
    I := M;                                        { Initialize I
                                                to index of node }
    F := I div 2;                            { Initialize F to
                                             index of parent node }
    while (I <> 1) and (Nums[F] < Nums[I]) do begin
          { Switch contents of node I with that of its parent F }
      OneArrayElt := Nums[F];
      Nums[F] := Nums[I];
      Nums[I] := OneArrayElt;
      I := F;                                    { Set I to index
                                                of its parent }

      if I > 1 then
        F := I div 2                       { Set F to index of
                                           parent of new node I }

      { end if }
    end  { while }
  end  { for }
end;  { CreateHeap }
```

The variable **OneArrayElt** is a temporary location to hold one array element while two elements are being switched and **N** is the number of array elements; these variables will be declared in the main heapsort procedure. The **CreateHeap** procedure will be nested within this main procedure.

After the initial heap has been created, the next step in the heap-sorting process is to switch the largest array element, which is now in the root, with the *last* element in the array (see Figure 8.23). The largest array element will then be in its final sorting position. During the remainder of the sorting process, this last largest array element will not be changed.

Figure 8.23

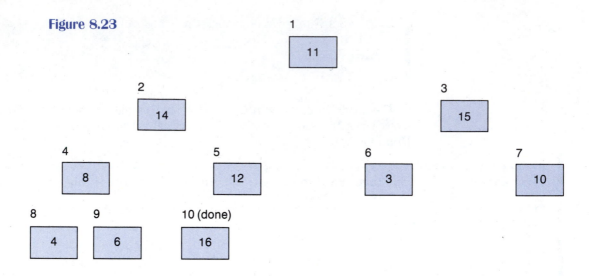

The next step in the heapsort is to adjust the elements **Nums**[1] through **Nums**[9] so that they form a new heap of nine elements. Remember that the first nine elements did form a heap; however, the last array element was switched with the first. Thus the first array element was changed, and it is likely that we do *not* still have a heap. Once we move the first element (if it has to be moved) to its new correct location so that **Nums**[1] through **Nums**[9] form a heap, the second largest number will be in the root. We then exchange the root with **Nums**[9], and the last two elements (**Nums**[9] and **Nums**[10]) are in their correct locations.

We then reform the heap containing **Nums**[1] through **Nums**[8] and exchange **Nums**[1] with **Nums**[8]. This process continues until finally we form the two-element heap consisting of **Nums**[1] and **Nums**[2]. After we switch **Nums**[1] and **Nums**[2], our sort is complete.

The pseudocode for the main **HeapSort** procedure follows.

Pseudocode

HeapSort Procedure

Create an initial heap containing the **N** array elements.
FOR each array element **J** from **N** DOWNTO 2
    Exchange element **J** with the root.
    Adjust the elements from 1 to **J** − 1 so that they reform a
        heap of **J** − 1 elements.
END FOR.

Before we write the Pascal code for procedure **HeapSort**, let us investigate the techniques we will use in procedure **AdjustHeap**, which will adjust the elements with indices from 1 to **J** − 1 so that they form a heap of **J** − 1

Figure 8.24

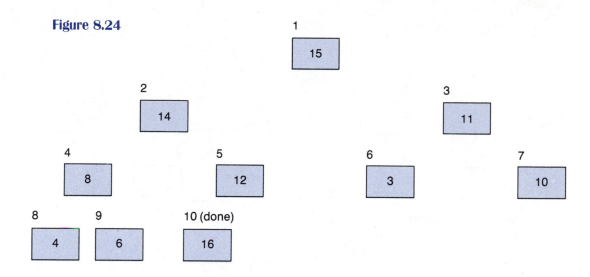

elements. Remember that after the initial heap is created, procedure **Heap-Sort** switches **Nums**[1] with **Nums**[10] (Figure 8.23). Procedure **HeapSort** then calls procedure **AdjustHeap** to adjust the elements **Nums**[1] through **Nums**[9] so that they again form a heap. Procedure **AdjustHeap** must move **Nums**[1] to its correct location. If **Nums**[1] is larger than or equal to both of its children, it is already in the correct location. Otherwise, it must be exchanged with the larger of its two children. Since **Nums**[3] (with a value of 15) is the larger of the two children and is also larger than **Nums**[1], **Nums**[1] and **Nums**[3] are exchanged (see Figure 8.24).

After this exchange, a check must be made to see if the 11 that is now at **Nums**[3] must be moved again. **Nums**[3] is compared with its two children, and if either child is larger than **Nums**[3], then **Nums**[3] must be exchanged with that child. However, **Nums**[3] is larger than each of its two children (**Nums**[6] and **Nums**[7]). Thus the 11 is in its correct location, and the nine-element heap consisting of **Nums**[1] through **Nums**[9] has been restored. Execution then returns from procedure **AdjustHeap** to procedure **Heap-Sort**, which exchanges **Nums**[1] with **Nums**[9] (see Figure 8.25).

Procedure **AdjustHeap** is again called, this time to adjust the elements **Nums**[1] through **Nums**[8] so that they again form a heap. For a heap to be formed, we must move **Nums**[1] (with a value of 6) to its correct location. The first step is to exchange **Nums**[1] with **Nums**[2] (the larger of the two children), creating the tree in Figure 8.26. **Nums**[2], which now has a value of 6, is then switched with the larger of its two children **Nums**[5], resulting in the tree shown in Figure 8.27. The process is now finished, because the only child for **Nums**[5] (which is **Nums**[10]) is already sorted.

Figure 8.25

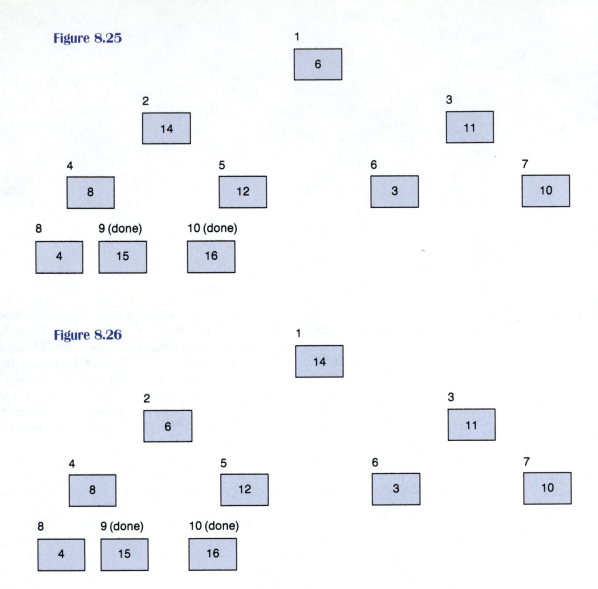

Figure 8.26

Figure 8.27

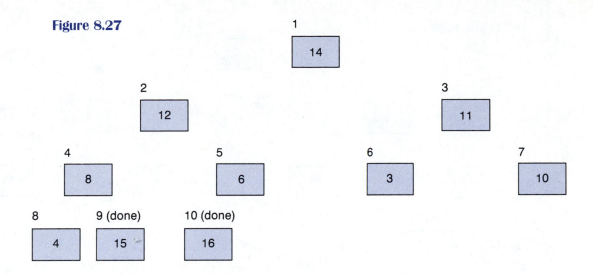

Execution returns from **AdjustHeap** to **HeapSort**, which then switches **Nums**[1] with **Nums**[8], creating the tree depicted in Figure 8.28. Procedure **AdjustHeap** is again called, this time to adjust the heap consisting of the array elements **Nums**[1] through **Nums**[7]. Since **Nums**[2] is the larger of the two children of **Nums**[1] and is also larger than **Nums**[1], **Nums**[1] is exchanged with **Nums**[2] (Figure 8.29). **Nums**[2] must then be switched with **Nums**[4] (Figure 8.30).

Figure 8.28

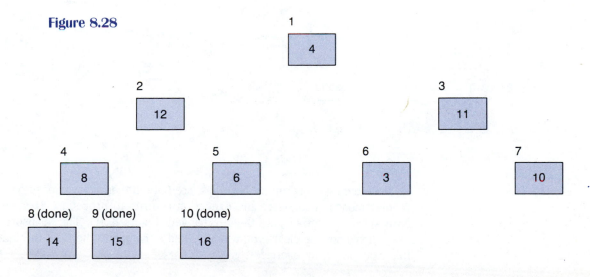

Figure 8.29

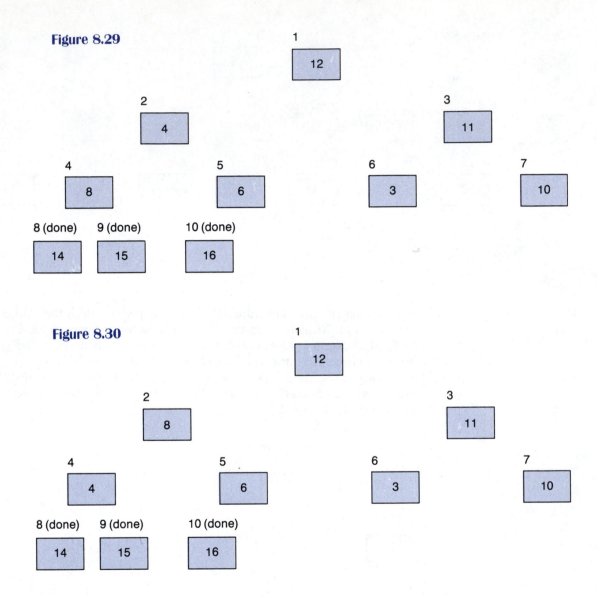

Figure 8.30

Since the two children for **Nums**[4] are both in their correct positions, the readjustment is complete, and execution returns to procedure **HeapSort**. **Nums**[1] and **Nums**[7] are then exchanged (Figure 8.31). The heapsort process should now be clear; you will be asked to complete the walk-through for this example in the exercises.

Figure 8.31

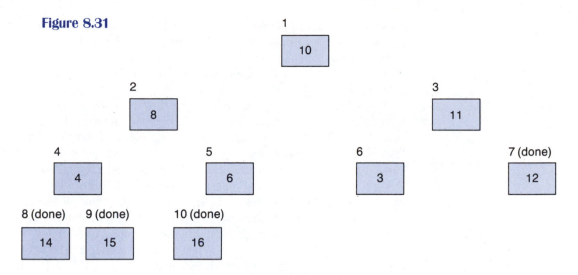

Let us now turn to the coding for procedure **AdjustHeap**. Remember that the procedure starts at the root with the comparison-and-replacement process. The index **M** of the last node that was replaced with the root is passed to **AdjustHeap**.

Pseudocode

> **AdjustHeap Procedure**
>
> Set local variable **ElementToMove** to contents of first array element.
> Initialize **Done** to false.
> Initialize **I** to 1.
> Initialize **S** to 2 (left child of root).
> WHILE **S** is less than **M** and not **Done**
>   IF index for right child, **S** + 1, is less than **M** THEN
>   IF contents of right child is larger than contents of left child THEN
>   Increment **S** to index of right child.
>   END IF.
>   END IF.
>   IF **ElementToMove** is larger than or equal to the value of child THEN
>   Set **Done** to true
>   ELSE
>   Switch contents of node **I** with that of its child (node **S**).
>   Set **I** to index of child (**S**).
>   Set **S** to index of left child of new node **I**.
>   END IF.
> END WHILE.

Notice that in the pseudocode for procedure **AdjustHeap Done** is initialized to false. This Boolean flag will be set to true if at any stage in the comparison a node is found to be larger than or equal to its largest noncompleted child. Then the index **I** is initialized to 1 (for the root) and **S** is set to the index of the left child of the root.

The **while** loop checks to make sure that the node for the child is less than the index of the previously completed node and also that **Done** is not true. Inside the loop is a check to see if the index of the right child is less than **M**. If so, there is another check to see if the contents of the right child is larger than the contents of the left child. If it is, **S** is incremented so that it is the index of the right child. Then if the value for **ElementToMove** (which was the value put in **Nums**[1]) is smaller than the value of the child (with index **S**), the element is moved down by switching the contents of the node with the contents of its child. Next, the indices are moved down by setting **I** to **S** and **S** to the index of the left child of the new node **I**. Then the process jumps back to the top of the **while** loop and continues until **ElementTo-Move** is in the correct position in the heap.

The Pascal coding for **AdjustHeap** follows.

```
{****************************************************************************}
{* AdjustHeap - Procedure to adjust the nodes with indices from 1     *}
{*          through M - 1 so that the nodes again form a heap.        *}
{*       var parameters -                                             *}
{*            None.                                                   *}
{*       value parameters -                                           *}
{*          M : Index of last node that was put into its final        *}
{*              position.                                             *}
{****************************************************************************}
procedure AdjustHeap(M : integer);
var
  ElementToMove : integer;                 { Index of element to move }
  I,                                                       { Index }
  S : integer;                                       { Child index }
  Done : boolean;                             { True when Nums[1]
                                                was not switched }

begin
  ElementToMove := Nums[1];
  Done := false;
  I := 1;
  S := 2;                                        { Initialize S to
                                                left child of root }

  while (S < M) and (not Done) do begin
    if S + 1 < M then                         { If index for right
                                                child is less than M }

      if Nums[S + 1] > Nums[S] then
        S := S + 1;
      { end if }
    { end if }
    if ElementToMove >= Nums[S] then
      Done := true
    { end if }
```

```
    else begin
          { Switch contents of node I with that of its child }
        Nums[I] := Nums[S];
        Nums[S] := ElementToMove;
        I := S;                                    { Set I to
                                                     index of child }
        S := 2 * I                                 { Set S to index
                                                     of left child
                                                     of new node I }

      end  { else }
    end  { while }
end;  { AdjustHeap }
```

We should now be able to write the Pascal code for the main **HeapSort**
procedure. We will make additional comments regarding procedure **Adjust-
Heap** after the listing for **HeapSort**.

```
{***********************************************************************}
{* HeapSort - Procedure to sort integer array Nums into ascending     *}
{*            order using a heapsort.                                  *}
{*      var parameters -                                               *}
{*          Nums : Entire integer array to be sorted.                  *}
{*      value parameters -                                             *}
{*          N : Number of elements in DataArray.                       *}
{***********************************************************************}
procedure HeapSort(var Nums : ArrayType; N : integer);
var
  OneArrayElt : integer;                           { One array element }
  J : integer;                                     { Index }

          ******************************************************
          **     Insert CreateHeap and AdjustHeap        **
          **     procedures here.                        **
          ******************************************************

begin
  CreateHeap;                                      { Create the
                                                     initial N-element heap }

  for J := N downto 2 do begin
            { Exchange element J with root }
    OneArrayElt := Nums[J];
    Nums[J] := Nums[1];
    Nums[1] := OneArrayElt;
    AdjustHeap(J)                                  { Adjust elements 1
                                                     through J - 1 so
                                                     that they reform a
                                                     heap of J - 1 elements }

  end  { for }
end;  { HeapSort }
```

In the **AdjustHeap** procedure the values for **ElementToMove** and **Nums**[S] are switched *each time* the element **ElementToMove** moves down the tree. The following two assignment statements accomplish this switch.

```
Nums[I] := Nums[S];
Nums[S] := ElementToMove;
```

It is not really necessary to execute the second assignment statement *each time* we move, since the value is safely stored in the variable **ElementTo-Move**. We could eliminate the second statement and make the final assignment of **ElementToMove** to the correct node only after the **while** loop in **AdjustHeap** was completed. This change would certainly improve the efficiency of the sort and will be included in the exercises.

The heapsort is one of the most memory-efficient advanced sorting methods that can be used. In addition to those used for the array, the only other memory locations required are those used for the index variables, **I**, **J**, **M**, etc.; for the two variables **OneArrayElt** and **ElementToMove**; and the required memory allocations used for the Pascal procedure calls. Since our version of the heapsort does not use recursion, very little memory is required for the procedure calls. We could even eliminate the memory required for the procedure calls by writing all of the code in the one procedure **HeapSort**, instead of calling the local procedures **CreateHeap** and **AdjustHeap**. This revision is left as an exercise.

It can be shown that the heapsort is of order N log N. However, it is a faster sort than the tree selection sort. Also, as discussed earlier, the heapsort uses less memory than the tree selection sort. Except for sorting of small arrays, the heapsort is an efficient sorting method.

Test runs of **Heapsort** (as listed above) yielded a sorting time of 0.354 second for a random array of 512 integers and 2.205 seconds for a random array of 2500 integers. Thus the **Heapsort** procedure is much faster than the **TreeSelectSort** procedure from Section 8.2 and slightly faster than the **ShellSort** procedure from Section 8.1. If the second assignment statement is moved out of the **while** loop in the **AdjustHeap** procedure as discussed earlier, these times improve to 0.342 second and 2.092 seconds.

Summary: Heapsort Method

1. Initialize the original array into a heap as follows.
   Consider the first array element to be a one-element heap.
   Rearrange (if necessary) the first two elements of the array so that these elements form a two-element heap.
   Rearrange (if necessary) the first three elements of the array so that these elements form a three-element heap.
   Repeat this process until all **N** elements form an **N**-element heap.

2. For array index values of **J** from **N** down to 2:
   Exchange the value in element **J** with the value in the root.
   Adjust the elements with indices from 1 to **J** − 1 so that they form a
      heap (of **J** − 1 elements).

Exercises

8.17 Complete the walk-through of procedure **HeapSort** for the example in this section on sorting the **Nums** array.

8.18 Rewrite program **TestSort** from Section 8.1 so that it creates a randomly generated **Numbers** array containing 512 elements. Then call procedure **HeapSort** to sort the array. Insert a **writeln** loop after the sort to make sure your sort is working. Then remove this loop and check the sorting time required. Repeat with an array of 2500 random numbers.

8.19 As discussed at the end of this section, eliminate the

```
Nums[S] := ElementToMove
```

statement for *each* move and include the correct final assignment statement for execution after the **while** loop is exited. Rerun the sorts in Exercise 8.18 and compare the new sorting times with that required there.

8.20 Redo Exercise 8.19 using integer arrays that are already in ascending order. Repeat for arrays in descending order.

8.21 Rewrite procedure **HeapSort** so that no procedure calls are made. That is, include the content of procedures **CreateHeap** and **AdjustHeap** as part of the normal code in **HeapSort**. Eliminate all unnecessary statements. Redo Exercise 8.19 using this version of **HeapSort**.

8.22 Redo Exercise 8.6 using the **HeapSort** procedure instead of **ShellSort**. Compare the sorting time with the sorting times found in Exercises 8.6 and 8.12.

8.23 Redo Exercise 8.10 using the **HeapSort** procedure instead of **ShellSort**. Compare the sorting time with the times found in Exercises 8.10 and 8.16.

8.4 Quicksort

One of the fastest and most commonly used routines for sorting large arrays is the *quicksort*. It was invented by C. A. R. Hoare, and the amount of code necessary is surprisingly small considering the quicksort's excellent speed.

In general, the quicksort involves selecting an element from an array and then rearranging all of the remaining elements into subarrays such that all elements that are smaller than the given element are put into one subarray and all elements that are larger than the given element are put into a second subarray. Thus the process puts all large elements (compared to the selected element) into one subarray and all small elements (compared to the element) into another subarray.

For example, suppose we have the following nine-element array.

$$8 \quad 22 \quad 30 \quad 16 \quad 20 \quad 18 \quad 12 \quad 14 \quad 25$$

Our first step in the quicksort is to select an arbitrary element from the array. Since we are free to select any element, it would appear that a middle element will be a good selection. The closer the value we choose is to the median value of the array, the more efficient the sort will be. For an array that is sorted or even almost sorted, the middle element is certainly a good choice, and for a random array, the middle element is as good a choice as any other.

Assume that we select the middle element, 20. The next step is to set up two pointers to the array. These pointers, which originally point to the first and last elements of the array, are really just array indices. The first pointer, which we will call I, will point to the first element. Thus $I = 1$. The second pointer, which we will call J, will point to the last element. Thus, in our example, $J = 9$.

$$8 \quad 22 \quad 30 \quad 16 \quad \textcircled{20} \quad 18 \quad 12 \quad 14 \quad 25$$
$$\uparrow \qquad\qquad\qquad\qquad\qquad\qquad\qquad\qquad\quad \uparrow$$
$$I \qquad\qquad\qquad\qquad\qquad\qquad\qquad\qquad\quad J$$

Now, *while I* points to an element that is *less* than the middle element, 20, we increment the value for I by 1. In this example, I originally points to 8. Since 8 is less than 20, we increment I by 1. Now I points to 22.

$$8 \quad 22 \quad 30 \quad 16 \quad \textcircled{20} \quad 18 \quad 12 \quad 14 \quad 25$$
$$\uparrow \qquad\qquad\qquad\qquad\qquad\qquad\qquad\qquad\quad \uparrow$$
$$I \qquad\qquad\qquad\qquad\qquad\qquad\qquad\qquad\quad J$$

Since 22 is not less than 20, we do not increment I again. On the other end of the array, *while J* points to an element that is *greater* than 20, we decrement J by 1. Since 25 is greater than 20, we decrement J. J now points to 14, and since 14 is not greater than 20, we do not decrement J again.

$$8 \quad 22 \quad 30 \quad 16 \quad \textcircled{20} \quad 18 \quad 12 \quad 14 \quad 25$$
$$\uparrow \qquad\qquad\qquad\qquad\qquad\qquad\qquad \uparrow$$
$$I \qquad\qquad\qquad\qquad\qquad\qquad\qquad J$$

We have now found two elements that should be exchanged, since 22 and 14 are both on the wrong sides of 20 for a finished sort. This is exactly what we do next in the quicksort. We exchange the elements pointed to by I and J.

$$8 \quad 14 \quad 30 \quad 16 \quad \textcircled{20} \quad 18 \quad 12 \quad 22 \quad 25$$
$$\uparrow \qquad\qquad\qquad\qquad\qquad\qquad\qquad \uparrow$$
$$I \qquad\qquad\qquad\qquad\qquad\qquad\qquad J$$

Each time that we switch two elements, we will then *increment I* by 1 and *decrement J* by 1.

8   14   30   16   ⑳   18   12   22   25
              ↑   ↑
              I   J

Our process now repeats. That is, while I points to an element less than 20, we increment I. However, 30 is larger than 20, so we do not increment I. On the other side, while J points to an element larger than 20, we decrement J; but since 12 is not larger than 20, we do not decrement J. As before, we have again found two elements that are on the wrong sides of 20. Thus, we exchange them.

8   14   12   16   ⑳   18   30   22   25
              ↑   ↑
              I   J

After the exchange, we must increment I and decrement J.

8   14   12   16   ⑳   18   30   22   25
              ↑   ↑
              I   J

The process now repeats. While I points to an element less than 20, we increment I. Since 16 is less than 20, we increment I.

8   14   12   16   20   18   30   22   25
                    ↑   ↑
                    I   J

I now points to 20. Since 20 is not less than 20, we do not increment I again. While J points to an element greater than 20, we decrement J. Since 18 is not greater than 20, we do not decrement J. We now exchange the elements pointed to by I and J.

8   14   12   16   18   ⑳   30   22   25
                    ↑   ↑
                    I   J

Since a switch has been made, we increment I and decrement J.

8   14   12   16   18   ⑳   30   22   25
                    ↑   ↑
                    J   I

We now have the situation where $I > J$. When the two pointers have passed each other, we know that our first rearrangement is complete. Notice that the array is now partitioned into two subarrays such that all elements in the first subarray are less than or equal to 20, and all elements in the second subarray are greater than or equal to 20.

Left Subarray	*Right Subarray*
8 14 12 16 18	(20) 30 22 25

To be more precise, for this **Nums** array

$$\textbf{Nums}[K] <= 20 \qquad \text{FOR } K = 1 \ldots I - 1$$
$$(K = 1 \ldots 5)$$

$$\textbf{Nums}[K] >= 20 \qquad \text{FOR } K = J + 1 \ldots N$$
$$(K = 6 \ldots 9)$$

Notice, also, that we can use J to be the ending index for the left subarray. Thus the indices for the left subarray are $1 \ldots J$ ($1 \ldots 5$). Similarly, we can use I to be the beginning index for the right subarray. The indices for the right subarray are $I \ldots N$ ($6 \ldots 9$).

$$\text{Left subarray indices} \qquad 1 \ldots J$$
$$\text{Right subarray indices} \qquad I \ldots N$$

In the above example, 20 ended up in the right subarray. However, depending on the array, the middle number could end up in the left subarray or it may end up between the left and the right subarrays. For example, suppose we have the following array and select 6 as the middle value.

$$1 \quad 2 \quad 7 \quad (6) \quad 8 \quad 9 \quad 9$$
$$\uparrow \qquad\qquad\qquad\qquad \uparrow$$
$$I \qquad\qquad\qquad\qquad\quad J$$

While I points to an element less than 6, we increment I. I then points to 7.

$$1 \quad 2 \quad 7 \quad (6) \quad 8 \quad 9 \quad 9$$
$$\qquad\quad \uparrow \qquad\qquad \uparrow$$
$$\qquad\quad I \qquad\qquad\;\; J$$

While J points to an element larger than 6, we decrement J. J then points to 6.

$$1 \quad 2 \quad 7 \quad (6) \quad 8 \quad 9 \quad 9$$
$$\qquad\quad \uparrow \;\; \uparrow$$
$$\qquad\quad I \;\; J$$

We now switch elements 7 and 6,

$$1 \quad 2 \quad (6) \quad 7 \quad 8 \quad 9 \quad 9$$
$$\qquad\quad \uparrow \;\; \uparrow$$
$$\qquad\quad I \;\; J$$

and then increment I and decrement J.

$$1 \quad 2 \quad ⑥ \quad 7 \quad 8 \quad 9 \quad 9$$
$$\uparrow \quad \uparrow$$
$$J \quad I$$

Since I and J have passed each other, the rearrangement is complete. The left subarray with indices of 1 through 3 contains the selected middle value.

Left Subarray	*Right Subarray*
1 2 6	7 8 9 9

This illustrates that the middle element chosen may end up in the left subarray.

Now, let us look at one more possibility. Consider the following subarray (which is already in order), in which 4 is selected as the middle value.

$$1 \quad 2 \quad 3 \quad ④ \quad 5 \quad 6 \quad 7$$
$$\uparrow \qquad\qquad\qquad \uparrow$$
$$I \qquad\qquad\qquad J$$

As before, while I points to an element less than 4, we increment I. I now points to 4.

$$1 \quad 2 \quad 3 \quad ④ \quad 5 \quad 6 \quad 7$$
$$\uparrow \qquad \uparrow$$
$$I \qquad J$$

While J points to an element larger than 4, we decrement J. J now points to 4.

$$1 \quad 2 \quad 3 \quad ④ \quad 5 \quad 6 \quad 7$$
$$\uparrow$$
$$I$$
$$J$$

As before, we must now switch the elements pointed to by I and J. In this case they are the same. Thus 4 is switched with itself, I is incremented, and J is decremented.

$$1 \quad 2 \quad 3 \quad ④ \quad 5 \quad 6 \quad 7$$
$$\uparrow \qquad \uparrow$$
$$J \qquad I$$

Since I and J have passed each other, this rearrangement is finished. Notice that for this array the middle number 4 ends up between the left and right subarrays.

Left Subarray		*Right Subarray*
1 2 3	④	5 6 7

What happens when other elements have the same value as the middle value will be investigated in the exercises. Regardless of the array, however, the rearrangement process results in the partitioning of the array. Thus it is common to refer to the rearrangement of elements of the array as a partitioning of the array.

Now that we have a grasp of the method used for this first rearrangement (or partitioning) step, let us investigate the coding of this first step before we discuss the remaining steps involved in the quicksort.

The coding for our **QSort** procedure follows directly from the steps used in our examples. Value parameters passed to the procedure will include **First**, which is the index of the first array element, and **Last**, which is the index of the last array element. In our original nine-element array example, **First** would be 1, and **Last** would be 9.

```
{*******************************************************************}
{* QSort - First rearrangement step of the quicksort procedure to  *}
{*         sort an array Nums of integer numbers into ascending     *}
{*         order.                                                   *}
{*         var parameters -                                         *}
{*             None.                                                *}
{*         value parameters -                                       *}
{*             First : First array index.                           *}
{*             Last :  Last array index.                            *}
{*******************************************************************}
procedure QSort(First, Last : integer);
var
  I,                                             { Array index }
  J,                                             { Array index }
  Mid,                                     { Middle array value }
  Save : integer;                      { Temporary save variable }
begin
  I := First;
  J := Last;
  Mid := Nums[(First + Last) div 2];             { Find middle index }
  repeat
    while Nums[I] < Mid do
      I := I + 1;
    { end while }
    while Nums[J] > Mid do
      J := J - 1;
    { end while }
    if I <= J then begin
             { Switch Nums[I] with Nums[J] }
      Save := Nums[I];
      Nums[I] := Nums[J];
      Nums[J] := Save;
      I := I + 1;
      J := J - 1
    end   { if }
  until I > J
end;  { QSort }
```

Now that we know how to code the first rearrangement step in the quick-sort, let us return to the nine-element array example and investigate the remaining steps in the complete sort. Recall that we had partitioned the array as follows.

Left Subarray	Right subarray
8 14 12 16 18	(20) 30 22 25

Also, remember that the range of indices for the left subarray was $1..J$, and the range of indices for the right subarray was $I..N$. As might be suspected at this point, the quicksort continues by rearranging each of these subarrays using the same method used for the first rearrangement step. Thus sorting the left subarray involves the same procedure as before except that now **First** = 1 and **Last** = 5. Sorting the right subarray involves the same procedure as before except that **First** = 6 and **Last** = 9.

This discussion suggests that recursive calls be made to the **QSort** procedure. Sorting the above left subarray requires the call

```
QSort(First, J)    { where First = 1 for this subarray }
```

Assume that this call has been made to **QSort**. **I** is set to 1, **J** is set to 5, and **Mid** is found to be 12.

$$8 \quad 14 \quad \textcircled{12} \quad 16 \quad 18$$
$$\uparrow \qquad\qquad\qquad\qquad \uparrow$$
$$I \qquad\qquad\qquad\qquad\quad J$$

Since 8 is less than 12, *I* is incremented.

$$8 \quad 14 \quad \textcircled{12} \quad 16 \quad 18$$
$$\qquad \uparrow \qquad\qquad\qquad \uparrow$$
$$\qquad I \qquad\qquad\qquad\quad J$$

J is decremented until it points to 12.

$$8 \quad 14 \quad \textcircled{12} \quad 16 \quad 18$$
$$\qquad \uparrow \quad \uparrow$$
$$\qquad I \quad J$$

The 14 and the 12 are switched.

$$8 \quad \textcircled{12} \quad 14 \quad 16 \quad 18$$
$$\qquad \uparrow \quad \uparrow$$
$$\qquad I \quad J$$

I is incremented, and *J* is decremented.

$$8 \quad \textcircled{12} \quad 14 \quad 16 \quad 18$$
$$\qquad \uparrow \quad \uparrow$$
$$\qquad J \quad I$$

Since *I* has passed *J*, this next rearrangement step is done, and we have the following two subarrays.

Left Subarray	Right Subarray
8 ⑫	14 16 18

When **QSort** is called again to sort this left subarray, the left subarray is partitioned into two smaller subarrays:

Left Subarray	Right Subarray
8	12

At this point, the left subarray contains only one element. Thus the calls to **QSort** to sort the left subarrays should stop. Remember that the *normal* range of indices for any left subarray is **First..J**. Therefore if **J** is not larger than **First**, the left subarray contains only one element, and there is certainly no sense in sorting a one-element subarray. Thus the recursive call to sort the left subarrays can be

```
if First < J then
   QSort(First, J);
```

When the left subarrays are completely sorted, then sorting of the right subarrays will start. However, because of the recursive order, the right subarrays must be sorted in the reverse order. That is, we start by sorting the last right subarray first. In our example the last subarray is

Right Subarray
12

Since this subarray contains only one element, the process should return to the next previous right subarray:

Right Subarray
14   16   18

A right subarray can be sorted with the recursive call

```
QSort(I, Last);
```

However, as with the left subarrays, a check should be made to make sure that **Last > I**. Thus the coding should be

```
if I < Last then
   Qsort(I, Last);
```

How do we *remember* the previous **I** and **Last** values? Well, remember we are making recursive calls. Also, remember that the value parameters **First** and **Last** and the local variables **I** and **J** are kept on the stack for each recursive call. Thus as the process backs through previous calls, the old **First**, **Last**, **I**, and **J** values can be retrieved.

We are now ready to complete the coding for the entire quicksort process.

We will use a control procedure called **QuickSort** to accept the array and the number of elements as parameters. Notice that the only difference between the first rearrangement and the complete quicksort procedure **QSort** is the addition of the two conditional recursive calls at the bottom.

```
{*********************************************************************}
{* QuickSort - Control procedure for procedure QSort.               *}
{*      var parameters -                                            *}
{*          Nums : Array of integer numbers.                        *}
{*      value parameters -                                          *}
{*          N : Number of elements in the array.                    *}
{*********************************************************************}
procedure QuickSort(var Nums : ArrayType; N : integer);
{*********************************************************************}
{* QSort - Recursive quicksort procedure to sort an array Nums of   *}
{*         integer numbers into ascending order.                    *}
{*      var parameters -                                            *}
{*          None.                                                   *}
{*      value parameters -                                          *}
{*          First : First array index.                             *}
{*          Last :  Last array index.                               *}
{*********************************************************************}
procedure QSort(First, Last : integer);
var
  I,                                              { Array index }
  J,                                              { Array index }
  Mid,                                       { Middle array value }
  Save : integer;                       { Temporary save variable }
begin
  I := First;
  J := Last;
  Mid := Nums[(First + Last) div 2];        { Find middle array value }
  repeat
    while Nums[I] < Mid do
      I := I + 1;
    { end while }
    while Nums[J] > Mid do
      J := J - 1;
    { end while }
    if I <= J then begin
            { Switch Nums[I] with Nums[J] }
      Save := Nums[I];
      Nums[I] := Nums[J];
      Nums[J] := Save;
      I := I + 1;
      J := J - 1
    end  { if }
  until I > J;
  if First < J then
    QSort(First, J);                            { Make recursive call
                                                  to QSort with
                                                  same First value and
                                                  Last value set to J }
```

```
   { end if }
   if I < Last then
      QSort(I, Last)                          { Make recursive call
                                                to QSort with
                                                value for First set to
                                                I and same Last value }

      { end if }
end;  { QSort }

begin  { QuickSort }
   QSort(1, N)                                     { Call QSort
                                                      to sort array }

end;  { QuickSort }
```

As may be seen from the code, the first recursive call

```
if First < J then
   QSort(First, J)
```

will be executed over and over to partition the left subarrays until finally the condition **First >= J** is reached. At this point, the **QSort** procedure can finally start completing execution for each recursive call. The only statement that remains to be executed is

```
if I < Last then
   QSort(I, Last)
```

This statement is a recursive call to **QSort** to partition the right subarray. Once this right subarray has been partitioned, the procedure returns to the previous call made by **QSort(First, J)** and again finishes execution of the procedure by calling **QSort** to sort the right subarray for that call. This process continues as execution backs out of the previous recursive calls. Notice that each time a right subarray is partitioned a left subarray may very well result which then has to be partitioned. A complete logical walk-through for **QSort** will be included in the exercises.

It can be shown that the quicksort method is of order N log N. A timed run of **QuickSort** to sort a randomly ordered 2500-element array **Nums** of integer numbers required only 1.16 seconds. For a 512-element array of random integer numbers, the sorting time was only 0.195 second. Thus the quicksort method is extremely efficient. Compared to the other sorts we have worked with both in Chapter 4 and earlier in this chapter, the quicksort is by far the fastest sort.

Recall that the closer the selected middle values are to the medians, the more efficient the process will be. Thus a potential hazard is the selection of middle values that are far from the median, which results in a large drop in efficiency. However, in actual practice, the selection of a large number of poor middle values is rare.

Some versions of the quicksort method select the first value of an array instead of the middle value. For randomly ordered arrays this causes no problems. However, for an array that is already ordered, this selection results in a highly inefficient sort which requires a large amount of memory because of the increased number of recursive calls. Thus the selection of the middle value is a good choice for all types of arrays.

Summary: Quicksort Method

1. Initialize **I** to **First** (the first array index).
2. Initialize **J** to **Last** (the last array index).
3. Select a middle element, **Mid**, in the array.

REPEAT

4. While the element at index **I** is less than **Mid**, increment **I** by 1.
5. While the element at index **J** is greater than **Mid**, decrement **J** by 1.
6. If **I** <= **J**, switch the array element at index **I** with the array element at index **J**.

UNTIL **I** > **J**

7. If **J** > **First**, call **QSort** to partition the left subarray from index **First** to index **J**.
8. If **I** < **Last**, call **QSort** to partition the right subarray from index **I** to index **Last**.

Exercises

8.24 If an array has more than one element with the same value as the middle value selected, will the multiple elements be put in the left subarray, the right subarray, both, or neither, or does it depend on the array? Illustrate your answer(s) with examples.

8.25 Walk through all steps in the complete sort of the nine-element array **Nums** that was used as an example in this section. Be sure to indicate the values for **First**, **Last**, **I**, and **J** for each partitioning stage.

8.26 Using a 2500-element array of randomly generated integer numbers, test the sorting time using the **QSort** procedure within program **TestSort** on your computer. Record this time and compare it with the sorting times using **ShellSort**, **TreeSelectSort**, and **HeapSort**.

8.27 Repeat Exercise 8.26 using a 512-element array of randomly generated integer numbers. Record the time and compare it with those for earlier sorts.

8.28 Repeat Exercise 8.26 with arrays of integer numbers that are already in ascending order. Repeat for arrays in descending order.

8.29 Revise **QuickSort** and **QSort** to sort the array of records in Exercise 8.6 according to social security number. Sort so that the social security numbers will be in ascending order. Record the execution time. How does this time compare with those of other sorts on this array of records?

8.30 Revise **QuickSort** and **QSort** to sort the inventory records in Exercise 8.10. Print the data before and after sorting. Then remove the **writeln** loops that print the data and check the actual sorting time. How does this time compare with the sorting times required for the sorting methods discussed earlier in this chapter?

8.5 Nonrecursive Quicksort

Since the quicksort method is quite efficient for sorting large arrays and is one of the most commonly used sorts, it is well worth the effort to investigate the possibility of improving its speed and/or memory requirements. Recall from Chapter 5 that it is possible to improve the speed and/or memory requirements of recursively designed programs by replacing the recursive calls with nonrecursive code. Also, an investigation of how the quicksort can be written without using recursion will provide the understanding necessary to code the procedure if a recursive language is not available.

In **QSort** there are two recursive call statements:

```
if First < J then
   QSort(First, J);
```

and

```
if I < Last then
   QSort(I, Last)
```

Since the last recursive call statement is right before the **end;** statement in the procedure, we can easily replace it. Remember that this recursive call will

1. Pass the formal parameter **I** to the parameter **First**.
2. Pass the formal parameter **Last** to the parameter **Last**.
3. Jump to the beginning of the procedure.

We could replace this recursive call by setting the value of **First** to **I** and then jumping to the top of the procedure. However, before coding this approach, let us take a look at the first recursive call,

```
if First < J then
   QSort(First, J)
```

This recursive call will also transfer execution back to the top of the procedure. It will pass the argument **J** to the parameter **Last**. However, it is very important to remember that during execution of any recursive procedure, copies of *all local variables* for each call are saved on a stack. Why is this important for us here? Recall that after we terminate the recursive calls to partition the left subarrays, we begin partitioning the right subarrays in reverse order. In order to partition these right subarrays we must know the **I** and **Last** values to use for these subarrays. This was automatically done for us with the Pascal recursive calls. However, if we do not use recursive calls, then we must save these **I** and **Last** values on a stack to simulate the recursive calls.

With these ideas in mind, we can now rewrite the pseudocode for **QSort**. We will name the modified procedure **QSort2**.

Pseudocode

QSort2 Procedure

Initialize stack.
Push value for **First** onto stack.
Push value for **Last** onto stack.
REPEAT
    Pop top stack value and assign it to **Last**.
    Pop top stack value and assign it to **First**.
    REPEAT
        Set **I** to **First**.
        Set **J** to **Last**.
        Find middle element value, **Mid**.
        REPEAT
            WHILE **Nums**[**I**] is less than **Mid**
                Increment **I** by 1.
            END WHILE.
            WHILE **Nums**[**J**] is larger than **Mid**
                Decrement **J** by 1.
            END WHILE.
            IF **I** <= **J** THEN
                Switch **Nums**[**I**] and **Nums**[**J**].
                Increment **I** by 1.
                Decrement **J** by 1.
            END IF.
        UNTIL **I** > **J**.
        IF **I** < **Last** THEN
            Push **I** value onto stack.
            Push **Last** value onto stack.
        END IF.
        Set **Last** to **J**.
    UNTIL **First** > **Last**.
UNTIL stack is empty.

Notice that the

Set **Last** to **J**.

statement sets up for partitioning of the next left subarray. **First** is still **First** for the next partition, so when execution goes back to the top of the procedure, the left subarray will be sorted from index **First** to index **J**. The

UNTIL **First** > **Last**

statement will continue the process of sorting the left subarrays until **First** > **J**. The sequence

IF **I** < **Last** THEN
    :
END IF.

will push the beginning and ending indices for the right subarray that must still be partitioned onto the stack (as long as the right subarray has more than one element).

The Pascal coding and test runs for **QSort2** are included in the exercises.

In general, the quicksort is usually quite efficient. However, remember that the continued selection of poor middle values can hurt the process. For example, in some of the worst cases, partitioning may cause the saving of a significant number of pairs of indices for subarrays that have a *very small* number of elements (as few as 1). Thus a large amount of memory may be wasted in order to save all these pairs of indices. We can partially solve this particular problem by always processing the smaller of the two subarrays and by pushing the indices for the larger subarray onto the stack for future processing.

This change is rather easy to code. We will replace the sequence

IF **I** < **Last** THEN
    Push **I** value onto stack.
    Push right value onto stack.
END IF.
Set **Last** to **J**.

with a check to see which subarray has fewer elements. Then we will stack the **First** and **Last** indices for the larger subarray and proceed to partition the smaller subarray. We will call the revised procedure **NonrecQSort**.

The Pascal coding for **NonrecQSort** follows.

```
{******************************************************************}
{* NonrecQSort - Nonrecursive quicksort procedure to sort an array  *}
{*            Nums of integer numbers into ascending order.         *}
{*      var parameters -                                            *}
{*          None.                                                   *}
{*      value parameters -                                          *}
{*          Nums : Array of integer numbers.                        *}
{*          N : Number of elements in the Nums array.               *}
{*      calls -                                                     *}
{*          InitStack : Procedure to initialize the stack.          *}
{*          PushStack : Procedure to push one data value onto the   *}
{*                      stack.                                       *}
{*          PopStack : Procedure to pop one data value from the     *}
{*                      stack.                                       *}
{******************************************************************}
procedure NonrecQSort(var Nums : ArrayType; N : integer);
```

```
var
  I,                                              { Array index }
  J,                                              { Array index }
  First,                                    { First array index }
  Last,                                      { Last array index }
  MidValue,                                 { Middle array value }
  Save : integer;                       { Temporary save variable }
begin
  InitStack(StTop, Empty);                   { Initialize stack }
  PushStack(1, StTop, Empty);              { Push 1 onto stack }
  PushStack(N, StTop, Empty);              { Push N onto stack }
  repeat
    PopStack(Last, StTop, Empty);        { Pop stack value Last }
    PopStack(First, StTop, Empty);      { Pop stack value First }
    repeat
      I := First;
      J := Last;
      MidValue := Nums[(First + Last) div 2];
      repeat
        while Nums[I] < MidValue do
          I := I + 1;
        { end while }
        while Nums[J] > MidValue do
          J := J - 1;
        { end while }
        if I <= J then begin
                { Switch Nums[I] and Nums[J] }
          Save := Nums[I];
          Nums[I] := Nums[J];
          Nums[J] := Save;
          I := I + 1;
          J := J - 1
        end  { if }
      until I > J;
      if J - First < Last - I then begin    { If left
                                             subarray has fewer
                                             elements than the right }

        if I < Last then begin
          PushStack(I, StTop, Empty);           { Push I onto stack }
          PushStack(Last, StTop, Empty)      { Push Last onto stack }
        end;  { if }
        Last := J
      end  { if }
      else begin
        if First < J then begin
          PushStack(First, StTop, Empty);    { Push First onto stack }
          PushStack(J, StTop, Empty)           { Push J onto stack }
        end;  { if }
        First := I
      end  { else }
    until First >= Last
  until Empty                               { Until stack is empty }
end;  { NonrecQSort }
```

Notice that the

IF **I** < **Last**

statement checks to see if the right subarray contains more than one element. If it does not, its indices will *not* be pushed onto the stack. Similarly, the

IF **First** < **J**

statement does the same for the left subarray. Since the procedure is nonrecursive, we will eliminate the control procedure that we used in Section 8.4.

The added overhead associated with always selecting the smaller subarray to process may cause an increase in sorting time for "normal" arrays. However, remember that we have eased the problems associated with the "abnormal" cases. Using program **TestSort**, the **NonrecQSort** procedure was used to sort a randomly generated 512-element file of integer numbers. The sorting time was 0.308 second. For a 2500-element array of random integers, the time was 1.674 seconds.

These times for a "normal" array are not as good as the times we found for the recursive version of the quicksort in Section 8.4. We should be able to improve this sorting time if we eliminate the procedure calls to **InitStack**, **PushStack**, and **PopStack**. Eliminating these calls should also decrease the amount of memory required for the quicksort process, since we will have eliminated all memory required for the procedure calls within the quicksort procedure. Coding this approach will be included in the chapter exercises.

Exercises

8.31 Walk through all steps in the complete sort of the nine-element array **Nums** using **QSort2**. Be sure to indicate the values for **First**, **Last**, **I**, and **J** for each partitioning stage.

8.32 Write the Pascal code for **QSort2** and repeat Exercise 8.26 using **QSort2** instead of **QSort**. Record the execution time and compare it with that found for **QSort**.

8.33 Repeat Exercise 8.27 using **QSort2** instead of **Qsort**. Record the execution time and compare it with the time for **QSort**.

8.34 Repeat Exercise 8.28 using **QSort2** instead of **QSort**. Run the procedure and compare the execution time with that found in Exercise 8.28.

8.35 Rewrite **QSort2** and redo Exercise 8.26. Compare the sorting times.

8.36 Rewrite **QSort2** and redo Exercise 8.10. Compare the sorting times.

8.37 Walk through all steps in the complete sort of the nine-element array **Nums** using **NonrecQSort**. Be sure to indicate the values for **First**, **Last**, **I**, and **J** for each partitioning stage.

8.38   Repeat Exercise 8.26 using **NonrecQSort** instead of **QSort**. Record the execution time and compare it with the times found for earlier sorts.

8.39   Repeat Exercise 8.27 using **NonrecQSort** instead of **QSort**. Record and compare the execution times.

8.40   Rewrite the **NonrecQSort** procedure to sort the array of records from Exercise 8.6. Record and compare the execution times.

Summary

In this chapter, four advanced array-sorting methods have been investigated. For larger arrays, each of these methods is significantly faster than the elementary sorting methods investigated in Chapter 4. However, except in the case of the recursive quicksort, the code for these advanced methods is longer than for the simpler sorts.

The sorting times required by the advanced methods to sort arrays of 512 and 2500 randomly generated integer elements are summarized in the following table:

	512 elements	*2500 elements*
Shellsort	.370 second	2.540 seconds
Tree Selection Sort	.487 second	3.171 seconds
Heapsort	.342 second	2.092 seconds
Recursive Quicksort	.195 second	1.160 seconds
Nonrecursive Quicksort (with subarray selection)	.308 second	1.674 seconds

The times for the nonrecursive quicksort are for the version that includes calls to the **InitStack**, **PushStack**, and **PopStack** procedures. As will be seen in the chapter exercises, these times can be reduced by having the codes for these procedures written directly within the quicksort procedure instead of having calls made to separately written procedures.

Very little memory, in addition to that needed for the array itself, is required by the Shellsort or the heapsort. However, the tree selection sort requires significantly more memory than that needed for the array itself. This is especially true if the number of array elements is not a power of 2. The recursive quicksort procedure requires memory for each of the recursive calls. The nonrecursive version of quicksort with no procedure calls uses less additional memory than the recursive version.

Even though these sorts are relatively efficient, the door is always open for more efficient sorting methods. If sorting is done on relatively large arrays and is done quite frequently, the time involved can become significant. The use of the best sorting method can save hours of computer time, and it is the programmer's responsibility to know the alternatives and to select the most appropriate technique or techniques.

Chapter Exercises

8.41 It is possible to reduce the execution time of **NonrecQSort** by eliminating the procedure calls to **InitStack**, **PushStack**, and **PopStack**. This can be done by directly entering the codes for these procedures in **NonrecQSort** instead of having the procedure calls. Rewrite **NonrecQSort** with these changes and repeat Exercise 8.32. Record and compare execution times.

8.42 Each line of a data file **DataF** contains a record of data according to the following format.

Columns		
1–7	Inventory number	(7 characters)
8–27	Description	(20 characters)
30–32	Quantity on hand	(Integer)
35–36	Reorder number	(Integer)
40–45	Cost of item	(Real)
50–55	Selling price	(Real)

(a) Write a program that reads the data into an array and then calls a Shell-sort procedure to sort the data into ascending order according to inventory number. Then write the sorted array data to a file **SortI**.

(b) Write the Shellsort procedure to sort the data into ascending order according to description instead of according to inventory numbers. Then write the sorted array data to a file, **SortD**.

8.43 Redo Exercise 8.42 using the other sorting procedures developed in this chapter:

> tree selection sort
> heapsort
> quicksort
> nonrecursive quicksort

Compare the sorting times.

8.44 Each line of a data file **DFile** contains a record of data according to the following format.

Columns		
1–20	Name	(20 characters)
21–64	Address	(44 characters)
65–76	Phone number	(12 characters)

(a) Write a program that reads the data into an array and then calls a Shell-sort procedure to sort the data into ascending order according to name. Then write the data from the sorted array to a file **SortN**.

(b) Instead of sorting by the name, write the Shellsort procedure to sort the data into ascending order according to phone number. Write the sorted data to a file **SortP**.

8.45 Redo Exercise 8.44 using the other sorting procedures developed in this chapter:

> tree selection sort
> heapsort
> quicksort
> nonrecursive quicksort

Compare the sorting times.

CHAPTER 9

Files

As you know, variables, arrays, sets, and records are all used to store data during the execution of a program. In this book we have also dealt with other structures, such as linked lists and trees, that are used to store data. However, none of these structures can be used to store data from one run of a program to the next. All of these variables and structures exist only while the program in which they are defined is executing; the memory space allocated to them by the program is released when the program ends. In order to store data so that they can be used for different runs of a single program or even for runs of different programs, most languages have a structure called a file in which the data can be stored. A *file* is a data structure consisting of a sequence of components all of the same data type. In order for data to be saved so that they can be used again, the data must be written to a file and the file must be stored on a peripheral storage device such as a disk or a tape.

In the first eight chapters, we used text files in all of our examples that used files. Recall that the identifier **text** is used for the built-in type declaration

```
type
  text = file of char;
```

In this chapter we will study the general file structure that is built into the Pascal language. Files are important in programming because they can provide permanent storage for data (usually on disk or tape). The amount of data stored in a file can be greater than the memory space allocated for the program. Files are considered to be data structures that are external to the program. They are the one structured variable type that cannot be used in an assignment statement. Files can be passed as parameters in procedures as long as they are declared as **var** parameters.

Files are not fixed in length, since they are stored externally to the program's memory. In Pascal, the components of a file are usually accessed in sequence and only one component of a file is accessible to a program at a time. The components of a file are accessed much more slowly than the components of other data structures. Access is slower because the file is stored externally to the memory set aside for a given program. Access of files on disk or tape is even slower, since these files are stored externally to the computer's memory.

One of the ways in which Pascal compilers differ is in how they handle files. Some Pascal compilers allow only physical files, whereas other compilers use physical and logical file names in the programs. The logical file name is the file name used by the program; the physical file name is the name of the file on the disk or other storage device. The programs that we have written use physical file names; this is similar to what is done on such systems as the Cyber and the Vax. In Section 9.6, programs are written for the IBM PC using the Microsoft Pascal compiler. This is one of the popular compilers for microcomputers that uses logical and physical file names. We discuss the way files are handled by several of the popular Pascal compilers in Appendix A.

There are two basic methods used to access the components of a file, sequential access and random access. In *sequential access* the values can be accessed only in the order in which they are stored in the file. In *random access* the values can be accessed in whatever order the programmer desires. Standard Pascal provides only sequential access; this is a major weakness of standard Pascal. However, since random access is required in many real-world applications, many Pascal compilers provide some version of random access, which will vary from one Pascal compiler to another. Some Pascal compilers, such as the Microsoft Pascal compiler, have added true random access capabilities. In Section 9.6 we will consider examples that illustrate random access using the Microsoft compiler.

9.1 Pascal Files

In Pascal, files of just about any data type can be created. As we have seen, files of type **char** can be created by using the declaration

```
var
   File1 : text;
```

where **text** is the built-in **type** identifier meaning

```
text = file of char
```

Files can also be **integer**, **real**, **Boolean**, or even **record**. A file is declared by using the statement

```
var
   File-identifier-name : file of Pascal-type;
```

For example, a file of integers can be declared using the statement

```
var
   IntFile : file of integer;
```

and a file of reals can be declared using the statement

```
var
   RealFile : file of real;
```

A file is a continuous stream of data stored in memory, on a disk, or on a tape. It can be pictured as follows.

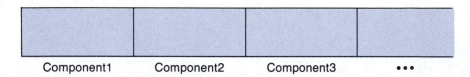

| Component1 | Component2 | Component3 | • • • |

The **type** of file declared establishes what each component of the file will be. For example, the declaration

```
var
   NumFile : file of integer;
```

establishes that each component of the file can store an integer. This file might be illustrated as follows.

Numfile

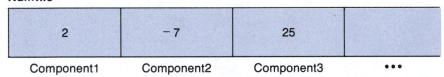

| 2 | −7 | 25 | • • • |
| Component1 | Component2 | Component3 | • • • |

Just as in the case of text files, each file has an associated *file pointer* and an associated *file window*. The file window is a block of memory that will hold one element from the file and that is accessible to the program. The file window is referenced by the program using an identifier name. In the above example the file is called **NumFile**, so the file window is referenced by the integer identifier **NumFile^**. The procedure **reset** is used to open a file for input, just as it is in the case of text files. When the file **NumFile** is opened for input with the statement

```
reset(NumFile);
```

the following occurs.

1. The file pointer is moved to the first component of the file.
2. The first component of the file is moved to the file window.

3. If the file **NumFile** has more than one element, the Boolean function **eof(NumFile)** is set to false.
4. The file window can now be referenced by an identifier. If **NumFile** is the file identifier, **NumFile^** is the identifier that references the file window.
5. The Pascal procedure **get(NumFile)** moves the file pointer to the next component of the file and moves that component to the file window. If the procedure is called and the file pointer encounters end-of-file, the Boolean function **eof(NumFile)** is set to true. (The Boolean function **eoln** only applies to text files; general files do not have end-of-line markers.)

The procedure **Rewrite** is used to open a file for output, just as it is used for text files. When the file **NumFile** is opened for output with the statement

```
Rewrite(NumFile);
```

the following occurs.

6. The Pascal procedure **rewrite** moves the file pointer to the beginning of the file. It empties the file window—that is, the file window contains no data. It also sets the Boolean function **eof(NumFile)** to true.
7. The Pascal procedure **put(NumFile)** is used for writing to general files. The **put(NumFile)** statement moves the element from the file window to the file. It also moves the file pointer to the next position in the file.

Let us illustrate these ideas with some examples. Suppose that we have the following file of integers being accessed by a simple summation program.

Nums

| 5 | 7 | 1 | −2 | 25 | |

When the program executes the statement

```
reset(Nums);
```

the file pointer is moved to the first integer of the file and that integer is moved to the file window.

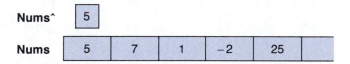

The program can now access the data item by referencing the file window identifier **Nums^**. For example, the statement

```
I := Nums^;
```

assigns the value 5 to the integer identifier I. The program can move the file pointer to the next element of the file and also move that element to the file window with the statement

```
get(Nums);
```

The block of code required to print the complete contents of the file **Nums** at the screen would be the following.

```
reset(Nums);
while not eof(Nums) do begin
  I := Nums^;
  writeln(I);
  get(Nums)
end; { while }
```

Note that the two statements

```
I := Nums^;
writeln(I);
```

can be replaced with the single statement

```
writeln(Nums^);
```

Let us examine these ideas with some more examples.

Example   If **Intfile** is a file of integers, write a program that will compute the sum of these integers and print the sum at the CRT.

On these simple examples the initial program documentation will not be included in order to save space. We will also omit the pseudocode and simply code the program.

```
program IntSum(IntFile, Output);
var
  Num, Sum : integer;                  { For computations }
  IntFile : file of integer;              { Data file }
begin
  reset(IntFile);
  Sum := 0;
  while not eof(IntFile) do begin    { Loop to compute Sum }
    Num := IntFile^;                 { Integer from window }
    Sum := Sum + Num;
    get(IntFile)                  { Next integer to window }
  end; { while }
  writeln(Sum)
end. { IntSum }
```

Example   Write a program that will create a file of integers. The file should contain the first 50 positive, even integers as data.

The first 50 positive, even integers are

$$2 \quad 4 \quad 6 \quad 8 \quad \ldots \quad 100$$

```pascal
program CreateIntFile(IFile);
var
  I, ENum : integer;              { For computations }
  IFile : file of integer;               { Data file }
begin
  rewrite(IFile);
    for I := 1 to 50 do begin      { Computation loop }
      ENum := 2 * I;
      IFile^ := ENum;           { Move integer to window }
      put(IFile)                 { Move integer to file }
    end { for }
end. { CreateIntFile }
```

The Pascal procedures **write**, **read**, **writeln**, and **readln** have been used throughout the text when we were doing input and output for text files. When we are dealing with files other than text files, the two procedures **readln** and **writeln** cannot be used, since text files are the only files that use end-of-line markers. However, the other two procedures, **read** and **write**, can be used with general files. In fact, these procedures are written using the procedures **put** and **get**. If **IntFile** is a file of integers and **Num** is an integer identifier, the statement

```pascal
read(IntFile, Num);
```

does the following.

1. It assigns the data from the file window of **IntFile** to the integer identifier **Num**.
2. It moves the file pointer to the next element of the file and moves that element to the file window. If no element exists, the Boolean function **eof(IntFile)** is set to true.

Thus the above statement is equivalent to the two statements

```pascal
Num := IntFile^;
get(IntFile);
```

Similarly, the statement

```pascal
write(IntFile, Num);
```

does the following.

1. It moves the data assigned to **Num** to the file window.
2. It moves the data from the file window to the file.

Thus the previous statement is equivalent to the two statements

```
IntFile^ := Num;
put(IntFile);
```

Each of the previous examples could have been written using **read** instead of **get** and **write** in place of **put**. We have used the procedures **get** and **put** in all of our examples in order to illustrate better the interaction among a file, its file window, and the Pascal procedures **reset**, **rewrite**, **get**, and **put**. Note, however, that the procedures **get** and **put** are not available with some Pascal compilers. These procedures are not available with the Turbo Pascal compiler, for example. In order for you to see how the two procedures **read** and **write** are used with other Pascal files, we will rewrite the two programs **IntSum** and **CreateIntFile** using **read** and **write** instead of **get** and **put**. The original versions of the programs are included beside the new versions in order to make the comparisons easier. The two versions of **IntSum** are as follows.

```
program IntSum(IntFile, output);
var
  Num, Sum : integer;
  IntFile : file of integer;
begin
  reset(IntFile);
  Sum := 0;
  while not eof(IntFile) do begin
    read(IntFile,  Num);
    Sum := Sum + Num
  end;  { while }
  writeln(Sum)
end.  { IntSum }
```

```
program IntSum(IntFile, output);
var
  Num, Sum : integer;
  IntFile : file of integer;
begin
  reset(IntFile);
  Sum := 0;
  while not eof(IntFile) do begin
    Num := IntFile^;
    Sum := Sum + Num;
    get(IntFile)
  end; { while }
  writeln(Sum)
end. { IntSum }
```

The two versions of **CreateIntFile** are as follows.

```
program CreateIntFile(IFile);
var
  I, ENum : integer;
begin
  rewrite(IFile);
  for I := 1 to 50 do begin
    ENum := 2*I;
    write(IFile, ENum)
  end { for }
end. { CreateIntFile }
```

```
program CreateIntFile(IFile);
var
  I, ENum : integer;
begin
  rewrite(IFile);
  for I := 1 to 50 do begin
    ENum := 2*I;
    IFile^ := ENum;
    put(IFile)
  end { for }
end. { CreateIntFile }
```

Study these examples carefully to make sure you understand exactly what happens when each statement in each program is executed. Compare the two versions of each program.

The **read** and **write** procedures can be used for any Pascal file, even files of some structured data type such as an array or a record.

Recall how the procedures **readln** and **writeln** work when text files are used. When the **writeln** procedure writes data to a file, the specified data item is written to the file, followed by an end-of-line marker. When the **readln** procedure is used, the specified data item is read from the file and then the file pointer is moved to the first character following the next end-of-line marker. It is important to understand these ideas when using text files.

Text files are files of characters, which means that all data is stored as a sequence of characters, each character being stored using the character code of the computer system. On most computer systems this is an 8-bit ASCII code; however, the Cyber computer systems use a 6-bit code and the large IBM systems use the 8-bit EPCIDIC code. Any time that we create a file using an editor we are creating a file of characters. Another method of storing data is to store all of the numeric data as binary data instead of as a string of characters. For example, the integer

59

would be stored as binary data in an 8-bit byte as

0 0 1 1 1 0 1 1

In a text file it would be stored as two characters in two consecutive bytes. On a system using the standard 8-bit ASCII code, the integer 39 would be stored as

3 5   3 9

These are the hex representations of the two 8-bit bytes.

One of the major reasons for using binary files rather than ASCII (text) files is that the I/O access time is much faster for binary files. For example, if integer numbers are stored in a text file, the **read** procedure has to read each number one character at a time and then convert the string of characters to a binary number. On the other hand, if the integer numbers are stored as a file of integers, each integer number is stored in its appropriate binary form and the **read** procedure simply has to move the number from the file to the program memory. No conversion is necessary. We will illustrate this difference on a file of 2500 random integer numbers. This program is written for a Cyber computer system. **SetRan** is the procedure to seed the random number generator and **Ran** is the function returning the generated random number.

```
{******************************************************************}
{* FileTestRead - This program will do the following.            *}
{*     1. Generate a text file of 2500 integer numbers.          *}
{*     2. Generate a binary file of 2500 integer numbers.        *}
{*     3. Use the system clock to compute the times needed       *}
{*        to read the numbers from the files and store them      *}
{*        in an array.                                           *}
{******************************************************************}
program FileTestRead(AscFile, IntFile);
{*$i'Random' *}          { Include library random number generator }
```

```
type
  NumFile = file of integer;
  ArrayType = array[1..2500] of integer;
var
  AscFile : text;           { ASCII file to contain 2500 integers }
  IntFile : NumFile;        { Binary file to contain 2500 integers }
  Nums : ArrayType;         { Array to store the 2500 integers }
  I, Num : integer;
begin
  rewrite(AscFile);
  rewrite(IntFile);
  SetRan(1);                        { Seed the random number generator }
  for I := 1 to 2500 do begin  { Loop to compute random numbers }
    Num := trunc(2500 * Ran + 1);          { Compute one number }
    writeln(AscFile, Num);                 { Store in ASCII file }
    IntFile^ := Num;
    put(IntFile);                          { Store in binary file }
  end; { for }
  reset(AscFile);
  writeln(clock);                    { Compute time for ASCII file }
  for I := 1 to 2500 do
    readln(AscFile, Nums[I]);
  { end for }
  writeln(clock);
  reset(IntFile);
  writeln(clock);                    { Compute time for binary file }
  for I := 1 to 2500 do begin
    Nums[I] := IntFile^;
    get(IntFile)
  end; { for }
  writeln(clock)
end. { FileTestRead }
```

A test run of the above program resulted in a time of 1.226 seconds for reading the data from the ASCII file **AscFile** and a time of 0.152 second for reading the data from the binary file **IntFile**—a significant difference. When the above program was modified so that the text file did not contain any end-of-line markers, the time did not change significantly; the time for reading the data from the text file was 1.210 seconds. In the exercises we will ask you to do similar tests for other size files.

Exercises

9.1   Explain what is meant by each of the following.
(a) File
(b) Main memory
(c) Auxiliary memory
(d) Internal file
(e) External file

9.2 Write the procedure that will make a copy of the file **File1**, which is a file of integers. Use the declaration

```
type
   IntFile = file of integer;
```

Write a program (driver) to test your procedure. Use the procedures **put** and **get**.

9.3 Write a procedure that will find the average of the integer numbers stored in **File1**. Use the procedure **get**. Write a driver and test your procedure.

9.4 Suppose that you have the following declarations.

```
type
   IntFile = file of integer;
var
   Num1 : integer;
   File1 : IntFile;
```

Each of the following blocks of code attempts to store an integer value in **File1**. Tell what is wrong (if anything) with each one.

(a)
```
readln;
read(Num1);
put(File1, Num1);
```

(b)
```
read(Num1);
get(File1);
File1^ := Num1;
put(Num1);
```

(c)
```
read(Num1);
File1^ := Num1;
put(Num1);
```

(d)
```
read(Num1);
Num1 := File1^;
put(File1);
```

9.5 Draw a diagram to show what will be stored for the following block of code.

```
rewrite(File1);
for I := 1 to 5 do begin
   if I mod 2 = 0 then
      File1^ := 1
   else
      File1^ := I;
   { end if }
   put(File1)
end; { for }
```

9.6 Write a procedure to count the number of integer items in **File1**. Write a driver and test your program.

9.7 Write a procedure to create a file of integers. The data are to be entered from the keyboard. The user is to decide how many data items should be entered. Use the **put** procedure.

9.8 Rewrite the procedure from Exercise 9.2 using the **read** and **write** procedures in place of the **get** and **put** procedures. Write a program and test your procedure.

9.9 Rewrite the procedure from Exercise 9.7 using the **write** procedure instead of the **put** procedure. Write a program to test your procedure.

9.10 Write a program to compare the amount of time needed to read 2500 randomly generated real numbers from an ASCII file with the amount of time needed to read these same numbers from a binary file. Write a program that is similar to the program **FileTestRead**.

9.11 Create two files, an ASCII file and a binary file. Obtain dumps of each of the files and compare how the data are stored. Compare these dumps with the dumps that were given in this section.

9.2   Files of Records

As we have seen, the data stored for use in programs are often grouped as records made up of fields of information, with each field of a different data type. One record contains the information associated with a single item or person.

We will consider some examples that use files of records. Consider the following data type.

```
type
   String20 = packed array[1..20] of char;
   EmpInfo = record
                  Name : String20;
                  Age : integer;
               end;
```

Example   Write a program to create a file in which each component is of type **EmpInfo**. The file is to contain 10 elements and the data are to be input from the keyboard.

```
{****************************************************************}
{* CreateEmpFile - Program to create a file of 10 records of  *}
{*                 type EmpInfo. The data are to be input     *}
{*                 from the keyboard.                         *}
{****************************************************************}
program CreateEmpFile(Input, EmpFile);
type
   String20 = packed array[1..20] of char;
   EmpInfo = record
                Name : String20;
                Age : integer
             end;
var
   TName : String20;                        { Name from keyboard }
   I, J,                                    { Indices for loops }
   TAge : integer;                          { Age from keyboard }
   EmpFile : file of EmpInfo;               { File to be created }
```

```
begin
  rewrite(EmpFile);                          { Open file for output }
  for I := 1 to 10 do begin
    writeln('Please input a name.');           { Input the name }
    writeln('Type in 20 characters.');
    writeln('   xxxxxxxxxxxxxxxxxxxx');
    for J := 1 to 20 do
      read(TName[J]);
    { end for }
    readln;
    writeln('Please input an age.');            { Input the age }
    writeln('   xx');
    readln(TAge);
                                      { Store data in record window }
    EmpFile^.Name := TName;
    EmpFile^.Age := TAge;
                                             { Move data to file }
    put(EmpFile)
  end  { for }
end. { CreateEmpFile }
```

Example   Write a program to read the data from the file that was created in the previous example and write the data back to a **text** file called **EmpData**.

```
{*****************************************************************}
{* TextCopy - Program to copy the file of records, EmpFile,  *}
{*            to a text file, EmpData.                       *}
{*****************************************************************}
program TextCopy(EmpFile, EmpData);
type
  String20 = packed array[1..20] of char;
  EmpInfo = record
              Name : String20;
              Age : integer
            end;
var
  TName : String20;                        { Name from record }
  I,                                        { Loop index }
  TAge : integer;                          { Age from record }
  EmpFile : file of EmpInfo;               { File of records }
  EmpData : text;                   { ASCII file to be created }
begin
  reset(EmpFile);                          { Open file for input }
  rewrite(EmpData);                        { Open file for output }
  for I := 1 to 10 do begin                { Loop to create file }
    TName := EmpFile^.Name;
    TAge := EmpFile^.Age;
    writeln(EmpData, TName, TAge);
    get(EmpFile)
  end { for }
end. { TextCopy }
```

Suppose a program is to use the data on an inventory for a hardware store. The data to be stored for each inventory item are the following.

Part description	15 characters
Code number	8 characters
Quantity	Integer
Cost	Real

Example   Give the **type** and **var** definitions needed to define a file of records in which each record will store information for one inventory item.

We will need the following declarations.

```
type
  String15 = packed array[1..15] of char;
  String8 = packed array[1..8] of char;
  Item = record
            Description : String15;
            CodeNo : String8;
            Quantity : integer;
            Cost : real
         end;
  ItemFile = file of Item;
var
  InvFile : ItemFile;
```

The storage of data in the file **InvFile** can be pictured as follows.

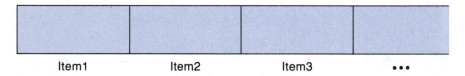

Item1   Item2   Item3   •••

Each item is made up of several words, organized as follows. The Description and the CodeNo are stored in several words depending on the system being used. The Quantity and the Cost normally are each stored in one word since they are stored in binary.

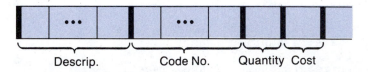

Descrip.   Code No.   Quantity Cost

In order to see how records of data are stored in binary files, you should create a file of records and obtain a printout of a dump of this binary file.

Let us now consider an example involving the copying of files. File copying is a frequent operation in data processing for several reasons. One is that programmers modifying a file normally make a backup copy to work on in-stead of modifying an existing file. Then if something goes wrong with the modification and the file is destroyed, the master file is still intact.

Another reason relates to the fact that it is not possible to alternate be-tween reading and writing during the accessing of data from a sequential file. Since the file is in either the **read** mode or the **write** mode during a particu-lar scan, we cannot alter a single component of a file by reading all of the components to reach it, modifying that particular component, and writing it back to the file. We must make a complete copy of the file and modify the particular component as we are making the copy. This is a very important re-striction for sequential files, and we will consider it again in Section 9.6 when we discuss direct access files. We can, however, **read** from one file and **write** to another file, as the next example illustrates.

Example A local business maintains the names and addresses of its customers on punched cards with this format:

Columns	1–20	Name
	21–40	Street address
	41–52	City
	53–62	State
	63–67	Zip code

The company wants to convert the storage medium from punched cards to magnetic tape. Write a program to read the data from the punched cards (a **text** file) and write the data to magnetic tape (a file of records).

```
{*****************************************************************}
{* CardToTape - Program to read the data from a text file and *}
{*              store them in a file of records.              *}
{*      files - CdFile : Text file containing the data.       *}
{*              TpFile : File of records where the data are   *}
{*                       to be written.                       *}
{*****************************************************************}
program CardToTape(CdFile, TpFile);
type
   String5 = packed array[1..5] of char;
   String10 = packed array[1..10] of char;
   String12 = packed array[1..12] of char;
   String20 = packed array[1..20] of char;
   EmpInfo = record
               Name : String20;
               Street : String20;
               City : String12;
               State : String10;
               Zip : String5
             end;
var
   I : integer;                              { Loop index }
```

```
    TName,                                       { Name for record }
    TStreet : String20;                       { Street for record }
    TCity : String12;                           { City for record }
    TState : String10;                         { State for record }
    TZip : String5;                         { Zip code for record }
    CdFile : text;                             { ASCII data file }
    TpFile : file of EmpInfo;               { File to be created }
begin
    reset(CdFile);                        { Open ASCII file for input }
    rewrite(TpFile);                    { Open binary file for output }
    while not eof(CdFile) do begin
      for I := 1 to 20 do                            { Read name }
        read(CdFile, TName[I]);
      { end for }
      for I := 1 to 20 do                          { Read street }
        read(CdFile, TStreet[I]);
      { end for }
      for I := 1 to 12 do                            { Read city }
        read(CdFile, TCity[I]);
      { end for }
      for I := 1 to 10 do                           { Read state }
        read(CdFile, TState[I]);
      { end for }
      for I := 1 to 5 do                         { Read zip code }
        read(CdFile, TZip[I]);
      { end for }
      readln(CdFile);                  { Next line, check for eof }
      TpFile^.Name := TName;               { Data to file window }
      TpFile^.Street := TStreet;
      TpFile^.City := TCity;
      TpFile^.State := TState;
      TpFile^.Zip := TZip;
      put(TpFile)                            { Record to file }
    end { while }
end. { CardToTape }
```

The code for this procedure could have been shortened if we had read the data directly into the file window of **TpFile**. We could do this by replacing the preceding block of code with the following block of code.

```
        reset(CdFile);
        rewrite(TpFile);
        while not eof(CdFile) do begin
          for I := 1 to 20 do
            read(CdFile, TpFile^.Name[I]);
          { end for }
          for I := 1 to 20 do
            read(CdFile, TpFile^.Street[I]);
          { end for }
          for I := 1 to 12 do
            read(CdFile, TpFile^.City[I]);
          { end for }
          for I := 1 to 10 do
            read(CdFile, TpFile^.State[I]);
          { end for }
```

```
         for I := 1 to 5 do
           read(CdFile, TpFile^.Zip[I]);
         { end for }
         readln(CdFile);
         put(TpFile);
       end { while }
```

When files of records are used, much less code is needed to write a procedure to make a copy of a file. We will ask you to write the procedure as one of the exercises.

Exercises

9.12   Give the **type** and **var** declarations needed to define a file of records in which each record will contain the following information.

Name	30 characters
Address	40 characters
Telephone number	10 characters
Age	Integer

9.13   A file called **Data** contains several records of information of the type described in Exercise 9.12. The file contains one record of information per line, with each line containing the data in the following format. The file is a text file.

Columns		
	1–30	Name
	31–70	Address
	71–80	Telephone number
	82–83	Age

Write a procedure that will create a file of records, called **TpFile**, containing the data from the text file **Data**.

9.14   Consider the first example in Section 9.2. Define a variable of type **EmpInfo** and rewrite the program so that it uses this variable and the procedures **read** and **write**.

9.15   Write a procedure to create a backup copy for the file **TpFile** from Exercise 9.13. The backup file should also be a file of records. Use the procedures **get** and **put**.

9.16   A teacher wants to establish a data file for a class so that the following information can be stored for each student.

Name	30 characters
Number of exams	Integer (maximum of 8)
Eight exam scores	Integer
Exam average	Real

Give the **type** and **var** declarations needed to define a suitable file of records.

9.17 Write a procedure to allow the user to create the file described in Exercise 9.16. The information to be entered by the user should be the names of the students, the number of exams, zeros for the exam scores, and zero for the average.

9.18 Write a procedure to allow the user to update the class file described in Exercises 9.16 and 9.17. The user will enter a set of exam scores, increment the number of exams, and recompute the averages.

9.19 Rewrite the program **TestFileRead** so that the files contain 500 integer numbers. Run the program and record the times. How much faster was the time for the binary file? Repeat the comparison for real numbers. Repeat the comparison for records of type **EmpInfo**. All records can be the same.

9.3 Sorting and Merging Files

When a file in which data are stored is too large to be stored in a structure internal to a program, a sorting method that only provides access to the components of the file one at a time can be used. Before we consider the sorting technique involved, we will first study a technique called *merging*, which will allow us to obtain a sorted file from smaller sorted files.

The process involved in merging two files is about the same as that involved in merging two file drawers of sorted cards into a third larger file drawer. If we were to merge the cards by hand, we would first open the three drawers and get the first card from each of the two drawers with cards. The "alphabetically" lower of the two cards would be placed in the third drawer, and another card would be taken from the drawer the lower card came from to take its place. This process would continue until one of the drawers was empty. Then, since all of the cards in the remaining drawer would be in order and would belong at the end of the third drawer, they could just be removed one at a time and placed in the new drawer. Another way to view this merging process is to think of the merge program as a traffic cop that always looks at the lead elements of each of the files. The smaller of the lead elements is the element that is let through (see Figure 9.1).

This process is easy and straightforward to program. We will illustrate the idea with an example. Suppose that **File1** and **File2** are two files of records, in which each record contains a name and an age. Suppose also that we have the following declarations in the main program.

```
type
   String20 = packed array[1..20] of char;
   EmpInfo = record
                Name : String20;
                Age : integer
             end;
   EmpFile = file of EmpInfo;
var
   File1, File2 : EmpFile;
```

Figure 9.1

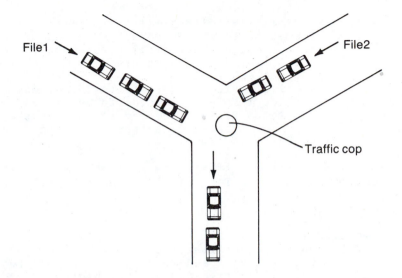

We will write a procedure to merge the two files **File1** and **File2** to a third file **File3** which is also of type **EmpFile**. We begin by writing the pseudocode.

Pseudocode

> **Merge Procedure**
>
> Open **File1** for input.
> Open **File2** for input.
> Open **File3** for output.
> WHILE (not EOF(**File1**)) and (not EOF(**File2**))
>   IF **Rec1(Name)** <= **Rec2(Name)** THEN
>   Move **Rec1** to **File3**.
>   Get new **Rec1**.
>   ELSE
>   Move **Rec2** to **File3**.
>   Get new **Rec2**.
>   END IF.
> END WHILE.
> WHILE not EOF(**File1**)
>   Move **Rec1** to **File3**.
>   Get new **Rec1**.
> END WHILE.
> WHILE not EOF(**File2**)
>   Move **Rec2** to **File3**.
>   Get new **Rec2**.
> END WHILE.

We can now code the procedure.

```
{*****************************************************************}
{* Merge - Procedure to merge two sorted files of records    *}
{*          into a larger sorted file of records. The data    *}
{*          are sorted on the name field.                     *}
{*       var parameters -                                      *}
{*            File1 : File of records to be merged.            *}
{*            File2 : File of records to be merged.            *}
{*            File3 : File of records to contain the merged,   *}
{*                    sorted data from File1 and File2.        *}
{*       value parameters -                                    *}
{*            None.                                            *}
{*****************************************************************}
procedure Merge(var File1, File2, File3 : EmpFile);
begin
  reset(File1);
  reset(File2);
  rewrite(File3);
      { Loop to merge File1 records with File2 records }
  while (not eof(File1)) and (not eof(File2)) do begin
    if File1^.Name <= File2^.Name then begin
      File3^ := File1^;
      get(File1)
    end { if }
    else begin
      File3^ := File2^;
      get(File2)
    end; { else }
    put(File3)
  end; { while }
            { Copy remaining records from File1 }
  while not eof(File1) do begin
    File3^ := File1^;
    put(File3);
    get(File1)
  end; { while }
            { Copy remaining records from File2 }
  while not eof(File2) do begin
    File3^ := File2^;
    put(File3);
    get(File2)
  end { while }
end; { Merge }
```

The sorting techniques that we have studied and used so far cannot be applied to files in which the amount of data to be sorted does not fit into the memory allocated to the program. This is a severe restriction compared to the possibilities offered by the array structure. Therefore, different sorting techniques have to be used with files or else a process must be devised to permit use of the sorting techniques we have discussed.

There is another important difference between sorting the data stored in an array and sorting the data stored in a file. In an array the elements can be accessed at random, whereas in a sequential file they must normally be accessed sequentially. With an array, all of the elements are in main storage, and it is not too difficult to swap any pair of elements. With a sequential file, only one element is available in main storage at any one time; thus sorts that are used on arrays cannot be used directly on files.

Merging is one of the fundamental operations used to sort a sequential file. This idea can be illustrated by considering a file of integer data items. Suppose that we have the following file.

13 24 3 4 10 55 35 5 68 12 33 70

We split the elements of the file into sequences of values that are already in order. These sequences are called *runs*.

<13 24> <3 4 10 55> <35> <5 68> <12 33 70>

The original file has five runs. Note that the end of a run is detected when the next value is smaller than the present value. Also, the end of the last run is the end of the file.

The next step is to *distribute* the runs of the original file into two temporary files. The first run is copied to **TempFile1**, the next run to **TempFile2**, the next run to **TempFile1**, and so on, until all of the runs have been distributed to the two temporary files. Our example produces the following.

Original file   <13 24> <3 4 10 55> <35> <5 68> <12 33 70>
TempFile1 <13 24> <35> <12 33 70>
TempFile2 <3 4 10 55> <5 68>

Note that since the end of a run is detected when the next element is less than the present element, the temporary file **TempFile1** has only two runs and can be viewed as follows.

TempFile1   <13 24 35> <12 33 70>

The next step is to merge the runs of the temporary files back into the original file. We will merge the first run of **TempFile1** with the first run of **TempFile2**, the second run of **TempFile1** with the second run of **Temp-File2**, and so on, until all of the runs of both temporary files have been merged back to the original file, producing the following.

TempFile1   <13 24 35> <12 33 70>
TempFile2   <3 4 10 55> <5 68>
Original file   <3 4 10 13 24 35 55> <5 12 33 68 70>

This distribution-merge process is repeated until the original file is completely sorted.

Distribute

Original file   <3 4 10 13 24 35 55> <5 12 33 68 70>
TempFile1   <3 4 10 13 24 35 55>
TempFile2   <5 12 23 68 70>

Merge

TempFile1	<3 4 10 13 24 35 55>
TempFile2	<5 12 23 68 70>
Original file	<3 4 5 10 12 13 23 24 35 55 68 70>

We can now outline the algorithm using pseudocode.

Pseudocode

MergeSort Procedure

REPEAT
   Open original file for input.
   Open **TempFile1** for output.
   Open **TempFile2** for output.
   Distribute original file to **TempFile1** and **TempFile2**.
   Open original file for output.
   Open **TempFile1** for input.
   Open **TempFile2** for input.
   MergeRuns TempFile1 and **TempFile2** to original file.
UNTIL sorted.

In order to complete the outline of the algorithm, we need to outline both the **Distribute** and the **MergeRuns** procedures.

Pseudocode

Distribute Procedure

REPEAT
   REPEAT
      Copy element from original file to **TempFile1**.
   UNTIL end of run.
   IF not end of file THEN
      REPEAT
         Copy element from original file to **TempFile2**.
      UNTIL end of run.
   END IF.
UNTIL end of file.

Since the statements

   Copy element from original file to **TempFile1**.
UNTIL end of run.

involve copying an element and determining if the element just copied represents the end of a run, we will write a procedure to accomplish these tasks. The following is the outline for this procedure.

Pseudocode

CopyElement Procedure

IF not end of file THEN
    Copy element from original file to **TempFile1**.
    Get next element.
    IF end of file THEN
       Set end of run to true.
    ELSE
       IF copied element > next element THEN
          Set end of run to true.
       ELSE
          Set end of run to false.
       END IF.
    END IF.
ELSE
    Set end of run to true.
END IF.

We will now outline the **MergeRuns** procedure. Notice that the **Merge-Runs** procedure will terminate when the number of runs in the original file is 1.

Pseudocode

MergeRuns Procedure

Initialize runs counter to 0.
WHILE (not end of **TempFile1**) and (not end of **TempFile2**)
    REPEAT
       IF **TempFile1**(element)(key) < **TempFile2**(element)
       (key) THEN
       Copy **TempFile1**(element) to original file.
       IF end of run THEN
          Copy **TempFile2**(element) to original file.
       END IF.
       ELSE
       Copy **TempFile2**(element) to original file.
       IF end of run THEN
          Copy **TempFile1**(element) to original file.
       END IF.
       END IF.
    UNTIL end of run.
    Increment runs counter.
END WHILE.
IF not end of **TempFile1** THEN
    Increment runs counter.
    REPEAT

> Move **TempFile1**(element) to original file.
>   Get next element.
> UNTIL end of **TempFile1**.
> END IF.
> IF not end of **TempFile2** THEN
>   Increment runs counter.
>   REPEAT
>   Move **TempFile2**(element) to original file.
>   Get next element.
>   UNTIL end of **TempFile2**.
> END IF.
> IF runs counter = 1 THEN
>   Set **Sorted** to true.
> ELSE
>   Set **Sorted** to false.
> END IF.

We can now write the procedure to sort a file using a merge sort. We will assume that our file is a file of inventory records that are to be sorted by the integer code number. We will assume that we have the following **type** declarations.

```
type
  String30 = packed array[1..30] of char;
  InvRec = record
             Desc : String30;
             CodeNo : integer;
             Num : integer;
             Cost : real
           end;
  InvFile = file of InvRec;
```

```
{********************************************************************}
{* MergeSort - Procedure to sort a file of records into           *}
{*             ascending order using a merge-sort technique.      *}
{*             The file is assumed to be a file of inventory      *}
{*             records and the data will be sorted on the key     *}
{*             CodeNo which is of type integer.                   *}
{*     var parameters -                                           *}
{*         Master : File of inventory records.                    *}
{*     value parameters -                                         *}
{*         None.                                                  *}
{********************************************************************}
procedure MergeSort(var Master : InvFile);
var
  TempFile1, TempFile2 : InvFile;    { Temporary files for runs }
  Sorted : boolean;
begin
```

```
  repeat                              { Loop to sort file }
    reset(Master);
    rewrite(TempFile1);
    rewrite(TempFile2);
    Distribute(Master, TempFile1, TempFile2);
    reset(TempFile1);
    reset(TempFile2);
    rewrite(Master);
    MergeRuns(TempFile1, TempFile2, Master, Sorted)
  until Sorted
end; { MergeSort }
```

We will now code the procedure **Distribute**.

```
{*******************************************************}
{* Distribute - Procedure to copy the runs in a file Master  *}
{*              to the two files TempFile1 and TempFile2. The *}
{*              files are expected to be files of inventory   *}
{*              records.                                      *}
{*      var parameters -                                      *}
{*          Mst : Master file containing the data to be       *}
{*                distributed.                                *}
{*          Tmp1 : Temporary file to contain every other      *}
{*                 run from Mst.                              *}
{*          Tmp2 : Temporary file to contain every other      *}
{*                 run from Mst.                              *}
{*      value parameters -                                    *}
{*          None.                                             *}
{*******************************************************}
procedure Distribute(var Mst, Tmp1, Tmp2 : InvFile);
var
  EndOfRun : boolean;
begin
  repeat                              { Copy until end of file }
    repeat                            { Copy until end of run }
      CopyElement(Mst, Tmp1, EndOfRun)
    until EndOfRun;
    if not eof(Mst) then
      repeat                          { Copy until end of run }
        CopyElement(Mst, Tmp2, EndOfRun)
      until EndOfRun;
    { end if }
  until eof(Mst)
end; { Distribute }
```

Before we code the procedure **MergeRuns**, we will code the procedure **CopyElement**, which is called by the procedure **Distribute**.

```
{*******************************************************}
{* CopyElement - Procedure to copy one element from the file *}
{*               Source to a file Dest. The procedure expects *}
{*               the files to be files of inventory records.  *}
{*               It checks for the end of a run in Source.     *}
```

```
{*        var parameters -                                    *}
{*            Source : File of inventory records containing the *}
{*                    runs to be copied.                        *}
{*            Dest : File where the run is to be copied.       *}
{*            RunDone : Boolean to return true if at end of run *}
{*                    and false otherwise.                     *}
{*        value parameters -                                    *}
{*            None.                                             *}
{****************************************************************}
procedure CopyElement(var Source, Dest : InvFile;
                      var RunDone : Boolean);
var
  TempRec : InvRec;                             { Temporary storage }
begin
  if not eof(Source) then begin
    TempRec := Source^;                         { Copy one record }
    get(Source);                                { Get next record }
    Dest^ := TempRec;
    put(Dest);
    if eof(Source) then
      RunDone := true
    else
      if TempRec.CodeNo > Source^.CodeNo then   { End of run ? }
        RunDone := true
      else
        RunDone := false
      { end if }
    { end else }
  end { if }
  else
    RunDone := true
  { end else }
end; { CopyElement }
```

We can now code the procedure **MergeRuns**.

```
{****************************************************************}
{* MergeRuns - Procedure to merge the corresponding runs in    *}
{*             the files Tp1 and Tp2 to the file Mstr. The     *}
{*             procedure counts the number of runs in Mstr     *}
{*             and returns a boolean to signal that the sort   *}
{*             is completed when the number of runs is 1.      *}
{*        var parameters -                                     *}
{*            Tp1 : File containing runs to be merged to Mstr. *}
{*            Tp2 : File containing runs to be merged to Mstr. *}
{*            Mstr : File to contain the merged runs from Tp1  *}
{*                    and Tp2.                                 *}
{*            Sorted1 : Boolean to return true when Mstr       *}
{*                    contains only one run and is therefore   *}
{*                    sorted, and to return false otherwise.   *}
{*        value parameters -                                   *}
{*            None.                                            *}
{****************************************************************}
procedure MergeRuns(var Tp1, Tp2, Mstr : InvFile;
                    var Sorted1 : Boolean);
```

```
var
   EndRun : boolean;                        { For end of run }
   NumRuns : integer;              { Number of runs counter }
begin
   NumRuns := 0;
                        { Loop to merge runs }
   while (not eof(Tp1)) and (not eof(Tp2)) do begin
      repeat                                    { Copy runs }
         if Tp1^.CodeNo < Tp2^.CodeNo then begin
            CopyElement(Tp1, Mstr, EndRun);
            if EndRun then
               CopyElement(Tp2, Mstr, EndRun)
            { end if }
         end { if }
         else begin
            CopyElement(Tp2, Mstr, EndRun);
            if EndRun then
               CopyElement(Tp1, Mstr, EndRun)
            { end if }
         end { else }
      until EndRun;
      NumRuns := NumRuns + 1
   end; { while }
   if not eof(Tp1) then begin       { Finish copying runs Tp1 }
      NumRuns := NumRuns + 1;
      repeat
         Mstr^ := Tp1^;
         get(Tp1);
         put(Mstr)
      until eof(Tp1)
   end; { if }
   if not eof(Tp2) then begin       { Finish copying runs Tp2 }
      NumRuns := NumRuns + 1;
      repeat
         Mstr^ := Tp2^;
         get(Tp2);
         put(Mstr)
      until eof(Tp2)
   end; { if }
   if NumRuns = 1 then                   { Check to see if done }
      Sorted1 := true
   else
      Sorted1 := false
   { end if }
end; { MergeRuns }
```

The **MergeSort** procedure is a very nice procedure to use for sorting files. There is one problem, however. When a file is stored on an external device such as a disk or tape, the access time for one record of data is much greater than when the record is stored in a structure in the program's memory area. Thus it may be more efficient to read the data into an internal structure, sort the data using one of our sorting techniques, and then write the sorted data back to the file. As we have pointed out, however, it is not always possible to store all of the data from a file in main memory at one time. Therefore, we will have to devise a technique that offers a compromise between the two extremes. We will assume that at most **Num** records can be stored in main memory and that the file **Master** contains at least **Num** records and at most 2 * **Num** records. The process is the following.

1. Read a fixed number of records from the file and store them in an array.
2. Sort the records in the array using one of the more efficient sorting techniques.
3. Write the sorted data back to a temporary file **File1**.
4. Read another fixed number of records from the file and store them in the array.
5. Sort these records using the more efficient sorting technique.
6. Merge the sorted records in the array with the sorted records in the file **File1** back to the file **Master**.

We can now outline the procedure that we will call **FileSort1**.

Pseudocode

> **FileSort1 Procedure**
>
> Open **Master** for input.
> FOR **I** = 1 TO **Num**
>   Read a record from **Master** and store it in **InvArray[I]**.
> END FOR.
> Sort the **Num** records in **InvArray** using the **QuickSort** procedure.
> Open **File1** for output.
> Write the records in **InvArray** to **File1**.
> Set **Count** to 0.
> WHILE not EOF(**Master**)
>   Increment **Count**.
>   Read a record from **Master** and store it in
>   **InvArray(Count)**.
> END WHILE.
> Sort the **Count** records in **InvArray** using the **QuickSort** procedure.
> Merge **File1** with **InvArray** back to the file **Master**.

Obviously, this is a very special case. There are certainly more general cases that we need to consider. Some of these will be dealt with in the exercises. The procedure to merge an array of records with a file of records will be a modification of the **Merge** procedure that we wrote in this section. You will be asked to write this procedure, **MergeArray**, as one of the exercises.
We can now code the procedure **FileSort1**.

```
{*****************************************************************}
{* FileSort1 - Procedure to sort a file of records into         *}
{*             ascending order. The file is assumed to be a     *}
```

```
(*            file of inventory records, and the data will be *)
(*            sorted on the key CodeNo which is of type       *)
(*            integer. The QuickSort procedure is called to   *)
(*            sort an array of inventory records. It is        *)
(*            assumed that the file contains at least Num       *)
(*            records and no more than 2 * Num records.        *)
(*      var parameters -                                       *)
(*          Mast : File of inventory records.                  *)
(*      value parameters -                                     *)
(*          None.                                              *)
(***************************************************************)
procedure FileSort1(var Mast : InvFile);
const
   Num = 100;
type
   ArrayType = packed array[1..Num] of InvRec;
var
   InvArray : ArrayType;               { Array to store records }
   Count,                                    { Array counter }
   I : integer;                                   { Index }
   File1 : InvFile;              { Temporary file for sorted records }
begin
   reset(Mast);
   for I := 1 to Num do begin         { Loop to store Num records }
      InvArray[I] := Mast^;
      get(Mast)
   end; { for }
   QuickSort(InvArray, Num);          { Sort array of records }
   rewrite(File1);
   for I := 1 to Num do begin         { Write records to File1 }
      File1^ := InvArray[I];
      put(File1)
   end; { for }
   Count := 0;
   while not eof(Mast) do begin       { Loop to store records }
      Count := Count + 1;
      InvArray[Count] := Mast^;
      get(Mast)
   end; { while }
   QuickSort(InvArray, Count);        { Sort array of records }
   reset(File1);
   rewrite(Mast);
   MergeArray(InvArray, Count, File1, Mast)
end; { FileSort1 }
```

Exercises

9.20 Rewrite the **Merge** procedure so that it can be used to merge two sorted files of inventory records. The key should be the code number, which is of type integer.

9.21 Write a procedure to merge an array of sorted records with a file of sorted records. The merged records are to be written to a second file. Assume that the records are inventory records that are sorted on the integer code-number field. The procedure should accept the array, the number of records in the array, and both files as parameters. Call the procedure **MergeArray**.

9.22 Rewrite the **MergeSort** procedure so that it accepts a file of integer numbers. Write a program similar to the **TestSort** program from Chapter 8. The program should generate a file of random integer numbers and use the system clock to calculate how long the procedure **MergeSort** takes to sort the file of integer numbers. Run the program twice, once for a file of 2500 integer numbers and once for a file of 512 integer numbers. Record the times to use for comparisons.

9.23 Rewrite the **FileSort1** procedure so that it accepts a file of integer numbers. Calculate the times for this procedure as you did in Exercise 9.22. When the file contains 2500 integer numbers the array should hold 1250 integer numbers, and when the file holds 512 integer numbers the array should hold 256 integer numbers.

9.24 Rewrite the **FileSort1** procedure so that it will work for any size file. You can use an array and two temporary files. The size of the array should not matter as long as it will fit into the program's memory area. Use the **Quick-Sort** procedure and assume that the file contains inventory records that are to be sorted on the integer code-number field.

9.25 Write a program that uses the **Merge** procedure to merge three sorted files of inventory records. The program should merge two of the files and then merge this resulting file with the remaining third file.

9.26 Rewrite the **Merge** procedure so that it will merge three sorted files of inventory records directly.

9.4 Master File Update

Business data processing involves the manipulation of large collections of data stored in files. In this section we will use some of the techniques that we have developed to illustrate what is involved in the very important problem of maintaining a master file of inventory data. *File maintainence* is a process that includes the operations of adding new records of information, deleting old records of information, and modifying existing records of information. Normally this process involves using at least two files: the *master file*, in which the data are permanently stored, and the temporary *transaction file*, which holds the data entered by the user from the keyboard. The transaction file normally holds records that are to be added, deleted, or modified in the master file. We will need the following **const**, **type**, and **var** declarations.

```
const
  Max = 100;
type
  String20 = packed array[1..20] of char;
```

```
ItemInfo = record
               Desc : String20;
               PtNo : integer;
               Quant : integer;
               Cost : real
            end;
PostInfo = record
               PNo : integer;
               Num : integer
            end;
ItemArray = packed array[1..Max] of ItemInfo;
PostArray = array[1..Max] of PostInfo;
InvFile = file of ItemInfo;
var
   InvMas : InvFile;
```

The first procedure that we will write will be a procedure to allow the user to add new inventory records to the master file. The procedure will allow the user to enter up to 100 records, which will be stored in an array. The data will then be sorted by part number and written to a temporary transaction file. Finally, the data in the transaction file will be merged with the data in the current master file to form the new master file.

```
{*******************************************************************}
{* AddItems - Procedure to add new inventory records to the       *}
{*            master inventory file. The user can add up to       *}
{*            Max new records.                                    *}
{*       var parameters -                                         *}
{*            IMas : Master file of inventory records.            *}
{*            NMas : New master file of inventory records.        *}
{*       value parameters -                                       *}
{*            None.                                               *}
{*******************************************************************}
procedure AddItems(var IMas, NMas : InvFile);
var
   Count,                              { Counter for added records }
   I : integer;                                       { Index }
   Done : boolean;                              { For input loop }
   Response : char;                         { For user response }
   TRec : ItemInfo;                     { Added inventory record }
   NItems : ItemArray;                        { Added records }
   NFile : InvFile;                 { File for records from array }
begin
   Count := 0;
   Done := false;
   AddInstructions;                         { Instructions to user }
   repeat                             { Loop to input new records }
      Count := Count + 1;
                          { Input description }
      writeln(' Please input the description.');
      writeln('   xxxxxxxxxxxxxxxxxxxx');
      for I := 1 to 20 do
```

```
      read(TRec.Desc[I]);
    { end for }
    readln;
                          { Input part number }
    writeln('Please input the part no.');
    writeln('  99999999');
    readln(TRec.PtNo);
                          { Input quantity }
    writeln('Please input the quantity.');
    writeln(  '9999');
    readln(TRec.Quant);
                      { Input cost }
    writeln('Please input the cost.');
    writeln('  999.99');
    readln(TRec.Cost);
    NItems[Count] := TRec;                { Store record in array }
    writeln('Do you wish to enter another record?');
    writeln('Enter Y - yes / N - no.');
    readln(Response);
    if Response = 'N' then
      Done := true;
    { end if }
  until Done or (Count >= Max);
                      { Check for full array }
  if Count >= Max then begin
    writeln('You have entered the maximum number of records.');
    writeln('Master file is now being updated.');
  end; { if }
  Quick1Sort(NItems, Count);          { Sort Items by part number }
  rewrite(NFile);
  for I := 1 to Count do begin          { Write records to file }
    NFile^ := NItems[I];
    put(NFile)
  end; { for }
            { Merge NFile with IMas to create NMas }
  Merge(NFile, IMas, NMas)
end; { AddItems }
```

The next procedure that we will write will be the procedure to allow the user to post the transactions that have been collected over a period of time. These would include any sales and any orders that have been received for items already included in the master file. As in the previous example, the procedure will allow the user to enter up to a fixed number of entries before the data will be processed. After the data have been entered and stored in an array, the data will be sorted, and then a merge process will be used in which the data in the array and the data in the master file will be compared a record at a time. If a match is found, the record will be updated and moved to a new file; if a match does not occur, the data from the master file will simply be moved to the new file. The process assumes that the data are stored in the master file in numeric order by part number. Any entered data items that are not found in the master file are stored in another temporary file so that the user can obtain a printout and check for any errors.

```
{***********************************************************}
{* PostItems - Procedure to update the master file with the   *}
{*             data from a collection of transactions. This    *}
{*             will include the data from items sold and from  *}
{*             the orders that have been received for items    *}
{*             that currently exist in the master file. The    *}
{*             data for any item entered that is not included  *}
{*             in the master file will be printed to an error  *}
{*             file. This is a text file that can be printed   *}
{*             by the user.                                     *}
{*       var parameters -                                       *}
{*             MFile : Master file of inventory records.        *}
{*             EFile : Text file to hold the part numbers for   *}
{*                     any records entered that are not in the  *}
{*                     master file.                             *}
{*       value parameters -                                     *}
{*             None.                                            *}
{***********************************************************}
procedure PostItems(var MFile : InvFile; var EFile : text);
var
  Count,                           { Counter for added records }
  I : integer;                              { Index }
  PResponse : char;                    { For user response }
  PtRec : PostInfo;                     { For added record }
  PArray : PostArray;                   { For added records }
  Done : boolean;                     { Control input loop }
  PFile : InvFile;                     { File to store records }
begin
  Count := 0;
  PostInstructions;                { Post instructions to user }
  Done := false;
  repeat                           { Loop to input records }
    Count := Count + 1;
                        { Input part number }
    writeln('Please input part number.');
    writeln('  999999999');
    readln(PtRec.PNo);
                        { Input quantity }
    writeln('Please input quantity.');
    writeln('Enter negative number for items sold.');
    writeln('  999');
    readln(PtRec.Num);
                        { Store record in array }
    PArray[Count] := PtRec;
    writeln('Do you wish to enter another transaction?');
    writeln('Enter Y - yes / N - no');
    readln(PResponse);
    if PResponse = 'N' then
      Done := true
    { end if }
  until Done or (Count >= Max);
                        { Check for full array }
  if Count >= Max then begin
    writeln('You have entered the maximum number of items.');
    writeln('Transactions now being processed.');
```

```
    end; { if }
    Quick2Sort(PArray, Count);          { Sort array by part number }
    reset(MFile);
    rewrite(PFile);
    rewrite(EFile);
    I := 1;
                    { Merge MFile with PArray to PFile }
    while (not eof(MFile)) and (I <= Count) do
      if MFile^.PtNo < PArray[I].PNo then begin
        PFile^ := MFile^;
        put(PFile);
        get(MFile)
      end { if }
      else
        if MFile^.PtNo = PArray[I].PNo then begin
          MFile^.Quant := MFile^.Quant + PArray[I].Num;
          PFile^ := MFile^;
          put(PFile);
          get(MFile);
          I := I + 1
        end { if }
        else begin
          writeln(EFile, PArray[I].PNo);
          I := I + 1
        end; { else }
      { end else }
    { end while }
                      { Copy rest of MFile to PFile }
    while not eof(MFile) do begin
      PFile^ := MFile^;
      put(PFile);
      get(MFile)
    end; { while }
                      { Copy rest of PArray to EFile }
    while I <= Count do begin
      writeln(EFile, PArray[I].PNo);
      I := I + 1
    end; { while }
    reset(PFile);
    rewrite(MFile);
                          { Copy PFile to MFile }
    while not eof(PFile) do begin
      MFile^ := PFile^;
      put(MFile);
      get(PFile)
    end { while }
end; { PostItems }
```

Our final task in this section will be to write the main program that will use the above procedures to maintain the master file of inventory records. In the exercises we will ask you to write the remaining procedures needed to complete the program.

```
{***************************************************************}
{* FileUpdate - Program to maintain a master file of inventory *}
{*             records. The program will allow the user to      *}
{*             add records to the file, post any transactions   *}
{*             and orders received, and print out a copy of     *}
{*             inventory.                                        *}
{*      files -                                                  *}
{*           InvMas : Master file of inventory records.         *}
{***************************************************************}
program FileUpdate(Input, Output, InvMas);
{***************************************************************}
{*              const, type, and var                            *}
{*              declarations go here.                           *}
{***************************************************************}
{*     Procedures UpdateInstructions, AddItems, Menu, SignOn,   *}
{*     PostItems, PrintInventory, ErrorInstructions,            *}
{*     Quick1Sort, Quick2Sort, PostInstructions,               *}
{*     AddInstructions, Merge, InvPrintInst, and MasFileInst    *}
{*     go here.                                                 *}
{***************************************************************}
begin
  SignOn;
  UpdateInstructions;                    { Instructions to user }
  Continue := true;
  repeat
    Menu;                                         { Menu to user }
    repeat
      readln(Choice);
    until Choice in ['a', 'p', 'r'];
    case Choice of
      'a' : AddItems(InvMas);
      'p' : PostItems(InvMas, ErFile);
      'r' : PrintInventory(InvMas, PtFile)
    end; { case }
    writeln('Do you want to repeat?');
    writeln('Enter Y - yes / N - no');
    readln(Response);
    if Response = 'N' then
      Continue := false;
    { end if }
  until not Continue;
      { Instructions to user for records not found }
  ErrorInstructions;
    { Instructions to user for obtaining inventory printout }
  InvPrintInst;
      { Instructions to user for saving new master file }
  MasFileInst
end. { FileUpdate }
```

In order to complete the program, we would have to write the procedures **SignOn**, **Menu**, **Merge**, **AddInstructions**, **PostInstructions**, **Update-Instructions**, **ErrorInstructions**, **InvPrintInst**, and **MasFileInst**. We would have to write the procedure to print out the data in the master inventory file of records, **PrintInventory**. We would also have to write two versions of the QuickSort procedure, **Quick1Sort** which is called by **AddItems** and **Quick2Sort** which is called by **PostItems**. We will ask you to write some of these procedures as exercises. Refer to Chapter 1, where similar procedures were written when we were building our **EmployeeList** program.

There are certainly other procedures that we could add to the program to make it more useful. For example, if we obtain a negative number when we are posting sales, we have a posting error and the user should be alerted to this fact. Another useful practice is to keep a field for the minimum number of items that should be kept on hand and then have the program check the number on hand against this number to see if more of a given item should be ordered. In the exercises we will ask you to modify the **FileUpdate** program to include some of these useful options.

Exercises

9.27 Write the procedures needed in the **FileUpdate** program to print instructions to the user.

9.28 Write the **PrintInventory** procedure that is called as one of the user options in the **FileUpdate** program.

9.29 Write the two versions of the QuickSort procedure, Quick1Sort and Quick2-Sort, that are needed for the **FileUpdate** program.

9.30 Using the procedures that you have written in Exercises 9.27, 9.28, and 9.29, finish writing the **FileUpdate** program. Create a file **InvMas** of inventory records, and then run and test the program.

9.31 Change the inventory record so that it contains an integer field for the minimum number of items to be kept on hand. Write a procedure that will print a list of the inventory items for which the number of items on hand is less than the minimum number of items to be kept on hand. The procedure should print the part number, the description, the minimum number, and the number on hand.

9.5 Hashing and Hashing Functions

One of the basic problems programmers face is the following: How can a given collection of data be organized on a given key so that the access of an item by the key involves the least amount of effort? We will assume for this discussion that the data are to be stored in an array of records. The problem is to establish an appropriate mapping or matching scheme between the keys of the data and the indices of the array. The location of the record in the array should depend only on the key and not on the location of other records in the table. Let us look at a very simple example.

Suppose that a small business has an inventory file consisting of at most 1000 data items and that each of the data items has a unique three-digit inventory number. In this simple case, the obvious way to match the inventory numbers (keys) with the locations of the corresponding records in the array is to use the inventory numbers for the indices of the array. Thus we can declare an array of 1000 records with indices ranging from 0 to 999, using the following declarations.

```
const
  Max = 999;
type
  String20 = packed array[1..20] of char;
  InvItem = record
                PartDes : String20;
                InvNo : 0..Max;
                Quantity : integer;
                Price : real
              end;
  InvList = packed array[0..Max] of InvItem;
var
  InvItems : InvList;
```

We will have an array in which **InvItems[I]** will contain the record for the inventory item whose inventory number (key) is also **I**.

If the business has only 500 items, much of the storage space is unused; that is, many of the locations in **InvItems** do not contain any inventory data. This waste of space, however, is offset by the advantage of direct access to each of the inventory items by its inventory number. Again we are faced with a tradeoff of space vs. time. The mapping or correspondence that we have established between the key of each inventory item and its position in the array is simply the identity mapping. By the identity mapping we mean that the nth inventory item is mapped (corresponds) to the nth position in the array.

In practice, we will almost never encounter anything quite this simple. Most situations will involve large files of data items in which the keys are several characters long. Most of the time these keys will be combinations of alphabetic characters and digits and not simply three or four numeric digits. If we had eight-digit inventory numbers, for example, the above method would involve using arrays with 100 million elements. This clearly would be unacceptable, because it is unlikely that the business would stock anywhere near this many items. Furthermore, the amount of wasted space would make this method highly inefficient if not impossible because of lack of memory space. We are faced with the problem of converting these eight-digit inventory numbers into a range of integers that will accommodate our collection of data. We would like to be able to do this in such a way that no two inventory numbers (keys) will be converted to the same integer. Let us consider one such attempt.

Suppose that a business has at most 10,000 inventory items and that these items have eight-digit inventory numbers. We can certainly define an array of 10,000 records to hold our inventory items; it will be large enough to store all of our data. We have the following declarations.

```
const
   Max = 9999;
type
   String20 = packed array[1..20] of char;
   InvItem = record
                ItemDes : String20;
                InvNo : integer;                    { 8-digit }
                Quantity : integer;
                Price : real
             end;
   InvList = packed array[0..Max] of InvItem;
var
   InvItems : InvList;
```

The problem now is to devise a method to match the inventory numbers (eight-digit) with the indices of the array (0..9999). Ideally there should be no duplications; that is, each inventory number should correspond to a unique index number. Unfortunately, obtaining this one-to-one correspondence is almost always impossible. We will attempt to develop methods that will come as close to this ideal as possible. We will also discuss what actions can be taken when this ideal is not achieved. Since our inventory numbers range from 0 to 99,999,999 and our array is indexed with subscripts from 0 to 9999, one method for matching inventory numbers with indices would be to use either the first four or the last four digits of the inventory number as the subscript. Suppose that we choose to use the first four digits. In this case, the inventory item with inventory number 12347296 would be stored in **InvItems**(1234).

We can now build a function that will accomplish the above transformation. The function that transforms the key (inventory number) into the corresponding array index is called a *hash function*. If H is our hash function and k is one of our keys (inventory numbers), then the computed index $H(k)$ is called the *hash of the key k*. In the above example, our hash function could be given by the formula

$$H(k) = k \text{ DIV } 10000$$

If we decided that we wanted to use the last four digits of the inventory number for our array index, the record with inventory number 12347296 would be stored in **InvItems**(7296). In this case, our hash function could be given by

$$H(k) = k \text{ MOD } 10000$$

In either case, our method would have one obvious flaw. Clearly, we cannot store two records of information in the same component of the array.

However, if we use the first four digits of the inventory number for the index, the items with inventory numbers 12347296 and 12340000 will both have 1234 as their computed index (hash). This situation is known as a *hash clash* or *hash collision*. We almost always will have and must expect to have some hash clashes. A *good hash function* is one in which the number of clashes is minimal and the inventory data items are spread uniformly throughout the array. To allow for clashes, an array must be somewhat larger than the number of inventory items. The larger the size of the array and therefore the range of the hash function, the less likely it is that two inventory numbers will yield the same hash value. As usual, we are faced with a tradeoff: leaving empty spaces in the array is inefficient in terms of space, but it reduces the number of hash clashes to be resolved and therefore is more efficient in terms of time. We will now consider some of the methods used to handle hashing clashes.

The basic problem can be illustrated with an example. Suppose that we have two part numbers, 12349700 and 12340000. When the indices are computed using the hashing function

$$\textbf{H(PNum)} = \textbf{PNum} \text{ DIV } 10000$$

both of the records are supposed to be stored at the location with index 1234. If the structure is an array of records called **InvItems**, this would be at the location

$$\textbf{InvItems}[1234]$$

The basic idea is to store one of the records at this location and use some method to compute the location for the second record. One way of doing this is to use the very next available location. For example, if we already have data stored as shown in Figure 9.2, the next available location is at 1237, and the record of information with part number 12340000 would be stored there. Such a method for resolving hashing clashes is referred to as a *rehashing* or *open-addressing* method. The problem is to build a function to allow us to locate the position in the array for our second item. In order to do this, we con-

Figure 9.2

	Key	Record
InvItems[1232]	12321221	
InvItems[1233]		
InvItems[1234]	12349700	
InvItems[1235]	12358291	
InvItems[1236]	12367110	
InvItems[1237]		

struct a function called a *rehash function*. If **RH** is our rehash function, **RH** accepts one array index and computes another. If **Key** is our part number and the location **H(Key)**, computed by our hashing function **H**, is already occupied, **RH(H(Key))** is computed in an attempt to find a location where the record may be placed. If the position **RH(H(Key))** is also occupied, it too is rehashed to see if the location given by **RH(RH(H(Key)))** is available. This process continues until a location is found or until it is determined that no available storage locations will be found with this method. In the above example, the rehash function should return the next index in the array up until the maximum subscript is reached and then it should return the first index, which we will assume to be 0. A little thought leads to the following formula for our rehash function.

$$\mathbf{RH(I)} = \mathbf{(I} + 1) \text{ MOD } 10000$$

For example,

$$\mathbf{RH}(156) = (157) \text{ MOD } 10000 = 157$$

and

$$\mathbf{RH}(9999) = (10000) \text{ MOD } 10000 = 0$$

A considerable amount of research has gone into developing methods for handling hashing clashes. There have been many techniques developed and a great amount of data gathered on the relative efficiencies and inefficiencies of various techniques (see, for example, Niklaus Wirth, *Algorithms + Data Structures = Programs*, Prentice-Hall, Inc., 1976). In this section we simply want to introduce you to some of these techniques and point out some of the advantages and disadvantages of the ones that we discuss. We will also consider some of these techniques in the exercises.

The method discussed above falls into a class of techniques that are referred to as *double-hashing* techniques. The techniques in this collection can all be developed by building the rehash function from two other functions. The two functions that are used are the *primary hash function* **H** and a *secondary probing function* **G**. The rehash function **RH** is then computed using the formula

$$\mathbf{RH(I)} = (\mathbf{H(Key)} + \mathbf{G(I)}) \text{ MOD } (\mathbf{Size} + 1)$$

where **I** varies over 1, 2, . . . , which represents the respective computations for a possible available index. Thus using this formula the sequence of generated indices would be

$$h_0 = \mathbf{H(Key)}$$

$$\begin{aligned} h_1 &= \mathbf{RH}(1) \\ &= (\mathbf{H(Key)} + \mathbf{G}(1)) \text{ MOD } (\mathbf{Size} + 1) \\ &= (h_0 + \mathbf{G}(1)) \text{ MOD } (\mathbf{Size} + 1) \end{aligned}$$

$$h_2 = (h_0 + \mathbf{G}(2)) \text{ MOD } (\mathbf{Size} + 1)$$

Different choices for the secondary probing function **G** give rise to different double-hashing techniques. For the secondary probing function **G** in our first example, we can use the following formula.

$$G(I) = I$$

The formula for the rehash function **RH** would now be the following.

$$RH(I) = (H(Key) + G(I)) \text{ MOD } (Size + 1)$$

When the secondary probing function **G** is linear, the method is called *linear probing*. The sequence of indices generated by repeated use of **RH** would be

$$h_0 = H(Key)$$

$$h_1 = (h_0 + G(1)) \text{ MOD } (Size + 1)$$
$$= (h_0 + 1) \text{ MOD } (Size + 1)$$

$$h_2 = (h_0 + G(2)) \text{ MOD } (Size + 1)$$
$$= (h_0 + 2) \text{ MOD } (Size + 1)$$

which is the same as the sequence we had before. For the previous example, if the part number is 12349700, this number is also the **Key**. Thus

$$Key = 12349700$$

and

$$h_0 = H(Key)$$
$$= 1234$$

If this position is occupied, we compute the next indices to be considered. These are given by the computations

$$h_1 = (h_0 + 1) \text{ MOD } (Size + 1)$$
$$= (1234 + 1) \text{ MOD } 10000$$
$$= 1235$$

$$h_2 = (h_0 + 2) \text{ MOD } (Size + 1)$$
$$= (1234 + 2) \text{ MOD } 10000$$
$$= 1236$$

One of the disadvantages of this method is that the entries in the structure tend to cluster around the primary keys. A *primary key* is one that is inserted directly, with no rehashing or secondary probing necessary. Ideally we would like to choose a function **G** that will spread the elements uniformly over the remaining set of available locations. Practically, however, this is too difficult a process, and we have to settle for methods that offer a compromise. These processes will be easy to compute and superior to the method of linear probing. We will discuss a few of these methods.

The first method, called *the method of quadratic probing*, uses the simple quadratic function as the probing function:

$$G(I) = I^2$$

If there is a clash at h_0, this method probes the structure using the sequence

$$h_0 + 1, \quad h_0 + 4, \quad h_0 + 9, \quad \ldots$$

The rehash function would be given by the formula

$$\begin{aligned} RH(I) &= (H(Key) + G(I)) \bmod (Size + 1) \\ &= (H(Key) + I^2) \bmod (Size + 1) \end{aligned}$$

The sequence of computed indices would be the following.

$$h_0 = H(Key)$$

$$\begin{aligned} h_1 &= (h_0 + G(1)) \bmod (Size + 1) \\ &= (h_0 + 1) \bmod (Size + 1) \end{aligned}$$

$$\begin{aligned} h_2 &= (h_0 + G(2)) \bmod (Size + 1) \\ &= (h_0 + 4) \bmod (Size + 1) \end{aligned}$$

Using our previous example,

$$Key = 12349700$$

$$\begin{aligned} h_0 &= H(Key) \\ &= 1234 \end{aligned}$$

$$\begin{aligned} h_1 &= (1234 + 1) \bmod 10000 \\ &= 1235 \end{aligned}$$

$$\begin{aligned} h_2 &= (1234 + 4) \bmod 10000 \\ &= 1238 \end{aligned}$$

$$\begin{aligned} h_3 &= (1234 + 9) \bmod 10000 \\ &= 1243 \end{aligned}$$

One of the nice features of this method is that the sequence of indices can be computed using the recurrence relations

$$\begin{aligned} G(I + 1) &= G(I) + D(I) \\ D(I + 1) &= D(I) + 2 \end{aligned}$$

with

$$G(0) = 0 \text{ and } D(0) = 1$$

We will ask you to justify these equations in one of the exercises. These recurrence relations allow us to compute the sequence of probing values without having to use the operation of squaring.

The method of quadratic probing has the advantages of being easy to compute and avoiding clustering around primary keys. The number of computations is essentially the same as for linear probing. The disadvantage of quadratic probing is that not all entries are searched. It is possible that this method will not encounter a free storage location even when there are locations that are still free. It can be shown that this disadvantage can be minimized if the size N of the storage structure is a prime number. When N is a prime number, the method of quadratic probing will visit at least half of the locations (Wirth).

A second method is referred to as the *midsquare method*. The basic outline of this method is as follows. Each index of the sequence is computed in two steps:

1. Compute the square of the previous index or key to obtain an integer keysquare.
2. Compute the index by choosing the middle digits from the integer keysquare.

For example, if the part number is 76329165, the first value of the sequence would be given by computing the hashing value using

$$\mathbf{H(PartNo)} = \mathbf{PartNo} \text{ MOD } 10000$$

which would yield

$$h_0 = 7632$$

In order to compute the next index of our sequence, we would first compute **KeySquare**:

$$\mathbf{KeySquare} = (7632)^2$$
$$= 58247424$$

The value for h_1 would be computed using the middle four digits of **KeySquare**, which would yield

$$h_1 = 2474$$

We will ask you to develop and use this method in the exercises.

A third technique, referred to as the *folding method*, involves using the given key or computed index to compute a binary value that can be broken into several segments. These segments are then combined to compute the value to be used for the next index in the sequence. There are two ways in which binary segments are combined. One of the ways is simply to add the segments together to form one binary value and then use it to compute the index. The other way is to combine the segments using the exclusive OR operation. The process involves the following four steps.

1. Use the given key or index to compute a binary value.
2. Break the binary value into several binary segments.
3. Compute the new binary value by combining the binary segments.
4. Compute the new sequence value from the new binary value.

Before we discuss this idea, let us review the operation of exclusive ORing. This is a bit-by-bit operation that is computed using the following table.

Exclusive OR

	0	1
0	0	1
1	1	0

We can illustrate this technique with an example. As before, suppose that our part number is 76329165 so the computed hashing value is 7632. We compute the binary value simply by using the binary representation for the hashing-sequence value. Assuming that we have a 16-bit representation, we would have the following conversion.

$$7632 = 0001110111010000$$

Assuming that our structure has 256 storage locations with indices 0-255, we will use 8-bit segments so that we will end up with an 8-bit binary representation for our next index. Although this assumption causes this example to be different from our previous examples, we make it in order to make our illustration easier to understand. In the exercises we will ask you to use this method on our previous example. We will compute the two binary segments simply by breaking the binary value for 7632 into two parts. Thus, we have

$$Seg1 = 00011101$$
$$Seg2 = 11010000$$

We can now compute our new binary value by either adding or exclusive ORing these two values. We have the following.

	ADDing	*ORing*
Seg1 =	00011101	00011101
Seg2 =	11010000	11010000
Hvalue =	11001101	11101101

In order to compute the next index in our sequence, we simply compute the corresponding integer value from the binary value of Hvalue. Thus the next index value would be

$$Index = 128 + 64 + 8 + 4 + 1 \quad = 128 + 64 + 32 + 8 + 4 + 1$$
$$= 205 \qquad\qquad = 237$$

As before, we will ask you to develop and use these techniques in the exercises. This technique is easier to develop using a language, such as C, that can be used at the bit level. Note, however, that this method is somewhat machine-dependent.

The method of rehashing has several problems. It assumes a fixed array size M. If the number of records grows beyond this size, a larger array must be declared, a new hash function must be defined, and all of the hash values for all of the records may have to be recomputed using the new function. Another problem is that it is very difficult to delete a record from the array. For example, suppose that the record R1 is stored at position p1 and a second record R2 has the same hashing value p1. The record R2 will be inserted in the first vacant position in the list of positions RH(p1), RH(RH(p1)), ... If the record R1 is deleted from the array, the element at p1 is empty. When we try to search for the record R2 we must start at position p1, and the search process may erroneously conclude that R2 is not stored in the array. There are, of course, ways around this problem.

There are many hashing functions, each with its own advantages and disadvantages. We have tried to illustrate some of these methods; some of the others will be developed in the exercises.

We will now illustrate a technique that combines the concept of hashing with the use of linked lists. This method is called *the method of chaining*. We will develop the idea behind the method of chaining, and we will write basic procedures for manipulating our collection of inventory data using a data structure that is built based on the concept of chaining. When clashes occur in the course of calculating the index from the part number of one of our inventory records, we will build a linked list to store all of the inventory records that have the same computed index. Thus, our structure will look something like Figure 9.3.

Figure 9.3

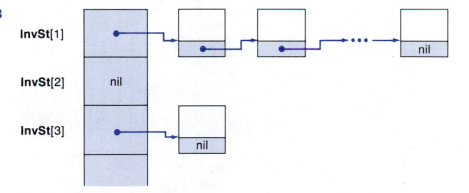

InvSt[1]

InvSt[2]   nil

InvSt[3]

To build such a structure, we will need to define an array of pointers to the elements of our linked lists. The elements of this array are sometimes referred to as *buckets*. We will need the following **type** and **var** declarations.

```
const
   Max = 999;

type
   String20 = packed array[1..20] of char;
```

```
                    InvRec = record
                                Description : String20;
                                CodeNo : integer;
                                Quantity : integer;
                                Price : real
                            end;
                    ElemPtr = ^InvElement;
                    InvElement = record
                                    Data : InvRec;
                                    Next : ElemPtr
                                 end;
                    InvStructure = array[0..Max] of ElemPtr;
                    FileType = file of InvRec;

                var
                    InvItem : InvStructure;
                    Master : FileType;
```

We will now build the basic procedures that we need to utilize the structure that we have declared. This structure will be an approximation of a direct-access structure. We begin by coding our hashing function. Let us assume that we will be using the first three digits of the code number of each inventory record as the index that is to be returned by our function. Thus we have the following.

```
{*********************************************************************}
{* Hash - Function to compute the index for the given inventory *}
{*        record. It is to return the first three digits of      *}
{*        the code number as an integer.                         *}
{*     value parameters -                                        *}
{*         Code1 : Code number used to compute the index.        *}
{*********************************************************************}
function Hash(Code1 : integer) : integer;
begin
  Hash := Code1 div 1000
end; { Hash }
```

One of the procedures that we will use will be a procedure to initialize all of our linked lists to empty. In order to initialize our linked lists to empty, we simply have to set all of the pointers in the array to **nil**. Our procedure will be the following.

```
{*********************************************************************}
{* Initialize - Procedure to set all of the elements in the     *}
{*              array to nil.                                    *}
{*     var parameters -                                          *}
{*         InvS : Array of pointers.                             *}
{*     value parameters -                                        *}
{*         None.                                                 *}
{*********************************************************************}
procedure Initialize(var InvS : InvStructure);
var
  I : integer;                                        { Index }
```

```
begin
  for I := 1 to Max do                  { Loop to initialize buckets }
    InvS[I] := nil
end; { Initialize }
```

We will now write the procedure to create our structure. This procedure will store all of the data in the file in the structure, and will call the two procedures **Initialize** and **Insert**.

```
{*****************************************************************}
{* CreateList - Procedure to create a direct access structure. *}
{*              The structure will consist of an array of       *}
{*              pointers, each pointer being a pointer to a      *}
{*              linked list. The data from the master file      *}
{*              will be stored in these linked lists. The data  *}
{*              items stored in each list will have the same    *}
{*              index where the index is computed from the      *}
{*              code number of each inventory record using the  *}
{*              hashing function.                               *}
{*      var parameters -                                        *}
{*          Mstr : Master file of inventory records.            *}
{*          InvStr : Array of pointers to the linked lists.     *}
{*      value parameters -                                      *}
{*          None.                                               *}
{*****************************************************************}
procedure CreateList(var Mstr : FileType;
                     var InvStr : InvStructure);
var
  Index : integer;                              { Array index }
  El : ElemPtr;                                 { General pointer }
begin
  reset(Mstr);
  Initialize(InvStr);                           { Initialize buckets }
  while not eof(Mstr) do begin       { Loop to create structure }
    new(El);
    El^.Data := Mstr^;
    get(Mstr);
    Index := Hash(El^.Data.CodeNo);             { Compute index }
    Insert(El, InvStr, Index)                   { Insert element }
  end { while }
end; { CreateList }
```

We will now code the **Insert** procedure.

```
{*****************************************************************}
{* Insert - Procedure to insert an element containing a record *}
{*          of inventory data into the structure.              *}
{*      var parameters -                                        *}
{*          None.                                               *}
{*      value parameters -                                      *}
{*          Elm : Pointer to the element to be inserted.        *}
{*          Ins : Array of pointers.                            *}
{*          Inx : Index where the element is to be inserted.    *}
{*****************************************************************}
```

```
procedure Insert(Elm : ElemPtr; var Ins : InvStructure;
                 Inx : integer);
begin
  Elm^.Next := Ins[Inx];
  Ins[Inx] := Elm
end; { Insert }
```

The next procedure that we will code will be the procedure to delete an element from the structure. The procedure will assume that we have a pointer, **Pt**, to the element that is to be deleted. We have two cases that we need to consider. Figure 9.4 illustrates the first case in which the element to be deleted is the first element of the list. In this case, all we have to do to delete that element is to make the array pointer point to the second element in the list. Figure 9.5 illustrates the second case, in which the element to be deleted is not the first element in the list. In this case we need to have another pointer to the element that is right before the element to be deleted (see Figure 9.6). We can then make this previous element point to the element following the element to be deleted. We will first write our outline.

Figure 9.4

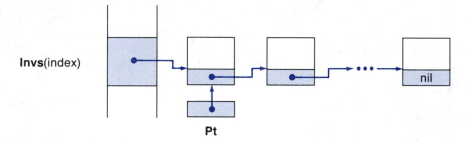

Figure 9.5

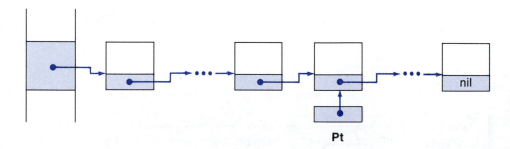

Figure 9.6

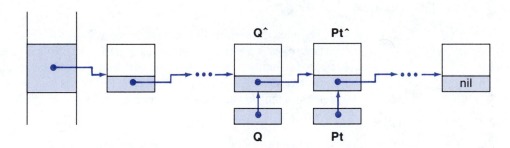

Pseudocode

Delete Procedure

Compute index from **Pt^(Data(CodeNo))**.
Set **Q** to **Inv(Index)**.
IF **Q** = **Pt** THEN
    Make **Q** point to element pointed to by **Pt^**.
ELSE
    WHILE **Q^(Ptr)** <> **Pt**
        Move **Q** to next element.
    END WHILE.
    Make **Q^** point to element pointed to by **Pt^**.
END IF.
Release memory for **Pt^**.

We can now code the procedure.

```
{*****************************************************************}
{* Delete - Procedure to delete an element from the structure. *}
{*      var parameters -                                        *}
{*          InvS : Array of pointers.                           *}
{*      value parameters -                                      *}
{*          Pt : Pointer to the element to be deleted.          *}
{*****************************************************************}
procedure Delete(Pt : ElemPtr; var InvS : InvStructure);
var
  Q : ElemPtr;                              { General pointer }
  Ind : integer;                            { Element index }
begin
  Ind := Hash(Pt^.Data.CodeNo);             { Compute index }
  Q := InvS[Ind];
  if Q = Pt then                            { If first element }
    InvS[Ind] := Pt^.Next                   { Unhook element }
  else begin
    while Q^.Next <> Pt do                  { Find list element }
      Q := Q^.Next;
    { end while }
    Q^.Next := Pt^.Next                     { Unhook element }
```

```
    end; { else }
    dispose(Pt)                                    { Release memory }
end; { Delete }
```

The next procedure that we will write will be the procedure to search the structure for an element containing a particular record of data. We will use the code number as the key for the search. The procedure will return a pointer to the element in the structure if there is one or a **nil** pointer if the element is not found. This is just one of the ways in which this procedure can be written.

```
{*******************************************************************}
{* Search - Procedure to search for an element of the           *}
{*          structure containing a particular inventory          *}
{*          record. The code number of the record is used for    *}
{*          the key.                                              *}
{*       var parameters -                                         *}
{*          FPt : Pointer to be returned. Points to the          *}
{*                element if found and is set to nil other-      *}
{*                wise.                                           *}
{*       value parameters -                                      *}
{*          CodeNumber : Code number of the record searched      *}
{*                for.                                            *}
{*          InvSl : Array of pointers.                           *}
{*******************************************************************}
procedure Search(var FPt : ElemPtr; CodeNumber : integer;
                InvSl : InvStructure);
var
  Index : integer;                          { For computed index }
  Done : boolean;                           { For search loop }
begin
  Index := Hash(CodeNumber);                { Compute index }
  FPt := InvSl[Index];
  Done := false;
  while not Done do                         { Search loop }
    if FPt = nil then
      Done := true
    else
      if FPt^.Data.CodeNo = CodeNumber then
        Done := true
      else
        FPt := FPt^.Next
      { end if }
    { end if }
  { end while }
end; { Search }
```

The next procedure that we will write will be the procedure to add a record of inventory data to the structure. We can use our **Insert** procedure to insert the element containing the new record of data into the structure.

```
{*******************************************************************}
{* Add - Procedure to store a record of inventory data in the   *}
{*       structure.                                              *}
{*          var parameters -                                     *}
{*             InvS2 : Array of pointers.                        *}
{*          value parameters -                                   *}
{*             InvDat : Record of inventory data to be inserted. *}
{*******************************************************************}
procedure Add(InvDat : InvRec; var InvS2 : InvStructure);
var
   Pt : ElemPtr;                                 { General pointer }
   Index : integer;
begin
   new(Pt);                                      { New element }
   Pt^.Data := InvDat;
   Index := Hash(InvDat.CodeNo);
   Insert(Pt, InvS2, Index)
end; { Add }
```

The last procedure that we will code will be the procedure to write the data stored in the structure back to the file of inventory records.

```
{*******************************************************************}
{* WriteList - Procedure to write the data stored in the        *}
{*             structure back to the master file.               *}
{*          var parameters -                                     *}
{*             Mast : Master file of inventory records.          *}
{*          value parameters -                                   *}
{*             InvS3 : array of pointers.                        *}
{*******************************************************************}
procedure WriteList(var Mast : FileType; InvS3 : InvStructure);
var
   I : integer;                                  { Array index }
   P : ElemPtr;                                  { General pointer }
begin
   rewrite(Mast);
   for I := 0 to 999 do begin                    { Loop for buckets }
      P := InvS3[I];
      while P <> nil do begin                    { Loop for each list }
         Mast^ := P^.Data;
         put(Mast);
         P := P^.Next
      end { while }
   end { for }
end; { WriteList }
```

In the exercises, we will ask you to write a program that will use these procedures to process a file of inventory records. We will also develop some other procedures that can be used with this inventory program.

Exercises

9.32   Suppose that the inventory numbers contain eight digits and that the middle four digits are to be used for the index. Write a hashing function that will compute this index.

9.33   Suppose that the inventory numbers consist of three alphabetic characters followed by four numeric characters. Write a hashing function that will return the last four digits, as an integer, for use as the index.

9.34   Suppose that the inventory numbers consist of eight alphanumeric characters. They can be any combination of letters and numeric digits. Write a hashing function that will compute and return an integer index in the range $0 .. \text{Size} - 1$. One way to do this would be to first use the alphanumeric characters to generate an integer number, which could be done by using the **ord** function.

9.35   Justify the equations for G(I) and D(I) that were discussed for the method of quadratic probing.

9.36   In order to show that the method of quadratic probing visits at least one half of the locations when $\text{Size} + 1$ is a prime, assume that $\text{Size} + 1$ is a prime and that the same location is reached at probe I and at probe J. This means that $h_0 + I^2$ has the same remainder as $h_0 + J^2$ when divided by $\text{Size} + 1$. Show that in this case J must differ from I by at least one half of $\text{Size} + 1$.

9.37   Write the procedures required to solve the problem of clashes through chaining using a binary-tree structure instead of the linked-list structure. The data are to be inserted into the tree structures in order by code number.

9.38   Using the method of linear probing, write a hashing function that will return the last three digits of the inventory number as the index. Write a rehash function that can be used to compute the next index when clashing occurs. Assume that the inventory number is a five-digit integer.

9.39   Write a procedure that will use the functions in Exercise 9.38 to store the data from a file **InvMas** of inventory records in an array of records. The array should have indices $0 .. 999$.

9.40   Write a procedure that will search the array of records created in Exercise 9.39. The procedure should search for a record with a particular inventory number and should use the functions that were written in Exercise 9.38.

9.41   Using the method of quadratic probing, write a hashing function and a rehash function that will return a three-digit index. Assume that the inventory number is a five-digit integer.

9.42   Write a procedure that will use the functions from Exercise 9.41 to store the data from the file **InvMas** in an array of records.

9.43   Write a procedure that will search the array in Exercise 9.42 for a record with a particular inventory number. The procedure should use the functions that were written in Exercise 9.41.

9.44   Using the midsquare method of probing, write a hashing function and a rehash function that will return a three-digit index. Assume that the inventory number is a five-digit integer.

9.45   Write a procedure that will use the functions from Exercise 9.44 to store the data from the file **InvMas** in an array of records.

9.46   Write a procedure that will search the array in Exercise 9.45 for a record with a particular inventory number. The procedure should use the functions that were written in Exercise 9.44.

9.47   Write a Pascal procedure that will compute the 16-bit binary representation of a four-digit integer number.

9.48   Write a Pascal procedure that will compute the Hvalue for the 16-bit binary returned in Exercise 9.47 by splitting the 16-bit binary into two 8-bit binaries and then adding. The result should be an 8-bit binary that ignores the carry.

9.49   Write another Pascal procedure that will compute the Hvalue for the 16-bit binary returned in Exercise 9.47. The Hvalue should be obtained by splitting the 16-bit binary into two 8-bit binaries and then using an exclusive OR to obtain the resulting 8-bit binary.

9.6   Random (Direct) Access Files

All versions of Pascal use sequential files, which are what we have been using up to this point in the text. Since *random access files* (also known as *direct access files*) are important in programming, some versions of Pascal support some version of direct file access. For example, UCSD Pascal and Microsoft Pascal both include random access files. The version of Pascal that is used on the Cyber supports segmented files, which have some but not all of the important attributes of random access files. In this section we will discuss random access files as they are used on the IBM personal computer with the Microsoft Pascal compiler.

The Microsoft Pascal compiler is one of the compilers for microcomputers that uses logical and physical file names. The logical file name is the file name used in the program and the physical file name is the name of the file on the disk. The logical file name is identified with the physical file name using the built-in procedure **assign**. If **DFile** is the logical file name used in the program and MASTER.DAT is the physical file name of the file on the disk, then these file names would be identified with the Pascal statement

```
assign(DFile, 'MASTER.DAT');
```

The physical file name can also include the drive containing the disk. Thus, if the disk containing MASTER.DAT is in drive B, then the statement would be the following:

```
assign(DFile, 'B:MASTER.DAT');
```

The basic problem with sequential files is that the file has to be either in the input mode or in the output mode and these modes cannot be concurrent. Recall that any time a sequential file is opened for output with the statement

```
rewrite(DFile);
```

the file **DFile** is empty as far as the program is concerned. This means that a record of information cannot be retrieved from the file, modified, and immediately put back in the file in the same position, as is possible with random access files. The other limitation of sequential files is that to access the 25th record of a file, a program must first process, one after the other, the first 24 records. With direct access files, the file pointer can be moved directly to the 25th component without processing of the first 24 components.

The basic procedure used to allow random access in Pascal is the **seek** procedure, which is used to move the file pointer to a particular record of the file. The format for using this procedure is the following.

```
seek(FileName, RecordNo);
```

Direct access files are composed of components, normally records, each of which is identified with a unique record number. In UCSD Pascal the first record is numbered 0, whereas in Microsoft Pascal it is numbered 1. Make sure to check the way the records are logically numbered when you are using random access files in any language or any version of Pascal that supports these files.

Before the **seek** procedure can be used, the file must be designated as being in the direct access mode and then opened for either input or output. The file **DFile** is designated as being in the direct access mode by using the statement

```
DFile^.Mode := Direct;
```

After the file has been designated as being in the direct access mode, it can be opened for input using the **reset** procedure with the statement

```
reset(DFile);
```

We can then move the file pointer to the 25th component of the file with the statement

```
seek(DFile,25);
```

The complete block of code required to access the 25th component of the file and move it to the file window is the following.

```
assign(DFile,'MASTER.DAT');
DFile.Mode := Direct;
reset(DFile);
seek(DFile, 25);
get(DFile);
```

When the command

```
reset(DFile);
```

is executed, the first component of the file is moved to the file window **DFile^**. Note, however, that even though the statement

```
seek(DFile, 25);
```

moves the file pointer to the 25th component of the file, the file window still contains the first record. In order for the twenty-fifth component of the file to be moved to the file window, the **seek** statement must be followed by the statement

```
get(DFile);
```

After the file has been declared to be in the random access mode with the statement

```
DFile^.Mode := Direct;
```

the file can be opened with either the **reset** or the **rewrite** command. The **reset** command, however, can only be used for files that already exist on a disk. The **reset** command cannot be used to create a new file. The **rewrite** command will open an existing file, or, if no file with the specified file name already exists on the disk, the **rewrite** command will create a new file with the specified name. If the **rewrite** command is used to open an existing file, the existing values in the file are still available for processing; they are not lost, as they are when the command is used on a sequential file.

After a file has been modified it must be closed in order for the information to be written to the file on the disk. The file DFile would be updated (closed) with the statement

```
close(DFile);
```

A random access file can have either a binary or an ASCII structure. By a binary structure we mean that the elements of the file are not single characters. The elements can be integers, reals, or even records as we discussed in Sections 9.1 and 9.2. For the ASCII structure, however, the basic components are single characters and the file is declared to be of type **text**. Each element of an ASCII file is a line or string of a fixed length. We will consider only files with binary structures. In our example each element will be a record.

For one record from the file **DFile** to be modified, the record must be brought from the file into main memory, the data stored in the record must be modified, and then the record must be moved from main memory back to the file. The block of code developed previously accomplishes the first of these steps. Assuming that the data have been modified, the following block of code moves the data back to the twenty-fifth position in the file.

```
seek(DFile, 25);
put(DFile);
```

We will now write some of the basic procedures that we can use to process the data in the file **DFile**, assuming that the file is a random access file of inventory records. The one problem that arises is that of determining which of the components of the file contains the record with a given code number. This is the same type of problem as we discussed in the section on hashing. We will assume that we have developed an appropriate technique for maintaining a separate file that matches the code number of each record with the record's position in the random file of records. At the beginning of the main control program, these values will be read and stored in an array. We need some **type** and **var** declarations.

Another one of the nice features of Microsoft Pascal is the built-in string structures to take the place of packed arrays of characters. These structures are created using **string** types that have the properties of packed arrays of characters. There is, however, one major difference. The number of characters in a string (i.e., the length of the string) may vary dynamically between zero and a specified upper limit, whereas the number of elements in an array is fixed. A string variable **Name**, to store up to 20 characters, would be defined with the statement

```
Name : lstring(20);
```

These string type identifiers cannot, however, be used to define parameters for procedures. We will have to define user-type identifiers as part of our global declarations. We will see how this is done as we write these declarations and the procedures.

```
const
  Size = 1000
type
  String20 = lstring(20);
```

```
         InvRec = record
                      Description : String20;
                      CodeNo : integer;
                      Quantity : integer;
                      Price : real
                  end;
         Positions = record
                         InvCode : integer;
                         FileNumber : integer
                       end;
         MatchArray = array[1..Size] of Positions;
         InvFile = file of InvRec;
         MatchFile = file of Positions;
      var
         DFile : InvFile;
         PosFile : MatchFile;
         Matches : MatchArray;
```

The user identifier **String20** is defined to use in place of the built-in type declaration 1string(20). We need this user-type identifier for defining parameters for our procedures.

We will assume that we have a file **Master.Dat** that contains **Size** records, some of which are empty. An empty record will contain the following information.

Description	20 blanks.
CodeNo	MaxInt
Quantity	0
Price	0.00

Pascal compilers have a built-in constant identifier **MaxInt**. The value of **MaxInt** is the largest possible integer value allowed by the Pascal compiler. On most 16-bit microcomputers this is 3267.

We will now write the procedures that we will need to add, modify, and delete one record of information from the file **MASTER.DAT**. We will first consider the **AddItem** procedure.

```
{***************************************************************}
{* AddItem - Procedure to add a record to a random file of     *}
{*           inventory records.                                *}
{*      var parameters -                                       *}
{*           InvMas : Random access file of inventory records. *}
{*      value parameters -                                     *}
{*           InvDat : Record to be added to the file.          *}
{*           Mats : Array of correspondences between code      *}
{*                  numbers and file record numbers.           *}
{***************************************************************}
procedure AddItem(var InvMas : InvFile;Mats : MatchArray;
                InvDat : InvRec);
var
  FNum : integer;                           { File record number }
begin
  for I := 1 to Size do            { Compute file record number }
```

```
    if Mats[I].InvCode = InvDat.CodeNo then
      FNum := Mats[I].FileNumber;
    { end if }
  { end for }
  assign(InvMas, 'MASTER.DAT');
  InvMas.Mode := direct;
  reset(InvMas);
  seek(InvMas, FNum);
  get(InvMas);
                          { Check for empty record }
  if (InvMas^.Description <> '              ') and
     (InvMas^.CodeNo <> MaxInt)  then
       writeln(' *** Data item already in file. ***')
  { end if }
  else begin                              { Store data in file }
    InvMas^ := InvDat;
    seek(InvMas, FNum);
    put(InvMas)
  end; { else }
  close(InvMas)
end; { AddItem }
```

We will now write the procedure to allow the user to delete a record from the file. The procedure will allow the user to input the part number from the keyboard. After the part number has been input, the array of matches will be searched for that part number. If a match is found, the corresponding record number will be used to delete the record from the file. This deletion will be accomplished by replacing the existing record with the empty record described earlier. If a match is not found, an error message will be printed and the user will have the option of reentering the part number.

```
{*******************************************************************}
{* DeleteItem - Procedure to delete a record from the file of   *}
{*              inventory records. The file is a random access  *}
{*              file. The PartNo of the record to be deleted    *}
{*              is to be input from the keyboard by the user.   *}
{*      var parameters -                                        *}
{*          InMas : File of inventory records.                  *}
{*      value parameters -                                      *}
{*          Mats1 - Array of matches for part numbers with      *}
{*                  file record numbers.                        *}
{*******************************************************************}
procedure DeleteItem(var InMas : InvFile; Mats1 : MatchArray);
var
  PartNo,                         { Part number from keyboard }
  RecNo,                           { File record number }
  I : integer;                        { Loop index }
  Done : boolean;                   { For search loop }
  Response : char;                 { For user response }
```

```
begin
  Done := false;
  repeat
                      { Input part number }
    writeln('Please input the part number.');
    writeln('   999999999');
    readln(PartNo);
                      { Search file for record }
    for I := 1 to Size do
      if Mats1[I].Code = PartNo then begin
        RecNo := Mats1[I].Number;
        Done := true
      end; { if }
    { end for }
    if Done then begin
      assign(InMas, 'Master.dat');
      InMas.Mode := direct;
      rewrite(InMas);
      seek(InMas, RecNo);
                      { Move empty record to file }
      InMas^.Description := '                        ';
      InMas^.CodeNo := MaxInt;
      InMas^.Quantity := 0;
      InMas^.Price := 0;
      put(InMas)
    end { if }
    else begin
      writeln('*** Record not found. ***');
      writeln('The part number was ', PartNo:1);
      writeln('Do you wish to try again?');
      writeln('Y - yes / N - no');
      readln(Response);
      if Response = 'N' then
        Done := true
      { end if }
    end { else }
  until Done;
  close(InMas)
end; { DeleteItem }
```

We will now write the procedure that will allow the user to modify the data for any of the inventory records contained in the file. As before, the user will be asked to input the part number of the record from the keyboard. The procedure will expect the user to modify each of the fields of the record if it is found. (In the exercises you will be asked to modify this procedure so that the user can choose which of the fields to modify.) If the record with the given part number is not found in the file, the user will be given the option to try again.

```
{*******************************************************************}
{* ModifyItem - Procedure to modify the data in one record of  *}
{*              the file of inventory records. The file is to  *}
{*              be a random access file. The part number of    *}
```

```
{*           the record is to be input from the keyboard.   *}
{*      var parameters -                                    *}
{*          InMas1 : Master file of inventory records.      *}
{*      value parameters -                                  *}
{*          Mats2 : Array of matches for part numbers with  *}
{*                  file record numbers.                    *}
{***********************************************************}
procedure ModifyItem(var InMas1 : InvFile; Mats2 : MatchArray);
var
  PartNo,                              { Part number from keyboard }
  RecNo,                                       { Record number }
  I : integer;                                   { Loop index }
  Found : boolean;                           { For search loop }
  Response : char;                        { For user response }
begin
  Found := false;
  repeat
                        { Input part number }
    writeln('Please input the part number.');
    writeln('  999999999');
    readln(PartNo);
                        { Search for file record }
    for I := 1 to Size do
      if Mats2[I].Code = PartNo then begin
        Found := true;
        RecNo := Mats2[I].Number
      end; { if }
    { end for }
    if Found then begin                      { Modify record }
      assign (InMas1, 'Master.dat');
      InMas1.mode := direct;
      reset(InMas1);
      seek(InMas1, RecNo);
      get(InMas1);
                        { Input new description }
      writeln('Please input new description.');
      writeln('  xxxxxxxxxxxxxxxxxxxx');
      for I := 1 to 20 do
        read(InMas1^.Description[I]);
      { end for }
      readln;
                        { Input new code number }
      writeln('Please input the new code number.');
      writeln('  999999999');
      readln(InMas1^.CodeNo);
                        { Input new quantity }
      writeln('Please input the new quantity.');
      writeln('  9999');
      readln(InMas1^.Quantity);
                        { Input new price }
      writeln('Please input the new price.');
      writeln('  999.99');
      readln(InMas1^.Price);
      seek(InMas1, RecNo);            { Store modified record }
      put(InMas1)
```

```
      end { if }
      else begin
        writeln('*** Part number was not found. ***');
        writeln('The part number was ', PartNo:1);
        writeln('Do you wish to try again?');
        writeln('Y - yes / N - no.');
        readln(Response);
        if Response = 'N' then
          Found := true
        { end if }
      end { else }
    until Found;
    close(InMas1)
end; { DeleteItem }
```

Another procedure that might be useful is a procedure to create a file of **Size** empty records. This procedure could also be used to convert an existing file to a file of empty records.

```
{****************************************************************}
{* CreateFile - Procedure to create a file of Size empty        *}
{*              records. An empty record will contain 20         *}
{*              blanks for the description and zeros in every    *}
{*              other field.                                     *}
{*        var parameters -                                       *}
{*            InMas2 : File to be created.                       *}
{*        value parameters -                                     *}
{*            None.                                              *}
{****************************************************************}
procedure CreateFile(var InMas2 : InvFile);
var
  I : integer;                                { Loop index }
begin
  assign (InMas2, 'Master.dat');
  InMas2.mode := direct;
  rewrite(InMas2);
                        { Create empty record }
  InMas2^.Description := '                    ';
  InMas2^.CodeNo := 99999;
  InMas2^.Quantity := 0;
  InMas2^.Price := 0;
                        { Create file of empty records }
  for I := 1 to Size do begin
    seek(InMas2, I);
    put(InMas)
  end; { for }
  close(InMas2)
end; { CreateFile }
```

In the exercises you will be asked to write a main program to use the procedures that we have just written.

We will now write a procedure that might be useful when the amount of memory available is limited. The procedure will allow us to do a binary search on a file of inventory records without having to bring the collection of records into main memory. The procedure will expect the part number to be passed in by the calling program and will return the record number if the appropriate record is found. If the record with the given part number is not found, the record number will be returned with the value 0.

We begin by outlining the procedure.

Pseudocode

BinFileSearch Procedure

Set **First** to 1.
Set **Last** to **Size**.
Open file for input.
Set **Found** to false.
Set **RecNo** to 0.
WHILE (**First** <= **Last**) AND (NOT **Found**)
   Compute middle index.
   Move file pointer to **Middle** record.
   Move record to file window.
   IF **PartNo** > record(**CodeNo**) THEN
      Set **Last** to **Middle** − 1.
   ELSE
     IF **PartNo** < record(**CodeNo**) THEN
        Set **First** to **Middle** + 1.
     ELSE
        Set **Found** to true.
     END IF.
   END IF.
END WHILE.
IF **Found** = True THEN
   Set **RecNo** to **Middle**.
END IF.

We can now code the procedure.

```
{********************************************************************}
{* BinFileSearch - Procedure to search a file of inventory        *}
{*                 records for the record containing a            *}
{*                 particular part number. The search process     *}
{*                 is a binary search.                            *}
{*       var parameters -                                         *}
{*            InMas] : File of inventory records.                 *}
{*            RecNo] : Record number to be returned if the        *}
{*                     record is found and to return the value    *}
{*                     0 if the record is not found.              *}
{*       value parameters -                                       *}
{*            PartNo] : Part number of the record searched for. *}
{********************************************************************}
```

```
procedure BinFileSearch(var InMas3 : InvFile; PartNo3 : integer;
                        var RecNo3 : integer);
var
  First, Last, Mid : integer;              { For search interval }
  Found : boolean;                         { For search loop }
begin
  First := 1;
  Last := Size;
  assign(InMas3, 'Master.dat');
  InMas3.mode := direct;
  reset(InMas3);
  Found := false;
  RecNo3 := 0;
                            { Search loop }
  while (First <= Last) and (not Found) do begin
    Mid := (First + Last) div 2;
    seek(InMas3, Mid);
    get(InMas3);
    if PartNo3 < InMas3^.CodeNo then
      Last := Mid - 1
    { end if }
    else
      if PartNo3 > InMas3^.CodeNo then
        First := Mid + 1
      { end if }
      else
        Found := true
      { end else }
    { end else }
  end; { while }
  if Found = true then
    RecNo3 := Mid;
  { end if }
  close(InMas3)
end; { BinFileSearch }
```

One of the questions that this procedure raises is its relative efficiency, in terms of run time, compared to that of storing all of the data in an internal data structure and then using a binary search on that structure. In the exercises you will be asked to perform this analysis.

Exercises

9.50 Using standard Pascal, write a procedure that will simulate a direct access read. Call the procedure **DirectRead**. The procedure should pass the file name, the record number, the record that is to be returned, and a Boolean as parameters. The Boolean is used in case the record number is larger than the number of records in the file.

9.51 Using standard Pascal, write a procedure that will simulate a direct access write. Call the procedure **WriteDirect**. Since a call to the **rewrite** procedure creates an empty file, the procedure will need to use a temporary file.

9.52   Consider the **ModifyItem** procedure written in this section. Rewrite the procedure so that it allows the user the option of modifying a single field.

9.53   Write a program that will compare the time required by the procedure **BinFileSearch** with the time required to read the data from a file and store it in an array, use a binary search of the array for the item, and then write the data back to the file. The test can be done for a file of randomly generated integer numbers if **BinFileSearch** is modified appropriately.

9.54   Rewrite the procedure **BinFileSearch** recursively.

9.55   Write a program that will compare the recursive binary file-search procedure from Exercise 9.54 with the procedure **BinFileSearch**.

Summary

The topic of this chapter was Pascal files. Files are used to store data so that the data can be used over again in different runs of a program or even in different programs. The basic file of characters (**text**) used in Pascal was reviewed, and then other types of files were defined and compared with text files. The more general file of records that can be defined in Pascal was discussed, and the ways in which such files could be used in our **EmployeeList** program from earlier chapters were explored.

Files allow us to store collections of data that are too large to be stored in an internal data structure for use in a given program. This chapter discussed some of the external sorting techniques, including merging of files, that can be used to maintain these large collections of data.

This chapter also introduced the topic of hashing. Complete coverage of this topic would require at least a complete book; this chapter merely covered some of the basic ideas and illustrated how they could be used in our program to maintain the collection of employee data. Some hashing techniques and hashing functions were developed.

Finally, the last section discussed the topic of random access files and how they are defined and used in Microsoft Pascal. Some basic procedures for these files were developed.

Chapter Exercises

9.56   Consider the collection of inventory data described in Program 1 in the chapter exercises in Chapter 1. Write the const, type, and var declarations needed to define a file of inventory records.

9.57   If your Pascal compiler supports random access files, then write a program that will read the data from the text file containing the inventory data and create a random access file of inventory records. Test the procedure.

9.58 Assume that we wish to create a small data base in which the data will be accessed directly from the random access file. Assume that we have at most 100 records and that each inventory number has seven characters, two letters followed by five digits. Write a hashing function that will return the last two digits of the inventory number to use as the position of the record in the random access file. Write a program that prints a sign-on message and then prints a message with the following choices:

0. Print the menu.
1. Create the data base (all data input from the console and stored in the random access file).
2. Create the data base (all data input from a text data file).
3. Write all data to a text file, sorted by inventory number.
4. Search the data base for an inventory item (binary search by inventory number using computed index).
5. Insert a new inventory item.
6. Delete an inventory item.
7. Exit.

Write all of the procedures that allow the above choices. The user should be allowed to continue making selections and have them executed until choice 7 is selected.

9.59 Add the following choices to the program from Exercise 9.58.

7. Modify any field in a given inventory item.
8. Print all inventory items for which the quantity on hand is less than the reorder quantity.
9. Exit.

Write the procedures that allow these new choices.

9.60 Consider the collection of address book data described in Program 2 of the review exercises in Chapter 1. Write the declarations needed to create a file of address book records.

9.61 Write a program to create and process a small data base for the address book data from Exercise 9.60. The data are to be stored in a file of records. The program should print a sign-on message and then print a menu with the following user options:

0. Print the menu.
1. Create an address data base (all data input from the console and stored in the file of records).
2. Create an address data base (all data input from a text data file).
3. Sort the data by name.
4. Print all address book data sorted by name.
5. Search for an address book record (by name).

6. Insert a new address book record.
7. Delete an address book record.
8. Exit.

Write all of the procedures that allow the above choices. Use any of the sorting techniques discussed in this chapter. The user should be allowed to continue making selections until choice 8 is selected.

9.62   Add the following options to the program from Exercise 9.61.

8. Search the address book data by phone number.
9. Modify any field in an address book record.
10. Search for all records with the same zip code.
11. Search for all records with the same last name.
12. Exit.

CHAPTER 10

Introduction to Graphs

A fascinating, but challenging, area of data structures and computer science is that of graphs. Graphs can be used for a wide variety of practical applications. For example, an airline may use graphs for scheduling of flights between cities, or an engineering company may use graphs to help with flow problems, or a telecommunications company may use graphs to help with communications links. These are only a few of the numerous potential applications for graphs.

All trees are graphs; however, in a tree there are several restrictions with regard to pointers. For example, the subtrees pointed to by any given node must be disjoint. Also, in a tree pointers are directed from a parent node to its children, but generally not from a child to its parent (except for threads). As we will see very shortly, in a graph we do not have these restrictions; any node can point to any other node.

A complete presentation of graphs would require at least an entire textbook. All that can be presented in a single chapter is an introduction. This chapter will cover the basic terminology associated with graphs, programming procedures used in creating and manipulating graphs, and an airline scheduling application using graphs.

10.1 Graph Terminology

Any graph consists of the union of two sets: a set of nodes and a set of pairs of nodes. For example, the graph in Figure 10.1 consists of the union of the set {A,B,C,D,E}, which contains the nodes, and the set {(A,B),

(A,C),(B,C),(B,D),(C,E),(D,E)}, which contains the pairs of nodes. Thus the graph is

$$\{A,B,C,D,E\} \cup \{(A,B),(A,C),(B,C),(B,D),(C,E),(D,E)\}$$

Notice that each pair of nodes in the graph is indicated by a line connecting the two nodes. For example, the pair (A,B) is indicated by a line drawn between the two nodes A and B. It is common to call each pair of nodes an *arc* or an *edge*. In this chapter we will refer to a pair of nodes as an arc. The selection of the arcs to be included in a graph is determined by the application.

Figure 10.1

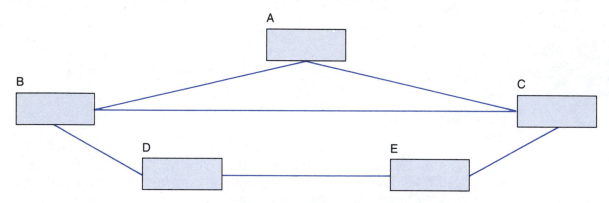

In Figure 10.1 no arrows appear on the lines between nodes. Thus no direction is implied. That is, no specific ordering of the nodes in each pair is indicated. In this case, the pair (A,B) is the same as the pair (B,A).

In certain applications, the ordering of the nodes in one or more of the arcs is important. For example, suppose that each node in Figure 10.2 represents an oil-line pumping station and each arc represents the flow of oil in a pipeline from one station to another. If we wish to represent an oil line *from* station A *to* station B, we draw a directed line from A to B, representing the arc (A,B). In this case the ordered pair (A,B) is not the same as the ordered pair (B,A). If the arcs in a graph are ordered, the graph is called a *directed graph* or an *ordered graph* or a *digraph*.

A tree is a directed graph because the pointers imply a direction from one node to another (parent to child). However, not every directed graph is a tree. Note that the directed graph in Figure 10.2 is not a tree, since nodes C and D both point to node E.

The ordering of the nodes is determined by the application. For example, if each node in a graph represents a day of the week (see Figure 10.3), we can imply that an ordered pair (A,B) means "A is the day before B."

If a node A is contained in an arc (A,B), A is said to be *incident* to arc (A,B). [Note that B is also incident to arc (A,B).] The *degree* of a node A is the number of arcs to which A is incident. For example, the degree of each node in Figure 10.3 is 2 because each node is contained in two different arcs. The *indegree* of any node A is the number of arcs in which A is the initial node. In Figure 10.3, the indegree of each node is 1. The *outdegree* of any node A is the number of arcs in which A is the terminal node. In Figure 10.3, the outdegree of each node is 1.

Figure 10.2

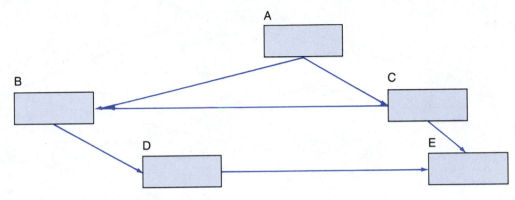

Figure 10.3

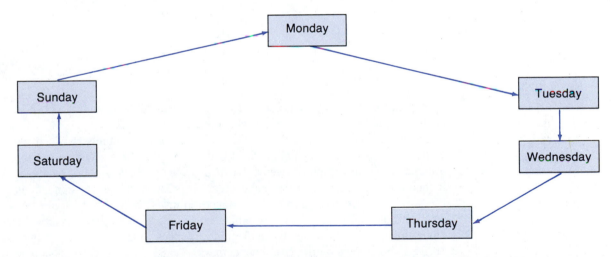

By following the arcs from one node through other nodes, we can form a *path* from one node to another. For example, in Figure 10.4 we can form a path from node A to node D by starting at node A, then going to node B, then going to node C, and finally going to node D. Formally, we define *a path of length m from node A to node B* to be a sequence of nodes

$$n_1, n_2, \ldots, n_{m+1}$$

such that n_1 = A, n_{m+1} = B, and all of the pairs (n_i, n_{i+1}) for i = 1, . . . , m are included in the graph. Thus in Figure 10.4 a path of length 3 exists from node A to node D, since there exists a sequence of nodes A, B, C, D such that (A,B), (B,C), and (C,D) are arcs in the graph.

Figure 10.4

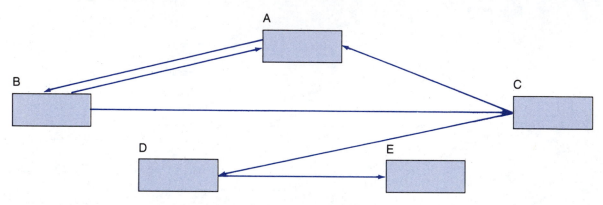

A path from a node back to itself is called a *cyclic path*. Thus the path A, B, A in Figure 10.4 is called a cyclic path. In fact, Figure 10.4 contains all of the following cyclic paths.

A, B, A

B, A, B

A, B, C, A

B, C, A, B

C, A, B, C

A path that is not cyclic is called *acyclic*. For example, the path C, D, E is acyclic because it does not cycle back to the initial node C.

In applications it is commonly desirable to associate a number, which we will call a *weight*, with each arc (pair of nodes). If a weight is assigned to each arc in a graph, the graph is called a *weighted graph* or a *network*. For example, if each node in a graph is a city and each arc represents a highway connecting the two cities, we could assign the distance (in miles) between the two cities as the weight for each arc. For example, in Figure 10.5 we have assigned a weight of 40 miles to arc (A,B), a weight of 50 miles to arc (A,C), etc. Figure 10.5 has no arrows on the lines connecting the cities, since we are assuming that we may travel in either direction between the two cities in any arc. We could also draw the same graph using two directed lines for each arc, as in Figure 10.6.

Now that we have discussed the basic terminology used with graphs, in Section 10.2 we will investigate the methods that may be used to implement graphs using Pascal.

Figure 10.5

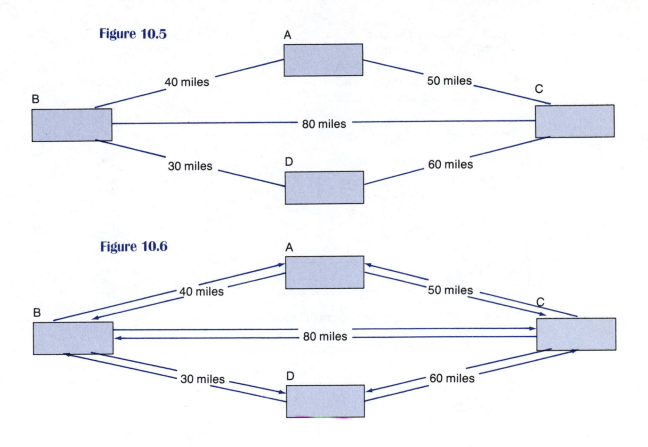

Figure 10.6

Exercises

10.1   Consider the graph below.
(a) Give the union (of nodes and pairs of nodes) that defines the graph.
(b) Is the graph a digraph? Why or why not?
(c) List the indegree of each node.
(d) List the outdegree of each node.
(e) List the degree of each node.

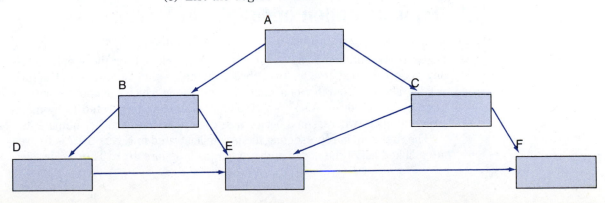

10.2   Consider the graph below.
(a) Give the union that defines the graph.
(b) Is the graph a digraph? Why or why not?
(c) List all cyclic paths.
(d) List all acyclic paths.

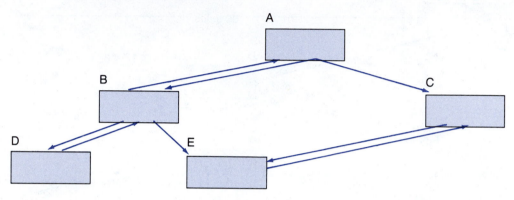

10.3   Consider the weighted graph below.
(a) Give the union that defines the graph.
(b) List the weight for each arc.

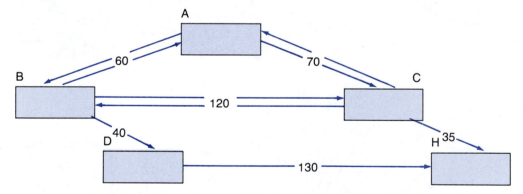

10.2   Implementation of Graphs in Pascal

Suppose that we wish to implement the graph in Figure 10.7 using Pascal. A linked representation using pointers can be developed for the graph. Since any node can point to one, two, three, or more other nodes, the structure will be different from that of a simple binary tree in which each node points to at most two children. Also, in a graph any node may be pointed to by more than one node, whereas in a binary tree each node has at most one parent.

The first step in representing the graph illustrated in Figure 10.7 is to create a linked list of the nodes in the graph, as in Figure 10.8. The "D" in each node stands for the node data. Each of the nodes in this linked list will be called a *header node*. The pointers from one node to the next are just used to create the linked list of nodes; they are *not* used to represent arcs in the graph.

Figure 10.7

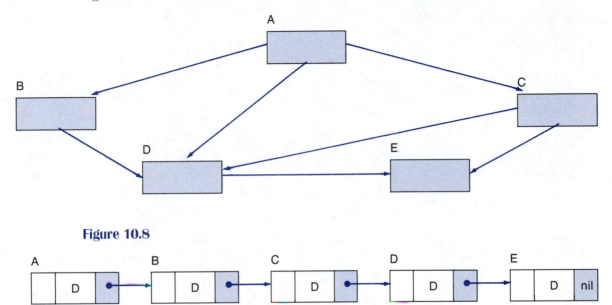

Figure 10.8

Notice that the first field in each node is blank. This field will be used to point to a linked list of the arcs in the graph that originate at the given node. Since (A,B), (A,C), and (A,D) are arcs for the graph in Figure 10.7, the linked list originating from A should include these three arcs. These arcs are indicated in the linked list by having *each* node in this list point to the final node in the arc (see Figure 10.9). Thus, pointers in the arc linked list for header node A point to B, C, and D. We will call each of the nodes in this linked list an *arc node*.

Completion of the graph involves inserting a linked list of arc nodes for each of the remaining header nodes. Figure 10.10 illustrates the complete linked representation for the graph in Figure 10.7.

The header nodes and the arc nodes are certainly different. Each header node contains a pointer to its list of arc nodes, data for the node, and a pointer to the next header node. Each arc node contains a pointer to the next arc and a pointer to a header node. If required for a specific application, the weight associated with a particular arc node can be included in each node by adding a new field to hold the weight.

Figure 10.9

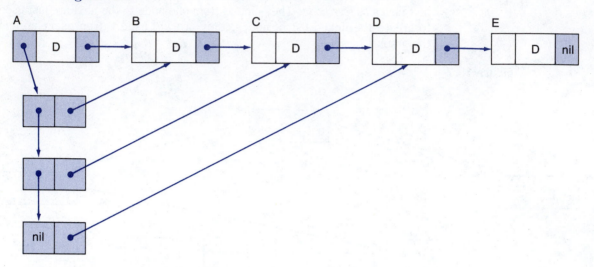

Figure 10.10

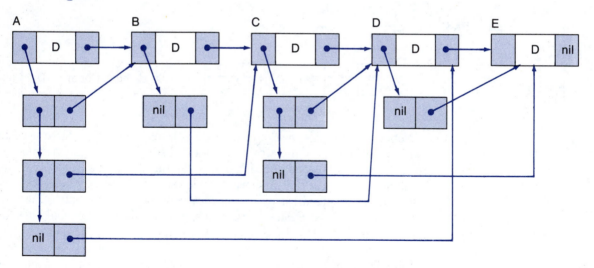

Let us now turn to the Pascal **type** declarations that can be used in the linked representation of a graph. Assuming that a weight is to be included in each arc node, we may use the following declarations.

```
type
    HeaderNodePtr = ^HeaderNode;
    ArcNodePtr = ^ArcNode;
    HeaderNode = record
                     PtrToArcNode : ArcNodePtr;
                     HNodeData : NodeData;
                     NextHeader : HeaderNodePtr
                 end;
```

```
ArcNode = record
        PtrToArcNode : ArcNodePtr;
        ArcWeight : ArcNodeData;
        PtrToHeader : HeaderNodePtr
     end;
```

HNodeData is the data item in each header node, and **ArcWeight** is the weight associated with each arc. Note that the header nodes are similar to, but still different from, the arc nodes. The type of data stored in each header node is normally different from the type of data stored in each arc node.

Each header node will then be represented as follows.

PtrToArcNode	HNodeData	NextHeader

PtrToArcNode is a pointer to the first arc node in the list of all arc nodes for which the header node is the initial node, and **NextHeader** is a pointer to the next header node in the list of header nodes. Each arc node will be represented as follows.

PtrToArcNode	ArcWeight	PtrToHeader

PtrToArcNode is a pointer to the next arc node in the list of arc nodes, and **PtrToHeader** is a pointer to the header node that is the terminal node in the arc that this arc node represents.

Suppose that we wish to create a graph in which each node represents a city and each arc represents a flight scheduled by a small airline between two of the cities (see Figure 10.11). Assume that the only data item in each header node (city) is the name of the city and that the weight for each arc node is the flight time in minutes for the flight between the two cities. Figure 10.11 illustrates the cities and the flights; however, it is *not* the Pascal linked representation for the graph. Since normal prevailing winds may make a difference in the approximate flight times, the flight time for arc (X,Y) from city X to city Y may be different than the flight time for arc (Y,X) from city Y to city X. The linked representation for the cities and flights (arcs) is illustrated in Figure 10.12.

In order to create the linked representation of the graph, we must

1. Create each header node.
2. Create each arc in the list of arc nodes for each of the header nodes.

To perform these steps we must have a source for the list of city names as well as a source for the list of flights and flight times. We will create one data file, **Names**, in which each line contains the name of one of the cities, and a second data file, **Flights**, in which each data line contains the names of two cities (for the flight from the first city to the second city) and the time (in minutes) required for the flight. Notice that the order of the cities in file **Flights** is important, since we will consider the flight to be from the first city listed to the second.

Figure 10.11

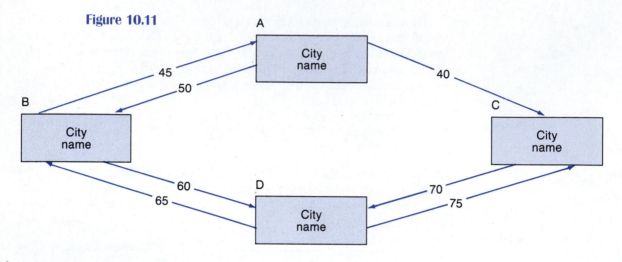

Figure 10.12

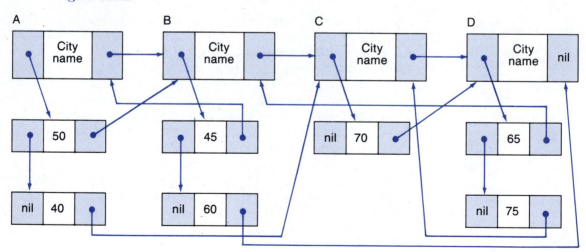

To implement the linked graph representation, we will make the following **type** declarations.

```
type
  String25 = packed array[1..25] of char;
  HeaderNodePtr = ^City;
  ArcNodePtr = ^Flight;
```

```
City = record
          PtrToFlight : ArcNodePtr;
          CityName : String25;
          NextCity : HeaderNodePtr
       end;
Flight = record
            NextFlight : ArcNodePtr;
            FlightTime : integer;
            Destination : HeaderNodePtr
         end;
```

Notice that the **type** for each arc node is **Flight** and that **Destination** is a pointer to the header node containing the name of the destination city.

A procedure **CreateLinkedGraph** to create the linked graph will begin by creating a header node and inserting the first city name from file **Cities** into this node. Just like the root in a tree, the pointer to this first header node will provide entry into the graph. After the creation of this first header node, each of the remaining city names will be read and inserted one at a time into a new header node. After the linked list of header nodes has been created, the procedure will then create the linked lists of arc nodes (flights) originating from the header nodes. This will be accomplished by reading each data line from file **Flights** and then calling a procedure **InsertArc** to insert the flight data into an arc node.

Pseudocode

> **CreateLinkedGraph Procedure**
>
> IF file CITIES is empty THEN
>   Print a message and return a value of NIL as pointer value
>   for **FirstNode**.
> ELSE
>   Create a header node **FirstNode**.
>   Read first city name and insert into **FirstNode**.
>   Set **PtrToFlight** and **NextFlight** pointers in **FirstNode** to
>   NIL.
>   WHILE not at EOF for file **Cities**
>   Create new header node and insert at end of header list.
>   Read next city name and insert in header node.
>   Set **PtrToFlight** and **NextFlight** pointers to NIL.
>   END WHILE.
>   WHILE not at EOF for file **Flights**
>   Read first city name, second city name, and flight time
>   from file **Flights**.
>   Call procedure to insert new arc node into graph.
>   END WHILE.
> END IF.

The Pascal coding for procedure **CreateLinkedGraph** follows.

```
{*********************************************************************}
{* CreateLinkedGraph - Procedure to create a linked graph in        *}
{*                     which each header node contains the name      *}
{*                     of a city and each arc node represents a      *}
{*                     flight between two cities.                    *}
{*        var parameters -                                           *}
{*              FirstNode :  Pointer to first header node.           *}
{*        value parameters -                                         *}
{*              None                                                 *}
{*********************************************************************}
procedure CreateLinkedGraph(var Firstnode : HeaderNodePtr);
var
  HNode,
  NextHNode : HeaderNodePtr;                   { Header-node pointers }
  OneCityName,
  FirstCity,
  SecondCity :  String25;                            { City names }
  I,                                                    { Index }
  Time : integer;                                  { Flight time }
begin
  reset(Cities);                               { Reset data files }
  reset(Flights);
  if eof(Cities) then begin
    writeln('The cities file is empty.');
    FirstNode := nil
  end  { if }
  else begin
    new(HNode);                      { Create the first header node }
    FirstNode := HNode;
    for I := 1 to 25 do                   { Blank out OneCityName }
      OneCityName[I] := ' ';
    { end for }
    I := 1;
                    { Read OneCityName from file Cities }
    while not eoln(Cities) do begin
      read(Cities, OneCityName[I]);
      I := I + 1
    end;  { while }
    readln(Cities);
    with FirstNode^ do begin           { Insert data into first node }
      CityName := OneCityName;
      PtrToFlight := nil;
      NextCity := nil
    end;  { with }
    while not eof(Cities) do begin
      new(NextHNode);                     { Create a new header node }
      for I := 1 to 25 do                  { Blank out OneCityName }
        OneCityName[I] := ' ';
      { end for }
      I := 1;
                      { Read OneCityName from file Cities }
      while not eoln(Cities) do begin
        read(Cities, OneCityName[I]);
        I := I + 1
      end;  { while }
```

```
      readln(Cities);
      HNode^.NextCity := NextHNode;      { Insert new node into list }
      HNode := NextHNode;
      with HNode^ do begin               { Insert data into new node }
        CityName := OneCityName;
        PtrToFlight := nil;
        NextCity := nil
      end   { with }
    end;  { while }
    while not eof(Flights) do begin
      for I := 1 to 25 do                { Read name of first city }
        read(Flights, FirstCity[I]);
      { end for }
      for I := 1 to 25 do                { Read name of second city }
        read(Flights, SecondCity[I]);
      { end for }
      readln(Flights, Time);                   { Read flight time }
        { Call procedure to insert new arc node into the graph }
      InsertArc(FirstNode, FirstCity, SecondCity, Time)
    end   { while }
  end   { else }
end;  { CreateLinkedGraph }
```

You will be asked in the exercises to modify the necessary code to handle the situation in which a city name is repeated in file **Cities**.

The **InsertArc** procedure should first search the list of header nodes for the node that contains the first city name. Then the linked list of arc nodes (flights) for this header node is traversed in order to find the end of the list. A new arc node is then created and inserted at the end of the list. (The case in which the arc node already exists will be considered in the exercises.) After the flight time is inserted into the new arc node and its **NextFlight** pointer is set to **nil**, the list of header nodes must again be searched to find the pointer to the node that contains the second city name. This pointer to the correct header node is then inserted as the **Destination** pointer in the new arc node. Since the search through the list of header nodes to find a city name is a commonly used process, we will write it as a separate procedure called **FindHNodePtr**.

```
{******************************************************************}
{* InsertArc - Procedure to insert a new arc node into a linked  *}
{*             graph.                                            *}
{*     var parameters -                                          *}
{*          None.                                               *}
{*     value parameters -                                       *}
{*          FirstNode :  Pointer to first header node.           *}
{*          BegCity : Initial city name in arc node.             *}
{*          EndCity : Terminal city name in arc node.            *}
{*          FlTime :  Flight time for the arc node.              *}
{******************************************************************}
procedure InsertArc(FirstNode : HeaderNodePtr; BegCity,
                 EndCity : String25; FlTime : integer);
```

```
var
  NewArcPtr,
  OneArcPtr : ArcNodePtr;                          { Arc-node pointers }
  OneCityPtr : HeaderNodePtr;                       { Header-node pointer }
begin
          { Call procedure to find the header node that contains
              the first city name }
  FindHNodePtr(FirstNode, BegCity, OneCityPtr);
  if OneCityPtr <> nil then begin
    new(NewArcPtr);                               { Create a new arc node }
    NewArcPtr^.FlightTime := FlTime;
    NewArcPtr^.NextFlight := nil;
          { Find the end of the arc-node list and insert new
              arc node }
    if OneCityPtr^.PtrToFlight = nil then
      OneCityPtr^.PtrToFlight := NewArcPtr
    { end if }
    else begin
      OneArcPtr := OneCityPtr^.PtrToFlight;
      while OneArcPtr^.NextFlight <> nil do
        OneArcPtr := OneArcPtr^.NextFlight;
      { end while }
      OneArcPtr^.NextFlight := NewArcPtr
    end;  { else }
          { Call procedure to find the header node that contains
              the second city name }
    FindHNodePtr(FirstNode, EndCity, OneCityPtr);
    if OneCityPtr <> nil then        { If found, insert pointer
                                        to the second city header node }
      NewArcPtr^.Destination := OneCityPtr
    { end if }
  end   { if }
end;   { InsertArc }
```

The **FindHNodePtr** procedure searches the linked list of header nodes for the node that contains a specific city name. If a node containing the given city name is found, the pointer to this node is returned; otherwise, a **nil** pointer value is returned.

```
{****************************************************************}
{* FindHNodePtr - Procedure to search the list of header nodes *}
{*                for a given city name.                        *}
{*      var parameters -                                        *}
{*          CityPtr : Pointer to header node that contains the  *}
{*                    given city name, if found. If not found,  *}
{*                    it is returned as nil.                    *}
{*      value parameters -                                      *}
{*          FirstNode : Pointer to first header node.           *}
{*          CityN : City name to be found.                      *}
{****************************************************************}
procedure FindHNodePtr (FirstNode : HeaderNodePtr; CityN : String25;
                        var CityPtr : HeaderNodePtr);
```

```
var
   HNode : HeaderNodePtr;                    { Header node pointer }
   Found : boolean;                      { Boolean flag to
                                           indicate if node is found }
begin
         { If city name is in the first header node, set found to
           true and return the pointer to the header node }
   if FirstNode^.CityName = CityN then begin
     CityPtr := FirstNode;
     Found := true
   end
   else begin
         { Else, search remaining header nodes for the city name }
     Found := false;
     HNode := FirstNode;
     while (not Found) and (HNode <> nil) do begin
       if HNode^.CityName = CityN then
         Found := true
       { end if }
       else
         HNode := HNode^.NextCity
       { end else }
     end;  { while }
     if not Found then
       CityPtr := nil
     { end if }
     else
       CityPtr := HNode
     { end else }
   end  { else }
end;  { FindHNodePtr }
```

Now that we have completed the procedures necessary to construct a linked graph, let us consider what we can do with the graph after it has been created. One obvious use is that of determining whether a direct flight exists between two given cities, and, if so, finding the flight time.

To accomplish this task, we will write a procedure called **FindArc** that will accept two city names and return a pointer to the arc node (flight). If the arc node is not found, a **nil** pointer will be returned. The calling program (or procedure) can then extract and print the flight time for the flight (assuming that one exists).

The first part of the procedure will resemble the **InsertArc** procedure, since it will call the **FindHNodePtr** procedure to locate the header node that contains the first city name. Then, if the header node is found, the linked list of arc nodes for that header node will be searched to find the arc node that contains the second city as its **Destination**.

```
{******************************************************************}
{* FindArc - Procedure to find an arc node containing the given   *}
{*           first and second cities. If the arc node is found,   *}
{*           the pointer to the arc node will be returned.        *}
{*           Otherwise, a nil pointer will be returned.           *}
```

```
{*        var parameters -                                        *}
{*          FoundArcPtr : Pointer to the found arc node (or nil   *}
{*                        if the arc node is not found).          *}
{*        value parameters -                                      *}
{*          FirstNode : Pointer to the first header node.         *}
{*          FirstCity : Name of the first city.                   *}
{*          SecondCity : Name of the second city.                 *}
{***************************************************************}
procedure FindArc (FirstNode : HeaderNodePtr; FirstCity, SecondCity :
                   String25; var FoundArcPtr : ArcNodePtr);
var
  OneArcPtr : ArcNodePtr;                       { Arc-node pointer }
  OneCityPtr : HeaderNodePtr;                { Header-node pointer }
  Found : boolean;                           { Boolean variable
                                               to indicate if found }
begin
          { Call procedure to find header node that contains
            the first city name }
  FindHNodePtr(FirstNode, FirstCity, OneCityPtr);
  if OneCityPtr = nil then
    FoundArcPtr := nil
  { end if }
  else begin
    if OneCityPtr^.PtrToFlight = nil then       { If no arc nodes,
                                                  return nil pointer }
      FoundArcPtr := nil
    { end if }
    else begin                                { Else, search arc nodes
                                                for second city name   }
      OneArcPtr := OneCityPtr^.PtrToFlight;
      Found := false;
      while (OneArcPtr <> nil) and (not Found) do
        if OneArcPtr^.Destination^.CityName = SecondCity then
          Found := true
        { end if }
        else
          OneArcPtr := OneArcPtr^.NextFlight;
        { end else }
      { end while }
      if OneArcPtr = nil then                  { If arc node not
                                                 found, return nil pointer }
        FoundArcPtr := nil
      { end if }
      else                                       { Else, return
                                                   arc node pointer }
        FoundArcPtr := OneArcPtr
      { end else }
    end  { else }
  end  { else }
end;  { FindArc }
```

Before we discuss any other procedures, we will write a program **Airlin1** that will create a linked graph for the airline example, allow the user to input two city names and then determine the time for the direct flight between the two cities (if a flight exists). The program will first call the **Create-LinkedGraph** procedure to create the linked graph. The user will then be asked if a search for a direct flight is desired. If so, the user will be asked to input the names of the first city and the second city. A call will then be made to the **FindArc** procedure to determine if the flight exists. If it does, a message indicating that the flight exists will be printed, and the flight time will also be printed. If the flight does not exist, a message to that effect will be printed. In either case, the user will then be asked if another search is desired. The process will continue until the user indicates that no other search is wanted.

The method used to input character data from the console varies according to the Pascal compiler and the computer system being used. You should determine the correct method(s) for the input of character data from the console for your particular Pascal compiler and computer system.

```pascal
{*********************************************************************}
{* Airlin1 - Program to create a linked graph of cities and then    *}
{*           to allow searches for direct flights and flight        *}
{*           times.                                                  *}
{*     files -                                                       *}
{*           Cities : Data file in which each line contains the      *}
{*                    name of one city.                              *}
{*           Flights : Data file in which each line contains the     *}
{*                     name of the original city, the name of the    *}
{*                     destination city, and the flight time.        *}
{*********************************************************************}
program Airlin1(Input, Output, Cities, Flights);
type
   String25 = packed array[1..25] of char;
   HeaderNodePtr = ^City;
   ArcNodePtr = ^Flight;
   City = record
            PtrToFlight : ArcNodePtr;
            CityName : String25;
            NextCity : HeaderNodePtr
          end;
   Flight = record
              NextFlight : ArcNodePtr;
              FlightTime : integer;
              Destination : HeaderNodePtr
            end;
var
   FirstNode : HeaderNodePtr;              { Header-node pointer }
   FirstCity,
   SecondCity : String25;                         { City names }
   Response : char;                       { User console response }
   FlightPtr : ArcNodePtr;                  { Arc-node pointer }
   Cities,                                 { File of city names }
   Flights : text;                          { File of flights }
```

```
                  ********************************************
                  **   Insert CreateLinkedGraph, FindArc,   **
                  **   FindHNodePtr, and InsertArc           **
                  **   procedures here.                      **
                  ********************************************

{*********************************************************************}
{* GetCityNames - Procedure to allow the user to input the first     *}
{*                city name and the second city name from the        *}
{*                console.                                            *}
{*        var parameters -                                           *}
{*            FirstCity : Name of the first city.                    *}
{*            SecondCity : Name of the second city.                  *}
{*        value parameters -                                         *}
{*            None                                                   *}
{*********************************************************************}
procedure GetCityNames(var FirstCity, SecondCity : String25);
var
  I : integer;                                            { Index }
begin
  for I := 1 to 25 do begin                  { Initialize first
                                               and second city arrays }
    FirstCity[I] := ' ';
    SecondCity[I] := ' '
  end; { for }
  writeln('What is the name of the first city?');
  I := 1;
  repeat
    read(FirstCity[I]);
    I := I + 1;
  until eoln;
  readln;
  writeln;
  writeln('What is the name of the second city?');
  I := 1;
  repeat
    read(SecondCity[I]);
    I := I + 1;
  until eoln;
  readln;
  writeln
end; { GetCityNames }


{*********************************************************************}
{*                       Main Control Module                        *}
{*********************************************************************}
begin
  CreateLinkedGraph(Firstnode);                  { Create linked graph }
  writeln('Do you wish to search for a direct flight (Y or N)?');
  read(Response);
  readln;
  while (Response = 'Y') or (Response = 'y') do begin
    GetCityNames(FirstCity, SecondCity);         { Get the city names }
            { Search for the arc node containing the flight }
    FindArc(FirstNode, FirstCity, SecondCity, FlightPtr);
```

```
   if FlightPtr = nil then
      writeln('A direct flight between ', FirstCity, ' and ',
           SecondCity, ' does not exist.')
   { end if }
   else begin
      writeln('A direct flight between ', FirstCity, ' and ',
           SecondCity, ' exists.');
      writeln('The flight time is ', FlightPtr^.FlightTime:0,
           ' minutes.')
   end;  { else }
   writeln;
   writeln('Do you wish to search for a direct flight (Y or N)?');
   read(Response);
   readln;
 end  { while }
end.  (* Airlin1 program *)
```

Note that the program checks only for direct flights between two cities. Searching for a flight that involves two or more subflights will be discussed in Section 10.4.

The efficiency of the program will be improved if the city names are inserted into the header nodes so that the names are in alphabetical order. Likewise, an increase in efficiency will result from the insertion of the arcs in each arc list so that the arcs are sorted according to the destination city names. These improvements will be discussed further in the exercises in Section 10.4.

Exercises

10.4   Make up a **Cities** file that contains at least four different city names. Walk through the **CreateLinkedGraph** procedure to see how each city name is inserted into a new header node.

10.5   Make up a **Flights** file that contains at least five flights for the cities in Exercise 10.4. Walk through the **CreateLinkedGraph** procedure (and the **InsertArc** procedure) to see how these arc nodes are inserted into the linked graph.

10.6   Run and test the **Airlin1** program for the following.
(a) All possible direct flights for the **Flights** file created in Exercise 10.5.
(b) Possible flights for which the first city does not exist.
(c) Possible flights for which the second city does not exist.
(d) Possible flights for which the two cities exist, but the flight does not.

10.7   Modify the necessary code to handle the case in which a city name is repeated in the **Cities** file. (Do not create new header nodes for repeated names.) Print an error message and ignore repetitions.

10.8   Modify the code to handle the case in which a pair of cities is repeated in the **Flights** file. (No arc should be repeated in the linked graph representation.)

10.3   Other Linked Graph Procedures

In addition to the procedures we have already discussed, there are other procedures that are helpful in working with linked graphs. For example, we could certainly use a procedure that will allow the deletion of an arc node from a linked graph. The procedure, which will be called **DelArc**, will search for an arc node containing two specified cities (first and last). If the arc node is found, it will be deleted and a Boolean **var** parameter **Found** will be returned as true. If the arc node is not found, **Found** will be returned with the value false.

```
{********************************************************************}
{* DelArc - Procedure to delete an arc node from a linked graph     *}
{*          given the first and last cities. The Boolean variable    *}
{*          Found will be set according to whether or not the arc    *}
{*          node is found.                                           *}
{*      var parameters -                                             *}
{*          Found : Boolean variable returned as true if the         *}
{*                  arc node is found; otherwise, false.             *}
{*      value parameters -                                           *}
{*          FirstNode : Pointer to first header node.                *}
{*          FirstCity : First city name.                             *}
{*          SecondCity : Second city name.                           *}
{********************************************************************}
procedure DelArc (FirstNode : HeaderNodePtr; FirstCity, SecondCity :
                  String25; var Found : boolean);
var
  OneArcPtr,
  NextArcPtr : ArcNodePtr;                       { Arc-node pointers }
  OneCityPtr : HeaderNodePtr;                    { Header-node pointer }
begin
  Found := false;
           { Call procedure to find the header node containing
             the first city name }
  FindHNodePtr(FirstNode, FirstCity, OneCityPtr);
  if OneCityPtr <> nil then           { If first city exists,
                                        search list for second city }
    if OneCityPtr^.PtrToFlight <> nil then begin
      OneArcPtr := OneCityPtr^.PtrToFlight;
      if OneArcPtr^.Destination^.CityName = SecondCity then begin
        Found := true;
        OneCityPtr^.PtrToFlight := OneArcPtr^.NextFlight;
        dispose(OneArcPtr)
      end { if }
      else begin
        NextArcPtr := OneArcPtr^.NextFlight;
        while (NextArcPtr <> nil) and (not Found) do begin
                    { If second city is found }
          if NextArcPtr^.Destination^.CityName = SecondCity then begin
            OneArcPtr^.NextFlight := NextArcPtr^.NextFlight;
            Found := true;
            dispose(NextArcPtr)
```

```
        end  { if }
        else begin
          OneArcPtr := NextArcPtr;
          NextArcPtr := NextArcPtr^.NextFlight
        end  { else }
      end  { while }
    end  { else }
   end  { if }
 { end if }
end;  { DelArc }
```

Note that two pointers **OneArcPtr** and **NextArcPtr** are used as we proceed down through the linked list of arc nodes, so that we can delete the arc node (pointed to by **NextArcPtr**) by patching the **NextFlight** pointer in **OneArcPtr**.

Another procedure we need is one to add a new city to the graph. Since this procedure, which we will call **AddCity**, is quite straightforward, it will be covered in the exercises.

We also need a procedure to delete a city. In order to delete a city, we must not only delete the header node containing the city, but also delete all arc nodes originating from this city. In addition, we must search *all* other linked lists of arc nodes for every arc node including the deleted city as its **Destination**, and then delete each of these.

Pseudocode

> **DelCity Procedure**
>
> Initialize **Found** to false.
> IF city name is found in one of the header nodes THEN
>   Patch pointer around this header node.
>   FOR each header node in list of header nodes
>   Search for and delete each arc node that contains city as
>   its **Destination**.
>   END FOR.
>   Dispose of header node to be deleted.
> END IF.

If a header node containing the city name to be deleted is found, this header node is removed from the linked representation by patching the pointer to this node (in the header-node list) around the node. If the node is the first header node, the **FirstNode** pointer is changed to point to the next header node; and since **FirstNode** is a **var** parameter, its new value will be sent back. However, assuming that we have done this patching, we cannot dispose of the header node until we have located and disposed of all arc nodes that contain the header node as their **Destination**. If we disposed of the header node first, then we would get invalid pointer references when checking arc nodes with the header node as their **Destination**.

The Pascal coding for the **DelCity** procedure follows.

```
{****************************************************************}
{* DelCity - Procedure to delete all references to a given city  *}
{*           in a linked graph.                                   *}
{*      var parameters -                                          *}
{*           FirstNode : Pointer to first header node.            *}
{*           Found : Boolean parameter returned as true if the city *}
{*                   is found; otherwise returned as false.       *}
{*      value parameters -                                        *}
{*           CName : Name of city to be deleted.                  *}
{****************************************************************}
procedure DelCity(var FirstNode : HeaderNodePtr; CName : String25;
                  var Found : boolean);
var
  OneCityPtr,
  NextCityPtr,
  FoundCityPtr : HeaderNodePtr;             { Header-node pointers }
  OneArcPtr,
  NextArcPtr : ArcNodePtr;                  { Arc-node pointers }
  ListP1Done,
  ArcListEnd : boolean;                     { Boolean variables }
begin
  Found := false;
               { If the city is in the first header node, set
                 FirstNode to the second header node }
  OneCityPtr := FirstNode;
  if FirstNode^.CityName = CName then begin
    FirstNode := FirstNode^.NextCity;
    Found := true;
    FoundCityPtr := OneCityPtr
  end  { if }
  else begin
            { Else, search for city in remaining header nodes }
    NextCityPtr := OneCityPtr^.NextCity;
    while (NextCityPtr <> nil) and (not Found) do begin
          { If header node is found, patch pointer around it }
      if NextCityPtr^.CityName = CName then begin
        Found := true;
        OneCityPtr^.NextCity := NextCityPtr^.NextCity;
        FoundCityPtr := NextCityPtr
      end  { if }
      else begin
        OneCityPtr := NextCityPtr;
        NextCityPtr := NextCityPtr^.NextCity
      end  { else }
    end  { while }
  end;  { else }
  if Found then begin
    OneCityPtr := FirstNode;
        { Search arc node lists for each header node and delete all
          arc nodes containing the given city as the destination }
    while OneCityPtr <> nil do begin
      if OneCityPtr^.PtrToFlight = nil then
        OneCityPtr := OneCityPtr^.NextCity
      { end if }
```

```
    else begin
      OneArcPtr := OneCityPtr^.PtrToFlight;
      ListP1Done := false;
      ArcListEnd := false;
     { While the first arc node in the arc node list contains the
       given city as destination, delete the arc node }
      while (not ArcListEnd) and (not ListP1Done) do begin
        if OneArcPtr^.Destination^.CityName = CName then begin
          OneCityPtr^.PtrToFlight := OneArcPtr^.NextFlight;
          dispose(OneArcPtr);
          if OneCityPtr^.PtrToFlight = nil then
            ArcListEnd := true
          { end if }
          else
            OneArcPtr := OneCityPtr^.PtrToFlight
          { end else }
        end { if }
        else
          ListP1Done := true
        { end else }
      end; { while }
     { Delete any remaining arc nodes in the list that contain
       the given city as destination }
      if not ArcListEnd then begin
        NextArcPtr := OneArcPtr^.NextFlight;
        if NextArcPtr = nil then
          ArcListEnd := true
        { end if }
        else
          while (not ArcListEnd) do begin
            if NextArcPtr^.Destination^.CityName = CName then begin
              OneArcPtr^.NextFlight := NextArcPtr^.NextFlight;
              dispose(NextArcPtr);
              NextArcPtr := OneArcPtr^.NextFlight
            end { if }
            else begin
              OneArcPtr := NextArcPtr;
              NextArcPtr := OneArcPtr^.NextFlight
            end; { else }
            if NextArcPtr = nil then
              ArcListEnd := true
            { end if }
          end { while }
        { end else }
      end; { if }
      OneCityPtr := OneCityPtr^.NextCity  { Go to next header node }
    end { else }
  end; { while }
  dispose(FoundCityPtr)
 end { if }
end; { DelCity }
```

One thing is missing in the Pascal coding of the **DelCity** procedure. When a header node that contains the given city name is found, the procedure disposes of the header node. However, even though the list of arc nodes for this header node is then eliminated from the linked representation, the procedure does not dispose of each of the arc nodes in this arc node list. The modifications necessary to rectify this omission will be covered in the exercises.

In procedure **DelCity**, the process of searching the arc node lists and deleting all arc nodes that contain the given city as the destination involves two stages. The first stage involves checking to see if the *first* arc node in the arc node list should be deleted (see Figure 10.13). If so, the pointer (**PtrToFlight**) in the header node must be patched around the node to be deleted to the next arc node, as shown in Figure 10.14. After the arc node is deleted, another check must be made to see if the *new* first arc node must again be deleted. This process is handled in a **while** loop which continues until the new first arc node is not to be deleted or the end of the arc node list is reached.

Figure 10.13

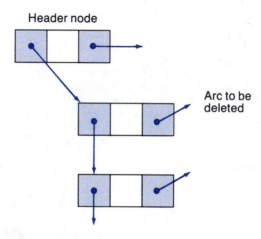

Header node

Arc to be
deleted

Figure 10.14

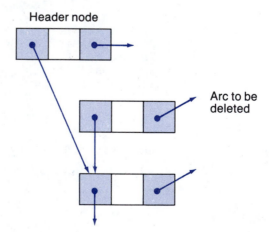

Header node

Arc to be
deleted

The second stage begins when the first stage has been completed. The second stage is a normal deletion process for all nodes within the list of nodes that should be deleted. Two pointers traverse down through the list and perform the required deletions. Note that the difference between the two stages is in the pointer that is patched to go around the node to be deleted. In the first stage, the **PtrToFlight** pointer in a header node is patched. In the second stage, a **NextFlight** pointer in an arc node is patched.

Exercises

10.9   Write the **AddCity** procedure to add a new city to the linked graph representation. Be sure to handle the case in which the city is already included.

10.10   Walk through the **AddCity** procedure written in Exercise 10.9 for
(a) A new city.
(b) A city that is already in the linked representation.

10.11   Write a test driver program that does the following.
(a) Creates a linked graph.
(b) Asks the user for any new cities (and inserts them).
(c) Asks the user for new arcs (and inserts them).
(d) Searches the linked representation for flights (input by the user).

10.12   Walk through the **DelArc** procedure for various pairs of cities.

10.13   Modify program **Airlin1** in order to check the **DelArc** procedure. Ask the user for flights to be deleted. Then search the linked representation to make sure the flights have been deleted.

10.14   Walk through the **DelCity** procedure for various city names.

10.15   Modify the **DelCity** procedure so that it disposes of all arc nodes in the arc node list for the header node that contains the given city name. Then modify program **Airlin1** in order to check the **DelCity** procedure. Ask the user for cities to be deleted. Then search the linked representation to make sure all references to the cities have been deleted.

10.16   Write an **Airlin2** program that does the following.
(a) Prints a menu of options for the user. The menu should include the following. (1) Search for a direct flight. (2) Add a new city. (3) Add a new flight. (4) Delete a city. (5) Delete a flight. (6) Exit.
(b) Allows the user to input a choice and then executes the choice.
(c) Performs parts (a) and (b) until choice 6 is entered.

10.4   Indirect Paths

So far, searches for flights in the airline example have been limited to direct flights between two cities. However, a normal airline cannot possibly schedule direct flights between each pair of cities that it serves. Thus flying from a city A to another city B may involve taking two or more flights by way of intermediate cities. For example, a passenger might take a direct flight from city A to city C, then take a second direct flight from city C to city D, and finally take a direct flight from city D to city B.

It is reasonable to assume that in scheduling such indirect flight paths, the airline will want to minimize the number of direct flights involved. In order to accomplish this a *breadth-first search* may be used. In a breadth-first search destination cities are investigated in the following order until the desired final city is found (assuming a flight path exists).

1. Direct flights from the original city
2. Indirect flights involving 2 direct flights
3. Indirect flights involving 3 direct flights
4. Indirect flights involving 4 direct flights etc.

For example, suppose that a flight is desired from city A to city C in Figure 10.15. In the breadth-first search, destination cities included in direct flights from city A are investigated first. Since there *is* a direct flight from city A to city C, the search is complete.

Figure 10.15

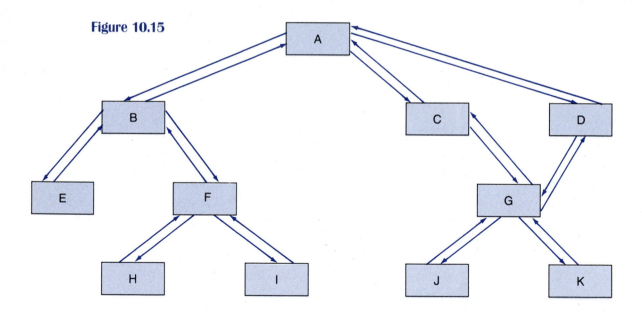

If a flight path from city A to city G is desired, the first step is to examine all direct flights from A:

A to B

A to C

A to D

Since city G was not found, the next step in the search is to examine all destination cities involving two direct flights from city A. This is accomplished by investigating destination cities involved in direct flights from cities B, C, and D. From city B, direct flights

B to E
B to F

are found. From city C, direct flights

C to F
C to G

are found. Since city G has now been found, the search can be terminated. The indirect flight path from A to G involves the following two direct flights.

A to C
C to G

In programming the breadth-first type of search, we will use a queue to control the order in which destination cities are examined. The names of destination cities will be pushed onto the queue as the cities are found in the search. For example, in the search for a path from A to G, the names for cities B, C, and D are pushed onto the queue.

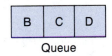

Queue

Since the desired final city (G) is not found, the name for city B is popped from the queue.

Then, the names for all cities that are destination cities in direct flights from B are pushed onto the queue.

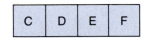

Since the desired final city (G) is again not found, the name for city C is popped from the queue.

Then the names for all cities that are destination cities in direct flights from city C can be pushed onto the queue. The first destination city from C is F. However, since the name for city F was previously pushed onto the queue, it is *not* pushed onto the queue again. The second destination city in a direct flight from C is G. Since G is the desired final city, there is no need to push it onto the queue.

There are some problems with this strategy. The first is how to determine whether a city name has been previously pushed onto the queue in order to avoid pushing the same city name more than once. All names presently in the queue could be searched. However, it is certainly possible that the name has already been popped from the queue. One solution to this problem is to add another field to each header node during the original creation of the linked representation for the graph; this field can hold a Boolean variable **Visited**. Then at the beginning of the breadth-first search, this added field can be initialized to false for each city (header node). As cities are visited during the search, this field is then set to true.

There is a second problem. The search process as described so far will determine whether a flight path *exists* between two cities. However, it would certainly be desirable to be able to print the city names involved in the flight path, along with the total flight time. What is needed is a method for going from the final city back through the direct flights until the first city is found. If flights are to be followed backwards, the first city for each direct flight must be known. Thus when city G is reached in the search process for our example, it must be known that this last direct flight originated at C. Similarly, it must be known that the direct flight ending at C originated at A.

One nonrecursive method for following flights backwards is to push onto a stack both the initial and the terminal names for each direct flight examined during the breadth-first search. The record pushed onto the stack for each flight can also contain the flight time for that direct flight. Thus each stack element will be a record consisting of the name of the destination city, the name of the initial city, and the flight time for the direct flight.

Destination city name	Original city name	Flight time

Stack data record

The following declarations can be made for the stack.

```
type
  StackPtr = ^StackElt;
  StackDat = record
               Destination : String25;
               Original : String25;
               FlightTime : integer
             end;
```

```
StackElt = record
           StData : StackDat;
           NextPtr : StackPtr
         end;
```

In the search for a flight path from city A to city G, the first record pushed onto the stack will be

B	A	40

(Note that the *name* for city B and the *name* for city A will be put in the record rather than B and A.) The search will next find destination cities C and D, and the stack will appear as follows.

D	A	30
C	A	30
B	A	40

Notice that the second record on the stack contains the information for the direct flight A to C, which will be needed for the final flight path. As the search continues and direct flights from B are investigated, the stack will become

F	B	45
E	B	40
D	A	50
C	A	30
B	A	40

Finally, when direct flights from C are examined, the stack will be the following. (Note that the flight from C to F is *not* pushed onto the stack. However, the flight from C to G *is* pushed onto the stack.)

G	C	60
F	B	45
E	B	40
D	A	50
C	A	30
B	A	40

The last record pushed onto the stack includes the information for the final direct flight (from C to G) in the flight path. The only problem with the above stack is that the direct flights in the final flight path (A to C and C to G) are in the wrong order on the stack. However, we must start at the top of the stack and work down through the stack in order to find all of the direct flights involved in the final flight plan (until the original city, A, is found). An easy solution to this problem is to create a final stack onto which the needed direct flights from the original stack are pushed (in reverse order). When the final stack is complete, we can then pop the direct flights from the final stack (now in the correct order) and print them. As these flights are popped from the final stack, a total flight time for the complete flight path can be easily computed and then printed.

Let us call the original stack the *search-time stack*, and the final reordered stack the *final stack*. The first step in the process of transferring the appropriate flight records from the search-time stack to the final stack will be to pop the top element from the search-time stack and then push it onto the final stack.

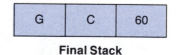

Final Stack

Since this record indicates a flight from C to G, the next step will be to keep popping records from the search-time stack until a record having C as the destination city is found. This record will be the flight from A to C and will now be pushed onto the final stack.

| C | A | 30 |
| G | C | 60 |

Since the initial city (A) in this last record is the original beginning city for the desired flight, the stacking process is terminated. By now popping each record from this final stack, it is quite easy to print the complete flight path and the total flight time.

Flight Plan from City A to City C

Direct flight from city A to city C
Direct flight from city C to city G
Total flight time = 90 minutes

Pseudocode

FindPath Procedure

Initialize Boolean variable **PathFound** to false.
IF original city specified is found in a header node and if there
    is at least one direct flight originating from this city THEN
    Call procedure to initialize Boolean variable **Visited** to false
    in each header node.
Initialize queue.
Initialize search-time stack.
Start at first arc originating from original city.
WHILE no path has been found and not at end of arcs
    IF destination node for arc has not been visited THEN
        Push name of destination city, name of original city,
            and flight time onto search-time stack.
        IF destination city in arc is final city desired THEN
            Set **PathFound** to true.
            Print data for direct flight.
        ELSE
            Push name of destination city onto queue.
        END IF.
    END IF.
    Go to next arc.
END WHILE.
IF path was not found THEN
    WHILE path has not been found and queue is not empty
        Pop one city name from queue.
        Start at first arc for this city (if it exists).
        WHILE not at end of arc list
            IF destination node for arc has not been visited
                THEN

Push destination city name, original city name,
and flight time onto search-time stack.
IF destination city (in arc) is final city desired
THEN
Set **PathFound** to true.
ELSE
Push name of destination city onto queue.
END IF.
END IF.
Go to next arc.
END WHILE.
END WHILE.
IF path was found THEN
Initialize final stack.
Call procedure to transfer desired flights from search-
time stack to final stack.
Call procedure to print total flight path and total flight
time.
END IF.
END IF.
END IF.
IF no flight path was found THEN
Print message that no flight path exists.
END IF.

There are three major stages in the **FindPath** procedure. If the first city in the desired flight is found in a header node and if the list of arcs for this city is not **nil**, the first stage is to see if there is a direct flight between the two specified cities. If so, the direct flight information is printed. If not, the second stage is to search for an indirect flight path between the two cities. If an indirect flight path is found, the third stage is to call a procedure to transfer the desired direct flights from the search-time stack to the final stack and then call a procedure to print the information for the indirect flight path.

```
{*****************************************************************}
{* FindPath - Procedure to find a flight path (direct or indirect) *}
{*            from one city to another. If a path is found, the    *}
{*            flight path and the total flight time are printed.    *}
{*            Also, a boolean parameter PathFound is returned as    *}
{*            true. If no flight path is found, a message is        *}
{*            printed and PathFound is returned as false.           *}
{*        var parameters -                                          *}
{*            PathFound : Boolean variable to indicate if path has  *}
{*                        been found.                               *}
{*        value parameters -                                        *}
{*            FirstNode : Pointer to first header node.             *}
{*            InitCity : Name of initial city in desired flight.    *}
{*            LastCity : Name of final city in desired flight.      *}
{*****************************************************************}
```

```
procedure FindPath(FirstNode : HeaderNodePtr; InitCity, LastCity :
                   String25; var PathFound : boolean);
type
  QueuePtr = ^QueueElt;
  StackPtr = ^StackElt;
  QueueElt = record
                 CityName : String25;
                 NextPtr :  QueuePtr
             end;
  StackDat = record
                 Destination : String25;
                 Original : String25;
                 FlightTime : integer
             end;
  StackElt = record
                 StData: StackDat;
                 NextPtr: StackPtr
             end;
var
  QFront,                                      { Beginning of queue }
  QTop : QueuePtr;                                   { Top of queue }
  StStackTop,                             { Search-time stack top }
  FStackTop : StackPtr;                          { Final stack top }
  QEmpty,                                      { Queue empty flag }
  StStackEmpty,                        { Search-time stack empty flag }
  FStackEmpty : boolean;                    { Final stack empty flag }
  OneCityPtr,
  FirstCityPtr : HeaderNodePtr;            { Header-node pointers }
  OneArcPtr : ArcNodePtr;                          { Arc pointer }
  OneCityName : String25;                            { City name }
  StDataItem : StackDat;                      { Stack data record }

              *************************************************
              **   Insert FindHNodePtr, InitStack,        **
              **   PushStack, PopStack, InitQueue,        **
              **   PushQueue, PopQueue,                   **
              **   InitVisitedFlags, TransferElts, and    **
              **   PrintFlightPath procedures here.       **
              *************************************************

begin
  PathFound := false;
  FindHNodePtr(FirstNode, InitCity, FirstCityPtr);
  if FirstCityPtr <> nil then
    if FirstCityPtr^.PtrToFlight <> nil then begin
            { Call procedure to initialize the boolean variable
              Visited to false in each header node. }
      InitVisitedFlags(Firstnode);
      FirstCityPtr^.Visited := true;
      InitQueue(QTop, QFront, QEmpty);
      InitStack(StStackTop, StStackEmpty);
                          { Start at first arc }
      OneArcPtr := FirstCityPtr^.PtrToFlight;
      while (not PathFound) and (OneArcPtr <> nil) do begin
        if OneArcPtr^.Destination^.Visited = false then begin
```

```
              OneArcPtr^.Destination^.Visited := true;
              StDataItem.Destination := OneArcPtr^.Destination^.CityName;
              StDataItem.Original := FirstCity;
              StDataItem.FlightTime := OneArcPtr^.FlightTime;
              PushStack(StDataItem, StStackTop, StStackEmpty);
              if OneArcPtr^.Destination^.CityName = LastCity then begin
                PathFound := true;
                writeln;
                writeln('A direct flight exists between ', InitCity,
                        ' and ', LastCity);
                writeln('The flight time is ', OneArcPtr^.FlightTime:0,
                        ' minutes.')
              end  { if }
              else
                PushQueue(OneArcPtr^.Destination^.CityName, QTop, QEmpty)
              { end else }
          end;  { if }
        OneArcPtr := OneArcPtr^.NextFlight
      end; { while }
      if not PathFound then begin                { If a direct path was
                                                   not found, search for
                                                   an indirect flight path }
        while (not PathFound) and (not QEmpty) do begin
          PopQueue(OneCityName, QFront, QEmpty);
          FindHNodePtr(FirstNode, OneCityName, OneCityPtr);
          if OneCityPtr^.PtrToFlight <> nil then begin
            OneArcPtr := OneCityPtr^.PtrToFlight;
            while (not PathFound) and (OneArcPtr <> nil) do begin
              if OneArcPtr^.Destination^.Visited = false then begin
                OneArcPtr^.Destination^.Visited := true;
                StDataItem.Destination :=
                    OneArcPtr^.Destination^.CityName;
                StDataItem.Original := OneCityName;
                StDataItem.FlightTime := OneArcPtr^.FlightTime;
                PushStack(StDataItem, StStackTop, StStackEmpty);
                if OneArcPtr^.Destination^.CityName = LastCity then
                  PathFound := true
                { end if }
                else
                  PushQueue(OneArcPtr^.Destination^.CityName, QTop,
                            QEmpty)
                { end else }
              end;  { if }
              OneArcPtr := OneArcPtr^.NextFlight
            end  { while }
          end  { if }
        end;  { while }
        if PathFound then begin                { If an indirect
                                                 flight path was found }
          InitStack(FStackTop, FStackEmpty);
            { Transfer desired flights from search-time stack
              to final stack }
          TransferElts(StStackTop, FStackTop, FirstCity, StStackEmpty,
                    FStackEmpty);
            { Print total flight path and total flight time }
```

```
         PrintFlightPath(InitCity, LastCity, FStackTop, FStackEmpty)
      end  { if }
   end  { if }
 end;  { if }
{ end if }
if not PathFound then begin
   writeln;
   writeln('No flight exists between ', FirstCity, ' and ', LastCity)
 end  { if }
end;  { FindPath }
```

During the first stage when a search for a direct flight between the two cities is being performed, the two names for each arc node checked are still pushed onto the search-time stack. If a direct flight is found, this is not really necessary. However, if a direct flight is not found and the search continues into the second stage, the names of the two cities for each arc node traversed must have been pushed onto the stack.

The Pascal coding of the **InitStack**, **PushStack**, **PopStack**, **InitQueue**, **PushQueue**, and **PopQueue** procedures will be assigned in the exercises. The **InitVisitedFlags** procedure initializes the **Visited** flag in each header node to false. The coding of this simple procedure will also be assigned in the exercises. Also, in the chapter exercises, you will be asked to redesign procedure **FindPath**, which is extremely long as written, so that it is replaced with two or more shorter procedures.

As discussed earlier, the **TransferElts** procedure transfers the arcs that will be in the final flight path from the search-time stack to the final stack. The final arc pushed onto the search-time stack will be the first arc transferred to the final stack. The last arc transferred will be the first flight in the final flight path. The Pascal coding for this procedure follows.

```
{********************************************************************}
{* TransferElts - Procedure to transfer the appropriate direct-    *}
{*                flight records from the search-time stack to      *}
{*                the final stack.                                  *}
{*     var parameters -                                             *}
{*         St1Top : Pointer to top of search-time stack.            *}
{*         St2Top : Pointer to top of final stack.                  *}
{*         St1Empty : Boolean variable to indicate if search-time  *}
{*                 stack is empty.                                  *}
{*         St2Empty : Boolean variable to indicate if final stack  *}
{*                 is empty.                                        *}
{*     value parameters -                                           *}
{*         FCity : Name of first city in flight.                    *}
{********************************************************************}
procedure TransferElts(var St1Top, St2Top : StackPtr;
                           FCity : String25;
                           var St1Empty, St2Empty : boolean);
var
  Done : boolean;
  OneStackRec,
  NextStackRec : StackDat;
```

```
begin
  Done := false;
  PopStack(OneStackRec, St1Top, St1Empty);           { Pop last arc from
                                                        search-time stack }
  PushStack(OneStackRec, St2Top, St2Empty);          { Push this arc
                                                        onto final stack }
  while not Done do begin                        { Transfer remaining
                                                    appropriate arcs      }
    PopStack(NextStackRec, St1Top, St1Empty);
    while NextStackRec.Destination <> OneStackRec.Original do
      PopStack(NextStackRec, St1Top, St1Empty);
    PushStack(NextStackRec, St2Top, St2Empty);
    if NextStackRec.Original = FCity then          { If find original
                                                     city then done    }
      Done := true
    { end if }
    else                                             { Else, continue }
      OneStackRec := NextStackRec
    { end else }
  end  { while }
end;  { TransferElts }
```

The **PrintFlightPath** procedure merely pops each arc from the final stack, prints the names of the two cities for the arc as a direct flight, and keeps a running total of the flight time required. The coding of this procedure is assigned in the exercises. For a complete program, the **FindPath** procedure may be substituted for the **FindArc** procedure in program **Airlin1**, to allow searches for both direct and indirect flights.

Although our airline program is starting to become useful, there are still many improvements and additions that could be made. First of all, the **FindPath** procedure will find *a* flight path (if it exists) that minimizes the number of direct flights. However, as soon as a path is found, the procedure stops. It does not check for any other potential flight paths between the two given cities. Obviously, the flight path found may or may not be the shortest path between the two cities.

Also, an actual airline program would normally include costs for the flights. In fact, there may be several different costs for *each* flight. In addition to the standard costs, there may be reduced costs for children and possibly different reduced costs for senior citizens, etc. The question of flight schedules is another issue that has not been addressed. We have included a flight time for the flight; however, each flight may depart at several times during the day. Thus each flight could be accompanied by a list of departure times. In addition, an airline must keep track of the seating on each flight. Thus some method of counting and scheduling of seats is certainly needed.

As all of this suggests, a complete airline scheduling program can become quite involved and intricate. Some of the above-mentioned additions and improvements will be assigned in the chapter exercises.

Exercises

10.17 Write the Pascal code for the **InitStack**, **PushStack**, and **PopStack** procedures.

10.18 Write the Pascal code for the **InitQueue**, **PushQueue**, and **PopQueue** procedures.

10.19 Write the Pascal code for the **InitVisitedFlags** procedure.

10.20 Write the Pascal code for the **PrintFlightPath** procedure. Print the final flight plan and the total flight time, as discussed in this section.

10.21 Create a **Cities** file and a **Flights** file. Walk through the **FindPath** procedure for each of the following.
(a) A direct flight.
(b) Several indirect flights.
(c) A possible flight in which the first city does not exist.
(d) A possible flight in which the second city does not exist.
(e) A possible flight in which both cities exist but no direct or indirect flight exists for the two cities.

10.22 Modify program **Airlin2** from Exercise 10.16 so that the **FindPath** procedure is used instead of the **FindArc** procedure to search for flights. Call the new program **Airlin3**. Test the program with the various types of flights listed in Exercise 10.21.

10.23 Modify the coding as necessary so that the list of header nodes will be sorted in ascending order according to the city names and also so that the arcs in each arc list will be sorted alphabetically according to the destination city name.

Summary

Graphs are a very interesting and useful application of data structures. A large variety of real-life application problems may appropriately use graphs for their structures.

A thorough study of graphs could well encompass one or more entire textbooks. Thus a single chapter can provide only an introduction to the subject. In addition to the basic terminology, Chapter 10 included a discussion of basic procedures used to create a linked representation of a graph and then to manipulate the linked representation. Although representations other than linked representations can be used for graphs, the linked representation provides greater flexibility and power. Since Pascal includes pointers, the linked representation for graphs is a particularly good choice when Pascal is being used.

In order to unify the discussion of graphs and the development of the basic procedures, an airline flight example was developed in this chapter. A complete airline scheduling program can be quite extensive and intricate; this chapter presented an introduction to the program, focusing on the creation and modification of the graph representation and procedures to allow the determination of both direct and indirect flight paths between cities.

Chapter Exercises

10.24   The **DelCity** procedure is extremely long. Redesign the procedure so that it is replaced with two or more smaller procedures.

10.25   The **FindPath** procedure is extremely long. Redesign the procedure so that it is replaced with two or more smaller procedures.

10.26   Modify the necessary code for the airline program so that each arc node also contains costs for that particular flight. Assume that the record contains three costs: regular flight cost (for adults), children's cost, and senior citizen's cost. When flight data are printed, all three costs should be printed for each flight.

10.27   Modify the code in the airline program so that each arc node also contains a count of the number of seats available for that flight (in addition to the costs from Exercise 10.26). When flight data are printed, the number of seats available should also be printed.

10.28   Modify the code in the airline program so that each arc node points to a linked list of departure and arrival times for that particular flight. Use some method of distinguishing between a.m. and p.m. times (such as military time or labels, etc.). When flight data are printed, the entire schedule should be printed for each flight. That is, for each succeeding flight the departure time selected should be the closest available to the previous arrival time.

10.29   Write a complete airline interactive program in which each flight includes all of the data described in Exercises 10.26 through 10.28. The program should allow searches to determine flight paths and availability of seats. It should then allow the making of reservations, which involves listing the passenger's name and reducing the number of available seats. The program should print an appropriately formatted schedule for the flight path for each customer, including the airline's name, the customer's name and address, etc.

Pascal Compilers

In this appendix we will discuss selected aspects of the following Pascal compilers:

CDC Cyber Pascal 6000
Microsoft Pascal
Turbo Pascal
PDP/11 and VAX/11 Berkeley Pascal
UCSD Pascal

These Pascal compilers vary in their handling of file names, character data, interactive input, and redirection of input/output. Our discussion will concentrate on these areas, since they are very important to the basic use of Pascal.

With regard to file names, it is important to know the difference between *logical file names* and *physical file names*. Physical file names are the actual file names used by the operating system. These are the names for files that are saved by the system on disk (or tape). Logical file names are names that are logical in the sense that they are used within the program in **read**, **readln**, **write**, **writeln**, etc., statements, but are not the actual names for files in the operating system.

Pascal considers a string of characters to be an array of characters. However, in three of the Pascal compilers the handling of character strings has been made much easier through inclusion of built-in string data types. These built-in string data types make the interactive input of character data much simpler. For each of the five Pascals, we will discuss the handling of character data (especially the interactive input of character data). Each of the three Pascals that have built-in string data types also includes an extensive library of string-handling functions and procedures. You should consult the appropriate Pascal manual for a listing and discussion of these routines.

Finally, in this appendix we will discuss the redirection of input and output and, for certain compilers, the piping of input and output. The methods used depend on the Pascal compiler and also on the operating system being used.

CDC Cyber Pascal 6000 (University of Minnesota)

The Cyber version of Pascal is a very basic and standard Pascal. No inherent string types exist. Even though sequential file processing is rather easy, there are no true direct (or random) file capabilities. The Cyber 6-bit subset character set does not include lower-case letters and the subset orders the character codes strangely. The codes for the space (blank) and the comma are greater than those for any of the letters. Thus in a string comparison,

SMITHS

is considered to be less than

SMITH

Therefore, character sorting in Cyber Pascal presents a challenge to the programmer.

File Names

Physical file names on the CDC Cyber can contain a maximum of seven characters, and each character must be a capital alphabetic letter or a numeric digit. File names used in a Cyber Pascal program are the actual physical system file names.

Physical file names that are included in the **PROGRAM** statement may be replaced with other physical file names by specifying the new file names in the command line. If desired, the predeclared file names **INPUT** and **OUTPUT** (which refer to input from the console and output to the console) may also be replaced by other physical file names. For example, suppose that the object (executable) file name is **SAMPLE1** and that the following **PROGRAM** statement is used:

```
PROGRAM SAMPLE1(OUTPUT, DFILE);
```

The following command will then execute the program, replace all references to the standard output file **OUTPUT** with the physical file **RESULT**, and replace all references to the physical file **DFILE** with the physical file **MYDFILE**:

```
SAMPLE1,RESULT,MYDFILE
```

Since the file **OUTPUT** was replaced with the file **RESULT**, all normal output that would have originally been written to the console will now be redirected to the file **RESULT**. Suppose that we do not wish to redirect the output from file **OUTPUT** to file **RESULT**; however, we still wish to replace all references to the file **DFILE** with references to the file **MYDFILE**. This could be done with the following command line:

```
SAMPLE1,,MYDFILE
```

Notice that the two commas must be used so that **MYDFILE** will replace the file **DFILE** rather than the file **OUTPUT**. All replacement file names must be included in the command line in the correct order.

Character Data and Interactive I/O

The Cyber Pascal 6000 has no predeclared string types. A string variable is declared either as an array of characters or as a packed array of characters. To read data from a data file or from the console into an array of characters (or a packed array of characters), the program must read one character at a time. However, if the variable is declared as a packed array, the entire array can be written just by specifying the packed-array name. For example, the following program will read 20 characters from data file **DFILE** into a packed array **NAME** and then print all characters in **NAME** back to the console:

```
PROGRAM SAMPLE2(OUTPUT, DFILE);
VAR
  DFILE : TEXT;
  NAME : PACKED ARRAY[1..20] OF CHAR;
  I : INTEGER;
BEGIN
  RESET(DFILE);
  FOR I := 1 to 20 DO
    READ(DFILE, NAME[I]);
  { END FOR }
    WRITELN(NAME)
  END.
```

Notice that since **NAME** was declared to be a packed array, the entire array can be easily printed with the statement

```
WRITELN(NAME)
```

If character data are to be input from the console rather than a data file, the file specification, **INPUT/**, should be included in the program statement. Then *before* the characters are read, a

```
READLN;
```

statement is included. Thus the following program could be used to input a 20-character **NAME** and then write it back to the console:

```
PROGRAM SAMPLE3(INPUT/, OUTPUT);
VAR
  NAME : PACKED ARRAY[1..20] OF CHAR;
  I : INTEGER;
BEGIN
  WRITELN('WHAT IS YOUR NAME');
  READLN;
  FOR I := 1 to 20 DO
    READ(NAME[I]);
  { END FOR }
  WRITELN(NAME)
END.
```

The

```
READLN;
```

statement will cause a question mark (**?**) to appear on the console. The program then allows the user to type in characters at the console, terminated by a carriage return. As the characters are typed, they are stored in an input buffer. The **FOR** loop then reads the characters one at a time from the input buffer until all 20 characters have been read. (Note that if more than 20 characters are typed, the extra characters will be ignored.)

In **SAMPLE3**, if the user does not input at least 20 characters, the program will abort during execution of the **FOR** loop. To avoid this problem, we could replace the **FOR** loop with a **WHILE** loop that reads characters until EOLN or until 20 characters have been input. We can then use a field-width specifier in the **WRITELN** statement to print the characters stored in variable **NAME**.

```
PROGRAM SAMPLE4(INPUT/, OUTPUT);
VAR
  NAME : PACKED ARRAY[1..20] OF CHAR;
  I : INTEGER;
BEGIN
  WRITELN('WHAT IS YOUR NAME');
  READLN;
  I := 0;
  WHILE (NOT EOLN) and (I < 20) DO BEGIN
    I := I + 1;
    READ(NAME[I])
  END;    { WHILE }
  WRITELN(NAME : I)
END.
```

Note that characters typed by the user (and placed in the input buffer) will be inserted into the packed array of characters, **NAME**, until EOLN is reached or until **I** has already become 20.

Redirection of Input and Output

As we have already seen, it is quite easy to redirect output (which would normally go to file **OUTPUT**) to another file. It is just as easy to redirect input so that the input comes from a system file rather than file **INPUT**. For example, in **PROGRAM SAMPLE5**, suppose that we wish to read the input from data file **DATAF**. That is, we wish to redirect the input so that it comes from file **DATAF**, rather than from standard file **INPUT**.

```
PROGRAM SAMPLE5(INPUT, OUTPUT);
VAR
  NAME : PACKED ARRAY[1..20] OF CHAR;
  I : INTEGER;
BEGIN
  FOR I := 1 to 20 DO
    READ(NAME[I]);
  { END FOR }
  WRITELN(NAME)
END.
```

This redirection will occur if we issue the command

```
SAMPLE5,DATAF
```

This command will replace the standard file **INPUT** with the file **DATAF** during execution. Notice that in **PROGRAM SAMPLE5** we used **INPUT** rather than **INPUT/**, since the input will really come from a file rather than be entered interactively. Also notice that the order of the code for reading is the same as it normally is for reading from a data file.

Microsoft Pascal (MS-DOS, PC-DOS)

The Microsoft version of Pascal is excellent and very complete. It includes built-in string types and an extensive library of string-handling routines. It is a truly professional implementation of Pascal which can be used for systems and applications software development.

The compiler generates machine-code **.OBJ** files that may be linked with the library to produce directly executable (machine-code) files with an **.EXE** extension. This approach is in contrast to that of Pascal compilers (such as UCSD Pascal) that generate p-code files, which must then be run with a p-code interpreter.

File Names

With the MS-DOS or the PC-DOS operating system, disk (physical) file names contain a maximum of eight characters followed by an optional file-name extension. The extension consists of a period followed by a maximum of three characters. Legitimate file-name characters include the following:

$$A–Z \ 0–9 \ \$ \ \& \ \# \ @ \ ! \ \% \ ` \ ' \ (\ ) \ - \ \{ \ \} \ \_ \ / \ \backslash$$

For example, the following are all valid disk file names under MS-DOS or PC-DOS:

```
MYFILE
MY_FILE
D_FILE_2
MYFILE.PAS
MY_FILE.PAS
D_FILE_2.DAT
```

The extension is used to identify the type of file. For example, Pascal source files are normally given the extension

```
.PAS
```

Executable files under MS-DOS and PC-DOS are normally required to have one of the two following extensions:

```
.EXE
```
(standing for *executable*)

or

```
.COM
```
(standing for *command*)

When a Pascal program is compiled using the Microsoft compiler, a machine-code file with an **.OBJ** extension is produced. The file can then be linked with the Pascal library to generate a directly executable file with a **.EXE** extension.

Within a Microsoft Pascal program, logical (rather than physical) file names are used in all the normal statements that reference files. These include all **reset**, **rewrite**, **read**, **readln**, **write**, **writeln**, etc., statements. When the program executes, actual physical (disk) file names must be assigned to the logical file names. Here, Microsoft Pascal is excellent, since it allows more than one method of assignment.

One approach to assigning a physical file name to a logical program file name is by using the command line. This is similar to the method used on the Cyber when one file name is substituted for another in the command line. The only exception is that physical file names cannot be substituted for the standard I/O files, **Input** and **Output**. (However, in this case redirection of input or output can be used in the operating system. We will discuss this redirection later.) For example, assume that we have the following program:

```
program Sample6(Output, DFile);
var
  DFile : text;
  Num1 : integer;
begin
  reset(DFile);
  readln(DFile, Num1);
  writeln('Num1 is ', Num1 : 0)
end.
```

If the executable file name is **SAMPLE6.EXE**, the command

```
SAMPLE6 MYDFILE.DAT
```

will execute the program and assign the physical (disk) file name **MYDFILE.DAT** to the logical program file name **DFile**. When the program executes, if the user has forgotten to supply the physical file name (or names) in the command line, a prompt (or prompts) will request input of the file name (or names).

A second method of assigning a physical file name to a logical file name is with the **assign** statement. For example, the Microsoft Pascal statement

```
assign(DFile, 'MYDFILE.DAT');
```

assigns the disk file **MYDFILE.DAT** to the logical file name **DFile**. The physical file name must be enclosed in single quotes since it is assigned to **DFile** as a string. When the **assign** statement is used, the logical file name is not included in the program statement. Thus a program might include the following:

```
program Sample7(Output);
var
  DFile : text;
  Num1 : integer;
begin
  assign(DFile, 'MYDFILE.DAT');
```

```
    reset(DFile);
    readln(DFile, Num1);
          .
          .
end.
```

It is also possible for the user to input the physical file name while the program is executing. The following code illustrates how this may be done. (The **lstring** data type used will be discussed shortly.)

```
program Sample8(Input, Output);
var
  DFile : text;
  DFileName : lstring(12);
  Num1 : integer;
begin
  write('What is the data file name? ');
  readln(DFileName);
  assign(DFile, DFileName);
  reset(DFile);
  readln(DFile, Num1);
        .
        .
  end.
```

The only problem with the above code is that the program will abort at the

```
reset(DFile);
```

statement if the physical file name input by the user for **DFileName** does not exist (on disk). This problem can be avoided by turning off the automatic I/O error abort, as illustrated in the following code:

```
program Sample9(Input, Output);
var
  DFile : text;
  DFileName : lstring(12);
  Num1 : integer;
  NameOK : boolean;
begin
  repeat
    write('What is the data file name? ');
    readln(DFileName);
    assign(DFile, DFileName);
    DFile.trap := true;
    reset(DFile);
    NameOK := (DFile.errs = 0);
    DFile.trap := false;
    Dfile.errs := 0;
    if NameOK <> 0 then
      writeln('File ', DFileName, ' does not exist!!!')
    { end if }
```

```
   until NameOK;
   readln(DFile,Num1);
        .
        .
 end.
```

The statement

```
DFile.trap := true;
```

traps the error code and blocks the automatic abort for the case in which the file does not exist. If the file does not exist, then

```
DFile.errs
```

is set to a nonzero value. After the reset statement, the programmer should be sure to reset **DFile.trap** to false so that succeeding I/O errors involving **DFile** will be handled normally. Also, **DFile.errs** should be set to 0; otherwise, after a bad reset, the program will abort at the next execution of the **assign** statement. Note that the user must input a correct physical file name before the program can exit the repeat loop and continue with the remainder of the program.

As can be seen from the preceding discussion, the Microsoft Pascal compiler is much more versatile than the Cyber Pascal in the handling of file names. The ability to enter physical file names during program execution allows much more flexibility in actual applications programming.

Character Data and Interactive I/O

Microsoft Pascal includes two built-in string types, **string** and **lstring**. The type

```
string(n)
```

is identical to the type

```
packed array[1..n] of char
```

where **n** is a positive integer from 1 to **maxint**. Assignments or comparisons with variables of type **string(n)** are limited to strings of exactly **n** characters.

The second string type,

```
lstring(n)
```

is similar to the type

```
packed array[0..n] of char
```

but not identical. As we shall see, variables of type **lstring(n)** are much more flexible. One major reason for this is that the value for **n** is a maximum length for the string rather than a specific required size. Thus, if we declare

```
var
  Name : lstring(20);
```

and read the data for variable **name** from the console, we are not required to input exactly 20 characters. We are allowed to input any number of characters up to the maximum of 20. The following code illustrates the simplicity of the use of the **lstring** type in interactive input of character data:

```
program Sample10(Input, Output);
var
  Name : lstring(20);
begin
  write('What is your name? ');
  readln(Name);
  writeln('Hello, ', Name, '.  I am pleased to meet you.');
end.
```

When the **lstring** variable **Name** is read, a dynamic length is assigned and stored as a character in **Name[0]**. The dynamic length is the actual length of the string. That is, the dynamic length is the actual number of characters typed before the return key is pressed. For example, if 15 characters are typed, the assigned dynamic length will be 15. If more than 20 characters are typed, the extra characters will be ignored, and the dynamic length will be set to 20.

The dynamic length can be accessed from **Name[0]**, which is of type **char**, or it can be accessed as

```
Name.len
```

which has a predeclared type of **byte**. **Byte** variables have a range of 0..255. Thus the maximum length of an **lstring** variable is 255 characters. The following statement would print the value for the present dynamic length of **Name**.

```
writeln('The length of your Name is ', Name.len : 0);
```

If desired, a program may read in the characters for an **lstring** variable (or a packed array of characters) one character at a time. However, as illustrated in the following program, the user must then set the value of **Name.len**. A variable assigned to **Name.len** should have a declared type of **byte** (or **word**).

```
program Sample11(Input, Output);
var
  Name : lstring(20);
  I : byte;
begin
  write('What is your name? ');
  I := 0;
  while (not eoln) and (I < 20) do begin
    I := I + 1;
    read(Name[I]);
  end;  { while }
  Name.len := I;
  writeln('Hello, ', Name, '.  I am pleased to meet you.');
  writeln('The length of your name is ', Name.len : 0)
end.
```

As characters are typed at the console, they are put into a buffer. An EOLN will occur when the return is pressed. While typing the input characters into the buffer, the user may backspace and make corrections. If desired, **Name** could have been declared to be a packed array of characters, as in standard Pascal. In Microsoft Pascal, the coding for the input of characters from the console follows the same ordering as the coding for the equivalent input from a data file. See program **Sample12**.

```
program Sample12(Input, Output);
var
  Name : packed array[1..20] of char;
  I : integer;
begin
  write('What is your name? ');
  for I := 1 to 20 do
    Name[I] := ' ';
  { end for }
  I := 0;
  while (not eoln) and (I < 20) do begin
    I := I + 1;
    read(Name[I]);
  end;  { while }
  writeln('Hello, ', Name : I,'.  I am pleased to meet you.')
end.
```

Any two variables of type **lstring** can be compared (as in a sort). Also, any **string** or **lstring** variable may be assigned to another **lstring** variable as long as the maximum declared length for the target **lstring** variable is at least as large as the **string** or **lstring** assigned.

For example, assuming that the declarations

```
    var
      Str1 : lstring[20];
      Str2 : lstring[10];
```

have been made, each of the following assignments is valid:

```
Str1 := 'Abcd efgh ijkl mnop ';  { Dynamic length of 20 }
Str2 := 'Hello';                 {  Dynamic length of 5 }
```

Also, the sequence

```
Str1 := 'Hello';                 {  Dynamic length of 5 }
Str2 := Str1;
```

is valid, because the length of the string assigned to **Str2** is not greater than 10. However, the sequence

```
Str1 := 'How are you?';          { Dynamic length of 12 }
Str2 := Str1;
```

should not be used, because the dynamic length of **Str1** is greater than 10.

It is possible to assign characters (one character at a time) to an **lstring** variable beyond the present dynamic length. However, any process such as **writeln** that uses the length would ignore these characters (unless the programmer changes the dynamic length). For example, in **Sample12** above, suppose the user types in a 10-character name. The value for **Name.len** is then automatically set to 10. Now suppose the following statement is executed:

```
Name[11] := 'Z';
```

No run-time error will occur. However, the value of **Name.len** is still 10. Thus a **writeln** statement to print **Name** will still print only the first 10 characters. However, if the statement

```
Name.len := 11;
```

 is included, a **writeln** statement to print **Name** will now print all 11 characters.

As can be seen from this discussion, **lstring** variables are very flexible, and thus they can be used in a wide variety of applications. Microsoft Pascal allows the programmer a great deal of freedom with these variables.

Input/Output Redirection

The standard files **Input** and **Output** are normally used in **terminal** mode. That is, these files are used for input from and output to the console (or terminal) device. In Microsoft Pascal, editing of the input line is allowed at the console, and EOLN is indicated when the return key is pressed. This is different from the case for normal text files, in which EOLN is indicated by a CR and LF pair of bytes.

The MS-DOS and PC-DOS operating systems allow redirection of the files **Input** and **Output**. Redirection of the output file occurs when all output that would normally go to the console is instead sent somewhere else, such as a file. Redirection of the input file occurs when the input comes from some source other than the console. Normally, this alternative source is a data file.

Redirection of output is quite simple. For example, the following command line will redirect the normal program output for program **MYPROG** to the file **RESULT.DAT**:

```
A>MYPROG >RESULT.DAT
```

The > indicates redirection for the file **Output**. Output could be also redirected to the first line printer by the following command:

```
A>MYPROG >LPT1:
```

Output could be redirected to a modem connected to serial port **Com1** by the command

```
A>MYPROG >COM1:
```

Redirection of the file **Input** is just as easy. For example, to get program input from a file **DATAF.DAT** instead of from the console, the following command may be used:

```
A>MYPROG <DATAF.DAT
```

Redirection of file **Input** is indicated with the < character.

We can include the redirection of both the **Input** and the **Output** file in the same command line. For example,

```
A>MYPROG <DATAF.DAT >RESULT.DAT
```

will result in the input coming from file **DATAF.DAT** and the output going to file **RESULT.DAT**.

In MS-DOS and PC-DOS it is also possible to pipe the output of one program into the input of a second program. The character used to indicate this piping is the | . The following command will pipe the output from **PROG1** into the input for **PROG2**:

```
A>PROG1|PROG2
```

If desired, the output from **PROG2** could then be sent to a file **RESULT.DAT** with the following command:

```
A>PROG1|PROG2 >RESULT.DAT
```

Turbo Pascal (MS-DOS, PC-DOS, CP/M-80, CP/M-86)

Turbo Pascal, written and distributed by the Borland Corporation, is actually a subsystem in which the user can use a built-in screen editor to create, modify, save, load, compile, and run programs. By just pressing the ″R″ key, the user can have a program compiled (in memory only) and then immediately executed. However, the user may also select a compiler option that generates and saves machine code in a directly executable file. Thus Turbo resembles both an interpreter and a compiler; either way, it is quite fast.

File Names

When used with the MS-DOS, PC-DOS, CP/M-80, or CP/M-86 operating system, physical disk file names consist of a maximum of eight characters followed by an optional name extension. The extension (or file identifier) consists of a period followed by a maximum of three characters. The normal assumed extension for Pascal source files is **.PAS**.

The **program** statement in Turbo Pascal is completely ignored. It is allowed, but has no effect; thus the listing of file names in the **program** statement is optional. However, for documentation and consistency with other Pascals, it is desirable to include them.

Logical file names are used within a Turbo Pascal program, and during execution actual physical file names are assigned to the logical file names with an **assign** statement. For example,

```
assign(DFile, 'MYDFILE.DAT');
```

will assign the physical file **MYDFILE.DAT** to the logical file name **DFile**. It is also possible to input the physical file during execution. For example, the following code could be used to input the physical file name to be associated with the logical file name **DFile**:

```
program Sample13(Input, Output, DFile);
var
  DFile : text;
  DFileName : string(12);
begin
  write('What is the data file name? ');
  readln(DFileName);
  assign(DFile, DFileName);
  reset(DFile);
     .
     .
end.
```

However, if the physical file name input does not exist, the program will abort at the reset statement. To avoid this, the **I** compiler directive is set to passive as follows:

```
{$I- }
```

When **I** is set to passive, an I/O error will not cause an automatic abort, but will suspend any further I/O until the standard function **IOResult** is called. This function returns a 0 value if the I/O operation was valid and a nonzero value otherwise. After the **IOResult** function is called, the error condition is reset, and further I/O operations may then be performed. The programmer should set the **I** directive back to active with

```
{$I+ }
```

as soon as possible. The following code illustrates the use of the **I** directive for the interactive input of a physical file name:

```
program Sample14(Input, Output, DFile);
var
  DFile : text;
  DFileName : string[12];
  OK : boolean;
begin
  repeat
    write('What is the data file name? ');
    readln(DFileName);
    assign(DFile, DFileName);
    {$I- }
    reset(DFile);
    OK := (IOresult = 0);
    {$I+ }
    if not OK then
      writeln('The file ', DFileName, ' does not exist.')
    { end if }
  until OK;
     .
     .
end.
```

We will discuss the **string** type in the next section. Turbo Pascal does not include a method for assigning physical file names to logical file names in the command line. However, if the MS-DOS or PC-DOS operating system is being used, it is possible to redirect and/or pipe the standard **Input** and **Output** files. This process is identical to that used with the Microsoft Pascal.

Character Data and Interactive I/O

Turbo Pascal includes a built-in **string** data type. As with the **lstring** data type in Microsoft Pascal, the dynamic length of the string variable may change during program execution. In the declaration, the user must specify a maximum length for each string variable. For example, the following declares **Name** to be a string variable with a maximum length of 20:

```
var
  Name : string[20];
```

The largest value that may be declared for a maximum string length is 255. There is no default string length; thus, the length must always be declared. The type

```
string[n]
```

is similar to the standard type,

```
packed array[0..n] of char
```

but not identical. The string type is much more flexible, since the length specified is a maximum instead of a required exact size. For example, the following code could be used to input a person's name:

```
program Sample15(Input, Output);
var
  Name : string[20];
begin
  write('What is your name? ');
  readln(Name);
  writeln('Hello,', Name,'. Nice to meet you.')
end.
```

If the number of characters input for **Name** is larger that the maximum size specified (20), the excess right-hand characters are truncated. The dynamic length of a string variable is stored as a character in the array at index location 0. For example, suppose that in program **Sample15** the user types in a name containing 16 characters; then

```
ord(Name[0])
```

will return a value of 16. The length may also be found by using the built-in **length** function as follows:

```
length(Name)
```

As with Microsoft Pascal, it is possible to assign characters to the string array at index locations beyond the present dynamic length. For example, suppose that the user inputs the following 10 characters for the **Name** variable:

```
Mary Smith
```

Then in the program the user could enter the following statement:

```
Name[11] := 'x';
```

However, since the dynamic length (stored in **Name[0]**) is still 10, the statement

```
writeln(Name);
```

will still only print

```
Mary Smith
```

In order for all 11 characters to be printed, the length needs to be changed.

```
Name[0] := chr(11);
```

A subsequent

```
writeln(Name);
```

would then print

```
Mary Smithx
```

A literal string of characters or a string variable may be assigned to any string variable as long as the destination string variable is declared to be large enough. If the destination string variable is not large enough, excess right-hand characters will be truncated. For example, in the code

```
var
   Str1 : string[10];
begin
   Str1 := 'abcdefghijklmnop';
   writeln(Str1);
```

the output from the

```
writeln(Str1)
```

statement will be only

```
abcdefghij
```

If desired, characters can be entered one at a time into a variable that has been declared to be either a string or a packed array of characters. However, the following code will cause unexpected problems:

```
program Sample16(Input, Output);
var
  Name : packed array[1..20] of char;
  I : integer;
begin
  for I := 1 to 20 do
    Name[I] := ' ';
  write('What is your name? ');
  I := 0;
  while (not eoln) and (I < 20) do begin
    I := I + 1;
    read(Name[I])
  end;  { while }
  readln;
  writeln('Hello, ', Name, '.  Nice to meet you.')
end.
```

With versions of Turbo Pascal prior to 3.0 the carriage return character (decimal value 13) will be read in as one of the **Name** characters (unless 20 or more characters are input prior to the carriage return). This will cause problems when **Name** is printed. This can be solved by reading each input character into a temporary variable **C** and then checking the character before it is assigned to one of the **Name** characters (see program **Sample17**).

```
program Sample17(Input, Output);
var
  Name : packed array[1..20] of char;
  I : integer;
  C : char;
begin
  for I := 1 to 20 do
    Name[I] := ' ';
  writeln('What is your name? ');
  I := 0;
  read(C);
  while (not eoln) and (I < 20) do begin
    I := I + 1;
    Name[I] := C;
    read(C)
  end;  { while }
  readln;
  writeln('Hello, ',Name, '.  I am happy to meet you.')
end.
```

This problem was corrected in version 3.0 of Turbo Pascal. However, there is still another problem with program **Sample17** (and program **Sample16**). Turbo Pascal allows three different logical console input modes:

CON:	Editing of input allowed.
TRM:	No editing of input allowed in versions prior to 3.0.
KBD:	No input echoed to the console.

The default mode is CON:. However, in this mode each **read** is treated as a **readln**. That is, once the variable items listed within the parentheses in the **read** statement are read, then the remainder of the line is ignored. Thus, since the **read** statement in program **Sample16** and program **Sample17** only specifies one character, then after that character is read, the remainder of the input line will be ignored. In order to continue reading the remaining characters from the same line, the **TRM:** mode must be specified. The **B** compiler directive (which must be inserted at the top of the block) is used to select either the CON: or the TRM: mode (see program **Sample18**).

$$\{\$B+\ \}\qquad \text{selects the CON: mode (the default)}$$
$$\{\$B-\ \}\qquad \text{selects the TRM: mode}$$

```
program Sample18(Input, Output);
{$B- }
var
  Name : packed array[1..20] of char;
  I : integer;
  C : char;
begin
  for I := 1 to 20 do
  Name[I] := ' ';
  writeln('What is your name? ');
  I := 0;
  read(C);
  while (not eoln) and (I < 20) do begin
    I := I + 1;
    Name[I] := C;
    read(C)
  end;  { while }
  readln;
  writeln('Hello ',Name, '.  I am happy to meet you.');
end.
```

Turbo Pascal allows the term **packed** for an array; however, it has no effect. Arrays of characters are automatically packed.

Input/Output Redirection

When Turbo Pascal is used with the MS-DOS or PC-DOS operating system, input and output can be redirected or piped in exactly the same way as with the Microsoft Pascal compiler (see the discussion in the Microsoft Pascal section).

VAX/11 and PDP/11 Berkeley Pascal

The Berkeley Pascal for the VAX/11 and PDP/11 minicomputers is a relatively standard Pascal. There are very few extensions and no built-in string types. It produces interpretive code and provides for fast translation at the expense of slower execution code. The Pascal package includes an execution profiler, a cross-reference program, and a debugger.

File Names

Under the UNIX operating system, file names can be long and can include an optional extension (file name identifier). Pascal source programs should have an extension of

.p. The following are examples of Pascal source-program file names:

```
myprog.p
prog3.p
```

By tradition, all system commands and file names are entered in lower case. File names used in the **program** statement are physical UNIX file names (other than the standard interactive files, **Input** and **Output**). If a logical file name that is not included in the program statement is used within a Pascal program, the user may associate a physical file name with the logical name with a **reset** or **rewrite** statement. For example,

```
reset(Data1, 'dfile1.dat');
```

associates the actual UNIX physical file name **dfile1.dat** with the logical name **Data1**. Similarly,

```
rewrite(Out1, 'result');
```

associates the UNIX physical file name **result** with the logical file name **Out1**.

It is also possible to associate a physical file name with either of the standard interactive files **Input** or **Output** in a **reset** or **rewrite** statement. For example,

```
reset(Input, 'dfile1.dat');
```

associates the physical file name **dfile1.dat** with the interactive file **Input**.

The following code illustrates how a user might input a physical file name during execution:

```
program Sample19(Input, Output);
var
  FileName : packed array[1..50] of char;
  Data1 : text;
  I : integer;
begin
  write('What is the data file name? ');
  I := 0;
  while (not eoln) and (I < 50) do begin
    I := I + 1;
    read(FileName[I])
  end;   { while }
  readln;
  reset(Data1, FileName);
      .
      .
      .
end.
```

The above program will abort if the physical file name (which is input) does not exist. Notice that no special ordering is needed to interactively read character data from the console. We will discuss further details regarding interactive input of character data in the next section.

The programmer can also replace a physical file name in the program statement with another physical file name by using either the **reset** or the **rewrite** statement in the same way as they were used in **Sample19**. For example, if **dataf.dat** is a physical file name included in the program statement, the statement

```
reset(dataf.dat, 'dfile1.dat');
```

will replace references to the physical file name **dataf.dat** with the physical file name **dfile1.dat**. The same may be done in a **rewrite** statement.

If a logical file name is used, but no association is made with a physical file name, the Pascal system will assign a temporary UNIX physical file of the form "temp.x" for some character x. The first such file name will be **temp.1**. For example, if **Data1** is a logical file name, the statement

```
reset(Data1);
```

will result in the creation of a temporary physical file to be associated with **Data1**. An advantage of this automatic assignment to a temporary file is that the temporary file will be removed from the system as soon as its scope within the program ends. (However, the file will not be automatically removed if a premature run-time error occurs while the file is active.)

It is also possible to include file names in the execution command line by using the function **argc** and the procedure **argv**. The function **argc** returns the number of parameters in the command line (including the executable file name). For example, if the execution command line is

```
obj dfile1.dat result1
```

argc will return a value of 3. The Pascal procedure **argv** has the form

```
argv(I, StrVar)
```

where **I** is an integer and **StrVar** is a string (packed array of characters) variable. The procedure assigns the Ith parameter from the command line to the variable **StrVar**. The Ith value is 0 for the first parameter and $N - 1$ for the Nth parameter. Thus, assuming that the command line given is

```
obj dfile1.dat result1
```

a call to procedure **argv**, such as

```
argv(1, StrVar);
```

will return the string (packed array of characters)

```
dfile1.dat
```

as the value for variable **StrVar**. For example, the following code could be used to associate the physical file name **dfile1.dat** with the logical name **Data1**, and the physical file name **result1** with the logical name **Out1**, given the preceding command line.

```
program Sample20(Output);
var
  Data1,
  Out1 : text;
  I : integer;
```

```
      FileName : packed array[1..50] of char;
begin
   argv(1, FileName);
   reset(Data1, FileName);
   argv(2, FileName);
   rewrite(Out1, FileName);
         .
         .
   end.
```

The above code assumes that the command line *does* include the two physical file names. The programmer should check to make sure that two file names were input by calling the function **argc** and making sure that the value it returns is 3. Recall that either of the two interactive files, **Input** or **Output**, can be associated with a physical file name by using a **reset** or **rewrite** statement. Thus if the line in **Sample20** had read

```
   reset(Input, FileName);
```

dfile1.dat would replace the interactive file **Input**.

As can be seen from the preceding discussion, Berkeley Pascal allows wide flexibility in the use of file names. As we will discuss later, UNIX also allows redirection of input/output and piping.

Strings and Interactive I/O

Berkeley Pascal does not include any built-in string functions. Thus the standard **packed array of char** data type for a string is used. Berkeley Pascal initializes each character position to the ASCII null character (numeric value of 0). One nice feature in the interactive reading of character data is that no special ordering of code is required. For example, the following code could be used to input a person's name:

```
program Sample21(Input, Output);
var
   MyName : packed array[1..30] of char;
   I : integer;
begin
   write('What is your name? ');
   I := 0;
   while (not eoln) and (I < 30) do begin
     I := I + 1;
     read(MyName[I])
   end;   { while }
   readln;
   writeln('Hello, ', MyName : I, '.  Nice to meet you.');
         .
         .
   end.
```

If the variable **MyName** is used only once, the field width specifier **I** in the statement

```
   writeln('Hello, ', MyName : I, '.  Nice to meet you.');
```

is really not necessary (since the remaining right-hand character positions in **MyName** are filled with ASCII nulls).

It is important that a **readln** statement be issued at the end of the reads for each input line. This is also true for the interactive input of numeric data. For example, the following code will cause a problem:

```
var
   Num : integer;
begin
   write('What is the number? ');
   read(Num);
   writeln('The input number was ', Num : 0);
```

However, the code

```
var
   Num : integer;
begin
   write('What is the number? ');
   readln(Num);
   writeln('The input number was ', Num : 0);
```

will work properly. The following code will also work properly:

```
var
   Num : integer;
begin
   write('What is the number? ');
   read(Num);
   readln;
   writeln('The input number was ', Num : 0);
```

If, in reading character data from a data file, the programmer ignores the EOLN, a blank will be returned for the EOLN character. However, normally the programmer will want to check for EOLN and, when it occurs, do a **readln**.

Redirection of Input/Output

The standard interactive files **Input** and **Output** are normally used for input from and output to the console. However, UNIX provides a way to redirect either the input or the output. For example, the statement

```
>result1
```

after the executable file name in the command line redirects the output from the program to the file **result1**. Similarly, the statement

```
<dfile1.dat
```

after the executable file name in the command line redirects the input so that it comes from a file **dfile1.dat**. For example, to run an executable program called **myprog**, get the input from **dfile1.dat**, and send the output to **result1**, the following command would be issued:

```
myprog <dfile1.dat >result1
```

It is also possible to pipe the output from one executable program to another. For example,

```
myprog | prog2
```

will pipe the output generated from **myprog** to the input of **prog2**.

UCSD Pascal (P-System)

The UCSD p-system is a general operating environment that facilitates computer-related activities ranging from word processing to program development and execution. The UCSD Pascal compiler generates intermediate p-codes instead of native machine code. Native machine code is binary machine code that is directly executable.

File Names

Under the p-system, a file is referred to by volume and by name. Each physical input/output device is called a volume. Examples of such devices are a printer, the console, and each disk. A file name includes up to 15 characters and must end with one of the extensions

```
.text
.code
.data
```

A file with an extension of **.text** is a readable character file (such as a source program file), formatted for use by the system's editor. Files with an extension of **.code** are either p-code or native-code files. A file with an extension of **.data** contains data for user programs in some format. The legitimate characters for file names include the following:

$$\text{A–Z, a–z}$$
$$\text{0–9}$$
$$\text{- / \_ .}$$

Here are some examples for physical (disk) file names under the p-system:

```
Prog1.text
System.wrk.text
Prog2.pas.text
Out_12.data
```

Within a UCSD Pascal program, logical rather than physical file names are used in all the normal statements that reference files. This includes all **reset**, **rewrite**, **read**, **readln**, **write**, **writeln**, etc., statements. When the program executes, actual (physical) disk file names must be assigned to the (logical) program file names.

A physical file name is assigned to a logical program file name when the file is opened, using the **reset** statement. For example, the UCSD Pascal statement

```
reset(Data_File, 'System.Data.text');
```

assigns the disk file **System.Data.text** to the logical file name **Data_File**. The physical file name must be enclosed in single quotes since it is a string. The logical file name does not have to be included in the **program** statement. Thus a program might include the following:

```
program Sample22(Input, Output);
var
   Data_File : text;
   Num1 : integer;
begin
   reset(Data_File, 'System.Data.text');
   readln(Data_File, Num1);
        .
        .
end.
```

It is also possible for the user to input a physical file name while the program is executing. String variables are used to read a file name from the keyboard; they will be discussed in the next section. The following code illustrates how the user can input the physical file name.

```
program Sample23(Output);
var
   FileName : string;
   Data_File : text;
begin
   write('What is your data file name? ');
   readln(FileName);
   reset(Data_file, FileName);
        .
        .
end.
```

The only problem with the above code is that the program will abort at the statement

```
reset(Data_File, FileName);
```

if the physical file name input by the user does not exist (on disk). To avoid this problem, the programmer can turn off the automatic I/O error abort by embedding one of the compiler compile-time options in the source code. The option to use is {$I−}. UCSD Pascal also includes a built-in integer identifier **IOResult** that returns an integer after each I/O operation. The integer value 10 is returned if the specified file is not found on the disk. The following program shows how to make use of these ideas.

```
program Sample24;
{$I-}
var
   F3 : text;
   Num3,
   Check : integer;
   FileName : string;
```

```
begin
  Check := 10;
  while Check = 10 do begin
    writeln('Please input the file name.');
    readln(FileName);
    reset(F3, FileName);
    Check := IOResult
  end;  { while }
  while not eof(F3) do begin
    readln(F3, Num3);
    writeln(Num3)
  end  { while }
end.
```

As can be seen from the above program, the UCSD Pascal compiler is very versatile in the handling of file names. The ability to enter physical file names during program execution allows flexibility in actual applications programming.

Character Data and Interactive I/O

UCSD Pascal includes a built-in string type, **string**. A string is stored as a packed array of characters and has a **length**. In a string variable, the length of the string can vary dynamically during the execution of the program. The function **length** returns the length of the string. The default length of the string is 80 characters, and the length can be modified by using the type declaration

```
string[n]
```

where **n** is a positive integer with a maximum value of 255. For example,

```
City : string[12];
State : string[2];
```

define string identifiers that can store sequences of characters of lengths up to 12 and 2, respectively. The statement

```
Title : string;
```

defines an identifier that can store up to 80 characters.

Values may be assigned to string identifiers using assignment statements, **read** or **readln** statements, or some of the built-in UCSD Pascal string procedures. The individual characters within a string are indexed from 1 to the length of the string. A string may not be indexed beyond its current dynamic length. For example, the following sequence would result in an "Invalid Index" run-time error.

```
Title := 'ABCD';
Title[5] := 'E';
```

String variables are compatible for assignment and comparison with any other string constant or variable, regardless of either static or dynamic length. A string variable may also be compared with a packed array of characters.

When a string is to be read by the UCSD Pascal procedures **read** or **readln**, characters are read into that string variable one at a time, up to but not including the EOLN (return).

UCSD Pascal has two types of files of characters, the standard text file and the file of type **interactive**. Files of type **interactive** are composed of characters, just like files of type **text**. The files **Input**, **Output**, and **Keyboard** are predefined files of type **interactive**. The file **Input** defaults to the console. The statement

```
read(Input, Ch);
```

where **Ch** is a character variable, will store the character typed at the console in **Ch** and will also echo this character back to the console. The file **Keyboard** is the non-echoing equivalent of **Input**. The statement

```
read(Keyboard, Ch);
```

will store the character typed at the console at **Ch**, but will not echo this character back to the screen. The file **Output** also defaults to the console. The statement

```
write(Output, Ch);
```

will print the character stored at **Ch** to the screen. The two statements

```
read(Keyboard, Ch);
write(Output, Ch);
```

are equivalent to the single statement

```
read(Input, Ch);
```

In UCSD Pascal, the procedures **read**, **readln**, **write**, and **writeln** may only be used with files of type **text** or **interactive**. **Interactive** files differ in behavior from text files when they are used with the procedures **read**, **readln**, and **reset**. In order to see the differences between these two files of characters, suppose that we have the following declarations:

```
var
   Ch : char;
   F1 : text;
   F2 : interactive;
```

When the file F1 is opened with the statement

```
reset(F1);
```

the file window, **F1^**, is loaded with the first character of the file. Thus for files of type **text**, the statement

```
read(F1, Ch);
```

is equivalent to the two statements

```
Ch := F1^;
get(F1);
```

(In UCSD Pascal on the IBM PC, the file window is referenced by **^F1** rather than **F1^**.)

In an interactive programming environment, it is not convenient for a user to have to type in the first character of an input file at the time the file is opened. In order to overcome this problem after a reset(F2) the statement

```
read(F2, Ch);
```

in made equivalent to the two statements

```
get(F2);
Ch := F2^;
```

when **F2** is a file of type **interactive**. This difference affects the way in which EOLN must be used when data are being read from a file of type **interactive**. The function EOLN becomes true only after the end-of-line character (return) is read. If this EOLN character is read, the character returned is a blank. The following two programs illustrate the differences between two files of type **text** and **interactive**. Even though the term **interactive file** is used, input and/or output are from the console, rather than from an actual file.

```
program ExText;
var
  F1,
  Y : text;
  Ch : char;
begin
  reset(F1, 'Source.text');
  rewrite(Y, 'Out1.text');
  while not eof(F1) do begin
    while not eoln(F1) do begin
      read(F1, Ch);
      write(Y, Ch)
    end;  { while }
    readln(F1);
    writeln(Y)
  end;  { while }
  close(Y, lock)
end.

program ExInteractive;
var
  F2 : interactive;
  Y : text;
  Ch : char;
begin
  reset(F2, 'console');
  rewrite(Y, 'Out2.text');
  read(F2, Ch);
  while not eof(F2) do begin
    while not eoln(F2) do begin
      write(Y, Ch);
      read(F2, Ch)
    end;  { while }
```

```
        readln(F2);
        writeln(Y)
    end;   { while }
    close(Y, lock)
end.
```

The statement

```
close(Y, lock);
```

is necessary in UCSD Pascal in order to make the output file permanent on the disk. In the first program, the file is called **Out1.text**, and in the second program, **Out2.text**. Instead of having the input coming from the console, the file **F2** in the second program could have been associated with a file on the disk.

Redirecting I/O

UCSD Pascal does not allow the assignment of physical file names to logical file names in the command line. It does, however, allow physical file names to be substituted for the standard **Input** and **Output** files. The **x(ECUTE)** command allows the user to specify options that will modify the system's environment. These include redirecting standard program I/O. The options that are used to redirect program input and output are the following:

PI=	redirect program input
PO=	redirect program output

The redirections apply only to the standard files **Input** and **Output**. Suppose that we have the following program:

```
begin
  writeln('This is a message.')
end.
```

Assuming that we have compiled the above program and have placed the executable code in the file called **Sample24.code**, we redirect the output from the program to a file called **Out24.text** on the disk with volume name **MyVol** as follows. (We choose the execute command from the command line by typing **x**.)

```
COMMAND:  e(DIT, r(UN, f(ILE, c(OMP, l(INK, x(ECUTE, a(SSEM, ? .. x
Execute what file? Sample24 PO=MyVol:Out24.text
```

This statement will execute the program **Sample4.code** and cause the output from the program to be written to the disk with volume name **MyVol** and to the file called **Out24.text**. Using the **PI=** option we could also substitute a physical data file for the input file.

Some Mathematical Formulas

In this appendix we will derive some formulas that are useful in algorithmic analysis. Some of these formulas will be justified with simple methods; the others will be justified using the powerful method of mathematical induction. The first two formulas that we will justify involve the sums of powers of integers and are useful in counting the steps executed by an algorithm. These two formulas are as follows:

$$1 + 2 + 3 + \cdots + n = \frac{n(n + 1)}{2}$$

$$1^2 + 2^2 + 3^2 + \cdots + n^2 = \frac{n(n + 1)(2n + 1)}{6}$$

The proof of the first identity is simple, but clever. We call the sum of the left-hand side S, write the sum down twice (once in each direction), and then add vertically.

$$
\begin{array}{ccccccccc}
1 & + & 2 & + & 3 & + \cdots + & (n - 1) & + & n & = S \\
n & + & (n - 1) & + & (n - 2) & + \cdots + & 2 & + & 1 & = S \\
\hline
(n + 1) & + & (n + 1) & + & (n + 1) & + \cdots + & (n + 1) & + & (n + 1) & = 2S
\end{array}
$$

Since there are n columns on the left, we have

$$n(n + 1) = 2S$$

and the identity follows.

We will use the method of mathematical induction to prove the second identity. The mathematical induction process is based on the following basic property of the natural (counting) numbers.

Axiom of Induction

Let N be a set of natural numbers satisfying the following two properties.
1. 1 is an element of N.
2. If the natural number k is an element of N, the successor of k (which is $k + 1$) is also an element of N.

Then N is the set of all natural numbers.

Every mathematical proof that is based on the above axiom of induction is said to be a proof by mathematical induction.

We are now ready to prove the second formula,

$$1^2 + 2^2 + 3^2 + \cdots + n^2 = \frac{n(n + 1)(2n + 1)}{6}$$

by mathematical induction. Let N be the set of all natural numbers for which the above equation is true. We must first show that 1 belongs to N — that is, that the equation is true for $n = 1$. For $n = 1$, we have

$$1^2 = \frac{1(1 + 1)(2 * 1 + 1)}{6}$$

$$= \frac{1(2)(3)}{6}$$

$$= 1$$

Thus 1 belongs to set N. Next we must show that if k belongs to set N, then $k + 1$ must also belong to N. Thus we assume that k does belong to set N, and we have the following:

$$1^2 + 2^2 + 3^3 + \cdots + k^2 = \frac{k(k + 1)(2k + 1)}{6}$$

We will use this result to show that $k + 1$ must also belong to set N. This means that we need to show that the following must also be true:

$$1^2 + 2^2 + 3^2 + \cdots + k^2 + (k + 1)^2 = \frac{(k + 1)((k + 1) + 1)(2(k + 1) + 1)}{6}$$

$$= \frac{(k + 1)(k + 2)(2k + 3)}{6}$$

Since the first k terms of the left-hand side are equal to

$$\frac{k(k + 1)(2k + 1)}{6}$$

we now have the following:

$$1^2 + 2^2 + 3^2 + \cdots + k^2 + (k + 1)^2 = \frac{k(k + 1)(2k + 1)}{6} + (k + 1)^2$$

$$= \frac{k(k + 1)(2k + 1) + 6(k + 1)^2}{6}$$

$$= \frac{(k + 1)[k(2k + 1) + 6(k + 1)]}{6}$$

$$= \frac{(k + 1)(2k^2 + 7k + 6)}{6}$$

$$= \frac{(k + 1)(2k + 3)(k + 2)}{6}$$

which is equivalent to what we wanted to show. Therefore, N must be the set of natural numbers. This proves that the original equation must be true for every natural number.

In mathematics we use a convenient shorthand symbol for a sum of terms. The Greek letter sigma,

$$\Sigma$$

is used, with the initial value written below the sigma and the final value written above the sigma. Thus the two preceding identities can be written as follows:

$$\sum_{k=1}^{n} k = \frac{n(n + 1)}{2}$$

$$\sum_{k=1}^{n} k^2 = \frac{n(n + 1)(2n + 1)}{6}$$

There are many other formulas used in mathematics; however, we will justify only two others that can be useful in working with trees. These formulas are as follows:

$$2^0 + 2^1 + 2^2 + \cdots + 2^{n-1} = 2^n - 1$$

$$1 * 2^0 + 2 * 2^1 + 3 * 2^2 + \cdots + n * 2^{n-1} = (n - 1) * 2n + 1$$

Using the sigma notation, these formulas become

$$\sum_{k=0}^{n-1} 2^k = 2^n - 1$$

$$\sum_{k=1}^{n} k * 2^{k-1} = (n - 1) * 2^n + 1$$

The first formula can be justified if we consider a more general equation that is encountered in a basic algebra course. If we expand

$$(x - 1)(1 + x + x^2 + \cdots + x^{n-1})$$

we obtain

$$x^n - 1$$

Thus we have

$$\frac{x^n - 1}{x - 1} = 1 + x + x^2 + \cdots + x^{n-1}$$

for every value of x except 1. Thus for $x = 2$ we obtain the desired result. Note that this formula will yield identities for the sums of powers of any integer except $x = 1$.

In order to prove the second formula, we use the above expression for $n + 1$ rather than n. We then have the following:

$$\frac{x^{n+1} - 1}{x - 1} = 1 + x + x^2 + \cdots + x^n$$

We now differentiate both sides with respect to x and find that

$$\frac{(x - 1)(n + 1)x^n - (x^{n+1} - 1)}{x - 1} = 1 + 2x + 3x^2 + \cdots + nx^{n-1}$$

Since the above formula is true for any value of x except 1, we may substitute $x = 2$. In order to obtain the above formula, we must simplify the left-hand side.

$$\frac{(2-1)(n+1)2^n - (2^{n+1} - 1)}{2-1} = (n+1)2^n - (2^{n+1} + 1)$$

$$= 2^n((n+1) - 2) + 1$$

$$= 2^n(n-1) + 1$$

This gives the desired result.

Logarithms and Logarithmic Functions

Before the development of electronic calculators and computers, logarithms were employed extensively in numerical computations. The primary reasons for the use of logarithms are to turn multiplication and division into addition and subtraction, and to turn exponentiation into multiplication. In this day and age, logarithms are rarely used in numerical calculations. However, they are still found in many applications, such as measuring the acidity or basicity of chemical solutions, the loudness of sound, the magnitude of earthquakes, and the magnitude of stars.

Logarithms are defined in terms of any real number a such that

$$a > 0 \quad \text{and} \quad a \neq 1$$

For any number $x > 0$, the logarithm of x to the base a is defined to be the real number y such that a raised to the y power is x. Thus we have

$$\log_a(x) = y \quad \text{if and only if} \quad x = a^y$$

From this definition, it follows that

$$a^{\log_a(x)} = x$$

and

$$y = \log_a(a^y)$$

This gives the fact that the two functions

$$y = a^x \quad \text{and} \quad y = \log_a x$$

are inverses of each other. Some other basic properties follow directly from the definition:

$$\log_a(1) = 0$$
$$\log_a(a) = 1$$
$$\log_a(x) < 1 \quad \text{if} \quad 0 < x < 1$$
$$0 < \log_a(x) < 1 \quad \text{if} \quad 1 < x < a$$
$$\log_a(x) > 1 \quad \text{if} \quad a < x$$

The graphs of the function $y = \log_2(x)$ and its inverse, $y = 2^x$, are the following:

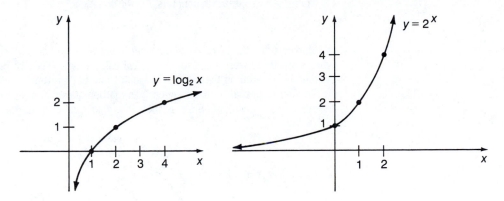

Some other basic properties follow from the definition:

1. $\log_a(xy) = \log_a(x) + \log_a(y)$

2. $\log_a\left(\dfrac{x}{y}\right) = \log_a(x) - \log_a(y)$

3. $\log_a(x^z) = z \log_a(x)$

We will illustrate how the above properties can be justified by proving the first one: Let

$$A = \log_a(x)$$
$$B = \log_a(y)$$

then

$$x = a^A$$
$$y = a^B$$

and

$$xy = a^A a^B$$
$$= a^{A+B}$$

Thus, again by definition,

$$A + B = \log_a(xy)$$

or

$$\log_a(x) + \log_a(y) = \log_a(xy)$$

Any positive real number a $(a \neq 1)$ can be chosen as the base for a logarithmic function. We rarely use the collection of functions

$$y = \log_a x \qquad \text{where } 0 < a < 1$$

Therefore, we will limit our discussion to the case where $a > 1$. When $a = 10$, that is, when the base of the function is 10, the function

$$y = \log_{10}(x)$$

is referred to as the *common logarithmic function*. The base 10 was used extensively when logarithms were used for numerical calculations. This, of course, was because our number system is the decimal (base 10) number system.

Another base that occurs frequently in mathematics and in other natural sciences is the number e, which is defined as the value approached by the expression

$$\left(1 + \frac{1}{n}\right)^n$$

as n gets larger and larger. We write

$$e = \lim_{n \to \infty} \left(1 + \frac{1}{n}\right)^n$$

and from the values of the above expression, e can be approximated to as many decimal places as needed. The following is an approximation of e to 20 decimal places.

$$e \approx 2.71828\,18284\,59045\,23536$$

Logarithms to the base e are called *natural logarithms,* and we write $\ln(x)$ instead of $\log_e(x)$ for the natural logarithmic function. Properties of this logarithmic function developed in the calculus make e the natural choice as a base. First, the derivative of the function

$$y = \ln(x)$$

is

$$\frac{dy}{dx} = \frac{1}{x}$$

Second, the inverse function of $y = \ln(x)$, that is,

$$y = e^x$$

has the derivative

$$\frac{dy}{dx} = e^x$$

In computer science in general and particularly in computer algorithms, logarithms with a base of 2 appear most frequently. This is because the number system used in computing is the binary number system. When we used logarithmic functions in this text, we always used a base of 2. We will now show that the same logarithmic functions to different bases differs only by the multiplication of a constant.

Suppose that we consider two logarithmic functions:

$$y = \log_a(x) \qquad \text{and} \qquad y = \log_b(x)$$

In order to obtain the relationship between these two functions, we start with the identity

$$x = a^{\log_a x} \quad \text{if} \quad x > 0$$

and take the logarithm to the base b of both sides.

$$\log_b(x) = \log_b(a^{\log_a x})$$
$$= [\log_a(x)][\log_b(a)]$$

Thus we have

$$\log_b(x) = [\log_b(a)][\log_a(x)]$$

The term

$$\log_b(a)$$

is a constant, since it does not depend on x, but only on the two bases a and b.

Let us now compare the graphs of the logarithmic functions with the graphs of the power functions. If we first compare the graphs of the functions

$$y = \log_2(x) \quad \text{and} \quad y = x \quad \text{and} \quad y = x^2$$

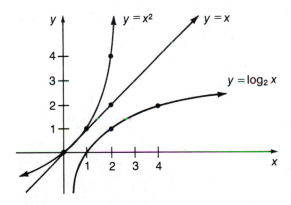

we see that the growth of each of the power functions is much faster than the growth of the logarithmic function. Furthermore, since any other logarithmic function is just a constant multiple of the function

$$y = \log_2(x)$$

this is true for any of the logarithmic functions.

If we compare the graph of the logarithmic function with the graphs of the power functions

$$y = x^{1/2} \quad \text{and} \quad y = x^{1/3}$$

we see that, for large values of x, the graph of the logarithmic function grows more slowly than the graphs of the power functions.

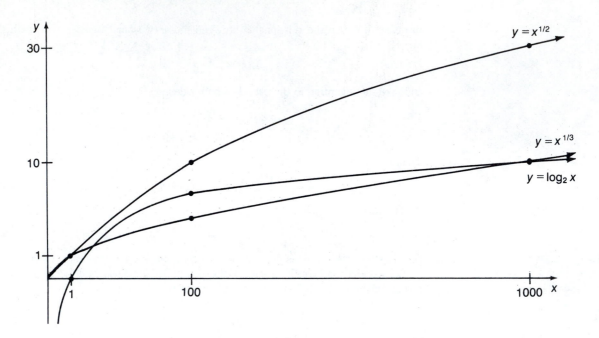

The derivatives for these three functions are as follows:

$$y = \log_2(x)$$

$$= \log_2(e) \cdot \ln(x) \qquad \frac{dy}{dx} = \log_2(e) \cdot \frac{1}{x}$$

$$y = x^{1/2} \qquad\qquad \frac{dy}{dx} = \frac{1}{2} x^{-1/2}$$

$$= \frac{1}{2} \cdot \frac{1}{x^{1/2}}$$

$$y = x^{1/3} \qquad\qquad \frac{dy}{dx} = \frac{1}{3} x^{-2/3}$$

$$= \frac{1}{3} \cdot \frac{1}{x^{2/3}}$$

Since the derivative gives the slope of the curve at each point, as x gets larger and larger, the slope of

$$y = \log_2(x)$$

will eventually get smaller than the slope of either of the other two functions. That is true because $1/x$ will get smaller faster than either

$$\frac{1}{x^{1/2}} \qquad \text{or} \qquad \frac{1}{x^{2/3}}$$

Answers to Selected Exercises

Chapter 1

1.1 For the IBM PC and compatibles using Turbo Pascal use the following:

Ring Bell   writeln(^G); {Ring bell}

For reverse video, normal video, and clear screen, the following special procedures in Turbo Pascal are called:

Clear Screen   ClrScr; {Clear text screen}
Normal Video   TextColor(7); {Wite text}
                       TextBackground(0); {Black background}
Reverse Video   TextColor(0); {Black text}
                       TextBackground(7); {White background}

1.4 Using MS-DOS or PC-DOS on an IBM PC compatible microcomputer with the work disk in drive B,

```
A>type b:ptfile.dat<Ctrl><P><Ret>
```

will print a copy of ptfile.dat at the printer. There are other ways to print a file.

In Turbo Pascal, the data will be written to the file on the disk where the name of the file (physical filename) needs to be identified with the filename (logical filename) used by the procedure **PrintData**. This identification is done using the **assign** procedure. At the end of the **PrintData** procedure the file needs to be closed. The following statements would need to be added:

```
begin
  assign(Pt, 'b:ptfile.dat');
  close(Pt);
end;  {PrintData}
```

1.8 In Turbo Pascal, if we use the built-in string-type identifiers, then the program can read a string at a time. We would need the following modifications in the type declarations.

```
type
  string11 = string[11];              {One soc. sec. num}
  string20 = string[20];              {One name          }
       ↓
  EmpArray = array[1..Max] of EmpInfo;
```

A37

The code for the **ReadData** procedure would now be rewritten as follows:

```
begin
  assign(Mas1, 'B:master.dat');
  reset(Mas1);
  Ct := 0;
  while not eof(Mas1) do begin
    Ct := Ct + 1;
    with Emps[Ct] do begin
      read(Mas1, Name);
      read(Mas1, SsNum);
      read(Mas1, PayRate)
    end { with }
    readln(Mas1)
  end; { while }
  close(Mas1)
end; { ReadData }
```

1.14 SMITH ALBERT   No commas, only one space.
      SMITH AL   Only one space
      SMITH ALICE   No change
      SMITH GEORGE   All uppercase
      SMITH ALEC G   All uppercase, no commas
      SMITH J R   No periods

1.19
```
const
  Max = 100;
type
  string7 = packed array[1..7] of char;
  string20 = packed array[1..20] of char;
  InvItem = record
              InvNum : string7;
              Descript : string20;
              Quantity,
              RecorderNum : integer;
              Cost,
              SalePrice : real
            end;
  AllItems = packed array[1..Max] of InvItem;
var
  Inventory : AllItems;
  InvMaster : text;
```

1.30
```
const
  Max = 100;
type
  string5 = packed array[1..5] of char;
  string10 = packed array[1..10] of char;
  string12 = packed array[1..12] of char;
  string14 = packed array[1..14] of char;
  string15 = packed array[1..15] of char;
  string20 = packed array[1..20] of char;
  AddItem = record
              Street : string15;
              City : string 14;
              State : string10;
              Zip : string5
            end;
```

```
AddBookItem = record
                  Name : string20;
                  Address : AddItem;
                  TeleNum : string12
              end;
AllItems = packed array[1..Max] of AddBookItem;
var
  AllAddresses : AllItems;
  AMaster : text;
```

Chapter 2

2.1 (b)
```
type
  ItemPtr = ^Item;
  Item = record
             Data : real;
             Next : ItemPtr
         end;
var
  First, P, Q : ItemPtr;
```

2.4

2.5 (a)

(b)

(c)

2.6   (a) 1   (b) 1   (c) 1   (d) 2   (e) 1
2   3   2   3   2
3   3   4   3
4   4   5   4
                  5   5

2.7   (a)

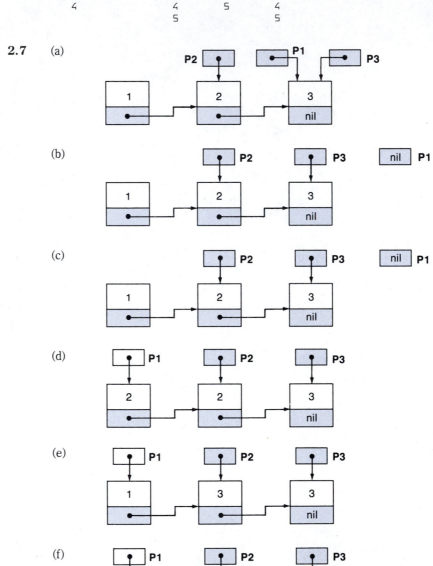

(b)

(c)

(d)

(e)

(f)

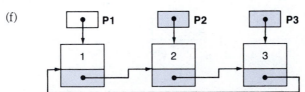

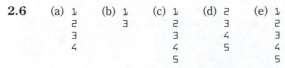

2.8
```
type
   CardPtr = ^Card;
   Card = record
              Suit : char;
              CardVal : integer;
              Next : CardPtr
          end;
var
   Hand1, Hand2, Hand3, Hand4,
   P, Q : CardPtr;
```
The Four **Hand** pointers will be used for separate linked lists for four players.

2.9
```
new(P);
P^.Suit := 'S';
P^.CardVal := 1;
```

2.36   The block of code

```
PrintMenu.
Input Choice.
Trap Choice
```

only has to be coded once.

2.40
```
type
   string7 = packed array[1..7] of char;
   string20 = packed array[1..20] of char;
   InvItem = record
                 InvNum : string7;
                 Descript : string20;
                 Quantity,
                 RecordNum : integer;
                 Cost,
                 SalePrice : real
             end;
   ItemPtr = ^Item;
   Item = record
              Data : InvItem;
              Next : ItemPtr
          end;
var
   InvMaster : text;
   InvHead : ItemPtr;
```

Chapter 3

3.1
(a) *Static data structure:* A data structure where the memory is allocated at the beginning of the program and cannot be changed while the program is running.

(b) *Dynamic data structure:* A data structure where memory can be allocated or deallocated while the program is running.

(c) *Stack:* A data structure where the last item stored is the first item accessed and the first item stored is the last item accessed.

(d) *Queue:* A data structure where the first item stored is the first item accessed and the last item stored is the last item accessed.

3.2
```
type
    ItemDate = char;
    ItemPtr = ^Item;
    Item = record
            Data : ItemData;
            Next : ItemPtr
          end;
var
  Front, Rear, P : ItemPtr;
  Empty : boolean;
  OneItem : ItemData;
```

3.3
```
type
  string11 = packed array[1..11] of char;
  string20 = packed array[1..20] of char;
  ItemData = record
            Name : string20;
            SocSecNum : string11;
            PayRate : real;
            InsCode : integer
          end;
  ItemPtr = ^Item;
  Item = record
            Data : ItemData;
            Next : ItemPtr
          end;
var
  Front, Rear, P : ItemPtr;
  Empty : boolean;
  OneItem : ItemData;
```

3.4
```
type
  string11 = packed array[1..11] of char;
  string20 = packed array[1..20] of char;
  ItemData : record
            Name : string20;
            SocSecNum : string11;
            PayRate : real;
            Age : integer
          end;
  ItemPtr = ^Item;
  Item = record
            Data : ItemData;
            RPtr,
            LPtr : ItemPtr
          end;
var
  First : ItemPtr;
```

3.18

(a) $3 + 7 * 8 - 5$
$3 + (7 * 8) - 5$
$3 + (7 8 *) - 5$
$(3 (7 8 *) +) - 5$
$(3 (7 8 *) +) 5 -$
$3 7 8 * + 5 -$

(c) $(3 + 7) * 8 - 5$
$(3 7 +) * 8 - 5$
$((3 7 +) 8 *) - 5$
$((3 7 +) 8 *) 5 -$
$3 7 + 8 * 5 -$

(f) $A - B * (C - D) / F$
$A - B * (C D -) / F$
$A - (B (C D -) *) / F$
$A - (B (C D -) *) F /$
$A (B (C D -) *) F / -$
$A B C D - * F / -$

3.19 (a) $3 + 7 * 8 - 5$
$3 + (7 * 8) - 5$
$3 + (* 7 8) - 5$
$(+ 3 (* 7 8)) - 5$
$- (+ 3 (* 7 8)) 5$
$- + 3 * 7 8 5$

(c) $(3 + 7) * 8 - 5$
$(+ 3 7) * 8 - 5$
$(* (+ 3 7) 8) - 5$
$- (* (+ 3 7) 8) 5$
$- * + 3 7 8 5$

(f) $A - B * (C - D) / F$
$A - B * (- C D) / F$
$A - (* B (- C D)) / F$
$A - (* B (- C D)) / F$
$A - (/ (* B (- (C D)) F)$
$- A (/ (* B (- C D)) F)$

3.20 (a) $3 7 8 * + 5 -$
$3 (7 * 8) + 5 -$
$3 \ 56 + 5 -$
$(3 + 56) 5 -$
$59 \ 5 -$
$59 - 5$
54

(e) $3 7 + 8 5 - *$
$(3 + 7) 8 5 - *$
$10 \ 8 \ 5 - *$
$10 (8 - 5) *$
$10 \ 3 *$
$10 * 3$
30

3.21 (a) $* - 2 3 5$
$* (2 - 3) 5$
$* (- 1) 5$
$(- 1) * 5$
$- 5$

(e) $- 1 - 8 2 3 * 4 5$
$- 1 - 8 2 3 (4 * 5)$
$- 1 - 8 2 3 \ 20$
$-1 (8 - 2) 3 \ 20$
$- 1 \ 6 \ 3 \ 20$
$- (6 / 3) 20$
$- 2 \ 20$
$2 - 20$
$- 18$

3.31
```
const
  Size = 100;
type
  QueueType = array[1..Size] of integer;
var
  IQueue : QueueType;
  QTop, QRear : integer;
```

3.34
```
type
  string7 = packed array[1..7] of char;
  string20 = packed array[1..20] of char;
  ItemData = record
               InvNum : string7;
               Description : string20;
               Quantity,
               ReOrderNum : integer;
               Cost,
               SellingPrice : real
             end;
  ItemPtr = ^Item;
  Item = record
           Data : ItemData;
           RPtr,
           LPtr : ItemPtr
         end;
var
  Head : ItemPtr;
```

Chapter 4

LINEAR SEARCH

4.4   Search for 27:

Moves		*Comparisons*	
1	Set Position to 0.	For I = 1 to 50	50 Comparisons
<u>1</u>	Move I to Pos.		
2	Moves	50 Comparisons	

Search for 55:

Moves		*Comparisons*	
<u>1</u>	Set Position to 0.	For I = 1 to 50	50 Comparisons
1	Move	50 Comparisons	

MODIFIED LINEAR SEARCH

Search for 27:

Moves		*Comparisons*	
3	Sets	Repeat	27 Comparisons
27	Increments	↓	
<u>2</u>	Sets	Until	
32	Moves		27 Comparisons

Search for 55:

Moves			
3	Sets		50 Comparisons
<u>50</u>	Increments		
53	Moves		50 Comparisons

4.5   Walk-through for 27.

Set **Pos** to 0	**Mid** = 63 div 2 = 31
Set **First** to 1	27 < **Mid**
Set **Last** to 50	Set **Last** to **Mid** − 1 = 30
Mid = 51 div 2 = 25	27 ≠ 31, **First** <= **Last**
27 > Mid	**Mid** = 56/2 = 28
Set **First** to **Mid** + 1 = 26	27 < **Mid**
27 ≠ 25, **First** <= **Last**	Set **Last** to **Mid** − 1 = 27
Mid = 76 div 2 = 38	27 ≠ **Mid**, **First** <= **Last**
27 < **Mid**	**Mid** = 53 div 2 = 26
Set **Last** to **Mid** − 1 = 37	27 > **Mid**
27 ≠ 38, **First** <= **Last**	Set **First** to **Mid** + 1 = 27
	27 ≠ **Mid**, **First** <= **Last**
	Mid = 54 div 2 = 27
	27 = **Mid**

4.6 Comparisons = C, Switches = S, Moves = M

Pass 1   5 9 1 7 4 3 2 6   C = 7   S = 1   M = 3
          ↑

Pass 2   1 9 5 7 4 3 2 6   C = 6   S = 4   M = 12
             ↑

Pass 3   1 2 9 7 5 4 3 6   C = 5   S = 4   M = 12
                ↑

Pass 4   1 2 3 9 7 5 4 6   C = 4   S = 3   M = 9
                   ↑

Pass 5   1 2 3 4 9 7 5 6   C = 3   S = 2   M = 6
                      ↑

Pass 6   1 2 3 4 5 9 7 6   C = 2   S = 2   M = 6
                         ↑

Pass 7   1 2 3 4 5 6 9 7   C = 1   S = 1   M = 3
                            ↑

                              Total   C = 28   S = 17   M = 51

	Compares	Sets	Moves
4.9 5 9 1 7 4 3 2 6	7	2	3
5 9 M 7 4 3 2 6	7	4	5
5 9 M 7 4 3 M 6	7	3	4
5 9 M 7 4 M M 6	7	2	3
5 9 M 7 M M M 6	7	1	2
M 9 M 7 M M M 6	7	4	5
M 9 M 7 M M M M	7	3	4
M 9 M M M M M M	7	2	3

Total   Comparisons = 56, Set Indices = 21, Moves = 29

4.13 Pass 1   5 9 1 7 4 3 2 6   C = 7   S = 6   M = 18

Pass 2   5 1 7 4 3 2 6 9   C = 6   S = 5   M = 15

Pass 3   1 5 4 3 2 6 7 9   C = 5   S = 3   M = 9

Pass 4   1 4 3 2 5 6 7 9   C = 4   S = 2   M = 6

Pass 5	1	3	2	4	5	6	7	9	C = 3	S = 1	M = 3
Pass 6	1	2	3	4	5	6	7	9	C = 2	S = 0	M = 0
Pass 7	1	2	3	4	5	6	7	9	C = 1	S = 0	M = 0
Total									C = 28	S = 17	M = 51

4.16

Pass 1	5	9	1	7	4	3	2	6	C = 7	S = 6	M = 18
Pass 2	5	1	7	4	3	2	6	9	C = 6	S = 4	M = 12
Pass 3	1	5	2	7	4	3	6	9	C = 5	S = 4	M = 12
Pass 4	1	2	5	4	3	6	7	9	C = 4	S = 2	M = 6
Pass 5	1	2	3	5	4	6	7	9	C = 3	S = 1	M = 3
Pass 6	1	2	3	4	5	6	7	9	C = 2	S = 0	M = 0
Pass 7	1	2	3	4	5	6	7	9	C = 1	S = 0	M = 0
Total									C = 28	S = 17	M = 51

4.18

									Comparisons	*Moves*
Pass 1	5	9	1	7	4	3	2	6		M = 1
Pass 2	5	9							C = 1	M = 2
Pass 3	1	5	9						C = 2	M = 4
Pass 4	1	5	7	9					C = 2	M = 3
Pass 5	1	4	5	7	9				C = 4	M = 5
Pass 6	1	3	4	5	7	9			C = 5	M = 6
Pass 7	1	2	3	4	5	7	9		C = 6	M = 7
Pass 8	1	2	3	4	5	6	7	9	C = 3	M = 4
Total									C = 23	M = 32

		Comparisons	Moves

4.19   5 9 1 7 4 3 2 6

			Comparisons	Moves
Pass 1	5			1
Pass 2	5 9		1	2
Pass 3	1 5 9		1	4
Pass 4	1 5 7 9		2	3
Pass 5	1 4 5 7 9		2	5
Pass 6	1 3 4 5 7 9		3	6
Pass 7	1 2 3 4 5 7 9		3	7
Pass 8	1 2 3 4 5 6 7 9		3	4
		Total	C = 15	M = 32

4.30 $N - 1$ comparisons

4.31 Time is of $O(N \cdot \log_2 N)$; then

$$\text{Time} = k \cdot N \cdot \log_2 N$$

Let

$$X = \log_2 N$$

then

$$2^X = N.$$

$$\log_{10}(2^X) = \log_{10} N$$
$$X \cdot \log_{10}(2) = \log_{10} N$$
$$\log_2 N \cdot \log_{10} 2 = \log_{10} N$$

Therefore

$$\text{Time} = k \cdot N \cdot \log_2 N = \frac{k \cdot N \cdot \log_{10} N}{\log_{10} 2} = \left(\frac{k}{\log_{10} 2}\right) \cdot N \cdot \log_{10} N$$

Time is of $O(N \cdot \log_{10} N)$ since $k/\log_{10} 2$ is a constant.

4.32 Selection sort not stable. $5_1 \quad 5_2 \quad 2 \rightarrow 2 \quad 5_2 \quad 5_1$
Bubble sort is stable.
Modified selection sort not stable. $5_1 \quad 5_2 \quad 2 \rightarrow 2 \quad 5_2 \quad 5_1$
Bubble sort with flag is stable.
Insertion sort is stable.

Chapter 5

5.11   Suppose the records in the data file contain the following social security numbers:

    123-23-1234   347-62-1998
    213-45-6781   458-32-1785
    345-78-2134

Also, suppose that the search is for the social security number 347-62-1998.

First call: *Second call:*

    First = 1   First = 4
    Last = 5   Last = 5
    Mid = 3   Mid = 4

Since **SearchNum** = **EList[4]** the number has been found. Thus **Position** is set to 4.

5.12   Assume that the data file is the same as in 5.11 and that the search is for the social security number 125-78-1234.

First call: *Second call:*

    First = 1   First = 1
    Last = 5   Last = 2
    Mid = 3   Mid = 1

Third call: *Fourth call:*

    First = 2   First = 2
    Last = 2   Last = 1
    Mid = 2

Since **First** > **Last**, the search ends and **Position** is 0.

5.26   For *each* recursive call, a copy of the value for each value parameter is pushed onto the stack. No copies for **var** parameters are pushed onto the stack.

Chapter 6

6.1   (a) Not a binary tree since node B has three children.
    (b) It is not a binary tree since the left and right subtrees of node C are not disjoint (node F is a child of both node D and node E).
    (c) It is not a binary tree since the left and right subtrees of node A are not disjoint (node D is a child of both node B and node C).

6.2   (a) Height is 4.
    (b) No, it is not balanced. Node S has only one child; node U has only one child; and all leaves are not at the same level.
    (c) The leaves are nodes W, T, X, and V.
    (d) The immediate predecessor of node U is node R.
    (e) The children of node R are nodes U and V.
    (f) The successors of node R are nodes U, V, and X.

6.3   (a) Inorder traversal: U, S, V, Q, P, R, W, T
    (b) Preorder traversal: P, Q, S, U, V, R, T, W
    (c) Postorder traversal: U, V, S, Q, W, T, R, P

6.25   (a) $* - 6\ 2\ 3$ (b) $6\ 2 - 3\ *$

6.26   It could be represented by the following tree:

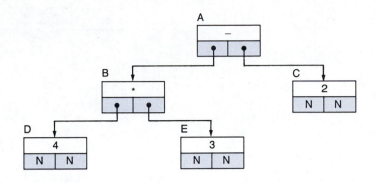

However, it could also be represented by the tree

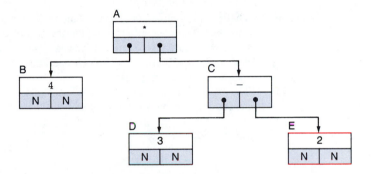

The problem is that we do not know whether it should be interpreted as

    (4 * 3) − 2   (as in the first tree)

or as

    4 * (3 − 2)   (as in the second tree)

6.27

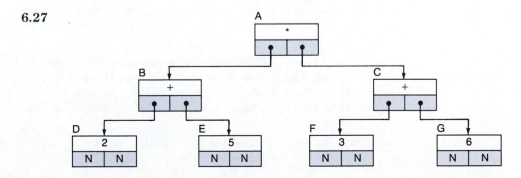

6.28

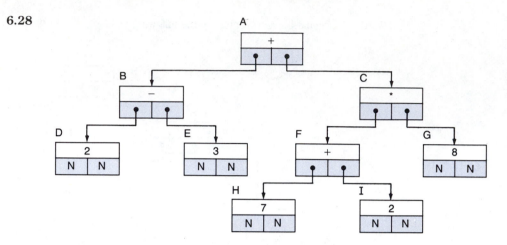

6.29 $2\,3 - 7\,2 + 8 * +$

6.40   The tree structure should be used for applications in which nodes may have more than one child. The tree structure is significantly better for applications in which the data is to become stored in a sorted order and in which searches are utilized (for finding data, deletions, insertions, etc.). Search operations in a binary tree are significantly faster than in a linked list.

6.41   The tree will then become a linked list. Thus the time required to search the tree is just as great as in a normal linked list. The problem can be solved by balancing the tree as new words are inserted. The methods used for this balancing are discussed in Chapter 7.

Chapter 7

7.26   Note that D has no children. The data key value to be deleted will be 8, and the pointer to node A (the root) will be the initial value for **Ptr**.

First call to **DelAndBal**: Since the data value to be deleted (8) is less than that in node **Ptr** (15) the procedure makes a recursive call to itself with the pointer to node B sent as **Ptr**.

Second call to **DelAndBal**: Since the data value to be deleted (8) is less than that in node **Ptr** (10) the procedure makes a recursive call to itself with the pointer to node D sent as **Ptr**.

Third call to **DelAndBal**: Since the data value to be deleted (8) is now equal to that in node **Ptr**, a temporary pointer **OneNode** is set to **Ptr**. Since the right pointer in **OneNode** is **nil**, the left pointer in **Ptr** is assigned to **Ptr** (note that this is **nil**). **OldDeleted** is then set to true. **OneNode** is deleted and this call to the procedure is completed.

   Return to previous calls: Since **OldDeleted** was set to true, the procedure to restore any right unbalance is called.

7.41   *Advantages*: If a tree is kept relatively balanced, the time required for searching is greatly reduced. Thus if we wish to search for an item in order to print its data, delete it, etc., the time required for the search is greatly reduced. Similarly, the time required to search for the correct location at which to insert a new node is significantly reduced.

   Disadvantages: There is certainly extra code and time involved in keeping a tree relatively balanced. If the number of nodes in a tree is relatively small, this extra time required may be more than the time saved during searches. Also, the code required to maintain tree balance is certainly more involved and more difficult to write.

7.43   *Advantages of a B-tree over an AVL tree:* Since a B-tree allows data items to be grouped into pages, there is less overhead required for maintaining balance than in an AVL tree. In an AVL tree each new item requires the creation of a new node and, possibly, a rebalancing of the tree. Since several items can fit into each page of a B-tree (and also counts for duplicate items) we do not have to create a new page for each item. The B-tree method can also be used with files (this will be discussed in Chapter 9).

   Disadvantages of a B-tree compared to an AVL tree: Since each page in a B-tree is declared as an array, memory space can be wasted, especially if several pages are not very full. Each node is created only as it is needed in an AVL tree. The searching methods used to search the array within each page may be more inefficient than the searching methods used in an AVL tree.

Chapter 8

8.24   *Example 1.* Assume we have the following array:

```
7   15   10   10   8   6
↑                    ↑
I                    J
```

In starting the sort, **I** will move, but **J** will not.

```
7   15   10   10   8   6
    ↑                ↑
    I                J
```

The values 15 and 6 are switched, **I** is incremented, and **J** is decremented.

```
7   6   10   10   8   15
        ↑        ↑
        I        J
```

In continuing the sort, neither **I** nor **J** moves. Then 8 and 10 are switched, **I** is incremented, and **J** is decremented.

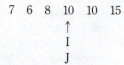

The value 10 is switched with itself, **I** is incremented, and **J** is decremented.

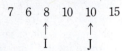

In this example, one of the 10's is in the right subarray, and the other 10 is in neither.

Example 2. Assume that we sort the following array:

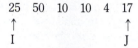

In starting the sort, **I** does not move, but **J** does.

```
25  50  10  10   4  17
↑               ↑
I               J
```

The values 25 and 4 are switched, **I** is incremented, and **J** is decremented.

```
 4  50  10  10  25  17
     ↑       ↑
     I       J
```

In continuing the sort, **I** does not move; neither does **J**. Thus, the values 50 and 10 are switched, **I** is incremented, and **J** is decremented.

```
 4  10  10  50  25  17
         ↑
         I
         J
```

Neither **I** nor **J** moves. Thus 10 is switched with itself, **I** is incremented, and **J** is decremented.

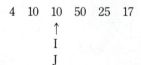

In this example, one of the 10's is in the left subarray, and the other is in neither.

Example 3. Suppose we sort the following array:

4   10   10   15
↑   ↑
I   J

In starting the sort, both **I** and **J** move.

4   10   10   15
      ↑   ↑
      I   J

The two 10's are switched, **I** is incremented, and **J** is decremented.

4   10   10   15
      ↑   ↑
      J   I

In this example one of the 10's is in the left subarray, and the other 10 is in the right subarray.

As can be seen from these examples, the resulting locations depend on the array to be sorted.

8.37   For the array

12   13   8   15

NonrecQSort will first initialize the stack and then push the values 1 and 4 onto the stack.

Stack top | 4 |
            |---|
            | 1 |

The outer **repeat** loop is entered, the value 4 is popped from the stack and assigned to **Last**, and the value 1 is popped from the stack and assigned to **First**. Note that the stack is now empty. The second **repeat** loop is then entered. **I** is set to 1, and **J** is set to 4. The array

12   13   8   15
↑   ↑
I   J

will now be sorted. **Mid** is found to be 13. The inner **repeat** loop is now entered. At first **I** and **J** are both moved.

12 13 8 15
    ↑ ↑
    I J

The values 13 and 8 are switched, **I** is incremented, and **J** is decremented.

12 8 13 15
   ↑ ↑
   J I

Control now exits the inner **repeat** loop. Since **First** (1) is less than **J** (2), the values 1 and 2 are pushed onto the stack.

Stack top

2
1

First is set to 3. Since **First** > **Last** we still remain in the second **repeat** loop. **I** is set to 3 and **J** is set to 4. The following subarray will now be sorted:

13 15
↑   ↑
I   J

Mid is found to be 13. **I** is not moved, but **J** is.

13 15
↑
I
J

The value 13 is switched with itself, **I** is incremented, and **J** is decremented.

   13 15
↑   ↑
J   I

Since **I** > **J** control now exits the inner **repeat** loop. Then, since the left subarray contains fewer elements (no elements) than the right subarray (1 element), **I** is compared to **Last**. Since **I** is not less than **Last**, no values are pushed onto the stack. **Last** is set to 2, and we exit the second **repeat** loop. Control now goes to the outside **repeat** loop and the values for **First** (1) and **Last** (2) are popped from the stack. Upon entry into the second **repeat** loop, **I** is set to 1 and **J** to 2. The subarray

12 8
↑ ↑
I J

will now be sorted. **Mid** is found to be 12. **I** is not moved, but **J** is

The values 8 and 12 are switched, **I** is incremented, and **J** is decremented.

Execution now exits the inner **repeat** loop. The left subarray has fewer elements than the right subarray. However, **I** (2) is not less than **Last** (2). Thus, no values are pushed onto the stack. **Last** is set to **J** (0). Since **First** (1) is >= **Last** (0) execution exits the second **repeat** loop. Then, since the stack is empty, the sort is complete.

Chapter 9

9.1　　*file*:　A data structure consisting of a sequence of components all of the same data type. A file is used to store data in order to preserve it beyond the life of a program execution.

main memory:　Memory that is allocated to a program for a given run.

auxillary memory:　Memory that is outside of the block of memory allocated to the program.

internal file:　A file that is stored in a program's main memory.

external file:　A file that is stored outside of a program's main memory.

9.4　　(a) May not want the readln; Must move the integer to the file window and then put it in the file.

```
read(Num1);
File1^ := Num1;
put(File1);
```

(b) Do you want

```
get(File 1);
```

(c) This is correct.

(d) Need to replace

```
Num1 := File1^;
```

with

```
File1^ := Num1;
```

9.5

1	1	3	1	5
I = 1	I = 2	I = 3	I = 4	I = 5
I mod 2 = 1	2 mod 2 = 0	3 mod 2 = 1	4 mod 2 = 0	5 mod 2 = 1

9.12

```
type
   String10 = packed array[1..10] of char;
   String30 = packed array[1..30] of char;
   String40 = packed array[1..40] of char;
   Item = record
            Name : String30;
            Address : String40;
            TeleNumber : String10;
            Age : integer
          end;
   DataFile = file of Item;
var
   DFile : DataFile;
```

9.16

```
type
   String30 = packed array[1..30] of char;
   ClassItem = record
                 Name : String30;
                 NumOfExams : integer;
                 Exam1, Exam2, Exam3, Exam4,
                 Exam5, Exam6, Exam7, Exam8 : integer;
                 Average : real
               end;
   ClassFile = file of ClassItem;
var
   DFile : ClassFile;
```

9.31

```
   ItemInfo = record
                Desc : String20;
                PtNo,
                Quant,
                MinOnHand : integer;
                Cost : real
              end;
```

9.32

Num = XXXXXXXX

Divide by 100   XXXXXX.XX
Compute integer part   XXXXXX
Divide by 10000   XX.XXXX
Compute integer part   XX
Compute decimal part   .XXXX
Multiply by 10000   XXXX

9.33

ABC1234

Store in an array Num.

Consider Num(4) through Num(7) and compute the integer value using the **ord** function and base 10 arithmetic.

9.35

$$G(I) = I^2$$
$$G(I + 1) = (I + 1)^2$$
$$= I^2 + 2I + 1$$
$$= G(I) + D(I) \qquad \text{where } D(I) = 2I + 1$$

Now

$$D(I + 1) = 2(I + 1) + 1$$
$$= 2I + 1 + 2$$
$$= D(I) + 2$$

Therefore

$$G(I + 1) = G(I) + D(I)$$
$$D(I + 1) = D(I) + 2$$

with $G(0) = 0$ and $D(0) = 1$

9.36   Let Size $+ 1 = P$ a prime.

$$h_0 + I^2 = K \cdot P + R$$
$$h_0 + J^2 = L \cdot P + R$$

Subtract

$$I^2 - J^2 = (K - L) \cdot P$$
$$(I + J)(I - J) = (K - L) \cdot P$$

Since P is prime, either $I - J$ or $I + J$ must be a multiple of P.

$I - J = mP$ certainly implies I is greater than $P/2$.
$I + J = mP$ implies that both I and J cannot be less than $P/2$.

9.47   Use successive divisions by 2 and keep the remainders. We illustrate with an example:

```
67  33  16  8  4  2  1  0
     1   1  0  0  0  0  1
```

Now rewrite in the reverse order and fill in the remaining bits with zeros.

```
0000  0000  0100  0011
```

9.56

```
const
  Max = 100;
type
  String7 = 1String(7);
  String20 = 1String(20);
  InvItem = record
               InvNum : String7;
               Description : String20;
               Quantity,
               ReorderNum : integer;
               Cost,
               SalePrice : real
            end;
  FileType = file of InvItem;
var
  Master : FileType;
```

Chapter 10

10.1
(a) {A, B, C, D, E, F, }∪{(A, B), (A, C), (B, D), (B, E), (C, E), (C, F), (D, E), (E, F)}
(b) Yes, it is a digraph. Each arc is an ordered pair of nodes.
(c) Node A: indegree of 2   Node D: indegree of 1
     Node B: indegree of 2   Node E: indegree of 1
     Node C: indegree of 2   Node F: indegree of 0
(d) Node A: outdegree of 0   Node D: outdegree of 1
     Node B: outdegree of 1   Node E: outdegree of 3
     Node C: outdegree of 1   Node F: outdegree of 2

(e) Node A: degree of 2   Node D: degree of 2
    Node B: degree of 3   Node E: degree of 4
    Node C: degree of 3   Node F: degree of 2

10.2   (a) {A, B, C, D, E} ∪ {(A, B), (A, C), (B, A), (B, D), (B, E), (C, E), (D, B), (E, C)}

(b) Yes. Each arc is ordered.

(c) A, B, A   D, B, D
    A, B, D, B, A   E, C, E
    B, A, B   C, E, C
    B, D, B

(d) A, B   B, A, C   D, B, A
    A, B, D   B, A, C, E   D, B, A, C
    A, B, E   B, D   D, B, A, C, E
    A, B, E, C   B, E   D, B, E
    A, C   B, E, C   D, B, E, C
    A, C, E   C, E   E, C
    B, A   D, B

10.3   (a) {A, B, C, D, H} ∪ {(A, B), (A, C), (B, A), (B, C), (B, D), (C, A), (C, B), (C, H), (D, H)}

(b) Weight of (A, B) is 60   Weight of (C, A) is 70
    Weight of (A, C) is 70   Weight of (C, B) is 120
    Weight of (B, A) is 60   Weight of (C, H) is 35
    Weight of (B, C) is 120   Weight of (D, H) is 130
    Weight of (B, D) is 40

Index